THE RAMAYA

Original works by
Hari Prasad Shastri

* * *

The Heart of the Eastern Mystical Teaching

The Search for a Guru

Wisdom from the East

Meditation - Its Theory and Practice

Yoga (Foyles Handbook)

A Path to God-Realization

Vedanta Light

Echoes of Japan

Scientist and Mahatma

Spring Showers (poems)

* * *

also from Shanti Sadan

SELF-KNOWLEDGE Yoga Quarterly
devoted to spiritual thought and practice

Book catalogue available on request
from Shanti Sadan, 29 Chepstow Villas, London W11 3DR

THE

RAMAYANA

OF

VALMIKI

Translated by

HARI PRASAD SHASTRI

VOLUME II

ARANYA KANDA

KISHKINDHA KANDA

SUNDARA KANDA

SHANTI SADAN

29 Chepstow Villas

London W11 3DR

First published 1957
Second impression 1969
Third impression 1976
Fourth impression 1985
Fifth impression 1992

ISBN 0-85424-031-4

*Originally printed in Great Britain
at the Burleigh Press, Bristol*

Reprinted by WBC Print Ltd., Bridgend, CF31 3YN

CONTENTS

Book III—Aranya Kanda

CONTENTS

CONTENTS

BOOK IV—KISHKINDHA KANDA

CONTENTS

CONTENTS

Book V—Sundara Kanda

CONTENTS

BOOK III

ARANYA KANDA

CHAPTER I

Rama is welcomed by the Sages of the Dandaka Forest

ENTERING the vast Dandaka Forest, the invincible Rama, master of his senses, saw a circle of huts belonging to the ascetics, strewn with bark and kusha grass, blazing with spiritual effulgence scarce to be borne by mortal eye, as the noonday sun is a source of torment to men.

This retreat, a haven to all beings, the ground of which was carefully tended, was frequented by many deer and multitudes of birds and rendered gay by the dancing of troops of apsaras.

Beautiful with its spacious huts, where the sacred fire burnt, surrounded by ladles and other articles of worship such as skins, kusha grass, fuel, jars of water, fruit and roots ; encircled by great and sacred forest trees, bowed with the weight of ripe and delectable fruits, the whole hermitage was hallowed by sacrificial offerings and libations and re-echoed to the recitation of Vedic hymns.

Carpeted with flowers of every kind, possessing pools covered with lotuses, it had been the retreat of former hermits, who subsisted on fruit and roots and who, wearing robes of bark and black antelope skins, their senses fully controlled, resembled the sun or fire. Now great and pious sages, practising every austerity, added to its lustre. Resembling the abode of Brahma, that hermitage resounded with the chanting of Vedic hymns, and brahmins, versed in the Veda, adorned it with their presence.

Beholding that sacred place, the illustrious Raghava, unstringing his bow, entered, and the august sages, possessed of spiritual knowledge, highly gratified, advanced to meet him.

Seeing that virtuous one, resembling the rising moon, with Lakshmana and Vaidehi of dazzling beauty, those ascetics of rigid vows received them with words of welcome and the dwellers in the wood were astonished at Rama's handsome mien, his youthful appearance, majesty and graceful attire and, struck with wonder, gazed unwinkingly on Raghava, Lakshmana and Vaidehi, as on a great marvel.

Then, those blessed sages, engaged in the welfare of all beings, conducted Rama to a leaf-thatched hut, where, offering him the traditional hospitality, those fortunate and pious men, resembling fire itself, brought water that he might wash his hands and feet. Experiencing great delight, those high-souled ascetics, bidding him welcome, gathered flowers, fruit and roots, placing the whole content of the hermitage at the disposal of that magnanimous hero.

Thereafter, those ascetics, versed in the sacred lore, with joined palms addressed him, saying :—

" O Raghava, a king is the defender of the rights of his people and their refuge; he is worthy of all honour and respect, he wields the sceptre, he is the Guru and partakes of a fourth part of the glory of Indra ; he enjoys the highest prerogatives and receives every homage. We, being under thy dominion, should be protected by thee, whether living in the capital or the forest ; thou art our Sovereign, O Master of the World !

" Having renounced all desire for revenge, subdued anger and mastered our senses, do thou protect us in the practice of virtue, as a mother protects the infant at her breast."

With these words they paid reverence to Rama, who was accompanied by Lakshmana, offering him fruit, roots, flowers and every product of field and forest, whilst other ascetics, resembling the fire in lustre, observers of sacred vows, honoured the Lord according to tradition.

CHAPTER 2

The Demon Viradha carries off Sita

HAVING received the homage of the ascetics, at dawn Rama paid obeisance to them and followed by Lakshmana, entered the forest, which abounded in every kind of deer and was frequented by bears and tigers.

There, trees, creepers and shrubs had been trampled underfoot, so that the paths were barely distinguishable and the reflection from the pools and lakes was dazzling; no birds sang in that whole demesne, which was filled with the humming of crickets.[1]

Followed by Lakshmana, Rama searched the depths of the forest with his gaze and in that wood, abounding in ferocious beasts, Kakutstha, accompanied by Sita, beheld a titan as large as a mountain creating a great uproar.

Of formidable aspect, hideous, deformed, his eyes sunk deep in his forehead, with a vast mouth and protruding belly, clad in a tiger skin, covered with blood and loathsome to look upon, he struck terror into the hearts of all beings; it appeared as if death itself were approaching with open jaws.

Three lions, four tigers, two leopards, four dappled deer and the head of a great elephant with its tusks, from which the fat ran down, hung from his spear.

Seeing Rama, Lakshmana and Sita, the Princess of Mithila, he rushed upon them in fury, like Time[2] at the destruction of the worlds. Then, creating a great uproar, causing the earth to tremble, he seized Vaidehi in his arms and began to carry her away, saying:—

"O Ye, wearing matted locks, clad in robes of bark, accompanied by a common consort, ye are about to die! Entering the Dandaka Forest, armed with weapons, bows and spears, whence have ye come, O Ascetics and why do ye dwell here in the company of a woman? Perverse and evil wretches, who are ye, bringing disrepute on the sages?

I am the Titan Viradha, this is my retreat and I roam the impenetrable forest, armed with weapons, feeding on the flesh of ascetics. This woman of lovely limbs shall become my wife and, in combat, I will drink the blood of ye both, O Miscreants!"

The daughter of Janaka, Sita, hearing the cruel and arrogant speech of the wicked-hearted Viradha, filled with dread, began to tremble like a palm shaken by the wind.

[1] The Commentaor explains that all this destruction was due to the presence of the demon Viradha and that the birds had deserted the place in fear of him.

[2] Time in the form of Death, the Destroyer.

Rama, seeing Viradha bearing the lovely Sita away, growing pale, said to Lakshmana :—

" O Friend, behold the daughter of Janaka, my chaste consort, an illustrious princess, reared in luxury, held fast in the arms of Viradha ! Alas ! Kaikeyi's desire has been fulfilled to-day ! O Lakshmana, the enthronement of her son did not suffice that designing woman, since she caused me to be banished to the forest despite the love my subjects bore me. Now she who reigns supreme in the midst of our mothers will be satisfied! That another should have laid hands on Vaidehi is the greatest of my misfortunes, worse even than the death of my sire or the loss of my kingdom, O Saumitri ! "

Hearing the words of Kakutstha, Lakshmana, his eyes streaming with tears, hissing like a wounded snake, said harshly :—

" O Kakutstha, O Protector of All Beings, who art equal to Indra himself, since I am thy servant, why dost thou lament as though thou hadst no defender ?

" Pierced by the shaft I am about to loose in my wrath, the Titan Viradha will die and the earth drink his blood. The bitterness, I felt towards Bharata for his desiring the throne, I shall expend on Viradha, as the God who bears the thunderbolt discharges it at a mountain ! With all the strength of mine arm, letting fly this sharp arrow, I shall pierce his breast! May he yield up his life and fall rolling on the earth ! "

CHAPTER 3

The Struggle between Viradha and the two Brothers

THEREAFTER Viradha spoke again, filling the forest with his voice :—

" Who are ye, where are ye going, answer me ! "

Then the illustrious Rama answered that titan, whose countenance was inflamed with anger, saying :—

" Know us to be two warriors of the race of Ikshwaku,

fixed in our vows, wandering in the forest; but now we would know who thou art, roaming here and there in the thickets?"

Thereupon Viradha said to Rama, whose strength was truth:—

"Hear and I will tell thee, O Prince of the House of Raghu! I am the son of Java and my mother is Satarhada. I am known among the titans throughout the world as Viradha. Having gratified Brahma by my penances, I obtained a boon and was rendered invulnerable to any weapon on earth; it is impossible to slay me by the use of arms!

"Forsaking this fair one, do ye, renouncing all hope, without turning back, go hence without delay and I will grant you your lives!"

Then Rama, his eyes red with anger, answered that hideous demon, the wicked Viradha, saying:—

"Wretch that thou art, cursed be thine evil design; assuredly thou art courting death, verily thou shalt find it in combat; stay but an instant and thou shalt not escape alive!"

Bending his bow and speedily placing two sharp arrows on it, Rama struck that demon with his pointed shafts and thereafter, stretching the cord tight, he loosed seven swift arrows, adorned with feathers and tipped with gold, equal in flight to Suparna and Anila.

Having pierced the body of Viradha, those fiery shafts, decorated with heron's plumes, fell to the ground hissing and stained with blood.

On receiving those wounds, Viradha loosed his hold on Vaidehi and brandishing his spear in fury hurled himself on Rama and on Lakshmana who accompanied him. Letting forth a mighty roar, grasping his spear, like unto the standard of Indra, his jaws wide open, he resembled death itself.

Then the two brothers rained a volley of flaming arrows on Viradha, who resembled time, death or fate, but that terrible demon, bursting into loud laughter, halting and opening his jaws, threw up those pointed arrows by virtue of the boon he had received. Restraining his breath and brandishing his spear, the demon Viradha again rushed on the two descendants of Raghu, whereupon Rama, the most skilful of warriors, with two arrows cut off that spear, which shone like lightning and resembled a flame in the sky.

Shattered by Rama's shafts, the spear fell to the ground, like a rocky ledge split by lightning. Thereat, unbuckling their swords, those warriors swiftly fell on Viradha like two black serpents, striking him heavily again and again.

Though hard beset, their formidable opponent beat them off vigorously with his fists, but they stood firm, whereupon he sought to lift them from the ground and Rama, guessing his intention, said to Lakshmana :—

" Let the demon carry us along the path as far as he wishes, O Saumitri ! Allow this Prowler of the Night to bear us according to his whim, since he is proceeding along our way."

Thereupon, the demon, proud of his strength, with great energy lifted them up and placed them on his shoulders like two striplings ; then having set the two descendants of Raghu on his shoulders, the demon Viradha, Ranger of the Night, emitting a great roar, strode off into the forest.

Entering that forest, abounding in trees of every kind, where diverse birds filled the air with their song and which was thronged with jackals, beasts and serpents, he resembled a great cloud.

CHAPTER 4

Rama and Lakshmana slay the Demon Viradha

SEEING the two brothers, the glory of the House of Raghu, being borne away, Sita, lifting up her arms, began to cry aloud, reflecting thus :—

' Rama, the son of Dasaratha, who is truthful, virtuous and guileless, is being carried away by a demon of terrifying aspect, I shall become a prey to bears, tigers and panthers ! '

Thinking thus, she cried out :—" O Foremost of Demons, I beg of thee, take me and spare those two descendants of Raghu ! "

Hearing Vaidehi's words, Rama and Lakshmana, full of valour, prepared to slay that wicked wretch, whereupon

Saumitri broke the left arm of that redoubtable demon and Rama the right; thereafter, that titan, resembling a mass of cloud, his arms broken, growing weak, suddenly fell to the ground unconscious, like a mountain struck by lightning.

Then the two brothers beat the demon with their fists and feet and picking him up, again hurled him to the ground; yet, though struck by innumerable arrows and wounded by their swords, the demon did not die.

Perceiving it to be impossible to slay that giant, like unto a mountain, the blessed Rama, the refuge of all who are in peril, spoke thus :—

" By virtue of his penances, O Tiger among Men, this demon cannot be overcome in combat by weapons, let us therefore cast him into a pit. O Lakshmana, as if for a great elephant, do thou dig a pit in the forest for this demon of formidable size."

Having thus commanded Lakshmana saying :—" Dig a pit ", the valiant Rama stood with his foot on the neck of the demon.

Hearing those words, the demon in humble accents addressed that descendant of Raghu, that Bull among Men, saying :—

" O Lion among Heroes, under the blows of a warrior whose strength equals that of Indra, I am dying. In mine ignorance, I did not recognize thee, O Lion amongst Men! I see now that thou art the noble son of Kaushalya. O Dear Child, thou art Rama and this is the fortunate Vaidehi and the illustrious Lakshmana.

" Through a curse, I had to assume the monstrous shape of a titan, but in reality I am the Gandharva Tumburu, who incurred the wrath of Kuvera. That glorious God, being propitiated by me, said :—' When Rama, the son of Dasaratha, overcomes thee in fight, then, assuming thy natural form, thou shalt return to the celestial region.' Owing to my lack of reverence for him, in anger the Lord Kuvera had denounced me for having conceived an attachment for the nymph, Rambha. By thy grace, I am delivered from this terrible curse and shall now return to mine abode. All hail to thee, O Scourger of thy Foes!

" O Dear Child, not far from here, at approximately four and half miles distance, dwells the virtuous Sharabhanga, a mine of austerity, a great and mighty rishi, effulgent as the sun. Go there, without delay; he will give thee most excellent counsel!

Having buried me in a pit, O Rama, go thy way in peace! Those demons who are about to die must according to a fixed law be buried in a pit."

Having spoken thus to Kakutstha, the courageous Viradha, pierced by many arrows, leaving his body, ascended to heaven.[1]

Then Raghava said to Lakshmana:—"Dig a pit for this demon of dreadful deeds, as for a great elephant in the forest." Having spoken thus to Lakshmana saying 'Dig a pit!', Rama who was endowed with great prowess, remained standing with his foot on the head of Viradha.

Then Lakshmana, taking up a pick, dug a great pit by the side of the demon, whose ears resembled conches and threw him into it, he letting forth dreadful shrieks the while.

Finding they were unable to kill that great titan with their sharp weapons, those two lions among men, having employed all their ingenuity, put an end to Viradha by burying him in the pit.

Viradha himself, a ranger of the forest, desiring to die at Rama's hands, had indicated to him how he should proceed, saying:—"I cannot be slain by weapons."

Hearing this, the idea had come to Rama to fling him into a pit, and while being cast into it, that all-powerful demon caused the forest to resound with his cries.

Having thrown Viradha into the pit, Rama and Lakshmana, their fears removed, rejoiced in that forest, like the sun and moon in the firmament.

CHAPTER 5

The Meeting with the Sage Sharabhanga and his Ascent to Brahmaloka

HAVING slain the mighty and terrible Viradha in the forest, the valiant Rama embraced Sita and comforted her; then addressing the resplendent Lakshmana, he said:—

[1] The following passages clearly indicate the resumption of the narrative on a later occasion.

"This impenetrable forest is dangerous and we are not its natural inhabitants; let us therefore seek out the Sage Sharabhanga without delay."

Raghava then turned his steps towards Sharabhanga's hermitage and, approaching that Sage, whose soul was purified by renunciation, he observed a great marvel.

In the sky, he beheld Indra, gorgeously attired in robes free from any particle of dust, his body shining like the sun or fire, mounted on a splendid chariot, followed by all the Celestials and innumerable high-souled sages like unto himself, who served as his escort. Bay horses were yoked to that aerial car, that shone like the rising sun and, luminous as the moon's disc, resembled a mass of white clouds.

Rama also observed an immaculate canopy with magnificent garlands and marvellous fans made of yaks' tails with handles of gold of great price, which two women of rare beauty, waved to and fro over the head of that God, whilst Gandharvas, Immortals, Celestial Beings and great Rishis, paid homage to him with sublime chants, as he hovered in space.

Seeing Shatakratu conversing with the Sage Sharabhanga, Rama pointed out the chariot to his brother and bade him gaze on the marvellous sight.

He said :—"O Lakshmana, dost thou behold that dazzling car of great brilliance shining like the sun in the skies ? Without doubt, these are the celestial bay horses of Indra of whom we have heard, who travels through space and who is constantly invoked at the time of sacrifice. Those youthful warriors wearing earrings, who in groups of hundreds, with swords in their hands, stand round him in the sky, with their broad chests and strong arms resembling maces, clad in magnificent purple, look like fierce tigers. On their breasts, gleam rows of pearls, and those lions among men, of handsome mien, appear to be twenty-five years old which is the age at which the Gods ever remain, O Saumitri. Tarry here a moment, O Lakshmana, so that I may discover who this great hero in the chariot really is."

Having uttered the words 'Tarry here' to Saumitri, Kakutstha advanced towards the hermitage of Sharabhanga.

Seeing Rama approaching, the Lord of Sachi, taking leave of the sage, said to the Gods :—

" Rama is coming hither, take me to mine abode 'ere he addresses me ; later he shall behold me ! When he returns victorious, having fulfilled his purpose, I shall readily show myself to him. It is for him to perform a great exploit impossible for any other to accomplish."

Thereafter, offering salutations to the ascetic, in all humility, the God who bears the thunderbolt, the Scourge of his Foes, ascended to heaven in his chariot, harnessed with horses.

When the God of a Thousand Eyes had departed, Raghava rejoined his consort and his brother and together they approached Sharabhanga, who was seated before the sacred fire. Embracing his feet, Rama, Sita and Lakshmana, on his invitation, seated themselves in the place assigned to them.

Questioned by Raghava concerning Indra's visit, Sharabhanga related everything to him.

He said :—

" O Rama, that magnanimous God wished to conduct me to Brahmaloka, the region I have attained by the merit of my penances, which is inaccessible to those who are not masters of themselves.

" Seeing thee approaching, know well, O Foremost of Men, that I had no desire to enter Brahmaloka 'ere I had enjoyed thy gentle presence in my hermitage. O Lion among Men, O Virtuous and Magnanimous Prince, having had intercourse with thee, I shall ascend first to the three lower heavens and thereafter to the highest. These worlds of unsurpassed beauty that have been conquered by me, these sublime abodes of Brahma, that are mine by right, do thou accept, O Lion among Men ! "

Hearing the words of the Rishi Sharabhanga, Raghava, that lion among men, versed in the Shastras, answered :—

" I also have conquered all the worlds, O Great Ascetic, but in obedience to my vow I desire to remain in the forest."

Thus addressed by Raghava, whose might was equal to Indra's, the eminently sagacious Sharabhanga spoke again, saying:—

" O Rama, the illustrious and virtuous Sutikshna lives in

this forest; that saint will tell thee what is best for thee to do.

"Follow the river Mandakini, that stream which is covered with a carpet of flowers, and thou wilt reach his dwelling place. There is the path, O Tiger among Men, but stay with me a moment yet, till I abandon this body as a snake casts off its slough."

Thereafter, having prepared a fire and poured clarified butter therein, Sharabhanga, that sage of supreme merit, entered the flames to the accompaniment of sacred formulas.

The hair of the magnanimous one was consumed together with his wrinkled skin, his bones, his flesh and his blood, whereupon, assuming a youthful and splendid appearance, Sharabhanga rose from the pyre like a flame.

Traversing the region where the sacrificial fires are tended by high-souled sages, as well as that of the Gods, he ascended to Brahma's abode.

That foremost of Rishis, of purified karma, there beheld the Grandsire of the World with those attendant on him, who, seeing that sage, addressed him, saying:—"Thou art welcome!"

CHAPTER 6

The Sages seek the protection of Rama

SHARABHANGA having ascended to heaven, the assembled ascetics presented themselves before Rama, the offspring of Kakutstha of flaming energy, and among them were those who had sprung from the nails and the hair of Brahma's body, also from the water in which his feet were bathed; there were those who lived on the moon's rays; those who subsisted on milled grain; those who did penance by standing in water; those who slept on the naked ground; those who lived in the open air the whole year round; those who subsisted on water and wind alone; those who never sought the shade; those

[1] Five Fires.—Four fires and the sun overhead. See Glossary also under Ascetics.

who underwent long fasts ; those who practised uninterrupted repetition of prayer ; those who gave themselves up to perpetual penance ; those who dwelt on the summit of high mountains ; those who had subdued their senses and those who lived between five fires.[1]

All these sages, fixed in Yoga, endowed with the powers of Brahma, gathered in Sharabhanga's hermitage in order to approach Rama.

Those virtuous companies of Rishis, having assembled there, addressed Rama, Foremost of the Good, who was conversant with his supreme duty, saying :—

" O Lord of the House of Ikshwaku and of the whole world, Warrior of the Great Car, thou art our defender and leader, as Maghavan is of the Gods.

" Thou art famed in the Three Worlds for thy valour and glory ! Filial devotion, justice and faith find their consummation in thee, O Lord. It behoves thee, who art cognisant with virtue, to pardon our temerity in approaching thee in order to make our supplication.

" It were a signal defect for a king to receive one-sixth of the revenue of his people, if he did not protect them as his own sons. Should he however defend those who inhabit his kingdom as his own life or as the lives of his offspring, to whom he is ever devoted, he will occupy an exalted position in the region of Brahma.

" The supreme blessedness acquired by those ascetics who live on roots and fruit is not equal to a quarter of that attained by the monarch who governs his subjects according to the law.

" Do thou become the defender of those countless brahmins who live in the forest who are without a protector, and so defend them from the cruel persecution of the titans.

" Come and behold the bodies of innumerable ascetics of pure heart, who have been slaughtered in diverse ways in the forest by titans.

" They have inflicted great carnage amongst the people who dwell on Lake Pampa, by the river Mandakini and on Chittrakuta. We are no longer able to endure the terrible plight of these sages, brought about in the forest by those titans of cruel deeds ; therefore we take refuge in thee ; protect us, O Rama, against those Prowlers of the Night, who seek our destruction. We have no asylum on earth but thee, O Valiant Prince; do thou save us from the titans."

Having listened to the sages, the virtuous Kakutstha answered them, who were rich in heavy penances, saying:—

"Do not entreat me thus; am I not the servant of the sages? It is solely to fulfil my duty, that I have entered the forest. It is in order to deliver you from the oppression of the titans and to carry out the commands of my sire that I am here. It is in your interest and for your happiness that I have come here of mine own will.

"My sojourn in the forest will be greatly to your advantage; I shall slay the titans, the enemies of the ascetics. Let the sages witness my prowess in combat and my brother's also, O Rishis!"

Having yielded to the entreaty of the ascetics, that hero, firm in his duty, accompanied by Lakshmana, directed his course towards the hermitage of Sutikshna, followed by the sages, who paid him every honour.

CHAPTER 7

The Meeting between Rama and Sutikshna

RAMA, the Scourge of his Foes, accompanied by his brother, Sita and the sages, approached the hermitage of Sutikshna, and having proceeded far and crossed many deep rivers he beheld a wonderful mountain as high as Mount Meru.

Thereafter those two scions of the House of Raghu went forward with Sita through a forest filled with many kinds of trees and having penetrated into that dense woodland, abounding in trees laden with flowers and fruit, Rama observed in a solitary spot a hermitage decorated with garlands and bark.

There he beheld the Sage Sutikshna, a mine of asceticism, his hair matted, covered with dust, seated in the lotus posture and addressed him, saying:—

"O Blessed One, I am Rama, who have come hither to

behold thee. Be gracious enough, O Virtuous and Illustrious Rishi, O Essence of Sanctity, to speak to me."

Seeing Ramachandra, the sage, foremost of the ascetics, took him in his arms and addressed him thus:—

"Be thou welcome, O Best of the Raghus, O Rama, chief of virtuous men. Henceforth this hermitage, which thou hast entered, has a protector. I have waited for thee, O Illustrious Hero, and for this reason did not ascend to the region of the Gods, leaving my body here on earth. I had heard that thou, being banished from thy kingdom, had gone to Chittrakuta, O Kakutstha!

"The Chief of the Gods, Shatakratu, came hither and approaching me, that mighty King of the Celestials made it known to me that I had conquered all the worlds by virtue of my good karma.

"All those blessings acquired by the divine sages through asceticism I offer to thee; do thou enjoy them with thy consort and Lakshmana."

To that great and illustrious sage of rigid vows and devout speech, Rama, the master of his senses, replied, as Vasava addresses Brahma, saying:—

"O Illustrious Sage, I myself have conquered the worlds; yet in accordance with the command received by me, I have elected to dwell in the great forest. 'Thou art possessed of everything, yet art engaged in the welfare of all beings', were the words of the ascetic Sharabhanga, that Gautama of great soul, to me."

Hearing Rama's words, the great Rishi, renowned throughout the world, graciously addressed him, saying:—

"Do thou live in this hermitage, O Rama, which is pleasant and frequented by companies of sages, where one may gather roots and fruit in all seasons, where herds of marvellous deer gather without injuring any and come and go enchanting all with their beauty. No harm is to be encountered here, save what the deer bring about."

Hearing the words of the great Rishi, the elder brother of Lakshmana, lifting up his bow and arrows, said:—

"O Blessed Lord, what could be more unfortunate than that I with my bow and sharp burnished arrows should slay those deer that gather here, and thus give thee pain; for this reason I shall not sojourn long in this sanctuary."

Having spoken thus, Rama became silent and performed his evening devotions; thereafter with Sita and Lakshmana he prepared to pass the night in Sutikshna's enchanting hermitage.

The evening having passed and night fallen, the magnanimous Sutikshna with his own hands distributed hulled grain, the traditional food of the ascetics, to those Lions among Men, having paid homage to them.

CHAPTER 8

Rama takes leave of Sutikshna

RAMA, having been treated with all honour by Sutikshna, passed the night in the ashrama with Saumitri, and waking at dawn bathed with Sita in the cool waters fragrant with the scent of lotuses.

At the proper time, having duly worshipped Agni and the Gods in that forest containing the retreats of the ascetics, Rama, Lakshmana and Videha's daughter, observing the sun had risen, approached Sutikshna with courtesy, saying:—

"O Lord, thou hast ministered liberally to us and paid us every honour, now we ask leave to depart, since the ascetics who accompany us wish us to press on without delay.

"It is our wish to visit all the retreats inhabited by holy men of devout practices in the Dandaka Forest. We therefore beg to take leave of these great sages, fixed in their vows, purified by penance and resembling clear flames.

"We desire to go hence 'ere the rays of the sun shine too fiercely and become unbearable, like one who has usurped royal prerogatives by unlawful means!"

Having spoken thus, Raghava with Saumitri and Sita, bowed down to the feet of the sage, and that Foremost of Ascetics, raising up those two heroes, clasped them affectionately to his heart and said:—

" Go thy way safely, O Rama, in the company of Saumitri and Sita, who follows thee like a shadow. Visit the entrancing solitudes of the Dandaka Forest, where those hermits dwell whose souls are purified by renunciation. Thou shalt see there woods abounding in fruit, roots and flowers, magnificent herds of deer, flocks of tame birds, tufts of lotus in bloom, tranquil lakes abounding in waterfowl, charming mountain springs and splendid cataracts falling from the hills with marvellous groves echoing to the peacock's cry. Go, O Child, and thou also, Sumitra's son ; then come again to this retreat when thou hast seen all."

Thus addressed, Kakutstha and Lakshmana answered :— " Be it so ! " and circumambulating the sage, prepared to depart.

Thereafter the large-eyed Sita handed those brothers their excellent quivers, bows and shining swords, and taking leave of the great sages the two descendants of the House of Raghu, of unsurpassed beauty, fastening on their quivers and bearing their bows and swords, swiftly set out with Sita.

CHAPTER 9

Sita implores Rama not to attack the Titans

When her lord, the Joy of the House of Raghu, having obtained the permission of Sutikshna was proceeding on his way, Sita, in gracious and gentle tones, addressed him saying :—

" Though thou art noble, a small defect by imperceptible degrees becomes great, but it is always possible to eschew evil, born of desire. There are three failings, born of desire; the first is the uttering of falsehood, but the other two are of graver significance, namely, association with another's wife and acts of violence committed without provocation.

" O Raghava, falsehood was never, nor could ever be, thy weakness ; nor yet, O Indra among Men, couldst thou, even in thought, covet another's wife ; this fault, destructive of virtue, was never thine, O Son of a King! Thou hast ever centred thine attention on thine own consort!

" Thou art righteous, humble and faithful to the commands of thy sire; in thee, justice and integrity flower in their fullness. All this is possible to those who have mastered their senses, O Long-armed Warrior, and thou art fully self-subdued, O Thou of Charming Presence!

" The third evil, which through ignorance leads men to bear hostility to one another without cause, now shows itself in thee! O Valiant Prince, thou hast vowed to the dwellers of the Dandaka Forest, whose defender thou art, to slay the demons without mercy, and for this reason, equipped with bows and arrows, thou hast set out with thy brother to the forest known as Dandaka. Seeing thee advancing thus my mind is filled with apprehension and I am pondering how to act in the most profitable manner for thy welfare in this world and the next. Thy departure for the Dandaka Forest does not find favour with me, O Hero; I will tell thee the reason.

" Entering the forest with thy brother, armed with bows and arrows, it may well be that, on seeing the titans, thou wilt loose thy shafts! As the proximity of faggots increases the violence of the fire, even so does the possession of a bow increase the strength and energy of a warrior!

" In former times, O Long-armed Prince, in a sacred forest frequented by deer and birds, dwelt a devout and virtuous ascetic. With the intention of obstructing his austerities, Indra, the Lord of Sachi, in the guise of a warrior, went to that hermitage, sword in hand. In this retreat, he left that excellent sword, requesting the sage, engaged in pious acts, to guard it as a trust. Receiving that weapon, he, fully conscious of the charge laid upon him, ranged the forest, carefully watching over the sword entrusted to him. Intent on preserving it, he ventured nowhere without that sword, either to gather fruit and roots or for other reasons. Constantly bearing this weapon and neglecting his penances, by degrees, that ascetic developed warlike inclinations. In time that foolish hermit, carrying the sword, began to enjoy nothing so much as violence and, losing his sobriety, was led astray and fell into hell.

" This, formerly, was the result of bearing arms! As contact with fire works change in a piece of wood, so the carrying of arms works alteration in the mind of him who carries them.

"From affection and reverence for thee, I draw thine attention to this matter. I do not venture to instruct thee. Equipped with bows as thou art, I ask thee to renounce all thought of slaying the titans in the Dandaka Forest without provocation. O Warrior! the world looks askance on those who strike without cause. It is the duty of warriors to protect those of subdued soul who are in peril. The bearing of arms and retirement to the forest, practice of war and the exercise of asceticism are opposed to each other; let us therefore honour the moral code that pertains to peace. Murderous thoughts, inspired by desire for gain, are born of the handling of weapons. When thou dost return to Ayodhya, thou wilt be able to take up the duties of a warrior once more. The joy of my mother and father-in-law will be complete, if during the renunciation of thy kingdom, thou dost lead the life of an ascetic. Thus happiness accrues to one who discharges his duty; through performance of one's duty, the whole world is conquered, duty constituting its very marrow. It is by the complete negation of self that the saints acquired bliss; happiness is not born of pleasure!

"O My Friend, with a pure heart fulfil thy duty in solitude; thou art conversant with the nature of the Three Worlds.

"It is through feminine weakness that I speak thus, for who would dare to instruct thee in thy duty? Having reflected carefully on what I have said, do what thou considerest best without further delay!"

CHAPTER 10

Rama reminds Sita of his Promise to the Ascetics

HEARING Vaidehi's speech, inspired by conjugal tenderness, Rama, his energy enhanced, replied to the daughter of Janaka, saying:—

"O Noble Lady, it is in appropriate words, dictated by thine affection, that thou hast sought to instruct me in the duties of my caste.

"How shall I answer thee, O Princess? Thou thyself hast said: 'Warriors bear their bows, so that the word "oppression" may not be heard on earth.' O Sita, it is on account of those ascetics of severe penances, beset with perils in the Dandaka Forest, who have sought my protection, that I have come hither. Dwelling in the forest at all times, where they live on fruit and roots, they are unable to enjoy a peaceful existence on account of the titans, O Timid Lady. These hermits of the Dandaka Forest are devoured by those terrible demons, who live on human flesh. 'Come to our aid' was the cry of those excellent Twice-born, and when I heard those words falling from their lips, I promised to obey them and answered 'Fear not'! It was a source of the greatest distress to me to see them kneeling at my feet, when it was I who should have been touching theirs."

"'What do you desire of me?', I enquired of that assembly of the Twice-born, whereupon, drawing near, they spoke the following words:—

"'In the Dandaka Forest, innumerable demons, assuming different forms, torment us cruelly. O Rama, do thou protect us! The time of the Homa sacrifice and the days of the full moon have come, O Irreproachable Prince! Thou art the sure refuge of all the saints and ascetics who harassed by the titans seek thy protection. By the power of our asceticism it were easy for us to destroy these Rangers of the Night, but we are loath to lose the fruits of austerity, earned over a long period.

"'Prolonged penance is subject to innumerable hindrances, and is exceedingly hard, O Rama! For this reason we refrain from pronouncing a curse on these demons, though they devour us. Tormented thus by the titans who frequent the Dandaka Forest, we implore thee and thy brother to protect us; thou art our support.'"

"Hearing these words, I promised my protection to the sages of the Dandaka Forest, O Daughter of Janaka!

"As long as I live, therefore, I cannot violate the promise given to the ascetics.

"I may yield up my life or even thee, O Sita, as well as Lakshmana, but I cannot be false to a vow made to brahmins.

"Even had I not promised them anything, O Vaidehi, it is my bounden duty to protect the sages; how much more so now!

"I am pleased with thee, O Sita, for one does not offer advice to those one does not love. Thy words are worthy of thee, O Beautiful One. By pursuing the path of duty thou hast become dearer to me than life itself."

Having spoken thus to Sita, the daughter of the King of Mithila, the magnanimous Rama, carrying his bow, continued to roam through those ravishing solitudes with Lakshmana.

CHAPTER II

Rama visits the different Retreats and hears of Agastya

WALKING ahead, Rama was followed by Sita, while behind her came Lakshmana, bow in hand. With Sita, they proceeded further, seeing many hills and plains, woods and enchanting rivers with geese and cranes frequenting their banks and pools covered with lotuses, abounding in waterfowl, and herds of deer, horned buffaloes in rut, bears and elephants, the destroyers of trees.

Having travelled a great distance, they beheld, as the sun was setting, a marvellous lake, some four miles in length, carpeted with lotus and water-lily blooms, graced with herds of wild elephants and abounding in geese, swans and teal.

From this enchanting lake of tranquil waters, the sound of singing and musical instruments could be heard, yet no one was visible there. Captivated, Rama and Lakshmana began to question a sage named Dharmabhrit, saying:—

"O Great Ascetic, this wonderful music, heard by us all, moves us strangely; what can it be? Be gracious enough to tell us."

Thus questioned by Raghava, the magnanimous sage began at once to relate the history of that magic lake.

He said:—"This lake, called Panchapsara,[1] is always filled

[1] Panchapsara—'Lake of Five Apsaras!'

with water and was created by the penances of the Sage Mandarkini.

" Practising a rigid asceticism, this great sage, lying in water for thousands of years, lived on air alone! Then the Gods with Agni at their head became agitated and, coming together, said to each other :—' This sage aspires to our state!' Thus did they speak, their minds full of apprehension.

" Then all the Gods, in order to destroy the merit of the sage acquired through his penances, sent down five of the most beautiful nymphs, whose complexion resembled lightning and, though the ascetic was fully conversant with what was good and evil, he was captivated by those nymphs and fell under the sway of the God of Love.

" These five nymphs became the wives of that sage, who constructed a secret dwelling in the lake for them. There they live happily, bringing delight to the ascetic, who by virtue of his penances has become youthful. They pass their time in dalliance and this is the cause of the entrancing music mingling with the tinkling of their ornaments."

Such was the strange tale recounted by that sage of pure soul.

Conversing thus, the illustrious Rama and his brother visited the circle of hermitages, strewn with kusha grass and bark, which were resplendent with the lustre of the brahmins. Accompanied by Vaidehi and Lakshmana, the Descendant of Raghu, Kakutstha penetrated into the blessed circle of those Lions among Men.

Received with delight and honoured by those great rishis, Rama roamed through the silent woods, that great warrior sojourning with the ascetics, sometimes for ten months, sometimes for a year, sometimes for four months or five or six months, sometimes for many months or a month and a half only, sometimes three months and sometimes eight. In this way, engaged in innocent pastimes, ten years passed away.

Having visited all the retreats of the ascetics, Rama returned to Sutikshna's hermitage and, receiving the homage of the sages, that Subduer of his Foes remained there awhile.

One day, as he sat at the feet of the ascetic, in all humility he addressed him, saying :—

" O Blessed One, I have heard that Agastya, that foremost

of sages, dwells in this forest, but it is so vast, that I do not know where his hermitage is to be found. Where does the retreat of that sagacious Rishi lie? By thy favour, O Blessed Lord, I, my younger brother and Sita wish to pay our respects to him."

Hearing the words of the virtuous Rama, that illustrious sage, Sutikshna, well pleased, answered the son of Dasaratha, saying:—

"It was my intention to speak of this to thee and Lakshmana, O Raghava and say: 'Do thou, with Sita, seek out Agastya.' Now thou thyself hast proposed it and it is well. I will now tell thee, O Rama, where that great Ascetic Agastya dwells.

"My Child, four miles from here to the south, thou wilt come to the hermitage of the brother of Agastya, situated in a fertile plain, covered with charming groves of fig, abounding in fruit and flowers, where the song of many birds may be heard. Innumerable lakes of tranquil water, carpeted by lotuses and frequented by swans, ducks and geese add to its beauty. Having passed the night there, do thou at dawn follow the path, through a glade, to the south and there thou shalt come upon Agastya's retreat, at four miles distance, in an enchanting spot planted with lovely trees. This place will charm Vaidehi as well as Lakshmana and thee, for this corner of the forest shaded by innumerable trees, is ravishing.

"Shouldst thou desire to visit that great ascetic, Agastya, then set out to-day, O Prince of Surpassing Wisdom."

At these words, Rama with Lakshmana and Sita, having made obeisance to Sutikshna, set out to seek the Sage Agastya.

Enjoying the marvellous woods and hills, which resembled a mass of clouds, and the lakes and rivers to be seen on the way, Rama proceeded quickly along the path pointed out by the sage Sutikshna, and full of delight that magnanimous One said to Lakshmana:—

"Assuredly, this must be the retreat of the illustrious brother of Agastya, that sage of blessed karma, that we now behold. Observe how along the woodland ride thousands of trees, bowed with the weight of their fruit and flowers, can be seen, and the pungent odour of ripe figs is borne on the breeze. Here and there heaps of fire-wood lie, with darbha grass, the colour of lapis lazuli; see also that column of smoke, like a plume of dark cloud, rising in the forest from a fire freshly lit in the hermitage.

" Having performed their ablutions in the sacred ponds, the Twice-born are offering flowers they themselves have gathered. The words spoken by Sutikshna have proved true O Friend. Here indeed is the retreat of Agastya's brother.

" In his desire to be of service to the worlds, by virtue of his austerities that great sage overcame death and set apart this quarter as a place of refuge.

" Here formerly the cruel demons Vatapi and Ilvala lived, two great asuras who together conceived a plan for slaying the brahmins.

" Assuming the form of a sage, the pitiless Ilvala, using the sanskrita language, invited the ascetics to partake of a feast. Preparing his brother disguised as a ram in a dish, he fed the Twice-born, according to traditional rites. When the ascetics had eaten, Ilvala cried out in a loud voice :—' O Vatapi, come forth.'

" At the sound of his voice, Vatapi, bleating like a ram, tearing the bodies of the ascetics, emerged.

" Thus thousands of brahmins were slain by those devourers of human flesh, who changed their shape at will and were full of deceit.

" At the request of the Gods, the great Rishi Agastya went to the feast and ate up the huge asura, after which Ilvala said:—' It is well,' and offering the guest water to wash his hands, cried out :—' Come forth O Vatapi ! '

" But as this Slayer of Ascetics was speaking thus, Agastya, that excellent sage, breaking into laughter, said to him :—

" ' How can that demon come forth, since I have consumed him ? Thy brother in the shape of a ram, has entered the abode of Yama.'

" Hearing that his brother was dead, the demon in anger rushed at the ascetic, hurling himself on that Indra of the Twice-born, but the sage, blazing with spiritual power, by a single glance consumed him, and he perished.

" This is the hermitage, beautified by lakes and groves, belonging to the brother of that sage, who in compassion for the ascetics performed that arduous feat."

While Rama was speaking thus to Saumitri, the sun set behind the mountain and the night drew on; duly performing his evening devotions, he entered the hermitage and offered obeisance to the ascetic.

Warmly received by that blessed one, Raghava passed the night there, having partaken of fruit and roots and, when morning came and the disc of the sun was visible, he paid homage to the brother of Agastya, saying :—

" Reverent Sir, I salute thee and thank thee for the peaceful night I have passed here, I will now go and seek out my spiritual preceptor, thine elder brother."

" So be it," replied the sage, whereupon the descendant of Raghu went along the path pointed out to him, enjoying the forest with the innumerable Nirvara, Panasa, Sala, Vanjula, Tinisha, Shiribilwa, Madhuka, Bilwa and Tinduka trees in full flower entwined with blossoming creepers, and trees ripped by the trunks of elephants, where monkeys disported themselves and which resounded to the warbling of a myriad birds.

Then the lotus-eyed Rama said to the valiant and heroic Lakshmana, who was following him :—

" From the glossy foliage of the trees and the tameness of the deer and the birds, we are undoubtedly not far distant from the retreat of that great and pure-souled Rishi of virtuous practices.

" This hermitage that removes all weariness, belonging to the Sage Agastya, well known among men for his virtue, with its groves filled with a rare fragrance, its robes of bark and garlands hanging here and there, frequented by herds of tame deer, the leafy boughs pervaded by countless birds, can now be seen by us.

" Having overcome Mrityu by his power, in his desire to do good to the whole world, he created this inviolate refuge in the south, which is eschewed by demons who fear to lay it waste.

" From the day that this region was rendered habitable by that virtuous ascetic, the demons have ceased to exercise their hatred and cruelty here. This fortunate land of the South, famed in the Three Worlds, associated with the name of that blessed sage, is no longer haunted by those wicked beings.

"The mountain Vindhya, foremost of its kind, that threatened to intercept the rays of the sun, dared not grow higher, submitting to Agastya's command and this enchanting retreat, frequented by deer, belongs to that long-lived one of exalted achievement. The virtuous Agastya, honoured by men, who is ever engaged in the welfare of all beings, will on our arrival accord us a great welcome.

"I wish to pay homage to that great ascetic personally and to pass the rest of mine exile in the forest with him, O Mild One! Here the Gods, Gandharvas, Siddhas and the great Sages, who live on a bare subsistence, constantly pay homage to the Sage Agastya, but dishonest, cruel, wicked and perverse men are not able to remain in the presence of that great ascetic.

"The Immortals, however, the Yakshas and those of the Serpent Race, the great Rishis also, dedicated to virtuous living, dwell here, and fixed in holiness, those exalted beings, discarding their worn-out bodies, assuming new ones, ascend to heaven in chariots resembling the sun.

"There the Gods fulfil the desires of the virtuous, granting them immortality, divine powers and every degree of majesty.

"We have now come to the hermitage, O Saumitri, do thou enter it and announce my arrival with Sita, to the Rishi."

CHAPTER 12

Agastya receives Rama into his Hermitage

Having entered the hermitage, Lakshmana, the younger brother of Raghava, approached a disciple of Agastya and said to him :—

"The eldest son of King Dasaratha, the illustrious Rama, has come with his consort, Sita, to pay homage to the sage. I am his younger brother, obedient and devoted to him and his humble servant; perchance thou hast heard of us?

"We have penetrated into this dangerous forest at the command of our royal sire. We three desire to see the blessed One, do thou make it known to him."

Hearing Lakshmana's words, the disciple said :—" So be it ! " and went to inform Agastya at the place where the sacred fire burned. With joined palms approaching that Foremost of Munis whose austerities had rendered him invincible, he conveyed the news of Rama's arrival to him.

In conformity with Lakshmana's words, the cherished disciple of Agastya said :—" The two sons of King Dasaratha, Rama and Lakshmana, have come to the hermitage with Sita. These two warriors, Conquerors of their Foes, have come to look on thee and to offer their services ; be gracious enough to instruct me in what should now be done ! "

Having heard from his disciple that Rama, followed by Lakshmana and the auspicious Vaidehi, were waiting, Agastya answered :—" How fortunate that after so long a time Rama has come to see me to-day. It was ever the desire of my heart to behold that great prince. Bid Rama welcome and ask him to enter together with his consort and Lakshmana who accompanies him ; let them be brought into my presence ; why has this not already been done ? "

Thus addressed by that mighty muni, learned in the spiritual tradition, the disciple saluted him with joined palms and said : " Be it so ! " Thereafter, issuing from the hermitage, he approached Lakshmana and addressed him, saying :— " Which of you is Rama? Let him enter and approach the sage."

Thereupon Lakshmana, moving nearer to the gateway of the hermitage, pointed out Rama and Sita, the daughter of Janaka, to him, and the disciple humbly communicated Rishi Agastya's message, conducting Rama into the hermitage.

Rama, accompanied by Sita and Lakshmana, entering the enclosure, which was filled with tame deer, observed the altars set up to Brahma and Agni and also the sacred places dedicated to Vishnu, Mahendra, Vivaswat, Soma, Bhaga, Kuvera, Dhatar and Vidhatar, Vayu, the God who holds the Thread in his hand,[1] the magnanimous Varuna, Gayatri, the Vasus, the Nagas, Garuda, Karttikeya and Dharma.

Escorted by the disciple, he saw all these and suddenly beheld the great sage himself. Seeing him at the head of the ascetics, blazing with the lustre acquired by the practice of

[1] Yama—The God of Death.

austerities, the valiant Rama said to Lakshmana, the increaser of his delight :—

" O Lakshmana, behold that blessed ascetic, Agastya, leaving the place of sacrifice ; it is with pride that I bow before that treasury of renunciation."

Speaking thus of Agastya, who shone like the sun, whilst he advanced towards him, the joy of the House of Raghu took hold of his feet and paid obeisance to him. Having saluted him, the virtuous Rama stood before him with joined palms, in company with Videha's daughter and Saumitri.

Thereafter, embracing Kakutstha and honouring him with water and a seat, questioning him as to his welfare, the saint bade him welcome according to the tradition of the forest. Offering oblations into the fire, and presenting his guests with the arghya, that ascetic entertained them with food and placing himself at the side of Rama, who, conversant with his duty, sat with joined palms, said to him :—

" O Prince, an ascetic who fails to offer proper hospitality will feed on his own flesh in the other world, as does one who bears false witness. O Lord of the Universe, Observer of Thy Duty, Warrior of the Great Car, who art worthy of all honour and respect, thou art come at last and art my beloved guest."

With these words, the Sage Agastya, as a symbol of homage, offered Rama fruits, roots, flowers, water and other things in great profusion, and said to him :—

" Here is a celestial and powerful bow, encrusted with gold and diamonds, that belonged to Vishnu. O Tiger among Men, it is the creation of Vishwakarma.

" Here also is the Brahmadatta dart, which is infallible and resembles the sun ; it is pre-eminent and was given to me by Mahendra ; here also are these two inexhaustible quivers, filled with sharp arrows that blaze like torches and here a mighty silver scabbard and a sword decorated with gold.

" With this bow, O Rama, Vishnu slew the great asura in battle and formerly acquired inexpressible glory amongst the dwellers in the celestial regions.

" This bow, these two quivers, the dart and the sword, pledges of victory, do thou accept, O Proud Warrior, and bear them as Vajradhara the thunderbolt."

Thus speaking, the illustrious and fortunate Agastya gave to Rama the whole panoply of weapons belonging to the mighty Vishnu, and once more addressed him :—

CHAPTER 13

Rama goes to Panchavati on the advice of Agastya

" O Rama, may happiness attend thee ! O Lakshmana, I am pleased with thee that with Sita thou hast come hither to pay me homage. Undoubtedly the long journey will have wearied you both, as also Maithili, whose sighs betray it.

" That youthful lady, who is unaccustomed to exertion, has come to the forest out of love for her lord, though the way is beset with difficulties ; therefore, O Rama, do that which will give her pleasure.

" Since the beginning of time, O Joy of the House of Raghu, it has been woman's nature to cling to a man in prosperity and abandon him in adversity. Swift as lightning in thought, sharp as a sword in speech, her moods comparable to an eagle's flight, such is woman ! But thy consort is wholly free from these defects, she is worthy of praise and is the foremost of those devoted to their lord ; amongst the Gods she is known as a second Arundhati. That region will be renowned where thou, Saumitri and this princess have sojourned, O Conqueror of Thy Foes."

Thus did the sage address Raghava, who, with joined palms, in humble accents, answered that ascetic who shone like a flame, saying :—

" I am overwhelmed with favour, since the foremost among ascetics is gratified with me, as also with my brother and my consort who accompany me.

" Do thou direct me to a place abounding in trees, and with abundant water, where we can dwell in peace and happiness."

Hearing Rama's words, that excellent and magnanimous sage, reflecting an instant, made this judicious reply :—

" My Dear Son, at eight miles distance from here, is a spot

known by the name of Panchavati, where roots, fruit and water abound and where there are many deer. Go thither and with Saumitri establish a hermitage, living there happily and carrying out the behests of thy sire.

"By the power of my penance and by virtue of the affection I bore for King Dasaratha, I am acquainted with thy history, O Irreproachable Prince. Though thou hast promised to remain with me in these solitudes, yet mine austerities have revealed to me the true desires of thine heart. Therefore I say to thee again: 'Seek out Panchavati!' It is an enchanting woodland, that will delight Maithili. That place, worthy of all praise, is not far from here, O Raghava, and is close to the Godaveri river; Sita will be happy there. Abounding in roots, fruit and every kind of bird, it is set apart, O Long-armed Hero, and is lovely, delightful and sacred. Thou of righteous ways, who art ever active and able to defend all beings, wilt dwell there, O Rama, in order to protect the ascetics.

To the north of the Madhuka woods, which thou art able to see from here, O Hero, thou wilt find a grove of fig trees. Scale the mountain ridges, not far distant, and thou shalt come upon the renowned Panchavati, lying there with its flowering woods."

Hearing the words of the Sage Agastya, Rama, accompanied by Saumitri, took leave of that illustrious ascetic, and having circumambulated him, paid homage to his feet and with his permission departed towards the solitudes of Panchavati, accompanied by Sita.

The two princes, invincible in combat, taking up their bows and strapping on their quivers, resolutely followed the path to Panchavati, pointed out by the great sage.

CHAPTER 14

Jatayu reveals his Lineage to Rama

As he was proceeding to Panchavati, that descendant of Raghu observed a large and powerful vulture. Seeing that bird in the woods, the two illustrious princes, Rama and Lakshmana, thinking him to be a demon in another form, said to him: "Who art thou?"

Then, in gentle caressing tones, the bird, as though addressing one dear to him, answered, saying: "Dear Child, know me to be the friend of thy sire!"

In deference to this relationship, Raghava paid obeisance to him, and enquired of him concerning his name and lineage, and he, hearing Rama's words, said:—

"In a former age there existed the Prajapatis, whom I will enumerate—the first of them was Kardama and immediately succeeding him was Vikrita, then came Shesha and Samshraya, the father of many powerful sons, thereafter came Sthanu, Marichi, Atri, Kratu who was full of energy, Poulastya, Angira, Pracheta, Pulaha and Daksha followed by Vivaswat and Arishtanemi; O Raghava, the renowned Kashyapa was the last of these. O Hero of Infinite Renown, we have heard that Prajapati Daksha had sixty lovely and illustrious daughters. Kashyapa wedded eight of these damsels of elegant waist, Aditi, Diti, Kalika, Tamra, Krodhavasa, Manu and Anila and well pleased, said to them: 'Do ye all beget sons, like unto myself, who shall be Lords of the Three Worlds.'

"Thereupon Aditi consented, O Rama, as did Diti, Danu and Kalika, but the others refused.

"Aditi became the mother of the Thirty-three Immortals. O My Son, Diti gave birth to the illustrious Daityas; it was to them that the earth with its seas and forests belonged.

"Danu gave birth to a son named Ashagriva, O Subduer of thy Foes, and Kalika gave birth to Naraka and Kalaka; and the five famous daughters, Kraunchi, Bhasi, Shyeni, Dhritarashtri and Shuki were produced by Tamra.

"Kraunchi begot the owls and Bhasi the vultures; Shyeni was the mother of the hawks and eagles possessed of great energy; Dhritarashtri, of swans, flamingoes and water-fowl.

"The beautiful Shuki begot Nata whose daughter was Vinata. O Rama, Krodhavasa brought forth ten daughters: Mrigi, Mrigimanda, Hari, Bhadramada, Matangi, Sharduli, Sheveta, Surabhi and Surasa, who were all endowed with beauty; finally Kadruka was born.

" O First of Men, Mrigi became the mother of all the deer ; Mrigamanda begot bears, buffaloes and yaks.

" Bhadramada had a daughter named Iravati who was the mother of Airavata, who is the guardian of the world.

" Hari gave birth to powerful lions and monkeys, lovers of the forest ; Sharduli begot chimpanzees and tigers. Of Matangi were born elephants, O Kakutstha, O Best of Men ! Shiveta gave birth to the elephants who support the earth.

" Two daughters were born of the Goddess Surabhi : Rohini, and the auspicious Gandharvi.

" Rohini produced cows, and Gandharvi brought forth horses. Sarasa was the mother of the hooded serpents, O Rama, and Kadru gave birth to all other snakes.

" Manu, wife of the magnanimous Kashyapa, gave birth to men, Brahmins Kshattriyas, Vaisyas and Shudras, O Lion amongst Men.

" According to tradition, from her mouth were born the Brahmins, from her breasts the Kshattriyas, from her thighs the Vaishyas and from her feet the Shudras.

" All the trees with succulent fruits were born of Anala.

" Vinata, whose grandmother was Shuki, herself begot Kadru and her sister, Surasa.

" Of Kadru were born thousands of serpents, the supporters of the earth, and Vinata had two sons, Garuda and Aruna.

" Know that I was born of Aruna, as also was Sampati, my elder brother. My name is Jatayu, the descendant of Shyeni, O Subduer of Thine Enemies.

" O My dear Child, I will take up my abode in thy vicinity, if thou so desire it, and keep watch over Sita, whilst thou art away with Lakshmana."

Raghava, having often heard of his father's friendship with the vulture, was filled with delight, and embraced him with affection, paying obeisance to him.

Having requested that powerful bird to keep watch over Sita, he went on towards Panchavati with him, accompanied by Lakshmana, firmly resolving to destroy his enemies and duly observing his daily devotions.

CHAPTER 15

Rama takes up his Abode in Panchavati

WHEN he had reached Panchavati, frequented by wild beasts and deer, Rama said to his brother Lakshmana, who was burning with energy :—

" O Dear One, we have reached the place described by the sage, this woodland of flowering trees, the much-loved Panchavati. O Thou who art full of resource, look about on every side and ascertain in which spot it is fitting for us to construct our hermitage. Let it be in the vicinity of a pool where the charm of the forest and the water adds to its beauty, where thou, Sita and I, may dwell in peace, where flowers, fuel and kusha grass abound."

Hearing the words of Rama, the offspring of Kakutstha, Lakshmana, with joined palms, in the presence of Sita, answered him :—

" Wert thou to live a hundred years, I should still be thy servant, O Kakutstha ! Do thou select some place favoured by thee and command me to build a retreat."

Well pleased with Lakshmana's compliance, that illustrious hero, looking here and there, chose a site which combined every advantage, and on that spot, taking the hand of Saumitri in his, said :—

" Here is a level place that is pleasant and surrounded by trees ; it is here that I desire thee to construct a retreat. Nearby is an enchanting river, rendered beautiful by lotuses, bright as the sun, exhaling a delicious fragrance, as described to me by that Rishi of pure soul, Agastya. This is the delightful river Godaveri, bordered with flowering trees, teeming with swans and waterfowl, geese enhancing its beauty and thronged with herds of deer, neither too near nor too far away, that come here to drink.

" And re-echoing to the cry of peacocks, lovely hills covered with blossoming trees containing many a cave, resembled great elephants with huge howdahs embroidered in gold, silver and copper, that are studded here and there with tiny mirrors.

"Sala, Tala, Tamala, Kharjura, Panasa, Nivara, Tinisha and Punnaga trees are their decoration, while Cuta, Ashoka, Tilaka, Ketaka and Champaka entwined with flowering creepers and plants, abound as also Syandana, Chandana, Nipa, Panasa, Lakuka, Dhara, Ashwakarna, Khadira, Shami, Tinduka and Patala trees. In this sacred place, this enchanting spot filled with deer and birds, let us dwell with Jatayu, O Saumitri."

Thus addressed by his brother Rama, Lakshmana, Slayer of Hostile Warriors, endowed with great energy, built him a retreat there without delay and constructed a spacious hut with walls of mud, supported by strong stakes made of long graceful bamboos, thatched with boughs of the Shami tree.

Creepers, kusha and sarpat grass strengthened it, while reeds and leaves were also used for the roof, its floor being well levelled.

Then the fortunate Lakshmana, having constructed that excellent hut, lovely to behold, went to the river Godaveri, and after bathing, gathered lotuses and fruit, returning to the hermitage to offer the flowers there and perform those traditional rites proper to the peace of that dwelling, thereafter leading Rama to the hut he had set up.

Seeing that charming retreat and the thatched hut, Raghava, who was accompanied by Sita, experienced intense delight.

Highly gratified, he pressed Lakshmana to his heart and in a voice full of tenderness and feeling, said to him :—

"I am pleased with thee; thou hast accomplished a great feat, O My Brother, for which as a token of satisfaction I now embrace thee. Whilst thou dost still live, with thy zeal, thy devotion and thy virtue, O Lakshmana, our illustrious sire is not dead."

Having spoken thus to Lakshmana, Raghava, the source of others prosperity, began to dwell happily in that region abounding in fruit. And ministered to by Sita and Lakshmana, that illustrious One lived there with them for some time, like the Gods in heaven.

CHAPTER 16

Description of Winter by Lakshmana

WHILST the magnanimous Rama was sojourning there, autumn passed away and the winter season set in.

One day at dawn, the issue of the House of Raghu went to the enchanting river Godaveri to perform his ablutions and the valiant Saumitri, pitcher in hand, following humbly with Sita, addressed him, saying :—

" Now that season dear to thee has come, O Amiable Prince, during which the whole year seems to clothe itself in splendour ! The ground is covered with frost and water is no longer pleasant to drink.

" Having offered ripened grain to the Pitris and the Gods, men are purified of their sins, their sacrifices having been made at the proper season. Desirous of the necessities of life, all are now abundantly supplied with milk and butter.

" Kings, dreaming of conquest, set out on their campaigns. The sun veering towards the southern region, beloved of Antaka, causes the north to resemble a woman, whose tilak mark is effaced. The Himavat Mountain, covered with snow, justly bears its name. Those clear days, when one seeks the sun and flees from shade and damp, are exceedingly pleasant, but now there is only faint sunshine, constant frost, piercing cold and deep snow. The long cold nights are with us, when it is no longer possible to lie in the open, and the Pushya star which served as a beacon is now obscured in the snow-laden air. The moon, that draws its brilliance from the sun, no longer shines, and its frozen disc is dim, like a mirror tarnished by the breath ; wrinkled by the cold, that orb's surface, though at the full, no longer sends forth its rays, like Sita, when her complexion, tanned by the sun, loses its radiance.

" Now that the snow is blended with its breath the west wind is icy, and the mornings are bitingly cold. The woods are shrouded in mist and the fields of barley and wheat, covered in rime, sparkle in the rising sun, while herons and cranes call in chorus. Fields of rice with ears resembling Kharjura flowers bend gracefully under the weight of the grain.

" With its rays scarcely penetrating the snow-laden clouds, the sun, long after it has risen, resembles the moon, but gradually gaining strength during the morning hours, rejoices the heart at noon, its rays shedding a pale beauty on the earth causing the woodland rides, covered with grass and drenched with dew, to sparkle.

" The wild elephant, suffering from extreme thirst, withdraws its trunk suddenly on coming in contact with the frozen water, and the waterfowl, standing on the banks, dare not enter the stream, like unto cowardly warriors, fearful of setting foot on the battlefield.

" Enveloped in dew at evening and wreathed in cold grey mist at dawn, the trees, bereft of flowers, seem to sleep. Streams are shrouded in fog and the cranes, their plumage hidden under the snow, can only be distinguished by their cries; the sands on the banks too are wet with snow.

" On account of the weakness of the sun's rays, the water remains in the hollows of hard rocks after the fall of snow and tastes sweet. The lotuses are nipped by frost, their stamens dried up, their petals fallen, only the stalks remaining, and in the grip of the bitter cold have lost all their beauty.

" O Lion among Men, at this season, in devotion to thee, the unfortunate and faithful Bharata is undergoing penance in the city. Renouncing kingdom, pomp and every pleasure, practising austerity, he gives himself up to fasting and restraint, and at this very hour is certainly making his way to the river Sarayu surrounded by his ministers in order to perform his ablutions.

" Brought up in luxury, exceedingly frail, tormented by the cold, how, in the last hour of the night, is he able to endure the icy water?

" With his large eyes resembling lotus petals, his dark skin and depressed navel, that great and virtuous Bharata, who is dutiful, truthful, restrained, his senses fully controlled, of sweet speech and gentle, that long-armed hero, the subduer of his foes, renouncing every pleasure, is wholly devoted to thee, O Rama.

" My Brother, the magnanimous Bharata, by living as if banished to the forest, in imitation of thee resident there, has conquered heaven, O Rama.

" It is said that a man resembles his mother and not his father. If it be so, how can a woman as cruel as Kaikeyi be his mother ? "

Thus spoke the virtuous Lakshmana in brotherly affection, but Rama, unable to brook their mother being blamed, answered him, saying :—

" She who occupies the second place among the queens, O My Friend, should not be disparaged in any way whatsoever. Do thou continue to speak of Bharata, the protector of the House of Ikshwaku.

" Though I have determined to dwell in the forest, yet my love for Bharata shakes my resolve and causes me to waver anew. I recollect his gentle and affectionate words well, sweet as amrita, delighting the soul. O when shall I be re-united with the magnanimous Bharata and the valiant Shatrughna, together with thee, O Joy of the House of Raghu? "

Lamenting thus, Kakutstha came to the Godaveri river, where he, his younger brother and Sita performed their ablutions ; then having offered water to the Gods and the Pitris, those sinless ones worshipped the rising sun and the Lord Narayana, thus purifying themselves.

Thereafter, Rama, accompanied by Sita and Lakshmana, appeared beautiful, resembling the Lord Shiva accompanied by Nandi and the Daughter of the Mountains.[1]

CHAPTER 17

The arrival of Shurpanakha at the Hermitage

HAVING bathed in the Godaveri river, Rama, Sita and Lakshmana left its banks and returned to the hermitage. On reaching their retreat, Raghava with Lakshmana performed their morning devotions and entered the leaf-thatched hut. In the hut,

[1] Girija, a name of Parvati.

that long-armed hero with Sita at his side dwelt happily, honoured by the great Rishis, and shone like the moon accompanied by the Chitra star.

One day, while Rama was reciting the traditional texts, a female demon chanced to pass that way, by name Shurpanakha who was the sister of Ravana.

Approaching Rama, she observed that he resembled a God, with his radiant countenance, his long arms, his large eyes like unto lotus petals, his majestic gait resembling an elephant's, matted locks crowning his head; youthful, full of valour, bearing the marks of royalty, his colour that of the blue lotus and alluring as the God of Love himself.

Beholding that hero, the equal of Indra, the Rakshasi was overwhelmed with desire. Rama was handsome, she hideous; his waist was slender, hers thick and heavy; he had large eyes, hers squinted; his locks were beautiful, hers were red; his whole appearance was pleasing, hers repellent. Rama's voice was sonorous, hers strident; he was fair and youthful, she old and haggard; he was amiable, she sullen; he was self-controlled, she unruly; he was captivating, she odious.

Consumed with passion, the Rakshasi said to Rama :—

" With thy matted locks and ascetic guise, bearing bow and arrows, why hast thou, accompanied by thy consort, come to these woods, which are frequented by demons? What is the purpose of thy journey? "

Hearing the words of the Rakshasi, Shurpanakha, that hero, the Scourge of his Foes, with perfect candour began to relate all.

He said :—" There was a king named Dasaratha, who was as powerful as a God. I am his eldest son, known among men as Rama; this is my younger brother, Lakshmana, my faithful companion, and this, my consort, the illustrious Sita, daughter of the King of Videha.

" Bound by the will of my sire and in order to carry out my duty, I have come to dwell in the forest.

" But now I wish to know who thy father is, who thou art, and what thy race? To judge by thy charms, thou art a Rakshasi! Tell me truly, what has brought thee hither? "

Hearing the words of Rama, the Rakshasi, tormented by the pangs of love, answered :—

"Hear O Rama and I will tell thee the truth! I am Shurpanakha, a Rakshasi, who can change her form at will. I wander about in the forest, striking terror in the hearts of all beings. My brothers are Ravana, of whom thou hast doubtless heard, and the powerful and somnolent Kumbhakarna, the virtuous Bibishana a stranger to our practices, and two others famed for their martial qualities, Khara and Dushana.

"I, who am more powerful than they, having seen thee, O Rama, wish to unite myself with thee, O Lord, O First of Men!

"I am endowed with power and able to range at will by thought alone; therefore do thou become my master. What is Sita to thee?

"Deformed, without beauty, she is not worthy of thee, whereas I should prove a well-matched partner, my beauty equal to thine own; do thou look on me as thy consort. This unsightly, grim-visaged human female, of lean abdomen, will be devoured by me this day in thy presence, together with that brother of thine.

"Thou and I shall wander on the summit of the mountains and through the forests together, exploring the whole region of Dandaka, according to thy whim."

Speaking thus, the Rakshasi threw impassioned glances at Rama, who, smiling, made the following astute reply.

CHAPTER 18

The Mutilation of Shurpanakha

SMILING a little, Rama, in gently mocking tones, answered Shurpanakha, who had been caught in the noose of love, saying:—

"I am already wedded and this is my beloved consort; the rivalry between co-wives would prove unbearable! My younger brother however who is of a happy disposition, of agreeable appearance, virtuous and chaste, is called Lakshmana and is full of vigour. He has not yet experienced the joys of a wife's company and desires a consort. He is youthful and attractive and would therefore be a fitting husband for thee. Take my brother as thy lord, O Lady of large eyes and lovely hips, and enjoy him without a rival, as Mount Meru, the sunlight."

Hearing these words, the Rakshasi, blinded by passion, leaving Rama, at once addressed Lakshmana, saying :—

" My beauty renders me a worthy wife for thee; therefore come and we will range the Dandaka Forest and mountains happily together."

Thus accosted by the Rakshasi Shurpanakha, Lakshmana, the son of Sumitra, skilled in discourse, smiling, gave this ingenious reply :—

" How canst thou wish to become the wife of a slave, such as I? I am wholly dependent on my noble brother, O Thou whose complexion resembles the lotus, who art pleasing to look upon and chaste? O Lady of large eyes, thou art a paragon, do thou become the consort of that matchless hero. Renouncing that ugly, evil and peevish old woman, whose limbs are deformed, he will certainly devote himself to thee! O Lady of ravishing complexion and lovely limbs, what sensible man would sacrifice that unrivalled beauty of thine for an ordinary woman?"

Thinking Lakshmana's words to be sincere and not understanding his jest, that cruel and misshapen Rakshasi, in the blindness of her passion once more addressed Rama, the Scourge of His Foes, who was seated in the leaf-thatched hut with Sita, and said :—

" Is it for this hideous, evil and peevish woman, who is old and deformed, that thou dost slight me?

" I shall devour her in thy presence to-day, and shall live happily with thee without a rival."

Speaking thus, the Rakshasi, whose eyes blazed like torches, hurled herself in fury on Sita, like a great meteor descending on the planet Rohini.

Then the mighty Rama restrained her, as, like the noose of death, she advanced towards Sita, and in anger addressed Lakshmana, saying :—

" It is unwise to taunt those beings who are vile and cruel,

O Saumitri. Take heed, see, Vaidehi is in danger, O Friend! Do thou maim this hideous demon of protruding belly, who is evil and filled with fury."

The valiant Lakshmana, highly incensed against the Rakshasi, thereupon drew his sword from its scabbard and, in the presence of Rama, cut off her ears and nose.

Her ears and nose severed, Shurpanakha uttered a terrible cry and ran into the forest. Being mutilated, the Rakshasi, streaming with blood, created a terrible uproar, like a tempest in the rainy season and, dripping with blood, that hideous monster, lifting up her arms, plunged howling into the deep woods.

Thereafter the injured Shurpanakha sought out her brother Khara of great might, who, surrounded by a troop of demons, was seated in Janasthana and threw herself on the ground before him, like a meteorite falling from heaven.

Wild with terror and covered with blood, Khara's sister, almost deprived of her senses, related everything concerning Raghava's arrival in the forest with his consort and Lakshmana and the circumstances of her disfigurement.

CHAPTER 19

Shurpanaka tells her brother Khara of her disfigurement

SEEING his sister lying on the ground, mutilated and streaming with blood, the demon, inflamed with anger, said to her :—

"Rise! Tell me why thou art distraught; master thy terror and narrate lucidly, who has disfigured thee in this fashion. Who has dared to touch a black and venomous serpent, stretched peacefully beside him, with his foot? That fool who has thus dealt with thee, is unaware that this day he has swallowed a virulent poison and placed the noose of death round his neck.

"Who has brought thee to this state, thou who art imbued with energy and courage, who art able to range everywhere at will, the rival of Antaka himself? How is it that thou art found in this sorry plight? Amongst Gods, Gandharvas, mighty Sages and other Beings, who is sufficiently powerful to have disfigured thee? I know of none in all the worlds who would dare to provoke me, save it be Mahendra, He of the Thousand Eyes, who overcame the demon Paka. To-day I shall exact the life of thy traducer with my death-dealing arrows, as swans suck out the milky substance that floats on the water.

"Struck down in the fight, mortally wounded by my shafts, whose foaming blood will the earth drink to-day? Whose limbs will the vultures, drawn by my summons, tear apart and devour with delight when they fall under my blows in combat?

"Neither the Gods nor the Gandharvas nor the Pisachas nor the Rakshasas shall be able to save that wretch from my grasp, in that fierce encounter.

"Compose thyself and in tranquillity, tell me who that miscreant is and who, abusing his power, has ill-treated thee thus?"

Having listened to her brother's words, Shurpanakha, beside herself with rage, answered weeping:—

"They are two most handsome and powerful youths, with large eyes resembling lotuses, clad in bark and black antelope skins, living on fruit and roots, their senses under control, practising penance and the brahmacharya vow, the sons of King Dasaratha, two brothers, Rama and Lakshmana, who bear the marks of royalty and resemble the King of the Gandharvas. I am unable to say if they be human beings or Gods. Between them, I saw a young and beautiful damsel of slender waist, adorned with many kinds of jewels, and it is on account of this youthful woman that I am reduced to this plight, like one uncared for and set at naught on account of her infidelity. I wish to drink the blood of this woman and those two youths on the battlefield."

Hearing his sister utter these words, Khara, mad with anger, called on fourteen demons of great strength, equal to Antaka himself, and said to them:—

"Two men furnished with weapons, clad in bark and black antelope skins, have ventured into the inaccessible Dandaka Forest in company with a youthful woman; do ye slay them and also that wretch herself. My sister desires to drink their blood! O Ye Rakshasas, this is my sister's dearest wish, go therefore with all speed and in your great might destroy them. On seeing the two brothers struck down by your blows, my sister will drink their blood on the field, with joy."

Receiving this command, the fourteen demons swiftly departed, accompanied by Shurpanakha, like clouds driven before the wind.

CHAPTER 20

Rama slays the Demons sent by Khara

The cruel Shurpanakha, having reached Raghava's hermitage, pointed out the two brothers and Sita to the demons, and they beheld Rama, full of valour, seated in his hut of leaves, in company with Sita, attended on by Lakshmana.

Seeing Shurpanakha and the demons who accompanied her, the illustrious descendant of the House of Raghu, Rama, said to Lakshmana who was burning with courage :—

" Stay a moment with Sita, O Saumitri, so that I may slay these demons who have followed the Rakshasi."

Hearing the words of Rama, versed in knowledge of the Self, that prudent offshoot of the House of Raghu answered with deference, saying : " Be it so."

Then the righteous Raghava, stretching his great bow, inlaid with gold, addressed those demons, saying :—

" We are the sons of Dasaratha, two brothers, Rama and Lakshmana, who have come with Sita to the inaccessible Dandaka Forest. Living on roots and fruit, with our senses under control, we practice penance and the brahmacharya vow and pass our days in the woods. Why do you seek to do us injury, wretches that you are? It is at the request of the Sages, that I have come hither to castigate you for your evil deeds on the field of battle. Halt where you stand and advance no further! If you desire to live, turn back, O Prowlers of the Night."

At these words, those slayers of brahmins, the fourteen demons, bearing spears in their hands, inflamed with anger, their eyes red, terrible to behold, filled with a fierce exultation, answered Rama, whose fiery glances and sweet speech manifested a courage they had not seen till that hour, and said :—

" For having incurred the displeasure of our master, the most magnanimous Khara, thou art about to fall under our blows in battle. What power hast thou single-handed to slay so many in the field; it is thou who shalt lose thy life to-day in this conflict. Our arms bearing maces, spears and darts will rob thee of thy strength, and thy bow shall fall from thy hand."

Thus speaking, the fourteen demons, brandishing their formidable weapons, hurled themselves on Rama, letting fly their spears at the invincible Raghava, but Kakutstha with as many arrows tipped with gold cut off those fourteen spears. And that illustrious warrior, full of wrath, taking out more arrows, which had been sharpened on stone, seized his bow and placing them on the string, made the titans his target.

Then Raghava, loosing those shafts, as Indra his thunderbolt, speedily pierced the breasts of those demons, and the arrows, all bloody, penetrated the earth like serpents disappearing into an ant heap.

With their breasts pierced by those arrows, the demons fell to the ground, like trees, whose trunks have been severed.

Bathed in blood, mutilated, bereft of life, they lay stretched on the earth, and Shurpanakha, seeing them thus, blind with rage, sped away, to seek out her brother Khara.

Wounded afresh, the blood coagulating like a tree exuding resin, Shurpanakha fell down before her brother and in his presence set up a mighty uproar, wailing and shrieking, raining tears, her features distorted.

Having seen the demons fall on the field of battle, Shurpanakha, returning in all haste to her brother Khara, described their deaths to him in every detail.

CHAPTER 21

Shurpanakha urges Khara to fight Rama

SEEING Shurpanakha beside herself, lying on the ground, having returned without accomplishing her design, Khara addressed her in harsh tones, saying :—

" Have I not placed those valiant demons, living on flesh at thy disposal,. for thy pleasure ? Why dost thou still complain ? They are zealous, loyal and have ever been my trusted servants. Though invincible, even had they to die, they would not disobey me. What is this ? I wish to know the reason why thou art rolling on the earth like a serpent, crying ' O, my Lord '. Why, since I am thy protector, dost thou lament like one abandoned ? Rise, rise ! Let us have no more of these tears and swoonings."

Thus did Khara, her brother, speak to that terrible Rakshasi to comfort her, and she, wiping away her tears, said :—

" When I came hither with my nose and ears severed, drenched in blood, which flowed forth like a river, thou didst console me. To please me, thou didst command fourteen valiant demons to slay the ruthless Rama and Lakshmana. These demons, incensed against Rama, armed with spears and pikes, have fallen victims to his murderous arrows, in combat. Witnessing those skilled warriors, felled to the ground in an instant and Rama's great exploit, I am filled with extreme fear.

" Trembling in every limb, terrified and beside myself, I take refuge in thee once more, O Prowler of the Night, seeing cause for apprehension on every side. Submerged as I am in the infinite ocean of distress, haunted by the crocodiles of affliction and the billows of fear, wilt thou not rescue me ? Under Rama's fiery arrows, the demons, eaters of flesh, who followed me, are lying on the ground.

" If thou hast any pity for me and for these demons, if thou art possessed of the courage and strength to meet Rama in battle, then, O Prowler of the Night, slay this thorn in the side of the demons, who has set up his hermitage in the Dandaka Forest.

" If thou dost not bring about the death of Rama, the Slayer of his Foes, this very day, I shall yield up my life in thy presence, dishonoured. I see clearly, that even supported by thy forces, thou art not able to meet Rama in pitched battle.

" Thou deemest thyself to be a great hero, but thou art not really so, thy prowess exists only in thine own conceited imaginings; therefore do thou leave Janasthana, in all haste, with thy companions, O Stigma of Thy Race ! Do thou return victor in the struggle, for, if thou hast neither the strength, nor the valour to slay these two men, how canst thou remain here ?

" Defeated by Rama's prowess, thou wilt surely die, for he is truly brave, that son of Dasaratha, Rama, and his brother also, who disfigured me is supremely valiant ! "

Thus, in the presence of her brother, did that Rakshasi lament again and again, beating her breast and, overcome with mortification, lost consciousness. Then, after a space coming to her senses, exercised with grief, she continued to cry out and strike her breast with her hands.

CHAPTER 22

Khara and his fourteen thousand Demons march against Rama

LISTENING to Shurpanakha's reproaches, Khara, burning with anger, seated amidst his warriors, answered fiercely :—

" Thy contempt incites me to ungovernable fury, I am beside myself and can no more endure this than it is possible to support salt poured into a wound. I hold Rama to be of no account and regard him as already dead. His offence will bring about his end this day ; therefore restrain thy tears, do not distress thyself further. I shall despatch Rama and his brother to the region of death, and thou, O Rakshasi, shalt to-day drink the warm blood of that one of evil deeds struck down by mine axe."

Overjoyed on hearing these words, falling from her brother's lips, Shurpanakha, in her folly, began to praise Khara, the Foremost of Titans.

First condemned, then extolled by her, Khara called on Dushana, the commander of his army, saying :—

" O Friend, make ready fourteen thousand trained titans who are obedient to my commands, full of martial ardour, who never retreat in battle, who resemble thunder clouds and who revel in cruelty and delight in slaying men.

" Do thou, with all speed, bring my chariot also, with bows, arrows, glittering swords, darts and javelins, that have been well sharpened. I wish to place myself at the head of those magnanimous titans, in order to slay the haughty Rama, O Skilful Warrior ! "

As he was speaking, Dushana harnessed excellent horses to the great car, that shone like the sun, whereupon Khara ascended the chariot resembling the peak of Meru, that was vast, inlaid with pure gold, with golden wheels and shafts set with emeralds. Decorated with symbols of good fortune, such as fish, flowers, trees, rocks, mountains, birds and stars, it was furnished with banners and spears, hung with delightful bells and yoked to excellent steeds.

Then Khara, chafing with impatience, as also Dushana, seeing that great host, furnished with chariots, shields, weapons and banners, cried to that multitude of demons :—"Advance ! "

Thereafter that mighty titan army, numbering fourteen thousand, equipped with formidable shields, weapons and banners, rushed out impetuously, amidst a great tumult.

Armed with hammers, picks, spears, sharp axes, sabres, discus and shining javelins, as well as darts, formidable clubs, immense bows, goads, swords, maces and thunderbolts, terrible to look upon, those ferocious titans, obedient to the commands of Khara, left Janasthana, and he, withdrawing himself a little, reviewed those titans of malignant aspect, who were rushing forth, and thereafter followed them.

Obedient to Khara's command, the charioteer mounted on the car of that Slayer of His Foes, spurring on his dappled steeds, whose harness was wrought with pure gold, advanced with all speed, causing the cardinal points and other regions to ring with the sound.

And Khara, in harsh tones, inflamed with anger, chafing with the desire to destroy his adversary, endowed with great strength, equal to Antaka, urged on his charioteer again and again, roaring like a great cloud about to let loose a stream of hail.

CHAPTER 23

The Titan Army advances amid evil Portents

At that time terrible portents appeared and from a dark cloud a shower of blood fell. The swift-footed steeds yoked to Khara's chariot, stumbled on the level road of the royal highway, strewn with flowers; the sun was covered with a black disc, edged, as it were with blood, like a circle of burning coals, whilst a frightful vulture settled on the standard with its golden support.

Birds and beasts of prey, roaming in the vicinity of Janasthana, emitted deafening cries, creating an appalling clamour, and near that region, terrible jackals gave forth fearful and blood-curdling howls, like fiends.

Immense and formidable thunderclouds resembling elephants with crushed Temples, showered down a rain of blood, which hid the entire firmament; a great darkness fell, causing the hair to stand on end, obscuring the four quarters. Dusk arrived before the appointed time, assuming a sanguinous hue and, as Khara proceeded, wild beasts and birds of terrifying aspect barred his path, whilst herons, hyenas and vultures raised a ghastly clamour.

Hideous jackals, a sign of misfortune in war, howled at the approaching army, flames darting from their jaws and a headless trunk, resembling a club, was seen close to the sun. Though the time of eclipse had not come, yet that golden orb was seized by the planet Swarbhanu; the winds blew violently and the sun was bereft of lustre; though not yet night, stars thick as fireflies appeared.

Birds and fishes dived into the depths of the lakes, on which the lotuses had withered, and in that hour the trees were bereft of flowers and fruit, and sombre dust-clouds arose without the stirring of the wind. Parrots called wildly 'Chichikuchi' and comets of sinister aspect fell without a sound; the earth with her mountains, woods and forests, shook.

As Khara, standing in his chariot, was raising his war-cry, his left arm twitched and his voice died away; glancing round on every side, his eyes were suffused with tears, his head throbbed, yet in his folly he did not turn back.

Witnessing these evil portents that caused his hair to stand on end, with a defiant laugh, Khara addressed that host of titans saying:—

"I hold these terrible portents, dreadful to behold, as nought compared with my power and disregard them as do the strong, the weak! I am able to shoot down the stars from heaven with my sharp arrows! I can subjugate the empire of death itself! Till by means of my powerful weapons, I have brought Rama low, who depends on his strength alone, as also Lakshmana, I shall not turn back. May my sister, for whose sake I have sworn to bring about the death of Rama and Lakshmana, drink the blood of these two. Till this hour, I have not known defeat on the field of battle; ye are witness to it, I do not utter falsehood! In my wrath I am able to slay the Chief of the Gods bearing the thunderbolt, mounted on the intoxicated Airavata, how much more am I able to slay these two mortals?"

Hearing those boastful words, the vast army of the titans, whom death already held in his noose, was filled with incomparable joy, and advanced full of vigour, anxious to join issue in battle.

Thereupon, the high-souled Rishis, Devas, Gandharvas and Charanas assembled and those virtuous beings said one to the other:—

"Reverence to the cows, the brahmins and all those who have acquired spiritual merit in the world!

" As Vishnu, bearing the discus in his hand, subdued the Asuras, so may Rama too triumph over the titans in this fight."

Repeatedly expressing this wish and many others, those illustrious Rishis and the Gods, stationed in the sky, gazed down on the army of the titans, that was about to be destroyed.

Then Khara in his swiftly-moving chariot rode out to the head of his army and those twelve of exceeding prowess: Karaviraksha, Parusha, Kalakarmukha, Hemamalin, Mahamalin, Sarpasya, Shyengamin, Prithugriva, Vajnashatru, Vihangama, Dirjaya, Krudhirashana, surrounded him, and Mahakapala, Sthulaksha, Pramatha and Trishiras, these four followed Dushana.

As a group of planets rush towards the sun or moon, so in their eagerness to enter the fight did that formidable army of of titans hurl themselves with tremendous impetus on the two princes.

CHAPTER 24

The Combat opens between Rama and the Titans

When Khara of great prowess advanced on Rama's hermitage, the two princes observed many dreadful portents, and Rama, deeply moved, said to Lakshmana :—" O Mighty-armed One, these inauspicious omens, causing terror to all beings, foretell the destruction of the demon hosts.

" Yonder dun-coloured clouds, resembling asses' skin, pass across the sky, raining blood in dreadful convulsions. Behold, O Lakshmana, smoke rising from mine arrows, as if they rejoiced at the coming contest, and my bow of beaten gold moving of itself, eager for action. Meseems the cry of wild birds that frequent the woods foretells danger, nay, that the very lives of our foes are in jeopardy. Assuredly a great battle will shortly take place ; the twitching of my left arm betokens it. O Hero, for us victory is imminent, and the defeat of the titans assured. Thy countenance is resplendent and exultant,

O Lakshmana! Those warriors who enter into combat with a rueful mien are lost.

"I hear the roar of those titans of cruel deeds and the sound of their drums. If a prudent man desires success and wishes to escape defeat, he should be forearmed against the future. Therefore, bearing thy bow and arrows, taking Sita with thee, repair to a mountain cave, screened by trees and difficult of access. O Lakshmana, do not oppose my commands, but, swearing obedience to my feet, go thither, O Friend, without delay. Thou art valiant and well able to strike down the titans, but I desire to slay these Prowlers of the Night single-handed."

Having spoken thus, Lakshmana, taking up his bow and arrows, withdrew with Sita to an inaccessible cave.

As Lakshmana entered the cavern with Sita, Rama rejoiced at his brother's submission and donned his coat of mail.

Clothed in armour that shone like fire, Rama resembled a mighty flame illumining the darkness, and that hero, standing erect, took up his bow and arrows and, by the twanging of the cord, caused the four cardinal points to re-echo.

Then the Gods, Gandharvas, Siddhas and Charanas gathered together to witness the struggle and the great-souled Rishis began to converse one with the other, saying:—

"May it be well with all the cows and brahmins found on the earth! May Raghava overcome the descendants of Poulastya in combat! May he be as victorious as Vishnu, who with his discus routed the foremost of the asuras!"

Having spoken thus, exchanging glances, they added:— "But how can Rama overcome those fourteen thousand demons of fearful deeds single-handed?"

Thereafter those Rajarishis and Siddhas, stationed in their aerial chariots, were moved with curiosity as to the outcome of the conflict and seeing Rama, splendidly accoutred, standing alone on the field of battle, all those beings were filled with apprehension; the peerless Rama, however, the doer of noble deeds, assumed the aspect of that high-souled and avenging God, Rudra!

Whilst the Gods, Gandharvas and Charanas were still conversing, the army of the titans, creating a fearful clamour, clad in mail, bearing weapons and banners, appeared on every side.

Uttering loud battle cries, jostling one another, twanging their bowstrings, opening their jaws wide, they shouted :—" We will destroy the enemy ! " This appalling tumult filled the forest and struck terror into the hearts of its denizens, who fled from the sound, not daring to look back.

Then the demon army, resembling a stormy sea, brandishing every kind of weapon, rapidly approached Rama, but he, an experienced warrior, looking round on every side, saw that army of Khara's advancing and went out to meet it, taking his arrows from their quiver and stretching his dread bow, letting forth a piercing shout presaging the death of the titans.

Dreadful to behold in his wrath, he resembled the fire at the dissolution of the world and seeing him filled with energy the forest deities fled away. In his anger, Rama resembled the Bearer of the Pinaka bow intent on destroying Daksha's sacrifice.

With their bows and weapons, their cars and their armour, which shone like fire, the hosts of those eaters of human flesh resembled a mass of dark clouds at the hour of sunrise.

CHAPTER 25

The Combat between Rama and the Titans continues

APPROACHING the hermitage, Khara, in company with those who preceded him, beheld Rama, the Destroyer of his Foes, full of wrath, armed with his bow and seeing that mighty warrior, bow in hand, Khara ordered his charioteer to drive upon him with his car.

Thus commanded, Suta drove his horses to where the illustrious Rama, wielding his bow, stood unmoved.

Beholding Khara advancing on Rama, the titans, uttering loud shouts, surrounded him on all sides, and he, stationed in his chariot amidst those Yatudhanas, resembled the planet Mars encircled by stars.

Loosing a thousand shafts, Khara emitted a tremendous war-cry and all the demons in fury showered various missiles on that invincible archer Rama, striking him in their frenzy with iron clubs, swords, spears and axes.

With their colossal stature and extraordinary power, they resembled mountains as they bore down on Kakutstha with their chariots and horses.

In their desire to overcome Rama, those demon hordes, mounted on elephants as high as the peaks of mountains, covered him with a hail of weapons, like great clouds letting loose their rain on the King of Mountains, and Raghava was hemmed in on all sides by those ferocious looking demons.

As at evening time Mahadeva is surrounded by his satellites, so was Rama beset by the lances of the titans, but that prince received the missiles hurled against him as the sea receives the rivers that empty themselves therein. As the Himalayas remain unmoved, when struck by lightning, so did he, when those dreadful weapons tore his flesh. Pierced in every limb, the blood gushing forth on all sides, he resembled the evening sun enveloped in cloud.

Beholding Rama encircled by thousands of titans, the Gods and sages were profoundly moved, but he, growing enraged, bending his bow like a sickle, let loose hundreds and thousands of pointed shafts, that could not be intercepted and carried death to those they pierced. As if in sport, on the battlefield Rama let fly countless arrows furnished with herons plumes, tipped with gold, destroying innumerable titans like the noose of death itself.

Unconcernedly loosed by Rama, those arrows passed through the demons' bodies and, stained with blood, flew through the air like blazing torches. Countless shafts drawn from Rama's quiver fell in hundreds and thousands, robbing the demons of their life's breath, their bows, their banners, their shields and their armour, their arms embellished with ornaments and their thighs resembling the trunks of elephants.

The arrows of Rama, discharged from the bowstring, cut down horses yoked to the chariots with their golden trappings together with the charioteers; elephants with their riders, horsemen with their steeds, were all transfixed by his shafts and despatched to the region of Yama.

Pierced by those pointed shafts, the Rangers of the Night, emitted terrible shrieks, and decimated by those death-dealing arrows, the demon host was unable to defend itself, as dried wood is ignited by the proximity of fire.

Then certain demon warriors, full of energy and zeal, in a paroxysm of rage, let fly lances, tridents and other weapons at Rama, but he, intercepting them, cut off the heads of those demons with his shafts, thus depriving them of their lives. They, having had their heads, their shields and their bowstrings severed, fell to the earth, like trees thrown down by the blast of Garuda's wings.

Then the remaining titans fled, seeking refuge from those death-dealing arrows with Khara, but Dushana, taking up his bow, rallied them and rushed on Rama as if he were Antaka himself; thereafter the titans, growing bolder, hurled themselves on Rama anew, armed with the trunks of Sala and Tala trees and huge rocks.

With lances, maces and snares, bearing darts, clubs and nooses in their hands, those great warriors covered the whole field with a hail of missiles, discharging volleys of trees and rocks. Thereafter the combat waxed furious, causing the hair to stand on end, and now it seemed as if Rama were the victor and again the demons appeared to triumph. Then, seeing himself beseiged on all sides, that mighty warrior Rama, covered by a hail of darts, sent up a terrific shout, placing the mantra-propelled Gandharva weapon on his bow, whereupon a thousand arrows sped from his bent bow, covering the ten regions.

With such skill did Rama discharge his arrows, that the demons were unable to distinguish when he drew them from their quiver and when he loosed them and his shafts caused darkness to spread over the sky and obscure the sun.

Slain in their thousands, the demons fell in heaps and the battlefield was strewn with corpses. Struck down, disembowelled, transfixed, torn and hacked asunder, they could be seen in their hundreds, and the ground was scattered with heads wrapped in turbans, arms encircled with bangles, thighs and torsos with their ornaments, horses, mighty elephants, shattered chariots, chowries, fans, umbrellas and standards of every kind, and beholding the slain, the remaining demons were afflicted and unable to withstand Rama, that captor of hostile citadels, further.

CHAPTER 26

Rama destroys the Titans and slays Dushana

SEEING his forces destroyed, the mighty-armed Dushana placed himself at the head of five thousand intrepid and invincible titans, to whom retreat was unknown.

Armed with pikes, sabres, rocks and trees, they let loose a hail of missiles on Rama from every side, without being able to wound him. Their onslaught was formidable and to all but Rama, deadly. The virtuous Raghava, however, met the attack with his arrows, his eyes closed, as unconcerned as a bull under heavy rain. Thereafter, growing wrath, he resolved to destroy the whole of Khara's army and, burning with energy, covered that host and its leader, Dushana, with his shafts, whereupon Dushana, the Slayer of His Foes, met Raghava with weapons that resembled thunderbolts. Then the heroic Rama, enraged, severed Dushana's mighty bow, slew the four steeds yoked to his chariot and cut off the head of his charioteer with a crescent-shaped arrow, thereafter piercing Dushana's breast thrice with his shafts.

Then Dushana lifted up his mace covered with gold, that resembled a mountain peak and was capable of destroying the army of the Gods. Studded with nails, smeared with the flesh of his foes, keen as a diamond, able to cut through the gates of hostile cities, that weapon, resembling a mighty snake, was wielded by that titan of evil deeds, who hurled himself on Rama.

Nevertheless, as Dushana rushed upon him, Rama cut off both his arms with his arrows, and that mace, loosed from his grasp, fell forward on the field like unto the banner of Indra, whilst Dushana, bereft of it, his arms severed, sank to the earth like a mighty elephant that, stripped of its tusks, succumbs.

Seeing Dushana lying on the battlefield, all beings, witnessing that conflict, cried out " Well done ! Well done ! " and paid obeisance to Rama.

Meantime, impelled by fate, the three generals, Mahakapala, Sthulaksha and the mighty Titan Pramathin rushed on Rama; Mahakapala brandishing a great trident, Sthulaksha bearing a harpoon and Pramathin, a huge axe. Seeing them advancing, Raghava, taking out some sharp steel-pointed arrows, went forward to meet them, as one receives a guest, and the Delight of the House of Raghu severed the head of Mahakapala with a single arrow and assailed Pramathin with innumerable shafts, whereupon he fell to the earth like an axed tree; thereafter, Rama blinded Sthulaksha with his sharp arrows and, inflamed with wrath, with five thousand shafts slew an equal number of Dushana's followers, sending them to the nether regions.

Hearing that Dushana and his warriors were lying dead, Khara, in great fury, addressed the leaders of the army, saying :—" Let all the titans attack that evil wretch, Rama, and strike him with weapons of every kind."

Speaking thus, Khara, full of wrath, flung himself on Rama, followed by Durjaya, Karaviraksha, Parusha, Kalakarmuka, Hemamalin, Mahamalin, Sarpashya, Syengamin, Prithagriva, Vajnasatru, Vihangama and Rudhinashana, those twelve valiant generals with their forces, who fell upon Rama, discharging their excellent shafts.

And Rama, endowed with supreme energy, with his gold and diamond encrusted arrows, despatched the remainder of Khara's forces, and those shafts, bereft of feathers, like golden stalks, resembling flames wreathed in smoke, laid those demons low, as lightning fells the giant trees. With a hundred ear-shaped arrows, Rama slew a hundred titans; and a thousand with as many shafts. Their breastplates and ornaments shattered, their bows broken, those Rangers of the Night fell on the earth, bathed in blood. Their hair dishevelled, covered with gore, they lay on the battlefield, like kusha grass scattered on the altar, and that great forest, strewn with the corpses of demons and befouled with their flesh and blood, resembled the region of hell.

Fourteen thousand demons of cruel deeds were slain by Rama, a mortal, single-handed and on foot! Out of the whole army only Khara of the great Car and the Titan, Trishiras survived, all others being slain by Lakshmana's elder brother, the illustrious Rama.

Thereafter, seeing that vast army destroyed in the great conflict, Khara, ascending his splendid chariot, advanced on Raghava with his mace upraised.

CHAPTER 27

Rama and Trishiras meet in Combat. Trishiras is slain

As Khara was advancing on Rama, the leader of the army, Trishiras approached him and said :—" O Lord, refrain from engaging Rama in combat and having recourse to me, who am possessed of prowess, witness his defeat. I swear to thee by my sword that I will slay Rama and avenge the death of the entire demon host. In this fight I shall be as Mrityu to him or he to me, but thou, O Excellent One, shouldst restrain thy martial ardour awhile and be a spectator only. Should Rama be slain, thou canst return home triumphant, but should I die, do thou enter the field against him."

Yielding to the persuasions of Trishiras, Khara said to him, who was already doomed :—" Go, engage Rama in combat!"

Thereupon Trishiras, like a triple crested mountain, advanced on Raghava in a glittering chariot yoked to excellent steeds and, as a great cloud pours down rain, so he discharged a volley of arrows, roaring the while like a kettledrum.

Seeing that demon drawing near, Rama loosed some pointed shafts and a terrible struggle ensued, so that it seemed as if a great lion and a mighty elephant were fighting together.

Trishiras, having pierced Rama's forehead with three darts, that hero, enraged, addressed him in biting accents, saying:—

"O Valiant Titan, the arrows thou hast loosed I bear on my brow as a wreath, do thou now receive the shafts from my bow."

Thereupon Rama let fly fourteen serpentine arrows striking Trishiras on the breast and with four further shafts brought down his four steeds, killing his charioteer with eight other darts and with a single arrow severing the up-raised standard in the front of his car. Then, as that Ranger of the Night was alighting from his shattered chariot, Rama pierced his breast with further arrows, depriving him of his senses, and that one of immeasurable prowess with his swift arrows cut off the three heads of Trishiras, causing the blood to flow from the stricken trunk, and the heads of that Ranger of the Night fell while he yet stood upright after the destruction of his forces.

Then the remaining titans, losing heart, sped away like deer stampeding on the approach of a hunter, and Khara, beholding them fleeing, waxing wrath, rallied them and rushed on Rama as Rahu on the moon.

CHAPTER 28

The Combat between Rama and Khara

SEEING that Dushana and Trishiras had been slain in the fight and witnessing Rama's prowess, Khara was filled with apprehension and reflected :—

"My vast army with my generals Dushana and Trishiras has been destroyed by Rama, single-handed."

Whereupon that Demon Khara, was seized with despondency and hurled himself on Rama, as the Titan Namuchi on Indra. Stretching his mighty bow, Khara discharged at Rama some blood-sucking arrows, resembling venomous snakes, and, mounted on his chariot, began to range over the battlefield, displaying his skill in the use of weapons, covering the four quarters with his shafts.

Beholding this, as Parjanya with his watery floods, Rama, armed with his mighty bow, filled the entire firmament with his irresistible shafts, which resembled tongues of fire, and all space was filled with arrows on every side, which had been loosed by Khara and Rama.

As those two heroes struggled together, the sun was obscured and darkness descended; then, like a mighty elephant struck with a goad, Rama assailed his opponent with Nalikas, Narachas and sharp-pointed Vikarnas, and that demon, standing in his chariot, bow in hand, resembled Death himself carrying his noose. At that moment Khara deemed the destroyer of his forces, endued with heroism, the extremely powerful Rama, to be overcome with fatigue, but Rama remained unmoved under Khara's assaults, as a mighty lion ignores the presence of an insignificant deer.

Then Khara, in his chariot blazing like the sun, drew near to Rama, as a moth approaches a flame and, displaying his skill, severed Rama's bow at the point where he held it, thereafter loosing seven mace-like shafts resembling Indra's thunderbolts, which shattered the armour of his adversary resplendent as the sun itself, so that it fell on the earth. Roaring like a lion, he let loose a thousand arrows, wounding Rama of unparalleled might, and in that conflict Khara set up a mighty shout.

Pierced by Khara's arrows, the body of Rama resembled a clear and smokeless flame, and that Destroyer of his Foes, in order to compass the titan's defeat, took up another great bow, stringing it with a mighty twanging. Holding aloft that prodigious bow, named Vaishnava, bestowed on him by the Rishi Agastya, Rama rushed on Khara, letting fly his arrows furnished with golden feathers and cut down his banner plated with gold, which fell from the chariot, as the sun falls on the earth, cursed by the Gods.

Highly provoked, Khara aimed at the heart of Rama and pierced him with four arrows, so that he resembled a great elephant under the deluge in the rainy season, and Rama, sorely wounded by his shafts, covered with blood, waxed wrath and that foremost of bowmen, with consummate skill, let fly six well-directed arrows. With one, he struck the head of Khara, with two others, his arms, and with the remaining three crescent-shaped darts, he pierced his breast. Thereafter that illustrious warrior, in his ire, let fly thirteen arrows sharpened on the whetstone, blazing like the sun; one severed the shafts of his adversary's car, four more felling the steeds; with a sixth he smote the head of his charioteer, and with three others that great and intrepid warrior, shattered the axles of the chariot; with the twelfth he severed Khara's bow at the point where he held it, and with the thirteenth arrow, that shone like lightning, Raghava, who was equal to Indra, transfixed Khara, as it were in sport.

His bow shattered, deprived of his chariot, his horses slain, his charioteer fallen, Khara, mace in hand, sprang to the ground and stood waiting.

Seeing Rama's feat of arms that was unsurpassed, the Gods and great Sages rejoiced and, assembling in the sky, with joined palms, extolling the wonderful exploit of that mighty warrior, offered obeisance to him.

CHAPTER 29

Rama and the Demon Khara taunt one another

THEN the illustrious Rama addressed Khara, who was standing mace in hand, bereft of his chariot, and in severe accents, said:—

"O Hero, with the support of this army of elephants, horses, chariots and men, thou hast adopted a course of action condemned by all. He who inflicts pain on others by oppressing them, who is ruthless and engaged in evil deeds, will never know happiness, even though he be Lord of the Three Worlds.

"O Ranger of the Night, one who, like a tyrant, works against the interests of others and resembles a vicious and marauding snake, is ultimately destroyed! He who, overcome by avarice or envy, pursues an evil course, without reflecting on the consequences, forfeits his life and comes to a miserable end, like a brahmany duck that feeds on hailstones.

" O Titan, how canst thou evade the consequences of the murder of those ascetics dwelling in the Dandaka Forest, enhancing their merit by the practice of virtue?

" Even if they attain to sovereignty, the wicked, engaged in cruel deeds, condemned by all men, do not enjoy it long, but fall like trees whose roots have been severed.

" O Dweller in the Darkness, as in its proper season the tree puts forth its flowers, so in the course of time evil actions produce bitter fruit.

" As a man who swallows poison soon succumbs, so does the sinner swiftly reap the fruits of his evil actions. It is to put down the instigators of evil, the oppressors of others, that I, under the orders of the King, have come hither. To-day my shining arrows shall penetrate thy flesh, as serpents enter an ant-heap, and thou shalt follow in the wake of those virtuous ascetics inhabiting the forest, whom thou hast slain without provocation. Soon those excellent sages, formerly slain by thee, shall in their aerial chariots return to behold thee lying in hell laid low by mine arrows. O Worst of Men, O Thou who art of an odious race, defend thyself as thou wilt, I shall presently cut off thine head like the fruit of a palm tree."

Hearing Rama's words, Khara, his eyes inflamed with anger, beside himself with rage, answered mockingly:—" O Son of Dasaratha, thou art but a common man; yet, having slain these insignificant titans in battle, thou dost extol thyself without reason. Those who are brave and valiant never boast of their prowess; only the scum of the warrior caste praise themselves as thou hast done. Where is the warrior who, on the battlefield, his death imminent, would hymn his own praise? Thou hast revealed thy worthlessness by this self-glorification, as brass wearing the semblance of gold reveals its true value in a fire of kusha grass.

" O Rama, armed with a mace, I stand immoveable on the field, like a mountain enriched by precious metals. Behold me with my mace, like unto Antaka himself, armed with his noose, about to end thy life; I shall destroy not only thee, but the Three Worlds! I could utter more, but refrain, lest our combat be intercepted as the hour of sunset is near. Fourteen thousand titans have fallen under thy blows; by slaying thee to-day I shall wipe away the tears of their relatives."

Speaking thus, Khara, filled with fury, hurled his marvellous gold-encircled mace at Rama. Leaving the hand of Khara, that massive and effulgent mace, resembling a blazing thunderbolt, consuming the trees and bushes to ashes, drew near to Rama, but he, as it was about to fall like the noose of death, shattered it to fragments with his arrows while yet in the air.

Crushed and broken, it fell to earth like a serpent stricken by the efficacy of herbs and the power of incantations.

CHAPTER 30

The Death of Khara

HAVING intercepted and shattered that great mace with his arrows, the ever virtuous Rama, though still wrath, spoke as if in jest:—

" O Titan, is this the extent of thy power? How strange that one so deficient in prowess should boast so loudly! Severed by my shafts, behold thy mace lies in pieces on the earth! Thou hast bragged to no purpose! Didst thou not declare: ' I will wipe away the tears shed for the death of the titans '? Vain words! As Garuda of old stole the nectar of immortality, I am about to deprive thee of thy life, thou vile and lying wretch! The earth this day will quaff the foaming blood issuing from thy throat, which my shafts have severed. Soon shall thy body, covered with dust, the arms extended, embrace the earth, as a frenzied lover embraces the woman he has won, after long delay.

" O Obloquy of Thy Race, on thy death the Dandaka Forest will become a refuge for those who are themselves a refuge; my shafts will rid the forest of all titans and the ascetics will wander about there without fear. To-day the titan women in sore distress, weeping and terrified, will fly this place. They who inspired terror in others, having evil-doers such as thou as their consorts, shall to-day taste the pangs of sorrow! O cruel, fallen and false-hearted Wretch, in fear of whom the sages, tremble as they pour forth their oblations into the sacred fire."

As Raghava, swayed by anger, uttered these words, Khara, foaming with rage, began to hurl abuses at him, saying :—

"Verily, despite thy boasting thou art filled with terror and in the face of death dost not know whether to speak or to be silent. Those about to die lose the power of their five senses and no longer know what is right and wrong."

Having spoken thus, that Ranger of the Night, Khara, scowling, looked round him for a weapon and, perceiving a great palm tree near at hand, forcibly uprooted it and whirling it with terrific energy hurled it at Rama, roaring : "Now thou art slain !"

Thereupon, Raghava with his weapon cut that tree to pieces and in an access of rage resolved to slay Khara. His body covered with sweat, his eyes inflamed, he pierced Khara with innumerable darts, so that rivers of blood gushed from his wounds, as do the torrents from the mountain Prasravana.

Stupefied by Rama's arrows and maddened by the smell of blood, Khara rushed at Rama, who, seeing him approach full of fury and covered with gore, retreated a few paces ; then, in order to slay him, he selected an arrow that shone like fire, resembling the Rod of Brahma. And that righteous One discharged that shaft at Khara, which had been conferred on the Sage Agastya by Indra, and like a thunderbolt it struck his breast so that he, consumed by the flame issuing therefrom, fell to the ground. As Rudra with his third eye consumed the demon Andhaka in the forest of Sweta, as Vritra was slain by the thunderbolt, as Namuchi by the foam, as Bal by Indra's mace, so did Khara fall.

Then the Gods and the Charanas assembled and, amazed and delighted, struck their drums, showering flowers on Rama and saying :—" In this great conflict Raghava, by means of his pointed shafts, has in an instant slain fourteen thousand demons, able to change their shape at will, with their generals, Khara and Dushana. Great indeed is this exploit of Rama, versed in the science of the Self. What valour ! His prowess resembles that of Vishnu himself !"

Saying this, the Gods returned from whence they had come.

Thereafter the Rajarishis and Paramarishis, accompanied by Agastya, joyfully paid homage to Rama and said :—

"It was for this that the Slayer of Paka, the mighty Purandara, visited the hermitage of the Sage Sharabhanga. It was for this that the great Rishis brought thee to this place, O Prince, that thou mightest compass the destruction of the titans of evil deeds. Thou hast fulfilled thy mission amongst us, O Son of Dasaratha; from to-day the virtuous sages may perform their devotions in the Dandaka Forest in peace."

Then that hero, Lakshmana, accompanied by Sita, issued from the mountain cavern and joyfully entered the hermitage, and the victorious and heroic Rama, honoured by the great Sages, returned to the ashrama, where Lakshmana paid him obeisance.

Seeing her consort returning victorious, having brought felicity to the ascetics, the happy Vaidehi embraced him. Beholding those hosts of demons slain, and that Destroyer of Enemy Hosts worshipped by the magnanimous sages, the daughter of Janaka began to minister to her lord and full of joy, embracing him afresh in her delight, experienced supreme happiness.

CHAPTER 31

Ravana hears of the Death of Khara and determines to slay Rama

THE Titan Akampana, speedily leaving Janasthana, repaired to Lanka in order to seek out Ravana, addressing him thus :—

"O King, the innumerable titans dwelling in Janasthana have perished and Khara himself has fallen on the field of battle; by some chance, I have been enabled to reach this place alive."

Hearing these words, Ravana, his eyes growing red with anger, bent his gaze on Akampana as if he would consume him, and said :—

"Who, seeking his own destruction, has dared to exterminate my people? None in the world will be able to protect him, not even Indra, Kuvera, Yama or Vishnu himself. No man can save him who has defied me! I am the Lord of Time, the Consumer of Fire, the death of Death itself! In my wrath I am able to reduce Aditya and Pavaka to ashes! Verily I can subdue the very wind in its course!"

On this, Akampana, with joined palms, in a voice strangled with terror, solicited the protection of that Ten-necked One, who was mad with anger, whereupon that Lord of the Titans gave him the assurance of safety, inspiring him with confidence, and Akampana thereafter addressed him boldly, saying :—

"There is a son of King Dasaratha, who is youthful, resembling a lion, broad-shouldered like unto a bull, possessing long arms, handsome, renowned and of immeasurable prowess; his name is Rama; it is he, who in Janasthana has slain Khara and Dushana."

At these words, Ravana, King of the Titans, breathing like a great serpent, enquired of Akampana, saying :—"O Akampana, when he came to Janasthana was Rama accompanied by the Leader of the Gods and all the Celestials?"

On hearing Ravana's words, Akampana began to describe the great and noble exploits of Raghava, saying :—

"O King, Rama is a mighty warrior, an invincible archer and the equal of Indra himself in prowess; his eyes are slightly red and his voice resembles a kettledrum, his countenance is like unto the full moon. Followed by Lakshmana, as Anila follows Pavaka, this is the fortunate leader of monarchs who has destroyed thy colony, as fire, fanned by the wind, consumes a forest! Rama was in no wise assisted by the Gods—of this there is no doubt—but his golden-winged arrows flying through the air, transforming themselves into five-headed snakes, destroyed the demons. O Mighty Sovereign, wherever they fled in their terror, they beheld Rama standing before them, and in this wise Janasthana was destroyed by him."

Hearing Akampana's words, Ravana cried out :—"I shall go to Janasthana and slay Rama and Lakshmana!"

Thereupon Akampana answered him, saying :—

"O King, hear from me the true measure of Rama's strength and prowess. Supremely virtuous and brave, none in the world is able to subdue him in his wrath. By means of his shafts, he is able to stem a river in its course and shatter the very firmament with its stars and planets; nay, if the earth were to be submerged, he could raise it up and, should he so desire it, change the boundaries of the sea and flood the continents with its waters. He is able to subdue all creatures and control the course of the wind itself; indeed that foremost of persons, having destroyed the worlds, can create a new universe. O Ten-necked One, as a sinner is not able to enter heaven, neither canst thou, nor thy titans, defeat Rama in combat. The Gods and titans together cannot overcome him; yet there is a way of destroying him, which I will now unfold to thee.

" Rama is wedded to one more beautiful than any woman on earth, and that slender-waisted damsel is known by the name of Sita. In the full bloom of youth, and possessed of well-proportioned limbs, she is a jewel adorned by jewels. In loveliness, she surpasses the celestial beings, nymphs and nagas. Having lured Rama into the forest, do thou carry her away! Bereft of Sita, Rama will not survive! "

The Lord of the Rakshasas was highly gratified to hear these words and, after a little reflection, said to Akampana :—" Be it so! To-morrow, accompanied by my charioteer alone, I shall, with a glad heart, bring back the Princess of Videha to this spacious palace! "

The following day, Ravana started out in his chariot, yoked to mules, and it was bright as the sun, illumining the four quarters. Following the path of the stars in its rapid course, it resembled the moon itself surrounded by clouds.

Proceeding to a great distance, he approached the hermitage of Taraka's son, Maricha, who entertained him with marvellous dishes unknown to man. Presenting him with a seat and water wherewith to wash his feet, that demon addressed him, saying :—" O Lord of the Titans, is it well with thee and thy people? O Sovereign, being ignorant of thine intention, thine unexpected and sudden advent fills me with apprehension! "

Then the resplendent and eloquent Ravana answered Maricha, saying :—

" O Friend! Rama, who is able to achieve that from which reason recoils, has destroyed the entire colony of Janasthana, heretofore impregnable, as also my generals, Khara and Dushana. Do thou, therefore, aid me in bearing off his consort, Sita."

Hearing these words of the King of the Titans, Maricha answered :—" O King, the man who has thus counselled thee concerning Sita is assuredly an enemy in the guise of a friend. By such advice, he has unquestionably affronted thee and is envious of thy great might.

" 'Bear Sita away!' who has uttered such words? Who seeks to cut off the head of the entire titan host? Without doubt the man who has thus counselled thee is thine enemy, since he desires thee to extract the poison fangs of a serpent with thy bare hands. Who is it who seeks to lead thee astray and strikes thine head whilst thou art sleeping happily?

" Raghava, that intoxicated elephant, may not be withstood on the field of battle. With the lineage of an illustrious House as his trunk, his valour the ichor, his outstretched arms the tusks, thou art wholly unable to pit thyself against him. Do not rouse that sleeping lion who hunts the titans as deer, the arrows of whose quiver are his talons, his sharp sword the jaws.

" O King of the Titans, do not hurl thyself into that dreadful and bottomless ocean called Rama, whose bow is the crocodile, the strength of whose arm is the quagmire, whose shafts are the rising waves, and whose battlefield is its waters.

" O Lord of Lanka, compose thyself and return in peace to thy capital. O Indra of Titans, continue to enjoy the company of thy consorts, and let Rama delight in his own, in the forest."

Hearing the words of Maricha, the ten-headed Ravana returned to the city of Lanka and re-entered his palace.

CHAPTER 32

Shurpanakha upbraids Ravana and urges him to destroy Rama

WHEN Shurpanakha saw those fourteen thousand titans of dreadful deeds slain by Rama single-handed on the field of battle, together with Khara, Dushana and Trishiras, she once more emitted dreadful shrieks and roared like thunder. Perceiving the incomparable prowess of Raghava, she became exceedingly agitated and proceeded to Lanka, Ravana's capital.

There she beheld Ravana shining in glory, surrounded by his ministers on the terrace of his palace, like Indra amidst the Maruts. Seated on his golden throne, blazing like a flame, Ravana resembled a great fire kindled on an altar, kept alive by sacrificial offerings. Unconquered by Gods, Gandharvas, Rishis or other creatures, that warrior, who resembled death itself with wide-open jaws, bore on his person the wounds inflicted by the thunderbolts in the war between Gods and titans and on his breast the marks of Airavata's tusks.

Having twenty arms, ten heads, a broad chest, wearing gorgeous attire and bearing the marks of royalty, he was adorned with a chain of emeralds and ornaments of fine gold and with his great arms, white teeth and enormous mouth resembled a mountain.

In the combat with the Gods, Vishnu had struck him a hundred times with his discus, and he bore the marks of other weapons from that great struggle, yet his limbs were intact and had not been severed. He who was able to churn up the seas, a feat not to be performed by any other, whose missiles were the mountain crests, he the scourge of the Gods, who transgressed every moral law, the ravisher of others' wives, the wielder of celestial weapons, the destroyer of sacrifices, who descended into the city of Bhogavati and subdued the serpent Vasuki, from whom, on his defeat, he stole the gentle consort; he who scaled Mount Kailasha and overcame Kuvera depriving him of his aerial chariot Pushpaka, which transported him wheresoever he desired; he who in his anger destroyed the garden of Chaitaratha, the lotus pool and the Nandana Grove and all the pleasurable retreats of the Gods, and with his vast arms, resembling the peaks of mountains, arrested the course of the sun and moon, twin scourgers of their foes, rising in splendour; practising asceticism in the mighty forest for a thousand years he offered his heads in sacrifice to Swyambhu and obtained the boon that neither Deva, Danava, Gandharva, Pisacha, Pataya nor Uraga should be able to slay him, but of man there was no mention;

proud of his strength, he stole the Soma juice, sanctified by mantras, before its pressing by the Twice-born in the sacrifice; this perverse wretch, Ravana of evil deeds, slayer of the brahmins, ruthless, pitiless, delighting in causing harm to others, was verily a source of terror to all beings.

The titan woman beheld her brother full of power, resplendent in gorgeous attire, adorned with celestial garlands, seated on his throne, resembling Time at the destruction of the worlds, that Indra of Demons, the proud descendant of Poulastyā and she, trembling with fear, in order to address him, drew near to the Slayer of his Enemies, who was seated amidst his counsellors. Distracted with terror and passion, Shurpanakha, who was wont to roam everywhere unafraid, now mutilated by the order of that magnanimous Ramachandra, displaying her ravaged features before Ravana, whose large eyes appeared to shoot forth flames, uttered these bitter words to him:

CHAPTER 33

Shurpanakha's Words to Ravana

FILLED with anger, Shurpanakha addressed Ravana, the Oppressor of the Worlds, in harsh accents, saying:—

"O Ravana, wholly devoted to pleasure and indulging in every whim without scruple, thou art oblivious of the great calamity that threatens thee. That monarch who is given up to lust and other dissipations and who is covetous, is disregarded by his subjects, as is the fire in the crematorium. That king who does not fulfil his duties at the proper season brings ruin on his state. The Prince who, committing excess, is ruled by his consorts and readily gives credence to other's counsel, is shunned as the mud of a river is shunned by an elephant. Those rulers who are unable to protect their lands or reclaim the territory wrested from them, live without glory, like mountains submerged in the ocean.

"At enmity with the Gods, the Gandharvas and the Danavas, who are masters of themselves, doing what ought not to be done and inconstant, how art thou able to rule as king?

"O Titan, thou art childish and thoughtless and art not conversant with that which should be known to thee; how canst thou govern? Those monarchs who have neither emissaries, wealth nor policy at their disposal, resemble a common man, O Prince of Conquerors! Since kings are informed by their spies as to what is taking place abroad, they are said to be far-sighted. Meseems thou dost not discharge thy duty and that the counsellors who surround thee are inexperienced, since thou art insensible to the destruction of thy people and their territory.

"Fourteen thousand titans of dreadful deeds with Khara and Dushana have been slain by Rama single-handed; Rama of imperishable exploits has freed the ascetics of fear, established peace in the Dandaka Forest and harassed Janasthana, but thou, who art covetous and a slave to lust, art unaware of the danger that threatens thy dominion. None will help that monarch in time of peril, who is mean, violent, dissolute, haughty and perfidious. Even his own relatives will overpower a king who is excessively vain, pretentious, boastful and irascible. That monarch who fails in his duty and, under the threat of danger is lulled into a false security, will in time of adversity be swept from his kingdom like a straw. Dry wood, turf or dust have some value, but a king who is degenerate is worthless and resembles a faded wreath or a worn-out garment. That monarch who is vigilant however, conversant with what is happening and virtuous, establishes his throne in perpetuity. The king who, even while sleeping, is yet awake to the ordering of his kingdom, who manifests his anger or approval at a fitting time, is revered by all.

"O Thou, whose emissaries have failed to inform thee of the great carnage among the titans, who art bereft of wisdom, O Ravana, thou art lacking in all these great qualities.

"Disregarding others, given up to the pleasures of the senses, not able to reap the advantage of time and place or discriminate between what is good and evil, having sacrificed thy kingdom, thou wilt soon perish."

Reflecting on the infirmities his sister had ascribed to him, Ravana, the Lord of the Titans, opulent, arrogant and powerful, became absorbed in thought.

CHAPTER 34

Shurpanakha urges Ravana to slay Rama and wed Sita

HEARING Shurpanakha's bitter words, Ravana surrounded by his ministers enquired angrily:—" Who is Rama? What, is his strength? How does he look and what is the measure of his prowess? Why has he penetrated into the lonely and inaccessible depths of the Dandaka Forest? With what weapons did he destroy the titans in that conflict, slaying Khara and Dushana as also Trishiras? Tell me truly, O Lovely One, who has disfigured thee?"

Thus addressed by the Lord of the Titans, Shurpanakha in a transport of rage began to relate the history of Rama.

She said: " Rama, the son of King Dasaratha, resembles the God of Love; his arms are long, his eyes large; clad in robes of bark and a black antelope skin, bearing a bow encircled with gold like unto Indra's, he lets fly blazing arrows resembling venomous snakes. Emitting a great shout, he discharges his formidable shafts, and in the struggle I could not distinguish him but beheld the host being decimated under the rain of his arrows, as the harvest is destroyed by the hail sent by Indra. In a short space, single-handed, standing alone, he slew fourteen thousand titans with Khara and Dushana, thus bringing peace to the sages in the Dandaka Forest and delivering them from fear. Chivalrous of soul, Rama, the Knower of Self, would not countenance the slaying of a woman and, having been mutilated at his command, I escaped.

" His brother, endowed with great valour, is renowned for his virtue; his name is Lakshmana and he is devoted to Rama. Full of fire, indomitable, victorious, powerful, intelligent and wise, he is his right hand and his very life's breath. And Rama's virtuous, tender and wedded wife, of large eyes, whose face resembles the full moon, is ever engaged in what is pleasing to her lord. With her lovely locks, well-formed nose, beautiful shoulders and her grace and dignity, one would deem her to be a forest divinity or Lakshmi herself. With a skin of the colour of molten gold, nails that are rosy and long, that surpassingly lovely woman is Sita, the slender-waisted Princess of Videha. No woman so beautiful has ever appeared in the world, either among the Gods, Gandharvas, Yakshas or Kinneras. He whose wife Sita becomes and whom she will warmly embrace will live in the world more happily than Purandara. With her natural amiability, her marvellous beauty, which is without equal on earth, she would prove a worthy consort for thee, and thou too art fit to be her lord. It was to bring thee this lady of shapely hips, softly rounded breasts and charming features, that I put forth my endeavours, when, O Mighty-armed One, I was mutilated by the ruthless Lakshmana!

"When thou dost behold Vaidehi, whose countenance resembles the full moon, thou shalt instantly be pierced with the darts of the God of Love. If thou desirest to win her, then set off speedily on thy right foot and lay siege to her heart. If, O Ravana, my counsel meets with thine approval, then, O King of the Titans, follow it without delay.

"Knowing the weakness of these people, O Valiant Chief of the Titans, make Sita, who is without blemish, thy consort. Hearing that Rama with his arrows that never missed their mark has slain the titans established in Janasthana, and of the death of Khara and Dushana, thou hast a duty to perform."

CHAPTER 35

Ravana visits the Demon Maricha once more

HEARING the words of Shurpanakha, causing his hair to stand on end, Ravana dismissed his ministers and began to reflect on what should or should not be done. Exploring the true significance of the undertaking and weighing the desirability and undesirability of the matter, he came to the conclusion

'Thus should I act', and, fixed in his resolve, went secretly to the splendid pavilion where his chariots were held in readiness, commanding his driver to bring out his car.

At his order, the zealous charioteer, in an instant, prepared that superb and marvellous chariot, and Ravana ascended the golden car set with gems, that coursed wheresoever he desired, to which mules in golden trappings, bearing the heads of goblins, were harnessed.

Mounted on that chariot, the wheels of which made a sound like thunder, the younger brother of Dhanada, the God of Wealth, proceeded beside the Lord of Rivers and Streams along the seashore.

Seated under a pure-white canopy with his white chanwaras, his ten heads the colour of lapis, wearing ornaments of pure gold, with ten necks and twenty arms, the younger brother of Dhanada, the enemy of the Gods, the slayer of the foremost among the ascetics, possessed of huge heads, like unto the Indra of Mountains with its ten crests, appeared beautiful, standing in his chariot, coursing at will like a mass of cloud, crowned with lightning and accompanied by a flock of cranes.

And that Great One, endowed with prowess, beheld the shores of the sea with its rocks and countless trees, laden with fruit and flowers of every kind, bordered by lakes of limpid water filled with lotuses, and spacious hermitages with their altars and groves of plantain trees lending brilliance to the scene, which was enhanced by blossoming Coconut, Sala, Tala and Tamala trees.

These places had been rendered illustrious by the presence of thousands of great Rishis of rigid penance and Nagas, Suparnas, Gandharvas and Kinneras; they were rendered pleasant by Siddhas and Charanas, who were fully self-subdued and those descendants of Brahma who derived their nutriment from the solar rays and those who lived on a bare subsistence such as the Ajas, Vaikhanasas, Mashas, Valakhilyas and Marichipas.[1] Countless nymphs of celestial beauty, adorned with garlands and jewels, beguiled them with every kind of pastime in which they excelled, and the auspicious consorts of the Gods honoured them by dwelling amongst them, whilst

[1] See under 'ascetics' in Glossary.

Danavas and other Celestial Beings who fed on Amrita frequented that place. Swans, cranes, pelicans and waterfowl disported themselves on the emerald sward, wet and shining with the sea mist; spacious cars festooned with celestial garlands from which strains of sweet music issued, flew here and there at the will of those who had conquered the worlds by their austerities, together with Gandharvas and Apsaras.

Ravana surveyed countless forests of sandalwood, whose roots were full of fragrant sap, delighting the olfactory sense, and groves of excellent Agallocha and Takkola trees with pear trees and bushes of black pepper and heaps of pearls lying on the shore, and coral reefs and gold and silver promontories, tumbling cataracts of crystal water and cities filled with grain and treasure, where the pearls of womanhood could be seen and which were thronged with horses, elephants and chariots.

On the shores of the ocean, the Lord of the Titans beheld a level and charming spot over which cool breezes blew resembling heaven itself, in the centre of which grew a great fig tree, like a bright cloud, where many sages sheltered, and on every side its branches stretched to a distance of several yojanas. It was there that the mighty Garuda brought a huge elephant and a giant tortoise in his claws, wishing to devour them among the branches, but the bough broke under the weight of that enormous bird, and the Vaikhanasas, Mashas, Valakhilyas, Marichipas Ajas and Dhumras being assembled there, Garuda had compassion on them and transported the branch together with the elephant and tortoise in one claw to a distance of one hundred yojanas, where that excellent bird regaled himself on their flesh.

Destroying the empire of the Nishadas with the severed branch, thus delivering the sages, his joy was re-doubled and his energy increased, whereupon filled with strength he resolved to steal the Nectar of Immortality. Having broken the iron bars, he entered the jewelled keep and bore away the Amrita from that place where it had been hidden by the mighty Indra.

It was this same Nyagrodha tree, frequented by groups of great sages, that still bore the marks of Suparna and was called 'Subhadra', that the younger brother of Dhanada now saw before him.

Passing over to the further side of that Lord of the Waters, the Ocean, Ravana saw a solitary hermitage, an ancient and holy retreat in the middle of a forest. There he found the Demon Maricha clad in a black antelope skin, wearing matted locks and given up to the practice of asceticism.

Ravana having approached him, Maricha, according to tradition, entertained him in many ways not known to man. Placing pure food and water before his sovereign, he humbly addressed him saying :—

" Is all well with Lanka, O Chief of the Titans ? With what purpose hast thou come hither again so speedily ? "

On hearing this enquiry, the mighty and eloquent Ravana answered in this wise :—

CHAPTER 36

Ravaṇa reveals his Project to the Demon Maricha

" O MARICHA, listen to me as I relate everything to thee ! O My Child, I am deeply afflicted and thou alone canst temper my distress !

" Thou art conversant with Janasthana, it was there that my brother Khara, the long-armed Dushana, my sister Shurpanakha and the powerful Ṭrishiras and other flesh-eating titans, prowlers of the night, had at my command taken up their residence, in order to harass the sages in that vast forest, who were engaged in their austerities.

" Fourteen thousand titans of terrible deeds, full of courage and supremely skilled, dwelt in Janasthana under the leadership of Khara. These powerful warriors assembled there, met with Rama in the field. Furnished with every kind of weapon, clad in mail, and headed by Khara, they were assailed by the infuriated Rama, without a single provocative word having been uttered, who directed the arrows of his bow against them, and under the fiery darts of a mere mortal, fighting single-handed and on foot, those fourteen thousand titans of great prowess fell ; Khara perished in that struggle and Dushana was laid low with Trishiras also; peace was thus established in the Dandaka Forest.

" Having been exiled to the forest with his wife by an outraged sire, that insignificant mortal, Rama, the obloquy of the warrior class, a man without moral principle, ruthless, passionate, fanatical, acquisitive and a slave to his senses, dwells in his hermitage, having forsworn his duty. Essentially unjust, seeking to harm others without cause, depending on his own strength alone, he has mutilated my sister by cutting off her ears and nose.

" I have resolved to carry off his consort, Sita, by force, who resembles a daughter of the Gods, and I now solicit thine aid in this undertaking. O Hero, I with my brothers have nothing to fear from the Gods, therefore do thou accompany me as a loyal ally; O Titan, thou hast no equal in pride and courage in battle and in strategy; thou art also a master, being versed in the laws of magic.

" Learn from me how thou canst best assist me! Assuming the form of a golden deer, flecked with silver, do thou pass to and fro near Rama's hermitage in the presence of Sita. Seeing that lovely doe, assuredly Sita will say to her lord and Lakshmana :—' Do ye capture it! '

" When they are far distant and, by good fortune, Sita is left alone, I shall bear her away without hindrance, as Rahu devours the splendour of the moon. The abduction of his consort will cause Rama to die of grief, and I shall regain my happiness and security in a heart wholly satisfied! "

Hearing these words concerning Sita, the benevolent features of Maricha wilted with terror and, passing his tongue over his dry lips, with a fixed gaze like unto one dead, he regarded Ravana. Filled with dread, knowing well the defence of the forest to be valiantly upheld by Rama, with joined palms Maricha addressed Ravana in words tending to his welfare :—

CHAPTER 37

Maricha seeks to persuade Ravana from his Purpose

HEARING the words of that Sovereign of the Titans, the wise and eloquent Maricha answered him, saying:—

" O King, those who have recourse to flattery are easy to find, but rare are those who are willing to listen to that speech which is severe yet salutory. Assuredly thou dost not know Rama and art not conversant with his great qualities, which equal those of Mahendra and Varuna.

" Thou art thoughtless and thy spies are incompetent; how canst thou dwell in security with thy titans, O Friend? Is not Rama in his wrath able to rid the world of titans? Will not the daughter of Janaka prove to be that which will determine thy death? Will not Sita become the cause of a great catastrophe?

" Will not the city of Lanka perish with thee and thy titans, since it has thee who followest the dictates of thy passions, who art a slave to thy senses and who knowest no restraint, as its lord? An unprincipled monarch, such as thou, is the slave of his desires and in his perversity heeds only evil counsels, thus placing his subjects and his kingdom in jeopardy.

" Rama has neither been disowned by his sire, nor is he unfaithful to his duty, nor is he avaricious nor wicked, nor the obloquy of the warrior caste. The son of Kaushalya is neither void of loyalty nor of other virtues, nor is he given to anger, nor does he seek to harm others. Knowing his father to be deceived by Kaikeyi, yet filled with filial devotion he said ' I will redeem his pledge ' and went into exile to the forest. To please Kaikeyi and his father Dasaratha, he renounced his throne and prerogatives in order to enter the Dandaka Forest. Rama is neither passionate nor is he an ignorant man, whose senses are unsubdued; what has been related to thee is false and should never have been uttered. Rama is duty personified; he is virtuous, and this great hero is the Lord of the World, as Indra is the Chief of the Gods. By virtue of her chastity and her devotion, Vaidehi protects Rama as Prabha the Sun, how canst thou think of bearing her away by force? Do not enter the inextinguishable fire of Rama, who on the battlefield employs his shafts as flames and his bow as fuel. No matter how great thine anger, it behoveth thee not to approach that invincible warrior, bearing his bow, his countenance inflamed with ire, furnished with every weapon, the Destroyer of his Foes!

"Unless thou art willing to forfeit thy kingdom, thine happiness and life itself, that is dear to all, do not approach Rama, who resembles Antaka himself. How canst thou bear away the daughter of Janaka from the forest, who is protected by Rama's bow of immeasurable power? The beloved spouse of that Lion among Men, whose chest is broad, is dearer to him than his own life, and she is wholly devoted to him. The Princess of Mithila of slender waist will never be torn from the arms of that great warrior who resembles a flame in a lit brazier.

"Why enter upon such a vain endeavour, O Great King? Should Rama single thee out on the battlefield, all would be over with thee. Since it concerns thy life, thy fortune and thy kingdom, heretofore invincible, take counsel with thy ministers with Bibishana at their head. In honour reflect and weigh carefully the merits and demerits, gain and loss, of this matter. Compare thy valour with that of Raghava! Consider what is to thine advantage and then do what thou thinkest right. It does not appear fitting to me, that thou shouldst meet the son of the King of Koshala on the battlefield. I counsel thee for thine own good, O King of the Night Rangers!"

CHAPTER 38

Maricha describes his first Encounter with Rama

"O KING, formerly I possessed great powers and ranged the earth in a body resembling a mountain, endowed with the strength of a thousand elephants. In colour like a dark cloud, wearing bracelets of fine gold, my brow encircled by a diadem, armed with a club, I sowed terror in the hearts of all creatures.

"Wandering in the Dandaka Forest, I fed on the flesh of ascetics, and the great and virtuous Sage Vishwamitra, alarmed, went in person to King Dasaratha and addressed that Indra among men, saying :—' Let Rama protect me with vigilance on the day of sacrifice! O Chief of Men, I fear Maricha exceedingly.'

"To these words, the righteous monarch Dasaratha answered that illustrious ascetic, Vishwamitra, saying :—' Raghava is not yet twelve years old and is not skilled in the use of weapons, but I myself will lead an army composed of four angas[1] against those Prowlers of the Night, O Thou Best of Ascetics and will destroy thine adversary in accord with thy desire!'

"Thus addressed by the King, Vishwamitra answered :—

"' Verily thou wert the refuge of the Gods and thine exploits are renowned in the Three Worlds, yet, however powerful thine army, none but Rama on this earth has the power to overcome these demons. Do thou therefore remain here, O Scourge of Thy Foes! Though still a child, Rama is fully able to subdue the demons, I shall therefore take him with me; may all be well with thee!'

"Having spoken thus, the Sage Vishwamitra, highly gratified, took the king's son with him to his hermitage.

"In the forest of Dandaka he initiated the traditional sacrifices, whilst Rama, with his bow strung in readiness, remained close at hand. Yet a child, with his dark skin of bluish hue and his shining glances, clothed in a simple tunic, bearing his bow, his locks tied in a knot, wearing a golden chain, he illumined the Dandaka Forest with his radiance, like unto the new moon about to rise.

"At that instant, full of power and proud of the boons won from Brahma, shining like a cloud and wearing golden earrings, I entered the hermitage. Seeing me, Rama took up his arrow and placed it on the string of his bow with care. In mine ignorance I passed him by, deeming him to be but a child and rushed towards the altar where Vishwamitra stood. Thereupon Rama let loose a sharp arrow fatal to his foes, and striking me, hurled me into the sea, a distance of a hundred

[1] Divisions—see Glossary.

yojanas ! O Friend, the valiant Rama, having no wish to kill me, spared my life, but overwhelmed by the violence of the blow I lost consciousness and was thrown into the depths of the sea. After a long while, recovering my senses, I returned to Lankà. Though my life had been spared, yet my companions, who went to mine aid were all slain by the child Rama of imperishable deeds, who proved himself a master in the science of archery.

" If, setting me aside, thou dost pit thyself against him, then thou shalt surely draw down an immediate, dreadful and inescapable retribution, not to be eschewed.

" The titans who know of nought but diversions and entertainments of every kind and who dream only of assemblies and festivities will be plunged in fruitless misery.

" On account of Sita, the City of Lanka, with its temples and palaces, encrusted with every kind of gem, will be razed to the ground under thine eyes.

" Even those who are pious and innocent, suffer for the misdeeds of others through their contact, as fish in a snake-infested lake.

" Their limbs perfumed with divine sandal-paste, wearing celestial ornaments, thou shalt see the titans lying on the earth on account of thy folly. The survivors with their consorts, save those who have been borne away, will flee in all directions, unable to find refuge. Under a hail of arrows, ringed in flames, thou shalt see the edifices of Lanka burnt to ashes.

" O King, there is no greater sin than consorting with another's wife ; thou hast thousands of concubines in thy train ; therefore, cleaving to thy lawful consorts, preserve thy line, thine honour, fortune, kingdom and thy life. If thou desirest to live happily with thy wives and friends, do not enter into conflict with Rama.

" If, despite my friendly counsels, thou dost bear Sita away by force, then thou and thy kinsmen, together with thine whole army will surely descend to the region of Yama under Rama's deadly shafts."

CHAPTER 39

Maricha again seeks to dissuade Ravana from pursuing his Design

" O Ravana I have told thee how my life was spared ; now hear what happened further.

" I was in no way daunted by this event and, accompanied by two demons, I entered the forest of Dandaka disguised as a deer. There I roamed about living on the flesh of ascetics, visiting the sacred retreats, the sacrificial fires and places of worship, sowing terror amongst the sages, whom I persecuted. Growing exceedingly rapacious, I slew those ascetics, drinking their blood and devouring their flesh, my cruelty rendering me the terror of all the inhabitants of the forest.

" As I roamed here and there throwing obstacles in the way of the religious rites, I encountered Rama living a life of asceticism with the blessed Sita and the mighty Lakshmana, engaged in pious practices and devoted to the welfare of all.

" Filled with contempt for the mighty Rama, who had retired to the forest, and reflecting : ' So he has now become an ascetic,' I, remembering my former defeat, filled with anger, rushed at him with lowered horns, in my folly desiring to kill him. But he, swift as Suparna or Anila, drawing his great bow, loosed three sharp and deadly arrows, and these dread shafts with burnished points resembling lightning, flew off as one, thirsting for blood.

" Knowing Rama's skill and prowess from former times and recognising the peril in which I stood, I ran away and escaped, but the two titans who accompanied me were slain. Having with supreme difficulty evaded Rama's arrows thus preserving my life, I retired to this place, adopting the path of an ascetic and practising Yoga. From that day, I behold Rama, clothed in bark, wearing a black antelope skin, bearing his bow, in every tree, like unto the God of Death himself carrying his noose ! In my terror, I see thousands of Ramas, O Ravana ! The whole forest assumes the form of Rama and even in deserted places I behold him! O Chief of the Titans, in sleep also he appear to me and I start up in fear. Such is the terror he inspires in me, that even those words beginning with the syllable 'Ra', such as 'Ratna'[1] and 'Ratha',[2] fill me with alarm.

"Having recognized the prowess of that descendant of Raghu, I am persuaded that thou art not able to withstand him in combat, when even Bali and Namuchi succumbed to him. Whether thou dost enter into conflict with him or makest thy peace, do not speak his name to me, if thou wouldst see me live!

"In this world, there are countless virtuous souls engaged in the practice of Yoga, fulfilling their every duty, who yet perish with those about them through another's fault. I too, therefore, should be doomed to die for another's misdeeds! O Ranger of the Night, do what thou deemest to be right, but follow thee I will not. Truly Rama, who is full of zeal, courage and prowess, will prove to be the destroyer of the titans of this world. Though the wicked-minded Khara of Janasthana was slain by him on account of Shurpanakha, how, in truth, is he to blame for that?

"I have uttered these words for thy good and the good of thy kinsmen; if thou disregardest them, thou and thy people will assuredly perish in combat with Rama!"

CHAPTER 40

Ravana's Wrath

As one about to die refuses a remedy, so did Ravana repudiate Maricha's judicious and opportune words and, having listened to this salutory discourse, replied in harsh and ill-considered accents, saying:—

"Thou Wretch, what thou hast spoken will bear no fruit, as seed that is sown on barren soil comes to nought, nor will it alter my determination to enter into combat with Rama, who is but a witless and insignificant creature.

[1] Ratna—Necklace.
[2] Ratha—Chariot.

" In thy presence I shall bear away the beloved wife of Rama, the slayer of Khara, who has renounced father, mother, kingdom and friends for a woman of no account. O Maricha, my mind is fixed; neither Gods nor titans nor Indra himself can alter my resolve.

" It is proper, when asked, to put forward the advantages and disadvantages of a project and what will best serve or injure a purpose; a wise minister, questioned by his sovereign, seeking his master's good, will answer with due deference, standing before him with joined palms, in words fitting to the occasion, but a gloomy discourse does not please a monarch, who, having regard to his dignity, is thereby affronted.

" Kings of limitless power represent the five Gods: Agni, Indra, Soma, Yama and Varuna, symbolising ardour, valour, gentleness, retribution and forgiveness; therefore at all times they should be honoured and revered. Thou, nevertheless, disregarding thy duty, dost only manifest arrogance. Thou to whom I have come as a guest hast treated me as a miscreant. I have not consulted thee regarding what is expedient or proper, O Titan, I ask thee for thy support in this enterprise. Hear how thou canst assist me.

" Assuming the form of a golden deer studded with silver, proceed to Rama's hermitage and pass to and fro before Vaidehi; after captivating her, thou canst depart. Seeing thee transformed into a deer by thy magic power, Vaidehi struck with wonder, will instantly call on Rama to capture thee. When Kakutstha is far away, having left the hermitage, do thou, imitating his voice, utter such cries as: 'O Sita! O Lakshmana!'

" At this call, urged on by Sita, Saumitri, in fraternal love, being perturbed, will hastily follow in Rama's wake. Kakutstha and Lakshmana being both far distant, I shall bear Sita away, as the thousand-eyed God carried off Sachi. Having accomplished this according to my design, I shall confer half my kingdom on thee, O Titan.

" O Friend, do thou pursue the path which leads to the success of this enterprise and I will follow in my chariot. Obtaining possession of Sita without a struggle by deceiving Rama, I shall return to Lanka with thee, my purpose fulfilled.

"If thou dost not obey me, even against thine inclination, O Maricha, I shall slay thee instantly! I shall compel thee! None can attain happiness and prosperity by opposing his sovereign's will. Verily by coming before Rama thou dost risk thy life, but certain death awaits thee if thou oppose me; therefore reflect carefully on what is most expedient, and do what thou deemest proper."

CHAPTER 41

Maricha counsels Ravana further

THUS commanded by the imperious King of the Titans, Maricha replied in bold and fearless tones, saying:—

"What wretch has counselled thee to take this course, which will lead to thine extinction, together with thy children, thy kingdom and thy counsellors, O Ranger of the Night? O King, who is that evil person, envious of thy good fortune, who seeks to open the portals of death to thee? Assuredly he is thine enemy, who in his impotence plots thy defeat under the blows of a superior antagonist. What miscreant of evil intent seeks to propel thee along the path of self-destruction? The counsellors, who do not dissuade thee from thy fell design, merit death and yet live. Upright ministers ever restrain a king, who following his own desires, enters on an evil path. Thou who should thus be guided art blind.

"By the grace of their sovereign, ministers attain justice, profit, pleasure and renown, but these objects are never found, O Ravana, if a king be lacking in virtue, and his people suffer nought but misfortune.

"O Thou, Foremost of Conquerors, the king is the root of the righteousness and good repute of his subjects, he should therefore always be protected by them. No kingdom survives under a sovereign who is violent, overbearing and intemperate, O Ranger of the Night. Those ministers who counsel violence perish with their chief, as a chariot is precipitated into an abyss by a reckless driver. Many pious persons in this world, engaged in their duties, have met with destruction with their relatives through the fault of others. A cruel despot is as unable to protect his subjects as a jackal is unable to defend a herd of deer. The titans, whose lord thou art, foolish, ruthless and a slave to thy passions, are doomed.

"It is not I who should be pitied for this unexpected calamity that has overtaken me, but thou, who with thine army will soon meet with destruction. Having been struck down by Rama, he will speedily despatch thee. My mission accomplished, I shall meet my death under the blows of thine adversary. Rest assured that I shall perish as soon as I appear before Rama and know well that the abduction of Sita will cost thee thy life as well as that of thy kinsmen.

"If thou succeedest in bearing Sita away from the hermitage with mine aid, it is the end of thee, of Lanka and of the titans.

"Though seeking thy good and desiring to be of assistance to thee, thou dost disregard my words, as those for whom the last hour has struck do not heed the counsel of their friends."

CHAPTER 42

Maricha assuming the form of a Deer goes to the Hermitage

HAVING addressed these bitter words to Ravana, Maricha, full of apprehension, said:—"Let us go, but know that when I come before that warrior furnished with arrows, sword and bow, which he will wield to my destruction, my life is forfeit! Nay, he who opposes Rama will not return alive! For thee he will prove the Rod of Death and thou shalt fall beneath his blows. In what way can I further thine evil design? Yet I will go. May prosperity attend thee, O Ranger of the Night!"

Highly gratified by these words, Ravana, embracing him warmly, addressed him in honeyed accents, saying:—

"This magnanimity is worthy of thee; now that thou art willing to accede to my request I know thee truly to be Maricha; heretofore another demon addressed me. Do thou with me ascend my winged chariot, encrusted with gems, to which mules with goblins' heads are harnessed. Having captivated Vaidehi in accord with my desire, fly thence, and she, being left alone, will be forcibly borne away by me."

" Be it so ", answered Tataka's son, whereupon Ravana mounted the chariot resembling a celestial car, and leaving that solitary place set out with all speed. Looking down on many villages, forests, mountains, rivers, kingdoms and cities, they finally reached the forest of Dandaka in which Rama's hermitage stood. Descending from the golden car, the Lord of the Titans, accompanied by Maricha, beheld Rama's retreat and taking that demon by the hand, Ravana said to him :—

" Here is Rama's hermitage shaded by palm trees ; now accomplish the purpose for which we have come hither."

Hearing Ravana's words, Maricha in an instant transformed himself into a deer and began to pace to and fro before Rama's hermitage.

Assuming a marvellous form, wonderful to behold, the points of his horns studded with gems, his skin dappled, his mouth like a red lotus, his ears azure-tinted, his neck outstretched, his belly of a sapphire hue, his flanks the colour of the Madhuka flower, shining like the filaments of the Kanja flower, his hoofs like emerald, his legs slender and well-proportioned, his haunches gleaming with all the colours of the rainbow, that demon in an instant had become a ravishing gazelle of iridescent hue, studded with every kind of gem, of exceeding beauty. The whole forest and Rama's enchanting retreat were filled with the radiance of that form, wonderful to behold, that had been assumed by the titan.

In order to capture the glances of Vaidehi with his shimmering colours, he strayed here and there in the grass among the flowers. His skin was stippled with hundreds of silver spots, giving him an enchanting appearance, as he wandered about nibbling the green shoots of the trees.

Approaching the circle of palm trees, he passed slowly here and there between the Karnikara trees in the hermitage, sometimes appearing in full view of Sita. That charming fawn of many colours strayed hither and thither in the vicinity of Rama's ashrama, coming and going at will, sometimes disappearing into the distance, then drawing near again, gambolling playfully, thereafter crouching on the earth, or following a herd of deer; then again it would appear at their head, and by every means this titan, in the form of a gazelle describing a thousand frolicsome circles, sought to attract the attention of Sita. The other fawns, approaching, snuffed its scent and then scattered in all directions, but that demon, who formerly had taken delight in slaying them, now, in order not to betray his real nature, abstained from molesting those who approached him.

Meantime Vaidehi of brilliant glances was engaged in gathering flowers, diverting herself in the midst of the Karnikara, Ashoka and Cuta trees that she loved so well. As she wandered here and there plucking the blossoms, that princess of tender looks, who did not merit exile in the forest, saw before her the fawn studded with precious gems, its limbs encrusted with diamonds and pearls. Beholding that doe, with its beautiful teeth and lips, its skin the colour of silver, the slender-waisted Sita opened her eyes wide in wonder and delight, and the marvellous fawn, seeing Rama's beloved consort, continued to pace to and fro before her, illumining the forest. Looking at that deer, never before seen by man, Sita, the daughter of Janaka, was amazed.

CHAPTER 43

Sita is enamoured of the Fawn

THEN the lovely Sita, of flawless limbs and skin of a pure golden hue, gathering flowers, beheld that ravishing fawn with gold and silver flanks, and highly delighted called to her Lord and Lakshmana, who were furnished with weapons, saying:— "O Prince, do thou come quickly with thy younger brother!" Thus she cried again and again, while continuing to watch the deer, and at her call those two lions among men, Rama and Lakshmana turned their eyes in that direction and beheld the fawn.

Astounded, Lakshmana exclaimed :—" Undoubtedly the titan Maricha has assumed the form of a deer. Kings who hunt in the forest, lured by this deceptive shape, are slain by him and, O Rama, this brilliant fawn, whose radiance rivals the sun, is the device of a magician ; such a deer does not exist on earth, O Master of the World, it is an illusion, born of cunning."

As Lakshmana was speaking thus, Sita with a delighted smile interrupted him and being wholly captivated by this phantom, said :—

" O Son of a King, this marvellous fawn has taken possession of my heart ; take it captive, O Great Warrior, it will serve as a plaything. Many beautiful creatures, lovely to look upon, range the forest in the vicinity of our hermitage, such as Chamaras, Srimaras and Rikshas, while troops of Prishatas, Vanaras and Kinneras disport themselves here, but O Long-armed Heroes full of grace and strength, I have never seen a wild creature whose brilliance and gentle nimble ways are equal to this wonderful fawn's. With its slender many-coloured body encrusted with gems, it illumines the whole forest around me with a lustre resembling the moon's. What beauty ! What resplendence ! What grace ! What radiance ! This marvellous fawn with its graceful limbs possesses me utterly. If thou art able to capture it alive, it will prove an object of supreme wonder in the hermitage and when our exile is over it will be an ornament to the palace of the queens.

" O Lord ! Prince Bharata and my mothers, seeing this celestially beautiful deer, will be struck with amazement. If thou art not able to capture this wonderful fawn alive, its skin will be most precious, O Lion among Men. I shall delight to sit on its golden hide, strewn with kusha grass. I crave pardon if this cruel wish may seem unworthy of a woman, but the beauty of the deer excites my admiration ! "

This graceful creature with its golden skin, its horns set with precious gems, shining like the rising sun or the Milky Way, captivated Rama himself, who, hearing Sita's words, yielded to her wish and gaily addressed Lakshmana, saying :—

" O Lakshmana, mark how this deer has excited Vaidehi's desire. On account of its supreme beauty this fawn will lose its life to-day. Neither in the forest, nor in the region of Nandana, nor in the solitude of Chaitaratha, nor anywhere on earth does such a fawn exist.

"See how, whichever way its velvety striped skin is brushed, it glistens. When it opens its mouth, its tongue shoots forth like a bright flame in a lit brazier or lightning from a cloud. With its head of emerald and crystal, its belly shining like mother of pearl, whose heart would it not steal away with its indescribable beauty? Who, on beholding this divine apparition, shining like gold, covered with every kind of gem, would not be charmed?

"It is for food and sport that kings, bearing their bows, hunt wild beasts in the forest, and many treasures of different kinds are found there by chance, such as pearls, diamonds and gold, increasing man's possessions, surpassing the imagination of Indra, and, O Lakshmana, this is the wealth spoken of by those who are versed in the Artha-Shastra.

"The slender-waisted Vaidehi will sit with me on the fleece of that marvellous deer; neither the skin of Kadali, Priyaka, Prabeni or Abiki compares in texture to that of this deer. Truly exquisite, this gazelle and its counterpart[1] in the heavens are both divine, the one amongst the stars and the other on earth, yet if thou art certain that this is an illusion created by the titan, O Lakshmana, I will destroy it. That cruel and evil-souled Maricha slew many great ascetics ranging in the forest; innumerable kings, armed with bows, hunting here, have fallen under his assaults when he assumed the shape of an illusive deer; let us therefore end his life.

"Formerly Vatapi oppressed the Sages here also, and, entering their stomachs, emerged, riving them, as the embryo of a mule may cause the death of its mother. One day that demon encountered the great Sage Agastya, gifted with divine powers and was devoured by him when presented in the form of an offering by his brother Ilwali; when the repast was concluded that titan called out 'Vatapi come forth' but the excellent Rishi, addressing Ilwali with a smile, said:—

"'Since being blinded by thy power, many illustrious sages

[1] This refers to the fifth lunar constellation Mrigashira, said to resemble a deer.

have fallen victim to thee on this earth; thy brother is now wholly consumed by me.'

"O Lakshmana, this titan will also be annihilated like Vatapi for having set me at nought, who am fixed in my duty and master of my senses. He shall meet his end, as did Vatapi who defied Agastya. Do thou remain here without absenting thyself and guard Sita with care. It is our first duty, O Delight of the House of Raghu! I shall either slay that deer or bring it back alive; till I return with the deer, which I shall do without delay, do thou remain here with Sita, O Son of Sumitra. She shall have the fawn; its skin will cost it its life this day. Now keep watch over Sita in the hermitage. Till with a single arrow I have brought down this dappled fawn and slain it, do thou stay here, O Lakshmana, with the mighty raven, Jatayu, who is strong and wise and ever engaged in pious acts, and protect Maithili in every way."

CHAPTER 44

Rama slays Maricha

HAVING issued this command to his brother, that invincible warrior, the Delight of the House of Raghu, endowed with great prowess, girded on his sword in its golden scabbard, and taking up his triply-curved bow, his personal insignia and two quivers filled with arrows, he set forth with long strides. Beholding that Indra among Men, the king of the beasts in fear disappeared only to re-appear once more.

Girt with his sword and bearing his bow in his hand, Rama ran in the direction of the deer and beheld it in all its beauty, close to him. Bow in hand, fixing his eyes on the fawn as it fled into the forest, he saw it sometimes taking a single bound, and then, in order to lure him on, allowing him to draw closer. Timid and fearful, it would leap into the air, at times becoming visible and then disappearing in the depths of the thickets.

As in the autumn, stray clouds pass across the moon's face, so that she sometimes shines in all her brilliance and at others seems far away, so appearing and disappearing, Maricha, in the form of a deer, enticed Rama far from the hermitage.

Kakutstha found himself, despite his exertions, thus beguiled and the fawn, feigning fatigue, would crouch in the grass or, the better to deceive him, join a herd of deer, but when Rama approached, it would take to flight once more, concealing itself, only to re-appear in the distance. Sometimes, in fear, it would make itself invisible, then, with Rama in desperate pursuit, it would appear in a far off thicket. Thereupon increasingly wrath, Rama drew out a death-dealing glittering arrow more brilliant than the sun's rays and placing it firmly on his bow, stretching it with great energy, let fly that shaft that resembled a fiery serpent.

Loosing that flaming arrow, which resembled a lightning flash, fashioned by Brahma himself, that marvellous shaft, pierced the heart of Maricha, who had assumed the form of a deer. Thereat, bounding into the air as high as a palm tree, the titan fell mortally wounded and lay on the earth, having but a few moments to live. On the point of death, emitting a terrible cry, Maricha abandoned his assumed form.

Recollecting the words of Ravana and reflecting on how to induce Sita to send away Lakshmana, so that in her isolation she might be borne away, Maricha, deeming the moment to be at hand, imitating Rama's voice, cried out " O Sita, O Lakshmana ! "

Stricken to the heart by that extraordinary arrow, discarding his deer's form, Maricha took on the huge shape of a titan. Then Rama, beholding that titan of formidable size, writhing on the earth about to die, his limbs covered with blood, remembered the words of Lakshmana and reflected :—" The illusion created by Maricha, spoken of by Lakshmana is manifest, it is Maricha whom I have slain. What will Sita not do on hearing the cry of the stricken titan : ' O Sita, O Lakshmana ' ? To what a pass will the mighty Lakshmana now have come ? "

Thus did the virtuous Rama reflect, his hair standing on end and, having slain the titan in the form of a deer and heard his cry, a great dread seized him.

That dappled fawn being slain, Rama speedily killed and seized the carcase of another deer and hastened towards the hermitage.

ARANYA KANDA

CHAPTER 45

Sita sends Lakshmana to Rama's Assistance

HEARING that cry of distress, which seems to come from her lord, Sita said to Lakshmana :—

" Dost thou not recognise the voice of Raghava ? Go quickly and see what has befallen him. Hearing his cry, my heart is filled with anxiety ; he must be in great peril to call out thus ; go to the assistance of thy brother, he is in need of thee. He has been overpowered by the titans like a bull by lions."

Recollecting Rama's command, Lakshmana withstood Sita's appeal and did not move, whereupon Janaki, highly provoked, said to him :—

" O Son of Sumitra, under the guise of affection thou dost show enmity towards thy brother, since thou dost not instantly proceed to his aid ! Because of me, Rama is about to die ! In thy desire to possess me, thou dost refuse to follow Raghava; thou dost welcome his death and hast no affection for him. It is for this reason that thou dost remain indifferent to his plight ; if he is in peril, of what use is my life ? It is on his account that I came hither."

Thus, weeping and overcome with grief, did Vaidehi speak, and Lakshmana answering her, who was trembling like a frightened doe, said :—

" O Vaidehi, neither serpents, titans, celestial beings, Gods, giants nor demons can overcome thy lord. Assuredly, O Princess, among Gods and Kinneras, wild beasts and goblins, there are none who can stand against Rama in battle. O Beautiful One, he who is equal to Indra is invincible. Do not speak thus ! I dare not leave thee alone in the forest without Rama.

" Even the Three Worlds and the Gods, with Indra Himself at their head, meeting Rama in combat, would be overcome by him, therefore calm thyself and banish all fear. Thy lord will soon return, having killed the marvellous deer ; that voice is assuredly not his, nor that of a God; it is an illusion, like the city of the Gandharvas and has been produced by the titan.

"O Vaidehi, thou hast been left in my charge by the magnanimous Rama. O Fair One, I dare not leave thee here alone. We are an object of hatred to the titans since the slaying of Khara and the destruction of Janasthana. The titans are able to simulate the voices of others in the great forest and delight in doing so in order to trouble the virtuous. O Vaidehi, have no anxiety!"

At these words, Sita, her eyes flashing with anger, answered:—

"O Thou Evil-hearted Wretch, Obloquy of thy Race, who delightest in Rama's misfortune! Is it a source of wonder that a villain such as thou, perverse, whose motives are concealed, should speak thus in the hour of Rama's distress? By an excess of perfidy, thou hast accompanied Rama to the forest and, practising guile, lusteth after me, while assuming the form of a friend! Or hast thou been engaged by Bharata as his agent? Thy design as also Bharata's, shall not succeed, O Saumitri! How should I desire another after serving the lotus-eyed Rama as my lord? Rather would I yield up my life in thy presence, O Saumitri; without Rama, I cannot maintain life on this earth for an instant."

Hearing these cruel words, causing him to shudder, Lakshmana, the master of his senses, with joined palms answered her, saying:—

"It is not for me to gainsay thee; thou art as a goddess to me. An ill-considered utterance from a woman causes no surprise. Negligent in her duty, fickle and peevish, woman is the cause of dissension between father and son; truly I am unable to endure these words of thine that pierce my ears like flaming darts, O Daughter of Janaka! O Vaidehi, may all the inhabitants of the forest bear witness that to my respectful address thou hast responded with such bitterness! It will go hard with thee this day for having set me at nought, I, who am obedient to the behests of mine elder brother! May all the Deities protect thee, O Lady of Large Eyes! Sinister portents present themselves to me! May I find thee safe when I return!"

At these words, the daughter of Janaka began to weep and scalding tears bathed her countenance as she answered :—

" If I am separated from Rama, I shall cast myself into the river Godaveri ! O Lakshmana, I shall hang myself or enter into the fire, but I shall never approach any man other than Raghava ! "

Thus protesting before Lakshmana, Sita, distraught, beat her breast with her hands and lamented.

In the face of her despair, Lakshmana, distressed, sought to comfort her, but she refused to answer the brother of her lord, whereupon he, bending low before her, set out to rejoin Rama, looking back again and again.

CHAPTER 46

Ravana approaches Sita

STUNG by Sita's bitter words, Lakshmana, in his ardent desire to rejoin his elder brother Rama, set out without further delay.

Thereupon Ravana, in the guise of a mendicant, availing himself of the opportunity, rapidly approached the hermitage with the purpose of seeking out Vaidehi. With matted locks, clad in a saffron robe and carrying a triple staff and loshta, that highly powerful one, knowing Sita to be alone, accosted her in the wood, in the form of an ascetic, at dusk when darkness shrouds the earth in the absence of the sun and moon. Gazing on Sita, the consort of Rama, Ravana resembled Rahu regarding Rohini in the absence of Shasi.

Beholding that monstrous apparition, the leaves of the trees ceased to move, the wind grew still, the turbulent course of the river Godaveri subsided and began to flow quietly. The ten-headed Ravana, however, profiting by Rama's absence, drew near to Sita in the guise of a monk of venerable appearance while she was overcome with grief on account of her lord.

Approaching Vaidehi in an honourable guise, as Saturn draws near to the Chitra star, Ravana resembled a deep well overgrown with grass. He stood there gazing on the glorious consort of Rama of incomparable beauty, Sita, with her brilliant lips and teeth, her countenance as radiant as the full moon, seated on a carpet of leaves, overwhelmed with grief, weeping bitterly.

On seeing the Princess of Videha alone, clad in a yellow silken sari, whose eyes resembled lotus petals, the titan, struck by Kama's arrow, joyfully accosted her, feigning the gentle accents of a brahmin. Praising her beauty, unequalled in the Three Worlds, which caused her to resemble Shri, he said :—

" O Thou, possessed of the brilliance of gold and silver, who art clad in a yellow silken sari and who, like a pool of lilies, art wreathed in garlands of fresh flowers, art thou Lakshmi bereft of her lotus or Kirti or a nymph of graceful aspect ? Art thou Bhuti of slender hips, or Rati disporting herself in the forest ?

" How even, sharp and white are thy teeth, how large thy slightly reddened eyes with their dark pupils, how well proportioned and rounded are thy thighs and how charming thy legs, resembling the tapering trunk of an elephant ! How round and plump are thy cheeks, like unto the polished fruit of the Tala trees ; how enchanting is thy bosom, decorated with pearls !

" O Lady of Sweet Smiles, lovely teeth and expressive eyes, as a river sweeps away its banks with its swift current so dost thou steal away my heart, O Graceful One. Slender is thy waist, glossy thine hair, thy breasts touching each other enhance thy loveliness ; neither the consorts of the Gods, the Gandharvas, the Yakshas nor the Kinneras can compare with thee. 'Till this hour, I have never seen any on earth so perfect ; thy youth, thy beauty and thy grace are unequalled in the Three Worlds !

" Seeing thee dwelling here in solitude distresses my heart. Come with me ! It is not fitting that thou shouldst remain here ; this place is frequented by ruthless demons, who are able to assume different forms at will. It is for thee to reside in sumptuous and delightful palaces in the vicinity of pleasant cities, surrounded by groves of sweet smelling shrubs and green trees, where thou canst wander clad in beautiful robes, decked in fragrant garlands, with a consort worthy of thy beauty, O Charming One. O Dark-eyed Lady of Sweet Smiles, art thou wedded to one of the Rudras, the Maruts or Vasus? Thou appearest divine to me, yet these are not the haunts of the Gàndharvas, Devas or Kinneras, but of the Titans. How hast thou come here?

"Dost thou not fear to live amidst monkeys, lions, tigers, deer, wolves, bears, hyenas and leopards? O Fair One, dost thou not tremble before those terrible elephants, maddened with the exudation of temporal juices, in this great forest? Who art thou? To whom dost thou belong? For what reason dost thou range the Dandaka Forest alone, which is frequented by terrible titans?"

With these flattering words did the evil-minded Ravana address Sita, and seeing him in the guise of a brahmin, she entertained him with the traditional hospitality due to an uninvited guest. Leading him to a seat, she brought water to wash his feet and offered him food, saying:—"Be pleased to accept this repast!" Seeing him in the form of a Twice-born with his loshta and saffron robe, unrecognizable in his disguise, Sita welcomed him as a true brahmin, saying:—

"Be seated, O Brahmin, and accept this water for washing thy feet, also this meal, composed of ripe fruits and roasted grain, prepared for thee, which please enjoy."

Thus did she receive him with hospitable words, but Ravana, his gaze fixed on the Princess of Mithila, determined to bear her away, thus preparing his own destruction.

Sita, anxiously expecting the return from hunting of her illustrious lord, with Prince Lakshmana, searched the vast and darkening forest with her eyes but was unable to see either Rama or his brother there.

CHAPTER 47

The Conversation of Ravana and Sita

THUS addressed by Ravana in the guise of a mendicant, who had resolved to bear her away, Sita reflected :—

'This person is my guest and a brahmin ; if I do not answer him he may curse me ! ' and thinking thus, she said:—

"May good betide thee ! I am the daughter of the high-souled Janaka, the King of Mithila, my name is Sita and I am the beloved consort of Rama. For twelve years, I dwelt in the palace of Ikshwaku, where all my desires were gratified and I enjoyed every comfort.

"In the thirteenth year, the king with the approval of his ministers decided to enthrone Rama. All being ready for the installation of Raghava, Kaikeyi, one of my mothers-in-law, requested a boon of her lord. Having gratified my father-in-law by her services, she extracted two promises from him, the exile of my husband and the installation of her son Bharata, saying :—'I shall neither eat drink nor sleep if Rama is enthroned and it will prove the end of my life.'

"The Lord of the Earth, my father-in-law, hearing her speak thus, offered her diverse gifts, but Kaikeyi refused them. At that time, my lord was twenty-five years old and I eighteen. Being loyal, virtuous, honourable and devoted to the good of all, my lord, Rama, endowed with long arms and large eyes, was renowned throughout the world. Our father King Dasaratha, blinded by passion, in order to please Kaikeyi, did not install Rama, and when he came before his sire, in order to receive the crown, Kaikeyi addressed the following bitter words to him :—" O Ramachandra, hear from me the decree issued by thy father. This great kingdom is to be given to Bharata and thou art to dwell in the forest for fourteen years. Now go hence, and save thy sire from the sin of perjury."

"Then the imperturbable Rama replied : 'So be it' and acted accordingly. My lord of firm vows, accustomed to give and not to receive commands, who ever speaketh truth without prevarication, hearing these words acquiesced and has fulfilled his vow to the uttermost. His brother, the valiant Lakshmana, a Lion among Men and the companion of Rama in combat, the Destroyer of his Foes, given to asceticism, bearing his bow, followed Rama into exile with me.

" Thus Raghava, fixed in his vow, wearing matted locks, accompanied by myself and his younger brother, penetrated into the depths of the forest of Dandaka. We have all three been banished from the kingdom by Kaikeyi and, depending on our own strength, wander about in the forest. Remain here awhile, O Foremost of the Twice-born, my lord will soon return with an abundance of roots and fruit and sufficient venison, having slain deer, kine and boar. But thou, O Brahmin, tell me who thou art and what thy name, family and lineage. Why dost thou range the Dandaka Forest alone? "

Hearing the words of Sita, the consort of Rama, the mighty titan replied in these harsh words :—

" O Sita, I am that Ravana, King of the Titans, in fear of whom the world, the Gods, titans and men tremble. O Source of Delight, since I beheld thee shining like gold, clad in silk, my consorts have ceased to find favour with me. Do thou become the chief queen of those countless women, stolen away from many quarters by me.

" Lanka, my capital, set in the midst of the sea, is built on the summit of a hill. There, O Sita, wander with me in the groves and thus forget the forest. O Lovely One, if thou dost become my wife, five thousand servants adorned with diverse ornaments shall attend on thee."

The blameless daughter of Janaka, being thus addressed by Ravana, was filled with indignation and answered that titan with contempt, saying :—

" I am dependent on my lord, Rama, who is as steadfast as a rock, calm as the ocean and equal to Mahendra himself, Rama, endowed with every good quality, who resembles the Nyagrodha tree in stature. I am dependent on that illustrious and noble warrior, whose arms are long, whose chest is broad, whose gait is like a lion's, nay, who resembles that king of beasts ; to him, the greatest of men, I give my whole allegiance.

To Rama, whose countenance resembles the full moon, the son of a king, master of his passions, of immeasurable renown and power, I shall ever remain faithful.

" O Jackal, thou desirest a she-lion but art no more able to possess me than grasp the light of the sun! Thou Wretch, who seekest to carry off the beloved spouse of Raghava! Verily thou dost imagine the trees that thou seest before thee to be made of gold,[1] that thou art seeking to draw the teeth of a famished and courageous lion, that enemy of the deer, or extract the fangs of a poisonous snake. Dost thou desire to lift up the Mandara mountain with thy bare hands or live at ease after drinking poison? Thou dost seek to rub thine eyes with a needle and lick a razor with thy tongue! Thou desirest to cross the ocean with a stone round thy neck or grasp the sun and moon. O Thou who seekest to bear away the beloved wife of Rama, thou art endeavouring to carry a blazing fire in thy robe or walk on iron spikes.

" The disparity between thee and Rama is as that between a jackal and a lion, a brook and an ocean, the nectar of the Gods and sour barley gruel; between gold and iron, sandal and mud, an elephant and a cat, an eagle and a crow, a peacock and a duck, a swan and a vulture. Even shouldst thou steal me, if that mighty archer, Rama, whose prowess is equal to the Lord of a Thousand Eyes, still lives, thou wilt no more be able to devour me than a fly can eat the clarified butter into which it has fallen."

Addressing that cruel Ranger of the Night thus, the guileless Sita shook like a leaf in the wind.

Perceiving her distress, Ravana, terrible as death, began to boast of his race, his power, his name and his exploits, in order to increase her fear.

[1] The trees of hell, said to be made of gold.

CHAPTER 48

Sita defies Ravana

PROVOKED by Sita's proud words, Ravana, scowling, answered her in fierce accents :—

" O Lady of Fair Complexion, may prosperity attend thee ! I am the brother of the Lord of Wealth, my name is Ravana. I am the mighty Dashagriva from whom, as all creatures before death, the Gods, Gandharvas, Pisachas, Patagas and Nagas flee in terror. I have subdued my blood-brother Kuvera, who for a certain reason I incited to combat and who, vanquished by me, fled in alarm from his sumptuous abode and sought refuge on Kailasha, the Lord of Mountains.

" By virtue of my prowess I robbed him of his marvellous chariot, Pushpaka, that moves according to one's will, and in it I range the skies. Seeing my dread visage, the Gods with Indra at their head flee in terror, O Maithili. Wheresoever I roam, the wind blows temperately and the rays of the sun resemble the moon's. Where I stay, the leaves of the trees become motionless and the rivers cease to flow.

" Beyond the sea stands my magnificent capital, Lanka, inhabited by powerful titans, equal to Indra's citadel, Amaravati.

" That beautiful stronghold, encircled by dazzling battlements with golden ramparts and gates of emerald, is a city of dreams.

" Filled with elephants, horses and chariots, echoing to the sound of bugles, it is embellished by pleasant gardens planted with diverse trees, yielding fruit of every desirable taste. O Sita, O Thou Daughter of a King, in that city thou shalt dwell with me, forgetting the lot of mortal women. There thou shalt taste celestial delights ! O Lady of exquisite countenance, think of Rama no more, who is but human and whose end is near. Placing his beloved son on the throne, King Dasaratha sent his heir of negligible prowess to the forest. What wouldst thou with that Rama, deprived of his kingdom, living as an ascetic in solitude, O Large-eyed Beauty? I, the Lord of all the titans, have come to thee in person, pierced by the shafts of the God of Love. It does not befit thee to disregard me. O Timid Lady, if thou dost pass me by, thou wilt repent, like Urvashi, who thrust away Puraravas with her foot. Rama is but a mortal and not equal to even a finger of mine in combat. By good fortune I have come to thee; do thou therefore yield thyself to me, O Fair One."

At these words, Vaidehi, her eyes flashing with anger, though alone, answered that Lord of the Titans boldly, saying:—

"Since thou claimest to be the brother of the God, Kuvera, who is held in veneration by all the Celestials, how dost thou dare to commit this infamous deed, O Ravana? Undoubtedly all the titans will meet with destruction, having so cruel, senseless and lustful a person as thee as their sovereign. The ravisher of Indra's consort, Sachi, may survive, but he who bears away the wife of Rama will never live in peace. O Titan, it were possible for the one who deprives the Bearer of the Thunderbolt of his consort of unsurpassed beauty to live on earth, but he who insults me will never escape death, were he to drink the water of immortality!"

CHAPTER 49

Sita's Abduction by Ravana

HEARING those words of Sita, the mighty Ravana, striking one hand on the other, revealed his gigantic form and, skilled in speech, addressed her, saying:—

"Methinks thou hast taken leave of thy senses, hast thou not heard of my great prowess and valour? Standing in space, I am able to lift up the earth; I can drink the waters of the ocean and destroy death himself in combat. With my shafts I can pierce the sun and cleave the terrestial globe. Thou, who dost allow thyself to be deceived by any trick and dost follow any whim, behold how I can change my shape at will."

Speaking thus, Ravana, full of wrath, his eyes glowing like

burning coals, resembled a flame, and discarding his benign aspect, he, the younger brother of Kuvera, assumed a terrible shape, resembling death itself.

With smouldering eyes, a prey to anger, resplendent in ornaments of fine gold, like a dark cloud, that Ranger of the Night appeared before her with his ten heads and twenty arms. Abandoning his ascetic disguise, the King of the Titans took on his native form; wearing a blood-red robe, he fixed that pearl among women, Maithili, with his gaze, thereafter addressing her, who resembled the sun, whose hair was dark and who was clothed in a robe and jewels, saying :—

" O Fair Lady, if thou desirest a master famed throughout the Three Worlds, then surrender thyself to me. I am a husband worthy of thee; do thou serve me forever! I shall do thee great honour nor will I ever displease thee. Renouncing thine attachment to a man, place thine affection on me. What binds thee to Rama, O Thou Foolish One who deemest thyself wise; he who has been banished from his domain, who has failed to fulfil his destiny and whose days are numbered, Rama, who on the injunction of a woman abandoned kingdom, friends and people to inhabit a forest frequented by wild beasts?"

Speaking thus to Maithili, who was worthy of tenderness and gentle of speech, that wicked titan, inflamed by passion, seized hold of her as Budha seizes Rohini. With his left hand he grasped the hair of the lotus-eyed Sita, and with his right, her thighs. Seeing Ravana with his sharp teeth like the peak of a mountain, resembling death itself, the Celestial Beings fled away in terror. Then instantly the great chariot belonging to Ravana, made of gold, to which braying mules were harnessed, appeared and, addressing Sita in harsh tones, he lifted her up and, clasping her, ascended the car.

Then the virtuous and unfortunate Sita, being overpowered by the titan, began to cry aloud, "Rama! Rama!" but he was far away in the depths of the forest. Though she possessed no love for him, Ravana, burning with passion, rose high into the air with her, as she struggled like the consort of the Indra of Serpents.

Seeing herself borne through the air by the King of the

Titans, Sita with piercing shrieks, distracted with anguish, cried out: "O Lakshmana, thou long-armed warrior, ever ministering to the satisfaction of thy superiors, dost thou not know that I am being carried away by a titan able to assume any shape at will? O Raghava thou, who art willing to renounce life and happiness in the cause of duty, dost thou not see that I have been borne away by one of unsurpassed wickedness? O Thou, the Scourge of Thine Enemies, art thou not accustomed to punish evildoers? Why dost thou not subdue the arrogance of this wicked titan? It is true that an evil deed does not bear fruit immediately, but time causes the grain to ripen.

"For this outrage, bereft of thy senses by fate, thou shalt, O Ravana, meet with a terrible retribution, bringing about thine end. Alas! The designs of Kaikeyi are crowned with success, since I, the virtuous consort of Rama am separated from that hero. I invoke Janasthana and the flowering Karnikara trees, so that they may tell Rama speedily that Sita has been borne away by Ravana! I appeal to the Godaveri river, that re-echoes to the cry of cranes and swans, to inform Rama that Ravana has stolen Sita away! Offering salutations to the forest Deities, I call upon them to tell my lord of mine abduction! I beseech all creatures, whatever they may be, whether beast or bird or those that inhabit the forest, to make these tidings known to Rama and to tell him that his tender spouse, dearer to him than life, has been forcibly borne away by Ravana. Were death himself my ravisher, that mighty-armed one, hearing this report, would rescue me by his prowess!"

In the extremity of her grief, the large-eyed Sita, uttering this lament, observed the vulture Jatayu, perching on a tree. Thereupon beholding him, the beautiful Sita, borne away by Ravana, who was filled with carnal desire, cried out in piteous tones:—

"O Noble Jatayu, see how I am being ruthlessly carried off by the wicked King of the Titans, like a woman bereft of her protector. Thou wilt not be able to resist him, for this cruel and evil Ranger of the Night is powerful, arrogant and furnished with weapons. Nevertheless, O Bird, do thou bear the tidings of mine abduction to Rama and Lakshmana and tell them all, omitting nothing."

CHAPTER 50

Jatayu attacks Ravana

JATAYU, who was fast asleep, awoke on hearing these words and beheld Ravana and the daughter of Videha.

Thereupon, the King of Birds, with his sharp beak resembling the peak of a mountain, perching on the tree, spoke softly to Ravana, saying :—

" O Dashagriva, I am conversant with the Puranas, firm in my vows, and follow the path of dharma. O Brother, it does not become thee to commit this infamy in my presence ! My name is Jatayu, the King of the Vultures ; she whom thou dost seek to bear away is the beautiful Sita, the faithful and illustrious consort of the Protector of the Worlds, that Lord of Men, Rama, the son of Dasaratha, who is equal to Varuna and Mahendra and ever engaged in the welfare of all beings.

" How can a king, fixed in his duty, look upon another's wife ? O Thou of mighty prowess, it is for thee particularly to defend the consorts of kings, therefore control thy base inclination to insult the wife of another. A noble person will ever eschew that which may bring reproach on him, and protects another's wife as if she were his own.

" O Delight of Poulastya, whether it concerns that which is expedient or agreeable, in the absence of the authority of the scriptures, men of honour follow the example of a king in matters of duty. A king represents duty, a king represents desire and is the supreme treasury of his subjects ; he is the root of good and evil.

" O King of the Titans, thou art wicked and fickle by nature; how hast thou obtained a kingdom, like unto a sinner winning the celestial abode ? It is hard for an unruly and passionate man to change his nature ; noble counsels are not long remembered by perverse persons. Since the mighty and virtuous Rama has never done a wrong in thy kingdom or capital, why dost thou seek to provoke him ? Is Rama of irreproachable action to blame if he slew the wicked Khara in Janasthana on account of Shurpanakha? Why dost thou seek to bear away the consort of that Lord of Men? Release Vaidehi this instant, lest, with his dread glance resembling a glowing brazier, he consume thee, as Indra reduced Vritra to ashes with his thunderbolt.

"O Ravana, thou art unwittingly carrying a highly venomous serpent in thy robe; without discerning it, thou art wearing the noose of death round thy neck. A man should only bear that weight which will not crush him and eat only that which does not give rise to sickness. Who will engage himself in an act which is neither praiseworthy, just, nor honourable, and which will cost him his life?

"O Ravana, I am sixty thousand years old and have ruled over the domain of mine ancestors with justice. I am exceedingly aged, thou art youthful and furnished with a bow, armour and arrows, mounted on a car, yet thou shalt not escape without injury, if thou seekest to bear Vaidehi away. Thou shalt no more be able to carry her away by force in my presence, than it is possible to destroy the wisdom of the Veda by logic.

"If thou art not afraid, O Ravana, then halt an instant and fight! Thou shalt fall on the earth as Khara before thee! Rama, clad in robes of bark, who more than once vanquished the Daityas and Danavas in the field, would soon have slain thee in combat. As for me, what can I do? The two princes are far away and undoubtedly thou art fleeing in all haste in fear of them, Thou Wretch! Yet while I still live, thou shalt not bear away the lovely Sita, the beloved consort of Rama, whose eyes resemble the petals of the lotus. Even at the risk of my life I shall render this service to the magnanimous Rama, as if to King Dasaratha himself. Stay! Stay! O Dashagriva, reflect but for a moment. O Ravana, I shall hurl thee from thy great chariot like a ripe fruit from its stalk! O Prowler of the Night, I challenge thee to fight to the last."

CHAPTER 51

The Combat between Jatayu and Ravana

WHILE Jatayu, the King of Birds, was speaking thus, Ravana, that Indra among Men, wearing golden earrings, his eyes red with anger, fell upon him and a terrible struggle ensued in the sky, resembling clouds impelled by the force of the wind; in that conflict Jatayu, King of Vultures, and Ravana, the Lord of the Titans, resembled two vast winged mountains.

Then Ravana began to shower innumerable steel-pointed shafts on the mighty King of the Vultures, but he, the chief of those whose wings are their chariot, received them unmoved and with his feet and sharp talons that foremost of birds inflicted countless wounds on the titan. Thereupon Dashagriva, filled with fury, anxious to destroy his adversary, taking out formidable shafts, equal to the God of Death, drew his bow up to his ear and pierced the vulture with those arrows, which, flying straight at their target, penetrated it with their steely points.

Seeing the daughter of Janaka, her eyes bathed in tears, in the titan's car, Jatayu, disregarding those shafts, hurled himself at his opponent and, with his claws that valiant prince of the feathered tribe broke that bow decorated with pearls and gems and the arrows also.

Thereupon Ravana, transported with anger, seized another bow and covered him with a hail of hundreds and thousands of arrows. Buried beneath those shafts, Jatayu resembled a bird in its nest, but flapping his wings, he broke through that cloud of arrows and with his sharp claws snapped that mighty bow; with a stroke of his wings he shattered Ravana's blazing shield, that resembled fire, and brushed aside the flaming darts that encompassed him.

Then Jatayu, in that conflict, slew the swift-coursing mules with demons' heads, harnessed with gold, and demolished the chariot of Ravana, furnished with a triple standard of bamboo staves, which was driven by thought alone, bright as fire, its steps studded with precious gems. With a single movement of his wings, Jatayu struck down the canopy, like unto a full moon, with the chowries and the titans who wielded them.

His bow shattered, bereft of his chariot, horses and charioteer, Ravana sprang to the ground, clasping Sita to his breast. Seeing Ravana descend, his car destroyed, all beings voiced their delight and praised the King of the Vultures again and again, paying obeisance to him.

Ravana, however, perceiving that winged hero to be failing through exhaustion and age, greatly encouraged, rose high into the air, clasping the daughter of Janaka to him. Though without a bow, his other weapons being broken in combat, possessing his sword alone, he clasped Janaki passionately to his breast. Then the King of the Vultures darted towards him, barring his passage, and said to him :—

" O Insensate One, thou art carrying away the beloved consort of Rama, radiant as lightning; it is to thy perdition that thou hast brought about her abduction. Like thirsty men drinking water, thou art swallowing poison, with thy friends, kinsfolk, ministers, army and people. Those who through want of discrimination fail to foresee the consequences of their acts soon perish, as thou too shalt meet thine end. Caught in the noose of death, whither wilt thou flee? Thou art like unto the fish that swallows the hook as well as the bait. Assuredly those two invincible heroes, Offspring of the House of Raghu, will not brook the violation of their domicile. The deed that thou hast basely committed will be denounced by the world, as the path frequented by brigands is eschewed by honest people. If thou art not a coward, fight, O Ravana, or pause an instant and thou shalt lie dead on the earth, as did thy brother Khara. Truly thou art engaged in that which will prove thy destruction, as one on the brink of death commits an impious deed. Those actions leading to evil are not undertaken even by the Lord of Creation, Swyambhu Himself."

Uttering these harsh words, the valiant Jatayu swooped on the ten-headed demon and, seizing him in his claws, tore his flesh like the rider of a restive elephant. Inflicting deep wounds, he plunged his beak into his back and tore his hair with his talons. Thus assailed by the Vulture King, the titan, trembling with rage, pressing Vaidehi to his left side, foaming with anger, struck Jatayu with the palm of his hand, whereupon the mighty vulture Jatayu, the Destroyer of his Foes, hurled himself on Dashagriva and with his beak tore off his ten left arms. His arms being severed, in an instant as many others sprang up again, like serpents issuing from an ant heap, spitting forth poison.

Then, in his anger, the mighty Dashagriva released Sita in order to beat off the King of the Vultures with his fists and feet, and a mighty struggle arose between those two intrepid combatants, the Chief of the Titans and the Foremost of Birds, until Ravana, drawing his sword, cut off the wings and feet of Jatayu, piercing the side of that champion of Rama. The Ranger of the Skies having sundered the two wings of that King of Vultures, Jatayu fell to the earth, at the point of death, and seeing him on the ground, bathed in blood, Vaidehi, exceedingly distressed, darted towards him, as to one of her own kin.

Then the Lord of Lanka beheld that noble bird of exceeding prowess, with his yellow breast and plumage resembling a dark cloud, lying on the earth, like an extinguished torch, whereupon the weeping Sita, daughter of Janaka, whose countenance was like unto the full moon, pressed that winged creature, victim of the wanton Ravana, to her breast.

CHAPTER 52

Jatayu being slain, Ravana resumes his Flight

BEHOLDING that King of the Vultures struck down by Ravana, she whose face was as fair as the moon, stricken with grief, burst into lamentation, crying :—

" Visions, omens, dreams and the cries of birds are the inevitable signs of good and evil fortune among men. O Kakutstha, because of me wild beasts and birds are fleeing away; dost thou not understand that a great calamity has befallen me? O Rama, this bird, out of pity for me, sought to deliver me and now lies dying on the earth owing to mine evil fate! O Kakutstha, O Lakshmana, hasten to mine aid!"

Thus did that lovely woman cry in her terror, as if they could hear her, and the Chief of the Titans, Ravana, continued to pursue her, who, far from her protectors, bearing a faded garland, was calling for aid. Clinging to the trees like a twining creeper, crying: "Save me! Save me!", she ran hither and thither pursued by the King of the Titans. Bereft of Raghava, who was far away in the forest, she was calling "Rama, Rama!" when Ravana, resembling death itself, to his destruction seized her by the hair.

At this outrage, the whole universe of animate and inanimate beings trembled and a profound darkness covered all. The wind grew still, the sun dim, and the Grandsire of the World, Swyambhu Himself, through his divine power seeing Sita overcome, exclaimed: "Our purpose is accomplished!" Perceiving violent hands laid on Sita, the illustrious Sages inhabiting the Dandaka Forest, recognising that the destruction of Ravana was now assured, were filled with joy!

The Lord of the Titans, however, laying hold of Sita who was weeping and crying out: "Rama! Rama! O Lakshmana!" ascended with her into the air.

Of the hue of molten gold, attired in a yellow sari, that daughter of a king resembled lightning athwart the clouds; her silken robe, streaming in the wind, lent Ravana the semblance of a blazing volcano, and the coppery and fragrant lotus leaves, falling from Vaidehi of incomparable beauty, covered him. Her yellow silken robe floating in the air resembled a cloud illumined by the setting sun, but her pure countenance, as she was being transported through space far from Rama, had lost its radiance, like a lotus detached from its stalk.

Resembling the moon that rises from the heart of a dark cloud, Sita, her fair brows crowned with lovely locks, appeared like a lotus in flower that had lost its brilliance.

With her sharp and brilliant teeth, glorious eyes, well-formed nose, sweet mouth and ruby lips, she resembled the moon, lovely to look upon, and transported through the air in Ravana's lap, her face, bathed in tears, shone as faintly as does that orb during the daylight hours.

The golden-hued Sita seen against the dark-bodied titan looked like the girth of gold encircling an elephant. Like unto the yellow lotus, the daughter of Janaka with her shining ornaments irradiated Ravana as lightning illumines a thundercloud, and accompanied by the clashing of her jewels the King of the Demons appeared like unto a muttering cloud.

As Sita was being borne away, the petals from her hair fell in a shower on the earth, and this rain of blossom, caused by Ravana's rapid flight, covered him also, as a wreath of stars encircles Mount Meru, and suddenly her anklet, encrusted with pearls, struck the earth like a flash of lightning.

Like rosy twigs she covered the dark limbs of the King of the Titans with a radiance equal to the golden girth of an elephant and, as a mighty meteor illumines the heavens with its splendour, so was she borne through the air by the younger brother of Vaishravana.

Her jewels, flashing like fire, fell tinkling on the earth, where they broke into pieces, like meteors falling from the firmament, and her chain of pearls, bright as the moon, fell from her breast, emitting a blaze of light, like the Ganges falling from heaven.

The trees, sheltering a myriad birds, buffetted by the following wind that swayed the topmost branches, seemed to whisper "Fear not!" and the lakes, carpeted with faded lotuses, filled with fish and stricken aquatic creatures, appeared to be weeping for Maithili as for a friend. Rushing in wrath from all sides, lions, tigers and other beasts and birds followed Sita's shadow, and the mountains too, with their cataracts like faces bathed in tears, their crests like arms upraised, seemed to lament for Sita, as she was being borne away. Beholding Vaidehi carried through the air, the glorious sun, oppressed with sadness, lost its brilliance and became but a pale disc.

"There is neither justice, equity, nor truth, nor sincerity, nor kindness, since the consort of Rama, the Princess of Videha, is being carried away by Ravana." Thus did the assembled beings lament, whilst the young of the wild creatures, forlorn and terrified, emitted plaintive cries. Lifting up their eyes, glassy with fear, again and again, the forest Deities, trembling in every limb, witnessed the anguish of Vaidehi, who was being borne away so cruelly and who was constantly looking towards the earth and crying in faint accents: "O Lakshmana, O Rama".

The guileless Vaidehi, her hair streaming behind her, her tilaka effaced, was borne away by Dashagriva to his own destruction, and Maithili with her beautiful teeth and gracious smile, bereft of her friends, not beholding Rama or Lakshmana, grew pale and felt herself wholly crushed under the weight of her despair.

CHAPTER 53

Sita censures Ravana

FINDING herself borne through space, Maithili, the daughter of Janaka, greatly alarmed and filled with distress, in an access of fear, her eyes red with tears and indignation, her voice broken by sobs, addressed that ferocious King of the Titans who was bearing her away, in plaintive tones, saying:—,

"O Base Wretch, art thou not ashamed of this act? Knowing me to be alone, thou hast laid hands on me and carried me away. O Sinful Being, thou it was who, seeking to abduct me, didst in the form of a deer lure my lord away by the power of illusion.

"The King of the Vultures, that friend of my father-in-law, who sought to defend me, lies slain! Verily thou hast shown great courage, O Last of the Titans! To thine eternal shame, thou didst not win me in fair fight but without disclosing thy name![1] Dost thou not blush to commit such an outrage? Wretch that thou art, to bear away a woman who is defenceless and the wife of another! Thy dishonourable exploit will be proclaimed throughout the worlds. Cursed be thou, O Infamous Barbarian, who boasteth of thine heroism! Cursed be such valour and prowess, O Thou, the Obloquy of thy Race,

[1] It was traditional to make one's name known before entering into combat.

cursed be thou in the world, for thy conduct! How should any restrain thee who fleest so precipitately? Halt but for an instant and thy life is forfeit! Shouldst thou come within the range of those two Kings of Men, thou wouldst not survive for a single moment even wert thou supported by an army! As a bird is not able to bear the blazing forest fire, neither couldst thou withstand the least of their shafts; therefore, for thine own good, release me instantly, O Ravana!

"Provoked by mine abduction, my lord with the aid of his brother will strive to destroy thee if thou dost not let me go. Thine evil intention, on account of which thou dost seek to bear me away, that vile purpose, will never find fulfilment; for even were I never again to see my lord, who is endowed with supreme wisdom and should fall a victim to an enemy, I should not survive long.

"Thou dost disregard thine own good and resemblest one who, in his last hour, chooses what is fatal to him; none who desires his end courts that which will save him. I see the noose of death about thy neck, since thou dost not tremble in this exigency, O Titan. Without doubt, thou shalt see those golden trees, with leaves like sharp swords and the dreadful river Vaitarani flowing with blood and the terrible forest and Shamali tree, with its flowers of refined gold and its leaves of emerald, bristling with iron thorns.[1]

"Having offered this affront to the high-souled Rama, thou shalt not survive the poison that thou hast swallowed, O Merciless One. Thou art caught fast in the noose of death; whither wilt thou turn for refuge from my magnanimous lord? He who, in the twinkling of an eye, without his brother, destroyed fourteen thousand demons in combat, how should that hero, issue of the House of Raghu, skilled in the use of every weapon, full of valour, not pierce thee with his pointed shafts, thou who hast carried away his beloved spouse?"

With these defiant words and others uttered in plaintive tones, Vaidehi, borne away in Ravana's arms, addressed him, though filled with grief and fear. Yet, despite her distress and lamentations, Ravana continued on his way, bearing that sweet and gentle princess, still struggling to break free.

[1] In the region of Hell.

CHAPTER 54

Ravana reaches Lanka with Sita

BORNE away by Ravana, Vaidehi, seeing none who would defend her, suddenly observed five powerful monkeys standing on the summit of a mountain.

Thereupon that large-eyed princess of surpassing charms, let fall among them her silken mantle, bright as gold and her rich jewels. Reflecting ' May they convey the tidings to Rama ', the beautiful Sita dropped her cloak and ornaments in their midst.

In his anxiety the red-eyed Dashagriva did not observe this proceeding but these excellent monkeys beheld the large-eyed Sita, who did not move her eyelids as she was crying out.[1] Then that Lord of the Titans, passing beyond the Pampa lake, his face turned towards Lanka, continued on his way, clasping the wailing Maithili. Although experiencing a transport of joy, Ravana in truth was carrying his own destruction in his arms, like a sharp-toothed and poisonous serpent.

Coursing through the air, he left behind forest, rivers, mountains and lakes and speeding on like an arrow shot from, a bow he passed over that sanctuary of whales and crocodiles, the indestructible abode of Varuna, the refuge of rivers, the ocean. Beholding Sita borne away, the waters became convulsed and the great serpents and fish were startled.

Then the voices of the Charanas and Siddhas could be heard in the sky, saying: " The end of Dashagriva is at hand ! ". Ravana however, who symbolised death itself, bearing the struggling Sita in his lap, entered the city of Lanka.

Reaching that capital with its broad and spacious highways, he entered the palace and penetrated into the inner appartments. It was there that the dark-browed Sita, a prey to grief and despair, was set down by Ravana in his own domain, as Maya sheds his illusion.

[1] Thus not betraying her intention to Ravana.

Then Ravana addressed those demons of dreadful aspect, saying :—

" Let none look on Sita without mine authority ! It is my will that she have pearls, rubies, robes and ornaments to the extent of her desire ! Whoever speaks harshly to her, either knowingly or unknowingly, will forfeit his life ! "

Having spoken thus to the titan women, Ravana left the inner apartment and began to reflect on what more should now be done.

Observing eight valiant, flesh-eating titans, that exceedingly powerful One, blinded by the boon he had received, after extolling their strength and heroism, said to them :—

" Equipped with every kind of weapon, betake yourselves with all speed to Janasthana, where Khara formerly dwelt and, summoning up your courage, banishing all fear, establish yourselves in that place, which is now a desert on account of the massacre of the titans. A great and mighty army was entrenched in Janasthana, which, with Khara and Dushana, was destroyed in combat with Rama. Since that time, an inordinate rage which I am unable to control has taken possession of me, precluding all rest. I wish to avenge myself on my sworn enemy, nor shall I sleep till I have slain him in fight. In the hour that I bring about the death of the slayer of Khara and Dushana, I shall rejoice, as a beggar on the acquisition of wealth.

" Established in Janasthana, keep me scrupulously informed concerning Rama and his movements. Without respite, let the Rangers of the Night take action and constantly strive to bring about Rama's end. Being acquainted with your valour, which I have often witnessed in the field, I have chosen you to repair to Janasthana."

Hearing these flattering and significant words of Ravana's, those titans, bowing down to him, left Lanka in a body and took the direction of Janasthana in all haste, having first made themselves invisible.

But Ravana, having secured Mithila's daughter and brought her to the palace, though he had thus incurred the hostility of Rama, gave himself up to transports of senseless joy.

CHAPTER 55

Ravana implores Sita to become his Consort

HAVING issued commands to those eight titans, renowned for their prowess, Ravana, whose perception was clouded, considered that he had prepared himself for every eventuality.

Brooding on Vaidehi, sorely pierced by the shafts of the God of Love, he hastened to his sumptuous apartments, inflamed with desire for her presence. Entering there, Ravana, the King of the Titans, observed Sita overcome with grief, surrounded by titan women, like a ship foundering in the sea at the mercy of a storm or a gazelle separated from the herd beset by hounds.

Then Ravana approaching that princess, whose head was bowed and who was disconsolate, compelled her to view that mansion resembling the abode of the Gods, containing many storeys and spacious apartments, inhabited by innumerable women and enriched by countless gems, whilst flocks of birds filled it with their carolling. Graceful pillars of gold, ivory, crystal and silver, encrusted with emeralds and diamonds could be seen and celestial gongs resounded there.

Ravana, in company with Sita, ascended the magnificent golden stairway, ornamented with burnished gold. Those lofty buildings possessed excellent windows of gold and ivory covered with golden trellises, and their marble floors were inlaid with precious stones that shed their lustre everywhere. Then Dashagriva showed Maithili the fountains and pools covered with lotuses and every kind of flower; all this did he bring to the notice of Sita who was overcome with grief; and after directing Vaidehi's attention to the splendours of the palace, that perverse wretch, with the intention of seducing her, said:

" O Sita, apart from the aged and the children, ten thousand titans, rangers of the night, all of whom are famed for their exploits, acknowledge me as their lord, and each among them has placed a thousand loyal servants at my disposal. This entire state, as also my life, is thine, O Large-eyed Lady. Thou art dearer to me than life itself! O Sita, become the queen of those numerous excellent women who are my wives. O Beloved, be my consort, it is to thine advantage. What boots it to consider aught else, do thou give my proposal thy consideration; it behoves thee to look favourably on me, who am burning with desire.

" Surrounded by the ocean, this city of Lanka, extending for a hundred yojanas, can never be taken by storm, even by the Gods themselves with Indra at their head. Among the Celestials, Yakshas, Gandharvas and Nagas, I can see none in all the worlds equal to me in prowess. Deprived of his kingdom, without possessions, dedicated to ascetic practices, travelling on foot, what canst thou hope from Rama, a mere man without resources?

" O Sita, I am a consort worthy of thee, do thou accept me; youth soon passes, O Darling; enjoy these delights with me. O Lady of charming mien, do not think of seeing Raghava again. How could he come hither even in thought? Who can fetter the impetuous wind in the sky or seize the pure flame of a brazier? None in the Three Worlds may snatch thee from mine arms. Do thou rule over this vast empire of Lanka and all beings, animate and inanimate; even I and the Gods shall be thy servants. Laving thyself in the crystal waters, be happy and live in delight. Thy former evil karma has been expiated by the time passed by thee in the forest. It is here that thou wilt be able to pluck the fruit of thy good deeds. In my company, O Maithili, enjoy these garlands with their divine fragrance and these magnificent ornaments. With me do thou disport thyself in the aerial chariot Puskpaka, bright as the sun, that was once Vaishravana's, which I won by my prowess in combat, that vast and beautiful car, swift as thought.

" Thy countenance, flawless and lovely to look upon, pure as a lotus, is wan on account of sorrow and has lost its radiance, O Lady of lovely limbs and gracious features."

Whilst he was speaking, the beautiful Sita covered her face that sparkled like the moon with the hem of her robe and allowed her tears to flow.

Thereat the sinful Ravana, that Ranger of the Night, addressed Sita who was sunk in thought and forlorn, her cheeks pale on account of grief, saying :—

" O Vaidehi, do not fear to contravene dharma ; the ceremony that shall consecrate our union is sanctioned by the Veda ! I press thy tender feet with my heads ; grant my prayer speedily ! I am thy slave and ever obedient to thee ! May these words, inspired by the torments of love, not prove fruitless ; never before has Ravana bowed his head before a woman."

Having spoken thus to Maithili, the daughter of Janaka, Dashagriva under the sway of destiny, thought : " She is mine ! "

CHAPTER 56

Sita is guarded by the Titan Women

HEARING these words, Vaidehi, though still distressed, ceased to tremble and placed a blade of grass between herself and Ravana, saying :—

" King Dasaratha, the indestructible rampart of justice, whose piety brought him renown, had a son, Raghava. Famed in the Three Worlds, that virtuous one, possessed of powerful arms and large eyes, is my God and my lord. It is he, that hero, born in the House of Ikshwaku, illustrious, possessing shoulders like unto a lion's, who, with his brother Lakshmana will rob thee of thy life !

" Hadst thou laid violent hands on me in his presence, he would have compelled thee to refrain and would have slain thee in single combat, even as he slew Khara himself in Janasthana. Those titans of grim visage, whom thou dost extol to me, valiant though they be, would be deprived of their power in Raghava's presence, as serpents yield up their poison before Suparna. Those golden shafts, loosed from the string of Rama's bow, would pierce their bodies, as the Ganges bears away her banks ! Though thou mayest not be slain by

Asuras or Gods, yet now that thou hast incurred the fury of Raghava, thou wilt not escape alive.

"Thou hast but a short time to live! Raghava will compass thine end! That life which thou deemest impossible to lose is as a beast's bound to the sacrificial stake! If Rama lets fall on thee his glance inflamed with ire, thou wilt instantly be consumed, O Titan, as Mamatha by Rudra! He, who is able to bring down the moon from the skies and destroy it or dry up the ocean, is assuredly able to deliver Sita. Thy life, thy prosperity, thy being and faculties are forfeit; Lanka, bereft of its inhabitants, will be left desolate through thy fault. Nay, this outrage will bring thee nought but misfortune, O Thou who in the absence of my lord didst bear me away by force, never more wilt thou know felicity!

"My illustrious lord, accompanied by his brother, depending on his own energy, does not fear to live in the Dandaka Forest. Thy prowess, thy strength, thine arrogance and thy presumption, will all be wiped out under the rain of his shafts in battle. When the hour, appointed by destiny for the destruction of beings, is at hand, they become mad under its sway. Mine abduction presages thine end and that of the titans and of those dwelling in the inner apartments. As an untouchable may not approach the sacred altar, furnished with ladles and vessels of worship at the time of sacrifice, so the legitimate spouse of one fixed in virtue, faithful to his vows, may not be approached by a sinner such as thou, O Last of the Titans!

"How should a royal swan, sporting amidst the tufts of lotuses with her mate, concern herself with a cormorant on the bank? Bind or destroy this insentient body[1], I have neither desire to preserve it nor my life, O Titan, for I will never submit to dishonour."

After speaking thus in her wrath, causing the blood to freeze, Vaidehi became silent, and Ravana answered her in menacing tones, saying: "Reflect well, O Lovely Princess; if thou dost not yield to me within the period of twelve months, my cooks shall cut thee to pieces for my morning repast."

[1] Implying that the body itself is inanimate when not energised by Consciousness.

Having spoken thus, Ravana, the Challenger of His Foes, exceedingly wroth, addressed those female titans in these words :—

" Ye terrible demons of ferocious aspect, who subsist on flesh and blood, do ye instantly crush the pride of this woman! "

When he had said this, those monsters of fearful aspect, joining hands, surrounded Maithili, and Ravana commanded those women, formidable to look upon, who walking struck the earth with such force that it shook, saying :—

" Do ye take Maithili to the centre of the Ashoka grove, and there, encircling her mount guard over her secretly, and sometimes by menaces and at others by soft speech seek in every way to break her will, as one would a female elephant."

Thus commanded by Ravana, those titan woman, taking hold of Maithili, dragged her to the Ashoka grove which was planted with trees covered with flowers of every kind and many fruits, able to satisfy every desire, where birds disported themselves in love.

And, as a gazelle in the midst of tigresses, Sita, the daughter of Janaka, her limbs giving way under her despair, fell under the sway of those titans.

Like a timid antelope taken in a snare, Maithili, the daughter of Janaka, overwhelmed with grief and fear, could find no relief. And threatened by those terrible monsters, the Princess of Mithila, unable to rest, remembering her lord and beloved brother-in-law, under the weight of terror and sorrow, swooned away.

CHAPTER 57

Rama sees Terrible Portents

HAVING slain Maricha, that titan able to change his shape at will who wandered about in the form of a deer, Rama took his way back to the hermitage with all speed, eager to behold Maithili and, as he hastened on, jackals began to howl mournfully behind him. Hearing those dismal sounds, causing him to tremble, Rama, seized with alarm, reflected: "Is Vaidehi safe and well or has she become a prey to the titans? The cry raised by Maricha in the guise of a deer, imitating my voice, if heard by Lakshmana, may cause him to leave Sita in order to come to mine aid! It may be that the titans have resolved to slay Sita and for this reason Maricha, in the form of a gazelle, lured me away! Having brought me a great distance, that titan fell a victim to my shafts and feigning my voice, cried out: 'O Lakshmana, I am slain!' Is all well with them, deprived of my presence in the forest? On account of Janasthana, I have rendered myself hateful to the titans, and many and dreadful are the portents I now see around me."

Reflecting thus on hearing the jackals' cries, Rama hurriedly made his way towards the hermitage, pondering on the means adopted by the titan in assuming the form of a deer to lure him far away from his dear ones.

Directing his steps towards Janasthana, his heart filled with apprehension, he observed the birds and beasts passing to his left, emitting fearful cries, and witnessing these dreadful signs Raghava beheld Lakshmana approaching, pale of mien. Already a prey to anxiety, Rama became even more distressed on seeing his brother thus cast down.

Observing that he had left Sita alone in the solitary wood frequented by titans, taking Lakshmana by the left hand, he spoke to him in a gentle voice, in sad and reproachful tones, saying:—

"Ah! Lakshmana, thou hast done wrong to come hither, leaving Sita unprotected. O My Friend, how can this prove auspicious? Assuredly the daughter of Janaka has been slain or even devoured by the titans who range the woods! Since so many evil portents have appeared to me, O Lakshmana, I question whether we shall find Sita, the daughter of Janaka, alive, O Lion among Men! Since this multitude of beasts and jackals are emitting fearful cries and the birds also, as they fly towards the south, I fear that all is not well with that king's daughter, O Hero of great prowess!

"That titan, wearing the form of a deer, deceived me and drew me far from the hermitage. Having slain him with difficulty, at the point of death, he revealed himself to me in his true form. My heart is heavy and bereft of all delight, and my left eye throbs. Undoubtedly, O Lakshmana, Sita is no longer there and has either been carried away or is dead or lost in the forest."

CHAPTER 58

Rama's Lament

SEEING Lakshmana, cast down and dejected, approaching without Vaidehi, the virtuous son of Dasaratha enquired of him, saying :—

" O Lakshmana, where is Vaidehi, who followed me to the Dandaka Forest and whom thou hast left alone to come hither? Where is that one of graceful form, the companion of my misfortune when I was banished from my kingdom and, dispirited, roamed the Dandaka Forest ; where is Sita, without whom I cannot live for an instant, my life's companion, who resembled a daughter of the Gods ?

" O Hero, separated from that daughter of Janaka, whose skin was like gold, I have neither a desire for the sovereignty of the Gods or the earth. O Lakshmana, Sita is dearer to me than life itself. O Saumitri, has my banishment been rendered void ? If, on account of Sita, I should die and thou return to the city alone, will it not prove the consummation of Kaikeyi's desires and she find felicity ? Will not Kaushalya, her son dead, become the abject slave of Kaikeyi when, having accomplished her design, she rules the dominion with her son ? If Vaidehi still lives, I will return to the hermitage, but if my virtuous spouse be dead, I shall yield up my life, O Lakshmana! If on returning to the ashrama the daughter of Videha, whose words were ever preceded by a smile, does not speak to me, I shall renounce my life.

" Tell me, O Lakshmana, if Vaidehi is living or no, or whether in consequence of thy leaving her that unfortunate creature has been devoured by the titans. Alas ! The wretched Sita, so tender and fragile, never having experienced unhappiness, will be wholly desolate in mine absence. Did that titan, full of cunning and craft, crying out ' O Lakshmana ', inspire thee with fear ? I surmise that Vaidehi, hearing that cry for help uttered in a voice resembling mine, besought thee to find out what had become of me and thou didst come hither with all speed. Thou hast done an irretrievable wrong in abandoning Sita in the forest, thus affording those cruel and ruthless titans an opportunity for avenging themselves. Those flesh-eating demons are aggrieved on account of Khara's death and now, without doubt, have slain Sita. Alas ! I am wholly submerged in an ocean of sorrow, O Destroyer of thy Foes ! What shall I do now ; I tremble before that which awaits me ! "

Thus immersed in the thought of Sita, that paragon among women, Raghava hastened towards Janasthana in company with Lakshmana.

Heaping reproaches on his younger brother, who was overwhelmed with distress, tormented by hunger, fatigue and thirst, Rama, sighing heavily, his countenance pale, a prey to despair, entered his hermitage and found it deserted.

Returning to the ashrama, that hero ran hither and thither where Sita was wont to disport herself and, recollecting those haunts where she used to roam, he became distracted, his hair standing on end.

CHAPTER 59

Rama reproaches Lakshmana

ISSUING from the hermitage, Rama, the Delight of the House of Raghu, continued to address Lakshmana in a faint voice, saying :—

" Having confided Maithili to thy care during mine absence in the forest, why didst thou abandon her ? Seeing thee appear alone, having left Maithili unprotected, my spirit was troubled, apprehending grave danger. O Lakshmana, watching thee approach from a distance unaccompanied by Sita, my left eye and arm twitched and my heart throbbed."

At these words, the son of Sumitra, who bore the marks of royalty, was seized with distress and said to the stricken Rama:—

"Nay, it was not of myself that I came hither, nor of mine own inclination that I left Sita and set out to meet thee, but I was urged thereto by her entreaties to come to thine aid.

"The cry, 'O Lakshmana, save me!' as if uttered by her lord, broke on Maithili's ears and she, hearing this despairing call, from affection for thee, weeping and filled with terror, said unto me: 'Go! Go!'. While she thus continued to urge me, repeating 'Go', I spoke to her, seeking to reassure her, saying: 'I know of no titan who can excite Rama's fear; it is not he, but another who calls, O Sita. How should that illustrious warrior, the inspirer of awe in the Gods themselves, utter so base and shameful a word as 'save me'? Who has imitated the voice of my brother and pronounced these cowardly words and for what motive? Assuredly it is a demon who, in his extremity, has uttered the cry, 'Help!'. O Lovely One, it does not become thee to tremble like a low-born woman! Take courage, calm thyself and banish thine anxiety. There is none born, nor yet to be born in the Three Worlds, who is able to triumph over Raghava in the field in open fight. He is incapable of being defeated in combat, even by the Gods with Indra at their head.'

"Thus addressed by me, Vaidehi, distracted and shedding tears, uttered these cruel words:—

"'O Lakshmana, in thine extreme perversity thou seekest to unite thyself with me on the death of thy brother but thou shalt never possess me! It is on Bharata's instigation that thou hast accompanied Rama, since, despite his despairing cry, thou dost not go to his aid. Concealing thy true purpose, thou hast treacherously followed Rama for my sake and for this reason dost refuse to assist him.'

"Hearing Vaidehi's words, I left the hermitage, my lips trembling, mine eyes inflamed with wrath."

When Saumitri had spoken thus, Rama, who was distracted with anxiety, said to him: "O Friend, thou hast done a great wrong by coming hither without Sita. Thou knowest well that I am able to defend myself against the titans, yet on account of a hasty word thou didst abandon Vaidehi.

"I am not pleased that thou didst leave her nor that thou hast come here on account of the reproaches of an indignant woman. Submitting to Sita and giving way to the impulse of anger has caused thee to contravene the spiritual law and disobey my command.

"That titan who assumed the form of a deer in order to lure me from the hermitage now lies stricken by mine arrows. Stretching my bow, I placed an arrow on it and loosed it, as it were in sport, laying him low.

"Discarding his deer's form and assuming the shape of a titan adorned with bracelets, he emitted cries of agony; thereafter feigning my voice, in accents capable of being heard afar off, he called out, and on hearing that sinister cry thou didst abandon Maithili and came hither."

CHAPTER 60

The Search for Sita

As Rama hastened on, his left eye began to twitch; he stumbled and was seized with a fit of trembling. Observing these inauspicious signs, he enquired repeatedly of Lakshmana:—

"Can all be well with Sita?"

Eager to see her again, he quickened his pace and hastened on, but when he reached the hermitage, he found it deserted and, filled with apprehension, began to run hither and thither, searching everywhere. To that descendant of Raghu, his thatched hut, without Sita, appeared like a lake bereft of lotuses, shorn of its beauty at the end of summer.

Seeing the deserted hermitage, with its trees that seemed to be weeping, its flowers faded, the deer and the birds melancholy, bereft of charm, wholly desolate, the forest Deities having forsaken it, the mats and deer-skins lying here and there, the grassy seats withered and trampled upon, Rama began to weep and cry out:—

"Hath that timid one been carried away or killed or devoured or is she drowned or has she hidden herself in the forest? Perchance she has not yet returned from gathering fruit and flowers or she has gone to bring back water from the pools or the river?"

Faint with seeking, without finding any trace of his beloved in the forest, running from tree to tree, scaling the hills, searching by river and stream, lamenting the while and overcome with grief, he appeared like one struggling in a morass!

"O Kedumbra Tree", he cried, "hast thou not seen my dear one, who cherished thee? If thou knowest aught, then tell me where the lovely Sita can be found? O Bilwa Tree! Say hast thou seen her, who wears a silken robe, who is as fair as the young green shoots and whose breasts resemble thy fruit? Or thou, O Arjuna Tree! Give me tidings of the one who loved thee, that daughter of Janaka; dost that frail creature still live? This Kadubha Tree knoweth for certain of Maithili, whose thighs resemble its fruit, and here stands the beautiful Vanaspati enveloped in flowering creepers, buds and leaves, in whose shade the bees hum, undoubtedly thou art the crown of trees! Surely this Tilaka who loved Sita knows where she is now! O Ashoka Tree, dispeller of grief, prove the truth of thy name and allay the pain pressing on my heart by disclosing my loved one to me without delay. O Tala Tree, have pity on me and if thou hast seen that fair damsel, whose breasts resemble thy ripe fruit, do thou tell me! O Jambu Tree, if thou hast seen my dear love, whose radiance resembles the Jambunada, then speak without fear, and thou, the first of the Karnikara trees, whose flowers are of surpassing loveliness, O Gentle One, say, hast thou seen my Beloved?"

Thus did the illustrious Rama question every tree, Cuta, Nipa, giant Sala, Panasa, Kuravasa, also Vakula, Punnaga, Candana and Ketaka trees, running hither and thither in the forest like one demented.

Thereafter he addressed the beasts, saying: "O Deer, do ye not know where Maithili is to be found, whose eyes resembled a gazelle's, who with her doe-like glances was followed by the fawns she had tamed? O Elephant, methinks thou dost know her, whose thighs resembled thy trunk: pray tell me, hast thou seen her? O Tiger, if thou hast seen my gentle spouse, whose countenance resembled the moon in radiance, then tell me fearlessly.

"Why art thou hiding, O My Beloved? I see thee, O Lotus-eyed One! Do not conceal thyself amidst the trees without replying! Stay! Stay! O Princess of lovely Limbs, hast thou no pity for me? Why dost thou mock me? It is not thy nature to yield thyself to this folly, O Lady of Fair Complexion, it is vain for thee to fly me, thy yellow sari renders thee easily distinguishable, I have seen thee! Stay, if thou hast any love for me! Alas! It is not she—my Sita of gracious smiles! Without doubt, she has perished since my grief leaves her unmoved!

"Assuredly that youthful woman has been devoured in mine absence; Sita, with her lovely countenance, exquisite teeth and lips, shapely nose and beautiful earrings, whose skin resembles the winter jasmine, has perished, and her beauty is extinguished, as the full moon under eclipse. The slender neck of my well-beloved, of the hue of sandal, adorned with a necklace, has been devoured, like that of one poor and helpless, possessing neither kith nor kin.

"O Mighty-armed One, dost thou not see my loved one anywhere? O Where hast thou gone, O Sita, O My Lovely One?"

Thus did Rama lament, and calling, ran from grove to grove, sometimes turning like a whirlwind, sometimes appearing like one who has lost his wits. Intent on finding his love, ranging the forest, scaling the mountain, exploring the rivers and waterfalls, he sped through the woodlands without rest.

Searching on every side without pause, seeking Maithili throughout the forest, hoping to find his Beloved, he became utterly exhausted.

CHAPTER 61

Rama's Plaint

SEEING the hermitage and the hut deserted, with the grassy seats strewn here and there and not finding Vaidehi anywhere, Rama, the son of Dararatha, lifting up his beautiful arms, uttered these sorrowful words :—

" O Lakshmana, where is Vaidehi, where has she gone? O Saumitri, who has carried away or devoured my dearest one? O Sita, if thou hast concealed thyself behind a tree and art mocking me, then bring this jest to an end; thou hast enjoyed my distress long enough! O Darling, the young gazelles with whom thou didst play, languish in thine absence, their eyes filled with tears. Without Sita I cannot live, O Lakshmana, I am overwhelmed with grief on account of her abduction. To-day I shall rejoin that great monarch, my sire, in the other world, who will reproach me, saying: 'How comes it that thou, having left me in order to redeem my vow, art come hither before the appointed time? O Slave of thy desires, thou art bereft of honour and loyalty, woe unto thee!'

" Without doubt, thus will my father address me in the other region! O Cruel One! distracted as I am and overwhelmed with sorrow, thou hast deserted me, as a fair name parts company with a swindler! O Lovely Princess, do not leave me! O Slender-waisted Lady, in the abyss in which thou hast plunged me, I shall yield up my life!"

Thus did Rama lament, desiring to behold Sita once more, but the unfortunate Raghava could not see the daughter of Janaka anywhere. Sunk in misery on account of Sita, he resembled a mighty elephant trapped in marshy ground in which it has set foot.

Then Lakshmana in his ardent desire to console him said:—

" O Hero, O Mine of Wisdom, do not grieve! Let us unitedly put forth our endeavours. This hill is famed for its many caves, and Maithili, who, enamoured of the woods often wandered in these thickets, has doubtless ventured into the deep forest or visited the lake covered with lotuses in bloom or she has gone to the river filled with fish and frequented by birds of beautiful plumage. Perchance she has hidden herself in the gorge to frighten us and to see if we will search her out. O Lion among Men, let us seek her without delay! O Fortunate Prince, if thou deemest her to be somewhere in the forest, we will leave no quarter unexplored; do not grieve, O Kakutstha!"

These words of Lakshmana, inspired by fraternal affection, comforted Rama, who with Saumitri began to search for Sita once more with a tranquil heart. But ranging the woods, hills, rivers and lakes on every side, searching the plateaus, caves and summits of the mountain, those two sons of Dasaratha could not find Sita anywhere, and having sought her in every part of that mountain Rama said to Lakshmana:—

"I see no trace of the lovely Vaidehi on this mountain, O Saumitri!"

Then Lakshmana in great distress addressed his brother, who was endowed with flaming energy, saying:—"It is by ranging the Dandaka Forest that thou wilt be re-united with Maithili, the daughter of Janaka, O Sagacious One, as Vishnu covered the earth on subduing Bali."

Being thus addressed by the valiant Lakshmana, Raghava, whose heart was heavy with sorrow, answered in piteous accents, saying:—

"The whole forest has been searched with care by us and the lakes where the lotus blooms and this mountain with its many caves and waterfalls also, O Prudent Prince, yet no trace of Vaidehi who is dearer to me than my life's breath can I find."

Thus mourning, Rama, overcome by anxiety, his heart contracted with grief, in an excess of anguish, swooned away. Trembling in every limb, his mind bewildered, stunned and broken, that unhappy prince heaving deep and burning sighs, in a voice strangled with sobs, cried out: "O Sita, O My Beloved!"

Thereupon Lakshmana, distracted with anxiety, sought to console his dear brother by every means, standing before him with joined palms.

But Rama gave no heed to the words that fell from Lakshmana's lips and, not beholding his dear Sita, continued to call upon her again and again.

CHAPTER 62

His Despair

In the absence of Sita, the lotus-eyed, righteous and mighty Rama, his mind distraught with suffering, tortured by love for her, though unable to see her, with bitter sighs, reproached her as if she were present, saying :—

" O Thou, whose youthful flowering is more graceful than the Ashoka branches, do not conceal thyself and increase my pain ! O Darling ! Thy thighs resemble the plaintain boughs which conceal thee, yet, O Goddess, thou canst not hide from me ! Laughing, thou hast taken refuge in the Karnikara grove, but enough of this jesting which is torturing me ! It is not fitting to sport thus in a hermitage, though I know laughter to be natural to thee, O Darling ! Return, O Large-eyed Damsel, thy hut is desolate !

" Alas ! It is certain that those titans have devoured my Sita or borne her away and it is for this reason that she does not appear ; she would never mock me thus in my sorrow, O Lakshmana !

" O Saumitri, observe these deer from whose eyes the tears fall and who seem to say that Sita has been devoured by those Rangers of the Night. O Noble Lady, where hast thou gone ? O My Chaste One, my Lovely One ! Alas ! The desires of Kaikeyi are fulfilled to-day ! I went into exile with Sita and shall now return alone. How shall I enter the palace of the queens bereft of her presence ? Will not the people say : ' He is a heartless wretch ! '

" By the loss of Sita, I shall bear the stigma of cowardice and when my exile is over, Janaka, the King of Mithila, will enquire of me as to our welfare. How shall I answer him ? The Sovereign of Videha, seeing me return without Sita, will be overwhelmed with grief on account of her death and become a prey to madness !

"No, I will never return to Ayodhya ruled over by Bharata; heaven itself would prove a desert without Sita. Do thou leave me in the forest and return to the opulent city of Ayodhya. As for me, I cannot live anywhere without Sita. Embracing Bharata tenderly, say to him in my name: 'It is Rama's command that thou rule the earth.' Making obeisance to our mothers, Kaikeyi, Sumitra and Kaushalya, with due respect, protect them with all thy might, taking counsel of the wise. O Destroyer of Thy Foes, it is for thee to recount to them the death of Sita and mine own, in every detail."

Thus did Raghava lament, while ranging the forest full of distress, far from Sita of lovely locks, whilst Lakshmana, his features blanched with terror, felt himself about to lose his reason in the excess of his grief.

CHAPTER 63

He continues to lament

THAT son of a king, stricken with sorrow and a prey to anxiety, separated from his dear one, having caused his brother distress, fell into deeper and deeper despondency. Sunk in an abyss of grief, Rama with burning sighs and deep groans addressed Lakshmana, who was overwhelmed with anxiety, in words inspired by his own affliction, saying:—

"There is none in the world I deem more wretched than I; misfortune after misfortune follow each other in uninterrupted succession; it is breaking my heart. Surely, formerly I either designed or executed innumerable evil acts and now their fruit has matured and greater and greater calamities beset me! The loss of my kingdom, separation from my relatives, the parting from my mother, the remembrance of these things adds to the sum of mine unhappiness. Yet those griefs were forgotten as also the privations of mine exile in the forest, but now the disappearance of Sita reawakens their memory as an almost extinct brazier suddenly bursts into flame.

" My youthful and timid spouse has been carried away through the sky by a titan, emitting heart-rending cries unceasingly in her terror, she who formerly was wont to converse so sweetly. Assuredly the breast of my Beloved, sprinkled with saffron of great price, is now soiled with blood and dust, yet I still live! Sita, whose speech was gentle, clear and sweet, whose beauty was enhanced by her curly locks, has grown pale, having fallen a prey to the titans and she has lost her radiance, as the moon in the mouth of Rahu. The neck of my beloved and faithful consort, decorated with a string of pearls, may even now have been severed by the titans in some deserted place, where they are drinking her blood. Deprived of my presence, surrounded by titans in the forest where they dwell and borne away by them, the unfortunate large-eyed Sita will be crying out pitifully like a wounded osprey.

" In this valley Sita of gracious mien, sitting beside me, addressed thee with gentle words and sweet smiles, O Lakshmana. Is she perchance wandering on the banks of this most beautiful of rivers, the Godaveri, so loved by her, but no, she was never wont to walk alone! She whose face resembled the lotus, her eyes like their petals, has gone to gather water lilies, but how is this possible, since without me she would never gather flowers?

" Has she entered the forest full of blossoming trees, frequented by flocks of birds of every kind? Alas, no! She was too timid to venture forth alone and would have died of fear! O Sun, witness of all that takes place on earth and of every act, be it good or evil, has my beloved wandered away or has she been abducted? O tell me, lest I die of grief! O Wind, nothing in the world is unknown to thee; say, has Sita, the flower of her race, lost her way or been carried off, or is she dead?"

Thus did Rama lament, a victim to grief and despair, and the valiant Saumitri, fixed in his duty, addressed him in words fitting to the occasion saying :—

" O Hero, abandon thy grief and take heart! Look on the disappearance of thy spouse with detachment and engage with vigour in thy search for her. Men of spirit do not allow themselves to be cast down, even in the face of extreme adversity."

Thus did the highly powerful Lakshmana speak, despite his distress, but Rama, the foremost of the House of Raghu, paid no heed to his words and once again gave himself up to his great sorrow.

CHAPTER 64

Rama's Wrath

STRICKEN with grief, Rama addressed Lakshmana in broken accents, saying :—" O Lakshmana, repair with all haste to the river Godaveri ; it may be that Sita has gone thither to gather lotuses."

At these words, Lakshmana immediately proceeded to the lovely river Godaveri and having visited the sacred fords, returning, spoke to Rama, saying :—

" I have searched all the holy places but I have not seen her anywhere nor does she answer to my call. Where can Vaidehi have gone ? I do not know where that lady of slender waist can be, O Rama."

Hearing Lakshmana speak thus, the unfortunate Rama, distracted with anxiety, ran to the banks of the Godaveri river and there cried out :—" Where is Sita ? "

But neither the spirits of the forest nor the river dared to inform Rama that she had been borne away by that Indra of Titans who merited death.

The Godaveri, recollecting the former exploits of the wicked Ravana, was restrained by fear from imparting what was known to her of Vaidehi's fate. The river's silence caused Rama to abandon all hope of seeing Sita again and overcome with despair at her disappearance he said to Saumitri :—

" The beloved Godaveri has no answer for me, O Lakshmana. What shall I say to Janaka or Vaidehi's mother when, returning without her, we meet once more ? Seeing me without Vaidehi, I shall become an object of odium to them.

" When, dispossessed of my kingdom, I was forced to live in the forest on wild fruits, my misery was assuaged by the

Princess of Videha. Where is she now? Far from my kinsmen, unable to find Vaidehi, how shall I pass the long nights without sleep?

" I have searched everywhere, by the Mandakini, in Janasthana and on the mountain Prasravana to find Sita. O Hero, observe the wild deer, full of energy, who regard me unceasingly and by their glances seem to wish to communicate with me."

Beholding them, that Lion among Men, Raghava, fixing his gaze on them cried :—" Where is Sita? " in a voice broken by sobs. Thus addressed by that Lord of Men, the deer rose and turned their heads towards the south, looking upward, thus indicating the path by which Sita had been borne away. Thereafter those deer, turning southwards, sometimes fixing their gaze on that Chief of Men and then looking towards the sky, emitted cries, running in front of the two brothers, seeking to attract their attention, and Lakshmana, understanding their movements and their cries, said to his elder brother :—

" O My Lord, since thou accosted these deer saying: 'Where is Sita?' they, rising up, have indicated a southerly direction, let us therefore follow that path; perchance we shall discover some trace of that noble lady or she herself."

" Be it so " answered Kakutstha, directing his step towards the south, followed by Lakshmana. Thereafter casting his gaze on the earth, he observed some flowers scattered on the ground and, exceedingly distressed, said to his brother :—

" O Lakshmana, I remember these flowers, for I gathered them in the forest and gave them to Vaidehi, with these she decorated her hair. Methinks the sun, the wind and the earth have preserved them for my pleasure."

Thereafter Rama addressed the mountain of innumerable torrents, saying :—

" O Lord of the Hills, hast thou seen that princess of lovely limbs, that gracious one I left in this charming grove? "

Thereupon, in tones of anguish he began to threaten that mountain, as a lion roars in the presence of a deer, and cried out :—" O Mountain, show me that lady whose skin resembles beaten gold or I will shatter thy crests."

Thus questioned by Rama concerning Sita, the Princess of Mithila, the mountain would fain have spoken but through fear of Ravana it remained silent; whereupon the son of Dasaratha addressed that rocky mass, saying :—

" My fiery arrows shall reduce thee to ashes, thou shalt be stripped of thy verdure, thy trees, and thy creepers, and none shall inhabit thee. O Lakshmana, this river too shall be dried up by me if it does not reveal where Sita may be found, whose radiance resembles the full moon in her course."

In his wrath, Rama would fain have consumed the mountain with his glance, when suddenly he beheld the imprint of the titan's foot on the ground and those of Vaidehi, who in her terror had run hither and thither before being dragged away by him.

Seeing the marks of Sita's feet and those of the titan, with the shattered bow, two quivers and parts of the chariot, Rama, his heart beating rapidly, said to his beloved brother :—

" See, O Lakshmana, the scattered fragments of Vaidehi's ornaments and the many garlands and the drops of blood shining like molten gold covering the earth on every side. It is certain, O Lakshmana, that the titans who change their form at will, have hewn the body of Sita to pieces, which they have now devoured. On account of Sita, a terrible struggle has taken place here, O Saumitri.

" This great bow, encrusted with pearls, marvellously inlaid, which is broken and lying on the earth, to whom can it belong, O Friend? To what titan or to what God, O My Child, does this golden armour belong, bright as the rising sun, enriched with emeralds and pearls, the pieces of which are strewn on the earth? Whose canopy is lying here, possessing a hundred staves, decorated with celestial garlands, its supports broken? And whose are these mules, harnessed with gold, having goblins' heads, terrible to behold, that have been slain in the fight? This chariot of war, shining like a flame, which is overturned and broken, to whom does it belong? These arrows too, a hundred fingers in length, of terrifying aspect, their golden tips blunted, lying in a hundred fragments and the two quivers filled with excellent shafts, whose are they?

" See the charioteer lying on the earth, the lash and reins still in his hands, who was his master? Without doubt these footprints are those of a mighty titan, O Lakshmana. Behold how under a thousand guises the bitter hatred of these titans, who are ruthless and able to change their form at will, is made manifest! Alas, the blessed Vaidehi has been carried hence or she is dead and has been devoured! If virtue was not able to protect Vaidehi from being carried away by stealth in the great forest and she has been devoured, O Lakshmana, how can even the great ones of this world offer me any solace? The supreme Creator of the Universe Himself, were He to manifest compassion, would be misunderstood and held in contempt by the world, and I, who am by nature gentle, who have subdued my senses and who exercise mercy, desiring the welfare of all, shall be thought wanting in valour by the Gods.

"O Lakshmana, my virtues shall be overshadowed to-day, as thou shalt soon witness, and my wrath be manifest in the destruction of the demons and all created beings! As the rising sun obscures the splendour of the moon, so will my great attributes be withdrawn and my naked splendour blaze forth; there will be no escape for any in the Three Worlds, neither Yaksha, Gandharva, Pisacha, Rakshasa, Kinnera, nor man, O Lakshmana. Soon shalt thou see mine arrows filling the firmament, the planets stayed in their courses, the moon veiled, fire and wind restrained, the brightness of the sun obscured, the crests of the mountains shattered, the lakes dried up, creepers and trees uprooted and the ocean drained.

"If the Gods do not bring back Sita to me, I shall blot out the Three Worlds! Then, O Saumitri they will be forced to acknowledge my prowess! None shall find refuge anywhere in space, O Lakshmana; to-day thou shalt see the universe pass beyond its bournes. With the help of the arrows loosed from my bow, which I shall stretch up to mine ear, no being will be able to survive; for Sita's sake I shall rid the world of goblins and demons and the Gods shall witness the power of these missiles, loosed in my wrath.

"The worlds of the Gods, Giants, Yakshas and Titans will be annihilated under the impact of my shafts. With mine arrows I shall shatter the defences of the Three Worlds, if the Gods do not restore Vaidehi to me as she was before she was borne away. If they do not bring back my beloved unharmed, I shall lay waste the entire universe and all contained therein. Until I find myself in Sita's presence once more, I shall let loose every weapon of destruction."

Having spoken thus, Rama, his eyes flashing with anger, his lips compressed and trembling, tied fast his robe of bark and deerskin and knotted his hair, whereupon that sagacious One resembled Rudra bent upon the destruction of Tripura.

Taking his bow from Lakshmana's hands, he drew it with might, selecting a terrible steel-pointed shaft resembling a venomous serpent, and the effulgent Rama, filled with wrath, the Scourge of his Foes, resembling the Fire at the destruction of the world, said :—

" As beings cannot escape old age, destiny or death, so is none able to restrain my wrath ! O Lakshmana, if I do not recover Sita this day in all her pristine beauty, I shall destroy the universe with its Gods, Gandharvas, human beings, Punnagas and mountains."

CHAPTER 65

Lakshmana seeks to pacify Rama

A PREY to grief on account of Sita's abduction, Rama, resembling the Fire of Dissolution, sought to bring about the destruction of the Worlds.

With burning sighs he contemplated the stringed bow, as Hara at the end of the world-cycle stands ready to consume the universe.

Seeing Rama transported with rage, hitherto never manifested by him, Lakshmana, his features pale with terror, addressed him with joined palms, saying :—

" Formerly thou wert ever gentle, of controlled mind and devoted to the welfare of all beings, do not now give way to wrath and renounce thy true nature. As the radiance of the moon, the brilliance of the sun, the velocity of the wind and the forbearance of the earth, so is thy glory manifested without equal and without end. Wherefore dost thou seek to destroy the worlds on account of one man's sin ?

"It is not yet known to whom this shattered chariot belongs nor because of whom nor between whom, the struggle, of which we see the traces, took place. This spot bears the marks of wheels and feet and is sprinkled with drops of blood; it is the scene of a desperate struggle, O Son of a King, but it is a fight between single combatants, O Most Eloquent of Men! I see no trace of a great army and it is not fitting that thou shouldst destroy the worlds on account of one man.

"Kings should always rule with justice, gentleness and moderation. Thou wast ever the refuge of all beings and their supreme asylum. Who would condone the bearing away of thy consort, O Raghava? Rivers, seas, mountains, Gods, Gandharvas and Danavas have no desire to displease thee, even as the officiating priest will not harm the one undertaking a sacrifice after he has performed the preparatory rites.

"O Prince, it is for thee to seek out Sita's abductor, followed by the great sages and by me with my bow. We will search the ocean, the hills, the forests, the deep caves and innumerable lakes filled with lotuses. We will enquire of the Gods and Gandharvas in every region, until we find the captor of thy consort. If the Chiefs of the Gods do not restore thy wife peaceably, then, O King of Koshala, adopt those measures that thou considerest fitting. If, through gentleness, humility and prudence, thou dost not regain thy spouse, O Indra among Men, then let loose thine innumerable golden-tipped arrows, resembling Mahendra's thunderbolts."

CHAPTER 66

Lakshmana seeks to inspire Rama with Courage

Overcome by grief and wailing like one orphaned, Rama, sick at heart, was plunged in misery, whereupon Lakshmana, the son of Sumitra, taking hold of his feet and pressing them, sought to console and comfort him, saying:—

"By great austerity and innumerable pious acts did the King Dasaratha obtain thee, as the Celestials acquired the

Nectar of Immortality. Bound to thee by thy virtues, that great monarch on thy departure returned to the heavenly region, thus have we heard from Bharata. If thou art not able to endure the calamity that has overtaken thee, then how should an ordinary man do so?

" O Chief of Men, take courage! What living being is not subject to adversity, which approaches like a flame and instantly passes away? Even so is the world. Did not Yayati, the son of Nahusha, fall from heaven overcome by ill fortune? In a single day the great Sage Vasishtha, the chief priest of our sire, was bereft of four hundred sons born to him; and the Mother of the World, the Earth herself, revered by all, is sometimes known to tremble, O Master of Koshala! The sun and moon, the eyes of the world, the very symbols of virtue by whom all things are ordered, suffer eclipse. Those great beings, the Gods themselves, are subject to fate, O Lion among Men; how much more man? It is said that even Indra and the Gods endure vicissitudes; it doth not behove thee, therefore, to lament.

" Even should Vaidehi be dead or carried away, O Raghava, it is not worthy of thee to yield to despair like a common man. Thine equals are never moved even in the greatest perils but look on all with equanimity, O Kakutstha!

" O Thou Best of Men, after due consideration, discriminate between that which is good and that which is evil; persons of right wisdom are ever cognizant of what is right or wrong. Owing to the element of uncertainty, one cannot at once distinguish the advantage or disadvantage of a deed, but if one fails to act the desired result will not take place. Thus hast thou often instructed me, O Hero, and who is able to teach thee anything? Not even Brihaspati himself. Even the Gods are powerless to fix the limit of thy wisdom, O Thou of Mighty Intellect.

" I would fain arouse the power that sorrow has quenched in thee! Having reflected on the strength of the Gods, of men and of thyself, O Lion of the Ikshwakus, prepare to overcome thine enemies! Of what use were it for thee to destroy the world, O Thou Best of Men? Seek out thy perfidious adversary and put an end to his life!"

CHAPTER 67

Rama encounters Jatayu

At these apposite words, full of wisdom, uttered by his younger brother Lakshmana, Raghava, regaining possession of himself, rallied his courage anew. Controlling his wrath, the long-armed Rama, leaning on his marvellous bow, said to Lakshmana :—" O My Friend, what should be done ? Whither shall we go, O Lakshmana ? How shall we find Sita again ? Let us consider these things carefully."

To these anxious enquiries, Lakshmana answered :—" It is for thee to search Janasthana which is inhabited by innumerable titans and covered with trees and creepers of every kind. There, inaccessible cliffs, chasms and caves are to be found and dark caverns inhabited by herds of wild beasts, the retreat of Kinneras and the resort of Gandharvas ; with me explore these places. As the mountains are not affected by tempest, neither can adversity daunt the wise such as thou, O Lion among Men."

Thus speaking, Lakshmàna began to scour the forest, and Rama, still chafing under adversity, advanced holding his bow on which was strung a formidable steel-pointed shaft, when suddenly he beheld Jatayu, that excellent King of Birds, resembling a mountain peak, lying on the earth covered with blood. Seeing that great vulture, like unto the crest of a mountain, Rama said to Lakshmana :—

" Without doubt, here is the titan, who, ranging the forest under the guise of a vulture, has destroyed Sita, the Princess of Videha ! Having satisfied himself by devouring that large-eyed princess, he is resting at ease ; I shall pierce him with my dread and fiery shafts that fly straight to their target."

Speaking thus, Rama, fixing a sharp arrow on his bow, ran towards him and in his ire it seemed he would destroy the earth, whose boundaries are the sea.

Vomiting blood, that bird then addressed Rama the son of Dasaratha, in the mournful accents of one about to die, saying :—

" O Thou of long life, that divinity whom thou seekest in the great forest, as one does a healing herb,[1] has been borne away by Ravana, as has my life also.

" O Raghava, in the absence of Lakshmana and thyself, that princess was seen by me, being dragged away by the all-powerful Ravana. Flying to the aid of Sita, O Lord, Ravana was thrown to the earth by me in the struggle that ensued, and his chariot and canopy shattered. With a stroke of my wing, I slew the charioteer, but being at the end of my strength, my two wings were severed by Ravana's sword, and he, seizing hold of Sita, the Princess of Videha, escaped into the air. That titan has left me here to die ; do not slay me, O Prince."

Receiving these precious tidings concerning Sita, Rama, dropping his great bow, embraced the King of the Vultures, and then, despite his resolve, fell to the ground overcome with grief and began to lament with Lakshmana. Seeing Jatayu alone in that perilous and isolated pathway, moaning unceasingly, Rama, overwhelmed with pity, said to Saumitri :—

" The loss of my kingdom, exile to the forest, the abduction of Sita and the death of this Twice-born, renders my fate such that it would consume fire itself. Even were the sea filled to the brim and I to enter it this day, that Lord of the Rivers would dry up on account of my misfortunes.

" Such is the adversity that encompasses me that there is none in all the worlds amongst animate and inanimate beings who is so wretched as I ! On account of mine evil karma, this childhood friend of my sire, the mighty King of the Vultures, lies dying on the earth ! "

Repeating these words again and again to Lakshmana who accompanied him, Rama began to caress Jatayu, passing his hand lovingly over the body of his father's friend. Thereafter taking the King of the Vultures, whose wings were severed and who was bathed in blood, in his arms, he said :—

" Where has Maithili gone, who is dearer to me than life ? " and having spoken thus, Raghava sank down on the earth.

[1] Lit : Oshadi or Oshadi Prastha 'the place of medicinal herbs'.

CHAPTER 68

Jatayu's Death

In the presence of the vulture, whom the terrible Ravana had struck down, Rama, full of compassion for all, addressed the son of Saumitri in these words :—

" This bird, who sought to defend my interests, has been mortally wounded in the struggle with the titan and for my sake now lies dying here. Its vital breaths are barely perceptible, O Lakshmana, its eyes are dim and it is unable to speak.

" O Jatayu, if it be possible for thee, then say what has become of Sita and how thou hast come to this sorry pass. For what reason has Ravana carried away my dear one ? How did that radiant and enchanting face, resembling the moon, appear at that time, O Best of the Twice-born. What words did Sita utter at that moment ? What is the strength, the appearance and the karma of that titan ? Where does he dwell, O Friend, answer me ! "

Beholding Rama lamenting like an orphan, the virtuous Jatayu answered in feeble accents :—

" Sita has been carried away by that Indra of Titans, Ravana, that evil wretch who resorts to the aid of sorcery and is able to loose the wind and the tempest. O Dear Child, I being exhausted, that Prowler of the Night severed my two wings and, thereafter taking hold of Sita, fled in a southerly direction. My breathing is laboured and my sight dim, O Raghava, I see before me the golden trees with leaves formed of Ushira.[1] The hour in which Ravana bore Sita away was that in which the loser soon recovers that which is lost, ' Vindya ' is its name, O Kakutstha, and Ravana was unaware of it. Like a fish that swallows the bait, he will soon perish ! Do not, therefore, despair of recovering Janaki ; thou wilt soon sport with her, having slain Ravana in battle ! "

While the vulture was thus replying to Rama, blood and morsels of flesh flowed from his beak and, on the verge of death, retaining his consciousness, Jatayu added :—" Ravana is

[1] Ushira—A hair-like grass said to grow on the trees in hell.

the son of Vishravas and the brother of Vishravana!" and thereafter yielded up his life.

"Speak! Speak further!" cried Rama, addressing him with joined palms, but the life-breaths, withdrawn from that vulture's body, were already dissipated. Thereupon the King of the Vultures fell on the earth, his legs, body and head stretched out and, beholding that bird resembling a mountain of vast proportions, that bird of reddened eyes, deprived of life, Rama, staggering under the weight of his misfortune, said to Saumitri in bitter tones:—

"Passing many years happily in the forest, the resort of titans, this bird has at length given up his life! Having lived innumerable years, he now lies here inanimate! None can withstand the course of destiny! Behold, O Lakshmana, this vulture who died in my service having sought to protect Sita, and who has been slain by Ravana of superior power. He renounced the dominion bequeathed to him by his ancestors and sacrificed his life for my sake. Undoubtedly the virtuous practise courage, devotion and the fulfilment of duty, even in the animal kingdom, O Saumitri! I did not feel so keen a grief for Sita's abduction as for the death of this vulture, who has sacrificed himself for me, O Scourger of Thy Foes!

"I hold this King of Birds in the same veneration as I did the illustrious and fortunate monarch, Dasaratha, O Saumitri! Do thou bring fuel that I may ignite the pyre of that King of Vultures, who died for me. Placing the body of that protector of the realm of winged creatures on the funeral pile, who has been destroyed by the cruel titan, I shall cremate it. O King of the Vultures, O Magnanimous Being, cremated and blessed by me, depart, and ascend to those regions, further than which it is not possible to go and which are the abode of those who habitually offer sacrifice, those heroes who never retreat on the battle field and those who distribute land in charity."

With these words, the virtuous Rama placed the King of Winged Creatures on the funeral pyre and, full of grief, ignited the flame as if performing the rite for his own kinsman.

Thereafter, the illustrious Rama, accompanied by Saumitri, entered the forest and, killing a few fat Rohi deer, strewed the flesh on the green grass as an oblation to that bird. Tearing off the flesh of those deer and kneading it into balls, he offered it to the vulture in that pleasant forest land, placing it on fresh grass. Thereafter, in order that Jatayu might soon reach the celestial abode, he recited those sacred formulas uttered by the brahmins, after which the two princes repaired to the Godaveri river to offer water in honour of the kingly bird. Following the traditional rites, those two Descendants of Raghu bathed and performed the Udaka[1] ceremony for the King of the Vultures, who, having fallen on the field of battle, had executed a glorious and difficult deed and now, blessed by Rama, had attained to the place prepared for him in the realm of the saints.

Thereupon those two princes, after offering the last rites in honour of that excellent bird, as if to their sire, entered the forest, their minds set on the recovery of Sita, like Vishnu and Vasava, the Sovereigns of the Gods.

CHAPTER 69

Rama and Lakshmana meet Ayomukhi and Kabandha

HAVING performed the purificatory rites in honour of Jatayu, the two princes entered the forest in quest of Sita, proceeding in a south-westerly direction. Armed with sword, bow and arrow, those offshoots of the House of Ikshwaku followed a hitherto untrodden path, overgrown with bushes, trees and creepers of various kinds, which was difficult of access, with dense thickets on either side and of sinister appearance; nevertheless the two mighty warriors pressed on through that vast and dangerous wood.

Having traversed Janasthana and covered a further three leagues, those brothers, endowed with great energy, penetrated into the thick woodlands of the Krauncha Forest, which resembled a group of clouds and presented a smiling aspect

[1] Udaka Ceremony—ritual presentation of water to the ancestors.

with its many brilliant flowers and the herds of wild deer and flocks of birds that inhabited it.

After exploring this forest, anxious to behold the Princess of Videha once more, sometimes halting to bewail her disappearance, the two brothers resumed their journey, and covering a distance of three leagues came to the hermitage of Matanga.

Having searched the whole forest filled with fearful beasts and birds and planted with innumerable trees and dense thickets, the two sons of Dasaratha beheld a cave in the mountain, deep as the region under the earth where eternal darkness reigns.

Then those two Lions among Men, approaching that cave, perceived the vast shape of a female titan of hideous appearance. Fearful of aspect, she was an object of terror to weaker creatures with her loathsome countenance, vast stomach, sharp teeth, immense stature and harsh voice.

This monster subsisted on the flesh of ferocious beasts and now appeared before Rama and Lakshmana, her hair dishevelled, and addressed them, saying :—

" Come let us pass the time in dalliance together." Thereafter she laid hold of Lakshmana, who had preceded his brother and added:—

" I am named Ayomukhi, I am thine ; do thou become my lord, O Hero ! Let us give ourselves up to a long life of pleasure on the summits of the mountains and among the islands in the rivers."

Hearing these words, the Slayer of his Foes, Lakshmana, full of wrath, drew his sword and cut off her ears, nose and breasts. Her ears and nose being severed, that terrible titan ran away with all speed, and when she had disappeared, the two brothers, Rama and Lakshmana, Scourgers of their Foes, hastily pressed on and entered the dense forest.

Thereafter the mighty Lakshmana, full of loyalty, charm and nobility, addressed his resplendent brother with joined palms, saying :—

" I am conscious of a violent throbbing in my left arm and my mind is filled with apprehension, whilst on every side I perceive inauspicious omens ; do thou therefore hold thyself in readiness, O Great One, and follow my counsel ; these different portents foretell imminent danger. The Vanchulaka bird is emitting fearful cries which indicate a speedy victory for us."

Thereupon the two brothers courageously began to explore the entire forest, when a terrible clamour arose appearing to rend the trees; such was the uproar that it seemed as though a mighty wind had suddenly swept through the forest.

Seeking to ascertain the cause of this disturbance, Rama, armed with a sword, bow in hand, advancing with his younger brother, beheld a titan of vast proportions, possessing huge thighs, standing before him. Headless, his mouth in his belly, covered with bristling hairs, in stature equal to a mountain, his complexion that of a dark cloud, terrible to look upon, his voice resounded like thunder.

Shining like a lit torch, he seemed to emit sparks; his single eye, furnished with yellow lids opening in his breast, was strange and hideous and this monster, possessed of enormous teeth, was licking his lips. Despite their ferocity and size, he fed on bears, lions, deer and birds, catching them with his great arms at a distance of four miles. With his hands he seized hold of flocks of birds and herds of deer, which he put into his mouth.

Having observed them a mile off, he obstructed the progress of the two brothers and stood awaiting them. That colossal, hideous and dreadful creature of sinister aspect, with his trunk and vast arms, fearful to behold, stretching out, seized the two valiant brothers and gripped them with all his strength.

On account of his coolness and courage, the valiant Raghava remained unmoved, but Lakshmana, being a mere stripling and volatile by nature, began to tremble, and that younger brother of Raghava said to him:—

"O Hero, behold how I have fallen into the power of this titan; do thou leave me as an offering to the evil forces and go thy way happily; thou wilt soon be re-united with Vaidehi, this is my firm conviction! O Kakutstha, when thou hast regained the kingdom of thy forbears and art installed on the throne, remember me!"

At these words, uttered by Lakshmana, the son of Sumitra, Rama answered:—"Have no fear, O Valiant One, persons of thy valour are never perturbed."

Meanwhile the headless titan, of huge arms, the foremost among the giants, said to them :—

" Who are you, whose shoulders resemble a bull's, armed with great swords and bows ? It is fortunate indeed for me that by chance you have come within my range in this dangerous place. Say for what reason you have come here, where I wait ravaged by hunger, ye who are armed with arrows, bows and swords and resemble bulls with pointed horns ? Having approached me, your death is imminent."

Hearing the words of the wicked Kabandha, Rama, his face growing pale, said to Lakshmana :—

" We have fallen from one danger into a greater one, O Hero ; this ill chance may cost us our lives without our being able to rejoin our beloved Sita. The power of destiny over all beings is inexorable, O Lakshmana ! See, O Lion among Men, how ill-fortune drives us to the last extremity ; there is nothing that weighs so heavily on man as destiny. Even the brave, the mighty, the great and skilful warriors on the field of battle, overtaken by destiny, are swept away like banks of sand."

Thus spoke that heroic and illustrious son of Dasaratha, filled with distress, his eyes fixed on Saumitri, while in his soul his composure was fully established.

CHAPTER 70

Rama and Lakshmana sever the Arms of Kabandha

SEEING the two brothers fallen into his arms as if into a snare, Kabandha said to them :—

" What ails you, O Foremost among Warriors ? Since I am tormented with hunger, fate has destined you for my food and for this reason has deprived you of your wits."

Hearing these words Lakshmana, though sore distressed, determined to display his valour and addressed Rama in words worthy of the occasion, saying :—

" We shall soon become the food of this vile demon, who with his vast and powerful arms subdues all beings; let us with our swords sever his arms with all speed, O Lord, or he will make an end of us. It is shameful for warriors to make away with those who cannot defend themselves like an animal deprived of its freedom that is led to sacrifice."

These words infuriated the demon, who opened his terrible mouth wide, preparing to devour them, whereupon the two brothers, choosing a favourable moment, as if in sport cut off his two arms at the shoulders, Rama cutting the right and Lakshmana with a vigorous stroke of his sword, the left. Thereupon Kabandha, his vast arms severed, emitting loud shrieks which resounded through the earth and sky like thunder, fell upon the ground. Beholding his two arms severed and the blood flowing in streams, the unfortunate demon enquired of those two warriors in feeble accents :—" Who are you ? "

Thus accosted, the supremely courageous Lakshmana began to extol the virtues of Kakutstha, saying :—

" This is Rama, the descendant of the House of Ikshwaku, known throughout the earth, and I am his younger brother, Lakshmana. Deprived of his kingdom by the Queen Kaikeyi, Raghava was exiled to the great forest, where he lived with his consort and myself. While this hero, mighty as a God, dwelt in that pastoral retreat, a titan bore away his consort, in search of whom we have come hither.

" And thou, who art thou, wandering in these woods emitting flames, thy thighs sunk into thy body ? "

On hearing Lakshmana, Kabandha, calling Indra's words to mind, answered joyfully :—

" Welcome to you, O Tigers among Men, beholding you is my salvation; for my good, you have cut off my arms. Do you hear, how, due to mine arrogance, I came to assume this monstrous shape. O Illustrious Ones, I shall relate all to you truthfully."

CHAPTER 71

Kabandha tells his Story

" O LONG-ARMED RAMA, formerly I was filled with unimaginable energy and courage; my beauty was famed throughout the Three Worlds and equal to the sun, the moon and Indra himself. Assuming a terrible form, I became an object of fear to all and struck terror into the hearts of the ascetics living in the forest.

" O Rama, on a certain occasion I incurred the wrath of a great Rishi named Sthulashira, whom I tormented in this loathsome shape, whilst he was gathering wild fruits. Fixing his gaze on me, he pronounced a terrible curse, saying:—' Do thou retain for ever this fearful form, assumed by thee in order to harm others!'

" Appealing to that provoked ascetic to rescind his curse, he took compassion on me and said: ' When Rama cremates thee in the lonely forest, having severed both thine arms, thou shalt regain thy great and wonderful form.'

" O Lakshmana, know that I am really the son of Danu, who was extremely handsome to look upon; my present appearance is due to a curse pronounced by Indra on the field of battle.

" By rigorous penances I gained the goodwill of Brahma, and he granted me the boon of longevity. Thereafter I was filled with pride and, thinking ' What can Indra do to me now', I challenged him to combat, whereupon he hurled his mace of a hundred edges at me. By the force of this weapon, my thighs and head were thrust into my body; I prayed to him to end my life, but he, saying: ' May the words of Brahma prove true', compelled me to go on living. Then I addressed Mahendra, saying:—' How shall I live without food, since thou hast thrust my head and thighs into my body?'

" Thereat, Indra caused my arms to extend over four miles and placed a mouth with sharp teeth in my belly. Ever since, stretching out my arms, I wander in the forest and seize hold of lions, tigers and deer and put them into my mouth. Then Indra said to me : ' When Rama and Lakshmana cut off thine arms, thou shalt attain heaven '.

" Since then, O Great One, I have laid hold on every living being I have found in the forest and have been awaiting Rama to sever my arms ; anticipating this, I have waited for death. Now, O Lord, thou hast come, be thou blessed ! None but thou can put an end to my life ; the words of the great Rishi have proved true, O Illustrious One. I will put my counsel at thy service, O Bull among Men, and, when I have received the consecration of fire, will form a pact of friendship with you both."

At these words of Danu, Rama, in the hearing of Lakshmana, answered him, saying :—

" Ravana has borne away mine illustrious consort, Sita, whilst I and my brother were absent from the hermitage. I am conversant only with the name of that titan but not with his form, nor are we acquainted with his strength, nor where he dwells. Helpless and distressed, we wander here and there in the forest ; it behoveth thee to show thy compassion to us. After gathering all the branches that are dry and have been broken down by elephants and digging a large pit, we will cremate thee at the time indicated by thee. Do thou tell us who has carried Sita away and where she is to be found. Render us this great service, if thou art acquainted with the truth."

Thus addressed by Rama, Danu, skilled in speech, answered Raghava, saying :—" I am not possessed of divine foresight, neither am I acquainted with the Princess Sita, but being cremated by thee, resuming my natural form, I shall be able to point out one to thee, who will know what has become of her. Without being consumed by fire, I am unable to tell thee who is acquainted with that titan who has carried Sita away. Through a curse, my foresight has been destroyed, O Raghava, and through mine own fault I have become an object of loathing to the whole world, but before the sun with his tired steeds withdraws behind the western horizon cast me into the pit, O Rama, and cremate me according to the traditional rites.

"Cremated by thee with due ceremonial, O Joy of the House of Raghu, I shall tell thee who is acquainted with that titan. It is for thee to seal a pact of friendship with him according to the law. O Raghava, that swift-footed hero will lend thee his assistance.

"For one reason or another, he has traversed the Three Worlds and there is nothing in the Universe that is not known to him."

CHAPTER 72

Kabandha tells Rama how to find Sita

After Kabandha had spoken thus, those two warriors, the foremost among men, Rama and Lakshmana, sought out a hollow on the mountain-side and ignited a fire. With the aid of glowing brands, Lakshmana lit the pyre that burst into flame on every side. The vast trunk of Kabandha began to melt in the heat of the fire like a lump of butter, and later the powerful Kabandha, scattering the ashes, rose up from the pyre wearing spotless raiment and a celestial garland, and that handsome demon, his limbs covered with diverse ornaments, ascended a chariot of dazzling beauty drawn by swans, in his splendour illumining the ten regions. Thereafter, standing in the sky, he addressed Rama, saying :—

"Learn, O Raghava, by what means thou shalt be able to recover Sita. There are six expedients[1] by which misfortune

[1] Six expedients :
Sandhi—making peace.
Vigraha—engaging in war.
Yana—marching against the enemy.
Ashana—maintaining a post against the enemy.
Daidibhava—sowing dissention.
Samshraya—seeking the protection of others.

may be combated, and in the light of which all things should be considered. He who has fallen into the worst misfortune may find solace if he has someone with whom to share his lot, but thou and Lakshmana are deprived of this consolation in the calamity that has befallen you through the theft of Sita. O Rama, thou who art thyself the foremost of friends art in need of a friend. After due reflection, I see no possibility of success for thee except by this.

" Hearken, O Rama, to what I am about to tell thee. There is a monkey named Sugriva, who was banished in anger by his brother Bali, the son of Indra. This sagacious and valiant Sugriva with four of his companions inhabits the lofty mountain Rishyamuka situated on the borders of Lake Pampa.

" This Indra among Monkeys, who is full of energy and prowess, of brilliant appearance, loyal, temperate, intelligent and magnanimous, skilful, courageous, wise and powerful, has been banished by his brother for the sake of the kingdom. He will surely prove thy friend and assist thee in thy search for Sita. O Rama, do not be disturbed on this account; that which is destined must come to pass. O Lion among the Ikshwakus, fate is inexorable!

" Do thou go hence with all speed, O Valiant Raghava, and seek out the powerful Sugriva. Without delay conclude an alliance with him and, swearing mutual loyalty in the presence of fire, unite thyself with that beneficent being. Thou shouldst not disregard that King of the Monkey Tribe, Sugriva, who is of a grateful disposition, able to change his form at will and worthy of thy friendship. Thou too wilt be able to accomplish his designs, but benefited by thee or no, he will execute thy purpose.

" This son of Riksharajas' consort and of Bhaskara, wanders about restlessly on the borders of Lake Pampa and is at war with Bali. Laying aside thy weapons, seek out the retreat of that monkey on the Rishyamuka Mountain without delay and enter into a bond of friendship with that inhabitant of the forest. That Foremost of Monkeys is conversant with all the haunts of the flesh-eating titans in the world and has thoroughly explored their retreats; there is nothing on this earth that is not known to him, O Raghava.

"As long as the many-rayed sun continues to shine, O Scourge of Thy Foes, he with his companions will search the rivers, the crags, the inaccessible mountains and the caves for thy consort. He will send out his monkeys of vast stature to scour every region in order to find Sita, separation from whom has rent thine heart. He will seek for Maithili of lovely limbs even in Ravana's own abode. Should thine irreproachable and beloved Sita have been taken to the summit of Mount Meru or abandoned in the nethermost hell, that Lion among the Monkey Tribe, having slain the titans, will restore her to thee."

CHAPTER 73

Kabandha's Counsel to Rama

HAVING revealed the way to recover Sita, the resourceful Kabandha counselled Rama in the following significant words, saying:—

"This is the path leading westwards to the Mount Rishyamuka, O Rama, abounding in blossoming trees; Jambu, Priyala, Panasa, Nyagrodha, Plaksha, Tinduka, Ashwattha, Karnikara, Cuta, Naga, Tilaka, Naktamala, Nilashoka, Kadamba, Karavira, Agnimukha, Ashoka, Raktachanda, Paribhadraka and many other trees grow there and, climbing or bending them by force, they should be used by you to sustain yourselves on the way with their sweet fruits.

"Passing through these flowery woodlands, O Kakutstha, thou wilt reach others resembling the Nandana Gardens, where, as with the northern Kurus, the trees bear fruit and produce honey in every month of the year and every season is represented simultaneously as in the forest of Chaitaratha. There, great trees with mighty branches, bowed under the weight of their fruit, resemble towering clouds on the mountain side. Lakshmana will climb those trees with ease or pull them down to offer thee the fruit equal in taste to the Nectar of Immortality. Ranging over those lovely mountains, wandering from hill to hill and wood to wood, O Hero, ye shall reach the lake Pampa covered with lotuses, free from boulders and gravel, whose level banks present no crevice and therefore no danger of falling. O Rama, its bed is sandy and it is covered with floating lilies; swans, ducks, herons and ospreys are heard calling sweetly on the waters of that lake; nor do they fear man, O Raghava, since none has ever hunted there. Do ye feed on these birds, fat as butter, O Rama, as well as on Rohita, Chakratunda and Nala.

" O Rama, the devoted Lakshmana will offer thee diverse and excellent fish, devoid of scale or fin, plump, possessing a single bone, which may be speared with arrows and roasted on the fire. And when thou hast feasted, Lakshmana, drawing pure water, fragrant with the scent of lotuses, fresh, limpid, sparkling like silver, shall offer it to thee on a lotus leaf.

" In the evening, ranging here and there, Lakshmana will point out to thee the great monkeys who dwell in the woods and in the hollows of the hills, and thou shalt see those wild and savage apes, roaring like bulls, coming to the borders of the lake to drink.

" Wandering abroad at dusk, thy grief will be assuaged on beholding the flowering trees and the auspicious waters of the lake, and thou shalt see the blossoming Tilaka and Naktamala trees with the red and white full-blown lotuses, which will dispel thy sorrow. No man has ever gathered those blooms nor do the garlands made of them ever fade away, O Raghava, for the disciples of the great ascetic Matanga lived there, who, proficient in penance, laden with the wild fruits they had collected for their Guru, covered the earth with drops of their perspiration from which these flowers have sprung; by virtue of their austerities these blooms never die.

" Those ascetics have now passed away but there still liveth one who served them, a mendicant woman named Shabari. O Kakutstha, she, who is ever fixed in her duty, is now extremely old and, on beholding thee who art honoured by the whole world, will ascend to heaven.

" O Rama, having reached the western bank of Lake Pampa, thou shalt see a lovely, isolated and concealed spot, which is Matanga's hermitage. There, in fear of his divine authority, no elephant dare enter, though there be many. This place is known as the Matanga Wood, O Raghava, and there, O Joy of the House of Raghu, where every variety of bird sings and which resembles the Garden of Nandana or a celestial grove, thou wilt be able to rest.

" The Rishyamuka mountain, covered with flowering trees and filled with birds, rises opposite Lake Pampa and is difficult of access, young elephants barring the way. This lofty mountain was formerly created by Brahma and a virtuous man who sleeps on its summit and dreams of treasure will find wealth on waking, whereas an evil-doer who attempts to scale it will be seized by demons while yet asleep. There too, the trumpeting of the young elephants who disport themselves in the Lake Pampa can be heard. O Rama, in that part of the hermitage where Matanga lodged them, wild elephants of vast size, streaming with crimson ichor, rush to the lake, full of ardour, like great clouds; there they slake their thirst in the cool waters, that are limpid, pleasant and extremely auspicious to those who bathe in them and which exhale a sweet fragrance. Having disported themselves, these elephants re-enter the thickets with the bears, panthers and wolves. Beholding them, as also the deer of gentle countenance resembling sapphire, who are harmless and do not fear man, thy grief will be assuaged.

" O Kakutstha, on this mountain, hewn out of the rock is a great cavern, difficult of access, covered on all sides with delightful fruits, and at the entrance is a great lake of cool water filled with every kind of reptile; there the virtuous Sugriva and his companions dwell, though sometimes he resides on the summit of the hill."

Having thus instructed the two princes, Rama and Lakshmana, Kabandha, resembling the sun in brilliance, wreathed in garlands, illumined the heavens with his splendour. Thereupon those two heroes, seeing that blessed One stationed in the sky, spoke unto him, saying :—" Go in peace ! " whereto Kabandha answered saying :—" Do ye proceed, ye will achieve your purpose ! "

Then Kabandha, having regained his pristine beauty, shining in grace and splendour, fixed his gaze on Rama and spoke again from the sky, saying :—" Enter into an alliance with Sugriva."

CHAPTER 74

Rama visits Shabari

THE two princes, following the instructions of Kabandha, proceeded along the path to the west leading to Lake Pampa. Wending their way, desirous of finding Sugriva, they gazed on the many trees laden with flowers and fruit, tasting of nectar, growing on the mountain-sides. Passing the night on a plateau, those two Descendants of Raghu reached the western bank of the Pampa abounding in lotuses and beheld Shabari's pleasant retreat.

Approaching that charming hermitage, shaded on all sides by innumerable trees, they beheld that perfected One who, seeing them, rose up and with joined palms touched the feet of Rama and the prudent Lakshmana and, according to tradition, offered water to rinse their mouths and bathe their feet.

Thereupon Rama addressed that female ascetic, fixed in her spiritual duty, and said :—" Hast thou overcome all obstacles to asceticism, O Thou of gentle speech ? Do thine austerities increase daily ? Hast thou subdued thine anger and thy need for food ? O Solitary One, hast thou observed thy vows and attained inner tranquillity ? Has thine attendance on thy Guru borne fruit ? "

Thus interrogated by Rama, the virtuous Shabari, revered by the Gods, extremely aged, standing before him, offered him homage and said :—

" Blessed by thy presence, I have acquired perfection and my asceticism is crowned. To-day my birth has borne fruit and the service of my Gurus has been fully honoured. To-day my pious practices have found fulfilment. O Foremost of Men, Greatest of the Celestials, worshipping thee, I shall attain the heavenly realm. O Gentle One, O Slayer of thy Foes, O Thou who dost confer honour on men, purified by thy compassionate regard, I shall, by thy favour, attain the imperishable worlds, O Subduer of Thy Foes.

" When thou didst set foot on the Mount Chittrakuta, those ascetics I served, ascending celestial cars of incomparable splendour, departed to heaven and those great sages, conversant with virtue, said to me :—

" ' Rama will visit thy holy retreat; do thou receive him and Lakshmana with traditional hospitality. On beholding him, thou shalt attain the highest sphere from whence none returneth.'

" O Foremost of Men, thus did those blessed ascetics address me, and for thee I have gathered the wild fruits of diverse kinds that grow on the borders of Lake Pampa."

Hearing these words, Raghava said to her, who had not been left in ignorance by her Gurus concerning the past and the future:—

" I have heard the truth about the greatness of thy Gurus from Danu and now I would fain witness it with mine own eyes, if thou judgest it fitting."

Listening to these words falling from Rama's own lips, Shabari, guiding the two brothers to the vast forest, addressed them, saying :—

" O Raghunanda, behold this forest resembling a dark cloud, filled with birds and beasts, known as the Matanga Wood. Here my Gurus of pure soul sacrificed unto fire, their persons consecrated by mantras through which they had purified them, thus consecrating the forest and rendering it a holy place. Here too is the altar facing the west, where, with hands trembling with fatigue, my worshipful preceptors offered flowers to their Gods. O Foremost of the Raghus, behold this altar of incomparable beauty, which, through the power of their penances, still sheds its lustre illumining the four regions. Behold also the Seven Seas, drawn here by virtue of their thought, since, through fasting and the weight of years, they were unable to walk. These robes of bark, left hanging on the trees by them at the completion of their ablutions, are still wet and the lotuses of azure hue offered by them in worship have not faded.

" Now thou hast seen the forest and hast heard all that thou didst desire to know; I will abandon my body so that I may approach those pure-souled ascetics whom I used to wait upon, to whom this hermitage belongs and whose servant I am."

Hearing these pious words, Rama, who was accompanied by Lakshmana, experienced great delight and exclaimed: "Wonderful it is!" Thereafter, addressing Shabari of ascetic practices, he said:—

"O Holy One, I have been fully honoured by thee; now repair whither thou wilt and be happy."

Having received permission from Rama to depart, Shabari, wearing matted locks, robes of bark and a black antelope skin, cast herself into the fire, thereafter rising into the air like a bright flame.

Adorned with celestial ornaments, wreathed in garlands, emitting a divine fragrance, sprinkled with sandal-paste and clad in celestial raiment, she appeared exquisite and illumined the heavens like a flash of lightning. By virtue of her meditations she ascended to those sacred abodes where her spiritual preceptors, those high-souled ascetics, dwelt.

CHAPTER 75

Rama reaches the Lake Pampa

WHEN Shabari had ascended to heaven through the merit of her spiritual prowess, Rama with his brother Lakshmana began to ponder over the pious influence of those great ascetics and, reflecting within himself on the divine authority of those holy men, Raghava said to his brother:—

"O Friend, I have now visited the retreat of those magnanimous sages of miraculous deeds, where deer and tigers roam, together with birds of every kind. O Lakshmana, we have performed our ablutions in the sacred waters of these seven seas and have offered oblations to our ancestors. Our evil karma has thereby been destroyed and prosperity made manifest; my heart is filled with peace. Methinks, O Lion among Men, that we shall soon meet with good fortune. Come, let us walk towards the enchanting Lake Pampa! The Rishyamuka Mountain may be seen in the distance; it is there that the four great monkeys with Sugriva, Surya's son, dwell in constant fear of Bali. I am impatient to see this Lion of the Monkey Tribe, Sugriva, for it is he who will ascertain where Sita can be found."

Thus did the heroic Rama speak, and Saumitri answered him, saying :—

" Let us repair thither without delay ; my heart too reaches out to that place." Thereupon, issuing from Matanga's hermitage, the mighty Rama, Lord of Men, accompanied by Lakshmana, proceeded towards lake Pampa.

On every side he saw innumerable trees in full flower and pools where small white cranes nested in the reeds, and peacocks, lapwings and woodpeckers, filling the forest with their cries, as also a multitude of other birds.

Enjoying the trees of varying fragrance and the many ponds, Rama, transported with delight, approached one whose waters, delicious to the taste, were drawn from the Matanga lake. There the two Descendants of Raghu stood in quiet recollection. Thereafter, grief once more invading the heart of Raghu, the son of Dasaratha, he entered the enchanting lake covered with lotuses.

Adorned on all sides with Tilaka, Ashoka, Punnaga, Vakula and Uddalaka trees, which were nourished by its waters, it was framed in charming groves and its waves, pure as crystal, on which hibiscus blooms floated, flowed over fine sand. Fish and turtle abounded there and the banks were embellished by trees intertwined with friendly creepers. Kinneras, Uragas, Gandharvas, Yakshas and Rakshasas frequented it and diverse trees and shrubs cast their shade over it. That lake was verily a jewel with its fresh and limpid waters, its lotuses and water-lilies lending it a coppery sheen, whilst clumps of nymphoae cast silvery reflections and the blue of sapphire was added by other flowers. Aravinda and Utpala blooms abounded round the lake, which was covered with innumerable lotuses, whilst groves of mango in flower lent their shade, and peacocks filled it with their cries.

Rama, the mighty son of Dasaratha, who was accompanied by Lakshmana, seeing the Lake Pampa adorned like a bride with Tilaka, Bijapura, Vata, Lodhra, Sukladruma, Karavira,

Punnaga in flower, bushes of Malati and Kunda, Bandira, Nichula, Ashoka, Saptaparna, Ketaka, Atimukta and diverse other trees of varying perfume, gave expression to his grief :—

" There stands on the right bank the mountain Rishyamuka, abounding in various metals and famed for the variety of its trees and flowers, spoken of by Kabandha, where the son of the magnanimous Riksharajas, the valiant Sugriva, dwells. ' O Foremost of Men, seek out the King of the Monkeys ', were his words."

Thereafter, Rama spoke to Lakshmana again, saying :—

" O Lakshmana, how will Sita be able to live without me ? "

Having spoken thus to Lakshmana, the foremost of the Raghus, tormented by his love, which precluded him from thinking of aught else, entered the marvellous Lake Pampa, having given voice to his sorrow.

Proceeding slowly, observing the forest, Rama, coming to Lake Pampa, surrounded on all sides with enchanting groves, filled with a multitude of birds, entered its waters with Lakshmana.

END OF ARANYA KANDA

BOOK IV.

KISHKINDHA KANDA

CHAPTER I

Rama describes the Spring and the Sentiments it evokes in him

DIRECTING his steps towards Lake Pampa, which was covered with lotuses of various kinds, Rama, who was accompanied by Lakshmana, his mind troubled, began to lament. Beholding that lake, his heart was filled with delight, and under the sway of love, he said to the son of Sumitra :—

" O Lakshmana, how beautiful is the Lake Pampa with its pure and limpid waves, its lotuses and flowering water-lilies, its many kinds of trees. Oh ! How delightful ! O Saumitri, observe the Pampa Woods, how pleasant they are to look upon, those magnificent trees resembling crested mountains. I am overwhelmed and stricken with grief on recollecting Bharata's distress and the abduction of Sita.

" Though my heart is heavy, yet the Pampa lake is still able to charm me, with its ravishing woods luxuriant with every kind of blossom and its fresh and delicious waters. The month of flowering lotuses[1] lends it an extreme beauty ; serpents and wild animals frequent it, whilst deer and birds abound. The thick grass, of a deep emerald hue, is sprinkled with different flowers that have fallen from the trees and resembles a bright carpet. On every side the tops of the trees, bending under the weight of their blossom, are wholly hidden by the creepers with their flowering fronds.

" O Lakshmana, it is the season of auspicious breezes and tender love, the fragrant spring month when flowers and fruit are brought to birth on the trees. See how lovely are these flowering woods, O Saumitri, showering down a rain of petals, like water from the clouds.

" In the enchanting valleys on the escarpments, innumerable trees, shaken by the wind, scatter their blossom on the earth. O Lakshmana, see how the breeze, agitating the myriad branches

[1] Lit. Padmas, Utpalas, Jhashas.

of the flowering trees, seems to play with the blossom that has fallen or is still on the trees. The God of the Wind frolics to the accompaniment of the humming of bees and to the song of the amorous nightingale, desiring, as it were, to make the trees dance. Emerging from the mountain caves, the wind gives forth a kind of music, shaking the trees violently from side to side, causing the extreme tips of their branches to meet, uniting them one with the other. The zephyr with soft caressing breath, diffusing the perfume of sandalwood, dispels all fatigue.

" Agitated by the wind, these trees seem to add their voices to the humming of the bees amidst the soft and fragrant groves.

" On the enchanting mountain plateaus, the crags, whose points touch, resplendent with large trees bearing beautiful flowers, sparkle with beauty, and the trees, tossed by the airy currents that stir them, their crests covered with blossom and crowned with bees, seem about to break into song.

" See, on every side, the marvellous blossoming of the golden Karnikara trees, resembling men robed in silk ! This season of Spring, O Lakshmana, with its choir of birds of every kind revives the pain caused by Sita's absence. In this overwhelming grief, pangs of love torment me. The gay trilling of the cuckoo tantalizes me ; the joyful Datyuhaka bird that sings from the waterfalls of the forest increases my pain, O Lakshmana ! Formerly when she heard its voice in our hermitage, my beloved, intoxicated with love and happiness, would call to me.

" See how the birds of varied plumage, giving forth every kind of note, seek refuge on all sides amongst the trees, bushes and creepers ! The females accompanied by the males flock together according to their kind and rejoice ; intoxicated by the Bhringaraja's exultant cries, they chirrup melodiously. Here, in the home of Sita, the assembled birds are made merry by the joyous song of the Datyuhaka responding to the cuckoo's call.

" The rustling of the trees rekindles the fire of my love, of which the bunches of the Ashoka blooms are the fuel, the humming of the bees the crackling, and the buds the golden tongues of flame.

" This fire of Spring is consuming me ! Nay, far from that lady of lovely eyelashes, beautiful looks and gentle speech, I cannot survive, O Saumitri ! The season that brings delight to the woods is the time she loved, and beyond all, she was enamoured of the forest echoing to the call of the cuckoo on every side, O Irreproachable Hero !

" The tender feelings I bear for my sweet One and the delights of Spring that increase them are a burning fire that will soon consume me utterly. I shall not live long separated from my spouse ; the beauty of these trees increases the pangs of my love. Being unable to see Sita any more intensifies my anguish, whilst the presence of Spring causes the sweat of desire to break forth on me. Thinking of that lady, whose eyes resemble a doe's, grief holds me in thrall ; the cruel Spring breeze from the woods tortures me, O Saumitri !

" Here and there, peacocks dance, spreading their brilliant wings in the breeze, and their tails, decorated with eyes, resemble crystal lattices. The females surrounding them are intoxicated with desire and this strengthens the love with which I am filled.

" See, O Lakshmana, on the mountain plateau, how the peacock dances and how the peahen, her heart intoxicated with joy, closely follows him ! He spreads his radiant wings and his cries seem to mock my pain, for in the forest his loved one has not been carried away by a titan and he can dance in these enchanting groves with his tender love. In this month of flowers, in Sita's absence, my stay here is unendurable !

" See, O Lakshmana, love is found even among lower animals! At this moment, the peahen is ardently attracted to the steps of the male ; even thus would the large-eyed daughter of Janaka follow my steps with renewed love, had she not been borne away.

" O Lakshmana, the flowers that bear down the forest branches with their weight in the autumn will produce no fruit for me and, though so lovely, will fall rotting to the ground with their swarms of bees.

" The birds at this time, in joyous flight, carolling in love, seem to call to one another, invoking deep transports of desire in me. If the Spring also reigns where my loved one, Sita, dwells, who has now fallen under the sway of another, she will be sharing my ardour. Yet if the Spring has not reached that place where she is, how will that dark-eyed lady be able to go on living in my absenec ? If this season has not come to where my gentle love resides, what will that fair-limbed lady do, who has been overpowered by a mighty adversary ? My youthful and beloved consort, whose eyes resemble lotus petals and who is gentle of speech, will certainly yield up her life at the first breath of Spring. In my heart, I feel assured that the gentle Sita will not be able to survive separation from me. Devotion to Vaidehi invades my entire being and my love is wholly centred on her.

" When I remember my gentle love, this caressing breeze, so fresh and cool, carrying the fragrance of flowers, is like a burning fire to me. The God of the Wind, who was ever welcome when Sita was present, is to-day a source of pain to me. In her absence, that bird flying through the air emitting cries, the crow now perching on a tree, makes a delightful sound.[1] This winged creature will prove a messenger and bring my remembrance to the mind of the large-eyed Vaidehi.

" Listen, O Lakshmana, to the birds' intoxicating chorus of love, as they warble in the flowery crested trees. That bee suddenly flying towards the young green shoots of the Tilaka tree, blown by the breeze, is like a lover trembling with desire. The Ashoka tree, that increases the torment of lovers, rises with its plumes of flowers waving in the wind, to tantalize me. Look, O Lakshmana, at the flowering mango trees, resembling those who are distracted by the pangs of love !

" O Saumitri, O Lion among Men ! See how amidst the magnificent range of trees that grow on the borders of Lake Pampa, the Kinneras wander about on every side ! Observe those Nalina flowers of subtle scent, O Lakshmana, gleaming on the water like unto the sun about to rise. See the calm surface of the Pampa Lake, fragrant with lotus and blue water-lilies, frequented by swans and waterfowl, and the stamens of the lotus flowers, bright as the dawn, that the bees have scattered on the waves.

[1] This refers to a crow cawing at the time of Rama's wedding, indicating that he would shortly be separated from her ; now the sound signifies reunion is near.

" How the Lake Pampa sparkles ! Waterfowl abound there in every season ; how wonderful are its woodland glades ! It is enchanting with its herds of elephants and deer, that love to come and bathe in it. The water-lilies rocking on the breast of the limpid waves, the waters whipped by the impetuous wind sparkle with beauty, O Lakshmana.

" Far from Vaidehi, whose eyes are as large as the petals of of the lotus, who ever loved the water-lilies, life has no attraction for me. O Perfidious Kama, now I am no longer able to rejoin her, thou seekest to evoke in me the memory of that sweet lady, whose speech was a thousand times sweeter still; it were possible to bear the love I feel for her, if the Spring with its flowers and trees did not increase my torment ! Those things that enchanted me, when I was with her, in her absence, have no further charm for me. On seeing the petals of the lotus cup, I say to myself : 'These resemble Sita's eyes', O Lakshmana. The fragrant breeze, blowing through the stamens of the lotus flowers and the trees, resembles her breath.

" O Saumitri, see how marvellous is the brilliance of the flowering trunk of the Karnikara on the ridges of the mountain to the right of Lake Pampa. Those ravishing trees with their flowers, stripped of leaves, seem to set the mountain ridges on fire ; whilst those growing on the banks of the lake, that irrigates them, give off a delicate perfume.

" Malatis, Mallikas, Karaviras and Padmas in flower, Ketaki, Sinduvara and Vasanti trees, Matulinga, Purna and Kunda bushes on every side ; Shiribilva, Madhuka, Vanjula, Bakula, Champaka, Tilaka, Nagavriksha, Padmaka, Ashoka with their azure flowers, Lodhra, Simhakesara, Pinjara trees are seen everywhere. Ankola, Kuranta, Shurnaka, Paribhadraka, Cuta, Patali, Kovidara, Mucukunda and Arjuna trees spread their blossom on the slope of the mountain. Raktakurava, Ketaka, Uddalaka, Shirisha, Shingshapa, Dhava, Shalmali, Kingshuka, Kurubaka with its red flowers, Tinisha, Naktamala, Candaka, Syandana, Hintala, Tilaka and Nagavriksha, these blossoming trees are entwined with flowering spiked creepers.

" See, O Saumitri, how they crowd together on the banks of Lake Pampa, their branches waving in the wind ; the creepers seem to be pursuing each other, resembling lovely women at play.

" The breeze passes through the trees from crag to crag, from wood to wood. Amongst them, some are in full flower and give off a soft fragrance, others, covered with buds, have a sombre air. What sweetness ! How pleasant ! What blossom!

" Amidst these trees on the borders of Lake Pampa, the bees seem to be resting in the heart of the flowers, staying a moment, then flying off again, quickly alighting elsewhere, greedy for nectar.

" The fortunate earth is heaped with masses of blossom that has fallen on the ground, resembling the covering of a couch. On the mountain sides unrolls a brilliant carpet of gold and red flowers of every kind, O Saumitri. At the end of winter all these trees are now in full flower, O Lakshmana. In this month of blossom, the plants open, vying with each other, and the trees, where the six-legged insects hum, seem to challenge one another, manifesting a great brilliance, their branches crowned with flowers.

" The Karandava bird plunging into the limpid waves, disporting itself with its mate, seems in some way to inspire love. Like that of the Mandakini, the beauty of the Lake Pampa is enchanting ; its perfections are famed throughout the world and, in proximity, ravish the heart.

" If I might find my gentle Love once again, and we could take up our abode here, I should not even covet Indra's realm or regret Ayodhya. Here, on these charming slopes, I should sport with her and neither my thoughts nor desires would lead me away.

" In the absence of my beloved, the trees of these woods, wholly covered with every kind of flower, almost deprive me of my reason.

" Gaze on this lake of limpid waters, O Saumitri, which is covered with lotuses, frequented by the Chakravaka bird, the abode of Karandavas, abounding in pelicans, herons and wild beasts and re-echoing to the warbling of birds; verily Lake Pampa is a paradise ! The myriad birds with their delightful antics and the memory of that youthful woman, my beloved, whose face shines like the moon, whose eyes resemble lotuses, all inflame my desire. I, who am separated from Sita, whose eyes resemble the doe's and the gazelle's, on seeing them disporting themselves there, am troubled, as it were.

"On that pleasant hillside, filled with flocks of birds, intoxicated with love, might I but see my gentle One, I should be content. O Saumitri, I should certainly live anew if Sita of slender waist were inhaling the auspicious air of Lake Pampa at my side. Fortunate is he, O Lakshmana, who drinks that pleasant air from the woods of Lake Pampa that carries the fragrance of the lotus and dispels all grief.

"How is that youthful woman, whose eyes resemble lotus petals, the beloved daughter of Janaka, able to bear the existence of a slave? What shall I say to that virtuous king, the faithful Janaka, when, in the presence of the people, he asks me if all is well with Sita?

"She who followed me to the dreary forest whither my father had banished me, that Sita, fixed in her duty, where is she, my beloved, now? Separated from her, how, in mine adversity, O Lakshmana, shall I be able to endure life? I am losing my reason! When shall I hear the incomparable voice of Vaidehi again? Though she found nought but misfortune in the forest, yet that youthful woman, in her tenderness, conversed sweetly with me, who was consumed with love, as if she had ceased to be unhappy and was full of joy. How shall I, in Ayodhya, reply to Kaushalya, O Prince, when that venerable queen asks me: 'Where is my daughter-in-law and what has befallen her?'

"O Lakshmana, return and seek out Bharata, our devoted brother; as for me, I can no longer continue living without the daughter of Janaka."

Thus did the magnanimous Rama lament, as if deprived of support, and his brother, Lakshmana, in judicious and measured words, answered him, saying:—"O Rama, summon up thy courage and be happy, do not grieve, O Thou, the Best of Men. Those in thy condition have nothing with which to reproach themselves and should not give way to despair. Calling to remembrance the grief caused by separation from that being who is dear to thee, banish all excessive attachment. In proximity to intense heat, even a damp net catches fire. Though he descend into hell or yet lower, Ravana will in no way survive his deed, O Beloved Rama. Let us first seek out this wicked demon; either he shall yield up Sita or he is lost. Should Ravana descend into the womb of Diti[1] with Sita, I shall slay him if he does not restore her to thee. Return to thy normal state, My Noble Friend, and throw off these mournful thoughts. Assuredly no success is gained by those who abandon their undertakings without making due efforts. Exertion is a powerful weapon, O Lord, there is no power superior to it. With effort, nothing is impossible in this world. Resolute men do not fail in their pursuits. By our efforts alone we shall recover Janaki. Do not permit thyself to be dominated by thy love or thy grief; cast it behind thee. Hast thou perchance forgotten the greatness of thy soul, the fixity of thy purpose and character?"

Thus spurred on by Lakshmana, Rama, who had allowed himself to be overcome by sorrow, banished his grief and distraction and regained his valour.

Calm and brave beyond imagining, Rama crossed the Pampa that was full of charm, enchanting with its trees of waving branches. When he had explored the whole forest with its waterfalls and ravines, the magnanimous Rama, agitated and overcome with grief, set out with Lakshmana, and with the joyous gait of an elephant intoxicated with Mada juice, the intrepid and magnanimous Saumitri, with rapid strides went on his way serenely, consoling Rama by his fidelity and valour.

As they neared the vicinity of Rishyamuka, the King of the Monkeys observed those heroes of unusual aspect and, despite his courage, trembled but made no move towards them. That magnanimous monkey, who walked with the dignity of an elephant, seeing those two brothers advancing, was filled with extreme apprehension and became distracted with fear.

In their terror at the sight of Rama and Lakshmana, those monkeys concealed themselves in that pleasant solitude, the refuge of the Deer of the Trees.[2]

1 The bowels of the earth.

2 Monkeys.

CHAPTER 2

Sugriva sends Hanuman to interview Rama

BEHOLDING those two illustrious brothers, Rama and Lakshmana, bearing great swords in their hands, Sugriva grew anxious and, with a beating heart, glancing round on every side, could find no place in which to take refuge. Seeing those two heroes, he moved about restlessly from place to place and, in his terror, felt himself about to swoon. Exceedingly perturbed, the virtuous Sugriva with his companions began to ponder on the varying aspects of the situation and that Chief of the Monkey Tribe, pointing out those two warriors, Rama and Lakshmana, to his ministers, said :—

" Without doubt, Bali has sent these two heroes to this wood, which is inaccessible to him, and they, assuming robes of bark, have come hither and have penetrated this stronghold."

Then those counsellors of Sugriva, perceiving the two skilful archers, sped away from that ridge to a higher crest, slipping off hurriedly behind their leader and thereafter they encircled that King of the Forest Dwellers. In close formation, they leapt from crag to crag, causing the rocks to tremble with their bounds. Jumping with extreme force, they broke down the flowering trees growing in that altitude and those amazing monkeys, leaping in every direction on that great mountain, struck terror in the hearts of the deer, the wild cats and the tigers.

Thereafter, the counsellors of Sugriva, assembling on that Indra of mountains, gathered round their sovereign with joined palms, and the eloquent Hanuman addressed Sugriva, who in his terror suspected some project of his brother's to be afoot, saying :—

" Let all banish fear of Bali ! There is nothing to inspire terror on this, the highest of mountains. I do not see any sign here of that cruel Bali of evil aspect, who has filled thee with apprehension and caused thy flight, O Bull among Monkeys. That cunning creature whom thou fearest, thy wicked elder brother, is not here, O Friend: I see no cause for thine apprehension. It is evident, O Plavamgama, that thy simian nature is asserting itself, since, by giving way to distraction of mind, thou art not able to see clearly. Thou art intelligent, experienced, able to read the expression of others and fully prepared for any eventuality, but a prince who gives way to agitation is not able to forestall any."

Hearing Hanuman's pregnant utterance, Sugriva answered him with greater calm saying :—

" Seeing those two long-armed warriors of large eyes, armed with bows and swords, resembling the offspring of the Gods, who would not be afraid ? I deem these two powerful heroes to be the messengers of Bali. Kings have many friends, and I do not feel able to trust them. Those who are cautious invariably find the weak spot in those who are over-confident. Bali is crafty in every enterprise. Those monarchs who are well-informed are able to overcome their enemies and should spy out their actions with the help of ordinary men.

" Go, O Plavamgama, in the guise of a common man and find out the intentions of these two strangers. Study their gestures, their manners and their speech ; observe their attitude and how they are disposed.

" By praise and repeated courtesies inspire them with confidence. Interrogate those two archers in my name, O Bull amongst Monkeys, and enquire of them for what reason they have come to these woods. Discover if their purpose be honest, O Plavamgama ; their speech and manner will betray them if they are ill-intentioned."

Thus commanded by Sugriva, the Son of Maruta prepared to seek out Rama and Lakshmana.

His master, through extreme fear, having rendered himself unapproachable, the monkey Hanuman of noble attributes, listening to his words with respect, answered : " Be it so ! " and went forth to meet the mighty Rama and Lakshmana who accompanied him.

CHAPTER 3

Hanuman's Meeting with Rama

At the command of the magnanimous Sugriva, Hanuman, with one bound, left the Mountain Rishyamuka and placed himself in the path of the two Raghavas.

Discarding his monkey form, Hanuman, the son of Maruta, by the power of illusion, assumed the guise of a wandering monk and, in gentle and pleasing tones, addressed those two brothers with humility, paying obeisance to them.

Approaching those two heroes, that Foremost of Monkeys praised them as they deserved, offering them every courtesy and in accord with Sugriva's wish spoke graciously to them, saying :—

" O Ascetics of renowned penance, who are full of faith and valour and who resemble the Rishis and the Gods, why have you come to this region, sowing fear amongst the herds of deer and other denizens of the forest, surveying the trees on every side that grow on the borders of Pampa, that lake of sparkling waves, the splendour of which you enhance with your radiance, O Heroes of Great Daring ?

" O Valiant Strangers, who are you, whose skin gleams like gold and who are clad in robes of bark, possessing strong arms, you who are sighing deeply and whose sight inspires fear in all beings ? You have the air of lions or warriors who are full of courage and heroism, armed as you are with bows, resembling Indra's, the Destroyers of your Foes ?

" Full of majesty and beauty, mighty as great bulls, your arms resembling the trunks of elephants, radiant, the first among men, youthful, illumining the king of the mountains with your effulgence, you who are worthy of ruling kingdoms and like unto the Gods, what purpose brings you here ? O Heroes, whose eyes are as large as lotus petals, who wear your matted locks coiled like crowns on your heads, who resemble each other, have you come hither from the celestial region? Verily the sun and moon have descended to earth of their own free will. O Broad-chested Warriors, ye who are men, yet have the aspect of divine beings, whose shoulders are like unto a lion's, who are endowed with great strength and resemble two bulls intoxicated with desire, whose large and massive arms look like clubs that should be adorned with every kind of ornament, yet bear none, it seems that you are both worthy of ruling the whole earth, whose decorations are the Vindhya and Meru mountains with their lakes and forests. How beautiful are your two shining bows, glistening with perfumed paste, covered with gold and shining like the mace of Indra; the two quivers also, filled with sharp death-dealing and formidable arrows resembling hissing snakes; your two swords of immense length and size, encrusted with fine gold that gleam like serpents that have just cast their slough! But why do ye not answer me?

"Sugriva is the name of that virtuous King of the Monkeys, that hero banished by his brother, who roams the earth in great distress. I have come here under the orders of that magnanimous one, the Chief of the Great Monkeys. The illustrious Sugriva desires your friendship. Know me to be his minister, a monkey, the son of Pavana, ranging where I please and coming here under the guise of a wandering monk from the Rishyamuka Mountain in order to please him."

Having addressed those two heroes, Rama and Lakshmana, in discreet and courteous terms, Hanuman fell silent and hearing that speech, the blessed Rama, delighted, addressed Lakshmana who stood beside him, saying:—

"This is the minister of the King of the Monkeys, the magnanimous Sugriva, whom I seek. O Saumitri, answer Sugriva's counsellor who is eloquent and warm-hearted and the subduer of his foes in courteous terms. Only one versed in the Rig-Veda and, who is conversant with the Yajur and the Sama Vedas, would speak thus. He has studied grammar thoroughly, and though he has spoken at length, it has been void of error. I see naught to offend, either in his mouth, his eyes, his brow, limbs, or attitude. His speech is neither lacking in fulness, depth, assurance or distinction; his voice issues from his breast in clear modulated tones. He expresses himself with admirable felicity without any hesitation; his tone is harmonious and moves the heart agreeably. What foe, having drawn his sword, would not be disarmed by the charm of that voice that enunciates each syllable so perfectly. O Irreproachable Prince, the king who employs messengers gifted with such talent is certain to succeed in all his undertakings, since they are enhanced at the very outset, by such eloquence."

On this, Saumitri addressed that eloquent minister of Sugriva's in well-chosen words, saying:—" O Sage, we have been told of the great attributes of Sugriva and are at this moment looking for that King of the Monkeys. That which he commands we will carry out on thine instructions, O Excellent Hanuman."

When he heard this gracious speech, that monkey, born of Pavana, who wished nothing more than that Sugriva should triumph, resolved to bring about a friendly alliance between Rama and his master.

CHAPTER 4

Hanuman bears Rama and Lakshmana into the presence of Sugriva

LISTENING to Lakshmâna's courteous words and marking the feeling of goodwill towards his master, Hanuman, deeming Rama would be willing to assist him, joyfully reflected that Sugriva's triumph was already assured.

He thought: " Undoubtedly the magnanimous Sugriva will not fail to regain his kingdom, for here is one who will enable him to accomplish his design."

Then the wholly delighted and eloquent Hanuman, the Foremost of Monkeys, said to Rama:—" What brings thee with thy younger brother to this perilous and inaccessible forest?"

On this enquiry, Lakshmana, prompted by his brother, related the history of Rama, the son of Dasaratha, to him.

"There was a king named Dasaratha, who was illustrious, fixed in his duty and, according to the law, the protector of the four castes. Without a foe, he himself hating none, he appeared to all living beings to be a second Brahma.

"The firstborn son of Dasaratha, who possessed every excellent quality, the refuge of all, endowed with royal virtues and of great majesty, was banished from his dominion and obedient to the behests of his sire, has come to dwell in the forest. Submitting to the paternal decree, he was followed by his consort, Sita, as the glorious sun by the sunset glow at evening.

"My name is Lakshmana. I, who am inferior to him in every respect, am his brother and accompany him as his servant. This dutiful prince, who is ever mindful of what should be done, is extremely learned and this hero, who spends his life in promoting the welfare of all beings, who is worthy of happiness and honour, deprived of supreme power, passes his days in the forest. A titan, who was able to change his form at will, carried off his consort, she being alone, and her abductor is unknown to us.

"The son of Diti, Danu, who, through a curse, had been forced to assume the form of a titan, imparted the name of Sugriva, the King of the Monkeys, to us. Now I have answered thine enquiries fully in all sincerity; Rama and I both seek the help of Sugriva. The distributor of all wealth, he, who has reached the peak of glory and was formerly the guardian of the worlds, has come to seek Sugriva's protection. The son of that instructor of his people, who was devoted to his duty, of whom Sita was the daughter-in-law, Rama, seeks the protection of Sugriva. The strong defender of the whole universe, that was formerly his highway, my Guru Rama, whom thou seest here, has come to seek refuge with Sugriva. He, under whose compassion all beings rest, Rama, has come to appeal to the goodwill of that King of the Monkeys. It is the eldest son of King Dasaratha, who was endowed with every good attribute and on this earth constantly showered honours on monarchs, Rama, renowned in the Three Worlds, who now seeks refuge in Sugriva, Lord of the Monkeys. Rama, a victim to grief, overwhelmed with affliction, has come as a suppliant! It is for Sugriva with the leaders of the monkey tribes to show favour to him."

Hearing Lakshmana, uttering this appeal, his tears flowing the while, Hanuman graciously replied :—

" Such suppliants, endowed with wisdom, who have mastered their anger and other passions and whose fortune has led them to his presence, are worthy to be brought before that Indra of Monkeys. He too is exiled from his kingdom and the object of his brother's enmity, who has carried off his consort and, after maltreating him cruelly, forced him to flee trembling to the forest. That offspring of Surya, Sugriva, will form a pact of friendship with you, and I shall accompany him in his search for Sita."

Having spoken thus in a gentle and kindly tone, Hanuman said to Raghava in friendly accents :—" Let us seek out Sugriva."

At these words, the righteous Lakshmana bowed courteously to him and addressed the virtuous Raghava, saying :—

" What this monkey, born of the Wind-God, has gladly told us, his master will carry out; it is here that thy purpose will find fulfilment, O Rama. Goodness is painted on his countenance; he speaks cheerfully and his words ring true."

Then that extremely intelligent son of Maruta, Hanuman, went away, taking the two heroes, the descendants of Raghu, with him. Abandoning the guise of a mendicant and assuming the form of a monkey, that great ape, taking those two warriors on his shoulders, departed.

Thereafter, that intelligent son of Pavana, who was renowned among the monkeys and endowed with great prowess, delighted to have accomplished his design, scaled the mountain with immense bounds taking Rama and Lakshmana with him.

CHAPTER 5

The Alliance of Rama and Sugriva

FROM the Rishyamuka mountain, Hanuman bounded to the Mt. Malaya and presenting the two valiant descendants of Raghu to Sugriva, said :—

" This is Rama, O Great and Wise King, who has come here with Lakshmana, his brother ; this true hero, born in the dynasty of Ikshwaku, is the son of King Dasaratha.

" Fixed in his duty, he is carrying out the behests of his sire, that great king who, gratifying the Deity of Fire, Agni, with the Rajasuya and Ashwamedha sacrifices, at those times distributed hundreds and thousands of cows in charity.

" On account of a woman, his son, Rama, who is present here, was exiled to the forest and, while that magnanimous hero was dwelling there, practising asceticism, Ravana carried off his consort ; he now seeks thy protection.

" These two brothers, Rama and Lakshmana, solicit thy friendship ; do thou receive these heroes, worthy of homage, with honour ! "

Hearing these words of Hanuman, Sugriva, the King of the Monkeys, who had now become easy of access, said to Rama:—

" This is a great fortune and the greatest of gains for me O Lord, that thou desirest to ally thyself in friendship with me, who am one of the Monkey Tribe. Should that friendship find favour with thee, then here is my hand, take it into thine and let us bind ourselves fast with a vow."

Hearing Sugriva's sweet words, Rama with a joyful heart clasped his hand and, happy in the thought of the alliance they were about to conclude, embraced him warmly.

Then Hanuman, the Subduer of his Foes, who had put off his monk's guise, assuming his own shape, kindled a fire by rubbing two pieces of wood together. The fire being lit and flowers cast into it, thus preparing it, he placed it between them,[1] full of joy and devotion.

Going round it they both worshipped the fire and thus Sugriva and Rama were united in friendship. Whereupon the hearts of the monkey and Rama were merry and, gazing upon each other, they were unable to have their fill.

" Thou art now the friend of my heart in joy and pain ! We are one ! " Thus spoke Sugriva in his satisfaction, as also Rama, and breaking off a branch from a Sala tree adorned with leaves and covered with flowers, Sugriva laid it down as it were a carpet and with Rama sat down upon it, whilst the

[1] The fire apparently being in a brazier.

delighted Hanuman, born of Maruta, in his turn, offered Lakshmana a branch of blossoming sandalwood.

Thereafter, full of happiness, Sugriva, his eyes wide with delight, said to Rama in sweet and gentle tones :—

" Cruelly persecuted, O Rama, I came hither in great fear, my consort having been wrested from me, and, in deep distress, I took refuge in this inaccessible part of the forest, where I now dwell, my mind distracted with terror.

" My brother oppresses me and is mine enemy, O Rama, O Great Hero ; do thou deliver me from the fear which Bali inspires in me ! Act, O Kakutstha. in such a way that my courage may be restored."

At these words, the illustrious and virtuous Rama, a lover of justice, smiling, answered Sugriva, saying :—

" I know well that the fruit of friendship is mutual aid, O Great Monkey ! I shall slay that Bali, who has carried off thy consort ! These pointed shafts that thou perceivest, these arrows bright as the sun, fly straight to their target. Decorated with heron's feathers and resembling Indra's thunderbolt, skilfully wrought, their points sharpened, resembling provoked serpents, they will pierce that perverse wretch with force. To-day thou shalt see Bali fall on the earth like a cleft mountain struck by these pointed darts, resembling venomous snakes."

Encouraged by Rama's words, Sugriva, overjoyed, spoke again, saying :—" May I by thy grace, O Valiant Lion among Men, regain my consort and my kingdom. O King, do thou restrain my wicked elder brother from harming me hereafter."

At the moment when Sugriva and Rama concluded their alliance, Sita's left eye, resembling a lotus, twitched,[1] as also did that of the Indra of Monkeys, which resembled gold, and that of the titan, Ravana, which was like a flame.

[1] A foreshowing of coming events.

CHAPTER 6

Sugriva shows Rama Sita's Cloak and Jewels

In his joy, Sugriva addressed Raghava, the delight of the House of Raghu, once again, saying: "I have learnt thine history from my servant, the best of counsellors, Hanuman, and why thou hast come to these sylvan solitudes, where thou residest with thy brother Lakshmana.

"Borne away by a titan, thy consort, Maithili, the daughter of Janaka, is grieving far from thee and the sagacious Lakshmana. That titan seeking an opportunity to do thee mischief, having slain the vulture, Jatayu, carried off thy consort, thus rendering thee unhappy. Thou shalt soon be freed from the sorrow that the abduction of thy loved one causes thee.

"Whether she is to be found in heaven or hell, I shall seek out that lady and bring her back to thee, O Conqueror of Thine Enemies! Know well, I speak truly, O Raghava. Sita is not destined to be the food of gods or titans; thy consort will prove to be a poisoned dish to them!

"Banish thy grief, I will bring thy dear one back to thee. As I surmised, it was undoubtedly Sita that I saw when that titan of cruel deeds bore her away. She was crying: 'O Rama! O Lakshmana!' in a pitiful voice and struggling in Ravana's arms, like the female of the Serpent King.

"Seeing me with my five companions standing on the summit of the mountain, she dropped her cloak and magnificent jewels, which we collected and preserved, O Rama. I will bring them to thee and thou wilt perchance be able to call them to remembrance."

On this, Rama answered Sugriva in all affection and said:—"Go quickly and bring them to me here without delay, O Friend!"

At these words, Sugriva, intent on pleasing Rama, ran in all haste to a deep cave in the mountain, and seizing the cloak and jewels, that monkey showed them to Rama, saying:—"These are they, O Raghava!"

Then Rama, taking the raiment and the sparkling jewels, found his eyes to be misty with tears, as the moon is veiled in cloud, tears that in his affection for Sita fell in torrents, and, losing his composure, he fell to the earth, sobbing: " O My Dear One! "

Pressing the precious jewels to his breast, heaving deep sighs like the furious hissing of a snake in its hole, his eyes streaming with tears, perceiving Lakshmana at his side, he began to lament bitterly, saying :—

" O Lakshmana, behold Vaidehi's cloak and jewels, which, while being carried away, she allowed to fall on the earth; without doubt, it was on this grassy slope that Sita, while being borne away, scattered her ornaments, their condition confirms it."

Hearing Rama's words, Lakshmana said :—" I do not recognize the bracelets or earrings, but I know the anklets, for I worshipped her feet alone."[1]

Then Rama said to Sugriva :—" In what place didst thou behold Vaidehi, my chaste spouse, dearer to me than life itself? What hideous titan bore her away? Where does that monster dwell, who has plunged me in this mourning? Having carried Sita away and kindled my wrath, he has forfeited his life and opened the portals of death. Say, who is this titan, who, in the forest, has by craft borne away my tender consort? O Chief of the Monkeys, to-day I shall dispatch him to the region of death."

CHAPTER 7

Sugriva consoles Rama

Thus, in his distress, did Rama speak, and the monkey, Sugriva, with joined palms, weeping, his voice shaken with sobs, answered him, saying :—

" Indeed I do not know where that wicked titan dwells, nor his strength, nor the extent of his valour, nor the tribe to which that vile monster belongs, but, O Subduer of Thy Foes, I beg thee in all sincerity to master thy grief.

[1] Implying that he never raised his eyes above her feet.

"By mine efforts, I shall succeed in restoring Maithili to thee! By slaying Ravana and his entire house and manifesting my personal courage to the uttermost, I shall act in such a way that thou wilt be happy 'ere long. Thou hast yielded to despair sufficiently, now exhibit thy native resolution! Men like thee should not give way to despondency!

"I too suffer greatly on account of separation from my consort, but I do not despair like thee, nor have I lost courage. Though but a common monkey, I do not indulge in complaint. How much less shouldst thou do so, O Magnanimous Hero, thou who art wise, valiant and illustrious!

"Thou shouldst resolutely restrain the tears that fall; it becometh thee not to lose patience, that quality that distinguishes men of nobility.

"A brave man has recourse to reason and does not allow himself to be moved either in adversity, consequent on separation from relatives, or on the loss of possessions, or at the time of death. But the man who is lacking in courage and gives way to despair inevitably succumbs to his grief, like an overloaded ship in the water.

"Bowing low before thee with joined palms, I beseech thee to summon up all thy fortitude and not yield to misery. Those who permit themselves to be overcome by grief never succeed, and their strength is decreased; do not therefore give thyself up to sorrow.

"He who is overwhelmed by despair is in danger. Banish thy sorrow, O Indra among Men, and revive thy courage; let it be fully restored! I speak to thee for thine own good, as a friend; I do not wish to instruct thee. Therefore for our friendship's sake, do not yield thyself up to grief."

Tenderly consoled by Sugriva, Rama wiped his face, which was wet with tears, with the corner of his tunic and, returning to his normal state as a result of Sugriva's words, the Lord Kakutstha, embracing him, said:—

"O Sugriva, thou dost fulfil the role of a devoted friend, that of being of service with dignity. O Friend, see how, through thy good counsel, I have become myself again. It is not easy to find such an ally, who is suffering the same adversity; therefore exert thyself to find Maithili and the cruel titan, that perverse Ravana, and tell me frankly what I should do. Thou art a rich field that the rains have visited; everything will succeed with thee. Further, the words I recently pronounced[1] with confidence, O Tiger among Monkeys, will without doubt come to pass. Never have I uttered a falsehood, nor shall I ever do so. I swear by the truth, that what I have said will come to pass!"

Hearing the words of that King of Men, the wise leader of the valiant monkeys felt in his heart that his purpose was accomplished.

CHAPTER 8

Sugriva implores Rama to help him against Bali

GRATIFIED on hearing these words, Sugriva joyfully addressed the elder brother of Lakshmana in this wise:—

"Undoubtedly I am favoured by the Gods, since I have a virtuous friend, full of great qualities, such as thou! With thy help, O Irreproachable One, it would be possible for me even to conquer the celestial realm, how much more regain my kingdom, O Lord! I am the object of reverence to my friends and kinsmen, O Rama, since, witnessed by the sacred fire, I have formed an alliance with thee! O Descendant of the House of Raghu, thou wilt soon find me worthy of thy friendship, but it does not become me to speak of mine own good qualities. It is in great heroes such as thou, masters of themselves, that affection, like true courage, remains fixed, O Best of Well-born Men! Silver, gold and precious gems are shared amongst friends as belonging to either; rich or poor, happy or wretched, destitute or gifted with good qualities, a friend is ever a friend. Good fortune, prosperity or country, O Irreproachable Hero, are all sacrificed for the sake of a friend; only devotion to him matters."

"True indeed," replied the blessed Rama to the handsome Sugriva, in the presence of Lakshmana, who equalled Vasava in wisdom.

[1] Concerning Bali.

The following day, Sugriva, seeing Rama standing by the valiant Lakshmana, scanned the forest hurriedly and, observing a Sala tree at no great distance, covered with flowers and heavy with luxuriant foliage, in which bees were humming, tore off a magnificent leafy branch, and spreading it on the ground sat down on it with Rama.

Seeing the two thus installed, Hanuman, in his turn, breaking off a branch of a Sala tree, invited the self-effacing Lakshmana to take his place there.

Beholding Rama seated at his ease on that lofty mountain, covered with flowering Sala trees, radiating serenity like a peaceful lake, Sugriva, in his delight, in soft and gentle tones, leaning towards his friend who was manifesting extreme joy, said to him in accents trembling with emotion :—

"Harassed by my brother, my declared enemy, O Rama, fear of Bali preys on my mind. O Thou who art the refuge of the world, I am without a defender, grant me thy support!"

Hearing these words, the illustrious and virtuous Rama, fixed in his duty, smiling, answered Sugriva, saying :—

"Administering relief is the fruit of friendship, harming others that of enmity! This very day, I shall slay the abductor of thy consort. Here are my winged shafts and fiery arrows, O Fortunate One, whose hafts, inlaid with gold, resembling Mahendra's thunder-bolt, have come from the forest of Karttikeya and are adorned with heron's plumes. Their smooth joints and sharp points lend them the appearance of angry snakes. Thou shalt see that enemy, thy brother called Bali, tainted with evil deeds, struck down with these arrows, like a mountain crumbling into dust."

Hearing Rama's words, Sugriva, the leader of the monkey army, felt an inexpressible joy. "Excellent! Excellent!", he cried. "O Rama, I have been overwhelmed with distress and thou art the refuge of the afflicted. Knowing thee to be mine ally, I have poured out my sorrow on thy breast. Having clasped thy hand in mine, witnessed by the fire, thou hast become the most valued friend of my life; by the truth I swear it. I have taken thee as my friend and speak to thee in confidence. The misfortune that has overtaken me constantly gnaws at my heart."

Thus spoke Sugriva, his eyes brimming, his voice strangled with sobs, unable to continue. Then, stemming the stream of his tears, that flowed like a raging torrent, Sugriva, in Rama's presence, mastering himself in an instant and, stifling his sobs, wiped his beautiful eyes. Thereafter, that illustrious monkey once again addressed Raghava, saying :—

" O Rama, formerly Bali, overwhelming me with insults, banished me from the kingdom. Seizing my consort, dearer to me than life itself, he bound my friends in chains. Then that perverse wretch sought to destroy me, O Rama, and often the monkeys themselves were bribed to that end, but I slew them. Full of apprehension on seeing thee, O Rama, I did not venture to go out to meet thee, being a prey to fear and yet in dread.

" These monkeys with Hanuman as their leader are my sole companions ; it is due to them that I am still alive, though the situation is grave. These loyal monkeys surround and protect me, accompanying me on all my journeys, remaining with me wherever I decide to stay.

" O Rama, of what use is it to speak further ? My elder brother, Bali, distinguished for his cruelty, is mine adversary. If he dies, at that very moment my misfortunes will be at an end. My happiness, nay, my very life, depends on his destruction. This is the only remedy for my woes. I tell thee this while yet overcome with grief ; happy or unhappy, a friend is ever the refuge of a friend ! "

At these words, Rama enquired of Sugriva, saying :—" I wish to know the source of this hostility, tell me the cause of your mutual enmity. When the reason for thine hatred is known to me, O Monkey, I will concern myself with thy relief. I shall reflect carefully on the matter and on its strength and weakness. Great is mine indignation to learn of thine ill-treatment, my heart beats faster, as in the rainy season the river's flow is augmented. Speak with serene confidence while I string my bow, and know that when I loose my shaft to strike thine adversary, he is already slain."

Hearing the speech of the magnanimous Kakutstha, Sugriva and his counsellors were highly gratified, and with a cheerful countenance Sugriva began to relate the real cause of his enmity with Bali to the elder brother of Lakshmana.

CHAPTER 9

The Story of Bali and Mayavi

" BALI is the name of my elder brother, the Scourge of his Foes. He was ever held in great esteem by my father and mother, and I, also, loved him. When his father died, he being the elder, the ministers, who thought highly of him, installed him as King of the Monkeys. During his rule over that immense empire of his ancestors, I lived in constant subjection to him, as one of his servants. On account of a woman, a great quarrel arose between Mayavi, the illustrious elder son of Dundubhi and Bali. One night, whilst others slept, Mayavi approached the gates of Kishkindha, roaring with anger and challenged Bali to fight. Roused from deep sleep by those formidable cries, my brother, unable to contain himself, went forth immediately, advancing in fury on that powerful titan in order to kill him. His wives and I tried to restrain him and I threw myself at his feet, but he repelled us all and went forth full of valour.

"Then, out of devotion, I followed him. Seeing my brother and me following within a short distance, the titan, in fear, fled in all haste. Struck with terror he ran on, but we ran even faster. The moon, that had risen, flooded the path with its light. Hidden by grass, a large hole in the ground came into view and the titan threw himself into it precipitately. We reached the edge and halted. Bali, who was overcome with rage, his senses perturbed, said to me :—

"' O Sugriva, remain here, without leaving the mouth of the cave, while I enter in order to engage the enemy and slay him! '

" Hearing these words I besought that Destroyer of his Foes to go no further but he, under the threat of a curse, told me not to move from there and disappeared into the cavern.

" After his entry into the cave, a whole year elapsed and I remained at my post without ; I imagined him to be dead and in my affection for him was deeply distressed and a prey to fearful presentiments, reflecting: 'I shall not see my brother again.'

"Then, for a long time, blood mixed with foam flowed from the cave and the roaring of the titan reached my ears, but I did not hear the cries of triumph that my elder brother emitted in the struggle. Thereafter on account of the various signs, I went away, thinking that my brother was dead, but first I blocked up the mouth of the cave with a rock as large as a mountain. O My Friend, overcome by sorrow, I offered up the ceremonial water for my brother and returned to Kishkindha.

"Despite mine efforts to keep the matter secret, the ministers learnt of it and having taken counsel together, they installed me as sovereign. I ruled the empire with justice, O Rama. In the meantime Bali, having slain his enemy, the titan, returned. Seeing me installed with all the insignia of royalty, his eyes became red with anger and he overwhelmed me with reproaches and bound my ministers in chains.

"Having slain his adversary, my brother returned to the city, and I, paying obeisance to that great warrior, offered him the traditional homage, but he did not respond to my cordial congratulations. I touched his feet with my forehead, O Lord, but Bali in his anger refused to pardon me."

CHAPTER 10

The Origin of Bali's Hatred of Sugriva

"In my desire to make peace, I tried to placate my brother, who, returning, was incensed against me.

"I said: 'By the grace of the Gods, thou art victorious and thine enemy has fallen under thy blows; without thee, I should be bereft of support, thou art my only defender, O My Protector, My Delight! Now accept this royal canopy of many supports, resembling the full moon about to rise. Take also these chanwaras from my hands!

"'O King! For a whole year I waited sadly beside the cave and, seeing blood flowing to the entrance and stopping there, my heart was filled with anguish and my mind deeply troubled. I then closed the opening of the cavern with a great rock and left that place to return to Kishkindha in deep distress. Seeing me, the people of that city and the ministers also placed me on the throne, without my desiring it. Therefore pardon me, thou who art our Sovereign. I was invested with royal dignity in thine absence and thus preserved the city, its ministers and inhabitants, from anarchy. This kingdom has been as a trust to me; I now render it back to thee, O Friend. Do not be wrath against me, O Destroyer of thy Foes! Placing my head at thy feet, O King, with joined palms, I appeal to thee. It was on the insistence of the ministers and the united populace, that I was placed on the throne, they reflecting that the country would be seized by an enemy in the absence of a monarch.'

"To this humble speech, Bali answered with invectives, saying:—'Cursed be thou!' and repeated the imprecation. Then, gathering his subjects and ministers together, he inveighed against me, in the midst of my friends, reproaching me with bitter words, saying:—

"'Know well, that in anger the great Titan, Mayavi, one night challenged me to a long-desired combat. Hearing his voice, I left my royal dwelling and was followed immediately by my unscrupulous brother, who is present here. In the night, seeing me followed by another, that great titan fled terrified and both of us pursued him closely. In his haste to escape, he entered a great cave, and, seeing that vast and fearful cavern, I said to my false-hearted brother: 'I cannot return to the city till I have slain my rival; do thou wait at the mouth of the pit till I have struck him down.' In the belief that he would remain there, I penetrated into that inaccessible cave.

"'While I was pursuing mine enemy, whose audacity rendered him truly formidable, a whole year elapsed, but at last I discovered him and slew him with his entire family. That titan, while being slain, roared aloud, and a stream of blood that spread all round, filled the cave, making it difficult to pass. Having happily slain my cruel adversary, I could not find the opening of the cave, the entrance having been closed. I called Sugriva again and again but there was no response and my situation was serious. By dint of kicking, I was able to roll back the rock and emerged, after which I returned to the city. That is why I am incensed against the wicked Sugriva, whose desire for the throne overcame his brotherly affection.'

" With these words, the monkey Bali, bereft of all sense of shame, chased me from the kingdom with but a single garment, having ill-treated me and carried off my consort, O Rama. Wretched and deprived of my companions, I took refuge on this lofty mountain, Rishyamuka, to which, for a particular reason, Bali has no access. This is the whole story of the origin of our intense hostility; I have not merited the great humiliation that has visited me, as thou now seest, O Raghava. O Thou who art the dispeller of fear, do thou take this dread of my brother from me and punish him in my name."

The virtuous prince, having heard the faithful Sugriva's narrative, smiling, answered him saying:—

" These arrows of mine, bright as the sun, never fail to reach their target and with their sharp points will strike down that evil Bali with force. As long as I do not behold this ravisher of thy consort, this wretch of perverse practices will live, but not an instant longer.

" I see thee to be plunged in an ocean of grief, as am I, and I shall aid thee to traverse it; thou shalt certainly regain thine erstwhile prosperity."

Hearing these words, that increased his joy and courage, Sugriva, in extreme delight, uttered the following memorable words.

CHAPTER II

Sugriva tells Rama of Bali's Exploits

HAVING listened to Rama's words, which inspired him with joy and courage, Sugriva paid obeisance to him, manifesting his gratitude, and said:—" In thy wrath, undoubtedly, thou art able to burn up the worlds with thy sharp arrows, like the fire at the end of the great cycle; yet reflect on the courage of Bali and, having heard me with attention, consider what should be done.

" 'Ere the sun rises, the indefatigable Bali strides from the western to the eastern ocean and from the northern to the southern sea. He is so powerful that he is able to break off the lofty mountain peaks, throwing them into the air and catching them again. In order to demonstrate his strength, he will snap in two innumerable trees of every kind in the forest.

" Once, there existed a giant, named Dundubhi, in the form of a buffalo, who resembled the peak of Mt. Kailasha and who was as strong as a thousand elephants. The thought of his own might intoxicated him and he was puffed up with pride on account of the boons he had received.

" That giant came to the sea, the Lord of Rivers, and approached that ocean of tumultuous waves, rich in pearls, saying:—' Let us enter into combat one with the other!' But that righteous Lord of the Waters, rising up in all his majesty, answered that titan who was driven on by destiny, saying:—' O Skilful Warrior, I am not able to take up thy challenge, but hear and I will tell thee of one who can match thee in fight.

" ' On a vast plain, the retreat of the ascetics, there lives a monarch of the mountains, named Himavat, the far-famed father-in-law of Shiva. He possesses great rivers, many ravines and waterfalls and is well able to satisfy thine overwhelming lust for combat.' Reflecting: ' The ocean holds me in dread', that foremost of titans sped to the forest of Himavat, as swift as an arrow loosed from a bow.

" Breaking off the great white cliffs, Dundubhi let them roll down, shouting with exultation. Then, like a mass of white cloud, Himavat of gentle and benign aspect, standing on the summit of the mountain, addressed that titan thus:—' Do not torment me, O Dundubhi, O Thou who delightest in justice! I am not concerned with the exploits of warriors but am a refuge of the ascetics.'

" Hearing these words of that righteous monarch of the mountains, Dundubhi, his eyes red with anger, answered:—

" ' If thou hast not the strength to fight and art paralysed with fear, then tell me who is able to match his prowess with mine, for I wish to enter into combat with him.'

" Hearing this, the wise Himavat, skilful in discourse, answered that powerful titan to whom he had spoken previously, saying :—

" ' The name of that hero of great intelligence, who dwells in Kishkindha, is Bali, the illustrious son of Shakra. That great sage is a skilful warrior and of thy stature, he is as well able to enter into combat with thee as Vasava with Namuchi. Go with all speed and seek him out, since thou art thirsting to fight; he has little patience and is ever full of martial ardour.'

" Having listened to the words of Himavat, Dundubhi in fury went to Kishkindha, Bali's city, and assuming the form of a terrible buffalo with pointed horns, resembling a thunder-cloud charged with rain in the sky, that powerful titan came to the gates of the capital. Causing the earth to tremble with his cries, he uprooted the trees near the entrance of the city, snapping them in two. Then, like an elephant, he burst open the gates.

" My brother, who was in the inner apartments, hearing the tumult, came out, full of impatience, surrounded by his wives, like the moon encircled with stars, and that leader of the monkeys, Bali, said to Dundubhi in clear and measured accents :—

" ' O Dundubhi, why dost thou obstruct the gateway of the city and bellow thus? I know who thou art. Have a care for thy life, O Warrior!'

" At these words of the sagacious King of the Monkeys, Dundubhi, his eyes red with anger, answered :—

" ' Do not address me thus in the presence of women, O Warrior! Accept my challenge and meet me in combat to-day, so that I can measure thy strength, though, O Monkey, I am willing to restrain my wrath for one night, to allow thee to indulge in the pleasures of love, according to thy whim, till the rising of the sun. Distribute alms, therefore, to thy monkeys and embrace them for the last time. Thou art the King of the Deer of the Trees, do thou load thy friends and people with favours. Look long on Kishkindha; enjoy the company of thy wives, for I am about to chastise thee for thine insolence. To slay a drunken man or one who is demented or whose strength has ebbed away or who is without weapons or defence, or one, like thee, given over to lust, is considered equal to infanticide in the world.'

"Dismissing all his wives, including Tara and others, my brother, restraining his wrath, smiling, answered that chief of the titans, saying:—

"'Do not make a pretext of my being inebriated if thou art not afraid to enter into combat with me! Know that in the present issue this intoxication is the wine of warriors!'

"With these words he threw off the golden chain that his sire, Mahendra, had given him and began to fight. Seizing Dundubhi by the horns, who resembled a mountain, that elephant among monkeys roared aloud and began to assail him with blows. Thereafter Bali with a tremendous shout threw him on the ground and blood began to flow from the stricken buffalo.

"Then betwixt the two combatants, Bali and Dundubhi, mad with anger, each desirous of overcoming the other, a terrible struggle ensued. My brother fought with matchless courage, equal to Indra's, dealing blows with his fists, knees, feet and also with rocks and trees. The duel between the monkey and the titan caused the latter to weaken, whilst the strength of the former grew. In the end, Bali, lifting Dundubhi up, let him fall on the earth and in this death struggle the giant perished.

"As he fell blood flowed in rivers from the veins of his body and that titan of vast limbs lay stretched on the ground, having rejoined the elements.

"Lifting up the inanimate corpse in his two arms, Bali with one throw sent it flying to a distance of four miles. From the titan's jaws, shattered by the violence of the fall, blood spouted forth and the drops were carried by the wind to Matanga's hermitage. Seeing that rain of blood, the Sage, displeased, reflected: 'What perverse wretch has dared to spatter me with blood? Who is this evil, perfidious and vile creature, this madman?'

" Thinking thus, that excellent Muni went out of the hermitage and beheld the buffalo, as large as a mountain, lying dead on the ground. By virtue of his austerities, he knew that a monkey was responsible for this deed and he pronounced a terrible curse on that ape who had thrown the corpse there saying:—

" ' May he never come here ! If that monkey who, with a stream of blood, has desecrated this wood where I have built my retreat, ever sets foot in this place, he will die ! Should that wicked wretch who has thrown the corpse of this titan here, breaking my trees, come within four miles of my hermitage, he shall assuredly not survive and his confederates, whosoever they may be, who have sought refuge in my forest, will not be permitted to remain here following this malediction. Let them go where they will, for I shall assuredly curse any who stay in these woods, that I have protected like mine own offspring, and destroy the foliage and young shoots, plucking the fruit and scratching up the roots. From to-day, every monkey that I see here will be changed into stone for the period of a thousand years ! '

" On hearing the words of the ascetic, all the monkeys that frequented those woods went away, and, beholding them issuing from the forest, Bali enquired of them, saying :—

" ' Why have ye all come here, ye dwellers in the Matanga Forest ? Happy are they who dwell in the woods ! '

" Then those monkeys told Bali, who wore a chain of gold, the cause of their departure and also of the curse that had been laid on them.

" My brother, hearing the monkeys' words, sought out that great Rishi and with joined palms attempted to appease him, but Matanga refused to listen to him and re-entered his hermitage.

" Trembling under the shadow of that curse, Bali began to roam about aimlessly, but, terrified of the malediction, that monkey did not dare approach the great mountain Rishyamuka or even glance in that direction, O Prince.

" Knowing he will never venture here, O Rama, I wander about these woods with my companions, free of all anxiety The heaped bones of Dundubhi, the victim of the arrogance, his strength inspired in him, are here and resemble the peak of a vast mountain. Bali in his might, stripped all the leaves from these seven giant Sala trees with their mighty boughs, one after the other. His strength is immeasurable, O Rama; I have now proved it to thee. In consequence, I do not see how thou canst overcome him in battle, O King."

Thus spoke Sugriva and Lakshmana, smiling, then enquired of him :—

"What can Rama do to convince thee that he is able to overcome him?" Sugriva then made answer :—

"If Rama is able to penetrate these seven Sala trees, that Bali pierced again and again, with a single arrow, then, by that sign, I shall know he can overcome him. At the same time, let him with a single kick send the carcase of the buffalo flying to a distance of a hundred bows' length."

Having spoken, Sugriva, the corners of whose eyes were slightly red, reflected awhile and then once more addressed Rama, the descendant of Kakutstha, saying :—

"Full of courage and audacity, renowned for his strength and energy, that powerful monkey has never been defeated in combat. His exploits are famous; the Gods themselves are not able to accomplish them. It was on remembering them, filled with terror, that I resolved to take refuge on the Rishyamuka Mountain. Thinking of that Indra among Monkeys and how invincible, irresistible and ruthless he is, I came here. Filled with distress and anguish, I wander about in these woods with my devoted and excellent companions, Hanuman and others. Thou art for me a glorious and illustrious friend, O Thou who art dear to thy friends, O Lion among Men! I take refuge with thee as in another Himavat; yet I am conversant with the strength of my wicked brother and his overbearing nature and I am not acquainted with thy skill as a warrior, O Raghava. Assuredly, it is not that I wish to test thee or humiliate thee nor inspire thee with fear by recounting his great exploits. Mine own cowardice is well known! O Rama, thine accents, thine assurance, thy temerity and thy stature truly manifest thy great power, which is like a fire concealed beneath the ashes."

Hearing the words of the magnanimous Sugriva, Rama began to smile and answered him, saying :—

"If thou dost not trust in our courage, O Monkey, I will instil thee with that confidence so essential in war."

Then with his foot, that mighty hero sent the dried up carcase of that titan flying. Seeing the carcase hurtling through the air, Sugriva once more addressed Rama, who was as radiant as the sun, in the presence of Lakshmana and the monkeys and in candid accents said :—

"O my Friend, when that corpse was fresh and its flesh intact, it was sent flying through the air by my brother, though he was weakened by inebriation and fatigue. Now stripped of flesh, as light as a straw, thou hast kicked it in play; it is therefore impossible for me to judge who is the more powerful, thou or Bali. Between a fresh corpse and dry bones, there is a great difference, O Raghava.

"I am therefore still uncertain, My Dear Friend, as to who is the stronger, thou or Bali, but if thou art able to pierce even a single Sala tree, then I should be able to judge who is superior and who inferior. Therefore stretch that bow, which resembles the trunk of an elephant and drawing the cord up to thine ear, discharge that great arrow, which I am sure will penetrate the Sala tree and by that sign I shall be satisfied. I implore thee, O Prince, to do me this great favour. As amongst the planets the sun is greatest and among mountains the Himalayas, just as among quadrupeds the lion is king, so among men thou art supreme in valour."

CHAPTER 12

The Fight between Sugriva and Bali

HEARING Sugriva's gracious speech, Rama, in order to inspire him with confidence, took up his bow and a formidable arrow, and taking aim, pierced the Sala trees, filling the firmament with the sound.

Loosed by that mighty warrior, the arrow, decorated with gold, passed through the seven Sala trees and entering the mountain, buried itself in the earth. In the twinkling of an eye that shaft with the speed of lightning, having pierced the seven trees with extreme velocity, returned to Rama's quiver.

Seeing those seven trees pierced by Rama's impetuous arrow, that Bull among Monkeys was extremely astonished and, overcome with joy adorned with all his ornaments, prostrated himself before Raghava with joined palms, his forehead touching the earth,

Amazed at Rama's prowess, he addressed that great warrior, skilled in the scriptural traditions, as also in the use of every weapon, who stood before him and said :—

" O Lion among Men, with thine arrows, thou art able to destroy all the Gods with their King in combat, why not Bali also ? O Kakutstha, who can resist thee on the field of battle, thou, who hast pierced seven Sala trees, the mountain and the earth with a single arrow ! Now my anxieties are dispelled and my satisfaction complete. Where could I find a friend such as thou, who art equal to Mahendra and Varuna ? For my sake do thou subdue mine adversary in the form of a brother, I implore thee ! "

Rama, embracing the handsome Sugriva, like unto Lakshmana, in his great wisdom answered him, saying :—

" Let us leave here without delay for Kishkindha. Do thou precede us. When we come to that city, O Sugriva, it is for thee to challenge Bali, who is a brother in name only."

Thereafter they started out in all haste for Kishkindha, Bali's capital. Concealing themselves behind some trees, they halted in a dense wood where Sugriva hurled defiance at Bali with a deep and challenging roar. His clothes tightly wrapped round him, he shouted with all his strength, shattering the silence of the firmament.

When the powerful Bali heard his brother emitting this tremendous clamour, he was livid with anger and rushed out like the sun rising over the mountain top. Then a terrible struggle ensued between Bali and Sugriva, resembling the clash of Mars and Jupiter, in the heavens.

With the striking of their palms like the clap of thunder and their fists that were as hard as diamonds, the two brothers, filled with fury, assaulted each other, whilst Rama, bow in hand, watched those two combatants, who resembled the Ashwins.

Not being able to distinguish between Bali and Sugriva, Rama was loath to loose his death-dealing shaft. Then Sugriva, overcome by Bali, seeing that Rama refrained from coming to his aid, ran towards the Rishyamuka Mountain. Exhausted, his limbs covered with blood, crushed by his brother's blows, who pressed him furiously, he took refuge in the vast forest. The mighty Bali, seeing him penetrating deep into the woods, said :—

"Go! I spare thee!" he himself not venturing to enter there, through fear of the curse.

Then Rama, accompanied by his brother and Hanuman, re-entering the wood, found the monkey Sugriva. When the latter perceived Rama returning with Lakshmana, he hung his head in shame and in a tearful voice, his eyes fixed on the ground, said :—

"After demonstrating thy strength, thou didst issue the command: 'Challenge thine adversary!' Thereafter thou didst allow him to defeat me. Why hast thou done this? O Raghava, thou shouldst have told me frankly: 'I do not wish to slay Bali,' then I would not have left this place." Thus in sad and reproachful tones did the great-souled Sugriva speak, and Rama answered him, saying :—

"O Sugriva, My Dear Friend, do not vex thyself but hear the reason why I did not discharge mine arrow. Thine ornaments, clothes, shape and gestures and those of Bali so resembled each other that there was no difference between you! The voice, colour, look, prowess and speech were wholly similar, O Monkey! Disconcerted by thine exact resemblance, O Best of Monkeys, I did not let fly my swift and dreadful death-dealing arrow, the slayer of the foe, for this reason. 'One must have a care not to destroy them both,' I reflected. In truth, had I made an end of thine existence, O Chief of the Monkeys, through ignorance or carelessness, then my stupidity and heedlessness would have been apparent. To kill one's ally is assuredly a great and heinous sin. Further, I, Lakshmana and the fair-complexioned Sita are all wholly dependent on thee; in the forest, thou art our refuge. Enter once more into combat, therefore, and fear nothing, O Monkey. In the twinkling of an eye, thou shalt see me piercing Bali with my shaft and striking him down; thou shalt see him writhing on the field of battle. Do thou, however, wear a distinguishing sign, O Chief of the Monkeys, by the help of which I may recognize thee in the thick of the struggle. O Lakshmana, these blossoming and beautiful Gajapushpi flowers, do thou place round the neck of the magnanimous Sugriva."

Plucking the blossoming Gajapushpi from where it grew, Lakshmana placed it round the neck of Sugriva. The creeper that the fortunate Sugriva wore round his neck was as bright as the sun and resembled a circle of cranes illumining a cloud over which they are planing. Sparkling with beauty and encouraged by Rama's words, Sugriva started on the road to Kishkindha with him.

CHAPTER 13

The Hermitage of Saptajanas

THE virtuous elder brother of Lakshmana, together with Sugriva, left the Rishyamuka Mountain and proceeded towards Kishkindha, which was maintained by Bali's valour, Rama bearing his golden bow and carrying his arrows that shone like the sun in his hand.

Sugriva, his neck adorned with a wreath of flowers, full of courage, strode before the magnanimous Raghava and Lakshmana, behind whom came the hero Hanuman with Nala, the valiant Nila and the illustrious general Tara, renowned among the monkeys.

They observed the trees bowed with the weight of their flowers and the rivers bearing their peaceful waters to the sea. The ravines and cliffs with their chasms, caves, peaks and charming dales, the lakes with their limpid waters of emerald hue, adorned with opening lotus buds, drew their gaze as they passed. Ducks, cranes, swans, woodcock and other waterfowl were heard calling, whilst in the clearings of the woods deer could be seen grazing on the tender grass and young shoots, without fear of the wild beasts that roamed everywhere.

Wild and ferocious elephants adorned with ivory tusks, who proved a menace to the lakes by causing the banks to crumble, wandered about here and there and intoxicated with Mada juice, striking their foreheads against the rocks, resembled moving mountains. Monkeys as large as elephants, covered with dust and every species of wild beast and bird were seen by the followers of Sugriva as they passed on their way.

Advancing thus in all haste, the Joy of the House of Raghu, Rama, seeing a grove of trees, enquired of Sugriva :—" What is this clump of trees like a cloud in the sky ? Indeed they seem like a mass of clouds ringed round by plantain groves ! Great is my curiosity concerning them, O My Friend. I wish to learn of thee what these are."

On this enquiry from Rama, Sugriva, still walking on, told him the history of that great wood. " O Rama ! It is a vast hermitage that removes all weariness and encloses many pleasant gardens and groves ; the roots, fruit and water are delicious. Under the name of Saptajanas, seven Munis of rigid vows lived there, lying in the water, their heads alone emerging from it. Every seven days they partook of food, which was the wind from the mountain on which they dwelt. After seven hundred years they ascended to heaven in their bodies. Through the power of their asceticism, this hermitage, encircled by a hedge of trees, is inaccessible even to the Gods and Asuras, as well as their leaders. The birds eschew it, as also the other beasts of the forest ; those who enter it unwittingly never return. Lovely melodies are heard issuing therefrom with the music of instruments and singing. Sometimes a divine fragrance is spread abroad from there, O Raghava, and three fires are lit ; it is their smoke that one can see from here ; the tops of the trees are enveloped in it like a golden cloud, resembling the plumage of a dove.

" These trees are magnificent with their tops crowned with smoke, like unto mountains of emerald crowned with rain clouds. Pay obeisance with reverence to them with joined palms, O Valiant Raghava, as also thy brother, Lakshmana. Those who offer salutations to those Rishis of pure soul experience naught that is grievous."

Then Raghava with his brother Lakshmana, with joined palms, offered salutations to those illustrious ascetics. Having paid reverence to them, the virtuous Rama, his brother Lakshmana and Sugriva with his monkeys went on happily.

Having left the hermitage of Saptajanas far behind, they beheld the inaccessible Kishkindha protected by Bali. Rama, his younger brother Lakshmana and the monkeys, famed for their valour, seizing their weapons, once more prepared to slay their enemy in that city which the son of the Chief of the Gods protected by his prowess.

CHAPTER 14

Sugriva again challenges his brother to fight

RETURNING to Kishkindha, Bali's city, they all concealed themselves behind the trees in the dense forest. Glancing round on every side, the Friend of the Woods, the thick-necked Sugriva began to exhibit signs of extreme anger and, surrounded by his kinsmen, let out a loud roar, challenging his brother to fight. Shattering the firmament with his war-cry which resembled a great thundercloud propelled by a high wind, that monkey, who was endowed with a leonine gait and resembled the rising sun, stepped forth.

Looking at Rama who was skilled in combat, Sugriva said to him :—" Behold Kishkindha, surrounded by its walls made of gold and a rampart of monkeys, that is bristling with instruments of war and from which innumerable banners stream. This is Bali's citadel. Now fulfil the promise formerly made to me of slaying him, O Hero, as the blessing of Spring visits the creepers."

At Sugriva's words, the virtuous Rama, the destroyer of his foes, answered :—" Thou art wearing that which will enable me to distinguish thee, this garland of Gaja flowers, placed by Lakshmana round thy neck ! This creeper worn by thee lends thee the brilliance of the sky in which the sun is surrounded by stars, O Warrior. To-day, O Monkey, I will deliver thee from the fear and hostility that Bali inspires in thee. Point out thine adversary in the guise of a brother,

O Sugriva! Till Bali is struck down in the forest, let him make merry, for when he crosses my path, he will not return alive. If he should do so, thou wilt be justified in reproaching me for not honouring my word.

"In thy presence, seven Sala trees were transfixed by me with a single arrow; rest assured that Bali will fall to-day on the field of battle under my shafts.

"No light word has ever passed my lips, even in adversity, nor ever shall, even were it to attain my purpose; therefore banish all anxiety.

"Like a field rendered fertile by the rains of Shatakratu, do thou challenge Bali of the golden diadem. O Sugriva, raise a shout that will cause that monkey, proud of his victory, whom thou wert unable to subdue before, and who is bellicose by nature, to come forth. Those who deem themselves brave are not able to endure the war-cry of their foes, above all in the presence of women."

Hearing Rama's words, the golden-hued Sugriva let out a deafening roar, rending the skies.

Terrified by the clamour, the kine ran hither and thither, like noble women exposed to danger of hostile attack through the negligence of their loved ones, and the wild deer fled away like maddened war horses wounded in battle, whilst the birds fell to the ground like planets whose virtue is exhausted.

Then that son of Surya emitted a roar resembling thunder, confident of his strength and radiant with courage, like the ocean whose waves are lashed by a tempest.

CHAPTER 15

Tara's Advice to Bali

HIS brother Bali, who was seated amidst his wives in the inner apartments, heard the cry of the great-hearted Sugriva and was filled with wrath. When he caught the sound of that uproar, causing terror to all beings, his feelings of lust changed to those of violent anger and, his limbs trembling with fury, he who formerly shone like gold suddenly lost his brilliance, like the sun under eclipse. Grinding his teeth, his eyes flashing with fire, he resembled a lake from which the lotuses have been uprooted. Hearing that unendurable cry, that monkey strode forth in great haste, stamping on the earth as if he wished to shatter it.

Then Tara, embracing him tenderly, once more avowed her devotion to him and, timid and troubled, addressed him in these words, the wisdom of which the future was to prove :—

" O Brave Warrior, this anger that has taken hold of thee is like a raging torrent ; do thou abandon it, as on rising in the morning thou dost throw aside a faded garland. Tomorrow at dawn, enter into combat with Sugriva, O Valiant Forest Dweller, for thou dost not yet know the strength or weakness of thine enemy. That thou shouldst set out immediately does not meet with my approval. Hear while I tell thee the reason why I seek to delay thee !

" Formerly Sugriva, in great anger, came hither and challenged thee to fight, but defeated and overwhelmed by thy blows, he fled. Having been assaulted and crushed in this wise, he now returns to challenge thee again, which rouses my suspicion. To roar thus in so insolent and arrogant a manner, so filled with wrath, is not done without a particular motive. To my mind, Sugriva has not returned alone but has an escort who is ready to rush to his defence ; hence this cry of defiance. Sugriva is a naturally clever and sagacious monkey and will never ally himself to one whose valour has not been tried. This, O Warrior, is what I have heard from the youthful Prince Angada ; take heed therefore and have a care ; it is to thine advantage ! He hath told me all that he has heard from his emissaries concerning Sugriva while journeying in the forest. Two sons were born to the King of Ayodhya, full of courage, invincible in combat ; they are of the House of Ikshwaku and are renowned ; their names are Rama and Lakshmana.

" These two indomitable heroes have sealed a pact of friendship with Sugriva, and this ally of thy brother is Rama, famed for his military exploits, the Destroyer of Enemy Hosts, who resembles the fire at the end of the world cycle. He dwells in the forest and is the supreme refuge of all the virtuous who seek his protection. He is the support of the oppressed, the unique repository of all glory and is conversant with both secular and spiritual learning; his pleasure consists in carrying out the behests of his Sire.

"As the King of the Mountains is a treasury of precious metals, so is he a mine of every good quality. It is peace and not war that thou shouldst seek with that magnanimous One, the invincible Rama, whose prowess on the battlefield is without limit. O Hero, I have no desire to oppose thee, but tell thee this for thy good. Therefore, heed my counsel! Do not seek a quarrel with thy younger brother, O Valiant Monarch. I am certain it is to thine advantage to contract a friendship with Rama. Reconcile thyself with Sugriva and put all thoughts of hatred far from thee. Thy younger brother is an inhabitant of the forest of amiable qualities. Whether he dwell here or there, he is bound to thee from every point of view, and I do not see any like him in the world. With gifts, honours and in other ways, bind him to thyself through kindness. Abandon thine ill-will and let him in future dwell near thee. The thick-necked Sugriva is a powerful, valuable and natural ally. Win back thy brother's affection; there is no other way to happiness for thee here. If thou dost desire to please me and recognizest my devotion to thee, then in the name of affection, O My Friend, I implore thee to act as I have counselled. Follow my advice which is salutary; trust me and do not give way to anger; live in peace with the son of the King of Koshala; do not quarrel with him, his valour is equal to Indra's."

In these words, which were full of wisdom and would have enabled him to save himself, Tara addressed Bali, but he refused to listen and, driven by the force of destiny, advanced to meet his death.

CHAPTER 16

Rama inflicts a mortal Wound on Bali

THUS spoke Tara, whose face was as radiant as the moon, and Bali answered her in tones of reproach, saying:—

" When my brother, who is above all mine adversary, challenges me in anger, how shall I endure it, O Lady of Lovely Countenance? The brave who are not accustomed to bearing insults and who never turn back in battle, O Timid One, would rather suffer death than such ignominy. I may not disregard the weak-necked Sugriva who, in his determination to enter into combat, has offered me so insolent a challenge.

" Have no anxiety on my behalf regarding Raghava, for he is conversant with dharma and pious by nature. How could he do wrong? Return home with thy companions! Why follow me further? Thou hast demonstrated thy tender devotion sufficiently! I am about to set out to fight Sugriva; control thine emotions. I shall punish his insolence, but I shall not take his life. I shall enter into combat with him, since he desires it, and, assailed by the blows dealt with my fists and the trunks of trees, he will flee. That coward will not be able to withstand my strength and prowess. O Tara, thou hast accompanied me far enough and shown thine affection for me sufficiently, now return, and I, having obtained satisfaction from my brother on the battlefield, will follow thee; I swear it by my life and race."

Then the virtuous Tara, embracing Bali and speaking tenderly to him, weeping, circumambulated him, keeping him on her right hand, and bidding him farewell according to the tradition and reciting the sacred texts so that he might return victorious, she re-entered the inner apartments, distracted with grief.

When Tara reached the inner sanctuary with the other women, Bali, distraught with anger, went out of the city, hissing like a great serpent. Full of ire, breathing heavily, he ran with all his strength, looking round on every side, eager to find his adversary.

At last he beheld that powerful monkey, the golden-hued Sugriva, clothed in excellent armour, full of confidence, resembling a brazier, and, seeing him inflated with pride, Bali wrapped his garments more tightly about him, a prey to extreme anger. Having thus girded up his apparel, his fists clenched, full of vigour, he advanced to meet Sugriva and engage him in combat. From his side, Sugriva, also doubling his fists in rage, went out to meet his brother who was wearing a crown of gold.

Then Bali, addressing Sugriva, whose eyes were red with anger, who was skilled in the art of fighting and was rushing towards him in fury, said :—

" With this clenched fist, its fingers tightly closed, I shall deal thee a blow that will cause thee to yield up thy life."

At these words, Sugriva, livid with anger, answered :—" It is mine that will drive the life's breath out of thee by caving in thy skull." Thereafter, violently assaulted by Bali, he hurled himself on him in fury, rivers of blood streaming from him, like a mountain from which torrents fall. Unperturbed, Sugriva, tearing up a Sala tree, struck his rival's body as lightning fells a mountain peak. Struck by the Sala tree which unnerved him, Bali resembled a heavily-laden ship, sinking with all its cargo in the waves. Endowed with terrific strength and as agile as Suparna, both fought like two formidable giants resembling the sun and moon in the sky. Each of these two destroyers of their foes sought to find the weak point of his enemy.

Bali excelled in strength and valour while the son of Surya, Sugriva, despite his great energy, was the weaker, and his courage beginning to dwindle, he ceased to boast and, enraged with his brother, made a sign to Rama.

The uprooted trees with their branches and crests, the blows from fists, knees and feet, fell thick and fast in the formidable struggle that resembled the duel between Vritra and Vasava. Covered with blood, the two monkeys, dwellers in the forest, whilst fighting resembled two thunderclouds clashing together with a great uproar.

Rama, observing Sugriva, the Prince of Monkeys, exhausted scanning the horizon without ceasing to struggle, and, seeing that he was almost overcome, selected an arrow for the purpose of slaying Bali, and that great hero stretched his bow and with that shaft, resembling a venomous serpent, held it ready, like Antaka, bearing the Wheel of Time. The twanging of the bowstring caused alarm among the birds, who flew away, as also the wild beasts who fled in terror as at the end of the world period.

Discharged by Rama with a sound like the crash of thunder, that formidable arrow of dazzling aspect pierced Bali's breast, and under its fatal impact the powerful and valiant King of the Monkeys fell to the earth, resembling Indra's banner ruthlessly thrown to the ground on the day of the full moon in the month of the constellation of Aries.

Stricken and senseless, Bali fell, his voice strangled with sobs which gradually died away. Rama, the strongest of men, discharged that formidable, fiery and death-dealing arrow, shining like gold, resembling Time itself at the end of the world, which shot forth like smoke issuing from the flaming mouth of Hara, and, streaming with blood looked like unto a blossoming Ashoka tree on the mountain-side, whereupon the Son of Vasava, like the banner of Indra that has been overthrown, fell senseless on the field of battle.

CHAPTER 17

Bali reproaches Rama

STRUCK by Rama's arrow, that doughty warrior fell to the earth, like a tree severed by an axe. With his ornaments of fine gold, his limbs paralysed, he sank to the ground, like the banner of the Chief of the Gods, its cord severed.

At the fall of the King of the Monkeys, the earth grew dark, resembling the firmament bereft of the moon. Though lying on the earth, the body of that high-souled Bali was neither robbed of its beauty nor of its life's breath, nor did his courage fail him, for that excellent golden necklace that Indra had bestowed on him preserved the life, strength and beauty of that Lord of Monkeys. Adorned with that golden chain, the heroic Monkey Chief appeared like an evening cloud tinged with the roseate hues of dusk! His chain, his body and the arrow piercing his heart blazed in triple glory, even after he had fallen. That arrow loosed by the valiant Rama from his bow, by its virtue opening the way to heaven, brought Bali supreme deliverance.

Lying on the field of battle, like a fire without flame, he resembled Yayati cast forth from the divine realms, fallen on the earth, his merits exhausted. Like the sun that Time, at the end of the world, throws down on the earth; unapproachable like Mahendra, inaccessible as Upendra, with his golden necklace, his broad chest, his vast arms, his mouth inflamed, his glances wild, that son of a mighty king lay. And Rama followed by Lakshmana, their eyes fixed upon him, approached that warrior lying there like a naked flame about to be quenched. Full of respect for that hero, who was gazing at them, the two valiant brothers, Rama and Lakshmana, approached with slow steps.

On perceiving them, the supremely courageous Bali uttered these harsh words, that seemed both restrained and just. Stretched on the earth, almost without lustre, mortally wounded, motionless, in words pregnant with meaning he addressed that warrior proudly, saying :—

" Striking me from behind, what merit dost thou hope to earn by this, O Thou who hast inflicted a mortal wound on me, while I was engaged in combat with another ? ' The virtuous Rama is full of nobility, generosity and valour; he is compassionate, devoted to the welfare of all beings, fixed in his duty; gracious, omnipotent and conversant with the rules of conduct and austerity; these are the praises sung of thee, these are the merits attributed to thee by the whole world!

" Self-mastery, forbearance, loyalty, fixity of purpose, goodwill and heroism are the virtues of kings, O Prince, as also the repression of evil deeds. It was reflecting on these virtues, believing them to be thine, that I came to fight Sugriva. ' Whilst I am filled with rage and engaged in combat with another, he will not attack me' was my conviction, even without knowing thee. Now I perceive that thou art a perverse creature, feigning piety whilst in truth thou art like a well concealed in the grass, without faith and resorting to evil deeds. Outwardly virtuous, wearing the cloak of integrity, thou art in reality a scoundrel, like a fire bidden by ashes, nor do I recognize thee behind the concealing mask of virtue.

"Since I have neither laid waste thy land, nor thy city and have not offered thee insult, why hast thou destroyed me —I who am guiltless and who have ever fed on fruit and roots, a monkey dwelling in the forest, who never sought to enter into combat with thee but who was engaged in fighting another? Thou art the son of a king and inspired confidence by thy benign aspect and, what is more, thou wearest the livery of sanctity; who of the warrior caste, conversant with what is good and evil, in the garb of a righteous man, would commit such a wicked deed?

"Thou art born of the House of Raghu and art spoken of as virtuous, how canst thou, assuming the guise of an ascetic, wander about thus? Equanimity of soul, liberality, forbearance, justice, loyalty, constancy and courage are the characteristics of a king, O Prince, also the meting out of punishment to the guilty.

"We live in the forest, O Rama, and are but wild beasts who feed on roots and fruits, which is natural to us; but thou art a man, O Prince! Land, gold and beauty are the causes of discord, but here in the woods, who will envy us fruit and roots? In temporal and spiritual matters, as well as in the dispensing of reward and punishment, a king should be wholly given up to the task of government and not dominated by any desire for pleasure, but thou art consumed by thy desires; irascible, restless, disregarding the royal code, thy bow is thy cherished argument! Thou dost not pursue the path of duty nor does thine understanding concern itself with the interests of the people; a slave to lust, thou dost permit thy senses to rule thee, O Chief of Men. In a word, Kakutstha, thou hast slain me, who never did thee any harm! How wilt thou answer in the assembly of the virtuous, having committed this reprehensible deed?

" The regicide, the brahmanicide, the slayer of the cow, the thief and the one who finds pleasure in the destruction of other beings, the unbeliever and the one who weds before his elder brother, all these enter hell. The informer, the miser, the one who slays his friend or defiles his Guru's bed, undoubtedly descends to the region of evil-doers !

" It is not permitted to the well-born to clothe themselves in my skin, nor may those, such as thou, partake of my flesh if they follow the tradition. There are five kinds of animals possessing five nails on each paw that may be enjoyed by the brahmin and the warrior, O Rama. They are the porcupine, the hedgehog, the deer, the hare and the tortoise. O Rama, men of worth will not touch my skin or bones nor eat my flesh.

" Alas ! I disregarded Tara, who, sagacious and prudent, offered me sound counsel, but in my folly, overpowered by fate, I did not heed it. O Kakutstha, like a virtuous woman who has married a man devoid of faith, the earth is without a protector, since thou art its protector. How canst thou be born of the magnanimous Dasaratha, seeing that thou art deceitful, mischievous, evil-hearted and treacherous ? Having exceeded the bounds of restraint, broken the law of the virtuous and disregarded the goad of justice, that elephant, Rama, has struck me down. Guilty of such an infamy, condemned by the wise, finding thyself in their presence, what wilt thou say?

" That valour that has been so greatly vaunted to us who are neutral, I do not see thee exercising against evil-doers ! If thou hadst fought me openly, O Prince, thou wouldst now find thyself in the presence of death, having been slain by me. Thou didst overcome me by taking me unawares, as a serpent bites a sleeping man, I who was else invincible. Thou art ruled by evil. In order to gratify Sugriva, thou hast struck me down.

" If thou hadst first confided thy purpose to me, I would have brought Sita back to thee in a day. Not only this, but I should have placed that wicked ravisher of thy spouse, the titan, Ravana, in thy power, a chain round his neck, having laid him low in combat. Even if Sita had been cast into the bottom of the sea or hell itself, I should have brought her back to thee at thy command, as Vishnu recovered the scriptures that had been borne away by Hayagriva.

" Sugriva would have obtained the throne legitimately on my departure to the celestial realm, whereas now he has acquired it wrongfully, since thou hast overcome me by craft on the field of battle. As death in this world is inevitable, I hold it as naught but how wilt thou justify thy conduct towards me ? "

Thus, pierced by an arrow, his features altered, did that magnanimous son of the Monarch of Monkeys speak whilst looking on Rama, who was as radiant as the sun, after which he fell silent.

CHAPTER 18

Rama answers Bali

SUCH was the speech, dictated by a sense of duty and his own interests, full of censure and harsh in tone, that Bali, who was mortally wounded, made to Rama. Resembling the sun shorn of its rays or a parched cloud or a fire that has been extinguished, that illustrious King of the Monkeys, endowed with justice and reason, having upbraided Rama with severity, was addressed by him in the following words :—

" O Bali, why dost thou inveigh against me like a child, since thou art wholly ignorant of the traditions of duty, profit and social convention ?[1] Without consulting thine elders, who are held in respect by the brahmins, in thy simian folly thou hast presumed to address me thus, who am filled with good-will towards thee.

" This earth belongs to the Ikshwakus, together with its mountains, forests and woods and they have jurisdiction over the wild beasts, birds and men. It is ruled by the virtuous Bharata, who is fixed in his duty and fully conversant with the law, with the proper means to acquisition of wealth and the right pursuit of pleasure and who is ever engaged in repressing evil-doers and recompensing the virtuous. It is the duty of a king to develop the art of government, be established in

[1] See Glossary under *Dharma, Artha, Kama.*

virtue, be endowed with valour and know how to estimate time and place. We other princes carry out his righteous commands and range the whole earth in our desire to promote the law. When that Lion among Men, Bharata who cherishes equity, rules the entire world, who would dare to commit an injustice? Fixed in our supreme duty, obedient to Bharata's will, in accord with the law, we put down transgression. Thou hast violated justice and thy conduct is condemned by all, lust being thine only mentor, ignoring as thou dost the royal path.

" One who pursues the path of duty should regard his elder brother, the one who has given him birth and the one who instructs him in wisdom as his three fathers. Righteousness demands that a younger brother, a son and a virtuous disciple should be regarded as one's own offspring; even for the virtuous, duty is subtle and not easy to grasp, the soul residing in the heart alone knows what is right and wrong.

" O Heedless Monkey, thou art surrounded by irresponsible simian counsellors, who are unable to control themselves, thus it is a case of the blind leading the blind, how canst thou learn from them? I am speaking frankly to thee; thou hadst no possible right to reproach me in my wrath. Learn now for what reason I struck thee down.

" Thou hast acted in opposition to the spiritual law. While Sugriva yet lives, thou hast had marital relations with Ruma, who is thy sister-in-law. O Perverse Wretch, in order to satisfy thy lust, thou hast transgressed the law of righteousness and, O Monkey, since thou hast not respected thy brother's wife, this retribution has followed thee. I see no other means of restraining him who acts contrary to the interests of his subjects and does not conform to the social code but by punishment, O King of the Monkeys!

" Being a warrior of an illustrious race, I am unable to brook thy villainy. The man who makes his daughter, his sister or his sister-in-law an object of lust, is punishable by death; this is the law!

" Though Bharata is the supreme monarch, we carry out his behests. How canst thou who hast broken the law, escape punishment? He who fails to listen to his instructor in the form of the law, will be judged according to the law by the King.

" Bharata seeks to repress dissolute customs, and we who carry out his commands fully try to bring to justice those who, like thee, overstep the boundaries of the law, O Chief of the Monkeys.

" Sugriva is my friend and equal to Lakshmana ; it is for the recovery of his wife and kingdom that he entered into a pact of friendship with me. In the presence of his ministers, I pledged my word ; how can a man like myself fail to meet these obligations ?

" For all these reasons based on the law, thou canst judge for thyself, whether thy punishment is merited or no. That it is wholly just, thou wilt be forced to admit and, further, that one is bound to help a friend if one acknowledges one's duty. Thou wouldst have done likewise if thou hadst followed the law. Two of the verses of Manu are specially devoted to these rules of conduct and are known to the authorities of the law ; I have been faithful to them. 'Those men who, having done wrong, submit to the penalty imposed by the king, are washed free from every stain and ascend to heaven like the good and those who do benevolent deeds. Further punishment or pardon exonerates the thief from his fault, but the king who does not put down vice himself assumes the guilt.'

" My worthy ancestor Mandhata voluntarily underwent a terrible expiation for a monk who was guilty of an offence similar to thine whom he pardoned. Other monarchs, in their folly, have also done wrong, but have practiced penance ; it is by this means that passion is subdued. But enough of recriminations ! Thy death has been decreed in accordance with the spiritual law, O Lion among Monkeys ; we are not acting on personal impulse.

" Listen to a further reason, O Valiant Bull among Monkeys; having grasped its significance, thou wilt no longer be able to reproach me. Neither did I follow mine own whim, nor did I act hastily, nor in anger.

" Snares, nets and traps of every kind, either open or concealed, are used to catch innumerable wild beasts, whether they be fleeing in terror, or, unafraid, are standing still. Whether these beasts are maddened with fear or no, they who feed on flesh run them through without pity while their back is turned; it does not seem to me that they are at fault. In this world, even royal Rishis, versed in their duty, indulge in the chase. This is why, with a single arrow, I struck thee down while engaged in combat with thy brother, O Monkey. What boots it, whether thou didst enter into combat with me or no, since thou art but a monkey.

"Unquestionably it is kings who dispense the unwritten law and happiness in life, O Best of Monkeys! One should never reproach them, nor address them disrespectfully, nor disregard them; they are Gods who, assuming human form, dwell on earth! But thou in thine ignorance of the law, dominated by anger, didst insult me, who have ever conformed to the established tradition of mine ancestors."

Hearing Rama's words, Bali, deeply mortified, no longer sought to denounce the son of Raghu, the task of duty now having been rendered clear to him, and with joined palms that King of the Monkeys answered him, saying:—

"Undoubtedly, O First of Men, what thou hast uttered is truth! To gainsay an eminent personage is not permitted to one who is of common stock. It was in ignorance that I formerly addressed thee in disrespectful terms. Do not hold it against me, O Raghava, thou who art conversant with the significance and implication of things and devoted to the welfare of all. In the serenity of thine understanding, that nothing disturbs, the working out of cause and effect are known to thee. O Thou whose speech accords with justice and who art conversant with duty, rescue me who am fallen and the first of those to transgress the law."

In a voice strangled with sobs, Bali, groaning, expressed himself with laboured effort, his eyes fixed on Rama, and resembled an elephant sinking in a morass.

"I am not concerned for myself or Tara or my relatives, as much as for my virtuous son, Angada, of golden bracelets. Beholding me no more, that unfortunate one, who has been so cherished from childhood, will pine away with grief, like a pool whose waters have dried up. He is yet young and his understanding has not yet matured; he is my only son and most dear to me. Tara is his mother, O Rama; do thou protect that powerful Angada.

"Show extreme kindness to Sugriva and Angada; be their guardian and their guide, O Thou who art fully conversant with the laws of righteousness and unrighteousness. What thou wouldst perform for Bharata and Lakshmana, do for Sugriva and Angada.

"See that Sugriva does not hold the sagacious Tara responsible for the fault I have committed or fail to treat her with respect. Under thy protection, let him govern the kingdom and, living obedient to thy counsels, he will attain heaven as well as rule the earth. As for myself, despite Tara's words, I wished to receive death at thine hands and came forth to enter into a duel with my brother Sugriva."

Having spoken thus to Rama, the now humble King of the Monkeys became silent.

Then Rama consoled Bali who was still fully conscious and spoke to him in a gentle voice, expressing the essence of spiritual and secular wisdom, saying:—

"Have no anxiety either on our behalf or thine own, O Best of Monkeys. We know what should be done, above all in that which concerns thee. He who punishes the guilty and he who is guilty and pays the penalty have both fulfilled the purpose of cause and effect and therefore eschew calamity. Thus, thanks to the punishment that frees them from all taint, they regain their immaculate nature by the very path which paved the way to the penalty.

"Put away grief, bewilderment and fear with which thine heart is filled; thou canst not avoid thy fate, O Chief of the Monkeys. What Angada was to thee, O King of the Monkeys, he will be to Sugriva and myself; do not doubt it."

The magnanimous Rama, intrepid in combat, uttered these words full of tenderness and benignity, in accord with righteousness, and the dweller in the forest answered him humbly, saying:—

"Pierced by thine arrow, my mind bewildered, I insulted thee without knowing what I was doing, O Lord, Thou whose immeasurable valour is equal to Mahendra's! Be pacified and pardon me, O Veritable Sovereign of the Monkeys."

CHAPTER 19

Tara's Grief

The mighty King of the Monkeys, who lay pierced by an arrow, did not reply further to Rama's judicious words. His limbs crushed by rocks, severly bruised by the trees that Sugriva had hurled at him, transfixed by Rama's shaft, at the point of death, he swooned away.

Tara, learning that he had been struck down by an arrow discharged by Rama in the struggle and receiving the distressing tidings that her lord lay dying, with a troubled heart hastily emerged with her son from the rocky cavern. The monkeys who followed Angada, however, on seeing Rama with his bow, ran away in fear.

Perceiving those monkeys fleeing in terror, like deer that scatter when the leader of the herd falls dead, Tara, though herself distraught, rallied the frightened monkeys, who sought to escape from Rama, as if his shafts had already been discharged at them, and said :—

" O Monkeys, you are the servants of that Lion among Monarchs ; why are you abandoning all and flying in disorder? Has Bali not been laid low by his wicked brother on account of the throne ? It was from afar that Rama loosed his far-reaching arrow ! "

Thus did the consort of Bali speak, and those monkeys, who were able to change their shape at will, answered with one voice in words fitting to the occasion, saying :—

" O Thou, who art the mother of a living son, return home and protect Angada ! Death, in the form of Rama, has struck Bali down and is bearing him away. Having launched a volley of immense trees and great rocks, Bali fell, borne down by arrows that resembled the lightning. Beholding that Lion among Monkeys overcome, him whose prowess was equal to Indra's, the whole army of monkeys has taken to flight. Let the warriors save the city and install Angada as king ! The monkeys will obey Bali's son, who will take his place. If these conditions do not meet with thine approval, O Lady of agreeable looks, then the monkeys will seek other inaccessible retreats. Amongst those who live in the forest, some have no wives, others have common wives, but we fear those who have been deprived of their wives and still desire them."[1]

As they were but a short distance away, that Lady of Sweet Smiles heard them and answered with dignity, saying:—

" Since that Lion among Monkeys is dying, of what use to me is my son or the entire kingdom ? I shall seek out the feet of that magnanimous hero whom Rama has slain with a single arrow."

Speaking thus, overcome with grief, beating her head and breast with her two hands and weeping, in her distress she rushed towards him and, still running, beheld her lord lying on the earth, he, the slayer of the foremost of monkeys, who never turned back in battle; he, who was able to hurl great mountains, as Vasava discharges his thunderbolt with all the fury of a storm, roaring the while like a great mass of thunder, clouds; he whose valour was equal to Shakra's; that hero pierced by a single arrow, lay on the earth, like the leader of antelopes a tiger has struck down for its prey, or like a place of sacrifice, held sacred by all, with its banners and its altars laid waste by Suparna on account of a serpent.

Then Tara beheld the .mighty Rama leaning on his bow, standing with his younger brother and the brother of her lord, and, beside herself with grief, she approached her spouse, who had fallen on the battlefield and, seeing him lying there, was overcome by distress and fell to the ground. Then, rising as if newly waking from sleep, seeing her lord caught in the noose of death, sobbing, she cried out: " O King ! "

Her piercing cries, resembling an osprey's, moved Sugriva deeply, as did the presence of Angada also.

[1] A reference to Sugriva.

KISHKINDHA KANDA

CHAPTER 20

Her Lamentations

SEEING her lord lying on the earth, pierced by that death-dealing arrow discharged by Rama, Tara, whose face resembled the moon, approaching him, embraced him. At the sight of Bali, who lay like an elephant wounded by an arrow, that monkey resembling a huge mountain or an uprooted tree, Tara poured out her heart, torn with grief, in lamentation :—

" O Thou who wert full of valour in combat ! O Hero ! O Best of Monkeys ! It is because of my recent importunities that thou wilt not now speak to me ! Rise, O Lion among Monkeys and rest on a comfortable couch ! Those great monarchs, thine equals, do not sleep on the earth ; or is the earth thy cherished love, since even in dying thou dost lie by her and scornest me ?

" Without doubt, O Warrior, thanks to thy great exploits, thou hast founded another and more glorious Kishkindha in heaven ! The pleasures we once shared in the woods and in the fragrant bowers are henceforth at an end. I am bereft of all joy and hope and sunk in a sea of sorrow, since thou, the King of Kings, art returning to the five elements.[1] My heart must be made of stone, since, seeing thee lying on the earth, grief does not cause it to break into a thousand pieces. Thou didst steal away Sugriva's consort and sent him into exile ; it is the fruit of this double fault that thou art now expiating, O Chief of the Monkeys !

" Intent on thy welfare, I submitted to thy senseless reproaches ; I, who in the desire to be of service to thee gave thee nought but wise counsel, O Indra of Monkeys ! Now, O Proud Lord, beguiled by their youthful and seductive beauty, thou art moving the hearts of the Apsaras. It is irrevocable fate which this day has put an end to thine existence ; thou whom Sugriva could not vanquish hast resigned thyself to its power !

[1] The body being said to rejoin the elements at death.

" Having without cause struck down Bali who was engaged in combat with another, though it is censurable, Kakutstha has no regrets. I who, till now, did not know distress, deprived of thy support, at the height of misfortune, must pass my life as a widow. What will the fate of Angada be, the object of my tenderness, a valiant though youthful prince accustomed to pleasure, now at the mercy of his paternal uncle, who is filled with anger against us ? Look long on thy virtuous Sire, O My Beloved Son ! Soon thou shalt see him no more.

" And Thou, O comfort thy son, give him counsel, embracing his brow before thou departest on thy last journey ! Assuredly Rama has accomplished a great feat in striking thee down, but he is guiltless, for all he did was to obey Sugriva. O Sugriva, rejoice, regain possession of Ruma and enjoy the kingdom without hindrance ; thy brother, thine adversary, is wounded unto death.

" But Thou, O My Beloved, why dost thou not answer my complaint ? See, thy numerous and lovely wives surround thee, O King of the Monkeys."

Hearing Tara's lamentations, those unfortunate women, placing Angada in their midst, emitted pitiful cries on every side. Then Tara spoke once again, saying :—

" How canst thou abandon Angada, O Thou whose powerful arms are decorated with bracelets, and go forth on thy last journey thus ? It is not meet to abandon a son who possesses thy virtues and is aimiable and handsome. If inadvertently I have offended thee, O Long-armed Hero, then forgive me ! O Chief of the Monkey Tribe, I lay my head at thy feet."

Thus did Tara with the other queens lament bitterly at the side of her lord and that lady of matchless beauty resolved to die of hunger lying on the earth at Bali's side.

CHAPTER 21

Hanuman's Speech

HANUMAN, however, the Leader of the Monkeys, gently tried to console Tara, who was lying on the earth like a star fallen from the heavens, and said :—

" The fruits of all that is done under the impulse of virtue or vice must be plucked after death, whether they be good or evil. O Unhappy One, for whom dost thou weep ? O Unfortunate One, whom dost thou bewail ? For whose life, that bubble, should one mourn ? Henceforth the youthful Angada should be the object of thy solicitude, since he alone survives. From now on, thou shouldst concern thyself on his account and render him fitting service. Thou knowest well how uncertain is the future of all beings ; therefore it is for thee to perform noble deeds here, who art conversant with thy duty and who art a stranger to common acts !

" He under whom hundreds and thousands of monkeys lived has now reached the uttermost bourne of his destiny, and since he fulfilled the injunctions laid down by the law and was distinguished for his impartiality, his liberality and his tolerance, he now dwells among the virtuous conquerors. Why shouldst thou mourn for him ? O Irreproachable One, thou hast now become the protectress of all the leading monkeys, thy son, and also this kingdom of the apes and bears. Little by little do thou console these two (Sugriva and Angada) who are afflicted, and under thy tutelage, O Fair Lady, let Angada rule the earth.

" To ensure the future and reflect on the present is the whole duty of a prince ; it is so decreed by destiny. Angada should be installed as King of the Monkeys and be anointed. Seeing thy son seated on the throne, thy peace of mind will be restored."

Hearing these words, Tara, who was torn with grief on account of her lord, answered Hanuman, who stood at her side, saying :—

" I would rather cling to the body of this hero than a hundred sons like Angada. I am not able to govern the monkeys nor is he; such a duty devolves on his paternal uncle, Sugriva. O Hanuman, it is not for me to confer the kingdom on Angada; the true relative of the son in succession to his father is the uncle, who stands as a second father to him and not the mother, O Foremost of Monkeys. There is nought better for me in this world or in the next than to take refuge near the King of the Monkeys, my lord; it is fitting for me to share the bed of him who has fallen facing the foe."

CHAPTER 22

Bali's last Words

BALI, whose breathing was scarcely perceptible and who was sighing faintly, glanced round and discerned his younger brother, Sugriva, before him. Addressing him whose victory had assured him of the possession of the dominion of the monkeys, he spoke in clear and affectionate tones, saying :—

" O Sugriva, do not approach me with any evil intent, I who was carried away by a fatal loss of understanding. It would seem to me, O My Friend, that it was not our destiny to live at peace with one another; though friendship is natural between brothers, yet with us it has been different. To-day, thou wilt regain the kingdom of the forest-dwellers, whereas I, mark well, am leaving this world and going to the region of death. Not only am I abandoning in an instant, life, kingdom and great prosperity but also a reputation without stain. At this supreme moment, I make an appeal to thee and, difficult though it is, it must be done, O Valiant Prince.

" See, stretched on the earth, his face bathed in tears, Angada, who is worthy of happiness, brought up in luxury and, though a child, possessing nought that pertains to childhood! Do thou protect him from all peril, he who is my son and dearer to me than life, the issue of my loins and whom I now abandon, though he does not merit abandonment. Be his father, his benefactor and his guardian in all circumstances and in danger be his refuge, as I have ever been, O Chief of the Monkeys!

" Born of Tara, that fortunate prince, thine equal in valour, shall precede thee in the destruction of the titans. That youthful Angada, Tara's son, that valiant hero, whose prowess is great, will manifest it in deeds of valour worthy of me. Further, when the daughter of Sushena (Tara), of profound discernment and conversant with future happenings, bids thee saying: 'Do this, it is right', do so without hesitation. There is no presentiment of Tara's that does not come to pass.

" Whatever Raghava proposes, do thou carry out with the same resolution; it were wrong to disobey him and he will punish thee for thy contempt. Take this golden chain, O Sugriva; the glorious Shri who dwells in it will leave it at my death."[1]

Hearing Bali's affectionate and brotherly words, Sugriva was bereft of joy and grew sad, resembling the moon in eclipse. Pacified by Bali and anxious to act in a fitting manner, on his brother's request, he took off the golden chain.

Having thus made over this mark of royalty, Bali, at the point of death, gazing on his son Angada, who stood before him, addressed him tenderly, saying :—

" Do thou act in a manner fitting to the time and place. Suffer pleasure and pain with equanimity; in joy and sorrow be obedient to Sugriva. Assuredly, O Long-armed Warrior, thou hast ever been cherished by me, but it is not by living thus that thou wilt earn Sugriva's respect. Do not ally thyself with those who are not his friends, still less his foes, O Conqueror of Thine Enemies! Be loyal to Sugriva, thy master, with thy senses fully controlled and ever be attentive to his interests. Be not inordinately attached to any nor hold any in contempt; both extremes are a great error, therefore pursue the middle course." With these words, suffering intensely from the arrow, his eyes staring wildly, his great teeth chattering, Bali expired.

Then a great tumult arose among the monkeys, thus deprived of their leader, and all the forest dwellers gave vent to lamentations, saying :—

[1] Shri or Lakshmi, the Consort of Vishnu and Goddess of Prosperity.

"Henceforth Kishkindha is nought but a desert, the King of Monkeys having ascended to heaven; his gardens are but a wilderness, as are the mountains and the woods. That Lion of Monkeys has passed away; the forest-dwellers are stripped of their glory.

"He engaged the illustrious and long-armed Golaba, the Gandharva, in a terrible battle lasting ten years and yet another five; that struggle did not cease day or night; then in the sixteenth year, Golaba was struck down, that foolhardy one falling under the blows of Bali of strong teeth. How has he who protected us from all peril fallen in his turn?

"That valiant Leader of Monkeys being slain, the forest-dwellers will not be able to find any safe place of refuge, like kine in the midst of a lion-infested forest."

On hearing these words, Tara, who was submerged in an ocean of grief, gazing on the face of her dead lord, fell to the earth, embracing Bali like a creeper clinging to an uprooted tree.

CHAPTER 23

Tara weeps over the Body of Bali

THEREUPON, smelling the face[1] of that King of the Monkeys, Tara, who was renowned throughout the whole world, addressed her dead consort, saying:—

"Not having followed my counsel, O Warrior, thou art now stretched on the rough, hard and stony ground. Hast thou then chosen the earth as thy love rather than myself, since thou now liest embracing it, whereas to me thou dost not utter a single word?

"Alas! Fate has favoured Sugriva, that valiant One, whose noble exploits will now cause him to be regarded as a hero. The Leaders of the Bears and Monkeys pay homage to thy prowess! Hearing their cries of distress and those of the

[1] A traditional salutation.

unfortunate Angada and myself, why dost thou not wake? Having been slain in combat, thou sleepest on that hard bed, the place where formerly thine enemies rested struck down by thy blows. O My Beloved, thou art the offshoot of a glorious race renowned for its heroism; thou, for whom war was but a sport, art gone, leaving me alone without a protector, O Proud Monarch! Nay, a wise man should never give his daughter in marriage to a warrior. Mark how I, wedded to a Kshatriya, am about to die, having been made a widow. My pride is humbled, and from this moment the path to everlasting life is closed to me. I am submerged in an ocean of grief without ground or bourne! How hard is my heart that, even seeing my dead lord, it does not break into a thousand fragments—my friend, my lord, naturally dear to me, that hero, who, falling on the field of honour under the blows of a warrior more powerful than he, has returned to the five elements. The woman who loses her consort, even if she have sons and be endowed with wealth, is yet a widow, say the wise. O Hero! Thou art lying enveloped in the blood that flows from thy limbs, as thou wert formerly with the scarlet silk of thy couch. Dust and gore covers thy body on every side, so that I cannot hold thee in mine arms, O Bull amongst Plavagas.

"To-day, Sugriva has achieved the purpose for which he engaged thee in this formidable struggle. A single arrow discharged by Rama freed him from all fear. That shaft that pierced thine heart now prevents me from embracing thy body and I can but gaze on thee, who art rejoining the five elements."

At that moment the General Nala drew out from the corpse the arrow which resembled an angry snake issuing from a mountain cave and glittered as he withdrew it, like the sun whose rays have been intercepted by the peak of a mountain. Thereupon streams of blood instantly began to flow again from those wounds on every side, resembling the water of a river that is stained by the sandstone washed down from a mountain.

Tara, wiping off the dust of combat with which he was soiled, washed her brave lord with the tears that welled up in her eyes, while she gazed lovingly down on him lying there, pierced by Rama's arrow, his limbs all covered with blood. Then, addressing her son Angada, whose eyes were red, she said to him :—

" Behold the bitter end of thy sire, O My Son ! How tragic it is ! This is the outcome of an hostility born of perfidy ! This body, gleaming like the sun about to rise, has entered the region of death. Embrace that proud monarch, O My Son ! "

At these words, Angada rising, seized hold of the feet of his father with his rounded arms, saying :—" It is I, Angada ! When I embraced thee formerly thou didst say ' Live long, O My Son ', why dost thou not speak to me thus now ? "

Then Tara said :—" Here I stand beside thine inanimate body, like a cow with its calf beside a bull that a lion has just slain ! I do not see the gift that the King of the Gods bestowed on thee when gratified by his victory over the Asura, that glorious chain of gold, why is this ? Thou shalt not be robbed of the insignia of royalty even after death, O Proud Monarch, for the King of the Mountains continues to glow after the sun has set.

" Thou didst not follow my sage counsel and I was unable to restrain thee. Thy death on the battlefield has brought about mine own and my son's also. The Goddess of Prosperity[1] has renounced both thee and me."

CHAPTER 24

Sugriva's Remorse

SEEING Tara submerged in the fathomless ocean of grief, Bali's younger brother was filled with remorse for his tragic end and overcome with distress, his face bathed in tears, in her presence, slowly approached Rama surrounded by his attendants.

Raghava, bearing all the marks of royalty, stood apart, full of dignity and majesty, bearing his bow and arrows, which resembled serpents, in his hands.

[1] Lakshmi who was said to have resided in the golden chain that Indra had bestowed on Bali.

Then Sugriva addressed him, saying:—" In accord with thy promise, O Indra among Men, thou didst accomplish this deed, the results of which are here made manifest. In the midst of my triumph, O Prince, in the presence of the slain, my spirit is troubled. On account of the dead monarch, his chief queen is wailing piteously, the city is giving vent to lamentation and Angada is plunged in affliction; all this, O Rama, robs sovereignty of any delight for me.

" At first, anger, resentment and extreme vexation caused me to view the death of my brother with satisfaction, but soon, in the presence of the corpse of that King of the Monkeys, a great sadness seized me, O First of the House of Ikshwaku. Now it is made clear to me that it would have been better to continue to live as I formerly did on the lofty summit of the Rishyamuka mountain, than slay my brother.

" 'I have no desire to destroy thee! Begone!' were the words that magnanimous warrior addressed to me. This utterance was worthy of him, O Rama, and I, by killing him, have acted vilely. How can any, even if he be devoid of virtue, approve the murder of a brother or balance the happiness experienced on attaining a kingdom with the grief suffered by his death. Unquestioningly he had no intention of slaying me, being too great of soul, but in my perversity I have robbed him of his life.

" In the struggle, when, under the blows of the trees, I was about to succumb and cried out, he at once reassured me, saying: 'Do not repeat thine impudence; go hence!'

" He was ever filled with brotherly affection, nobility and justice, whereas I was full of anger, envy and the natural characteristics of a monkey.

" That which should be excluded from one's thoughts, feelings, desires and conduct is what I have harboured in murdering my brother, a crime equal to the slaying of Vishwarupa by Indra. But Indra's guilt was shared by the earth, the trees and the waters as well as women, whereas who is able to share mine? Who would wish to bear the weight of the sin of a Deer of the Trees?

" I am not worthy to be held in honour by the people, nor to be allied to the kingdom, still less do I merit the throne, having committed such an infamous deed that entails the destruction of one of mine own race.

"I have perpetrated a vile and ignoble act, condemned by the whole world. An overwhelming sorrow fills me, as torrential rain fills a ravine. I am crushed by the bank of a river that has been trodden down by an intoxicated elephant, whose back and tail are the murder of my blood-brother, whose trunk, eyes, head and tusks are the remorse bearing me away.

"This sin, the weight of which is intolerable, O Prince, O Son of the House of Raghu, has destroyed all that is best in my heart, as fire consumes gold, leaving only dross. The company of the great leaders of monkeys, O Prince, are half dead through my fault and also on account of the violent despair of Angada.

"Rare indeed is a son as obedient as Angada, but a son is easily acquired; where however in the world can one akin to a blood brother be found, O Hero? To-day, if Angada, that Chief of Warriors, and his mother live, she, though overcome with grief will surely care for him, for bereft of him she would die. As for me, I wish to enter the blazing pyre in order to regain the affection of my brother and his son.

"Those leaders of monkeys will set out in search of Sita whenever thou commandest. O Son of that Indra among Men, I, the Destroyer of my Race, who am no longer worthy to live after committing this outrage, bid thee farewell, O Rama."

Hearing the words of the wretched Sugriva, Bali's brother, that noble descendant of the House of Raghu, Rama, began to weep, he, the Destroyer of Hostile Armies, for his mind was troubled. Thereafter, glancing here and there, that support of the earth, the protector of the world, Rama, in the midst of his distress, observed Tara groaning under the load of her affliction.

The chief queen of that Lion among Monkeys, of lovely eyes, was lying beside her lord, whom she held in her arms. Then the first of the ministers raised up that valiant consort of the King of the Monkeys, and she, trembling as they separated her from her lord, whom she was embracing, beheld Rama, whose radiance equalled the sun's, standing with his bow and arrows in his hand.

Adorned with all the distinguishing marks of royalty, that large-eyed prince, whom she had never yet beheld, that first of heroes, was recognized by Tara, whose eyes resembled a doe's, and she reflected 'It is Kakutstha!'

Then that noble and unfortunate lady, who had so suddenly been plunged into affliction, tottering, approached the one who was the equal of Indra, inaccessible and all powerful. The venerable Tara, her beautiful frame wasted with grief, drawing near to the pure-souled Rama, who by his valour ever attained his end in combat, addressed him thus:—

"Thou art of immeasurable courage, unapproachable, master of thy senses and of supreme faith; thy fame is imperishable, thou art full of wisdom and the support of the earth! Thine eyes are the colour of blood; thou bearest a bow and arrows in thine hand; thou art endowed with great strength and strong limbs; thou hast renounced the concerns of the body in this world in order to enjoy divine attributes. The shaft with which thou didst pierce my beloved lord, now use to destroy me also. When I am dead, I shall be reunited to him; without me, Bali will never be happy, O Hero. Far from me, even in heaven, amidst the red-haired Apsaras, whose locks are braided in various ways and who are gorgeously attired, he will not be happy, O Thou whose eyes resemble the pure petals of the lotus.

"Thou knowest well that he who is separated from his loved one is wretched! On account of this, slay me, so that Bali shall not suffer in mine absence. If, in the greatness of thy soul, thou shouldst reflect 'I will not be guilty of slaying a woman', say to thyself, 'She is part of Bali himself' and strike me down. It will not be a woman whom thou hast put to death, O Son of that Indra among Men! By virtue of the law and according to the different Vedic texts, women are not other than the higher self of man. Therefore the wise say that the gift of a woman is assuredly the greatest of gifts. In this wise thou dost give me back to my dear one in order that I may fulfil my duty to him, O Warrior; by this offering thou shalt not incur the sin of slaying me.

"Filled with sorrow, bereft of support, left desolate, thou shouldn'st not spare my life. The more so that far from that sagacious Prince of Monkeys, whose joyful gait resembled an elephant's, with his glorious golden chain, the insigna of supreme majesty, I shall not live long, O Prince."

Thus spoke Tara, and in order to console her, the magnanimous Lord addressed her with wisdom and understanding, saying :—

" O Consort of a Hero, do not grieve ! The whole universe is ordered by the creator ; similarly it is established that the sum of good and evil is ordained by Him, nor do the Three Worlds, obedient to His will, transgress His fixed laws. Because of this, thou wilt attain supreme happiness and thy son become heir-apparent to the kingdom. The Lord has ordained this in the order of things ; the consorts of heroes do not complain."

Thus comforted by the magnanimous and powerful victor of his foes, the wife of the valiant Bali, the gorgeously-attired Tara, ceased to lament.

CHAPTER 25

Bali's Funeral Rites

FULL of compassion for Sugriva's distress and that experienced by Tara and Angada, Kakutstha, who was accompanied by Lakshmana, in order to console them, said :—

" It is not by weeping that the happiness of the departed is assured ! Carry out your immediate duty without delay ! By shedding tears, you have observed the demands of social convention ; it is vain to seek to avoid fate. Time[1] is the driving force that orders the world's events ; it is Time that creates all conditions here below. None is the real agent of action and none truly causes action to take place. The world abides by virtue of the dictates of its own inner being. Time is its source, stay and goal. Time does not overstep its own bounds, nor does it suffer decrease. Self-dependent, there is neither kinship nor friendship in it, nor is it restrained by any, nor has it any cause. Assuredly, he who sees clearly is aware of the working of Time. Duty, prosperity and pleasure are subject to Time ; it is on this account that Bali attained his

[1] Time in the form of Destiny.

own true state. The King of the Plavagas has reaped the fruit of his works, acquired by his merits, through his integrity and liberality. He has attained heaven on account of his observance of duty and he has taken possession of it by sacrificing his life. The Sovereign of the Monkeys has reached the highest state. Thou hast mourned long enough; now perform the last rites."

When Rama ceased speaking, Lakshmana, the Slayer of His Foes, spoke sagely to Sugriva, who was distraught, saying:—

"O Sugriva, inaugurate the obsequies without delay with the assistance of Tara and Angada. Issue the order that a large quantity of dry wood be gathered together with the sacred sandalwood, for the funeral pyre. Banish indecision; this city depends on thee. Let Angada bring garlands and robes of every kind, together with butter, oil, perfumes and all that is requisite.

"O Tara, do thou find a palanquin without delay; prompt action is always praiseworthy, the more so at such an hour. Let those who are skilful and strong, accustomed to palanquins, hold themselves in readiness to bear Bali away."

Having spoken thus to Sugriva, the on of Sumitra, Lakshmana, the Slayer of His Foes, took up his position beside his brother.

Hearing Lakshmana's command, Tara with a beating heart hastened to the cave, bent on finding a litter, and soon returned with one borne by strong monkeys to whom the work was familiar.

It was indeed magnificent, well-cushioned and resembling a chariot, the sides being marvellously decorated and enriched with carved wooden figures. Resting on wonderful supports, it was gorgeously fitted like a palace belonging to the Siddhas and was furnished with windows and balconies that were spacious and embellished with carvings, a work of extreme artistry. Large and well constructed of wood from the mountain-side, priceless ornaments, strings of pearls and splendid crowns gave it a dazzling appearance and it was covered with clay, painted red and sprinkled with sandal-paste. Festooned with wreaths of lotuses, shining like the dawn, it was strewn with innumerable flowers.

Beholding it, Rama said to Lakshmana :—" Let Bali's body be placed upon it with all speed and let the funeral ceremony proceed." Then Sugriva, weeping, assisted by Angada, raised Bali's body and placed it on the litter. Having laid the corpse on its couch, he covered it with ornaments of every kind together with wreaths and cloths. Thereafter, Sugriva, the King of the Monkeys, commanded that the last rites of his noble brother should be carried out on the banks of a river.

The great monkey leaders preceded the litter, scattering jewels of every kind in profusion. Every honour due to a king of this world was offered by the Vanaras to their lord that day.

Then the funeral rites began immediately, Angada, Tara and the others surrounding the master they had lost. On their side, the women who had lived subject to his authority gathered together crying : " O Hero, O Hero ", thus bewailing the death of their lord.

All the wives of Bali, who had been widowed, with Tara at their head, accompanied their deceased sovereign, lamenting pitifully. Their cries were heard in the depth of the forest and re-echoed through the woods and among the rocks on every side. Then on a deserted sandbank surrounded by water, formed by a torrent issuing from the mountain, innumerable monkeys, inhabitants of the forest, constructed a pyre, and those excellent bearers reverently lowered the litter from their shoulders and all stood round, plunged in mourning.

Seeing her lord lying on the funeral bed, Tara, taking his head in her lap, a prey to extreme grief, began to lament :—

" O Illustrious and Mighty Prince, O My Dear One, look on me ! Why dost thou not cast a single glance on all those who are plunged in sorrow ? Thou smilest even in death, O Noble Hero, and thy countenance resembles the rays of the rising sun ! Death, in the guise of Rama, has struck thee down, O Monkey ! A single arrow discharged by him on the field of battle has made us all widows. Thy wives, present here, who no longer know how to leap, O Indra among Kings, have come this painful road step by step on foot, is it not known to thee ? Dost thou no longer love these women whose radiant looks resemble the moon ? Why dost thou not look on Sugriva, O King of the Monkeys? Here are thy counsellors, O Sovereign, also Tara and the others and the leading citizens surrounding thee, all plunged in grief. Dismiss thy ministers as thou wert wont to do, O Vanquisher of thy Foes, and we will go to the woods with thee in happy dalliance."

Then the women, themselves overwhelmed with affliction, caused Tara to rise.

Assisted by Sugriva, Angada, sobbing, bore his sire to the funeral pyre, his mind distraught with grief, and, igniting the flames according to the traditional rites, keeping his father on his right hand, he circumambulated him, sorrowfully watching him setting forth on his last journey.

Having performed the ritual acts in honour of Bali, that Bull among Monkeys, accompanied by Sugriva and Tara, performed his ablutions.

Associating himself with Sugriva's loss, the mighty Kakutstha, sharing his grief, officiated at the funeral rites.

The body of Bali, chief of heroes, full of glory, whom that descendant of Ikshwaku had slain with his marvellous arrow, having been cremated, Sugriva, whose splendour resembled a clear flame, approached Rama and Lakshmana who accompanied him.

CHAPTER 26

Sugriva is installed as King

THE chief ministers encircled Sugriva, who was clad in dripping garments and overcome with grief. Approaching the illustrious Rama of imperishable exploits, he stood before him with joined palms like the Sages before the Grand-sire of the World.

Then Hanuman, the son of Maruta, who resembled a mountain of gold, his face shining like the rising sun, addressed him with profound reverence in the following words:—

"May it please thee, O Kakutstha, to reinstate Sugriva in the vast and impregnable kingdom of his mighty ancestors.

Be gracious unto him, O Lord, and permit him to return to his magnificent capital. May he regulate his affairs with the co-operation of his many friends.

"After the purificatory bath of perfumes and aromatic herbs of every kind, he will pay thee homage and bestow gifts and garlands and precious gems, scents and herbs on thee. Thou shouldst enter this marvellous cave, carved out of the mountain, and unite these monkeys with a master, thus making them happy!"

Hearing Hanuman's words, Rama, that Destroyer of Hostile Warriors, answered him with wisdom and eloquence, saying:—

"Most beloved Hanuman, in accordance with the behests of my sire I may not enter a village or city for fourteen years. Let Sugriva, that Bull among Monkeys enter that prosperous and glorious city and be installed as king according to the traditional rites!"

Having spoken thus to Hanuman, Rama said to Sugriva:—

"Thou who art conversant with thy duty, proclaim that noble and valiant hero, Angada, heir-apparent to the kingdom. He is the eldest son of thy elder brother and equal to him in courage; Angada has a valiant heart and deserves to be thine heir. It is now Shravana, the first month of the rainy season,[1] that brings the floods; it is no time for military exploits therefore return to thy capital. As for me, I shall live on the mountain with Lakshmana. This cavern, carved out of the rock, is large and airy and possesses a lake whose crystalline waters abound in lotuses of every kind. When the month of Kartika[2] has come, make ready to slay Ravana, this is our pact; meantime, O Friend, return to thine home and receive the royal anointing, thus gratifying thy friends."

Thus dismissed by Rama, Sugriva, that Bull among Monkeys penetrated into the enchanting city of Kishkindha of which Bali had been the supreme lord.

Following their sovereign, thousands of monkeys prostrated themselves, touching the dust with their foreheads, and Sugriva, full of valour, called on them to rise, addressing his subjects with affection.

[1] July–August.

[2] October–November.

That mighty warrior thereafter entered his brother's private apartments and, having come there, the powerful hero, Sugriva, that Bull of Forest-dwellers, was proclaimed king by his friends, as was formerly the God of a Thousand Eyes.

Then they brought him a white canopy, decorated with gold, and two magnificent whisks of yak's tails with gleaming golden handles, also gems of every kind and grain and grass, together with blossoming branches, flowers and rich stuffs, white unguents, fragrant garlands, wild flowers and those that grow in water, sacred sandalwood, varied and numerous perfumes, roasted grain, gold, panic seed, honey, butter, curds, a tiger skin and wonderfully wrought sandals.

Thereafter six lovely young girls, bringing scents, tallow and red and yellow pigments,[1] entered joyfully and distributed gems, raiment and food among the foremost of the twice-born.

Those versed in the sacred formulas then prepared heaps of kusha grass and, igniting a fire, poured out the Soma, purified by the recitation of traditional prayers. Then Sugriva, seated on a gorgeous golden-based throne, covered with rich draperies and a magnificent three-tiered baldaquin, decorated with marvellous garlands, facing the East, was enthroned.

Those Lions among the Forest-dwellers had visited the banks of rivers and streams, far and wide, as well as the sacred places and the seas, in order to draw pure water which they brought back in pitchers of gold.

Employing golden vases and the polished horns of bulls, Gaja, Gavaksha, Gavaya, Sharabha, Gandhamadana, Mainda, Dvivida, Hanuman and Jambavan in accordance with the tradition laid down in the scriptures and on the instructions of the Sages, poured the clear and fragrant water over Sugriva, as formerly the Vasus bathed Vasava of a Thousand Eyes.

When the enthronement was completed, all those illustrious leaders of the monkeys raised a shout of joy again and again. Thereafter, in order to follow Rama's counsel, Sugriva, the King of the Monkeys, embracing Angada, installed him as heir-apparent.

Angada received the investiture, and those magnanimous Plavagas acclaimed him crying "Excellent! Excellent!",

[1] Pigments. Yellow Gorocala used for Tilak; red Manahshila, a form of red arsenic.

praising Sugriva and the great-souled Rama and Lakshmana. All were overjoyed on this auspicious occasion ; a large and merry crowd, fully satisfied, filled the streets, carrying banners and standards in the enchanting city of Kishkindha, which had been hollowed out of the mountain.

Having informed the illustrious Rama of the great coronation ceremony and being reunited with his consort, Ruma, the heroic leader of the monkey army took possession of his kingdom, like the Chief of the Immortals.

CHAPTER 27

Rama describes Prasravana

THE monkey Sugriva, having been crowned king, returned to Kishkindha, whilst Rama retired to the Mountain Prasravana.

That mountain resounded with the cries of tigers and deer, and the roaring of the lions that frequented it was heard day and night ; bushes, diverse creepers and innumerable trees were to be seen everywhere. It was inhabited by bears, lynxes and many kinds of monkeys and resembled a mass of clouds sparkling with light and beauty. On the summit was a large and spacious cave, which Rama, who was accompanied by Saumitri, chose as a dwelling for himself.

Having contracted an alliance with Sugriva, Rama, the irreproachable descendant of the House of Raghu, addressed his brother Lakshmana, the increaser of his delight, in appropriate and significant words, saying :—

" O Saumitri, Destroyer of Thy Foes ! We should establish ourselves in this agreeable rocky cavern during the rainy season. This peak, the most lofty on this mountain, is enchanting, O Prince ! White, black and dun-coloured crags adorn it and metals of every kind abound, while its rivers swarm with frogs ; it is filled with innumerable trees and charming creepers, where a variety of birds warble and splendid peacocks can be heard ; Malati, Kunda, Sinduvara, Shirishaka, Kadamba, Arjuna and Sarja trees embellish it with their blossom.

" Here is a lovely pool, festooned with flowering lotus, adjoining the cave, O Prince. Where the rock is hollowed out, it inclines to the north east, which will make our stay more agreeable, whilst on the west it is higher and we shall be sheltered from the winds. At the entrance, O Saumitri, is a smooth black stone like a piece of antimony washed in oil; to the north, O Friend, the crest of the mountain is magnificent and looks like a mass of polished collyrium or a stationary cloud. To the south, it stretches like a white veil, resembling Mount Kailasha, rich in metals, which give it a dazzling appearance.

"Observe this river of translucent water like unto Jahnavi on the Mount Trikuta! Candana, Tilaka, Sala, Tamala, Atimuktaka, Padmaka, Sarala and Ashoka trees embellish it; Vanira, Timida, Bakula, Ketaka, Hintala, Tinisha, Nipa, Vetasa and Kritamalaka trees grow on its banks, adorning it on every side, like a woman attired in rich raiment and precious gems.

"Innumerable flocks of birds fill it with their various notes and waterfowl enliven it with their amorous frolics. The river has created enchanting islands which are frequented by swans and cranes; its smiling aspect calls to mind a beautiful woman wearing innumerable ornaments. Here it is carpeted with blue lotuses, there shining with the red and in the distance white water-lilies may be seen. Ducks sport here in their hundreds, whilst peacocks and curlews fill this river, full of charm and colour, with their cries, and groups of sages frequent it.

"See how the Sandal and Kadubha trees grow in clusters of five, as if planned by an intelligent will. Ah! What an enchanting spot! O Saumitri, Thou Scourger of Thy Foes, let us enjoy it to the full and make our retreat a happy one. Kishkindha too is not far from here, that marvellous city of Sugriva's, where songs and the sound of musical instruments are heard, O Most Illustrious of Conquerors! It is the monkey warriors sporting to the sound of drums.

"Having recovered his consort and his kingdom, that monarch of the monkeys, Sugriva, surrounded by his companions, is assuredly celebrating his return to full prosperity."

With these words, Rama with Lakshmana took up their abode on the Mountain Prasravana, where there were innumerable caves and woods.

Yet despite the beauty and abundance of fruits, Rama was unable to find the least pleasure there. Remembering the woman who had been torn from him and who was as dear to him as his very life's breath, the more now, when the moon was rising over the summit of the mountain, he was unable to sleep, passing the nights on the couch, sighing, his spirit troubled, a prey to constant grief.

Seeing Rama desolate and a victim to profound melancholy, Lakshmana, who was equally afflicted, addressed him in affectionate words, saying :—" Cease to mourn, O Hero, thou shouldst not distress thyself thus. One who grieves is never successful, thou knowest it well. In this world, one should have faith and trust in God, pursue virtue and engage in action, O Raghava ! If thy mind is agitated, thou wilt never be able to overcome that titan, thine adversary, in combat, for he is a crafty fighter.

" Banish thy grief and persist in thine endeavour ; it will be thine to triumph over this demon and his entire family. O Rama, thou canst overthrow the earth with its oceans, forests and mountains, how much more Ravana ! Wait but till the autumn, for it is now the rainy season, then thou shalt destroy him, his kingdom and his kinsfolk. Truly I desire to rekindle thy dormant valour, as at the hour of sacrifice the fire buried beneath the ashes is revived by glowing libations."

This salutary and opportune counsel of Lakshmana's was received by Rama with respect and he answered in tender and friendly accents, saying :—

" O Lakshmana, inspired by devotion, thou hast spoken to me with wisdom and courage. Henceforth I shall manifest that valour no danger is able to subdue. I shall wait for the autumn and in accord with thy counsel depend on Sugriva's willing co-operation and the state of the rivers. He who has rendered a service merits repayment ; the ungrateful who do not honour an obligation lose the respect of the good." With joined palms, Lakshmana listened with approval to this judicious speech and addressed Rama, who had regained his cheerful mien, saying : " Thou speakest truly, O Chief of Men; without fail, that monkey will bring about that which thou desirest. Meantime, while awaiting the autumn, endure the rains, resolving to slay thine adversary. Restraining thine anger, let us pass these four months of autumn together, dwelling on the mountain frequented by lions, and then hold thyself in readiness to destroy thine enemy."

CHAPTER 28

Rama describes the Rainy Season

HAVING slain Bali and enthroned Sugriva, Rama, who was dwelling on the Malyavat plateau, said to Lakshmana:—

"Now the rainy season is here, see how the heavens are laden with clouds as large as hills. After nine months, the sky, by the action of the sun's rays, has sucked up the waters of the ocean and is now giving birth to the showers.

"Ascending to heaven by the stairway of the clouds, one might decorate the sun with garlands of Kutaja and Arjuna blossom. The sky appears like one wounded, bound with the rags of moisture-laden clouds, stained with the vivid tints of the setting sun, bordered with red. With the gentle breeze as its breath, the saffron colour lent by the twilight and its yellow clouds, the sky seems like one who is sick with love. Tormented by the sun's rays, the earth is shedding tears, like Sita racked by grief. Emerging from the heart of the clouds, cool as camphor, redolent with the fragrance of Ketaka flowers, the balmy winds can, as it were, be sipped from the palms of the hands.

"This mountain of blossoming Arjuna trees, planted with Ketakas and anointed by showers of rain, resembles Sugriva freed from his foes. These mountains, that the dark clouds clothe as with antelope skins, catch the rain drops as the sacrificial thread, their caverns filled with the wind lending them a voice; they resemble studious brahmin disciples reciting the holy Veda.

"Whipped by lightning like unto golden thongs, the sky seems to be crying out in pain. The flash that convulses the breast of that sombre cloud is to me like Sita struggling in the arms of Ravana. When covered by dense cloud, the quarters of the sky, so dear to lovers, are blotted out, together with the moon and the stars.

" On the ridges of the mountain, as if drowned in tears, these Kutaja trees in full flower, that sighed for the rain, rekindle love in me in the midst of the grief that overwhelms me.

" The dust has settled and a cold wind blows ; the heat of the summer is allayed ; the martial undertaking of kings is suspended, and travellers have returned to their own country.

" Now the waterfowl, in their haste to regain the Manasa lake, have left with their dear companions. Chariots and other conveyances no longer venture on the roads, deeply rutted by continuous rain.

" Sometimes visible, sometimes invisible, the sky, sown with clouds, looks like a ocean encircled with hills. The streams carrying away the Sarja and Kadamba blossom assume a yellow hue from the metallic deposits of the rocks and pass swiftly on amidst the cry of peacocks.

" The Jambu fruit, full of savour and gilded like a bee, is pleasant to the taste, and ripe mangoes of many tints fall to the ground shaken by the wind. Clouds like high mountains, having the lightning as their banner and cranes for their garlands, give forth a reverberating sound, like great elephants intoxicated with Mada juice who are about to fight.

" The grassy slopes of those forest tracts, revived by the rain where delighted peacocks dance, gleam brightly under the moon at night. Charged with an immense weight of water, clouds surrounded by cranes emit a muttering sound and in constant movement journey on and on, sometimes resting on the mountain tops. In their joyous circling flight, cranes, in love with the clouds, resemble an enchanting garland of lotus flowers suspended in space at the mercy of the breeze.

" The earth with its fresh grass strewn with tiny ladybirds, looks like a woman, whose limbs are swathed in a bright green cloth flecked with red.

" Sleep falls gently on Keshava;[1] the river runs swiftly to rejoin the sea ; the crane is happy to be united with the cloud ; fair ones approach their lovers with joy.

[1] Tradition holds that the Lord Narayana fell into the cosmic sleep in the rainy season, prior to the rebirth of Brahma, who issued from his navel.

" See how the groves are rendered gay by the dance of peacocks and how the Kadamba trees are covered with flowers ; bulls, filled with desire, follow the cows and the earth is rendered charming by forests and fields of grain.

" Rivers rush onwards, clouds discharge their rain, frenzied elephants are trumpeting, the woods grow more fair, lovers yearn for their loved ones, peacocks dance and the monkeys have regained their zest for life. Drunk with the aroma of the blossoming Ketaka trees, amongst the thundering waterfalls, the great elephants mix their amorous trumpeting with the peacocks' cries.

" Flowers, bruised by the downpour, are expelling their nectar, that the bees gaily plundered from the branches of the Kadamba, trees and now it is falling drop by drop. With their abundant fruit resembling ashes, full of savour, the boughs of the Jambu tree are swarming with bees.

" Following the woodland track amidst the hills, the chief of the elephants, hearing the roar of thunder behind him, halts in his tracks, thirsting to fight and, deeming it to be a challenge, turns back in fury.

" Filled now with the humming bees, now with blue-necked peacocks that dance or great elephants in rut, the woods take on a thousand varying aspects.

" Abounding in Kadamba, Sarja, Arjuna and Kandala trees, the forest with the ground saturated with water, resembling wine and the intoxicated peacocks that cry and dance, takes on the appearance of a banqueting hall. The raindrops, like pearls, falling in the folds of the leaves, rest there happily, and the many coloured birds drink of them, delighted by this gift from the King of the Gods.

" The soft humming of the bees, the joyous croaking of the frogs blended with the rumbling thunder of the clouds, resembling the roll of drums, create a veritable orchestra in the forest.

" The peacocks with their richly decorated tails are the choir, some dancing, some calling, here and there clinging to the tops of the trees.

" Roused by the sound of thunder, frogs of different shapes and colour waken from hibernation and whipped by the rain, croak loudly.

"The rivers, frequented by waterfowl, bear away their crumbling banks proud of their speed, and happy in their fullness, rush towards their lord, the ocean.

"Sombre clouds charged with fresh rain melt into each other and resemble the rocks scorched by the forest fire whose bases cohere with those that are equally laid bare.

"Elephants wander in the midst of the charming groves, that are filled with the cries of intoxicated peacocks in the grass sprinkled with ladybirds and planted with Nipa and Arjuna trees. Ardently embracing the lotuses, whose stamens are flattened by the recent showers, the bumble bees eagerly drink the nectar from these and from the Kadamba blossom that has been laid waste. Bull elephants in rut and leaders of kine disport themselves in the forest; the king of beasts bounds through the thickets and the kings of men are enraptured and forget their cares and anxieties whilst the Chief of the Gods is disporting himself in the clouds. Torrents of rain loosed from the sky, causing the seas and rivers to overflow, flood the streams, lakes and ponds together with the entire earth. With sheets of rain falling and the wind blowing with extreme violence, the banks of the rivers are swept away and the waters surge onwards so that the familiar paths can no longer be trodden.

"Like kings bathed by their servants, great mountains stand under the downpour from the clouds, which resemble ewers emptied by the King of the Celestials assisted by the Wind God, and seen thus, stand forth in all their native splendour.

"The sky, overcast with cloud, renders the stars invisible; the earth is saturated with the recent rains and the four quarters are shrouded in darkness. The summits of the mountains washed by the rain sparkle, their great cataracts twisting and falling like strings of pearls. Obstructed in their course by the jutting rocks, these mighty waterfalls precipitate themselves from the heights into the valleys like necklaces of pearls that break and scatter. Those rushing torrents, bathing the lower reaches of the rocky crests, fall into immense chasms, where they find themselves imprisoned and spray, resembling strings of pearls, which celestial nymphs have broken in the violence of their emotions, are scattered in unparalleled showers on every side.

" Only when the birds withdraw to the trees and the lotus closes, whilst the evening jasmine opens, can one divine that the sun has set behind the Astachala Mountain. Kings postpone their warlike expeditions and even the army, already on the march, halts ; hostilities cease, for the roads are water-logged. It is the month of Prausthapada,[1] when the brahmins who chant the Veda, the singers of the Sama Veda, begin their studies.

" Assuredly Bharata, the King of Koshala, having collected the revenue and completed the storing of provisions, is now engaged in celebrating the festival of the month of Ashada.[2]

" The Sarayu river must be overflowing its banks and the current increasing in velocity, like the shouts of acclamation with which Ayodhya will greet my return.

" Sugriva will be listening with joy to the sheets of rain falling, since he has overcome his adversary, recovered his consort and regained his vast kingdom; but I, O Lakshmana, separated from Sita, exiled from my immense dominion, resemble the bank of a river that has been carried away by the current and precipitated into an abyss.

" My grief is without bourne, the rains close every avenue and Ravana appears to me a formidable and invincible foe. Unable to travel on these impassable roads, I wish to make no demands on Sugriva despite his devotion, who after prolonged suffering is reunited with his spouse ; I do not desire to press for an interview on account of the urgency of his private concerns.

" As for that, when he has rested and the time is ripe, Sugriva will of himself remember the help he has promised me, there is no doubt of it. Because of this, I wait hopefully, till the rivers and Sugriva are favourable to me, O Thou who bearest the auspicious marks of royalty !

" A favour obliges a man to show gratitude ; the ungrateful who fail to honour an obligation wound the heart of honest men."

Lakshmana, standing with joined palms, fully concurred with these words to which he listened with extreme respect;

[1] Prausthapada—August–September.

[2] Ashada—June–July.

then addressing the magnanimous Rama with a joyful air, he said :—

" O Prince, the King of the Monkeys will not delay in carrying out the desire thou hast expressed ! Wait for the autumn and let the rainy season pass, re-affirming thy resolution to overcome thine adversary."

CHAPTER 29

Hanuman urges Sugriva to honour his Promise

HANUMAN observed that the heavens had become serene, free from lightning or cloud, filled with the cry of cranes and marvellously illumined by the light of the moon.

Sugriva however, having attained his end, had become indifferent to his duty and proper responsibilities, allowing his mind to engage in lower pursuits. His ambitions fulfilled, he ceased to harbour any solicitude concerning his affairs and gave himself up to enjoyment with women, satisfying every capricious desire.

Having realised his hopes and his fears being allayed, he passed the time by day and by night with his favourite consort Ruma and also Tara who was equally dear to him, as the Lord of the Gods disports himself among the troops of nymphs and musicians. Leaving the administration of the state to his ministers without supervision, his realm not being in peril, he became a slave to sense pleasures.

Seeing this, the resourceful Hanuman, the eloquent son of Maruta, conversant with what ought to be done and knowing the appropriate time for the performance of duty, approaching the King of the Monkeys, who well understood what was placed before him, spoke to him with confidence, in well chosen words inspired by respect and affection, words that were pleasing, full of good sense, practical, true, salutary, in accord with the law and duty, expedient and diplomatic. Even such was the speech of Hanuman, which he addressed to the King of the Monkeys.

He said :—

" Thou hast recovered thy throne and thy glory and added to the prosperity of thine house; it now remains for thee to concern thyself with thy friends; this is thy duty! He who, recognizing the fitting moment, conducts himself honourably towards his friends, sees the increase of his glory and his power.

" He who treats with equal regard, wealth, sceptre, friends and life itself, O Prince, acquires a vast empire. Let this be thy conduct, establish thyself in the path of honour, this is what thou shouldst do for thy friends in accordance with thy vow.

" He who does not abandon everything in order to occupy himself with the interests of his friends, whatever his aim, enthusiasm or undertakings, is courting failure.

" In the same way, he who allows the occasion for coming to the assistance of his friends to pass is worthless, even if he achieve great things. We are losing this opportunity of serving the interests of our friend Raghava, O Vanquisher of Thy Foes. Let us occupy ourselves with finding Vaidehi. Rama has not reminded thee that the time appointed has gone by, though he is fully conversant with the hour; albeit hard pressed, that sagacious prince has graciously resigned himself, O King!

" It is to Raghava that thou owest the prosperity of thine House, he wields immense influence, his power is immeasurable, his personal attributes incomparable. Render back the service he has done to thee, O Chief of the Monkeys, call together the leaders of thy people! The delay is not yet serious, as long as Rama does not call upon thee to redeem thy promise, but if thou defer till he constrain thee by force, it will be too late.

" Even had he done nought for thee, it would be thy duty to assist him in his quest, O Chief of Monkeys! How much more so after the service he has rendered thee in re-establishing thee on thy throne and slaying Bali.

" Thou art powerful and thy courage is extreme, O Thou who rulest the monkeys and the bears, therefore thou art under a greater obligation to assist Rama.

" Without doubt the son of Dasaratha is able to overcome the Gods, the demons and the great serpents with his arrows, he is merely awaiting the fulfilment of thy vow. It was not without risking his life that he bestowed such happiness on thee. Let us scour the earth and, if need be, the sky, in search of Sita. Neither the Devas, Danavas, Gandharvas or Asuras accompanied by the hosts of Maruts, nor the Yakshas are able to make him tremble, much less the titans.

" It is imperative, O Prince of the Tawny-coloured Ones, that thou shouldst try to please Rama with thine whole soul, who is endowed with that power that formerly succoured thee.

" We will not hesitate to enter the subterranean regions beneath the waters nor ascend into the sky if thou commandest it, O King of the Monkeys ! Do thou decree who shall proceed and how and in what order. There are more than ten million monkeys of indomitable strength ready to serve thee, O Irreproachable Prince ! "

Hearing these apposite and reasonable words, Sugriva, in his rectitude, made a supreme decision.

Wisely commanding Nila of inexhaustible valour to gather the troops from every quarter, he said :—

" Do thou muster mine entire army with its leaders and generals, whom none can resist, and bring them here immediately. The Plavagas who are stationed on the frontiers are skilled and brave, let them come here, see to it personally that I am instantly obeyed. He who does not present himself within fifteen days from now will be summarily executed, none shall escape.

" With Angada, seek out the veterans, carry out my orders scrupulously."

Having made all these arrangements, the Chief of the Monkeys, the valiant Sugriva, returned to his private apartments.

CHAPTER 30

Description of Autumn

SUGRIVA re-entered his palace, and the sky being free from cloud, Rama, who, during the rainy season, had been overcome by the intensity of his grief, gazing on the pure and tranquil moon and the marvellously clear autumnal nights, perceiving that Sugriva was leading a life of pleasure and reflecting on his own loss, also that time was passing, fell into a profound melancholy.

Though he soon mastered his mood, yet the wise Raghava remained absorbed in the thought of Sita, and seeing the sky free from cloud taking on a serene aspect, re-echoing to the call of cranes, he began to lament in sorrowful accents. Seated on the jutting ridge of a mountain rich in gold, under the autumnal sky, his thoughts went out to his beloved spouse and he reflected :—

" What joy can my youthful wife experience now, she, who loved the call of the cranes in the forest and imitated their note ? In mine absence, how can that tender maid take any delight in the tufts of flowers shining like pure gold, she, who formerly wakened to the cry of the swans ? What felicity can Sita of soft speech and tender form enjoy now ?

" When she hears the cry of the wild geese, travelling in skeins, what will become of that princess, whose eyes are as large as lotuses ? I feel no happiness without Sita, whose eyes resembled the doe's, when wandering by river, lake and forest, and my beloved in her tenderness will suffer cruelly in mine absence, through the desire that the beauty of autumn inspires." Thus did that son of a King lament like unto the Saranga bird when it solicits water from Indra.

At that moment, Lakshmana, who had gone out in careful search of fruits, returned from the enchanting mountain slopes and perceiving his elder brother absorbed in sorrowful thoughts, his mind distraught, alone in that solitude, the sagacious Saumitri, who was deeply distressed by the grief of his unfortunate brother, said to him :—

" Why, O Noble Prince, hast thou become a slave to love ? Why this reversion of thy former resolution ? Thy distress precludes thee from reflecting calmly ; tranquillity of mind is essential to carrying out any design ; after mature consideration, the time ordained together with the strength of thine ally should be utilised by thee for carrying out thy project without delay, O Friend !

" Nay ! The daughter of Janaka supported by thee, will not be of easy access to the foe, O Protector of the Human

Race. None may approach a blazing fire without being burnt, O Valiant Warrior ! "

On this, Rama answered the indomitable Lakshmana in characteristic accents that were worthy of him, saying :—

" Thy words are practical and wise, full of good sense and in accord with duty and the law. We should reflect on how to act without delay ; this quest must be pursued ; when one is powerful, invincible, youthful and valiant, one should have no misgivings concerning one's success."

Then recollecting Sita, whose eyes were as large as lotus petals, Rama with a downcast mien again addressed Lakshmana, saying :—

" The Thousand-eyed God, having saturated the earth with water and caused the grain to germinate, his task accomplished, is now resting. The clouds, which amidst a deep and prolonged rumbling spread over the mountains, forests and cities, letting loose their showers, are stationary, O Prince. The fury of the thunderclouds, resembling intoxicated elephants, black as the leaves of the blue lotus, darkening the ten regions has abated. Swollen with water, the clouds have visited the fragrant groves of Kutaja and Arjuna trees with wind and rain and have now disappeared in their airy flight, O My Friend. The clamour of the herds of elephants, the cry of the peacocks and the sound of the rain have ceased, O Irreproachable Lakshmana.

" Washed by dense clouds that have removed their impurities, the mountains with their magnificent escarpments shine forth illumined by the moon's rays.

" Autumn now manifests her grace in the branches of the Saptacchada trees, in the light of sun, moon and stars and in the gait of the majestic elephants, and her influence appears everywhere. In the tufts of lotuses opening to the first rays of the sun, in the scent of the Saptacchada flowers, in the music of the humming bees, autumn shines in all her splendour.

" The geese with their large and graceful wings, friends of the God of Love, have just arrived, covered with the pollen of the lotuses and are walking to and fro on the sandy banks of the rivers, disporting themselves with the swans.

" In the intoxicated elephants, in the kine, in the tranquilly flowing rivers, autumn is reflected in her myriad aspects.

Seeing the sky bereft of cloud, the peacocks in the woods, shorn of their caudal beauty, are no longer attracted to their chosen ones and having lost their brilliance, their delight has evaporated and they appear absorbed in their own thoughts.

"The tall trees of sweet fragrance, the tips of whose branches are bent under the weight of their blossom, shining like gold, enchanting to look upon, seem to light up the depth of the forest.

"Accompanied by their females, the great elephants, frequenters of the pools covered with lotuses and the woods, who formerly stood amidst the flowers, intoxicated with ichor, now walk with a slow and languid pace, merged in amorous sport.

"The sky has cleared and is as bright as a drawn sword; the water in the river flows slowly; a breeze, refreshing the white water lilies, blows and those regions delivered from the darkness shine forth.

"Freed from mud by the growing warmth of the sun, the soil is covered with a thick dust that the wind carries to a great distance.

"It is the time when kings, at enmity with each other, start on their campaigns.

"Shining with beauty with which the autumn has endowed them, exulting, their limbs powdered with dust, mad with desire and thirsting to fight, the bulls bellow amidst the kine.

"Sharing his love, the noble she elephant, eager and affectionate, with a slow tread circles round the bull intoxicated with ichor and follows him in the woods.

"Bereft of their tail feathers, their marvellous natural adornment, wandering on the banks of the rivers, the peacocks, as if scorned by the cranes, move about forlornly, in flocks.

"With their formidable cries, the chief of the elephants strike terror in the ducks and geese standing in the pools covered with flowering lotuses and, having sprinkled themselves with water again and again, begin to drink.

"On the rivers, free of mud, with their sandy banks and peaceful ripples frequented by herds of kine, re-echoing to the cry of cranes, herons frolic joyously.

"The sound of the rivers, the clouds, the waterfalls, the winds, the cry of the peacocks and the croaking of frogs has ceased. Many coloured venomous serpents, greatly emaciated, deprived of food during the rains, tormented with hunger emerge from their holes where they have been confined so long.

" The evening, caressed by the rays of the trembling moon, casts aside her veil, revealing her roseate countenance with its stars, in an ecstasy of joy. The night, whose gentle face is the full moon, resembles a youthful woman, the clusters of stars her smile and charming mien ; lit by the orb at its full it seems as if wrapped in a white mantle.

" Gorged with ripe grain, an enchanting flock of cranes joyfully crosses the sky in rapid flight, blown by the breeze like a garland of flowers tastefully interwoven.

" The waters of the great lake, with a solitary swan floating there asleep amidst countless waterlilies, resembles the heavens free from cloud, illumined by the full moon and a myriad stars. With their girdle of swans, their wreaths of blue and white lotus in flower, the great lakes are surpassingly beautiful and resemble lovely women decorated with jewels.

" At break of dawn, blending with the sound of the breeze blowing through the reeds, resembling the notes of a flute, the deep roarings in the caverns, increased by the wind and the bellowing of bulls, seem to answer one another.

" The river banks adorned with flowering grasses, stirred by a gentle breeze, resemble bright linen cloths from which the stains have been washed away.

" Bumble bees, roaming at will in the forest, gorged with nectar, heavy with the pollen of lotuses, where they have rested, in an excess of joy accompanied by their loved ones, follow the God of the Wind, in the woods.

" The calm waters, the flowering grasses, the cry of curlews, the ripened paddy fields, the gentle breeze, the immaculate moon, are all celebrating the departure of the rainy season.

" To-day the rivers, wearing their silver fish as girdles, flow by slowly, like lovely women, moving languidly, having passed the night in love.

" With the geese, aquatic plants[1] and the reeds that cover them like woven shawls, the rivers, sparkling, resemble the faces of women.

[1] Aquatic plants, literally Shaivala—Vallisneria Octandra or Blyza.

" In the forest, adorned with arches of blossom and full of the joyous humming of bees, the God of Love, to-day, impatiently wields his fiery bow.

" Having saturated the earth with their profuse showers and filled the lakes and rivers, preparing the soil for the harvest, the clouds have disappeared from the sky.

" Little by little, the rivers in autumn uncover their banks, like chaste brides disclosing their charms.

" O My Friend, the waters having subsided, the rivers re-echo to the cry of ospreys and flocks of geese abound in the ponds.

" It is the time, O Beloved Prince, when kings declare war on each other and thirsty for conquest enter upon their campaigns. The inception of hostilities for monarchs has begun, O Prince, and I do not see Sugriva making ready for an expedition of this kind.

" Asana, Saptaparna, Kovidara trees are in full flower as also the Bandhujiva plant and the Tamala trees on the mountain slopes.

" O Lakshmana! Behold the sandy banks of the rivers abound in swans, cranes, geese and osprey that are seen on every side. The four months of rain that have passed seemed to me like a hundred years, so filled with grief was I on account of Sita's absence.

" Like the Chakravaka bird with its mate, she followed me in the forest and the dreadful loneliness of the Dandaka solitudes seemed to that youthful woman a garden of delight. Though far from my beloved, overcome with sorrow, bereft of my kingdom and an exile, yet Sugriva shows no pity for me, O Lakshmana!

" ' He is without support, deprived of his kingdom, affronted by Ravana, unhappy, exiled, that amorous prince has taken refuge with me.' Thus will Sugriva speak, O My Friend, and in his perversity, he, the King of the Monkeys, holds me in contempt, I, the Scourge of My Foes. Having fixed a time to set out in search of Sita and entered into a formal contract to do so, this false one, having obtained his ends, has forgotten his pledge.

" Do thou enter Kishkindha and in my name, address that Bull of the Monkeys, the wretched Sugriva, the slave of domestic bliss, saying :—' He who, having raised the hopes of those who have sought his help in adversity and who formerly rendered him a service, fails to fulfil his promise to them, is considered the least of men in this world but that valiant one, who for good or evil loyally honours his given word, he is the best of men.

" ' Even the carnivorous beasts refuse to feed on the flesh of those ungrateful beings, who, having obtained their end, do not assist their friends to do so in their turn.

" ' Assuredly thou desirest to behold the gleam of my gold backed bow, resembling a series of lightning flashes, stretched ready for combat. Then shalt thou hear the dread twanging of my bowstring like unto the clash of thunder, when in wrath, I range the field of battle.'

" Having brought my renowned valour to his remembrance, O Illustrious Prince, thou, who art my companion, it would be strange if he did not pause and reflect. O Thou Conqueror of Hostile Cities, since he, the King of the Plavagas, has gained his desire, he no longer recollects the time chosen, and the King of the Monkeys, wholly given over to pleasure, does not appear to be aware that four months have passed. Drinking and roystering with his ministers and his court, Sugriva does not trouble himself about us, who are filled with anxiety.

" Go and address him, O Valiant Hero, inform him of our displeasure and speak to him in those terms, which are inspired by my wrath, saying :—' The Gate of Death, through which Bali passed, is not closed ! O Sugriva, honour thy pledge, for fear that thou mayest follow in the path taken by him ! ' Thy brother died alone, struck down by mine arrow but if thou failest in faith, I shall destroy thee together with thine whole House.'

" O Greatest of Men, say all that will further our desire, we must not delay, O Prince. Say to him ' Honour the promise thou didst make to me, O King of the Monkeys, recollect that virtue is eternal or, losing thy life this day, thou shalt fall into the jaws of death, where my shafts shall despatch thee to seek out Bali ! ' "

Seeing his elder brother, who was afflicted in his great misfortune, in the throes of violent anger, Lakshmana, burning with courage, the promoter of the glory of Manu's Race, profoundly distressed, felt a deep resentment towards the King of the Monkeys.

KISHKINDHA KANDA

CHAPTER 31

Lakshmana goes to Kishkindha

THE offspring of that Indra among Men, the son of a king, then spoke to his elder brother, who, full of tenderness, cheerless, despite his natural gaiety and full of distress, had but now expressed his desire to him :—

" Nay, that monkey is not a civilized being ; he does not consider the immediate consequences of his acts nor will he enjoy the glory of the monkey realm ; it is not fitting he should take advantage of circumstances in this wise. In his stupidity, he has become the slave of domestic bliss without calling to mind the debt he owes to thee ; let him therefore die and seek out Bali ; the throne should not be conferred on one devoid of virtue. I am unable to contain my violent rage ; I shall slay that disloyal Sugriva immediately. That son of Bali with the leaders of the monkeys shall this day assist us to recover the princess."

Then Rama, the Destroyer of Warriors, in terms that were prudent and appropriate, addressed Lakshmana, who bow in hand desired to follow up his words with action and who full of ire was burning to fight :—

" Nay, thine equals in this world do not commit such an outrage,[1] the warrior who nobly masters his anger, is the greatest of heroes. Do not belie thy natural integrity, O Lakshmana ! Recollect the feelings of joy that the alliance with Sugriva formerly aroused in thee. Speak to him in moderate tones, omitting all harsh expressions, regarding his delay and his tardiness."

Thus counselled by his elder brother, that Lion among Men, the valiant Lakshmana, the Slayer of Hostile Warriors, entered the town of Kishkindha. The sage and virtuous Lakshmana, eager to carry out what was agreeable to his brother, filled with indignation, entered the abode of that monkey, bearing in his

[1] That is slay a friend.

hand his bow, resembling Indra's, high as the peak of a mountain, like unto Mt. Mandara.

Faithful to the behest of Rama, his younger brother, the equal of Brihaspati, reflected in himself how he should address and answer Sugriva and, filled with ire on account of his brother's anguish and displeasure, Lakshmana advanced like a loosened tempest, uprooting Sala, Tala, Ashwakarna and other trees in his impetuous strides, like a great elephant shattering the mountains and crushing the rocks under his feet, thus cutting short he distance to his goal.

That Tiger among the Ikshvakus then beheld the splendid city of the King of Monkeys, the inaccessible Kishkindha, hollowed out of the mountain and filled with warriors. His lips trembling in his fury against Sugriva, Lakshmana beheld those formidable looking monkeys ranging round the city and seeing that foremost of men, those monkeys resembling elephants, tore up parts of the mountain, rocks, boulders and great trees. Lakshmana, observing them seizing hold of these missiles, felt his anger redoubled, like a brazier lit with innumerable brands, and they, beholding that infuriated warrior, who resembled the God of Death himself at the dissolution of the worlds, fled in their hundreds on all sides.

At that, those Foremost of Monkeys, returning to Sugriva's palace, informed him of Lakshmana's approach and of his anger, but that King of the Monkeys who was passing his time in dalliance with Tara paid no heed to what those Lions among Monkeys were saying.

Thereupon, under the orders of the ministers, those monkeys, their hair standing on end, large as mountains or elephants or clouds, issued out of the city and terrible to behold with their nails and teeth, their jaws like tigers, stationed themselves in the open. Many had the strength of ten elephants, others were ten times as strong and some were endowed with the strength of a thousand elephants.

Lakshmana, who was enraged, recognized that Kishkindha, filled with these monkeys, who were armed with trunks of trees and endowed with great valour, was difficult of access. And emerging from the walls and ditches, these monkeys stood courageously in the open field.

In the face of Sugriva's debauched indifference and the provocative attitude of the monkeys, the valiant Lakshmana, guardian of the interests of his elder brother, was seized with fresh anger, and that lion among men, heaving deep and burning sighs, his glances flashing with fury, resembled a brazier belching forth smoke.

With his pointed darts as the flickering tongue, his military ardour the poison, his bow the coils, he resembled a five-headed snake or the blazing fire at the end of the world or the enraged serpent king.

Then Angada, who had gone out to meet him, in his terror, suffered extreme discomfiture and that illustrious warrior Lakshmana, his eyes red with anger, commanded him saying :—
" O Child, inform Sugriva of my advent and tell him that the younger brother of Rama has come. O Conqueror of thy Foes, tormented by his brother's grief, Lakshmana waits at thy gate. Do thou seek to prepare that monkey by addressing him in this wise and return with all speed to inform me of his answer, O Dear Child."

Hearing these words spoken by Lakshmana, Angada, filled with distress, went to seek out his uncle, who now occupied his father's place and said to him : " Saumitri is come ! "

Then Angada, overwhelmed by the harsh accents of that hero, his countenance bearing the traces of profound distress, went away, first offering obeisance to the feet of the king in great reverence and thereafter to those of Ruma.

That valiant prince, having touched the feet of his father, then made obeisance to his mother also and finally pressed the feet of Ruma having informed Sugriva of what had taken place.

Sugriva, heavy with sleep and fatigue, did not wake up but lay in a drunken stupor, sexual indulgence having dulled his reason.

Meantime, seeing Lakshmana, fear troubling their hearts, the monkeys welcomed him with shouts to appease his wrath. Beholding him near at hand, they raised a great clamour, resembling a huge wave or the growl of thunder or the roaring of lions; and this great tumult roused that red-eyed monkey adorned with garlands who was bemused with liquor, his mind bewildered.

Recognizing his voice, two ministers of that king of the monkeys, accompanied by Angada, approached him. Both were of noble and venerable appearance and were named Yaksha and Prabhava. Ingratiating themselves by their speech that went straight to the point and sitting down near the king, who resembled Indra, the Lord of the Maruts, they said to him :—

" There are two brothers, full of nobility and power, Rama and Lakshmana, who in human form are worthy of the kingdom they confer on others. One of them, bow in hand, stands at the door ; beholding him, the monkeys, terrified, are raising a great clamour. This brother of Raghava, Lakshmana, his spokesman, charged by him to communicate his wishes, has come at Rama's command and the son of Tara, the beloved Angada, has been sent to thee in all haste by Lakshmana, O King, as his deputy, O Irreproachable Prince.

" That valiant warrior Lakshmana stands at the door, his eyes inflamed with anger and consumes the monkeys with his glances, O King. Go quickly and place thy head at his feet with all those who belong to thee, O Great Monarch, so that his anger may be instantly appeased.

" That which the virtuous Rama desires, do thou carry out scrupulously so that his wrath be softened ; execute his wishes with care, O King, fulfil thy pledge and be true to thy word ! "

CHAPTER 32

Hanuman's Speech

At these words of Angada and his ministers, Sugriva, learning of Lakshmana's anger, rose from his seat and came to himself.

Having considered the different aspects of the matter, he addressed his counsellors, who were versed in the sacred formulas, with which he too was conversant and of which he was a strict observer, saying :—

" I have neither spoken nor acted wrongfully; why is the brother of Raghava, Lakshmana, incensed against me, I ask myself? Evilly disposed persons, enemies ever looking for an occasion to charge me with imaginary crimes, have set the younger brother of Raghava against me. It behoves ye all to reflect on the matter wisely in order to discover the cause of his anger. Assuredly I do not fear Lakshmana any more than Raghava, but a friend who becomes angry without reason invariably creates anxiety. It is easy to contract a friendship, but extremely difficult to sustain it, for owing to the fickleness of the mind a friendship can be broken for the most trivial reason. Because of this, I am apprehensive in regards to the magnanimous Rama, for I have not been able to render back a proportionate service to him for that which he has done for me."

Sugriva having spoken, Hanuman, that foremost of monkeys, answered according to his understanding, saying:—

"It is in no way surprising, O Chief of the Monkey Tribes, that thou art unable to forget the significant and unexpected service rendered to thee by Rama. Assuredly that hero, for thy well-being, fearlessly slew Bali, equal to Indra in power. Undoubtedly Rama's feelings have been wounded, which is evidenced by his sending his brother Lakshmana, the increaser of his happiness, as his deputy, to thee. O Thou, the most skilled in discerning the seasons, autumn is here in all her glory, the Saptacchada and Shyama trees being in full flower, but thou, given up to pleasure, doth not perceive it. The sky, free from cloud, is filled with brilliant stars and planets, and on all the regions, lakes and rivers, calm prevails.

"The time has come to inaugurate the search for Sita of which thou art conversant, O Bull among Monkeys. Finding thee forgetful, Lakshmana has come to inform thee that the hour is at hand. Grieving over the abduction of his spouse, the magnanimous Rama will speak harshly to thee through the lips of this hero; is it a cause for wonder? Having acted improperly towards him, I see no other means tending to thy welfare but to offer obeisance to Lakshmana and crave his pardon.

"It is the duty of counsellors to utter what is true freely to a king and it is for this that after mature reflection I have spoken thus.

"Armed with his bow, Rama, in his wrath, is able to subdue the whole world as also the Gods, the Asuras and the Gandharvas. It is unwise to provoke one of whom subsequently forgiveness must be craved, the more so, when the recollection of a favour received places one under the obligation of gratitude. Therefore incline thine head before this man with thy son and thine entourage, O King, and remain faithful to thy promise, as a woman to her husband's will. It is ill-advised of thee to oppose Rama's behests, even in thought, for thou art well aware of this man's power. whose prowess is equal to Indra and the Gods."

CHAPTER 33

Tara pacifies Lakshmana

At Angada's request, and in accord with Rama's command, Lakshmana, the slayer of hostile warriors, entered the beautiful city of Kishkindha situated amidst caves.

Seeing Lakshmana approaching, the highly powerful monkeys of immense size guarding the gate, stood with joined palms and beholding the son of Dasaratha filled with wrath, breathing heavily, dared not obstruct his entry.

Then that mighty warrior, gazing about him, beheld that great city decorated with jewels and flowery gardens and rendered magnificent by heaps of precious stones with which it was filled; abounding in spacious buildings and temples, with jewels of every kind in abundance offered as merchandise, it was embellished by flowering trees covered with every desirable fruit.

Born of the Gods and Gandharvas, monkeys, able to change their form at will, wearing celestial garlands and raiment, added to the beauty of the city by their charming appearance.

Fragrant with the scent of sandalwood, aloes and lotus, the broad highways were also filled with the intoxicating odour of Maireya and Madhu[1].

[1] Wines made from honey.

Lakshmana beheld great mansions also, as high as the Vindhya and Meru mountains, and streams of pure water flowing through the city. He surveyed the enchanting abodes of Angada, Mainda, Dvivida, Gavaya, Gavaksha, Gaja, Sharabha, Vidhumati, Sampati, Suryaksha, Hanuman, Virabahu, Subahu and the great souled Nala, Kumuda, Sushena, Tara, Jambavan, Dadhibaktra, Nila, Sunetra and Supatala, dwellings like unto white clouds adorned with fragrant garlands and filled with jewels, grain and lovely women.

The magnificent and inaccessible abode of the King of Monkeys, like the palace of Mahendra, stood on a white rock and was decorated with pinnacled domes resembling the peaks of Mt. Kailasha. Trees in full flower, bearing fruits of every kind of delicious flavour, had been planted there and resembled blue clouds, enchanting with their cool shade, celestial blooms and golden-hued fruit.

Valiant monkeys, bearing weapons in their hands, guarded the resplendent gateway, the arches of which were of fine gold adorned with magnificent garlands.

The mighty Lakshmana entered Sugriva's palace without hindrance as the sun enters a great cloud, and having traversed the seven courtyards, filled with conveyances and seats, he beheld the inner apartments of that Chief of the Monkeys abounding in gold and silver couches with rich coverlets and fine seats.

On entering there, he heard sweet music blending with the rhythmic cadence of singing to the accompaniment of stringed instruments; and in the private apartments of Sugriva, many a high-born woman, distinguished for her youth and beauty, sumptuously attired, crowned with flowers and engaged in weaving garlands was observed by the high-souled Lakshmana. He noted too, that there were none of the king's attendants, who were not richly apparelled, happy, well fed and eager to offer their services.

Hearing the sound of the women's anklets and girdles, the virtuous Lakshmana became confused and incensed by the tinkling of those ornaments ; and that hero stretched the cord of his bow so that the twanging resounded on all sides. Thereafter the valiant Lakshmana, indignant on Rama's account, withdrew into a corner and stood silent, reflecting on his presumption in entering Sugriva's private apartments. Hearing the twanging of the bow, Sugriva, the King of the Monkeys, recognizing the presence of Lakshmana, began to tremble on his splendid throne.

He reflected : ' As Angada previously informed me, Saumitri, through brotherly solicitude, has undoubtedly come hither.'

Then that monkey, informed by Angada, his tidings now made doubly sure by the sound of the bow, understood that Lakshmana had come and he grew pale, his heart being filled with apprehension, and Sugriva, the King of the Monkeys, addressed Tara, of charming appearance, in well considered words saying:—

" O Lady of Lovely Eyebrows, what cause for displeasure has the younger brother of Rama, who is gentle by nature? Why has he come hither like a raving madman? Dost thou know the reason of this prince's anger? Assuredly that lion among men cannot be enraged without cause. If we have unwittingly displeased him, then considering the matter carefully, inform me without delay or go thyself to him.

" O Lovely One, by thy sweet speech seek to conciliate him. Seeing thee, his mind will become tranquil and his anger be allayed, for great warriors do not permit themselves to treat women with harshness. When thy gentle words have soothed him and his mind and senses are under control, then I, in my turn, will approach that prince, whose eyes are as large as lotus petals and who is the conqueror of his foes."

On this, Tara, swaying slightly, her eyes bright from the drinking of wine, her girdle loosened, hanging by a golden thread, wearing the insignia of royalty, with downcast looks approached Lakshmana. And when that great warrior beheld the consort of the King of the Monkeys, he, restraining his wrath in the presence of a woman, bowed his head, conducting himself like an ascetic.

Under the influence of wine and observing the benign attitude of that Prince, Tara, discarding all diffidence, addressed him in a conciliatory manner, in words calculated to gain his confidence and said :—

" From whence springs this anger, O Son of a King? Who has failed to carry out thine orders? What reckless person has approached the forest where the trees are dry with a flaming torch ? "

Mollified by this soft speech, Lakshmana replied with studied courtesy :—

" Why, given over to lust, does thy consort neglect his duty and his own true interests ? And thou, who art devoted to him, why dost thou not give the matter thy consideration ? He has become indifferent to the affairs of the kingdom and of ourselves and our displeasure. Surrounded by parasites, O Tara, he gives himself up to sensual enjoyments.

" The four months appointed as the term of waiting have passed, but the King of the Monkeys in an orgy of drunkenness and pleasure, is unaware of it. Assuredly dissipation is not a proper means to the observance of one's duty and obligations. Intemperance brings in its train the loss of wealth, virtue and the capacity for enjoyment.

" Not to requite a service received is to fail wholly in one's duty and to lose a good friend is immensely injurious to one's higher interests. From the point of view of prosperity, the greatest of virtues is friendship that is rooted in loyalty and justice ; he who fails in these is not fixed in his duty. This being so, what should therefore be done, O Thou, who art conversant with the path of duty ? "

Hearing these just and reasonable words, expressed with gentleness, Tara assured the prince of the certain fulfilment of his enterprise and again addressed Lakshmana saying :—

" O Son of a King, this is not the time for recrimination, thou shouldst restrain thine anger against my lord ; he has thine interests at heart, forgive his folly, O Warrior.

" O Prince, how can a man endowed with every good quality be indignant with one who is lacking in them ? Which of thine equals, despite his good character, would give way to wrath ? I know the reason for the displeasure of Sugriva's valiant ally, I am conversant with the service that you have both rendered us and which we must return. I know further, O Best of Men, that one must master one's passions. I am aware in what company Sugriva has yielded to lust, which is the cause of the present procrastination that incites thy wrath. When man yields to desire he forgets time and place as also his duty and what should rightfully be done. Do thou pardon this Leader of the Monkey Race, who, at my side, without shame, gives himself up to sensual enjoyment to which he is the slave. Even the great Rishis, devoted to the practice of asceticism, when carried away by desire, lost control of their minds, how should this monkey, therefore, volatile by nature, when overcome by passion, not become a slave to pleasure, king though he be ? "

Having addressed these words of profound understanding to Lakshmana, whose courage was immeasurable, the gentle Vanari, with a troubled look, on account of her conjugal affection, then added for the good of her lord :—

" O Most Excellent of Men, though overcome by desire, Sugriva has long since made preparation to thine advantage. Already hundreds, thousands and millions of valiant monkeys, able to change their form at will, inhabiting every kind of tree, have come here.

" Be pleased to enter, therefore, O Long-armed Warrior; the chaste conduct of a sincere friend authorizes him to look on the wives of others."

At Tara's invitation and urged by a desire to carry out the commands that had been laid upon him, that illustrious hero, the conqueror of his foes, entered the inner apartment.

There, seated on a golden throne, covered with a rich cloth, he beheld Sugriva, resembling the sun itself, his person decked with celestial ornaments, of a godlike beauty and dignity. Wearing superb raiment and wreaths he looked like Mahendra himself, on every side he was surrounded by women adorned with crowns and jewels meet for goddesses, and his reddened eyes gave him the appearance of Antaka.

Of the hue of fine gold, clasping Ruma firmly in his arms, seated on a magnificent throne, that large-eyed hero saw before him the mighty Saumitri of expansive eyes.

CHAPTER 34

Lakshmana reproaches Sugriva

SEEING that indomitable lion among men, Lakshmana, entering full of wrath, Sugriva was troubled and, observing that Son of Dasaratha breathing heavily and burning with indignation on account of the calamity that had overtaken his brother, the King of the Monkeys rose and, leaving his golden seat that resembled the highly decorated standard of Indra, his eyes inflamed, approached Prince Lakshmana and stood before him like the mighty Kalpa tree.[1] Thereupon the women, lead by Ruma, followed him, like a cluster of stars surrounding the moon.

Then Lakshmana, filled with ire, said to Sugriva standing amidst the women with Ruma at his side, like the moon surrounded by stars :—

" That king who is endowed with great and noble qualities and is compassionate, who has subdued his senses and is grateful and loyal, obtains renown in the world, but the monarch who is rooted in unrighteousness and is unjust to his friends who have rendered him assistance, is the object of opprobrium.

" To utter a falsehood with reference to a horse is to be guilty of the death of a hundred horses, in regard to a cow of a thousand cows, but to utter a falsehood in regard to a man is to destroy one's self as well as one's kindred.

" That ungrateful wretch, who, having gained his end, does not render service for service, is guilty of the murder of all beings, O King of the Plavagas ; this is the text recited by Brahma on beholding one who was guilty of ingratitude ; it is known throughout the world, O Plavamgama. He who kills a cow or drinks intoxicating liquor or is a thief or violates his vow is still able to expiate his sin, but for him who is guilty of ingratitude, no expiation is possible.

" Thou art an ignoble, false and ungrateful wretch, O Monkey, for having obtained what thou didst seek from Rama without requiting his services. Having achieved thy desire through

[1] Kalpa—The Wish-fulfilling tree.

Rama, is it not thy duty to do everything in thy power to recover Sita? Yielding thyself up to sensual delights, untrue to thy promise, Rama does not know thee for the serpent croaking like a frog, that thou art.[1]

" In his compassion for thee, O Wicked Wretch, the magnanimous Rama enabled thee to regain the kingdom of the monkeys. Thou hast failed to acknowledge the benefits conferred on thee by the high-souled Raghava, therefore pierced by sharp arrows thou shalt follow Bali. The path thy brother took at death is not yet closed! Honour thy promise, O Sugriva, do not follow in his wake. Since thou dost not behold the Prince of the Ikshwakus loosing his fiery shafts, thou art still able to remain serene and happy, without concerning thyself about his anxieties."

CHAPTER 35

Tara defends Sugriva

THUS spoke Lakshmana, the son of Sumitra, inflamed with anger and Tara, whose face was as fair as the moon, answered him saying:—

" O Lakshmana, the King of the Monkeys has not merited this harsh language, particularly from thy lips. Sugriva is not ungrateful nor false nor worthy of condemnation nor, O Hero, does he utter what is not true nor is he an impostor!

" The valiant monkey, Sugriva, has not forgotten the assistance rendered to him by Rama on the field of battle, which no other was able to give. With the aid of the magnanimous Rama, Sugriva has regained his glory and the lasting dominion of the monkey realm and has been restored to Ruma and myself once again, O Scourge of thy Foes!

" Having been subject to cruel adversity and now enjoying the summit of good fortune, he has become insensible to the arrival of the time for the fulfilment of his promise, as was the Sage Vishwamitra of old. For ten years, that virtuous Sage was

[1] The meaning being " croaking like a frog to attracts frogs."

attached to the nymph Ghritachi and failed to perceive that time was passing, he, who was skilled in discerning time.[1]

"Sugriva had been deprived of physical pleasures over a long period, he was exhausted and had not experienced any relaxation, O Lakshmana, therefore Rama should pardon him. And thou, O Lakshmana, shouldst not give way to wrath like an inferior person without ascertaining what has taken place. Virtuous people like thee, O Lion among Men, do not give way to immediate and unreasoning anger. In all humility, I appeal to thee on behalf of Sugriva to control the grief that gives rise to this anger in thee. It is my firm conviction that Sugriva is ready to renounce Ruma, Angada, myself, kingdom, wealth, grain and herds to please Rama. Having slain that vile demon, Sugriva will restore Sita to Rama, as the moon is re-united with Rohini.

"In Lanka there are hundreds, thousands and millions of irrepressible demons able to change their shape at will; without destroying these formidable beings, it is impossible to overcome Ravana, by whom Maithili has been borne away. Sugriva is unable to defeat those demons of terrible exploits without the support of auxiliaries, O Lakshmana. This was Bali's considered opinion, that resourceful and experienced monarch of the monkeys. Knowing nought of the matter, I heard it from his lips.

"In order to render thee assistance, the foremost of the monkeys have been summoned for this enterprise with innumerable carefully selected troops. Awaiting those valiant and powerful monkeys, chosen to assure the success of Rama's undertaking, the King of the Monkeys has not yet left the city.

"O Lakshmana, some time ago Sugriva, wisely ordered that these monkeys should come together this very day. Thousands and millions of bears and hundreds of Golangulas[2] as well as innumerable kotis[3] of monkeys, burning with energy, will be at thy disposal to-day.

"Therefore O Conqueror of Thy Foes, subdue thy wrath. Seeing thy face distorted with anger and thine eyes inflamed,

[1] This story is told in Balakanda.
[2] Golangula—a black monkey with the tail of a cow.
[3] Koti—a crore or ten millions.

the wives of these foremost of monkeys, far from being reassured, are suffering all the anguish of their former fear."

CHAPTER 36

Lakshmana is reconciled to Sugriva

BY nature gentle, Lakshmana listened to those just and gracious words of Tara with deference.

Perceiving the magnanimous acceptance of her speech, the King of the Monkeys threw off his fear as one discards wet clothing. Thereafter Sugriva tore off the gaudy and variegated garland from his neck and threw it away, his intoxication being dissipated and that Chief of the Monkeys addressed the redoubtable warrior Lakshmana with humility, thus gratifying him, and said :—

" O Saumitri, I had lost my fortune, my fame and the kingdom of the monkeys which by Rama's favour have been wholly restored to me. Who is able to equal this or render it back even in part to that divine Rama, renowned for his exploits, O Prince? The virtuous Raghava will recover Sita and slay Ravana by his own valour alone ; as for me, I shall merely accompany him. What need of assistance has he who, with a single arrow pierced seven giant trees and a mountain, penetrating deep into the earth ? He by the sound of whose stretching bow the earth with its mountains quakes, what need has he for aid ? I shall follow that Indra among Men, O Lakshmana, when he goes forth to destroy his adversary, Ravana, together with his House.

" If I have betrayed his friendship or confidence in some measure, may he pardon me ; is there any without fault ? "

These words of the magnanimous Sugriva pleased Lakshmana who addressed him affectionately, saying :—

" Assuredly my brother will not lack support, O Prince of the Monkeys, above all, O Sugriva, with thy co-operation, who art full of humility. Such is thy valour and sincerity, that thou art worthy of enjoying the unequalled prosperity of the monkey realm.

"With thine aid, undoubtedly, O Sugriva, the illustrious Rama will soon slay his enemies in battle. Virtuous, mindful of what should be done, intrepid in the field, thou utterest noble words that are worthy of thee, O Friend. Who else, recognizing his fault, at the height of his power, would speak thus, O Bull among the Monkeys, save mine elder brother and thee?

"Thou art equal to Rama in courage and strength! Thou has been ordained his ally by the Gods, O Chief of the Monkeys. Why delay further, O Hero, let us go forth together and offer consolation to thy friend, who is afflicted on account of separation from his consort.

"O Sugriva, forgive those reproaches that I addressed to thee on account of Rama's profound distress."

CHAPTER 37

Sugriva assembles his Troops

HEARING the words of the magnanimous Lakshmana, Sugriva said to Hanuman who stood near:—

"Call together all those who inhabit the heights of the Mahendra, Himavat, Vindhya, Kailasha and Mandara mountains, as also those from the peaks of Mt. Pandu and the Five Hills; those who dwell on the mountains that are bright as the dawn; those who inhabit the furthest shores of the sea in the western region and those on the mountains in the mansions of the sun; those formidable monkeys who have taken refuge in the Padmachalu woods; those monkeys resembling clouds of collyrium, who possess the strength of the lord of elephants, who dwell on the Anjana hill; those possessing the splendour of gold, inhabiting the caves of the Mahashaila mountains and those who frequent the slopes of Mt. Meru, as well as those dwelling on Mt. Dhumra; those who possess the brilliance of the rising sun, of immense bounds, who, on the Mt. Maharuna, drink the heady wine Maireya; those who dwell in the vast, fair and fragrant forests with their charming glades, where the ascetics' hermitages are found. With the aid of the fleetest of monkeys summon them all from every quarter of the world by means of gifts and conciliation, Already I have sent out messengers who are famed for their agility, yet, in order to expedite matters further, let them be followed by other emissaries.

"Bring those leaders of monkeys also, who are lazy or given over to pleasure. If they have not responded to my appeal in ten days, they will suffer the death penalty for infringing the royal command. Let those lions among monkeys under my dominion carry out my orders with all speed in their hundreds, thousands and millions.

"Resembling mountains of mist shrouding the heavens, let those excellent monkeys of terrifying aspect come at my call. Let all the monkeys who are acquainted with the way, scour the earth; call them together at my command with all speed."

At the words of the Monkey King, the Son of the Wind dispatched groups of intelligent monkeys to every quarter. Setting out to that region traversed by Vishnu, by the paths frequented by birds and stars, the monkeys, under the commands of their sovereign set forth immediately.

Scouring the seas, mountains, forests and lakes, they called all the different monkeys together to help Rama. When these monkeys heard of Sugriva's order, a very death warrant, they, in fear, at once set out for Kishkindha.

Those of the Plavagama Tribe, who were as black as collyrium, filled with energy, came from the Mt. Anjana to the number of three kotis to join Rama. Those who frolicked on the high hills, where the sun sets, shining like gold, offered themselves in ten kotis. From the heights of Mt. Kailasha, monkeys whose colour resembled a lion's mane, came to the number of a thousand and those who lived on fruit and roots, who dwelt on Himavat came in tens of millions, whilst those terrible apes of fearful deeds, resembling burning coals, descended in haste from the Vindhya mountain in thousands of millions. Those who dwelt on the shores of the white sea, the dwellers of the Tamala forests and those who fed on coconuts could not be numbered.

From woods, caves and rivers, a vast army of monkeys issued forth, who seemed able to drink up the sun's rays. Now those mighty monkeys, who had gone out in all haste to spur others on, found a great tree growing on the summit of Mt. Himavat. In ancient times on that divine and sacred peak, a great sacrifice had been performed which found favour with Mahadeva, who satisfies all the desires of the Gods. Thereafter many varieties of fruit and roots resembling ambrosia had sprung up in that quarter from the sacred offerings of grain and seed,[1] and those who partook of them had no need of further sustenance for the period of a whole month.

Then those foremost among the monkeys gathered those celestial fruits and roots with medicinal herbs from that place of sacrifice and they brought fragrant flowers also to please Sugriva.

Having called all the monkeys of the world together, those chosen messengers returned with speed at the head of their troops and soon those fleet and spirited monkeys had returned to Kishkindha, where Sugriva was; and they presented him with the fruit, herbs and roots that they had gathered, saying :—

"We have scoured the mountains, rivers and forests; all the monkeys of the earth have come at thy call."

These words pleased Sugriva, the King of the Monkey Tribe, who freely accepted all the gifts they had brought.

CHAPTER 38

Sugriva goes to meet Rama

SUGRIVA, having accepted the gifts presented to him, thanked the monkeys and dismissed them all.

Having sent away those thousands of monkeys, who had performed their task, he deemed his mission, as that of the mighty Raghava, well nigh accomplished.

Thereupon Lakshmana addressed the redoubtable Sugriva, the foremost of monkeys, with a deference which moved him, saying :—"O Friend, be pleased to set out from Kishkindha."

[1] That had been scattered there.

Hearing these words spoken by Shri Lakshmana, Sugriva filled with joy answered :—" Be it so, let us go forward, I am at thy command."

Having thus spoken to the illustrious Lakshmana, Sugriva dismissed Tara with the other women and thereafter summoning the leaders of the monkeys in a loud voice addressed them, saying :—" Come hither ! "

At the sound of his voice all those admitted to the presence of women came immediately and stood with joined palms before the king, whose brilliance equalled the sun's and who said to them :—

" Go with all speed and bring a litter, O Monkeys ! " At this command they set out with rapid strides to seek that marvellous litter and, when it was made ready, the supreme Sovereign of the Monkeys said to Saumitri :—" Be pleased to ascend the litter. O Lakshmana ! "

Speaking thus, Sugriva with Lakshmana mounted the golden litter that shone like the sun and was supported by a large number of monkeys. A white canopy was spread over Sugriva's head and magnificent fans made of yaks tails were waved about him. Eulogized by bards, to the sound of conches and trumpets, he set out in regal state. Surrounded by hundreds of war-like monkeys bearing weapons in their hands he proceeded to the place where Rama dwelt and, having arrived at that excellent spot, that illustrious prince descended from the litter with Lakshmana and approached Rama with joined palms. Then the monkeys, grouped about him, did likewise and, seeing that great army of monkeys resembling a lake covered with lotus buds, Rama was well pleased with Sugriva.

Raising the King of the Monkeys, who had prostrated himself before him and whose forehead touched his feet, the virtuous Rama embraced him to demonstrate his affection and esteem and requested him to be seated. Thereafter seeing him seated on the ground, Rama said :—

" He who divides his time judiciously between duty, pleasure and the legitimate acquisition of wealth and honours his responsibilities in these things is truly a king, O Best of Monkeys ; but he who neglects his duty, his true interests and legitimate pleasures is like one who sleeps on the top of a tree and does not wake up till he has fallen. The monarch who is ever ready to destroy his foes and delights in showing favour to his friends, who plucks the fruit of the threefold food,[1] has fulfilled his duty.

"The time has now come to act, O Scourge of Thy Foes, therefore take counsel with thy ministers, O King of the Apes!"

Thus addressed, Sugriva answered Rama, saying:—"I had lost fame and fortune together with the entire monkey realm, O Long-armed Warrior but, through thy favour have received them again by thine and thy brother's grace, O Great One, O Greatest of the Conquerors. He who does not acknowledge a service done to him is an object of contempt.

"These energetic leaders have gone out in their hundreds to summon all the monkeys in the world, O Slayer of thy Foes. Monkeys, bears and apes full of valour, of ferocious aspect, familiar with the woods and inaccessible forests, monkeys that are born of the Gods and Gandharvas, able to change their shape at will, are on their way followed by their troops, O Rama.

"These monkeys are proceeding here surrounded by hundreds and thousands,[2] by millions and tens of millions; these monkeys and their chiefs, who are as valiant as Mahendra and resemble mountains in stature, are coming together from the Meru and Vindhya ranges. They will unite with thee to fight the demon Ravana and, laying him low on the battlefield, will restore Sita to thee."

Seeing the preparations made by that valiant monkey, in accord with his desire, the illustrious prince was delighted and his countenance resembled the blue lotus in flower.

[1] The three ends of life, duty, wealth and legitimate pleasures.

[2] Lit. Arvuda—a hundred millions.
Sanku—is a thousand Arvudas.
Madhya is an Arvuda ten times; Antya is a Madhya ten times; Samudra is a Madhya twenty times and a Paradha a Samudra thirty times.

CHAPTER 39

The Arrival of Sugriva's Forces

THUS spoke Sugriva, standing with joined palms before Rama, and that most virtuous of men, taking him in his arms, embraced him saying :—" It is no wonder that Indra sends the rain, nor that the sun with its thousand rays dispels the darkness from the sky, O My dear One, nor that the moon by its brilliance makes the night clear, nor that thine equals create the happiness of their friends, O Scourge of Thy Foes. To find nobility of character in thee is not strange ; I know thee by the affectionate tenor of thy speech. With thy support, O My Friend, I shall vanquish all my foes on the battlefield ; thou art mine ally and shouldst assist me.

" To his own destruction, did that vile demon bear Maithili away, as Anuhlada[1] carried away Sachi, having first deceived her sire.[2] Ere long, I shall pierce Ravana with my sharp arrows as Shatakratu, that slayer of his enemies, slew the haughty father of Paulomi."

At that moment, darkness covered the firmament and veiled the fiery brilliance of that orb of a thousand rays ; a pall of dust hung over all regions, and the earth with its mountains, forests and woods trembled. The entire earth was covered with innumerable monkeys resembling kings of men and who, having sharp teeth, were gifted with great strength. In the twinkling of an eye, those foremost of monkeys surrounded by troops, numbering hundreds of kotis, endowed with extreme energy, roaring like thunder, gathered from the rivers, mountains and seas with others who inhabited the forests.

Monkeys the colour of the rising sun or white like the moon or of the tint of lotus stamens or pale, having their home on the golden mountain, appeared in tens of thousands in attendance on that renowned and valiant monkey Shatavali. Then the puissant

[1] Anuhlada—A son of Hiranya-kasipu, a Daitya, father of Prahlada. His story is to be found in the Puranas.

[2] Puloman—a Danava who was slain by Indra when he attempted to curse him for ravishing his daughter Sachi.

sire of Tara, who resembled a golden hill, appeared at the head of many thousand kotis. Thereafter the father of Ruma, father-in-law of Sugriva, who resembled the filaments of a lotus and was like a youthful sun, arrived accompanied by other thousands of kotis of monkeys; and that foremost of monkeys, Kesharin, Hanuman's illustrious sire, appeared in company with many thousands of monkeys. And Gavaksha, King of the Golangulas, endowed with dreadful power came, surrounded by millions of monkeys ; Dhumra also, the destroyer of his foes, advanced with two thousand bears endowed with terrific speed. Thereafter the leader of herds, Panasha of exceeding prowess came, accompanied by three million mighty and dreadful warriors and he was followed by Nila of immense stature, who resembled a mass of collyrium, with ten kotis of monkeys. And bright as a golden mountain, the heroic Gavaya arrived with five kotis of monkeys, and in his devotion to Sugriva the brave chief Darimukha brought a thousand kotis. Thereafter the two powerful Ashwiputras, Mainda and Dvivida presented themselves with a thousand million monkeys. The brave warrior Gaja conducted an army of three kotis of monkeys, and the illustrious king of the bears, called Jambavan, came at the head of ten kotis, placing himself under Sugriva's command. The renowned Rumana followed with a hundred kotis of intrepid monkeys in all haste. A hundred thousand million monkeys followed Gandhamadana, and an infinite number were under the command of Prince Angada, who, like his father, was full of courage. Thereafter, shining like a star, came Tara of supreme valour, accompanied by five kotis of monkeys from a great distance and there followed Indrajanu, a brave and skilful general, who in his turn presented himself at the head of eleven kotis, and also Rambha with an ayuta[1] of soldiers; and there followed the monkey leader Durmukha, that valiant one full of phenomenal courage, with two kotis of monkeys, resembling the peaks of Mt. Kailasha. Hanuman himself was accompanied by thousands of monkeys and the supremely brave Nala was followed by the inhabitants of the woods to the number of an hundred, a thousand and an hundred monkeys. The fortunate Darimukha was escorted by ten kotis of monkeys and with loud shouts took his place beside

[1] Ayuta—Ten thousand, a myriad or a number not to be counted.

Sugriva. And Sharabha, Kumuda, Vahni and Rambha came, those monkeys who were able to change their shape at will, with their forces of incalculable numbers covering the entire earth, its mountains and forests. All the monkeys inhabiting the earth gathered round Sugriva, leaping, gambolling and roaring, and those Plavagamas surrounded Sugriva like massed clouds round the sun. Full of courage and energy, they gave voice to repeated shouts of acclamation, bowing their heads in salutation to the King of Monkeys. Others, the leaders of armies, according to tradition, approached the king and stood by his side with joined palms; and Sugriva standing in extreme devotion before Rama, informed him of the arrival of the monkeys and then addressed his generals, who were burning with zeal, saying:—" O Chiefs of Monkeys, station your forces duly on the mountain near rills in the woods and let each ascertain the exact number of his troops."

CHAPTER 40

Sugriva sends his Monkeys to the East in search of Sita

THEN the Lord of the Monkeys, his purpose accomplished, said to that lion among men, Rama, the destroyer of hostile hosts :—

" Here, gathered together, are the foremost of monkeys inhabiting my dominions, who are equal to Mahendra and are able to transport themselves anywhere at will. These ferocious monkeys, resembling giants and titans, of immeasurable prowess, renowned for their exploits, bellicose, valiant, indefatigable and supremely sagacious in all their deliberations, have come with their vast forces.

" O Rama, these untold millions, who inhabit various mountain tracts, traversing land and sea, have come to place themselves at thy service. All are intent on their master's welfare and obedient to thy behests ; they are at thy command, it is for thee to dispose of them as thou wilt. Though I am fully conversant with thy design, yet do thou order all as thou judgest best."

Thus spoke Sugriva and Rama, the son of Dasaratha, taking him in his arms, said to him :—

" O Dear and Wise Friend, let us learn if Sita still lives or no and ascertain in what country Ravana dwells. Then, having come to where Videha's daughter is to be found, we will adopt those measures that circumstances dictate, the hour having been fixed.

" O Lord of the Monkeys, it is not for me to command this expedition nor for Lakshmana; it is thou who must direct it; thou shalt be its leader. Do thou, O Lord, take the command thyself in this matter, thou art fully acquainted with my purpose, O Hero. Thou, the second of my friends,[1] art full of courage, wise, knowing how to choose the fitting moment, devoted to my true interests, supremely loyal and accomplished."

Thus addressed, Sugriva, in the presence of Rama and the sagacious Lakshmana, said to his general, Vinata, who resembled a great hill and whose voice resounded like thunder :—

" O Foremost of Leaders, who art accompanied by monkeys as bright as the sun and moon, thou art able to turn time and place to advantage and art skilled in conducting thine affairs ! Taking with thee hundreds and thousands of apes, explore the eastern region with its forests, woods and mountains, in search of Sita, the Princess of Videha and also Ravana's stronghold. Search among the mountain fastnesses, the forests and rivers for Rama's beloved consort, the daughter-in-law of King Dasaratha ; search by the beautiful Bhagirathi, the Sarayu, the Kaushiki and the Kalindi, the enchanting Yamuna and the great hills bordering the Saraswati, the Sindhu and the Shona of ruby waters, the Mahi and Kalamahi with their splendid wooded hills.

" Look for them in the Brahmamalas, Videhas, Malavana, Kashikoshalas, and Magadhas, the Pundras and Angas, lands where the silkworm and silver mines abound and on the mountains and cities skirting the sea. Search through the houses in Mandara, amongst those people whose ears resemble cloths reaching to their nether lip, whose faces are black and dreadful, who are one-footed, though fleet withal, and whose bodies do not deteriorate ; those also who feed on human flesh, and the Kiratas, hunters who are golden-hued, of pleasing

[1] The first being Lakshmana.

looks, possessing thick hair worn in a knot, who subsist on raw fish and those creatures, tiger-men, terrible to behold.

"O Dwellers in the woods, search carefully in all these places that are accessible by climbing and swimming and the Island of the Seven Kingdoms Yava, also and the islands Suvarna and Rupayaka, full of gold mines, called the gold and silver islands. Beyond these, is the mountain Shishira, whose peaks reach to the heavens, and which is inhabited by Gods and Giants. Seek here in the mountain fastnesses, cascades and forests for the glorious consort of Rama.

"Thereafter you will reach the red and swiftly flowing river Shona ; from there descend to the seashore, where the Siddhas and Charanas dwell. In these enchanting sacred spots, seek everywhere for Ravana and Sita. Explore the forests, mountain sprung rivers, wild tracts and cavernous heights. It behoves you to examine the terrible islands in the ocean, where great waves arise and, whipped by the tempest, let forth a thunderous roar. There dwell Asuras of immense size, who by Brahma's permission, seize the shadows of birds flying over the sea. Arriving at that vast ocean, that resounds like clouds at the time of the dissolution of the universe, frequented by huge serpents, keep careful watch and crossing over that sea, called Lohita, whose red waters are terrible to behold, you will come upon the mighty knarled Shamali tree. There, constructed by Vishwakarma, like unto Mt. Kailasha, decorated with every kind of gem, towereth the abode of Garuda. Terrible demons resembling hills of diverse forms, named Mandehas, hang suspended from the rocks there. Day after day, at the rising of the sun, those demons tormented by that planet, fall into the water, struck by Brahma's energy and then suspend themselves on the rocks once more.

"Proceeding further, you will come to the sea, named Kshiroda, that resembles a white cloud with its waves shining like a necklace of pearls. In its centre rises the great white mountain Rishabha, planted with trees, bearing fragrant blossoms and a lake named Sudarshana covered with dazzling silver lotuses having golden stamens, where flamingoes abound. Vibudhas, Charanas, Yakshas and Kinneras in the company of troops of Apsaras, disport themselves on the shore of that lake.

" Leaving the Kshiroda Sea behind, O Warriors, you will come to the Jalada sea which is a source of terror to all beings. There the Rishi Aurva[1] created a shining object by the power of his anger, which was transformed into the head of a horse by Brahma. Its heat is unequalled and its food is the universe of movable and immovable beings. There the cries of the creatures of the sea, who are unable to bear the flames, can be heard wailing in its vicinity.

" To the north of the Svadu Sea rises the high mountain Jatarupashila, covering thirteen yojanas, of the splendour of gold. There, O Monkeys, you will behold the supporters of the earth, the serpent resembling the moon, with eyes as large as lotus petals, worshipped by the Gods, and possessing a thousand heads, the divine Ananta of dark hue sleeping on the summit of the mountain. There stands a golden palm tree with three branches resembling a standard set upon an altar. This is the boundary of the Eastern region set up by the Gods.

" Reaching up to the heavens, measuring a hundred yojanas, the mountain, Udaya, rises with its golden peak, beautiful with its Sala, Tamala and flowering Karnikara trees bright as the sun.

" There also is the peak Saumanasa four miles in breadth and forty in height. From there in former days, Vishnu, the supreme Lord, measured the earth with three strides, the second being Mt. Meru.

" The sun passing from Jambudwipa on the north and reaching the summit of Saumanasa, again becomes visible to the dwellers in Jambudwipa. It is there that the great Rishis, Vaikhanasas, bright as the sun, perform their austerities.

" This is the island Sudarshana, where the sun rises, giving light to all beings. Search for Janaki and Ravana on these mountain fastnesses and in the forests and woods. Here, when the sun shines on the Shaila mountain, the east appears roseate. Because the sun rises there, Brahma established it, in ancient times, as the gateway of the world, called the East.

[1] A miraculously born sage who castigated the warrior class, but on the persuasion of his ancestors, cast his anger into the sea, where it assumed the form of a being with a horse's head.

In other versions it was said to be the subterranean fire that consumes the world at the end of the cycle and is represented as a flame with a horse's head.

Here you should look for Sita and Ravana on the mountain breast, in the caves and by the waterfalls.

"Beyond is the impassable eastern quarter inhabited by the Gods, bereft of sun and moon, covered by darkness. Search for the princess in all those rocks, woods and streams that I have made known to you, but, O Foremost of Monkeys, you are only able to proceed thus far. Beyond is the region without sun or bourne of which I have no knowledge. Proceeding in search of Vaidehi and Ravana's abode, having reached the mountain Udaya, return, when a full month shall have passed. Do not exceed the period; he who does so, will be punished by death.

"Having attained your end, and met with Maithili and with care explored the favourite region of Mahendra, which is covered with woods and thickets, return satisfied."

CHAPTER 41

Sugriva sends out other Monkeys to explore the Southern Region

THEN having sent away that mighty host of monkeys to the east, Sugriva dispatched another well tried army to the south.

Appointing Angada leader of those heroic monkeys, that hero, the lord of the monkey bands, conversant with the countries that had to be explored, sent out those endowed with speed and valour: Nila, the Son of Agni, and the monkey Hanuman, the exceedingly energetic Jambavan, Suhotra and Sharari, Sharagulma, Gaja, Gavaksha, Gavaya, Sushena, Vrishabha, Mainda, Dvivida, Gandhamadana, Ulkamukha and Ananga, the two sons of Hutashana.

And the King of the Monkeys began to describe those regions that were difficult of access to those simian chiefs, saying:—

"You will first behold the Vindhya ranges, possessing a hundred peaks covered with trees and shrubs of every kind, and the enchanting river, Narmada, frequented by mighty serpents, and the wide and charming stream, Godavari, with its dark reeds, and the captivating Krishnaveni; the regions of Mekhalas and Utkala and the city of Dasharna also; Abravanti and Avanti,

Vidarbhas and Nishtikas and the charming Mahishakas. You will see too, the Matsyas, Kalingas and Kaushikas, where you should search for the princess and the Dandaka Forest with its mountains, rivers and caverns and the Godavari, also examine the districts of Andhras, Paundras, the Cholas, Pandyas and Keralas. Then repair to the Ayomukha Mountain, rich in ore, with its marvellous peaks and flowering woodlands; that mountain, possessing lovely forests of sandalwood, should be carefully searched by you.

" Thereafter you will behold that divine river of pure waters, the Kaveri, rendered gay by troups of Apsaras. On the summit of the mighty Mountain Malaya, bright as the sun, you will behold Agastya, the foremost of Rishis. By the permission of that high-souled one, you will cross over the great river, Tamraparni, abounding in crocodiles. Ravishing forests of sandalwood cover the islands of these waters flowing to the sea, which resemble a youthful bride going to meet her lover.

" Proceeding further, O Monkeys, you will see the golden gates set with pearls of the city of the Pandyas; then in order to ensure the success of your enterprise, you will approach the sea and ascertain your ability for crossing it. In the centre of the ocean, Agastya has set that foremost of mountains, Mahendra, its slopes covered with trees. Entirely made of gold it extends deep down into the waters; the abode of Gods, Rishis, Yakshas and Apsaras, thronged by innumerable Siddhas and Charanas and of surpassing loveliness, it is visited by the thousand-eyed God at each new moon.

" On the other side of the sea is an island, four hundred miles in length, inaccessible to men and splendid to look upon; search there with particular care, it is the abode of the wicked Ravana, who merits death, the Lord of the Titans, in splendour equal to Indra himself.

" In the middle of the ocean dwells the female titan named Angaraka, who procures her prey by seizing the shadow of those who fly in the air. Your doubts at rest, search there for the consort of that king of men whose glory is limitless.

" Beyond that island in the sea there rises a lovely hill on which Celestial Beings dwell, named Pushpitaka, bright as the rays of sun or moon, lapped by the waves of the ocean, whose peaks seem to pierce the heavens. Of these, one all golden, on which the day's orb lingers, the ungrateful and the unbeliever may not behold. Inclining your heads to that peak, offer salutations and search on. After this you will come to another mountain, difficult of access, named Suryavan extending over fourteen yojanas and, beyond this, the mountain Vaidyuta, ever green, with trees bearing every desirable fruit in all seasons. Partaking of these delectable fruit and roots and drinking the honey, pass on, O Monkeys.

" Beyond there is the Mountain Kunjara which delights the eye and heart, where Vishwakarma constructed the abode of Agastya. Extending over four miles, this stately golden edifice adorned with many kinds of gems rises to the height of ten yojanas. There also is the city of Bhogavati, the abode of the Serpent Race, with spacious streets, incapable of being captured, guarded by formidable snakes and sharp-toothed highly-poisonous serpents, where the dread King of the Serpents, Vasuki, dwells. Search that city with care in every hidden place wheresoever it may be.

" Going beyond, you will find the beautiful Rishabha Mountain in the form of a bull, filled with gems where excellent Goshiraka, Padmaka, and Harishyama trees and those possessing the brilliance of fire are seen. Approaching the sandalwood forest by no means should you enter there, for a certain Gandharva, named Rohita, protects it with five other Celestial Beings resplendent as the sun, named Shailusha, Gramani, Shiksha, Shuka and Rabhru.

" Thereafter you will see the retreat of those ascetics, whose splendour resembles the sun, moon and fire ; this is the end of the earth where those who have won the heavenly regions, dwell. Beyond is the dread abode of the Pitris, which is inaccessible. There Death has his city, enveloped in abysmal gloom, O Bulls among Monkeys. Pursue your explorations thus far ; but those who go beyond never return.

" Having searched all those regions which are accessible to you, seeking for some trace of the princess, he who shall return within a month saying ' I have seen Sita ' will pass his days in happiness, enjoying prosperity equal to mine, in the midst of every delight. None will be dearer to me ; I shall cherish him as a relative and, however great the number of his faults, he will become my friend.

"Your strength and vigour are immeasurable and you are born in families endowed with great qualities; strive manfully therefore to find the princess; set forth on this mission of supreme importance and demonstrate your heroism."

CHAPTER 42

Other Monkeys are sent to explore the Western Region

HAVING despatched those monkeys in a southerly direction, Sugriva, addressing the leader, Sushena, who resembled a cloud, with bent head and joined palms approached his father-in-law, Tara's sire, who was endowed with great prowess, and spoke to him also. Then he issued orders to Maricha, the son of Maharshi and the mighty ape, Archismat, surrounded by the foremost of monkeys, possessing the splendour of Mahendra and like unto Vainateya in brilliance, and also to Maricha's offspring, the Marichas, the mighty Archirmalayas, that all these sons of the ascetic[1] should march towards the region of the West, saying:—

"O Ye Monkey Chiefs, let two hundred thousand monkeys, led by Sushena, set out in search of Vaidehi! Scour the countries of the Saurashtras, the Bahlikas and Chandrachitras abounding in antimony and other provinces and populous places and fair and pleasant cities and Kukshi, dense with Punnaga trees and filled with Bakula and Uddalaka trees, as well as the tracts covered with Ketakas and the auspicious streams whose cool waters flow towards the west.

"Explore the forest of the ascetics and the mountain woodlands; there, having searched the tracts resembling deserts, the towering cliffs and the mountain ranges, extremely difficult of access, proceed further, when you will behold the sea, which abounds in whales and crocodiles, O Monkeys.

[1] Marichi.

"Then the apes shall disport themselves amidst the groves covered with Ketakas and dense with Tamala and coconut trees. Look for Sita and Ravana's stronghold there, in hills and woods, on the shores of the sea and explore Murachipattana and the delightful cities of Jatapura, Avanti and Angalapa as also the forest of Alakshita and all these spacious kingdoms.

"There, where the river Sindhu joins the ocean, is a high mountain named Somagiri, possessing a hundred peaks and covered with tall trees. On its slopes dwell the Sinhas[1] who carry whales and elephants to their nests. These are found on the mountain ridges and on the extensive plateaus, where wild elephants range, gratified with food, whose trumpeting resembles the roar of thunder. The monkeys, able to change their shape at will, should scour that golden summit, towering to the sky and covered with graceful trees.

"In the middle of the sea rises the golden summit of the Mountain Pariyatra, extending over a hundred yojanas. There dwell thousands of powerful Gandharvas, effulgent as fire, formidable and mischievous, resembling flames. O Valiant Monkeys, do not approach them nor seek to eat the fruits from that region. These fruit trees are guarded with ferocious vigilance by those mighty Gandharvas, nevertheless you should search for Janaki there, nor have you ought to fear if you preserve your monkey form.

"There is a mighty hill, the colour of emerald, shining like a diamond, named Vajra, covered with trees and creepers, an hundred yojanas in height and area; carefully search all the caves of that mountain.

"In the fourth quarter of the ocean is the Mt. Charavat; there Vishwakarma forged the discus Sahasrara, which together with the conch was taken possession of by Shri Vishnu when he had slain Panchajana and the Danava Hayagriva. In those deep caverns and amidst those charming slopes, search for Ravana and Videha's daughter with care.

"Beyond, rising from the depths of the sea, is the mighty mountain, Varaha with its peak of pure gold which measures four and sixty yojanas. On it is the golden city named Pragjyotisha where the giant, Naraka, dwells. There do you

[1] Lit. "Flying lions," possibly eagles or prehistoric birds.

search for Ravana and Vaidehi among the beautiful plateaus and huge caves.

" Passing beyond that foremost of mountains, revealing glimpses of the gold in its depths, you will come to the Mountain Sarvasauvarna with its many fountains and waterfalls ; there elephants, wild boar, lions and tigers roar ceaselessly on every side, filling it with their clamour day and night. Then there is the mountain named Megha where the Gods crowned the fortunate Mahendra, he of the bay horses, the Vanquisher of Paka. Having passed that mountain protected by Mahendra, you should repair to a range of sixty thousand golden hills, bright as the rising sun, casting their light on every side and embellished with blossoming golden trees. In their midst rises the monarch of mountains, Meru, the foremost of hills, on whom Aditya, well pleased, conferred a boon saying :—

" ' By my grace all the mountains under thy protection shall be golden by night and day and those Gods who inhabit thee, the Gandharvas and Danavas, shall both assume the radiance of gold.'

" At dusk, the Vishwadevas, the Vasus, the Maruts and the Celestials gather to adore the Sun-god and worshipped by them the sun sinks below the horizon traversing forty thousand miles in the space of an hour, when it withdraws behind the mountain range. On the summit of that mountain rises a palace resembling the sun in splendour, consisting of countless towers, which was built by Vishwakarma and is graced by various trees filled with birds. It is the abode of the magnanimous Varuna, who bears the noose in his hand.

" Between the Meru mountain and the Astachala Range there is a great Tala tree with ten crests, made of pure gold, which shines with extreme brilliance on a marvellous base. Search all the inaccessible places on this mountain, as well as the lakes and rivers for Ravana and Vaidehi.

" It is there that the virtuous Merusavarni dwells, sanctified by his asceticism and equal to Brahma himself. Bowing down, you should make enquiries of the Maharishi Merusavarni, who resembles the sun, concerning Mithila's daughter.

" From the end of the night, all those regions, that the sun illumines till it sets behind the Astachala mountains, should be searched by you, O Bulls among the Monkeys, but of that which lies beyond which is covered in darkness and without bourne, we know nought!

"Search for Sita and Ravana in this region as far as the Astachala Mountain and at the end of a month, return; those who tarry beyond this term will die. My father-in-law of long arms gifted with great prowess, I appoint as your leader; you should abide by his commands and listen to all he says; he is my spiritual preceptor. All of you are valorous and well able to ascertain the wisdom of a course, still you will be doing your duty in accepting him as your leader. In this wise, explore the western quarter. Having requited the good that has been done to us, we shall attain our end. Do you also determine what is pleasing to Rama and, in accord with time and place, execute it."

Then those monkeys and their leaders with Sushena at their head, having given a due hearing to the wise counsel delivered by Sugriva, offered salutations to him and set out for the quarter protected by Varuna.

CHAPTER 43

Searchers are sent to the Northern Region

HAVING directed his father-in-law to the western region, the Lord of the Apes spoke to that heroic monkey Shatavali, in words fraught with his own and Rama's interests:—"With an escort of a hundred thousand rangers of the woods, the sons of Vaivasvat and thy counsellors, do thou explore the northern region, O Hero, which is crowned with the snowy peaks of Himalaya, and search everywhere for Rama's illustrious consort there.

"O Most Circumspect of Beings, having executed this task and done that which is pleasing to the son of Dasaratha, we shall have honoured our obligation and achieved success. The magnanimous Raghava has rendered us a great service and, if we can make some return, our life will not have been lived in vain. To render assistance to any in need is to make one's life fruitful, even if one is under no obligation to do so; how much more if one is able to repay one's benefactor. Reflecting on this, those who value our well-being and happiness should do all in their power to discover Janaki.

"Rama, the foremost of men, revered by all beings, the conqueror of hostile citadels, is united with us in friendship. Endowed with courage and discrimination, do you explore these numerous and dangerous regions, rivers and mountains.

"Search the lands of the Mlecchas, Pulindas, Shurasenas, Prasthalas, Bharatas, Kurus, Madrakas, Kambojas and Yavanas. The cities of Shakas should be visited by you as well as the Varadas, thereafter do you explore Himavat. In the tracts of Lodhras and Padmakas and in the Devadaru woods, search on every side for Ravana and Vaidehi. Reaching the Soma hermitage, frequented by Devas and Gandharvas, proceed to the mountain named Kala, possessing spacious plateaus. In the midst of these mountainous tracts, in the valleys and caverns search for that illustrious lady, Rama's irreproachable consort. Having traversed that golden breasted mountain, you should scale Mt. Sudarshana and further Mt. Devasakha, the refuge of birds, filled with every variety of winged creature and covered with trees of differing fragrance. Amidst its golden rocks, fountains and caves, search for Ravana and Videha's daughter.

Going beyond this mountain, you will come upon an open space, measuring four hundred miles in extent, devoid of mountains, rivers and trees, nor are any living beings to be found there. Speedily traversing this desert you will reach the stainless Kailasha Mountain which will fill you with delight. There, resembling a pale cloud, you will see the charming domain of Kuvera, of burnished gold, constructed by Vishwakarma, where lies a great lake covered with flowering lotuses and lilies, frequented by swans and ducks, where troops of Apsaras disport themselves. There the King Vaishravana, adored by the whole world, the gracious dispenser of riches, sports with the Guhyakas[1]. Amidst these mountains, bright as the moon, as also in the caverns, search carefully for Ravana and Sita.

[1] Hidden Beings attendants on Kuvera.

Coming to Mt. Krauncha, with exceeding circumspection, enter its inaccessible caverns, which are well known to be extremely hard to penetrate. There dwell certain great and illustrious Rishis, effulgent as the sun, adored by the Gods, whose forms they assume. You should explore the other caves, plateaus and peaks of the Krauncha Mountain thoroughly. Then the tree-less Manasa peak will be seen, the abode of birds, and the scene of Kama's austerities, where no way for any creature, God or Titan exists; this mountain should also be searched by you. Beyond this is the Mainaka Mountain where the great giant Maya has built his abode; this place with its plateaus, plains and woods must also be searched by you. Women with the faces of horses dwell there.

" Going beyond there, you will reach the abode of the Siddhas, where the ascetics—Valakhilyas and Vaikhanasas are. Pay obeisance to those great beings, whose austerities have cleansed them from all sin and, in humility, enquire of them concerning Sita. There is the Vaikhanasa lake covered with golden lotuses, the resort of beautiful swans, bright as the dawn. The elephant of Kuvera, Sarvabhauma by name, in the company of she-elephants, wanders about in that region.

" Beyond that lake is a sky bereft of moon, sun, stars and clouds but it is illumined as if by so many solar rays, through the effulgence of god-like Sages crowned by asceticism, who rest there. Leaving that region behind, you come to the river Shailoda, on whose banks the Kichaka reeds grow, by the help of which the Siddhas cross to and fro. There are the Uttara Kurus, with whom those who have acquired spiritual merit take refuge. There are lakes there, whose waters are covered with golden lotuses and innumerable rivers abounding in dark green leaves and pools of the hue of the rising sun, embellished by clumps of crimson lotuses. Pearls and gems of great price and masses of blue flowers possessing golden stamens cover those tracts and rivers with floating islets, where gold abounds and high banks scattered with precious stones, are seen. The trees there, thronged with birds, bear fruit and flowers at all seasons, charged with delectable juices and distilling delicious perfumes, fulfilling every desire. Other excellent trees give rich attire of different kinds and ornaments of pearls, emeralds and other gems desired by men and women; some also bear fruit which can be partaken of in every season. Some trees bring forth precious couches bedecked with costly and variegated coverlets and others furnish enchanting garlands, costly drinks and various kinds of viands. Women possessed of every accomplishment distinguished for their youth and beauty, are there, sporting with Gandharvas, Kinneras, Siddhas, Nagas, and Vidyadharas of great splendour; and all those of righteous deeds engaged in pleasure and those who enjoy what is pleasant and useful, sojourn there with their wives.

"There the continual sound of musical instruments, blended with sweet laughter, is heard, giving delight to all beings: there is none there who is not happy or wants for any desirable object and every day the enchantment of that place increases.

"Beyond that region is the Northern Sea. There in the bosom of the deep rises the Somagiri Mountain of immense size. Though bereft of the sun, yet on account of the brilliance of the Soma mountain, that land is as bright as if Vivasvat himself had warmed it with his luminous rays. There dwells the Soul of the universe, Shambhuinin, in his cosmic form as the eleven Rudras surrounded by Brahmarishis.

"O Foremost of Monkeys, you should not venture beyond the region of the Uttara Kurus, nor is there any way for creatures to do so. That mountain, named Soma, is incapable of being scaled, even by the Gods. Sighting this mountain, turn back speedily. You may proceed so far, O Foremost of Monkeys, but the region beyond, where unending night broods, is unknown to us.

"You should search all those places, which I have described to you, and also those I have omitted to mention. O You who are equal to the wind and fire, by discovering the place of concealment of Videha's daughter, you will be doing what is exceedingly pleasing to the son of Dasaratha as well as to me! Having achieved your purpose, do you with your relatives, honoured by me and having acquired every distinction, your enemies slain, range the earth, the support of all beings, O Monkeys."

CHAPTER 44

Rama gives his Ring to Hanuman

SUGRIVA disclosed his plan to Hanuman in particular, being supremely confident that this leader, the foremost of monkeys, would accomplish his purpose.

Then the monkey king, the lord of all the dwellers in the woods, well pleased, addressed the son of the Wind-God, the peerless Hanuman, saying :—" Nowhere on the earth, in the air or sky, in the celestial regions or in the depths of the sea, do I know of any obstacle that can impede thy course, O Best of Monkeys ! All the worlds with the Asuras, Gandharvas, Nagas, Men and Gods, as well as the mountains and the seas are well known to thee. In motion, speed, skill and energy thou art the equal of thy sire, O Valiant One, and there exists no creature on this earth that is like thee in vigour, O Hero of infinite resource ! Reflect therefore on how Sita may be found ! In thee, O Hanuman, repose strength, wit, courage and policy in conjunction with the knowledge of time and place."

Realizing that success in the venture depended on Hanuman and that Hanuman himself was chosen on account of his exploits, Rama reflected : " This Lord of the Monkeys has supreme confidence in Hanuman and Hanuman too is sure of success ; he who has been tested by his deeds and who is considered worthiest by his master is certain to accomplish his purpose."

Thereupon that mighty warrior, Rama, considering that his ends were already gained, felt a great felicity flooding his mind and heart and that scourge of his enemies, highly gratified, gave Hanuman a ring inscribed with his name that would be a sign to the princess and said to him :—

" O Foremost of Monkeys, by this token, the daughter of Janaka will not fail to recognize thee as my messenger. O Warrior, thy resolution, thy courage and thine experience as also Sugriva's words seem to me to predict success."

Thereupon, taking the ring and placing it to his forehead, that foremost of monkeys, offering obeisance to the feet of Rama, prepared to depart. Taking with him a mighty band of monkeys, that hero, the son of Pavana, resembling the moon in a cloudless sky encircled by stars, set forth.

And Rama addressed that mighty warrior saying :—" O Thou endowed with the strength of a lion, I depend on thy valour; by summoning up thy great resources, do all in thy power, O Son of the Wind, O Hanuman, to bring back the daughter of Janaka."

CHAPTER 45

The Departure of the Monkeys

SUMMONING all the monkeys, the Lord of the Apes, Sugriva, spoke to them touching the success of Rama's enterprise, and said :—

" O Chiefs of the Monkeys, knowing my commands, go forth and search those regions indicated by me." Whereupon, covering the earth like locusts, the army started out. During the month fixed for the search for Sita, Rama and Lakshmana remained on the mountain Prasravana.

The valiant Shatavali set out with all speed for the north, that marvellous region where the monarch of the mountain rises[1] whilst the leader of the monkey bands, Vinata, went towards the east. Tara,[2] Angada and others, in company with that monkey born of Pavana, marched towards the southern region inhabited by Agastya; and Sushena, that lion among monkeys, went to the west, that fearful region protected by Varuna.

Having despatched the generals of his forces to each of the quarters, that king of the monkey hosts experienced supreme satisfaction.

Under the orders of their sovereign, all the monkey leaders departed in great haste, each in the direction assigned to him and, full of valour, those monkeys shouted, cheered, howled and

[1] Mount Meru.
[2] The General Tara.

chattered, rushing on and on amidst a great uproar. Having listened to the instructions of their monarch, the leaders of these monkeys cried: " We shall bring Sita back and slay Ravana ". Some said: " I alone shall defeat Ravana in open combat and having laid him low, shall deliver the daughter of Janaka, still trembling with fear, saying to her ' Rest here, thou art weary '." Others said: " Singlehanded I shall recover Janaki even if it be from the depth of hell; I shall uproot the trees, cleave the mountains, penetrate the earth and churn up the ocean." One said, " Without doubt I can clear four miles in one bound! " and another, " I can clear a hundred," and yet another, " I am able to leap more than a hundred. Neither on earth, in the sky nor on the sea nor mountains nor in forests, not even in the nether regions can anything bar my progress ".

Thus in turn did the monkeys, proud of their strength, speak in the presence of their king.

CHAPTER 46

Sugriva narrates his Travels through the World

THE leaders of the monkeys having departed, Rama enquired of Sugriva saying:—" How is it that thou knowest all the quarters of the earth? "

Then Sugriva, bowing low, said to Rama: " Hear me and I will tell thee all.

" When Bali pursued the giant Dundubhi, in the form of a buffalo, in the direction of the Malaya mountain, Mahisha[1] entered a cave in that mountain and Bali, desirous of slaying that Asura, followed him.

" I remained obediently at the entrance of the cave, but a whole year passed and Bali did not re-emerge. Then the cavern was filled with foaming blood which gushed forth, and seeing this, I was terrified and consumed with a burning grief on account of my brother. Distracted, I reflected: ' My elder

[1] Another name of Dundubhi, meaning " great or powerful animal," a buffalo.

brother is certainly dead ' and I placed a rock, as large as a hill, at the mouth of the cave, thinking ' The buffalo will not be able to come out and will die' ; after which I returned to Kishkindha giving up all hope of Bali being alive.

" There obtaining the mighty kingdom with Tara and Ruma, surrounded by my friends, I began to pass my days in peace.

" That bull among monkeys, however, having slain Dundubhi returned, and trembling with fear, in all humility, I made over the crown to him.

" That wicked wretch, however, beside himself with rage, wishing to slay me, followed me whilst I sought to fly with my ministers. It was then that, hotly pursued by him, I passed by various streams, forests and cities. The earth appeared to me like the reflection of a whirling firebrand seen in a mirror or a puddle.[1]

" Journeying towards the eastern region, I beheld many kinds of trees, beautiful mountains, charming caverns and lakes. I saw the Udaya Mountain rich in gold and the white sea, the abode of Apsaras. Pursued by Bali, flying on and on, O Lord, I turned and continued my course then, changing my direction once more, I made for the south, covered by the Vindhya Forest and embellished with sandal wood trees. Thereafter, seeing Bali among the woods, on the mountains, I went westwards still followed by him.

"It is thus that I grew conversant with every kind of region and finally reached the Astachala Mountains. Beyond that most beautiful and elevated of ranges I turned to the north and passed Himavat, Meru and the Northern Sea.

" Unable to find refuge from Bali, the sagacious Hanuman said to me :—' O King, I recollect now that the Lord of the Monkeys was formerly cursed by the Sage Matanga in this very hermitage. If he should enter this asylum, his head will be split into a hundred pieces ; we can, therefore, take up our abode here without anxiety.'

" O Son of a King, I, thereupon, went to the Rishyamuka Mountain, nor did Bali dare to come there for fear of the Sage Matanga. This is how, O King, I visited every part of the world and took refuge in this cave."

[1] Lit.: Made by the imprint of a cow's hoof.

CHAPTER 47

The Return of the Monkeys

In order to find Vaidehi, those leaders of monkeys, in obedience to their sovereign's will, speedily went forth in all directions to their destinations, and they explored lakes, streams, plains, cities and tracts rendered impassible by torrents. Then those chiefs of the monkey bands searched the regions described by Sugriva with their mountains, woods and forests. Engaged during the day in seeking for Sita, when night fell, they stretched themselves on the ground, and coming to trees covered with fruits in all seasons, they slept there.

Counting the day of their departure as the first, at the end of a month, giving up hope, they returned to their king on the Prasravana mountain.

Having scoured the eastern region with his forces, the mighty Vinata returned without having seen Sita. Thereafter the great monkey Shatabali came back disappointed with his forces, having scoured the whole of the northern quarter. And Sushena, at the end of the month, ranging the western region without success, presented himself in company with his monkeys before Sugriva.

Coming before Sugriva who was seated with Rama on a ridge of the Prasravana Mountain, and paying obeisance to them, Sushena said: "We have searched all the mountains, deep woods, valleys, ravines and the countries situated on the shores of the sea. All the places described by thee have been scoured by us, as also all the jungles intertwined by creepers abounding in thickets that are impassable and the hilly districts. Huge animals have been encountered by us, which we have slain, and we have searched these densely wooded regions again and again, O Lord of the Monkeys. It is Hanuman, who is mighty and nobly born, who will discover Maithili; the son of the Wind has undoubtedly gone to where Sita has been taken."

CHAPTER 48

Angada slays an Asura

THE monkey Hanuman, accompanied by Tara[1] and Angada, swiftly set out to the quarter assigned to him by Sugriva. With all those leaders of monkeys, he travelled a great distance and explored the woods and caves of the Vindhya Mountains. Rugged crags, impassable rivers, lakes, vast jungles, groves, innumerable hills covered with forests were searched by the monkeys on every side, without their being able to find Maithili, the daughter of Janaka, anywhere.

Subsisting on various roots and fruits, they were overcome by fatigue in that uninhabited and waterless region amidst the fearful ravines and solitary places. Having searched that immense area extremely hard of access, with its mighty forests, containing caves, all those foremost of monkeys fearlessly penetrated into another equally inhospitable region, where the trees yielded neither fruit, flowers nor foliage and where the streams were dried up and even roots were rare. There, neither buffaloe nor deer, nor elephants, tigers, birds nor any other animals, that are found in the forest, could be seen. There were neither trees, grass, plants nor herbs, and in that place there were no pleasant pools with flowering or fragrant lotuses and no bees to be observed.

There dwelt the fortunate Sage, Kandu, a treasury of asceticism, of truthful speech, whose austerities had rendered him invincible and who was irascible, having lost his young son at the age of ten years in the forest. Filled with wrath on account of his death, that great-souled One had laid a curse on the entire vast forest, rendering it unfit to harbour any creature. This inaccessible region, deserted by beasts and birds, the hidden recesses of the woods, the mountain caves and the bends of the rivers were carefully searched by the monkeys in order to carry out Sugriva's desire, but they were unable to find the daughter of Janaka or her abductor, Ravana, there.

[1] The General Tara.

Having entered a wood, overgrown with creepers and briars, they beheld a terrible titan, of dreadful deeds, cherishing no fear, even for the Gods. Seeing that formidable titan, who stood erect like a great hill, the monkeys pressed close to each other girding up their loins.

Then that mighty Asura said to them " You are lost ! " and, clenching his fists, rushed upon them in fury, but Angada, the Son of Bali, thinking it was Ravana, struck him with the palm of his hand with such force, that he fell to the earth like a great hill, vomiting blood. When he had ceased to breathe, the triumphant monkeys searched that mountain cavern; and having satisfied themselves that it had been thoroughly explored, those dwellers of the woods entered into another fearful cave. After having searched that place also, they emerged exhausted and wholly dispirited sat down at the foot of a solitary tree.

CHAPTER 49

The Monkeys search the Southern Region in vain

THEN the eminently wise Angada addressed all the monkeys and, though himself fatigued, exhorted them to take courage, saying : " We have searched the forests, mountains, rivers and impenetrable wilds, valleys and caverns with care, without finding the daughter of Janaka, Sita, or that wicked wretch, the titan, who bore her away. A great part of the time assigned to us by Sugriva, whose commands are inexorable, has elapsed ; therefore, banishing languor, despondency, torpor and fatigue, together let us examine every region once again. Search in such a way that Sita may be discovered by us. Perseverance, ability and ardour are said to conduce to success ; I therefore address you thus :—O Dwellers in the Woods, explore the whole inaccessible forest to-day without counting the cost, success will wholly depend on your exertions ; to permit yourselves to be overcome by fatigue or give way to sleep is not fitting. Sugriva is irascible and inflicts harsh punishments ; he is ever to be feared, as also the magnanimous Rama. I speak in your own interests; therefore, if you concur, act accordingly or let someone point out what alternative will benefit us all, O Monkeys."

Hearing Angada's words, Gandhamadana, though faint from thirst and fatigue, spoke in clear accents, saying :—" That which Angada has said is worthy of him and is appropriate and timely, let us act upon it! Let us search the hills, caves, rocks, desert places and waterfalls, in accord with the instructions given by Sugriva; let us scour the forest and the mountain ridges together!"

Then the monkeys, rising, full of valour, began to range the south covered by the Vindhya forests, afresh. Scaling the mountain that resembled an autumnal cloud, rich in silver, with its innumerable peaks and valleys, those foremost of monkeys, eager to find Sita, ranged the enchanting Lodhra forests and the woods of Saptaparna trees. Ascending to the summit of the mountain, though endued with immense energy, they were overcome with fatigue, yet they did not see Vaidehi, the beloved consort of Rama, anywhere. Having surveyed that hill with its innumerable ravines, as far as eye could see, the monkeys looking on every side, descended and, reaching the base, harassed and beside themselves, halted for an instant under a tree; then finding themselves less fatigued, they prepared to explore the southern region again.

Thereafter the chiefs of the monkeys, with Hanuman at their head, began to range the Vindhya hills once more.

CHAPTER 50

Hanuman and his Companions enter the Rikshabila Cavern

THE Monkey Hanuman, in company with the General Tara and Angada, once again explored the deep woods and ravines of the Vindhya range. Those monkeys searched the caverns which resounded with the roar of lions and tigers as well as the inaccessible and mighty torrents. Finally they came to the south-western summit of the mountain and, while they rested there, time passed.

That region is hard to explore on account of the vast extent of the forests and the dangerous ravines and caverns; nevertheless the Son of the Wind examined it all thoroughly. Separated from each other by a short distance, Gaja, Gavaksha, Gavaya, Sharabha, Gandhamadana, Mainda, Dvivida, Hanuman and Jambavan, the youthful Prince Angada and Tara, dwellers of the woods, began to search those regions in the south covered by the mountain range.

While they were exploring this place on every side, they observed the opening to a cave named Rikshabila, difficult of entry, guarded by a giant. Tortured with hunger and thirst and overcome with exhaustion they espied this cavity overgrown by trees, bushes and creepers, from which herons, swans, geese and waterfowl were issuing, dripping with water and covered with the pollen of lotuses.

Drawing near to that fragrant cave, difficult of access, those monkeys were struck with astonishment and desired to enter it. Then those foremost of monkeys, seeing signs of water, full of joy, approached that subterranean chamber abounding in every kind of creature, resembling the abode of Indra, which was impenetrable and fearful to behold.

And Hanuman, the son of the Wind-god, who resembled the peak of a mountain, said to those redoubtable monkeys, who dwelt in the woods and forests :—" We have explored the southern region covered with a chain of mountains ; we are exhausted with fatigue and unable to find Maithili. From yonder cave, swans, cranes, herons and waterfowl are emerging on every side, drenched with water. Without doubt there is a well or pool to be found there for these trees at the mouth of the cave are green."

Hanuman having spoken thus, all the monkeys entered into the dark cave, bereft of sun and moon, that caused their hair to stand on end. They heard the roar of lions and the sound of deer and birds and those invincible monkeys felt their courage and prowess fail; moving with the speed of the wind and despite the darkness, their sight being unimpaired, they penetrated deep into the cave and beheld a luminous, enchanting and marvellous region filled with different kinds of trees of varying fragrance. Pressing close to one another, they advanced four miles into the interior and fainting with fatigue, bewildered, seeking for water, they continued to descend into the darkness. Emaciated, their faces woe-begone, spent, despairing of their lives, those monkeys then beheld a light. Happily they approached that spot and saw trees glistening like gold, possessing the brilliance of fire, and they beheld Salas, Talas, Tamalas, Punnagas, Vanjulas, Dhavas, Champakas, Nagavrikshas and Karnikaras in full flower with clusters of golden blossom, crimson buds, twigs and creepers adorning them, dazzling as the dawn, their trunks being of emerald and their bark luminous. There were also lakes of blue lotus, abounding in waterfowl, there, and great golden trees encircled that place, that shone like the first light of dawn and fishes of gold and enormous lotuses were to be seen in pools of tranquil waters. Gold and silver palaces were to be found there with little windows of refined gold festooned with chains of pearls, the floors paved with silver and gold and encrusted with pearls and diamonds.

And the monkeys beheld splendid mansions everywhere and trees laden with fruit and flowers that shone like coral and precious gems and golden bees and honey in abundance. Couches and marvellous seats of immense size, decorated with gold and diamonds, drew their gaze, as well as gold and silver vessels, heaps of aloes and sandal, pure foods, fruits and roots, costly vehicles, delicious syrups, priceless raiment and great piles of woollen cloths and wonderful skins.

Whilst wandering here and there about that subterranean chamber, those courageous monkeys beheld a woman at a short distance from them. Attired in robes of bark and a black antelope skin, that ascetic, given to fasting, shone with a great effulgence.

Astonished, those monkeys halted suddenly and Hanuman addressed her saying :—" Who art thou ? To whom does this cavern belong ? "

Bowing down to that aged woman, Hanuman, who resembled a mountain, with joined palms, enquired of her: "Who art thou ? To whom does this retreat, this cave and its jewels belong ? "

CHAPTER 51

The Tale of the Ascetic

HAVING spoken thus to that blessed ascetic given to the practice of austerity, who was clad in bark and a black antelope skin, Hanuman added :—

" We entered this cave enveloped in darkness being wholly exhausted with hunger and thirst and overcome with fatigue ; having penetrated into the depths to seek for something to eat, we have become distracted on seeing all these marvels so that we have almost taken leave of our senses.

" To whom do these golden trees belong, that shine like the sun about to rise and these pure foods, roots and fruits ; these mansions of gold and silver with their windows of gold refined in the crucible and their network of pearls ? Who has produced these golden trees covered with marvellous flowers and fruit emitting a delicious fragrance, the golden lotuses that float on the pure waters, the golden fish and the turtles ? Are they sprung from thy power or do they owe their existence to another ? It behoves thee to tell us, who are ignorant in the matter."

Hearing the words of Hanuman, the virtuous ascetic, engaged in the welfare of all beings, replied to Hanuman saying :—" O Foremost of Monkeys, Maya is the name of the magician of great powers, by whom this entire golden grove has been constructed. He who created this enchanting and celestial place was formerly the chief architect of the Giants.[1] Having practised austerity for a thousand years in the vast forest, he obtained a boon from the Grandsire of the World, in virtue of which he attained complete mastery in his art, as well as an absolute control over the materials required therein. Having accomplished everything , that wonderful one, commanding every enjoyment, for a time lived happily in the mighty forest. Thereafter he conceived a great passion for the nymph Hema, whereupon Purandara hurled his thunderbolt at him and slew him.

[1] Danavas or Daityas.

"Then Brahma bestowed this marvellous forest with his golden mansion on Hema with the perpetual enjoyment of her desires. I, Swayamprabha by name, the daughter of Merusavarni, guard this dwelling belonging to Hema, who, skilled in the arts of dancing and singing, is my dear friend, O Foremost of Monkeys! By her favour, this vast forest has been given into my hands. Now tell me for what purpose and with what motive you have come hither? Why are you roaming in these inaccessible woods? Having partaken of these fruits and roots and drunk of the pure water, tell me all."

CHAPTER 52

Swayamprabha frees the Monkeys from the Cave

THAT virtuous ascetic, greatly mystified, addressed all those leaders of monkeys who were now rested, saying :—

"O Monkeys, if, satisfied by the fruits, your fatigue is alleviated, I would fain listen to your story if it is fit to be heard by me."

Hearing these words, Hanuman, the Son of Maruta began to relate all with perfect candour, saying: "The Sovereign of the whole world, Rama, who is equal to Mahendra and Varuna, the illustrious son of Dasaratha, retired to the Dandaka Forest in company with his brother Lakshmana and his consort Vaidehi. The latter was forcibly carried away by Ravana.

"His friend is that valiant monkey named Sugriva. By that monarch, the foremost of monkeys, we have been sent hither and with the assistance of those led by Angada, we have been dispatched to search the southern region inhabited by Agastya and protected by Yama. We have been commissioned to search for Sita, the daughter of Videha and the demon Ravana, who is able to change his form at will. Having scoured the forests and the seas of the south, overcome with hunger, we sat down at the foot of the trees. Our faces drained of colour, absorbed in thought, we were sunk in an ocean of anxiety which we were unable to cross.

"Casting our eyes round, we observed a huge cave hidden by trees and creepers and enveloped in gloom. Now swans, geese and osprey flew out from that cave their wings dripping with water, and I said to those monkeys, 'Let us enter there!' which all agreed to do. Anxious to accomplish our purpose, we went in grasping each others hands, thus forcing an entry into that dark cave; this is our purpose and the reason why we have come hither. Having come here, famished and exhausted, we, who were sorely tried by hunger, have been entertained on fruits and roots with the traditional hospitality. Thou hast saved us, who were weary and suffering from starvation; now say what service the monkeys may render thee in return?"

Thus addressed by the apes, the all-knowing Swayamprabha replied to those monkey leaders, saying: "I am well pleased with all these excellent monkeys; I am but fulfilling my duty and have no need of anything."

Thus answered in words filled with nobility and virtue, Hanuman addressed that irreproachable lady saying: "We have all found refuge with thee, O Virtuous Ascetic, but the time fixed by the magnanimous Sugriva has run out since we entered the cave, it behoves thee, therefore, to assist us to leave this place. If the commands of Sugriva be disregarded, it will mean death for us. Please deliver us all; the fear of Sugriva afflicts us. Great is the task that has been undertaken by us and if we remain here, that work of ours will not be accomplished."

Thus addressed by Hanuman, the ascetic answered him saying:—"For a living being to emerge from this cave alive, is hard, but by the power of my asceticism acquired through self control I shall deliver all the monkeys from this subterranean chamber. Do you all close your eyes, for none will succeed in issuing from this place if their eyes remain open."

Then, desirous of going out, all those magnanimous monkeys instantly closed their eyes covering them with their hands, possessed of slender fingers, and in the twinkling of an eye, the ascetic transported them outside the cave and having saved them from danger, in order to encourage them, said:—

"This is the auspicious Vindhya Mountain covered with trees and herbs, there the Prasravana Mountain and the great ocean. May good fortune attend you! I go to my abode, O Foremost of Monkeys."

With these words Swayamprabha re-entered the cave.

CHAPTER 53

Angada and his Companions consider what Course to take

THEN the monkeys beheld that awe-inspiring ocean, the abode of Varuna, shoreless, thunderous and abounding in huge billows.

Now the month fixed by the king as the term set for the search had passed while they were exploring that mountain fastness, the miraculous creation of Maya. Sitting down at the foot of the Vindhya Mountain amidst the blossoming trees, those high-souled monkeys anxiously began to reflect among themselves.

Perceiving the spring trees bending beneath the weight of flowers interlaced by hundreds of creepers, they were filled with apprehension. Recognizing the advent of spring and knowing the time appointed for their task had run out, each in turn sank to the ground.

Then that monkey having the shoulders of a lion, with plump and long arms, the youthful Prince Angada, endowed with wisdom, duly honouring the aged apes and other dwellers in the woods, spoke thus :—

" At the command of the monarch of the monkeys, we set out and, while we sojourned in the cave, a full month has passed away, O Monkeys. The month Ashvayuj[1] was the time fixed, which was not to be exceeded. This is known to you ! What should now be done ? Receiving the mandate from your master, you who are his trusted men, politic, devoted to his welfare, skilled in every work, incomparable in its execution and renowned in every quarter, have set out on this campaign with me as your appointed leader. Now, having failed to attain our objective, we shall certainly die, of this there is no shadow of doubt. Who, failing to execute the commands of the King of the Monkeys, can live at ease ? The time allotted by Sugriva has run out, all that remains is for us, the dwellers in the woods, to die fasting. Stern by nature, jealous of his authority, he will not forgive us if we return having transgressed his orders. He

[1] September–October.

will regard it as a crime if we come before him without news of Sita; it is therefore better to allow ourselves to die of hunger here than give up all hope of seeing our sons, wives, wealth and homes. It were preferable to die here than perish ignominously at the hands of Sugriva. Further, I was not installed as heir-apparent by Sugriva but by Rama, that king among men of immortal exploits. Entertaining enmity to me of old, the king, finding me at fault, will determine to take my life by cruel means. Of what use is it to meet death in the presence of my friends who will witness the last moments of my existence? I shall remain here on the sacred shore of the sea for the last supreme fast."

Hearing the words of the crown prince, all those monkeys, exclaimed in sympathy:—

" Sugriva is harsh by nature and Raghava is devoted to his tender spouse. The king, perceiving that the time has past without our having been successful in our undertaking and that we have not found Vaidehi, will certainly put us to death in order to do what is agreeable to Rama. Those who fail (to execute his commands) may not enter the presence of a king. Having come hither as the principal servants of Sugriva, we must either find Sita or obtain information concerning her or else we must enter the region of Yama, O Hero."

Hearing the monkeys speak thus in their terror, the General Tara said:—" Of what use is it to yield to despair? Let us re-enter the subterranean chamber and take up our abode there. That place abounding in flowers, food and water, which has been created by the power of illusion, is inaccessible. There we need not fear Purandara Himself or Raghava or the King of the Monkeys."

At these words to which Angada himself assented, all the monkeys with renewed confidence, cried:—" Without delay, let us from now on employ those means that will save us from death."

CHAPTER 54

Hanuman seeks to discourage Angada from his Design

WHEN the General Tara, who was as radiant as the moon, had spoken thus, Hanuman deemed that Angada had already usurped supreme authority. He knew the son of Bali to be endowed with the eightfold intelligence, the four powers and the fourteen qualities,[1] to be possessed of valour, energy and martial ardour, waxing in glory like the moon in the bright fortnight, the equal of Brihaspati in wisdom, in bravery resembling his sire and obedient to Tara's counsel as Purandara regards the instruction of Shukra.[2]

Thereupon, Hanuman, versed in all branches of learning, resolved to win over Angada, who had become lax in the service of his sovereign and bring him back to the right path. Reflecting on the four means for bringing about peace, he chose the second, that of sowing dissension amongst the monkeys by subtle suggestion ; when the disaffection was general, he sought to instil fear in Angada's heart, by harsh words uttered in severe tones :—

He said :—" O Son of Bali, surely thou art a warrior more skilful even than thy sire and art able to govern the monkey kingdom as well as he, but, O Foremost of Monkeys, the apes were ever fickle by nature. Bereft of their wives and sons, they will never suffer thy rule. This I declare to thee in the presence

[1] Eightfold Intelligence—The quality of accepting the truth and what is right, cherishing it, remembering it, propagating it. Knowledge of the positive and negative side of a matter. Knowledge of the ultimate essence.

Four Powers—Physical power, mental power, power of resource, power of making friends.

Fourteen Qualities—Knowledge of Time and Place. Endurance. Empirical knowledge. Skill. Physical strength. Power to conceal one's counsel. The honouring of one's obligations and promises. Heroism. Appreciation of the enemy's strength and one's own in relation to it. Gratitude. Beneficence to one's dependents or suppliants. Non-acceptance of insult. Freedom from uncontrolled movements. Poise.

[2] Shukra—Indra's spiritual preceptor.

of all! Neither by conciliation, gifts nor penalties shalt thou succeed in drawing Jambavan, Nila, the mighty ape, Suhotra, or myself to thy side. One who is strong can overcome the weak and usurp his place, therefore, he who is weak should, for his own safety, never incur the enmity of the strong. This cave, that thou deemest to be a safe refuge and which is said to be impregnable, can easily be penetrated by Lakshmana with his arrows. Formerly this tiny rift was made by Indra hurling his thunderbolt against it, but Lakshmana will pierce it like a leaf by means of his keen arrows. He possesses innumerable arrows of this kind, whose impact resembles lightning, capable of shattering the mountains themselves.

" O Scourge of Thy Foes, as soon as thou dost install thyself in that place, the monkeys, remembering their wives and sons, will decide to forsake thee. Pining for domestic happiness, ever restless, anxious and weary of their pitiable plight, they will abandon thee. Thereafter, bereft of friends, relatives and those who seek thy welfare, even the trembling of a blade of grass will fill thee with terror.

" Lakshmana's arrows, irresistible in flight, keen, formidable and of exceeding velocity, will transfix thee where thou hast sought to conceal thyself.

" If, however, assuming a humble guise, thou, with us, dost present thyself before Sugriva, he will establish thee in the kingdom and restore thee as rightful heir. A virtuous monarch, firm in his vows, honorable and loyal, he desires thy welfare and will assuredly not kill thee. Thy paternal uncle is devoted to thy mother and wishes to do what is agreeable to her, this is the purpose of his life and she has no other son, therefore, O Angada, return with us."

CHAPTER 55

The Monkeys decide to die of Hunger

HEARING Hanuman's speech uttered with humility, filled with wisdom and justice and reflecting honour on Sugriva, Angada answered him saying :—

" Stability, purity of mind and disposition, compassion, rectitude, daring and perseverance are unknown to Sugriva. He who, while her son was living, united himself to the beloved queen of his elder brother, on whom he should rightfully have looked as a mother, is to be condemned. What does he know of morality who, while his brother was in the grip of an Asura, closed up the opening of the cave ? What gratitude will he manifest who, having clasped his hand in friendship, forgot the favours received from his great benefactor, Raghava, of imperishable deeds ? Where is righteousness in one who directed us to search for Sita here, not from fear of disloyalty but of Lakshmana ? Who would trust that fickle, impious and ungrateful wretch, more especially those sprung from his own race ? Whether he be possessed of good qualities or no, having established me in the kingdom, will he suffer the son of his enemy to live ? How can I, whose counsels have been disclosed, who have been found guilty, who am powerless, poor and weak, expect to survive if I repair to Kishkindha ? In his desire to retain the throne, Sugriva, who is wily, cunning and cruel, will assuredly place me in chains. For me death through fasting is preferable to being tortured and confined. Let all the monkeys abandon me here and return home. I vow I shall never reenter the city but shall stay here and fast to the end ; death is better for me.

" Bowing to the king and also to the mighty Raghava, enquire after their welfare for me and bring news of my health and state to my adopted mother Ruma. To Tara, my real mother, offer consolation, for she is compassionate and pious and naturally full of love for her son. When she learns of my death, she will certainly yield up her life."

Having said this, Angada, making obeisance to the elders, his countenance woe-begone, weeping, spreading out some kusha grass sat down on the ground ; as he sat there, those foremost of monkeys groaned, burning tears falling from their eyes. Thereupon surrounding Angada, condemning Sugriva and praising Bali, those monkeys resolved to starve themselves to death and, seating themselves on the seashore on heaps of darbha grass, pointing towards the south, those excellent monkeys sipping water, facing the east, resolved to die, saying :—"This is better for us ! "

As they spoke of the exile of Rama, the death of Dasaratha, the carnage in Janasthana, the slaying of Jatayu, the abduction of Vaidehi, the killing of Bali and the wrath of Raghava, those monkeys were filled with fear ; and while those innumerable monkeys, resembling the peaks of mountains sat there, the whole region with its torrents and caverns resounded with their lamentations like the roll of thunder in the skies.

CHAPTER 56

The Intervention of Sampati

WHILE the monkeys remained seated on the mountain plateau resolved on their last great fast, the King of the Vultures by chance came to that place. That long-lived bird, the fortunate brother of Jatayu, was renowned for his strength and prowess.

Issuing from a cave on the mighty Vindhya Mountain, he observed the monkeys seated there and, highly gratified, said:— " Every man reapeth the fruit of his former acts, on account of this, after a long time, this food comes to me. I shall eat up these monkeys one by one as they die."

Eyeing those apes, the Vulture expressed himself thus, and hearing the utterance of that famished bird, Angada, full of apprehension, addressed Hanuman in faint accents, saying :—

" Behold, on account of Sita, Death, the descendant of Vivasvat, has come to this place to destroy the monkeys. Rama's purpose not having been effected nor the mandate of the king obeyed, this calamity has overtaken the monkeys unaware. Thou art conversant in detail with all that Jatayu, that Prince of Vultures did for the sake of Sita. All beings, even those born of the mating of beasts, desire to please Rama at the cost of their lives as we have done. On account of Rama's love and compassion, people bear each other affection and pity. The blessed Jatayu voluntarily laid down his life for the good of Rama; we too, exhausted and about to die, came to this forest to render a service to the Son of Raghu. We have searched the woods in vain for Maithili. Happy is that Prince of Vultures who was slain in combat by Ravana for he is freed from the fear of Sugriva and has attained the supreme abode. The death of Jatayu and King Dasaratha and the abduction of Sita has placed the monkeys in jeopardy. The sojourn of Rama and Lakshmana in the forest with Sita, Raghava's slaying of Bali with an arrow, the slaughter of innumerable demons by Rama in his wrath, all owe their origin to those boons granted to Kaikeyi."

Hearing these piteous words and seeing the monkeys stretched on the ground the magnanimous King of the Vultures was deeply moved and that sharp beaked bird cried out:—

"Who is it who, causing my heart to tremble, speaks thus of the death of my brother, dearer to me than life itself? How did the demon and the vulture come to fight in Janasthana? It is after a long time that I hear the name of my brother spoken. I wish to descend from this lofty mountain height. I am well pleased to hear of my youthful and valiant brother, renowned for his exploits. I wish to learn of the death of my brother, Jatayu, O Foremost of Monkeys, and how King Dasaratha, whose elder son is Rama, beloved of his elders, came to be his friend? I am unable to fly in consequence of my wings having been scorched by the rays of the sun. Assist me to descend from this mountain, O Conquerers of your Foes!"

CHAPTER 57

Angada's Narrative

THOUGH the voice of Sampati faltered on account of grief, the Chiefs of the Monkeys did not trust him, doubting his intentions.

Seated for the purpose of fasting to death, the monkeys, seeing that vulture, framed the following resolution, saying :—

" Let us help him to descend and he will then devour us all ; should he do so, while we are seated here fasting, we shall have achieved our purpose and shall speedily attain success."

Having thus resolved, they assisted the vulture to descend from the summit of the mountain and Angada addressed him saying :—

" There was a great King of the Monkeys named Riksharajas, the founder of our race ; he was my grandsire, O Bird. He had two virtuous sons, Bali and Sugriva, both were exceedingly powerful. My father Bali, was famed throughout the world for his exploits.

" Now it happened that the Sovereign of the whole earth, the descendant of Ikshwaku, the great and illustrious car warrior, Rama, the son of King Dasaratha, obedient to the injunctions of his sire, fixed in the path of righteousness, entered the forest of Dandaka with his brother Lakshmana and his consort Vaidehi. His spouse was forcibly borne away from Janasthana by Ravana and the friend of Rama's father, the Prince of Vultures, Jatayu, observed Sita, Videha's daughter, being carried through the air. Having shattered Ravana's chariot and released Maithili, that vulture being old and exhausted finally fell under Ravana's blows. Slain by the powerful Ravana, he had his funeral rites performed by Rama himself and attained the celestial abode. Then Raghava allied himself with my paternal uncle, Sugriva, and slew my sire, who had banished him from the kingdom with his ministers.

" Having killed Bali, Rama installed Sugriva as Lord and Monarch of all the Monkeys. We have been sent by him in all directions under Rama's orders to search for Sita but we have not found Vaidehi, as by night one is unable to perceive the splendour of the sun. Having explored the Dandaka Forest, we, through ignorance, penetrated into a cave through a rift in the earth. That cavern was constructed by the illusive power of Maya and there we passed the month fixed by the King of the Monkeys, as the term appointed; while executing the commands of Sugriva, we exceeded the time fixed and from fear have seated ourselves here, resolved to die of hunger, for, if we return to face the wrath of Kakutstha, Sugriva and Lakshmana, we shall surely be put to death!"

CHAPTER 58

Sampati tells the monkeys of Sita's Place of Concealment

HEARING the pitiful narrative of the monkeys, who had resolved to give up their lives, the vulture in mournful accents, with tears in his eyes, answered them saying:—

"O Monkeys, you have told me, that Jatayu, my younger brother, was slain in combat by Ravana, who was his superior in strength. Old and bereft of my wings, I can only resign myself to these tidings for I no longer have the power to avenge my brother's death.

"Formerly, when Indra slew the demon Vritra, my brother and I, wishing to prove which of us was superior, soared into the sky, drawing nearer and nearer to the sun with its aureole of rays. Flinging ourselves into the currents of air, we rose rapidly higher and higher, but the sun having reached its zenith, Jatayu grew faint. Seeing my brother tormented by the sun's rays, I covered him affectionately with my wings, for he was suffering greatly, whereupon they were scorched and I fell on the Vindhya Mountain, O Foremost of Monkeys, where I remained, not knowing what had befallen him."

Thus addressed by Sampati, Jatayu's brother, the eminently sagacious Prince Angada answered:—"If thou art indeed the brother of Jatayu and hast heard what I have related, then tell us, dost thou know aught of that titan's abode ? Say, if thou knowest, whether the retreat of that short-sighted, vilest of demons, Ravana, is near or far away ? "

Then the illustrious elder brother of Jatayu answered in words worthy of him, causing delight to the monkeys, and said : " O Monkeys, my pinions being burnt, I am a vulture bereft of strength, yet by my words alone, I shall render Rama a signal service.

" I know the realm of Varuna and those covered by Vishnu's three strides. I am also conversant with the wars between the Gods and Asuras and the churning of the ocean, from whence the Amrita issued. Though age has deprived me of strength and my vitality is ebbing away, this mission of Rama's must be my first concern.

" I saw a young and lovely woman, beautifully attired, being carried off by the wicked Ravana and that beautiful creature was crying out ' O Rama ', ' O Rama ', ' O Lakshmana '. Tearing off her ornaments she cast them on the earth ; her silken cloak, resembling the rays of the sun striking on a mountain summit, shone against the dark skin of the demon like a lightning flash irradiating a cloudy sky. Since she was calling ' Rama ', ' Rama ' I believe her to have been Sita. Now hear me, and I will tell you where the abode of that demon is to be found.

" The son of Vishravas and brother of Kuvera, that demon, named Ravana, resides in the city of Lanka, constructed by Vishwakarma, which lies a full hundred yojanas from here on an island in the sea, furnished with golden gateways and ramparts of Kancana gold, with lofty palaces gleaming with Hema gold adorning it. A great wall, bright as the sun, encircles it, and it is there that the unfortunate Vaidehi, attired in a silken cloth, is confined in Ravana's inner apartments, carefully guarded by demon women. It is there you will find Sita.

" Four hundred miles from here on the southern shore of the sea dwells Ravana. O Monkeys, hie thither speedily and demonstrate your valour ! By supernatural means, I know that having seen that place you will return. The first course is the path taken by the fork-tailed shrikes and others living on grain ; the second by those who live on insects and fruit ; the third by cocks; the fourth by herons, hawks and birds of prey; the fifth by vultures; the sixth by swans endowed with strength, energy, youth and beauty and the last by eagles; we have all derived our origin from Vainateya,[1] O Foremost of Monkeys. I shall avenge that execrable deed of that eater of flesh (Ravana) as also his cruelty to my brother.[2]

"Resting here, I am able to see Ravana and Janaki, for we all possess the supersensual sight of Suparna.[3] It is by virtue of our nature and on account of the food we eat, that we can see clearly to a distance of four hundred miles. We are instinctively drawn to search for our food at a distance, whilst other birds scratch it up with their claws at the foot of the trees where they roost, their sight being limited.

"Do ye look about for a means to cross over the salty waves; having found Vaidehi, return, your purpose accomplished. Now I desire to be taken by you to the shore of the sea, the abode of Varuna; I will there perform the water ritual for the spirit of my high-souled brother, who has gone to the celestial abode."

At those words those mighty monkeys carried Sampati, whose wings had been burnt, to the shore of the ocean, after which they brought back that King of the Birds to the Vindhya Mountain; and, having received the information concerning Sita, they experienced great joy.

CHAPTER 59

He encourages them to pursue their Quest

HEARING these words, sweet as nectar, uttered by the Vulture King, the monkey chiefs were filled with relief.

Then Jambavan, the foremost among the apes, with all the monkeys, rising from the ground, said to the Vulture King:—"Where is Sita? Who has seen her? Who has carried away Mithila's daughter? Do thou tell us all this and thus be the

[1] Vainateya—The Eagle Garuda, said to be Vishnu's messenger and vehicle.

[2] Implying by sending the monkeys he would be avenged on Ravana.

[3] Suparna—another name for Vainateya or Garuda.

means of saving the dwellers in the woods. Who is able to forget the power of the arrows of Dasaratha that fly with the speed of lightning and those that are loosed by Lakshmana?"

Then Sampati, once again consoling those monkeys who had risen from their fasting and who were all attention to what was being related concerning Sita, well pleased, said to them:—

"Hear how I came to learn of Sita's abduction at this place and who it was that told me where that large-eyed lady could be found! It is a long time since I fell on to this inaccessible mountain, many miles in extent. Now I am old and feeble in life and limb; in this condition my son, named Suparshwa, the best of birds, brought me food regularly. If the Gandharvas are extremely pleasure loving and the serpent race prone to anger and the deer exceedingly timid, we, in our turn, are voracious.

"One day, tormented with hunger, I demanded food and my son flew off at sunrise to procure it, but returned at night without any flesh. He, the increaser of my delight, had grown tired of searching for nourishment and in order to propitiate me said in all sincerity:—

"'My dear father, wishing to bring thee thine accustomed portion, I flew into the air and stationed myself near the approach of the Mahendra Mountain in order to obstruct the passage of thousands of creatures who range the sea. There I was, looking down, guarding the pass, when suddenly I observed someone resembling a mass of collyrium, carrying a woman as beautiful as the dawn. Seeing them, I resolved to seize them for my prey, but he humbly implored me in peaceful accents to let him pass. None on earth, not even the wicked, devour the peaceful willingly, how much less a creature like myself! He passed on quickly, pushing away the air, as it were, with his energy. Thereafter, those beings that inhabit space approached me and paid obeisance to me and the great Rishis said to me:—

"'"By good fortune Sita still lives! It is well for thee that he has passed by thee with this woman."

"'Then the glorious Siddhas addressed me and informed me that it was Ravana, the King of the Demons, whom I had seen with the consort of Rama, the son of Dasaratha, the daughter of Janaka, who, her silken attire torn, overcome with an excess of grief, her hair falling about her, was calling the names of " Rama " and " Lakshmana ". Thus, O My Father, is how the time has passed.'

" All this did Suparshwa tell me, and even on hearing it I did not consider exerting my strength, for without wings, how can a bird undertake anything? But hear how I can help you with my word and knowledge, so that you can manifest your prowess! By my speech and my experience I will do what is agreeable to you. I shall make the concern of the son of Dasaratha my concern, do not doubt it. Possessed as you are of intelligence, energy and wisdom, incapable of being overcome even by the Gods, you have been sent here by the King of the Monkeys. The arrows of Rama and Lakshmana furnished with heron plumes are able to destroy the Three Worlds. Although the ten-necked Ravana is endowed with strength and energy, yet assuredly none can resist your united efforts! There is no need for further delay. Now accomplish your purpose. The wise, such as you, are not dilatory in their undertakings."

CHAPTER 60

The Story of the Ascetic Nishakara

WHEN the vulture had offered oblations of water for the spirit of his brother and performed his ablutions, the monkey chiefs sat down on that marvellous mountain, placing him in their midst.

Then Sampati, in order to reassure them, said cheerfully to Angada, who was seated surrounded by all the monkeys who escorted him :—" Listen to me with attention and in silence, O Monkeys, and I will tell you truly how I came to know of Maithili.

" A long time ago, I fell on the summit of the Vindhya Mountain, O Irreproachable Prince, my wings scorched by the heat of the sun, which consumed them with its rays. On regaining consciousness at the end of six days, faint and bereft of strength, looking round, I was unable to distinguish anything. Nevertheless on scanning the lakes, rocks, rivers, ponds, woods and countries, my memory returned and I reflected, 'This mountain filled with cheerful birds, containing deep caves and innumerable ridges is certainly the Vindhya Peak on the shores of the southern sea.'

" Here lay a sacred hermitage revered by the Gods themselves, where a Sage named Nishakara, of severe austerities, dwelt; since that time, that saint conversant with virtue has ascended to heaven.

" I passed eight thousand years on this mountain. Then not having seen that ascetic, crawling slowly and painfully down from that high peak to the ground covered with sharp pointed grass, eager to see that sage, I rejoined him with great difficulty. Formerly Jatayu and I visited that sage many times.

" In that neighbourhood, soft and fragrant breezes blew and there was no tree without flowers or fruit. Approaching that sacred hermitage, desirous of seeing the blessed Nishakara, I waited at the foot of a tree. Then, at a distance, I beheld that Rishi, blazing with effulgence, who, having performed his ablutions, was returning towards the north.

" As all living beings surround a giver, so was he surrounded by bears, srimaras, tigers, lions and snakes of various kinds. And when they observed that the saint had entered his hermitage, they all went away, as when a king retires, the ministers who have escorted him withdraw.

" The Sage, on seeing me, was pleased, and retiring into his hermitage for a while, came out again and enquired as to my welfare. He said :—' O My Friend, on account of thy discoloured plumes, I am unable to recognize thee ; thy two wings have been scorched by fire and thy frail frame is shaken by gasps. In former times, I knew two vultures resembling the wind in speed, who were brothers, able to change their shape at will. Thou art, I know, the elder, Sampati, and Jatayu is thy younger brother. Both assuming human shape were wont to massage my feet with their hands.

" ' By what disease hast thou been afflicted ? From whence comes the loss of thy wings ? Who has inflicted this punishment on thee ? Do thou tell me all ! ' "

CHAPTER 61

Sampati tells his Story to the Sage Nishakara

THEREUPON Sampati related to the ascetic the whole of his fearful, arduous and rash act of flying towards the sun :—

" O Blessed One, the wounds I have received, the shame I feel and the exhaustion I experience, all prevent me from entering into a lengthy narrative.

" From pride in our power of flight, Jatayu and I, in order to test each other's powers, vowing in the presence of the sages on Mt. Kailasha that we would follow the sun till it set behind the Astachala Mountain, flew into the sky. Reaching a great height together, we looked down on the earth with its various cities that appeared like chariot wheels. Sometimes the sound of musical instruments reached us, at others the tinkling of ornaments. In certain places we saw many damsels clad in red who were singing.

" Passing rapidly through the air, we followed the path of the sun and observed a forest intersected with green rides ; the mountains appeared like pebbles and the rivers like threads binding the earth ; Himavat, Vindhya and that mighty mountain, Meru resembled elephants standing in a pond.

" Nevertheless we were perspiring freely and were filled with anxiety and extremely fatigued, no longer being able, in our bewilderment, to distinguish between the south, west or the quarter presided over by Fire ; the earth seemed to us to have been consumed by flames, as at the end of the world period. My mind and my eyes failing, with a violent effort I fixed them on the sun and with great difficulty succeeded in doing so. The blazing orb seemed to us much larger than the earth in extent, and at that instant, Jatayu, without speaking to me, began to fall. Seeing this, I flew down from the sky and covered him with my wings, in consequence of which my brother was not burnt, but I, in my arrogance was scorched and thrown out of the wind's course. I surmised that Jatayu had fallen in

Janasthana, but my wings scathed, deprived of strength, I fell on the Vindhya Mountain.

" Bereft of my dominion, my brother, my wings and my power, I now long to hurl myself headlong from the summit of this mountain and put an end to my existence."

CHAPTER 62

Sampati learns where Sita is from the Sage Nishakara

" HAVING spoken thus to that foremost of Sages, in my distress, I began to weep, and that blessed One, reflecting for a while, said to me :—

" ' Thy two wings with their feathers will grow again and thou wilt recover thy sight, thine energy and thy prowess. Having learnt it from the Puranas and foreseen it by mine ascetic power, I know that a great event is about to take place.

" ' It concerns a certain king, named Dasaratha of the race of Ikshwaku, to whom a son, full of valour, will be born by the name of Rama. He will repair to the forest with his brother Lakshmana, having been constrained to do so by his sire.

" ' The son of Nairriti, Ravana, the King of the Titans, incapable of being slain by Gods or Danavas, will bear off his consort from the forest of Janasthana. And, albeit tempted by delicious viands and objects of enjoyment and desire, that noble and illustrious one, overcome by grief, will not partake of them. Then Vasava learning of this will offer her ' payasa ' resembling ambrosia that the Gods themselves only obtain with difficulty. Receiving this food, Maithili, knowing it to come from Indra, will offer part of it to Rama, by pouring it on the ground, saying :—' Whether my husband or his younger brother still live or have attained the celestial state, may this food be acceptable to them.'

" ' Rama's envoys having been sent hither, it will be for thee to inform them of the facts relating to Sita, O Airy Traveller ! Do not go hence for any reason, but whither canst thou go in this condition ? Wait for the time and place ; thou shalt recover thy wings. I am able this very day to furnish thee with wings but by waiting here thou canst render a service to the worlds. Even so, thou shalt be doing thy duty to the two princes, the brahmins, thy spiritual preceptors, the sages and Indra. I also am desirous of beholding the two brothers, Rama and Lakshmana, after which I shall yield up my life.'

"Thus did that great Rishi, conversant with the nature of all things, speak to me."

CHAPTER 63

The Wings of Sampati grow once more

"HAVING consoled me with these words and many others, the eloquent ascetic took leave of me and re-entered his hermitage. Thereafter I crawled slowly out of the cave and scaled the Vindhya Mountain to wait for you. Since that time, a whole century has passed, and, keeping the words of that hermit in my heart, I await the time and place.

"Nishakara has ascended to heaven and I, distracted by many thoughts, have been consumed with grief. When the idea of death comes to me, I put it away, remembering the words of the Sage. The determination he inspired in me to preserve my life dissolves my distress, as a flame in a lit brazier dispels the darkness.

"Though fully conversant with the power of the evil-hearted Ravana, yet I approached my son saying:—'Hearing her lamentations and knowing these two princes to be deprived of her, how is it that thou didst not free Sita?' In my affection for King Dasaratha I was displeased with my son."

As Sampati was speaking thus to the monkeys, his wings suddenly began to grow again in the presence of those dwellers in the woods. Thereupon seeing his body covered with tawny feathers, he experienced an immense joy and said to those monkeys:—"By the grace of Nishakara, that Sage of immeasurable power, my wings, that had been scorched by the sun's rays, have grown again and the prowess I possessed in my youth has returned. To-day I have regained my strength and vigour. Do you spare no effort to find Sita; the recovery of my wings is a pledge of your success."

Having spoken thus to the monkeys, Sampati, the foremost of birds, anxious to ascertain his powers of flight, flew up to the mountain top. Hearing his words, those mighty monkeys were delighted and confident of their success, prepared to demonstrate their valour.

With the speed of the wind those foremost of monkeys, intent upon finding Sita, the daughter of Janaka, set out towards the south to the quarter dominated by Abhijit.[1]

CHAPTER 64

The Monkeys are disconcerted at the sight of the Ocean

THUS informed by the King of the Vultures, the monkeys, endowed with the strength of lions, began to leap about, emitting cries of delight.

Hearing from Sampati that Ravana would be slain, the happy monkeys reached the sea, anxious to discover Sita. And coming to that place, those redoubtable warriors beheld the ocean, the mirror of the whole world.

Arriving at the northern side of the southern sea, those exceedingly powerful and heroic monkeys halted there. And seeing the ocean which at times appeared to be asleep, at others playful, sometimes covered with huge waves and thronged with aquatic animals, causing their hair to stand on end, those foremost of monkeys were amazed and became despondent. Beholding that ocean incapable of being traversed, even as the sky itself, the monkeys began to lament, crying: "What is now to be done?"

Then the foremost of the monkeys, the mighty Angada, seeing the despair of the army at the sight of the sea, began to reassure those warriors afflicted with terror, saying:—

"One should never give way to agitation, of all things it is

[1] Abhijit—the name of a constellation. Some Commentators translate it as meaning "he who is to be conquered" implying the region in which Ravana was to be found.

the most fatal: agitation destroys a man even as a provoked serpent doth a child. He who, when the time is ripe for displaying his valour, becomes agitated, will grow weak and fail to attain his object."

The night having passed, Angada took counsel with the older monkeys, and that monkey host surrounding him resembled the hosts of the Maruts surrounding Vasava. Who, save Bali's son or Hanuman was capable of maintaining discipline amongst those troops?

Having called the elders together in company with the army, the fortunate Angada, the subduer of his foes, saluting them, spoke words fraught with good sense, saying:—

"Who amongst you is of sufficient stature to cross the ocean? Who is able to carry out the commands of Sugriva, the conqueror of his foes? Which valiant monkey can leap the four hundred miles and deliver the leaders of the monkeys from their great anxiety? By whose favour shall we, crowned with success and content, return and behold our wives, our sons and our homes? Who will enable us to meet Rama, the mighty Lakshmana and that dweller in the woods, Sugriva, with a light heart? If there be any monkey capable of leaping over the ocean, then may he show his blessed form to us and deliver us from fear!'

Hearing Angada's speech, no one uttered a word and the entire monkey host appeared stunned. Then that foremost of monkeys once more addressed them saying:—

"O Ye Excellent Warriors, of tried valour, unimpeachable family and worthy of honour, say how far each of you is able to leap over the sea without any being able to hinder you!"

CHAPTER 65

The Leaders of the Monkeys each state what they are able to accomplish

HAVING listened to Angada's words, those Chiefs of Monkeys, each in turn, began to dilate on what he was able to accomplish—Gaya, Gavaksha, Gavaya, Sharabha, Gandhamadana, Mainda,

Dvivida and Angada as also Jambavan. Gaya speaking first, said :—

" I can leap a hundred miles ! " and Gavaksha said :—" I can leap two hundred ! " Then the monkey Sharabha said to his companions :—" I am able to leap three hundred miles, O Monkeys ! " thereafter Rishabha said, " I can undoubtedly cross over four hundred miles ! " and the mighty Gandhamadana said " I can leap five hundred miles ! " In his turn the monkey, Mainda, said " And I, six hundred miles " and the illustrious Dvivida " Without difficulty I can leap over seven hundred miles ! " Then Sushena, full of energy, the best of monkeys said, " I declare that I can leap eight hundred miles ! "

And as they were speaking thus, the oldest of them, Jambavan, offering salutations to them all, spoke in this wise:—" Formerly I, also, had the power of motion but now I am advanced in years. Nevertheless in the present situation, nothing should be overlooked to assure the success of both Rama's and the King of Monkeys' mission : I shall therefore leap three hundred miles. There is no doubt whatever about this." Then Jambavan, addressing all those monkeys, added : " Alas ! I have assuredly not the strength for that ! Of old, I circumambulated the eternal Vishnu when he covered the world in three strides at the sacrifice of Virochana's son ; now, however, I am old and tire quickly. When I was young, my energy was great and unmatched ; to-day, I can only go as far as I have told you, which is not sufficient to bring success to our undertaking."

Thereupon the sagacious Angada, bowing to that mighty monkey, addressed him in pregnant words, saying : " I am able to leap these four hundred miles easily but should I be able to return ? Nothing is certain ! "

Thereat Jambavan answered that excellent monkey and said : " O Foremost of Monkeys, thy power of motion is well known, but art thou able to cross over eight hundred miles ?[1] It is not fitting that thou shouldst do so. My Dear Son, the master must in no way be commanded by his servants ; it is for thee to order this expedition. Thou art our leader and our only good. The head of the army is, as it were, the wife, who should constantly be protected ; this is thy rôle, O Dear Child. One

[1] That is, there and back.

should take care of the root of a thing, this is the practice of men of experience; the root being sound, the juices that have for their purpose the maturing of the fruit will be safeguarded. Thou art the essential part of this undertaking and, O Subduer of Thy Foes, thou, furnished with wisdom and valour, art the principle underlying it. Thou art our superior and the son of our superior, O Excellent One; with thy support we shall be able to accomplish our mission."

Thus, in his great wisdom, Jambavan spoke and that mighty monkey born of Bali, Angada, answered him saying:—

"If I do not go nor any among these powerful monkeys does so, then undoubtedly we must begin our supreme fast once more, for if we return without having fulfilled the commands of that lord of the monkeys, then I do not see how we can hope to preserve our lives. Whether he show clemency or wrath, he is the chief of the monkeys and to disregard his will means death. In this matter no other alternative is possible; therefore it is for you who are able to see clearly to reflect upon it."

Thus spoke Angada and that powerful and heroic monkey, Jambavan, answered him in felicitous words saying:—

"O Warrior, this mission will be carried out without obstruction! I will call on the one who is able to accomplish it."

Thereupon that heroic monkey sent for the foremost of the apes, Hanuman, who was sitting tranquilly apart.

CHAPTER 66

Jambavan appeals to Hanuman to sacrifice himself for the good of all

PERCEIVING the discouragement of that great army composed of hundreds and thousands of monkeys, Jambavan said to Hanuman:—

"O Warrior, foremost among the multitude, thou who art versed in the scriptures, why art thou sitting apart, silent? In courage and strength, thou art the equal of Rama and Lakshmana and of the King of the Monkeys himself, O Hanuman!

" Arishtanemi's[1] son, the mighty Vainateya, the illustrious Garuda is the foremost of all winged creatures. Many a time I have seen that all-powerful bird of immense wings and exceeding energy bearing away serpents from the ocean ; the strength that is in his wings resembles the might and vigour of thine arms; none can withstand thee. Thine energy, intelligence, courage and loyalty sets thee apart from the rest of beings, therefore prepare thyself to cross the ocean.

" The most noble of all the Apsaras, Punjika-Thala, under the name of Anjana, became the wife of the monkey Kesarin. She was renowned in the three worlds and her beauty was unequalled on earth. As a result of a curse, O Friend, she was born in the monkey race, able to change her form at will.

" Once that daughter of the king among the monkeys, Kunjara, having assumed the form of a woman radiant with youth and beauty, adorned with garlands of various kinds, clad in silk, was wandering about on the summit of a mountain, which resembled a mass of clouds in the rainy season.

" And it happened that the God of the Wind stole away the red-bordered yellow robe of that large-eyed maiden, who stood on the mountain top. Then Maruta perceived her rounded, well-proportioned thighs and her breasts touching each other and her amiable and pleasing mien. Beholding that youthful woman of lovely limbs and slender waist, her whole being radiant with beauty, he was filled with desire and beside himself, enveloping that irreproachable lady in his arms, Manmatha embraced her.

" In her distress, Anjana, faithful to her conjugal vows, cried out :—' Who desires to sever the ties of a woman devoted to her lord ? ' Hearing these words, the Wind-God answered, ' I do not wish to wrong thee, O Lady of Lovely Hips, let not thy heart be troubled. By embracing thee and entering into thee thou shalt bear a son endowed with strength and intelligence, of immense energy, of noble nature, possessed of vigour and courage and in agility and speed equal to myself.'

" These words pleased thy mother and she gave birth to thee in a cave, O Foremost of Monkeys.

[1] Arishtanemi—A name of Garuda meaning " the felly of whose wheel is unscathed ".

"While still a child, thou didst see the sun rise over the great forest and taking it to be a fruit sought to seize it. Bounding into the air, thou didst mount up for a thousand yojanas, O Great Monkey and, though the burning rays of the sun beat upon thee, thou didst not falter. Seeing thee rushing through space, Indra, full of wrath, hurled this thunderbolt at thee, whereupon, falling, thou didst fracture thy left jaw on the point of a rock from which arises thy name, Hanuman.[1] Observing thee in this state, Vayu the Destroyer, the Bearer of Fragrance,[2] in the height of anger, ceased to blow throughout the Three Worlds.

"Then all the Gods were distressed on account of the calamity that has befallen the worlds and these Lords of the Universe sought to pacify the wrathful Wind-god, whereupon Pavana being placated, Brahma accorded thee the boon of invulnerability in combat. Seeing how thou didst sustain the impact of the thunderbolt, that God of a Thousand Eyes was pleased with thee and also conferred an excellent boon on thee, saying:—'Thou shalt not die till thou desireth to do so! Thou, endowed with extreme vigour, the son of Kesarin, resembling the Wind God in energy, art born of his loins and equal to him in speed'. O Friend, we are lost, but thou, possessed of skill and courage, art in our midst a second Lord of the Monkeys.

"In the time when Vishnu covered the world with three strides, I, O Child, circumambulated the earth with its mountains, forests and woods, one and twenty times. Then commissioned by the Gods, we gathered all the herbs which (when cast into the sea) produced the nectar of immortality and at that time our strength was great. Now I am old and my prowess has deserted me, but thou, endowed with every virtue art amongst us. Employ thy valour, O Hero, for thou are most fitted to do so. Bestir thyself and cross the vast ocean, O Redoubtable Monkey; the entire monkey host is eager to behold thy prowess. Arise and leap over the mighty sea, for thou surpasseth all beings in motion. Canst thou remain indifferent to the despair of all the monkeys? Put forth thy strength, as did Vishnu when traversing the Three Worlds with three strides, O Lion among Monkeys!"

[1] Hanuman—"He of the fractured jaw".

[2] The Wind-god.

Thus exhorted by the foremost of monkeys, Hanuman, renowned for his great might, the son of the Wind, assumed a form preparatory to crossing the sea that gladdened the hearts of those monkeys.

CHAPTER 67

Hanuman prepares to go to Lanka

SEEING that extremely agile leader of monkeys stretching himself in preparation for crossing the four hundred miles of sea, the monkeys, renouncing all despondency, were filled with delight and began to shout and praise the heroism of Hanuman.

And, struck with amazement, beings from every sphere rejoiced unitedly, even as when they beheld the Lord Himself displaying his powers, when taking the three strides.

Thus acclaimed, the mighty Hanuman expanded in size and waved his tail in pleasure, demonstrating his strength. Applauded by the older monkeys and filled with energy, he assumed an unparalleled shape, like a lion that stretches himself at the mouth of a rocky cavern, and that Son of Maruta began to yawn and the mouth of that intelligent monkey resembled a blazing brazier or a smokeless fire.

Rising in the midst of those monkeys, his hair standing on end for joy, he paid obeisance to the older leaders and said to them :—

" I am the son of him who shatters the mountain peaks and is the friend of fire, the mighty and incommensurable Vayu, who circulates in space, Maruta, of impetuous bounds, rapid pace and great soul. A thousand times am I able without pausing, to encircle Meru, that colossus that seems to lick the heavens. With my strong arms, churning up the sea, I can inundate the world with its mountains, rivers and lakes ; with my thighs and legs, I can cause the ocean, the abode of Varuna with its great denizens, to overflow. I can encircle Vainateya, revered by all, who feeds on serpents, a thousand times while he courses once through space. What is more, I am able to reach the sun which rises in glory crowned with rays, before it sinks in the west and return without touching the earth. I can leap beyond the stars and planets, suck up the ocean and rive the earth ; I can shatter the mountains with my bounds and in the immeasurable energy of my leaping I can cause the sea to overflow. When I mount into the sky, flowers from countless shrubs and trees will be borne away by me on my aerial course this day and studded with flowers my path shall resemble the Milky Way.

" And, O Monkeys, all beings shall behold me coursing through the air, encompassing the firmament, now rising, now descending, as it were devouring space. I shall scatter the clouds, shatter the mountains and dry up the ocean with my constant leaping. My powers are equal to the eagle's or the wind ; I know of none that surpasses the King of the Birds, the Wind-god or myself. In the twinkling of an eye, I shall float through the air like lightning from a cloud. While crossing the sea, my form will resemble Vishnu's taking his three strides. My heart foretells that I shall encounter Vaidehi, therefore rejoice. Equal to Maruta in motion and Garuda in speed, I shall cover ten thousand miles ; this is my firm conviction. I am able to wrest the 'amrita' from Indra, armed with his thunderbolt or from Brahma himself. Be assured, that having turned Lanka upside down, I shall return ! "

That monkey of immeasurable vigour roared thus, and astounded, the monkeys gazed on him with joy ; and hearing those words that dissipated the distress of his kindred, that foremost of monkeys, Jambavan, transported with delight, said :—" O Hero ! O Son of Kesarin ! O Offspring of the Wind ! Thou hast dispelled the immense anxiety of thy fellows, and these foremost of monkeys assembled here will perform acts tending to thy welfare. By the grace of the Sages, the approval of our elders and the blessing of our spiritual preceptors do thou cross the ocean. We will stand on one foot awaiting thy return. On thee depend the lives of all the inhabitants of the woods ! "

Then that tiger of the monkeys said to those rangers of the woods :—" None in this world will be able to sustain the force of my leaping. Here is the mountain Mahendra with its compact mass of rocks and high escarpments, it is from its summit that I shall spring. With its trees of varied fragrance that cover it and its many crags, it will be able to bear my weight, when I prepare to leap over four hundred miles."

With these words that monkey, the scourge of his foes, born of Maruta, whose equal he was, scaled that monarch of mountains, carpeted with flowers of every kind and grassy swards ranged by deer, containing flowering creepers and trees laden with fruit and blossoms, frequented by lions and tigers and herds of intoxicated elephants maddened with ichor; there flocks of birds trilled and waterfalls tumbled on every side.

Ascending that mountain, that foremost of monkeys, equal to Mahendra in power, began to wander from one crest to another and crushed between the arms of that high-souled one, that great mountain emitted a loud clamour, like a mighty elephant that has been attacked by a lion and waters gushed out from the scattered rocks and deer and elephants were seized with fear, whilst the giant trees shook.

Its spacious uplands were deserted by the pairs of Gandharvas engaged in drinking and dalliance, the birds flew away and the bands of Vidyadharas fled from the high plateaus; the huge serpents hid themselves in terror and the cliffs and spars broke away. With its serpents hissing, their bodies half issuing from their holes, the mountain shone, as if decorated by pennants. The Rishis in fear and agitation fled from that support of the earth so that it resembled a wayfarer in a vast forest, deserted by his companions.

And that agile and valiant monkey, endowed with great speed, the destroyer of his foes, filled with an exalted purpose, had already reached Lanka in thought.

End of Kishkindha Kanda

BOOK V.

SUNDARA KANDA

CHAPTER I

The Departure of Hanuman

THEN that Scourge of His Foes, Hanuman, prepared to follow the path of the Charanas[1] in quest of the place to which Sita had been borne away by Ravana.

Desirous of accomplishing this difficult feat without hindrance, impossible to any other, that powerful monkey, stretching out his head and neck like a bull, frightening the birds, uprooting the trees with his breast and destroying innumerable creatures, like a lion overflowing with energy joyfully bounded over the grassy slopes resembling the sea.

On that mountain plateau, frequented by the Chiefs of the Serpent Race, embellished by blue, red, yellow, rose and various coloured metals, thronged with Celestial Beings, Yakshas, Kinneras and Gandharvas, able to change their form at will, that foremost of monkeys stood like a Naga in a lake.

Then, having paid homage to the Sun-god, Mahendra, Pavana, Swyambhu and all beings, he prepared to set out on his journey. Turning towards the east and saluting his sire, the resourceful Hanuman, having resolved to cross the ocean to fulfil Rama's purpose, in order to reach the southern region, expanded his body under the eyes of the leaders of the monkeys, as the sea increases under the full moon.

Assuming an immense stature, desirous of traversing the ocean, he pressed the mountain with his hands and feet and that immoveable peak shook under his weight and all the blossom from the tops of the trees fell in a shower wholly covering it with a mass of fragrant blooms.

Under the extreme pressure of that monkey's weight, water gushed forth from the mountain like ichor from the temples of an elephant in rut. Trampled underfoot by that mighty forest

[1] Path of the Charanas or the Path of the Wind—His sire being the Wind-God.

dweller, the mountain let loose innumerable streams of gold, silver and collyrium and, from that rocky mass, enormous boulders detached themselves containing red arsenic so that it resembled a brazier wreathed in smoke.

Crushed on every side by the monkey, those creatures, dwelling in the caverns, bruised and stifled, emitted strange cries and the formidable clamour created by them filled the whole earth and other regions.

Great serpents, rearing their distinctive hoods, vomited fire and bit the rocks with their fangs and those great crags, split by the venom, broke into flames and were shivered into a thousand fragments. The medicinal herbs also, which grew there, were affected by the poison which they were unable to neutralise.

Then the ascetics, terrified, reflecting that the mountain was being riven by great Beings, fled away, as well as the Vidyadharas with their attendant women. Forsaking their golden seats, goblets and precious vessels with the ewers of gold in the feasting hall; abandoning the priceless sauces, wines and viands of every kind and the hides and swords with guards of Kanaka gold; intoxicated, their necks encircled with jewelled chains, adorned with garlands and red sandal paste, their eyes resembling blue lotuses, they rose into the air; and those fair Ones, wearing strings of pearls, rings and bracelets, startled, ascended smiling into the sky, close to their loved ones.

Witnessing this great marvel, Maharishis and Vidyadharas stood in the firmament gazing down on the mountain and they heard those pure-minded ascetics saying: "This Hanuman, born of the Wind, endued with great energy, desirous of crossing the ocean, the abode of Varuna, in order to carry out Rama's purpose and that of the monkeys, is eager to reach the further shore, a most difficult feat."

Hearing the words of the ascetics, the Vidyadharas beheld that foremost of monkeys on the mountain, bristling and quivering like a flame, emitting a great roar like the rumble of thunder. Then raising his tail which twitched convulsively, like a snake shaken by an eagle, he waved it to and fro and, lying curled across his back, it resembled a great serpent borne away by Garuda.

And that monkey, stiffening his arms like unto two immense clubs, girded up his limbs and, crouching down, contracted his neck and arms, summoning up all his strength and courage. Scanning the path he was to take and examining the distance to be covered, he drew in his breath, pressing his two feet firmly on the ground and that elephant among monkeys, Hanuman, flattening his ears, leapt forward and, full of energy, addressed the forest dwellers, saying:

"As an arrow loosed by Raghava flies with the speed of the wind so shall I course to Lanka which is guarded by Ravana. If I fail to find the daughter of Janaka there, I shall repair with the same speed to the region of the Gods, where, if despite mine efforts I do not recover Sita, I shall bring back the King of the Titans in chains. Either, achieving success, I shall return or uprooting Lanka from its foundation, I shall bear it hither, together with Ravana."

With these words, Hanuman, the foremost of monkeys, without pausing for breath, deeming himself to be a second Suparna, sprang into the air and, such was the force of his leap, that the trees growing on the mountain, tossing their branches, were sent spinning on every side.

In his rapid flight, Hanuman bore away those trees with their flowering boughs filled with lapwings intoxicated with love, into the empyrean. Carried away by the impetus of his tremendous bound, those trees followed in his wake, like relatives accompanying their dear one setting out on a journey to a far country. Uprooted by the force of his motion, Sala and other forest trees followed in Hanuman's wake, like an army its leader. Surrounded by countless trees, the crests of which were laden with blossom, the monkey Hanuman, resembling a glorious mountain, was wonderful to behold. And those great trees, full of sap, fell into the sea, as formerly the mountains in fear of Indra plunged into Varuna's abode.

Covered with flowers of every kind, as well as young shoots and buds, that monkey shone like a cloud or a hill aglow with fireflies. Torn away by his leaping, those trees, scattering their blossom here and there, plunged into the sea, like friends who, having escorted one of their company, return. Borne away in their fragility by the wind produced by the monkey's impetuous flight, which had detached them from their stems, the multi-coloured flowers fell into the sea.

Covered with a drift of fragrant blooms of diverse tints, that monkey, in his flight, resembled a mass of clouds embellished by lightning and the waters strewn with the blossom of his leap, looked like the firmament when the enchanting stars appear. His two arms outstretched in space, resembled two five-headed serpents issuing from the summit of a mountain.

Sometimes that mighty monkey seemed to be drinking up the ocean with the multitudinous waves and sometimes it seemed as if he would swallow the sky itself. As he thus followed the wind's path, his eyes, shining like lightning, sparkled like two fires that have been kindled on a mountain.

The eyes of that tawny-hued one resembled the sun and moon in juxtaposition, and his coppery nose lent his countenance the same hue as the solar orb at the approach of dusk; his uplifted tail caused that offspring of the wind to appear like the raised banner of Indra. With his coiled tail and white teeth, that exceedingly sagacious son of Anila, Hanuman, shone like the star of day encircled by a halo of rays and his plump form, of a coppery hue, caused him to resemble a mountain which is being excavated for its deposits of red ochre. Bounding over the waters, the air imprisoned in the armpits of that leonine monkey, emitted a sound like thunder.

As in space, a meteor from a higher region rushes through the skies so did that elephant of monkeys appear or like a great bird soaring into the air or a great tusker tightly-bound by a girth, whilst the reflection of his body cast on the deep resembled a vessel foundering in a storm.

Wherever that great monkey passed, the sea rose tumultuously under the force of his bounds and, rushing on with extreme speed, with his breast like a great prow, he caused the salty sea to surge mountainously. Pushing those high heaving billows before him, that lion among monkeys seemed to be separating heaven and earth; the waves that rose up resembled Mount Meru and Mandara and, breasted by him in his impetuous course, the waters lashed by his speed, overspread the sky like autumnal clouds. Whales, crocodiles, huge fish and turtles were uncovered in turn, like the limbs of one shedding his attire, and sea serpents, beholding that lion among monkeys travelling through space took him to be Suparna himself.

The shadow of that great monkey, forty miles in extent and thirty wide, grew larger in the rapidity of his flight and, resembling a mass of white clouds, falling on the salty waters, looked exceedingly beautiful. That supremely illustrious and mighty monkey of vast body appeared like a winged mountain as he followed his aerial path without rest.

Wherever that mighty elephant among the monkeys passed, the sea was instantly transformed into a fountain and, following the path of the birds, Hanuman, like the King of the feathered tribe, thrust aside the massed clouds like the Wind-god himself. Great clouds, red, blue, pale or dark, scattered by the monkey's flight, looked exceedingly beautiful and he, now entering into them, sometimes hidden sometimes visible, resembled the moon.

Seeing that Plavaga[1] coursing with such speed, the Gods, Gandharvas and Danavas began to rain flowers on him and, as he sailed on, the sun refrained from tormenting him and the wind ministered to him for the sake of Rama's enterprise.

Then the Rishis praised that dweller of the woods as he was coursing through the sky and the Gods and Gandharvas extolled him in song. Seeing him bounding in space, Nagas, Yakshas and Rakshasas of various races lauded that excellent monkey and the ocean, ever solicitous for the honour of the House of Ikshwaku, reflected :—" If I do not lend assistance to this Lord of Monkeys, I shall be an object of obloquy to all those gifted with speech ; was I not reared by Sagara, the foremost of the race of Ikshwaku ? This monkey is their counsellor, it is therefore incumbent on me not to let him perish in the waves. It behoves me to act in such wise that he may rest and, thus relieved by me, he will happily traverse the remaining way."

In this magnanimous thought, the sea addressed that most excellent of mountains, the golden-hued Mainaka, which was covered by waves, saying :—

" Thou hast been placed here by the King of the Celestials, as a rampart against the Asuras inhabiting the nether regions.

[1] Plavaga.—One who moves by leaps and bounds.

Their power is well known and, lest they rise up anew from that hell of immeasurable dimensions, thou art here to prevent their escape. Nevertheless thou art able to move upwards and downwards and from side to side. I command thee, therefore, O Best of Mountains, to rise up. That lion among monkeys, performer of mighty exploits, engaged in Rama's service, overcome with fatigue is passing over thee; thou art witness of his exertions, now lift thyself up!"

Hearing the Ocean's words, the golden-breasted Mountain Mainaka with its tall trees and creepers, instantly rose from its watery bed and, as the sun with its burning rays divides the cloud, that great mountain, which the waters had concealed, on Sagara's request, exposed its golden peaks inhabited by Kinneras and great serpents, shimmering like the sun at dawn, as if it were licking the skies. The summits of that high mountain, shining like a sword, possessed the brilliance of gold and its gilded crests emitted a dazzling light lending it the lustre of a thousand suns.

Beholding that mountain suddenly emerge before him from the middle of the sea, Hanuman reflected: 'This is an obstacle', and that mighty and impetuous monkey crushed that stony mass with his breast as the wind scatters the clouds; then that foremost of mountains, recognizing the power of Hanuman, shouted for joy. Thereupon, assuming the form of a man, stationing himself on his own summit, with a glad heart he addressed Hanuman saying:—

"O Most Excellent of Forest Dwellers, thou hast undertaken an arduous task, take thine ease on my crest and continue without fatigue. The ocean king was born in the House of Raghu and, seeing thee engaged on Rama's behalf, offers obeisance to thee. To render service for service is the divine decree. Desirous of serving Raghu's race, he is worthy of thy consideration. To do thee honour, the Sea God adjured me thus:—

"'Traversing a hundred yojanas through the air, this monkey is worn out by his exertions, let him rest awhile on thy summit and continue his way without fatigue.' Do thou therefore remain here, O Best of Monkeys and repose thyself. Having feasted on these many sweet and fragrant fruits and roots, proceed on thy course at thy leisure. O Foremost of Monkeys. the sum of thy virtues is well-known in the Three Worlds. O Son of the Wind, of all the Plavagas who abound in energy, I esteem thee to be the chief, O Lion among Monkeys! Even an ordinary man is honoured as a guest by one conversant with his duty, how much more one such as thou? Thou art the Son of Maruta, the Foremost of the Celestials and dost equal him in speed, O Best of Monkeys! In honouring thee, who art conversant with virtue, one is honouring thy sire, therefore thou dost merit my reverence. Hearken, there is a further reason for this:

"In olden times, Dear Child, the mountains, endowed with wings, began to range the four quarters with the speed of Garuda, and journeying thus, the companies of Celestials, ascetics and other Beings trembled with fear lest they should fall. Then, highly enraged, the God of a Thousand Eyes, the performer of an hundred sacrifices severed the wings of those hundreds and thousands of mountains with his thunderbolt.

"When, full of wrath, the Lord of the Celestials approached me, brandishing his mace, I was suddenly swept away by that high-souled Wind-god. O Foremost of Monkeys, I was thus cast into the salty waves and, retaining my wings, was preserved unhurt by thine ancestor. On account of this, thou art an object of adoration to me and this is the powerful bond which unites us, O Chief of the Monkeys. The time for honouring the benefit conferred having come, it behoves thee to accord this felicity to the Ocean and myself, O Illustrious One! Repose thyself therefore and accept our homage, who are worthy of thy respect, O Venerable Hanuman! Happy am I to see thee here!"

Thus accosted by Mainaka, the foremost of mountains, that excellent monkey answered, saying:—"I am grateful for thy welcome but time presses and I have vowed not to rest on the way; day is declining, let nothing disturb thy serenity."

Then, touching the mountain with his hand, that lion among monkeys, smiling, sailed on through the air, whereupon the mountain and the ocean offered him their respect and gave him their blessings. Rising high into the sky, he looked down on the mountain and the vast ocean and proceeded unsupported in the pathway of the wind.

Seeing Hanuman achieve this difficult feat, the Celestial Beings and the ascetics acclaimed him; then the Gods present, in their turn, applauded the action of that golden mountain of beautiful slopes, as did Indra, the Thousand-eyed Deity also, and supremely gratified, the consort of Sachi paid homage to that illustrious mountain personally, saying:—

"O Lord of Mountains, I am extremely pleased with thee! I grant thee full security, proceed therefore where thou desirest, O Friend. Thou hast fearlessly offered assistance to Hanuman, who was exhausted after crossing four hundred miles of sea, despite every hazard. It is on Rama's behalf, the Son of King Dasaratha, that the monkey has undertaken this journey and thou hast welcomed him to the best of thy power, I am well pleased with thee!"

Beholding the King of the Gods, Shatakratu highly gratified, that foremost of mountains experienced supreme felicity and having received that boon from Indra, resumed its former place. Then Hanuman, in a short space, sped over the sea.

Thereupon the Gods, Gandharvas and Siddhas with the ascetics called upon Surasa, the Mother of Serpents, who resembled the sun, saying:—

"The effulgent Son of the Wind is crossing the main, it is for thee to delay him awhile Assuming the form of a terrible Rakshasi, as high as a mountain, with monstrous jaws and coppery eyes, do thou reach up to the sky. We desire to test his strength and measure his fortitude to see if he is able to overcome thee or if he retires discomfited."

At these words, Surasa, having been honoured by the Gods, rose from the ocean in the form of a female demon, deformed and hideous, inspiring terror in all beings and, staying Hanuman in his flight, addressed him saying:—

"O Foremost of Monkeys, thou hast been destined by the Lords of the World to be my food, I am about to devour thee, do thou enter my mouth! This boon was formerly granted to me by Dhatar."

With these words she opened her vast mouth wide, placing herself in Maruti's path.

Having listened to Surasa's speech, Hanuman, smiling, answered her:—

" Rama, the Son of Dasaratha, who retired to the Dandaka forest with Lakshmana his brother, and Vaidehi his consort, as a result of a certain exploit, became the enemy of the demons. His beloved wife, the illustrious Sita was subsequently carried away by Ravana. I have been sent to her on Rama's behalf, to whom thou shouldst proffer assistance, O Thou who inhabitest his dominion. Having found Maithili and rejoined Rama, whose deeds are memorable, I shall return and enter thy mouth, this I promise thee in good faith."

Thus addressed by Hanuman, Surasa, who was able to change her form at will, answered :—" None shall pass me alive, this is the boon I have received." Then seeing him continue on his way, the Mother of Serpents added :—" I have received this favour from Brahma, first enter my mouth then go thy way."

Thereafter, extending her capacious jaws, she placed herself in front of Maruti. Surasa's words incensed that lion among monkeys and he said :—

" Open thy mouth wide enough to swallow me." Having said this in anger, Surasa extended her jaws to the width of forty miles and Hanuman increased his girth accordingly ; thereat Surasa enlarged her mouth to fifty miles, and seeing the jaws of Surasa wide open with its long tongue, terrible to look upon, resembling a mountain, measuring fifty miles, Hanuman enlarged himself to that extent also. Then Surasa increased her mouth to sixty miles and the heroic Hanuman to seventy, whereupon Surasa widened her jaws to eighty miles, and Hanuman, resembling Fire[1] itself, to ninety miles. Then Surasa enlarged her mouth to the extent of an hundred miles and Hanuman, reducing his body like a cloud to the size of a thumb's breadth entered into her mouth and, re-emerging from it, standing in space, addressed her saying :—

" O Dakshayani, salutations to thee, I have entered thy mouth, now I go to seek out Vaidehi. Thy boon has been honoured ! "

Seeing Hanuman emerging from her mouth like the moon from the mouth of Rahu, that goddess, assuming her own form, said to the monkey :—

" Go, O Best of Monkeys ! Accomplish thy mission. Thou

[1] Lit. : The Fire-god.

hast done well, O Friend! Now restore Sita to the magnanimous Raghava!"

Seeing this third supremely difficult feat accomplished by Hanuman, all beings extolled that monkey, crying: 'Excellent! Excellent!' paying obeisance to him; and he, flying into the sky, with the speed of Garuda, went on across the sea, the abode of Varuna, coursing through the air which was filled with clouds, where birds ranged and which was frequented by Vidyadharas and shining vehicles drawn by lions, elephants, tigers and winged serpents. And Maruti, scattering the clouds like the wind itself, sailed on like Garuda through that firmament, which was illumined by flashes of lightning, resembling the five fires, inhabited by beings, who, by their merits had conquered heaven, occupied by the Deity of Fire bearing the sacrificial oblations. Adorned by the constellations of planets, the sun, the moon and hosts of stars; thronged with Maharishis, Gandharvas, Nagas and Yakshas; pure, stainless, immense; inhabited by Vishvavasu; trodden by the elephant of the King of the Gods, that orbit of the sun and the moon, the canopy of the world, stretched by Brahma over the earth, was visited by countless heroes and aerial beings.

Mighty clouds, shining with the tints of Kalaguru,[1] red, yellow and black, sparkled with brilliance as they were dispelled by Hanuman and he, penetrating those cloudy battlements, emerged once more as the moon in the rainy season disappears and re-appears in the clouds. Everywhere the son of Maruta could be seen cleaving the air like the King of the Mountains furnished with wings.

Seeing him sailing through space, a female demon of immense size, named Singhika, who was able to change her form at will, said to herself:—'To-day, after a long time, I shall be able to satisfy my hunger! That great creature has appeared in answer to my wish!'

Reflecting thus in her heart, she seized Hanuman's shadow, and he, feeling it held fast, thought: 'My power has suddenly been dissipated like a mighty barque which is retarded in its course by an adverse wind!' Then looking round on every side, Hanuman perceived that immense being rising from the

[1] Kalaguru—Agallochum: A species of sandal paste.

salty waves. Seeing that monster, the Son of the Wind-god, reflected :—' This is without doubt that creature of wonderful form, possessed of exceeding power, given to securing its prey by means of their shadow, who was described to me by the monkey king.' Concluding by her action that it was Singhika, that sagacious monkey expanded his frame to gigantic proportions so that he resembled a mass of cloud during the rains.

When the demon saw the enlarged body of that mighty monkey, she extended her jaws so that they resembled the sky and the nether regions and, roaring like thunder, hurled herself upon him, but marking the proportions of her mouth and the vulnerable parts of her body, that intelligent monkey, hard as a diamond, contracting his limbs, threw himself into her jaws.

And the Siddhas and Charanas beheld him diving into her mouth, disappearing like the moon devoured by Rahu at the time of eclipse. And Hanuman, with his sharp nails tore the entrails of that demon and, with the rapidity of thought, emerged, having slain her by his acuteness, endurance and skill and, having overthrown her, began to expand once more. Thereafter that hero among monkeys suddenly regained his power, whilst Singhika, deprived of life by him, torn asunder, sank into the waves, Swyambhu having created him for her destruction.

Perceiving Singhika speedily overcome by him, all the beings who range the skies addressed that foremost of monkeys saying: " Tremendous is this deed that thou hast performed this day! Mighty was this monster whom thou hast slain. O Illustrious Monkey, now pursue the purpose dear to thine heart without hindrance. He, who like thee, possesses the four attributes: fixity of purpose, circumspection, wisdom and ability, does not fail in his enterprise O Indra among Monkeys ! "

Honoured by those whose wishes are fulfilled, as he merited to be, that monkey flew into the sky like Garuda, the devourer of serpents. Then, having reached the further shore, Hanuman looking round on every side, observed countless woods a hundred miles distant and, as he went on, that leader of forest dwellers saw an island adorned with trees of various kinds and thickets belonging to the Malaya mountains ; and he surveyed the sea and the lands bordering it and the trees growing on its shores as also the mouths of the ocean's consorts.[1]

Gazing down on his own body which resembled a great cloud covering the sky that self-contained monkey reflected: "Observing mine immense stature and the rapidity of my flight the demons will be seized with curiosity concerning me."

Thinking thus, in his great prudence, he contracted his body, which was the size of a mountain and assumed his ordinary form as one whose wits have been scattered resumes his normal state. Abandoning his gigantic dimensions, he took on his native form, as did Vishnu, the depriver of Bali's power, when he made the three strides.

Constantly mindful of his mission, Hanuman, who was able to assume various graceful forms, having crossed the sea, a feat not to be accomplished by any other, reduced his body to its former size.

Thereafter that high-souled One, resembling a cloudy pavilion, alighted on the summit of the glorious mountain Samva, of many splendid peaks which was covered with Ketaka, Uddalaka and Narikela trees.

Reaching the shore of the sea, the monkey beholding Lanka on the top of the foremost of mountains, descended, having assumed his native form, causing agitation among the deer and birds.

Through his valour having traversed the ocean heaving with waves and abounding in Danavas and Pannagas, Hanuman, alighting on the further shore, beheld Lanka which resembled the city of Amaravati.

CHAPTER 2

Hanuman's Arrival in Lanka

HAVING crossed the unconquerable sea, that mighty monkey, standing on the summit of the Trikuta Mountain, surveyed

[1] Ocean's Consorts: Probably estuaries.

Lanka and that ape endowed with great prowess was covered by a shower of blossom that fell from the trees on every side, nor did that fortunate monkey, who had just traversed many hundreds of miles of sea without pausing for breath, experience any fatigue.

'I am able to journey many hundreds of miles, what then is this ocean measuring four hundred miles only?' Thus thinking, that foremost of monkeys, endowed with great energy, turned quickly towards Lanka, having crossed the mighty ocean and he passed between green fields and dense thickets fragrant with the scent of honey and traversed the mountainous district covered with trees and blossoming woods. Stationing himself there, the Son of the Wind-god beheld forests and groves and Lanka itself perched on the summit of the mountain.

Sarala, Karnikara, Kharjura trees in full flower with the balmy Priyala, Muchulinda, Kutaja, Ketaka and Priyangu trees heavy with scent; Nipa, Saptachchada, Asana, Kovidara and Karavira trees laden with buds and flowers, whose crests, waving in the wind abounded with birds, were seen by him and ponds filled with swans and waterfowl and carpeted with white and blue lotuses; flower gardens with ornamental fountains and marvellous parks planted with every kind of tree which yielded fruit and flowers in every season.

Drawing nearer to Lanka, which was protected by Ravana, surrounded by a moat embellished with blue and white lotuses, the auspicious Hanuman noted that a strong guard had been placed round it since Sita's abduction; and demons with formidable bows ranged it on every side and that great and marvellous city was encircled by a golden wall, its buildings as high as mountains, resembling autumn clouds.

The main highways were lined with tall white buildings with hundreds of turrets decorated with flying pennants and banners. Most wonderful, with its golden archways festooned with climbing plants, the city of Lanka appeared to Hanuman to be like the city of the Gods. Built on the summit of a mountain, with its palaces of dazzling white, it resembled an aerial city. Constructed by Vishwakarma and ruled by the Lord of the Titans himself, it seemed to that monkey to be suspended in the sky with its ramparts as the thighs, the stretches of water and woods, the raiment, Shataghnis[1] and spears the hair, the terraces the diadem, Lanka resembled a woman, a creation of Vishwakarma's thought.

Reaching the northern gate resembling Mount Kailasha, which seemed to cleave the skies and support the firmament with its splendid lofty towers and, observing that city thronged with ferocious titans, like a cavern full of venomous snakes, protected by the ocean and, recollecting that terrible adversary, Ravana, the monkey reflected :—

'Even should the mighty armed Raghava succeed in reaching this dread and impregnable city protected by Ravana, what could he do ? It is not possible to enter into negotiations with these demons nor could one win them over by bribes nor succeed in sowing dissension among them nor overcome them in fight. Among the monkeys, only four have power to reach this place—Bali's son, Nila, the sagacious Sugriva, and I. But first let me ascertain if Vaidehi still lives or no ; after seeing Janaka's daughter, I shall consider these matters further.'

Then that elephant among monkeys, stationed on the summit of the mountain, bethought himself how he could discover Sita, the delight of Rama. 'In this shape I shall not be able to enter the city guarded by valiant and ferocious demons nor outwit those warriors full of courage, energy and prowess. In order to find Janaki, I must enter the city by night at a favourable moment, in a form which will not attract attention so that I may carry through this great enterprise.'

Beholding that city, inaccessible even to the Gods and Asuras, Hanuman, sighing deeply, reflected within himself : 'How can I succeed in finding Maithili, the daughter of Janaka, without being discovered by the perfidious Ravana, Lord of the Demons ? How may the work of Rama, who is cognisant of the Self, not be brought to nought ? How may I see the daughter of Janaka alone and in secret ? Undertakings fail in the face of hindrances raised by time and place or through the fault of an incompetent messenger, as darkness is dispelled by the rising sun. When it concerns that which should be undertaken or avoided, the best laid plans may come to nought through the heedlessness of a

[1] See Glossary of Weapons.

messenger nor do they appear in all their splendour; a presumptuous messenger may spoil all!

'How shall I act so that there shall be no incompetence on my part? How may my crossing of the ocean bear fruit? If I am discovered by the demons, the project which the sagacious Rama has formed, who desires the destruction of Ravana, will miscarry. Even if I assume the form of a demon I cannot remain here long without being discovered by them, how much less in some other shape. Even the wind is not able to circulate here unrecognized, I deem. Nothing escapes the vigilance of these formidable titans. If I remain here in my native form, I shall be courting disaster and the purpose of my master will be frustrated, therefore, reducing my size, I shall enter Lanka as a monkey in order to carry through Rama's design. Entering this inaccessible city by night, I shall penetrate into every dwelling in order to find Janaka's daughter.'

Having thus resolved, Hanuman, eager to find Vaidehi, waited for the sun to set.

When the day's orb had sunk behind the Asta Mountain, Maruti reduced his body to the size of a cat, extraordinary to behold and, in the dusk, the mighty Hanuman, springing up, entered that marvellous city traversed by wide streets with rows of houses adorned with golden pillars and balconies, which lent it the appearance of a city of the Gandharvas.

Then he beheld that capital containing seven and eight storied buildings with marble floors inlaid with golden mosaic and golden archways, lending it a great brilliance and, seeing the unimaginable splendour of Lanka, in his eagerness to find Vaidehi, he experienced both sadness and delight.

With its garlands of palaces rivalling each other in whiteness and the arches interlaced with gold of great price, that magnificent city protected by Ravana was encircled by intrepid warriors of great prowess.

And the moon at its full with its flocks of stars seemed to be ministering to Hanuman and, with its myriad rays, filled the worlds with its light. Then that hero among monkeys gazed on the moon shining like a conch-shell, white as milk or a lotus stalk that, floating all luminous in space, resembled a swan swimming on a lake.

CHAPTER 3

Hanuman enters the City

HAVING rested on Mount Samva of lofty summits, that resembled a great cloud, Hanuman, the son of Maruta, that lion among monkeys, confident of his own strength, entered Lanka by night, with its wealth of ravishing groves and waters, guarded by Ravana; that enchanting city with its dazzling palaces resembling autumn clouds, where the sound of the sea could be heard, the breezes of which it inhaled day and night.

Prosperous, surrounded by great forces, resembling Vitapavati with its white gates and decorated arches, protected by infuriated elephants, splendid as Bhogavati filled with huge serpents, similar to the city of Indra, embellished by hosts of stars, resounding to the clamour of blustering winds, encircled by a golden rampart, re-echoing to the pealing of innumerable bells and adorned with banners, that city was approached by Hanuman in exaltation, his heart full of wonder.

And he surveyed it on every side, with its golden gates, the lintels of emerald and the pavements studded with pearls, crystal and gems; with its steps inlaid with precious stones, and floors of lapis lazuli, the grilles of refined gold and parapets of silver; the stairways of crystal that, free from dust, were possessed of emerald treads. And there were charming rooms, which, on account of their elegance, seemed to be built in the air.

The cries of curlews and peacocks could be heard and geese frequented that place whilst swans floated majestically on the lakes; everywhere the sound of the beating of drums and the tinkling of ornaments resounded and, beholding Lanka that resembled Vasvakara and seemed to be built in space, the monkey was filled with rapture.

Gazing on that splendid city belonging to the Lord of the Titans, that no other surpassed in opulence, the sagacious Hanuman reflected:—'This capital, protected by Ravana's warriors is not to be subdued by force and is only accessible to Kumuda, Angada and that mighty monkey, Sushena or

Mainda and Dvivida or the offspring of Vivaswata or the monkey Kushaparva or Rikshya, that foremost of monkeys, or myself.'

Thereafter, recollecting the valour of the long-armed Raghava and the prowess of Lakshmana, the confidence of that monkey was restored.

And that mighty monkey surveyed Lanka, the capital of the Lord of the Titans, that had the sea as her raiment, cow sheds and stables for her pendants, the armouries her breasts, decked out like a woman, where darkness was dispelled by the bright light of torches and the gleaming of the stars.

And as that tiger among monkeys, son of the great Wind-god, entered the city, the Deity who presided over the capital protected by Ravana, she of monstrous aspect, rose up and barred the way of that heroic son of Vayu. Emitting a great roar, she challenged the offspring of the Wind-god, saying :—

" O Dweller of the Forest, who art thou and for what purpose hast thou come hither ? Answer truthfully if thou dost value thy life ! Under no pretext wilt thou be able to obtain entry into this Lanka protected by the forces of Ravana, which patrol it on every side."

Then the valiant Hanuman answered her, who stood before him, saying :—" I shall tell thee all about that on which thou questioneth me anon but say first who thou art in this hideous form and why thou dost admonish me in anger, O Irascible One."

Hearing Hanuman's words, the Goddess of Lanka, able to change her shape at will, waxed wrath and in harsh tones addressed the son of the Wind-god, saying :—

" Obedient to the mandate of the magnanimous Ravana, the King of the Titans, I guard the city. None may pass me, yet if any should contrive to enter here, he will soon fall under my blows, deprived of his life breaths. I am the city of Lanka itself, and whatever betide I shall remain true to the words I have uttered ! "

Hanuman, born of Maruta, the foremost of monkeys, stood motionless like a rock and beholding her in the form of a woman, that lion among monkeys, endowed with intelligence and courage, spoke to her thus :—

" I wish to behold this city with its turrets, walls and arches, and have come hither for this purpose. Great is my desire to see it and explore its woods, groves and gardens, as also its great buildings."

Hearing these words, the presiding Deity of Lanka, who was able to change her form at will, was still further provoked and answered in anger :—

" O Insensate One, O Last of the Monkeys ! without overcoming me, thou canst not behold this city to-day, which is ruled over by the King of the Titans."

Then that lion among forest dwellers replied to that female ranger of the night, saying :—" After viewing the city, O Auspicious One, I shall return from whence I came."

On this, Lanka emitted a terrible cry and struck that excellent monkey with the palm of her hand. Under the force of her blow, the valiant Son of Maruta let out a roar and closing the fingers of his left hand, pushed her away with his fist. Reflecting ' She is a woman ' he controlled his anger, nevertheless the demon fell to the ground instantly, her face distorted and, seeing her lying on the earth, Hanuman, who was full of courage and nobility, had compassion on her, she being but a woman.

Thereupon, Lanka, exceedingly agitated, addressed that monkey in low and faltering accents, saying :—

" O Mighty-armed One, have pity on me ! Spare me, O Best of Monkeys ! Those endowed with strength and prowess, stay their hand betimes ! O Thou of great might, thou hast overcome me by thy valour ! Hear the following truth from me which was proclaimed by Swyambhu who prophesied saying : ' In the hour that a monkey overcomes thee by force, the titans will cease to be invincible.'

" That time, fixed by Swyambhu has come, as is shown by thy presence here to-day ! The truth ordained by the Self-create is unalterable. The destruction of the unrighteous King Ravana together with all the titans is imminent, in consequence of the abduction of Sita. Therefore, O Best of Monkeys, do thou enter this city, which is protected by Ravana, and accomplish all thou desirest. Entering this splendid city, protected by the Lord of the Titans, which is doomed, go about freely wheresoever thou wilt, in search of the chaste daughter of Janaka."

CHAPTER 4

Hanuman observes the City and its Inhabitants

By his valour, the mighty Hanuman, foremost of monkeys, having triumphed over Lanka, that splendid city, able to change her form at will, without passing through the gate, leapt over the wall and, by night, penetrated into the centre of the capital.

Hanuman, faithful to the interests of the King of the Monkeys, having found his way into that city, thus placed his left foot on the heads of his foes;[1] and that excellent son of Maruta, entering by night, proceeded along the royal highway strewn with flowers and continued to advance through that enchanting capital where the sound of musical instruments blended with laughter.

That magnificent city with its innumerable dwellings bearing the mark of the mace and the goad, with windows of diamond, resembled the sky adorned with clouds. Lanka belonging to the titans, with its opulent mansions like white clouds, adorned with lotuses and swastikas, hung with garlands, highly decorated, was viewed by Hanuman with delight, who ranged it on Rama's behalf and in the interests of Sugriva.

That illustrious monkey passing from house to house, observed the many dwellings of varying forms, on every side and listened to the melodious chanting in triple modulation, of women sick with love, who resembled celestial nymphs. He heard the tinkling of their girdles and the clashing of their anklets, as they ascended the stairways of those dwellings belonging to the great Ones, and here and there the sound of clapping of hands and the clicking of castanets. He heard also the intoning of sacred formulas in the dwellings of the titans and the recitation of those occupied in the study of the Veda.

He also saw titans who were singing the praises of Ravana in a loud voice, a great company of them being stationed on the royal highway which they obstructed; and he observed a large

[1] Placed his left foot . . . implying that he thereby initiated the defeat of the titans.

concourse of spies in the central courtyard, who had been initiated, some with matted locks, some shaven, some wearing deerskins and some stark naked, bearing handfuls of darbha grass, braziers, picks, clubs and staves, and others in rags, who had only a single eye or ear or breast which twitched ; and some were dwarfs, hideous to behold ; and there were bowmen, swordsmen and warriors bearing clubs and iron bars or effulgent in curious armour ; some were neither exceedingly fat nor too lean nor unduly tall nor short nor extremely fair nor dark nor humpbacked nor dwarfed ; some were deformed, some handsome, some distinguished and there were also standard bearers and some who carried flags and every kind of weapon.

And Hanuman observed that some were armed with spears, darts, harpoons, arrows, slings and other weapons and many ranging about at will wore garlands and were daubed with paste, sprinkled with perfume, clothed in rich stuffs and adorned with magnificent jewels ; some of these mighty warriors were furnished with javelins and maces and hundreds and thousands of them were garrisoned in the central courtyard, engaged in guarding the private apartments with vigilance by order of their king.

And he saw the famous palace of the Lord of the Titans, built on the summit of the mountain, with golden arched gateways, surrounded by a moat, embellished with pale lotuses and completely encircled by a rampart, resembling heaven itself ; and it was marvellous, resonant with pleasant sounds and filled with the neighing of superb steeds and well-bred beasts and the noise of chariots and elephants ; and there were four tusked elephants resembling great clouds and many herds of deer.

Then the monkey entered that palace protected by the Titan King, guarded by thousands of mighty Yatudhanas, the portals of which were richly decorated with beasts and birds and he penetrated to the inner apartment encircled with walls of Hema and Jambunada gold, its ceilings adorned with pearls and gems of great price and pervaded by the fragrance of aloe and sandalwood.

SUNDARA KANDA

CHAPTER 5

Hanuman ranges the City without finding Sita

THEN the fortunate Hanuman beheld that brilliant orb of the night in the midst of the stars covering all beings with its light, like a bull inflamed with desire in the midst of a herd of cows, and that heroic monkey gazed on that moon, floating in the sky, white as the sheen of a conch or a lotus stalk, that star of cooling rays which destroys the sorrows of the world, draws up the tides and sheds its light on all beings. That brightness which shines on the summit of Mount Mandara and at dusk sparkles on the sea, as well as on the lotuses of the lakes, now blazed from the face of that nocturnal planet.

Like a swan on its silvery nest or a lion in a cave of the Mandara Mountain or a warrior on a proud elephant so was the splendour of the moon in the heavens. Like a humpbacked buffalo with pointed horns or the lofty Mountain Shveta with its high peaks or an elephant with gold-encircled tusks, so did the moon appear with its clearly defined prominence.

Just as the great orb of the sun dissolves the ice and frost on muddy pools so was darkness dispelled by the brilliance of the auspicious moon, whose symbol is the hare, so that even the dark patches on its surface appeared bright. Like the King of Beasts issuing from his cave or the lord of elephants entering the deep woods or a sovereign of men ranging his dominions so did the moon appear in its full splendour.

The brightness of its rising had dispelled the night, accentuating the swarthiness of the titans, those eaters of flesh, and awakening thoughts of love in the lover.

Women, whose melodious voices had charmed the ear, having disported themselves, now slept in the arms of their lords, whilst titans of strange and terrible deeds went forth marauding.

And the sagacious Hanuman beheld mansions where intoxication and folly reigned, where chariots, horses and golden seats were seen everywhere in luxurious and warlike abundance .

He beheld titans in violent debate, raising their great arms, discoursing wildly, railing at each other and exchanging acrimonious words; and some were striking their breasts and brandishing great bows, whilst others adjusted their attire or embraced their consorts.

And Hanuman observed courtesans performing their toilet, whilst others slept and incomparably lovely women laughing or frowning in anger. Here gigantic elephants trumpeted, there worship was being performed, whilst warriors were uttering threats, so that the city resembled a lake filled with angry serpents.

And he beheld in that place, persons full of intelligence, able debators, pious men, leaders of fashion and observers of ritual, and beholding those magnificent beings, endowed with every attribute in accord with their nature, Hanuman was delighted; such was their splendour, that even those who were ugly, appeared fair.

And he saw their consorts, full of nobility and of great beauty, worthy of adornment, like unto stars in the excellence of their conduct, who were filled with affection for their protectors, some casting tender glances, others exchanging tokens and some drinking.

And by night, Hanuman observed lovely women being embraced by their paramours, affecting modesty or passion, like birds sporting with their mates, whilst others, in their homes, lay peacefully on the breasts of their lords, full of tenderness, and faithful to their conjugal duty.

Some, lying without raiment, deserted by their lovers, had the radiance of gold and were marvellously beautiful with their golden skins, graceful limbs and complexions like the moonlight.

And Hanuman saw other women in their homes experiencing the height of joy with their lords, full of delight, decked with flowers, charming the hearts of their consorts with their beauty. These lovely women of radiant countenance, resembling the moon, possessing marvellous eyes with sweeping lashes and slanting lids and adorned with innumerable jewels, seemed to Hanuman to resemble flashes of lightning.

But of the nobly-born Sita, offspring of a royal House, fixed in the path of virtue, resembling a delicate flowering creeper or the frail Sadhujata plant, sprung from the mind of Brahma Himself, he could find no trace. Sita, established in the path of chastity, her gaze ever fixed on Rama, ever absorbed in his contemplation, his very mind and heart itself, exalted above all women, a prey to burning grief, her bosom wet with tears, she who was formerly adorned with priceless ornaments, Sita with her charming lashes and enchanting throat, resembling a blue-necked peahen disporting itself in the woods, or the blurred outline of the moon or a golden ingot covered with dust or a scar left by a wound or a golden arrow snapped by the wind.

And that monkey, after his long search, not finding Sita, consort of that lord of men, Rama, the foremost of those skilled in speech, was overcome with grief and bereft of all courage.

CHAPTER 6

Hanuman explores Ravana's Palace

WANDERING here and there at will on the roofs of the houses, that monkey, able to assume any form he chose, ranged the city of Lanka, and that auspicious one came to the abode of that Lord of the Titans, encircled by a shining wall, sparkling like the sun and guarded by terrible demons, as is a mighty forest by lions.

And that foremost of monkeys beheld that marvellous palace with its fretted archways, inlaid with silver and embellished with gold, abounding in splendid courts and gateways, filled with the drivers of elephants and indomitable warriors, irresistibly swift horses harnessed to chariots and curious waggons, covered with lion and tiger skins, that were embossed with images of gold and silver and hung with jingling bells.

Strewn with precious stones and furnished with rich seats, this was the favourite haunt of the Maharathas and their meeting place. Rare deer and birds of every species and variety abounded here, whilst disciplined sentries protected it. Everywhere noble and distinguished women could be seen and the palace was filled with the tinkling of their ornaments ; there the foremost of the titans dwelt and it was decorated with royal symbols and fragrant with sandalwood. Crowded with great beings, like a forest filled with lions, resounding to the beating of gongs, tambourines and the blare of conches, it was also the place of worship of the titans, where offerings were made at the times of the moon's change ; sometimes, in fear of Ravana, silent as the sea and sometimes resounding like the waves, that vast abode belonging to the mighty Ravana was strewn with precious gems, and that great monkey beheld it blazing in splendour and filled with elephants, horses and chariots.

'It is the jewel of Lanka' reflected that illustrious monkey, Hanuman, wandering about the outskirts of the palace and he began to range the dwellings of the titans and their gardens, and he bounded into the abode of Prahasta and then plunged courageously into the palace of Mahaparshwa ; thereafter, that mighty monkey entered the residence of Kumbhakarna which resembled a mass of clouds and also that of Bibishana ; then in turn he visited the dwellings of Mahodara, Virupaksha, Vidyujjibha and Vidyunmala and with a bound he entered the house of Vahudanshtra and that of Suka and the intelligent Sarana. Then the mansions of Indrajit, Jambumala and Sumala were explored by that foremost of monkeys and thereafter he passed on to the abodes of Rashmiketu, Suryasachu and Vajrakaya ; and next the offspring of the Wind-god searched the habitations of Dhumraksha, Sampati, the grim Vidyudruna, Phana, Vighana and Sukanabha, Shakra, Shatha, Kapatha, Hrasvakarna, Danshtra and the demon Lomasa, Yudhyonmatta, Matta and the horseman, Dhwajagriva, Sadin, Vidyujjibha and Vijibha, as also that of Hastimukha and of Karala, Vishala and Sonitaksha. The illustrious Son of Maruta then searched the dwellings of other prosperous titans one after the other, marking their affluence.

And having searched all the residences belonging to those titans in every way, that fortunate monkey approached the palace of the king. Then the foremost of monkeys observed demon women of menacing looks, prowling outside the apartments where Ravana slept, bearing darts and maces in their hands and equipped with spears and clubs and he beheld innumerable bands of them in the abode of the titan king and gigantic demons brandishing weapons of every kind. He beheld steeds of exceeding swiftness, red, white and black and wonderfully bred elephants, vanquishers of hostile tuskers, trained for every suitable purpose and equal to Airavata himself in conflict and these elephants, the destroyers of hostile armies resembled scurrying clouds or moving hills and their trumpeting was like the crash of thunder.

Then that monkey, the son of the Wind-god, beheld thousands of the titan host in that palace and cars of gold and glittering mail which shone like the rising sun; he saw also many litters of different shapes, and bowers, picture galleries, gymnasiums, mountains constructed of wood, pavilions and entertainment halls. And in that palace belonging to Ravana, was a charming edifice as beautiful as the Mandara Mountain and pens for peacocks and banners and flagpoles. Heaps of jewels lay about and a great accumulation of treasure had been brought there by the exploits of those valiant titans so that it resembled the palace of Kuvera. On account of the lustre of those gems and the resplendence of Ravana himself, that palace glittered like the sun with its myriad rays.

And that monkey chief beheld couches and seats of gold, and vessels wrought with pearls overflowing with wines,[1] and the dimensions and magnificence of that place caused it to resemble the mansion of Kama or the abode of Kuvera, and that palace resounded with the tinkling of anklets and girdles, with drums and cymbals and other musical instruments and was thronged with women as lovely as pearls and surrounded by great ramparts.

CHAPTER 7

Description of the Aerial Chariot Pushpaka

THEN that mighty monkey continued to explore those dwellings fitted with golden windows, studded with emeralds, resembling a mass of clouds in the rainy season rent by lightning and traversed by flocks of cranes. And he beheld various halls and

[1] Overflowing with Wines—Lit.: Madha and Asava—spiritous liquors made of honey, molasses or the blossom of Bassia Caryola, or according to some, grapes.

buildings stored with conches, bows and weapons of war, furnished with turrets as high as hills, and these mansions, containing treasure of every kind were held in regard by both Gods and titans and were flawless and constructed by Ravana by his own power.

Hanuman having scoured the mansions of that Lord of Lanka meticulously furnished with every comfort as if Maya had created them, thereafter visited the palace of that King of Rakshasas himself, which surpassed all others and resembled a mass of towering clouds. Of incomparable loveliness, it seemed as if heaven itself had descended on earth and its beauty was dazzling. Teeming with innumerable gems, trees of every kind covered it with flowers like the summit of a mountain on which snow has fallen; beautiful women served as its ornaments and it shone like a cloud riven by lightning; such was its splendour that it resembled a marvellous chariot drawn through the skies by ravishing swans.

Like the peak of a mountain rich in ore or the firmament adorned by the moon and stars or like clouds of many hues, it glistened with innumerable gems. Artificial rocks made of clay, resembling mountain ranges, planted with counterfeit trees laden with heaps of flowers, fashioned with stamens and leaves could be seen there and improvised dwellings, dazzlingly white, with pools covered with flowering lotuses possessing golden stamens, and diverse groves and ravishing fountains.

The monkey gazed on the vast aerial chariot named Pushpaka, which, gleaming like pearl, planed above the highest buildings and contained birds made of emerald, silver and coral and serpents marvellously fashioned of various metals and life-sized horses and birds with charming beaks and wonderful wings which contracted and expanded, their plumage like that of Kama himself, posed on gold and coral flowers; and there were elephants with tapering trunks, bearing lotus leaves, engaged in showering water on the Goddess Lakshmi, who, seated in a pool, held lotuses in her fair hands.

Such was the marvellous creation which met the astonished monkey's gaze, which resembled a mountain of charming caverns or a tree from whose hollows delicious fragrance escapes in the springtime.

Yet that monkey searching that exalted city, protected by the ten-headed Ravana, was unable to find the daughter of Janaka, so highly regarded and deeply afflicted and who had been conquered by the virtue and valour of her lord. And not finding Janaka's daughter, despite his investigations and the vigilance of his search, the illustrious Hanuman, who was virtuous and generous of soul, felt a burning anguish take possession of his heart.

CHAPTER 8

A further Description of the Aerial Chariot Pushpaka

HALTING there, the intelligent monkey, born of Pavana, regarded that splendid chariot encrusted with gold and gems more carefully. Fashioned of plated gold, embellished with lovely images, regarded by Vishwakarma himself as an incomparable artistic achievement, travelling in space like a guiding light in the orbit of the sun, it was immeasurably resplendent. No detail of that car had been executed unskilfully, no ornament but appeared to be a jewel of great price nor was there anything surpassed by the chariots of the Gods, every part being excellently wrought.

By the merit of his asceticism and contemplation Ravana had obtained it and it repaired wheresoever its master directed it by the power of his thought. Irresistible and swift as the wind, a source of happiness to those magnanimous beings given to pious deeds, who had reached the peak of prosperity and glory, capable of ranging the firmament, containing many apartments and furnished with innumerable works of art, captivating to the mind, stainless as the autumnal moon, resembling a mountain with splendid peaks, borne by thousands of demons whose cheeks were graced with earrings, voracious eaters, of large unwinking eyes, who travelled through space with exceeding velocity day and night, that aerial chariot, Pushpaka, splendid to look upon, covered with flowers, fairer than spring itself, drew the gaze of that Prince of Monkey Warriors.

CHAPTER 9

Hanuman searches the Harem

WITHIN these precincts, a magnificent building, remarkable for its spaciousness and splendour, arrested the attention of Hanuman, the son of Maruta; it was two miles in width, four in length and belonged to the King of the Titans himself.

And Hanuman, the slayer of his foes, ranging here and there in search of the Princess of Videha, the large-eyed Sita, beheld that goodly residence where the titans dwelt together and he approached the palace of the king, surrounded by three and four tusked elephants and guarded in its entire length by warriors bearing weapons in their hands. He beheld that dwelling, thronged with titan women, consorts of Ravana, and also the daughters of kings who had been forcibly carried away by him, which resembled an ocean teeming with crocodiles, sharks, whales, enormous fish and serpents, agitated by the force of the tempest. And the splendour of the abode of Vaishravana, Chandra and Harivahana was reflected in Ravana's palace, a splendour that was unequalled and changeless and the prosperity of the residences of Kuvera, Yama and Varuna were rivalled, nay surpassed, by that of the titan's abode.

In the centre of that palace, the offspring of the wind, saw yet another edifice, well constructed and furnished with innumerable grilles. Formerly created in heaven at Brahma's wish by Vishwakarma, that noble car embellished with gems was called Pushpaka, which Kuvera had acquired by prolonged austerities and of which the King of the Titans, having vanquished him by his might, took possession. And that mighty monkey ascended that splendid car, containing figures of wolves made of Kartasvara and Hiranya gold and adorned with slender pillars of dazzling splendour, furnished with private rooms and gleaming pavilions, resembling the Meru and Mandara Mountains, licking the skies and blazing like the sun.

This masterpiece of Vishwakarma had many golden stairways and a superb and marvellous ceiling; it contained balconies and galleries of deep blue sapphire and other precious gems; the floors were encrusted with rare pearls which rendered it blindingly beautiful; built of red sandalwood and shining like pure gold, it resembled the rising sun and subtle perfumes rose therefrom.

That mighty monkey, stationed there, smelt the rich odour of wines and viands which rose on every side, and those ambrosial and penetrating fumes seemed to him to be the embodiment of Anila herself and were inhaled by him as coming from an intimate friend, and that aroma seemed to say to Hanuman " Come hither where Ravana is to be found ", and he proceeded further and beheld a vast and glorious hall.

Now that spacious apartment was very dear to Ravana, who looked on it as a greatly cherished woman and its jewelled stairways and galleries of pure gold gave it a dazzling appearance, the floors being of crystal with inlay of ivory, pearl, diamond, coral, silver and gold. It was adorned with many jewelled pilasters, which were symetrical, straight, elegant and inlaid with exceeding artistry and it was supported by tall pillars of equal size resembling wings so that the building seemed to be flying in the air and the floor was covered by a carpet, wide and four-cornered like the earth[1] and patterned as with varied countries, kingdoms and dwellings, and there the song of birds could be heard and it was pervaded by a celestial fragrance.

Hung with rich tapestries, darkened by incense fumes, spotless and pure as a swan, garlanded with leaves and flowers lending it the resemblance of Kamadhenu, bringing delight to the heart, colour to the cheek, giving birth to prosperity and banishing all sorrow, the apartments of the King of the Titans gratified every sense, as if it were a mother.

Entering that abode protected by Ravana, Hanuman asked himself: " Can this be paradise or the region of the Gods or Indra's capital or the state of supreme bliss ? " and he examined the golden lamps, which resembled gamblers

[1] Four-Cornered—The ancient Hindu belief was that the earth was four-cornered.

absorbed in their dice, who, defeated by their opponents, are plunged in thought, and Hanuman perceived that the brilliance of the lamps and the lustre of Ravana and the splendour of the decorations, illumined the appartment.

He beheld innumerable women, lying on the rugs, attired in every kind of raiment with wreaths on their heads, who, under the influence of wine, had fallen asleep, having ceased to disport themselves, half the night being spent. And, on account of the silence, that great company, decked with ornaments, the tinkling of which was no longer audible, resembled a vast lake filled with lotuses where the sound of the swans and the humming of bees has ceased.

Maruti gazed on the faces of those lovely women with eyes and mouths shut fast, emitting a flower-like fragrance and they resembled lotuses that, folding their petals at evening, wait for the dawn to open them once more or like water lilies which the bees, intoxicated with love, visit continually. With just cause did that noble and mighty monkey compare them to nymphoeae, for the harem was bright with their radiance, as the starry heavens on a serene autumnal night and, in their midst, the King of the Titans blazed like a fair moon, encircled by attendant stars.

Then that monkey said to himself: " Those planets that have fallen from the firmament, their merit exhausted, are all re-united here ", and in sooth, those women in their grace, beauty and magnificence shone like dazzling meteors.

Some lay wrapped in slumber into which they had fallen in the midst of dancing and feasting, their hair and crowns in disarray, their ornaments scattered here and there; others amongst those lovely beings had lost their anklets and the tilaka mark on their foreheads had been effaced; some had allowed their garlands to fall aside, some had broken their pearls and, their raiment in disorder, their girdles loosened, resembled disburdened mules, whilst others, bereft of earrings, their garlands torn and crushed, looked like flowering creepers trodden under foot by great elephants in the forest.

Sometimes the loosened pearls, like the scintillating rays of the moon, lay between the women's breasts like sleeping swans, whilst chains of emerald resembled drakes or those of gold looked like Chakravata birds. And those women were like unto rivers, their thighs being the banks, where swans, geese and other waterfowl disport themselves or, sleeping, resembled streams, the golden bells on their girdles, the ripples, their faces, the lotuses, their amorous desires, the crocodiles, their grace, the banks.

On their tender limbs the marks of the ornaments looked like bees, whilst the veils of others, rising and falling with their breath, fluttered gracefully before their faces like bright streamers of many-coloured yarn and the earrings of others vibrated gently with the circulating air.

Their subtly perfumed breath impregnated with the aroma of sugar-sweetened wines which they had drunk, caused Ravana delight and, some of his consorts, in dream, savoured the lips of their rivals again and again, deeming them to be the king's. Passionately devoted to their lord, these lovely women, no longer mistresses of themselves, offered their companions marks of their affection. Some, in their rich attire, slept leaning on their arms laden with bracelets, some rested on their companions' breasts, some on their laps, their bosoms, their thighs and backs, and under the influence of wine, clinging amorously to one another, those women of slender waist, slept, their arms intertwined.

Those groups of damsels enfolding one another, resembled a garland of flowers visited by amorous bees or, like creepers opening to the caress of the vernal breeze that intertwine, forming clusters of blossom or the interlocking branches of great forest trees full of swarming bees; thus seemed this gathering of Ravana's consorts. And on account of the proximity of these women, sleeping close to one another, it was impossible to distinguish to whom the jewels, veils and garlands covering their limbs, belonged.

While Ravana slept, the beauty of those women resembling golden lamps, seemed to watch over him and there were daughters of Rajarishis, Giants and Celestial Beings, who had become his consorts and that war-like titan king had acquired them after subduing their relatives, though some had followed him of their own accord from love. None had been forcibly borne away who had not been attracted by his prowess and qualities and none had belonged to another, save the daughter of Janaka whose heart was set on Rama; none was devoid of nobility, beauty, intelligence and grace and each was the object of Ravana's desire.

Then the lord of the monkeys, endowed with virtue, reflected: "If the consort of Raghava were as one of these women, the King of the Titans would indeed be blessed to-day, but Sita is far superior to them on account of her great qualities, which is evident, since for her sake that mighty monarch of Lanka has committed this wicked deed.

CHAPTER 10

Hanuman sees Ravana surrounded by his Wives

LOOKING round, Hanuman observed a splendid dais, worthy of the Gods, made of crystal encrusted with pearls, furnished with couches of emerald mounted on ivory and gold and covered with rich and priceless rugs. And he saw a white canopy, in that place, festooned with celestial garlands that gleamed like the moon.

And he observed a magnificent couch inlaid with gold, flaming like fire and bearing garlands of Ashoka flowers, around which figures were waving fans to and fro, creating cooling draughts and perfumes of every kind wreathed it with delicious fragrance. Spread with soft woollen cloths and decked with chaplets of flowers, it was adorned on every side.

And there, resembling a thundercloud, the Sovereign of the Titans lay with bright and flashing earrings, reddened eyes, golden raiment, his limbs smeared with saffron and fragrant sandal, like a purple cloud at dusk, riven with lightning. Adorned with celestial ornaments, magnificent to behold, able to change his form at will, as he lay asleep he resembled the Mandara Mountain with its trees, groves and bushes without number. Having ceased from dalliance, decked with priceless ornaments, the delight of the titans and dear to all the titan women, his feasting over he lay sleeping on the golden bed, breathing like a serpent.

And Hanuman, filled with awe, shrank back in fear, and stationed himself on a landing of the stairway, pressing himself against the inner wall; then that courageous monkey looked down on that lion among titans lying there in a drunken stupor. And as the King of the Titans lay sleeping, his luxurious couch resembled a great waterfall by which a mighty tusker in mustha is resting.

Hanuman looked down on the two outstretched arms, encircled with golden bracelets of that gigantic monarch, resembling the standards of Indra, which had formerly been pierced in combat by the sharp tusks of Airavata and torn by the discus of Vishnu and the great shoulders that had been lacerated by Indra's mace. Those vast arms, firmly set with well-formed, powerful muscles and thumbs and nails bearing auspicious marks, rings coverings the fingers, those arms, thick as clubs, rounded like the trunk of an elephant, that lay along the opulent couch as it were two snakes with five heads, smeared with sandal of the colour of hare's blood, fresh, extremely rare and of a delicious fragrance massaged by women of sovereign beauty with precious unguents, those arms that had caused Yakshas, Pannagas, Gandharvas Devas and Danavas to cry out in terror, that monkey gazed upon as they lay along the couch, like two great and angry reptiles sleeping in a cave on the Mandara Mountain. And with his two great arms, the Chief of the Titans resembled Mount Mandara with its twin peaks.

The scent of the Mango or Punnaga tree, impregnated with that of the Bakula blended with the savour of viands and the aroma of wine, issued from the vast mouth of that Monarch of Titans during sleep and seemed to fill the whole apartment. His diadem was decorated with rubies and precious stones, gleaming with gold and he was adorned with earrings, smeared with red sandal, his well-developed chest bearing a string of pearls; a white silken cloth, flung aside, revealed his scars and he was covered with a costly yellow coverlet. Like a mass of light he lay, hissing like a serpent so that it seemed as if an elephant lay asleep in the deep waters of the Ganges. Four lamps, set on golden pillars, cast their light to the four sides as lightning reveals the surface of a mass of cloud.

Then that foremost of monkeys saw the wives of that great monarch of the titans sleeping at the foot of their lord, their faces bright as the moon, wearing precious earrings and fresh garlands. Skilled musicians and dancers, they lay in the arms and on the breast of that Indra of Titans, attired in beautiful raiment, and the monkey gazed on those women wearing golden bracelets and earrings set with diamonds and emeralds, their faces fair as the moon, illumined by the reflection of their glittering earrings, lighting the hall as stars illumine the firmament.

Overcome with drinking and amorous dalliance, those slender-waisted wives of the King of the Demons lay fast asleep where they had been seated; and one, possessed of lovely limbs, skilled in the dance, slept there, wearied by her graceful motions, whilst another, embracing her Vina, looked like a lotus that had fallen into the water clinging to a passing raft; a third dark-eyed maiden held her Mankuka in her lap, as a youthful woman would her child, while yet another with graceful limbs and shapely bosom, slept with her tambourine pressed to her heart, as one embraces his love after a long absence. This one, with eyes like lotuses had fallen asleep clasping her Vina, as a beautiful girl enfolds her beloved one affectionately in her arms. Here one of restrained sense lay beside her lute which she encircled with her arms, resembling one affianced lying by the side of her chosen one; there, one whose limbs gleamed like Kanada gold, dimpled, ravishing, her eyes heavy with wine, though sleeping, was striking her drum. One of slender waist and flawless beauty, worn out by feasting, slept with a cymbal in her lap and yet another held a Dindima and had another slung on her back so that she looked like a young mother with her husband and her child. One, with eyes large as lotus petals, clasping her Adambara tightly to her breast, had fallen asleep under the influence of wine and yet another, her water vessel overturned, resembled a flowery wreath that is sprinkled with water to keep it green; another, falling under the sway of sleep, with her hands covered her breasts resembling two golden cups, and one, with eyes like lotuses, fair as the moon, had fallen asleep embracing one of her companions possessed of lovely hips. Peerlessly beautiful women, clasping musical instruments, pressed them to their bosoms like lovers their chosen ones.

And that monkey beheld a marvellous bed set apart, on which one of these lovely women lay, richly attired, adorned with pearls and precious gems, who seemed to lend radiance to that magnificent apartment. Clad in silk bright as Kanaka gold, Ravana's favourite Queen, Mandodari by name, that slender-waisted woman of gracious features, lay fast asleep, adorned with ornaments and, seeing her, that offspring of the Wind-God said to himself: " This one, endowed with the wealth of youth and beauty may be Sita " and he rejoiced exceedingly. Thereafter, in his delight, he leapt into the air, waving his tail and manifesting his joy by his antics, frolicking, singing, climbing up the pillars from whence he dropped to the ground, thus demonstrating his monkey nature.

CHAPTER II

Description of the Banqueting Hall

THEN that mighty monkey dismissed this thought concerning Sita and began to reflect further:

" Separated from Rama, that lovely woman would be unable to sleep, eat or adorn herself nor would she submit to any other, were he King of the Celestials himself, for Rama has no equal even among the Gods; this is therefore some other."

In this conviction, that foremost of monkeys began to search the banqueting hall anew, anxious to discover Sita.

Leaning on their tambourines, drums and Celikas, or stretched on luxurious couches, all these women slept soundly, worn out with playing, singing, dancing and drinking. And that leader of monkeys saw thousands of women beautifully adorned, some having fallen asleep discussing each other's charms, some debating the art of singing, some skilled in discerning time and place, discoursing on circumstance, some given over to merriment and, elsewhere also, he observed beautiful and youthful women who had fallen asleep talking of beauty, or, full of perspicacity, deciding what was opportune. And in their midst, the Lord of the Titans, resembled a bull in a spacious stall, surrounded by graceful kine. Encircled by those women, that King of the Titans looked like a mighty tusker accompanied by female elephants in the forest.

In the abode of that powerful Titan King, that lion among monkeys searched the banqueting hall throughout, furnished with every desirable object and he beheld the flesh of buffalo, deer and bear in separate dishes together with peacock and fowl on golden platters, that had not been broached, and percupine, deer and peacocks, seasoned with curds and sochal salt and goats, leverets and fish half consumed, with portions of dressed venison and sauces. There were wines of superior vintage and rare dishes with salted pies spiced with vinegar and diverse confections capable of stimulating the appetite. Costly bracelets and anklets were scattered here and there and fruit was arranged in small dishes, whilst flowers were spread about, lending the whole floor an air of splendour, and elegant couches and seats set round that place of feasting caused it to shine like fire. In addition, meats of every kind and flavour, seasoned with diverse substances and dressed by skilful cooks, were placed round the hall and Hanuman observed delicious beverages made of a variety of ingredients, some from sugar, some distilled from fruit and flowers or impregnated with fragrant powders.

The vast floor reflected the innumerable garlands, golden vessels, crystal bowls and cups lying everywhere and looked exceedingly beautiful and that mighty monkey saw golden wine jars studded with gems, some of which were full of wine, some half full and some wholly drained; and there were many wines that had not yet been served and various kinds of viands that remained untouched.

Elsewhere he saw many couches that were unoccupied, and some, where women of unsurpassed beauty slept, clasping each other in their arms. One of these youthful women had forcibly possessed herself of another's quilt and, wrapping herself therein, had fallen asleep. The gentle breathing of these women barely stirred their attire or the garlands that adorned them but caressed them as it were and a gentle breeze, laden with the odour of sandal and the sweet-tasting Sidhu, with the diverse floral wreaths and flowers, perfumed bark prepared for ablutions and incense, spread over the aerial car, Pushpaka.

And in that residence of the titan there were women of incomparable beauty, some dark-skinned, some the colour of Kancana gold, who, overcome by slumber and worn out with dalliance, resembled sleeping lotuses.

Thus that mighty monkey searched every quarter of Ravana's private apartments without seeing Janaki anywhere and, having scanned the faces of all these women, he was filled with apprehension, fearing lest he had failed in his purpose. Then he reflected: " Beholding the wife of another while she is sleeping, is undoubtedly an infringement of the moral law, verily to look on another's wife was never my intention but here I have seen one who hath lusted after the wives of others."

Then another thought came to that sagacious monkey, single-mindedly bent on the execution of his duty: "All these consorts of Ravana have been beheld by me without their knowledge yet I find no fluctuation in the tenor of my mind. The mind is the motive power of every movement of the senses, whether it be good or evil and mine remains untroubled; further, how could I search for Sita otherwise? It is amongst women that one should look for women; every being is to be sought amongst its own kind, none searches for a woman among deer. Therefore with a pure heart I have explored Ravana's inner apartment but I have not seen the daughter of Janaka."

And Hanuman scrutinized the faces of the daughters of Devas, Danavas and Nagas, without finding Sita and, not finding her in that place, he left the banqueting hall and began to search elsewhere. Leaving that place of feasting, the offspring of the Wind-god began to look for Sita in another quarter.

CHAPTER 12

Hanuman becomes despondent

REMAINING in the precincts of the palace, Hanuman searched the arbours, galleries and the sleeping apartments, eager to discover Sita but without being able to find that lady of gracious appearance there; and, not finding the beloved of that descendant of Raghu, the mighty monkey reflected:—

"Since, despite mine exertions I am unable to find the daughter of Mithila, assuredly Sita is no longer alive. That youthful and virtuous woman, anxious to defend her honour, has been slain by the wicked Lord of the Titans for remaining faithful to her conjugal duty or the daughter of King Janaka has died of fright on seeing those consorts of the Sovereign of the Titans, who are deformed, sallow-skinned, misshapen and who possess huge heads and monstrous forms. Failing to discover Sita, my valour has been expended in vain and a large part of the term allotted to the monkeys has run out; I dare not present myself before Sugriva, who is powerful and given to meting out harsh punishment. I have explored the inner apartments thoroughly but the gentle Sita was not to be found there and I have spent myself in vain. Further, on my return, the assembled monkeys will enquire of me saying: "O Valiant Hanuman, having reached the further shore, what didst thou accomplish there, tell us?"

Not having seen Janaka's daughter, what shall I answer? The term fixed having passed, assuredly it is meet that I should fast to death, and what will the aged Jambavan and Angada say with all the assembled monkeys since I have crossed the ocean to no purpose? Yet perseverance is the root of success, perseverance is the root of prosperity, perseverance brings supreme felicity, therefore I will search all those places still left unexplored by me. Moreover it is my intention to put forth fresh efforts and investigate all those regions not yet visited by me and the banqueting halls, the gardens, the sports pavilions, the courtyards, dwellings, highways, alleys and chariots, though already searched by me, shall be examined once again.

Having thus resolved, Hanuman set about exploring the basements, temples and many-storied dwellings, going up and down, to and fro, opening doors and closing others, entering here and making an exit there, till there was not even the space of four fingers left unscrutinized by him. And he visited the galleries running inside the ramparts and terraces supported by stanchions and the groves and lotus pools and he saw there hideous and monstrous female titans of every shape but not the daughter of Janaka; and the illustrious consorts of Vidyadharas fell under his gaze but not the beloved of Raghava.

Hanuman beheld there also the daughters of Nagas, of lovely limbs, whose faces shone like the full moon, who had been forcibly brought there by the Lord of the Titans, but not the cherished daughter of Janaka and, not seeing her among all those lovely women, a profound despair seized that warrior born of Maruta.

Reflecting that the exertions of all those leaders of monkeys and the crossing of the ocean had proved vain, the son of Anila became extremely anxious and descended from that aerial car. Thereafter Hanuman, born of Maruta, grew pensive and a great melancholy invaded his soul.

CHAPTER 13

Hanuman's Dilemna

DESCENDING on to the ramparts from the aerial car, that leader of monkeys, the agile Hanuman, resembled a flash of lightning athwart the clouds and, having searched the apartments of Ravana without finding Sita, Videha's daughter, he said to himself:—

" Seeking the object of Rama's affection, I have explored Lanka again and again without finding the daughter of Janaka of immaculate form! Many times have the marshes, pools, lakes, streams, rivers, banks, forests and inaccessible mountains been scoured by me without any trace of Sita being found!

"The King of the Vultures, Sampati, affirmed that Sita was in Ravana's palace but I do not see her there, how can this be? Or has the daughter of Videha, Maithili, born of Janaka, who was carried away against her will, being wholly helpless surrendered to Ravana? Or perchance, fearing Rama's arrows, in his rapid flight, that titan has allowed Sita to slip from his grasp or she seeing herself borne away on the path of the Siddhas and beholding the ocean, has yielded up her life? Who can say whether that noble large-eyed lady has not succumbed on account of the great speed assumed by Ravana and the pressure of his arms?

"It may happen that, while Ravana flew over the sea, the daughter of Janaka struggling to free herself, fell into the waves, or alas, far from her lord, seeking to defend her honour, was devoured by that vile Ravana. May not that innocent dark-eyed lady have become the food of those impure consorts of that Indra of demons? Ever absorbed in the contemplation of Rama, whose countenance resembles the moon, has she breathed her last, bewailing her lot and crying: 'O Rama! O Lakshmana! O Ayodhya!', or, having been banished to the dungeons of Ravana's palace, is that youthful woman grieving like a caged bird? How could the slender-waisted consort of Rama, born of the blood of Janaka, possessing eyes like lotus petals, submit to Ravana? But whether she be slain or is lost or has died, I dare not speak of it to Rama. To tell him would be an offence, yet it is also wrong to withhold it from him; what should I do? I am perplexed! In such a dilemna, how shall I act?"

Thus thinking, Hanuman added:—"If, without finding Sita, I return to the city of that lord among monkeys, in how far will my courage have availed me? My crossing of the ocean has come to nought as also my entry into Lanka and my survey of the titans. When I come to Kishkindha, what will Sugriva and the assembled monkeys say to me or those twin sons of Dasaratha? If I approach Kakutstha with these fatal tidings saying: 'I have not found Sita', he will give up his life. Hearing these cruel, terrible, heartrending and barbarous words, he will not survive and, when his mind has been withdrawn into the five elements, the sagacious Lakshmana, deeply attached to Rama, will also cease to exist ! Then, hearing that his two brothers are dead, Bharata will yield up his life and Shatrughna will renounce his existence also. Beholding their sons dead, their mothers, Kaushalya, Sumitra and Kaikeyi will undoubtedly surrender their lives and, seeing Rama's plight, his grateful and loyal friend, Sugriva, will give up his life. Then the grief-stricken Ruma, distracted and crushed with sorrow, will perish on account of her lord and the Queen Tara, already inconsolable on account of Bali's end, worn out by suffering will be unable to continue living. The loss of his parents will lead the youthful Angada to the brink of death and, overwhelmed by the passing of their leader, the inhabitants of the woods having been cherished with gentleness, gifts and regard by their illustrious monarch, will strike their heads with their fists and die.

" Thenceforth, those foremost of monkeys will no longer assemble to disport themselves in the woods, among the rocks and caves, but with their sons, wives and servants, in despair on account of their master's death, will hurl themselves from the height of the rocks into the abysses and chasms. And they will take poison or hang themselves or enter the fire or fast to death or fall on their own weapons. It is certain that a great calamity will follow my return and the House of Ikshwaku and the inhabitants of the forests will meet with destruction.

" But, if I do not return, those two virtuous and great car-warriors as also the swift-footed monkeys will continue to live in the hope of receiving tidings of Sita, and I, not having found Sita, shall exist by that which falls to my lot, living a life of privation and subsisting on fruit and roots in the forest.

" Preparing a funeral pyre on the shores of the sea, in a place abounding in roots, fruits and water, I shall enter the flames or allow myself to die of hunger and, without fail, offer my emaciated frame as food for the birds and beasts of prey. In my belief, this is the death the sages envisaged for themselves; either I must find Janaki or enter the sea.

" My bright garland of glory, so nobly plaited and begot of courageous acts has perished because I have not been able to find Sita. I shall therefore become an ascetic living under the trees but return I will not without having seen that dark-eyed damsel. If I go back without finding Sita, neither Angada nor the other monkeys will survive. Yet incalculable ills lie in store for one taking his own life ; if however I continue to live, I may achieve success, therefore I shall maintain my existence ! If I live, the re-union of Rama and Sita may be effected."

Revolving these innumerable and painful considerations in his mind, that lion among monkeys sought to prevent himself from being overcome by despair. Summoning up all his courage, that mighty monkey said to himself :—

"I shall slay Dashagriva the terrible Ravana and thus avenge the abduction of Sita or, crossing the sea, I shall drag him before Rama as a beast is offered up to Pashupati."

Reflecting thus, that monkey, who was filled with anxiety and grief, not having been able to find Sita, thought : "So long as I do not find the illustrious consort of Rama, I shall not cease from searching the city of Lanka on every side. If, according to Sampati's words, I bring Rama hither, Raghava, not beholding his consort, will burn all the monkeys with the fire of his wrath. Therefore I shall stay here, living a life of abstinence with my senses under control lest all men and monkeys perish through my fault.

"Here is a great Ashoka grove, containing huge trees, which has not yet been searched by me. Having paid reverence to the Vasus, the Rudras, the Adityas, the Ashwins and the Maruts, in order to increase the torment of the titans, I shall enter it. Having vanquished the demons, I shall restore the divine Sita, the delight of the House of Ikshwaku to Rama as the fruit of austerity is bestowed on an ascetic."

Having thus reflected for a space, the mighty offspring of the Wind-god suddenly rose and said : "Salutations to Rama accompanied by Lakshmana and Anila ! Salutations to Chandra, Agni and the Maruts !"

After paying obeisance to all the Gods as also to Sugriva, the offspring of the Wind-god, surveying the four quarters, in imagination as it were advanced towards that magnificent grove and began to consider what should be done further.

He reflected: "This Ashoka Grove which is sacred with its dense thickets must be filled with titans, its trees are surely protected by trained guards and the blessed Vishvatam himself refrains from blowing vigorously here. In Rama's interests I shall contract my form so that I may not be detected by Râvana. May all the Gods, as also the hosts of sages, confer success on me! May Swyambhu, the Celestial Beings, as also the ascetics, the God of Fire, the God of the Wind, the Bearer of the Thunderbolt, Varuna, the Moon and the Sun, the high-souled Ashwins and all the Maruts grant me success! May all beings and the Lord of all Beings and those unknown, who are met with on the way, confer success on me!

"When shall I behold that noble and irreproachable queen with her arched nose, pearly teeth, sweet smile and eyes resembling lotus petals, bright as the King of the Stars, O when?

"O how will that frail and virtuous one, ruthlessly borne away by that wicked and vile wretch, the scourge of human beings, who masks his savagery under an alluring disguise, disclose herself to me?"

CHAPTER 14

The Ashoka Grove

HAVING meditated for a space, Hanuman, who had rejoined Sita in thought, leapt from the rampart on to the surrounding wall and trembling with delight, that mighty monkey, standing there, beheld every variety of tree and flower, it being early spring He saw Sala, Ashoka, Bhavya, Champaka, Uddalaka, Nagavriksha, Mango and Kapimukha trees in flower with clumps of Amras intertwined with hundreds of creepers. And Hanuman, leaping down into that enchanting grove, like an arrow shot from a bow, entered that garden resembling the rising sun which re-echoed to the song of birds, planted with gold and silver saplings and containing flocks of birds and deer with trees of varying fragrance which filled him with wonder.

Abounding in trees of every kind, laden with flowers and fruit, where cuckoos called deliriously and swarms of bees hummed, where all creatures expressed happiness in their movements, where the cries of the peacock could be heard and waterfowl teemed, the heart of the beholder was ravished.

And Hanuman, searching for that princess of beautiful and faultless limbs, woke the birds that had been sleeping sweetly and blown by the wind set up by the wings of those birds in flight, a shower of variegated blossom fell, covering Hanuman, the son of the Wind-god in the midst of the Ashoka Grove lending him the loveliness of a hill covered with flowers. Then all the creatures beholding that monkey, as they darted from all sides, thought: " It is the God of Spring ".

Wholly hidden in blossom which had fallen from the trees, the earth looked like a bride covered with jewels and, shaken in diverse ways by the motion of that impetuous monkey the trees rained down a shower of multi-coloured blooms. And those trees, whose tops were stripped of leaves, from which both blossom and fruit had fallen, looked like gamblers who have staked their raiment and possessions only to lose all. Buffetted by Hanuman's leaping, those lovely trees speedily let their flowers, leaves and fruit fall to the ground and, deserted by the birds, no longer able to seek shelter there, on account of the shaking administered by Maruti, presented their bare branches only, so that the Ashoka grove, battered by the blows of the monkey's feet and tail, resembled a youthful woman with her locks dishevelled, the brightness of her lips and teeth dimmed, her tilaka mark effaced and her arms and legs scarred. And in his haste, that monkey snapped the clusters of creepers as the wind dispels the clouds during the rainy season.

Ranging here and there, that monkey observed places that were paved with gold and silver with ponds filled with translucent water, their steps encrusted with valuable gems, pearls and coral, their floors being of crystal and the banks set with trees of Kancana gold which emitted a dazzling light.

These pools were covered with clumps of lotuses and lilies whilst waterfowl enhanced their beauty and they re-echoed to the cry of Natyuhas, swans and geese; broad and beautiful streams, bordered on every side by trees, fed them with their waters which resembled Amrita and glided under variegated shrubs decorated by hundreds of creepers, the ground being carpeted by rhododendron and oleander flowers.

Then that foremost of monkeys beheld a high hill, bright as a cloud crowned with lofty peaks, many kinds of trees and filled with caves, and it was one of the wonders of the world! And he beheld a river falling from those heights, like a youthful woman tearing herself from her lover's arms in order to leave him and the branches of the trees, sweeping the water, looked as if the companions of that damsel were detaining her, whilst further down, Hanuman beheld that stream returning on its course, as if the maiden, appeased, were reconciled to her beloved.

Thereafter at some distance from the river, a pool filled with lotuses, frequented by birds of every kind drew the gaze of that lion among monkeys, Hanuman, born of Maruta; and he saw a fountain of fresh water with enchanting steps made of precious gems, its basin strewn with pearls, which was embellished on every side with countless herds of deer, ravishing groves, and mansions built by Vishvakarma himself, adorned with artificial woods and trees laden with fruit and flowers, their branches spreading like umbrellas giving shade, whilst the ground beneath was paved with gold and silver.

And that great monkey beheld a single golden Shingshapa tree surrounded by a golden dais and he saw many flower beds and trees which resembled flames, the radiance of which rivalled Mount Meru and caused him to think they were made of gold. Seeing those beautiful golden trees, with their flowering crests, buds and shoots agitated by the wind, emitting a sound like the tinkling of many ornaments, Hanuman was astounded.

Climbing quickly into that many-leafed Shingshapa tree Hanuman reflected: "From here I may perchance behold Vaidehi, that unhappy being who sighs for Rama's presence and who, filled with grief, wanders aimlessly to and fro. Without doubt, this Ashoka Grove embellished by Candana,

Champaka and Vakula trees, belongs to the wicked Ravana. Here by this lovely pool frequented by birds, that princess and royal spouse, Sita, will certainly repair. She, the beloved of Raghava, accustomed to wander in the woods, bereft of Rama, will assuredly come hither. That lady, whose eyes resemble a doe's, tormented with grief on account of separation from Rama, fond of roving in the woods, will certainly walk in this grove. She, the chaste and virtuous wife of Rama, Janaka's daughter, who ever loved the creatures of the forest, anxious to offer up her devotion, will come to this river of translucent waters, for this purpose.

" Truly this beautiful grove is worthy to be the abode of that chaste consort of the king of men, Rama. If that goddess, whose countenance resembles the moon, still lives, she will inevitably visit this river of cool waters."

Thus reflected the high-souled Hanuman, expecting the consort of that lord of men to appear and, concealing himself in the Shingshapa tree covered with leaves and flowers, gazed out over the whole scene.

CHAPTER 15

Hanuman sees Sita

SEATED in the tree, glancing round in quest of Sita, Hanuman surveyed the entire grove filled with trees intertwined with creepers and redolent with celestial odours. Manifesting every aspect of beauty, possessing the splendour of the Nandana Gardens, it was inhabited by various animals and birds, embellished by palaces and temples and re-echoed to the call of the cuckoo. Adorned with pools filled with golden lotuses and silvery waterlilies, furnished with seats and cushions, buildings and courtyards, with its ravishing trees laden with fruit and flowers in every season and the blossoming Ashoka trees, it resembled the effulgence of the rising sun.

Seated there, Maruti never wearied of gazing on those lovely woods, whose foliage was almost concealed by hundreds of birds disporting themselves there and the beauty of those

Ashoka trees, bending under the weight of their flowers, so that their blossoming seemed to extend to their very roots, dispelled all sorrow. The entire region seemed ablaze with the brilliance of the Karnikara and Kimshuka trees in flower; the giant-rooted Punnaga, Saptaparna, Champaka and Uddalaka blazed forth in blossom and there were thousands of Ashoka trees some of a golden colour, some like flames of fire and some as dark as collyrium so that the whole place resembled the Garden of Nandana or the enchanting domain of Chaitaratha or even surpassed them. This celestial unimaginably beautiful region was like a second heaven, having flowers for its constellations or a fifth ocean, its pearls being the blossom scattered there. Planted with trees, which bloomed in every season, emitting honeyed scents, that garden was filled with the cries of birds and beasts and redolent with exquisite scents, a delicious spot, equal to that King of Mountains, a second Gandhamadana.

Now, in that Ashoka Grove, that lion among monkeys observed, at a short distance, a splendid temple as white as Mount Kailasha, flawless, supported by a thousand pillars, its steps of coral, its floors of refined gold, dazzlingly beautiful, blinding to the eyes and of such a height that it seemed to kiss the sky.

Then, all at once, he beheld a woman, in soiled raiment, surrounded by female titans and she was emaciated through fasting, sorrowful, heaving frequent sighs, immaculate as the moon's disc in its first quarter, resplendent with a radiance which now shone but dimly so that she seemed like a flame wreathed in smoke.

Clad in a soiled robe of yellow silk, divested of every ornament, she resembled a lotus pool stripped of its flowers. Oppressed, racked with grief and tormented, she was like unto Rohini pursued by Ketu. Her face bathed in tears, distressed, worn out by privation, plunged in anxiety and separated from her kith and kin, no longer able to behold Rama and Lakshmana but only the titans, she appeared like a gazelle surrounded by a pack of hounds.

With her long hair resembling a black serpent, hanging down her back, she looked like the earth with its dark blue forests in the rainy season. That large-eyed lady, worthy of happiness, not having known adversity till that hour, sunk in woe and emaciated was attired in soiled raiment.

Then Hanuman, beholding her, for many reasons deduced that it was Sita and reflected :—" That princess, borne away by the titan, able to change his shape at will, must be this woman before me."

Her face shone like the full moon and she possessed beautiful brows and gracefully rounded breasts ; by her radiance she dispelled the darkness in all regions ; her neck was of a bluish tint, her lips like the Bimba fruit, her waist slender and her carriage full of dignity, her eyes, resembling lotus petals equalled those of Rati, the beloved spouse of Manmatha, lovely as the moon, adored by all.

Now that youthful woman of graceful form was seated on the ground practising austerity like a female ascetic and that timid lady was heaving frequent sighs like the consort of the Serpent King.

Entangled in a mighty web of sorrow, her beauty was veiled like a flame enveloped in smoke or a traditional text obscured by dubious interpretation or wealth that is melting away or faith that is languishing or hope that is almost extinguished or perfection unattained on account of obstacles or an intellect which is darkened or fame tarnished by calumny.

Distracted by her separation from Rama, tormented by the presence of the female titans, her eyes, like a young doe's ranged here and there searching everywhere in her distress. Tears streamed from her eyes with their arched brows and dark lashes and, her features altered, she sighed again and again. That unfortunate one, worthy of every decoration, now bereft of all, covered with stains, resembled the King of the Stars obscured by heavy cloud. Beholding Sita in that pitiable state, Hanuman was perplexed as one whose learning is lost for lack of sustained endeavour and, seeing her without ornaments, he recognised her with difficulty as a text that is wrongly construed. Beholding that large-eyed and irreproachable princess, Hanuman concluded from her many distinctive characteristics that it must indeed be Sita.

Perceiving on her person such ornaments as had been

described by Rama at the time of his departure, such as the Svadangstras and jewelled armlets, which were now darkened by dust and neglect, nevertheless, they appeared to Hanuman to be those mentioned to him and he reflected :—" Those which wère cast off by Sita on the way, I do not see but those she preserved are certainly here.

" The rich silken mantle shining like Kanaka gold, which she let fall, was found by the monkeys caught in a tree and the valuable ornaments cast off by her fell on the earth with a tinkling sound. The robe she now wears is exceedingly worn but its colour remains and resembles her own radiance. Here is the one for whom Rama has suffered torment through affection, pity, grief and love: through affection in consequence of his beloved spouse being borne away; through pity, by his inability to protect her who is dependent on him; through grief, at her loss, and through love by his separation from her. Verily from the grace of her person and her beauty, that resembles his, this lady of dark eyes must be his spouse.

She has her mind fixed on him, and he on her, it is on account of this that they are able to survive. Indeed the Lord Rama has achieved a great feat by still existing separated from her and not yielding up his life in grief."

Having beheld Sita, the Son of Pavana allowed his thoughts to fly to Rama, to whom he silently offered obeisance, and to that princess also.

CHAPTER 16

Hanuman's Reflections on seeing Sita

HAVING offered obeisance to Sita who was worthy of homage, and also to Rama of gentle conduct, that bull among monkeys became absorbed in thought once more.

Reflecting awhile, his eyes full of tears on account of Sita, that sagacious monkey, Hanuman, gave voice to his distress in the following words :—

" None can withstand the force of destiny, since Sita, the consort of the illustrious brother of Lakshmana ever obedient to his preceptors, has met with this misfortune. Conversant with the prowess of Rama and the sagacious Lakshmana, that divine lady is no more perturbed than is the Ganges at the approach of the rainy season. In character, age, conduct and family, they are equal and Raghava is worthy of Vaidehi, that one of dark eyes, who is his."

Seeing Sita, radiant as newly minted gold and who resembled Lakshmi beloved of the worlds, Hanuman approaching Rama in thought, said :—

"On account of this large-eyed lady, the mighty Bali was slain, and Kabanda, equal to him in strength; for her, the mighty demon Viradha, despite his renowned prowess, also succumbed in the forest under the thrusts of the valiant Rama, as Shambara under Mahendra's blows. It was for her that fourteen thousand demons of outstanding exploits were pierced by Rama's arrows resembling tongues of fire in Janasthana. Khara too was brought low on the field of battle; Trishiras was overthrown and the mighty Dushana also by the righteous Raghava. And it was on her account that that supreme and inaccessible kingdom of the monkeys belonging to Bali was acquired by Sugriva, renowned in the Three Worlds; it is for this large-eyed damsel, that the effulgent Lord of the Waters has been crossed by me and this city explored. Methinks that if Rama had turned the whole earth, with its boundaries, upside down for her sake, it were fitting! Were the dominion of the Three Worlds on one side and Sita, born of Janaka, on the other, the former would not equal a fraction of the latter; such is the virtuous daughter of the magnanimous King of Mithila, who is wholly devoted to her lord. She, as a field was being dug, rose from a furrow which the blade of the plough had turned, covered with dust which gleamed like the pollen of a lotus; she, the eldest daughter-in-law of King Dasaratha, who was full of courage and nobility and was never known to retreat in battle; she, the beloved consort of the faithful and dutiful Rama, knower of his own Self, is now in the power of the titans.

"Renouncing every pleasure, actuated by love of her lord, disregarding the inevitable privations, she entered the beautiful forest to live on fruit and roots, ever engaged in the service of her spouse and considered herself to have attained the peak of felicity there, as if it were the palace itself. This lady, whose limbs resemble Kanaka gold and who was ever wont to smile when conversing, now suffers unimaginable woes and Raghava, like a thirsty man panting for a stream, sighs for the sight of that noble woman oppressed by Ravana. Re-united with her, Raghava will enjoy felicity once more, as a king who has been deprived of his throne rejoices on regaining it.

"Deprived of all comfort and pleasure, far from her kinsmen, she preserves her life in the hope of seeing Rama and being re-united with him. Oblivious of the titans and the trees covered with fruit and flowers, her spirit is wholly absorbed in the thought of Rama. For a woman the greatest decoration is her lord and Sita, though incomparably beautiful, no longer shines in Rama's absence. It is only Rama's heroism that makes it possible for him to continue living separated from his consort and prevents him from being overwhelmed with grief. This lady of dark eyes, resembling the moonlight, worthy of happiness, is now utterly wretched and my heart is troubled. Patient as the earth, this lady whose eyes resemble lotuses, who was formerly protected by Rama and Lakshmana, lying at the foot of a tree, is being guarded by demons of hideous aspect. Like a waterlily snapped by the frost, the daughter of Janaka, her beauty faded, is fainting under the rain of misfortunes and, like a doe separated from the herd, is fallen into this distress. The Ashoka trees with their boughs bending under the weight of their blossom seem to increase her grief, as also the moon of pure beams that is rising in this spring season."

Reflecting thus, that valiant monkey, being convinced that it was Sita, stationed himself in the Shingshapa tree.

CHAPTER 17

Description of the Female Titans who guarded Sita

THEN the moon, pure as a waterlily, rose in the stainless heavens, sailing through the firmament like a swan floating on blue waters.

As if to aid him with her light, that pure and clear orb covered the Son of Pavana with her cool rays.

Thereupon that monkey beheld Sita endowed with a moon-like countenance who, under the load of grief, resembled a heavily laden ship foundering in the waves. And gazing on Vaidehi, Hanuman, born of Maruta, observed a number of grim-visaged titan women at a distance, some with but a single eye or ear, some with ears concealing their visage, some without ears, some with noses on their foreheads, some possessed of disproportionately large heads and long necks, some with sparse hair and others covered with hair so that they appeared to be wrapped in a woollen cloth; the ears and brows of some were set low, and their breasts and bellies protruded; others were knock-kneed, stunted, humpbacked, crooked, dwarfed, unkempt, their mouths set awry, their eyes inflamed, their faces fearful to behold Hideous, irascible, quarrelsome, they were armed with spears, darts, hammers and mallets and some had snouts like bears or the muzzles of deer or the faces of tigers, camels, buffalo, goats and jackals and some had the feet of elephants, camels, horses and the heads of some were sunk in their breasts.

Some had a single hand or foot, some the ears of asses, horses, kine and elephants or some the ears of monkeys. Some had enormous noses, some crooked noses and some none at all, some had noses like the trunks of elephants, some had their noses fixed in their foreheads, through which they breathed like beasts. The feet of some were like elephants and some had the feet of kine, some were hairy; some had huge heads, gigantic faces and long tongues; some had the heads of goats, elephants, cows, pigs, horses, camels and donkeys.

These titan women of formidable appearance held spears and maces in their hands, they were ill-humoured and rejoiced in discord. Their hair was black as soot or smoke-coloured, their aspect repellant and they feasted continually, regaling themselves on wine and meat without surcease, their bodies being spattered with blood from the flesh they consumed.

That foremost of monkeys surveyed those titan women whose appearance caused his hair to stand on end and who were seated in a circle round the many-branched tree under which the divine and irreproachable Janaki stood. And the graceful Hanuman beheld that daughter of Janaka bereft of her radiance, consumed with grief, her locks soiled with dust, like a star which has fallen on the earth its merits exhausted, Sita, famed throughout the worlds for her fidelity, yet with little hope of being re-united with her lord.

Stripped of her jewels, she whose chief ornament was her devotion to her lord, held captive by Ravana, appeared like a female elephant separated from the herd who has been attacked by a lion or like the moonlight enveloped in cloud at the end of the rainy season. Her beauty dimmed, she resembled a stringed instrument that one has ceased to pluck and has laid aside. Far from her lord, that illustrious one had fallen under the sway of the titans without having merited it. Sunk in an ocean of grief, surrounded by those titan women in the midst of the Ashoka Grove, she looked like Rohini about to be devoured by Rahu and, beholding her there, Hanuman thought she resembled a creeper divested of its blooms. Having lost her radiance, her limbs covered with dust, with her hidden grace she looked like a lotus spattered with mud.

The monkey, Hanuman, beheld that youthful woman, whose eyes resembled a doe's, clothed in a soiled and tattered cloth and though that blessed one was shorn of her beauty, yet her soul did not lose its transcendency, upheld as it was by the thought of Rama's glory and safeguarded by her own virtue.

Beholding Sita, whose eyes, wide with fear, resembled a doe's, casting her glances here and there like a fawn and consuming the trees and their leaves with her sighs, like a mountainous wave rising from the ocean of adversity, incomparably beautiful with her slender limbs and graceful form, bereft of ornaments, Maruti experienced a great felicity; and Hanuman wept tears of joy at this fortunate meeting and silently offered obeisance to Rama.

Having bowed down to Rama and Lakshmana, the valiant Hanuman, filled with happiness on having beheld Sita, remained there wholly concealed.

CHAPTER 18

Ravana goes to the Ashoka Grove

SURVEYING the woods filled with flowering trees, desirous of beholding Sita closely and the night being almost spent, towards dawn, Hanuman heard the chanting of the Vedas by those among the titans conversant with the holy Shastras and the six supplementary portions.[1]

Then the mighty ten-headed Lord of the Titans awoke to the sound of auspicious music, delightful to the ear and, waking, that great and powerful king, his garlands and attire in disarray, remembered Vaidehi. Passionately enamoured of her, that titan filled with pride could not restrain his desire.

Thereupon, adorned with every kind of ornament, gorgeously robed, he entered the Ashoka Grove filled with innumerable trees, laden with fruit and flowers of every kind with pools embellished with lotuses and lilies, enlivened by birds of rare beauty ecstatic with love and sculptured wolves wonderful to behold.

Dashagriva gazed on those avenues with their arches of gold and gems, thronged with deer of every sort and carpeted with the fruit that had fallen on the earth. And one hundred damsels, daughters of the Gods and Gandharvas, followed in the train of the son of Poulastya, resembling the nymphs who follow Mahendra and some carried lamps of gold whilst others bore chanwaras and fans in their hands. Some carrying water in golden ewers, walked ahead, others following with a golden seat and round cushions and one on his right bore a cup encrusted with gems and filled with wine whilst another carried a canopy resembling a swan, golden-ribbed like the moon and having a handle of fine gold.

In this way, the most beautiful of Ravana's wives, their eyes heavy with sleep and wine followed their august lord like

[1] Grammer, Prosody, Astronomy, Pronunciation, the meaning of unusual terms and Ritual.

flashes of lightning following a cloud. Their bracelets and necklets of pearl, swung to and fro, their sandal-paste was effaced and their hair hung loose while drops of perspiration stood on the brows of those women of lovely mien who stumbled on account of the effects of wine and sleep, and the sweat had caused the flowers that adorned them to wither and their locks were full of shreds from their garlands; in this way, those women of tender appearance full of pride and affection, followed the King of the Titans.

And that powerful lord, the slave of his desires, his heart fixed on Sita, proceeded at a slow pace.

Then the monkey heard the sound of the bells on the women's girdles and anklets, and the joy of Maruta beheld Ravana of inconceivable prowess, whose energy and valour were unimaginable, as he entered the gate; and he was illumined on all sides by the innumerable lamps, fed with fragrant oil, which were carried by those damsels and, intoxicated with pride, desire and wine, his eyes of a coppery red, he looked like Kandarpa himself bereft of his bow. He adjusted his magnificent cloak, decorated with flowers, stainless as the foam of Amrita when churned, and which flung back was held by a clasp.

Hanuman, concealed behind the curtain of leafy branches, stared at him as he approached and from his hiding place, that elephant among monkeys beheld that mighty king, Ravana, surrounded by beautiful and youthful brides, with majestic strides enter that grove, which re-echoed to the cry of deer and birds. Already intoxicated, adorned with priceless ornaments, possessing pointed ears resembling darts, full of energy, that Son of Vaishravas, the Lord of the Titans, appeared surrounded by lovely women, as the moon amidst the stars, and that illustrious monkey, beholding him, reflected:—

"This is the long-armed Ravana who was formerly sleeping in that sumptuous apartment in the centre of the city."

Then the valiant Hanuman, born of Maruta, despite his great courage and though highly effulgent, found himself eclipsed by Ravana's glory and effaced himself among the leafy branches. Ravana however, eager to see that dark-eyed Sita of faultless limbs, whose breasts touched each other, and whose tresses were black, strode on.

CHAPTER 19

Sita's Grief

BEHOLDING Ravana, the Lord of the Titans, endowed with youth and beauty, wearing gorgeous raiment and priceless jewels, that irreproachable princess trembled like a palm agitated by the wind and, covering her breasts and belly with her hands, seeking to conceal them, shrank away.

Dashagriva gazed on Vaidehi, who was guarded by companies of female titans and that unfortunate One, given over to grief, resembled a ship foundering in the sea.

Seated on the naked ground, Sita who was fixed in virtue, resembled a branch severed from a tree that has fallen to earth. Her limbs covered with a soiled cloth, she, who was worthy of ornaments, now no longer adorned, resembled a lotus stalk stained with mud and, though radiant, her beauty was dimmed.

In imagination, she took refuge with that lion among men, Rama, her mind a chariot drawn by the steeds of resolution and that charming princess, devoted to Rama, emaciated, weeping, separated from her kinsfolk, was a prey to anxiety and grief and saw no end to her misfortune. Rocking herself to and fro, she resembled the female of the King of the Snakes under the spell of an incantation or the planet Rohini pursued by Dhumaketu or a saintly and virtuous woman of a noble house who finds herself, through marriage, placed in a low-born family. She resembled a great reputation that has been lost or a faith that has been disregarded or a mind that has become clouded or a hope destroyed, a future shattered, an order misinterpreted, a region obliterated at the destruction of the world or an offering rejected by the Gods, a night on which the full moon is obscured by clouds or a lotus pool laid waste, an army bereft of its warriors, a moon under eclipse, a dried up river, an altar which has been desecrated or a flame that has been extinguished or a lotus pool bereft of flowers, its birds struck with terror agitated by the trumpeting of elephants.

In separation from her lord, consumed with grief, she appeared like a river whose waters have run dry and on account of her limbs not having been washed, she resembled night during the period of the waning moon. That lovely and graceful woman, accustomed to a palace filled with precious gems, now, with wasted limbs, resembled the stalk of a lotus freshly plucked and wilting in the sun.

As the female elephant which has been captured, chained to a stake, grieving for its mate, sighs again and again, so seemed she. Her long dark tresses, utterly neglected, lay along her back so that she appeared like the earth covered with a dark forest at the end of the rainy season. Tortured by hunger, sorrow, anxiety and fear, emaciated, desolate, weakened by abstinence and given over to austerity, stricken with grief, resembling a goddess, her hands were joined offering prayers to Rama for the destruction of Ravana.

And beholding that blameless Maithili with her beautiful dark eyes and graceful lashes, Ravana, to his own destruction, sought to seduce her.

CHAPTER 20

Ravana begs Sita to wed him

THEREUPON Ravana approaching Sita, who was helpless, surrounded by female titans and vowed to a life of austerity, with sweet words and courteous gestures said to her :—

" O Thou whose thighs resemble the trunk of an elephant, who, beholding me dost seek to conceal thy breasts and thy body as if thou didst fear me, O Lady of large eyes, I love thee. Be gracious to me, O Thou of charming looks, who art adored by all the world ! There is no man present here nor any titan able to change his form at will therefore banish the fear which I inspire in thee, O Sita.

"It has ever been the unquestioned and special privilege of titans to unite themselves with the wives of others, either taking them of their own free will or bearing them away by force. In spite of this, O Maithili, I shall not lay hands on thee since thou hast no affection for me but, for myself, I am completely under thy sway, therefore trust in me and respond to my love. O Goddess, have no fear of me, take courage, O Dear One, and do not let thyself be consumed with grief. To wear but a single plait, to lie on the earth in soiled attire and fast unnecessarily does not become thee. In my company, O Maithili, do thou enjoy garlands, perfumes, sandal, ornaments, wine, rich beds and seats, singing, dancing and music. Thou art a pearl among women, do not remain in this condition, adorn thyself as heretofore. Having united thyself with me, O Lady of Lovely Form, what will not be thine?

"Thine enchanting youth is passing away, which like the water of a river, once gone, does not return. O Thou of Fair Looks, the creator of thy loveliness, Vishvakrita, after devising thee, ceased from his work for I see none who is equal to thee in loveliness and grace! Who, having seen thee, resplendent with beauty, could withstand thee O Vaidehi? Even Brahma Himself is moved, how much more other beings? O Thou whose countenance resembles the moon, on whatever part of thy body mine eyes rest, my gaze is riveted. O Maithili, do thou become my consort and renounce this thy folly. Become the foremost queen of these innumerable and lovely women who belong to me. O Timid One, all the treasure I have won throughout the worlds I offer thee as also my kingdom. O Sportive Damsel, for thy sake, having subjugated the entire earth with its many cities, I will confer them on King Janaka. None on this earth can withstand my prowess; behold mine immeasurable valour in battle! Did not the Celestials and the Demons find me irresistible on the battlefield as I broke through their ranks shattering their standards?

"Therefore yield to my desire and attire thyself in splendid robes, letting brilliant gems adorn thy person. O Timid One, enjoy every comfort and luxury according to thy pleasure, divert thyself and distribute land and treasure to others. Live happily depending on my support and exercise supreme authority. By my favour, all thy relatives shall share thy felicity. Observe my prosperity and glory, O Gentle Lady, what canst thou hope from Rama who is clothed in robes of bark? O Fortunate One, Rama has been deprived of his kingdom and is bereft of his might, he practises asceticism, his couch is the bare earth, indeed it is doubtful whether he still lives. O Vaidehi, Rama will never be able to find thee, thou who resemblest a star veiled by dark clouds preceded by cranes. Raghava will never rescue thee from my hands, as Hiranyakashipu was not able to recover his consort Kirti, who had fallen under the sway of Indra.

"O Lady of Sweet Smiles, O Thou of lovely teeth and beautiful eyes, thou dost ravish my heart as Suparna carried away a serpent. Although thy robe is torn and stained and thou art stripped of ornaments, seeing thee, my mind turns away from all my other consorts. O Daughter of Janaka, do thou hold sway over all the women in my harem, who are endowed with every accomplishment. O Princess of raven locks, these women, the foremost among the beauties of the world, shall be thy slaves and attend on thee as the Apsaras attend on Shri. O Graceful Princess, enjoy the pleasures of the world with me and the riches of Kuvera to the utmost of thy desires. O Goddess, neither in asceticism, strength, prowess, wealth nor fame is Rama equal to me. Therefore drink, eat, enjoy thyself and indulge in every pleasure. I shall confer on thee immense wealth, nay, the whole world.

"Do thou satisfy all thy desires in my company, O Timid One, and let thy relatives share thy felicity also. Adorned with dazzling golden bracelets, O Beautiful One, in my company range the groves of flowering trees on the shores of the sea where the black bees hum."

CHAPTER 21

Sita rejects Ravana's Advances with disdain

HEARING the words of that terrible titan, Sita, overwhelmed with grief, answered in a faint and feeble voice. The unfortunate Sita, afflicted and trembling, faithful to her lord and anxious to preserve her virtue, her heart fixed on Rama, placed a straw between Ravana and herself and with a sweet smile answered him, saying:—

"Take back thy heart and set it on thine own consorts. As a sinner may not aspire to heaven, so shouldst thou not expect to win me. That which should never be done and is condemned in a woman faithful to her lord, I shall never do. Born in a noble House, I have been joined to a pious family."

Having spoken thus to Ravana, the virtuous Vaidehi, turning her back on him, continued:—

"It is not meet that I become thy wife since I am united to another. Do thy duty and follow the rules laid down by men of integrity. The wives of others, like thine own, are deserving of protection, O Prowler of the Night. Do thou furnish a good example and enjoy thine own consorts. That wretch who, in the inconstancy and levity of his heart, is not satisfied with his own wives, will be brought to misery by those of others. Either no pious men exist here or thou dost not follow their example, since thy mind is perverse and turns from what is virtuous; or the wise having uttered sage counsel, thou, to the destruction of the titans, dost ignore them.

"Prosperity, kingdom and city are all brought to nought in the hands of a vicious monarch who is not master of himself, hence Lanka, overflowing with treasure, having thee for her king, will suffer destruction 'ere long. O Ravana, that wicked being who brings about his own downfall, succumbs, to the delight of all. When thou meetest with thine end, this evil deed will cause the oppressed to say: 'Fortunate are we that this great tyrant has fallen.'

"Thou art not able to tempt me with wealth and riches; as the light of the sun cannot be separated from the sun so do I belong to Raghava. Having rested on the arm of that Lord of Men, how should I depend on any other? Like unto the spiritual truth known to a brahmin faithful to his vows, I belong to the Lord of the World alone and am lawfully wedded to him. It is to thine own advantage to restore me to Rama, wretched as I am, like unto a she-elephant anxiously awaiting her mate in the forest. It behoveth thee to seek Rama's friendship, that lion among men, if thou desireth to preserve Lanka and dost not wish to bring about thine own destruction. He is wise, conversant with every duty and ever eager to serve those who seek his protection; form an alliance with him if thou desirest to survive. Seek to conciliate Rama, who is full of devotion to those who take refuge in him and humbly conduct me to him once more. If thou dost bring me back to the greatest of the Raghus, thy well-being is assured but if thou dost act otherwise thou art doomed. Thou mayest evade the thunderbolt of Indra, even death himself may overlook thee but there will be no refuge for thee from the fury of Raghava, that lord of men, when thou dost hear the terrible twanging of Rama's bow resembling the thunderbolt hurled by Indra. Soon shall those arrows, bearing the impress of Rama and Lakshmana, like serpents with flaming jaws, penetrate Lanka and those shafts, decorated with heron's plumes, shall cover the whole city annihilating the titans. As Vainateya bears away great reptiles, so shall that eagle, Rama, speedily bear away the titans.

" And like unto Vishnu wresting the radiant Shri from the Asuras by covering the worlds in three strides, so shall my lord, the destroyer of his foes, recover me from thee.

" This cowardly deed has been perpetrated by thee in order to revenge thyself for the destruction of Janasthana and the hosts of the titans. In the absence of these two brothers, those lions among men who had gone forth hunting, didst thou carry me away, O Vile Wretch; but, dog that thou art, thou didst not dare stand before those tigers, Rama and Lakshmana! Wealth and friends will be of no avail to thee in conflict with them and thou shalt be defeated as the one-handed Vritra who entered into combat with the two-handed Indra.

" Soon shall my protector, Rama, accompanied by Saumitri, draw out thy life's breaths, as the sun with its rays dries up shallow water.

Whether thou takest refuge in the abode of Kuvera or terrified, descendest into Varuna's realm, thou shalt assuredly perish, struck down by the son of Dasaratha, like a mighty tree felled by lightning."

CHAPTER 22

Ravana's Threats

To this stern speech from the gracious Sita, the King of the Titans replied harshly :—

" In the world it is said the more gentleness one manifests towards a woman, the more responsive she becomes, but the more kindness I show to thee the more thou dost repulse me. Verily only the love I bear thee restrains my wrath, as a skilful charioteer controls the horses who seek to leave the road. Mighty indeed is the power of love, for even if the object of his affection invoke his anger, man covers her with pity and tenderness. It is on this account, O Lady of lovely mien, that I do not slay thee, thou dost merit death and dishonour, thou who delightest in asceticism without reason. For each and every harsh word which thou hast addressed to me, thou meritest a dreadful end, O Maithili."

Having spoken thus to Sita, the Princess of Videha, Ravana, Lord of the Titans, filled with indignation, added :—" I shall grant thee two months as the term assigned to thee, after which thou must share my bed. If thou should'st refuse, my cooks shall mince thy limbs for my morning repast."

Hearing these threats addressed by the King of the Titans to Janaki, the daughters of the Gods and Gandharvas were exceedingly perturbed and, by the expression of their lips and eyes and their gestures sought to reassure Sita thus menaced by him.

Encouraged by them, Sita, fortified by her virtue and her pride in Rama, addressed Ravana, the Lord of the Titans, in his own interests, saying :—

" It appears that there is none in this city who desires thy welfare and therefore seeks to prevent thee from this despicable deed. Who in the Three Worlds would desire to possess the chaste consort of the high-souled One, who resembles Indra's Sachi ? O Vilest of Demons, how wilt thou escape the consequences of this insult offered to Rama's consort, he whose valour is immeasurable? Like unto an infuriated elephant, encountering a hare in the forest, so shalt thou, the wretched hare, meet with that elephant Rama. Thou dost not fear to rail at the Chief of the Ikshwakus so long as thou art not in his presence. Why do not those cruel, terrible, coppery eyes of thine fall out, looking on me so lustfully, O Ignoble Creature? O Contemptible Wretch, when thou didst threaten the spouse of that high-souled Rama, the daughter-in-law of King Dasaratha, why did not thy tongue dry up? O Ten-necked One, by the power of my asceticism, I could reduce thee to ashes instantly had I Rama's mandate. On account of my consuming virtue and ascetic observances, I could never have been wrested from Rama, were it not that thine evil act was to be the cause of thy destruction, O Dashagriva! Assisted by the brother of Kuvera and proud of thine own heroism, thou didst lure Rama from the hermitage and succeed in bearing me away by stealth."

Hearing Sita's words, Ravana, the King of the Titans, cast ferocious glances at her. Like a mass of black clouds, with his enormous arms and neck, endowed with an elephantine gait, his eyes smouldering, his tongue like a darting flame, of immense stature, wearing a plumed diadem, covered with necklaces, sprinkled with perfume, decked with garlands and, bracelets of gold, his waist encircled with a dark blue belt so that it resembled the Mandara mountain encompassed by the snake at the time of the churning of the ocean; with his vast arms, the Lord of the Titans looked like a mountain with twin peaks. Adorned with earrings gleaming like the rising sun, he resembled a hill between two Ashoka trees enveloped in crimson flowers and buds or like the wish-fulfilling tree or spring incarnate or an altar in a crematorium.

Then Ravana cast furious glances from his bloodshot eyes at the Princess of Videha and, hissing like a serpent, addressed her, saying:—"O Thou who art attached to that wretch without resource or moral sense, I shall destroy thee to-day as the sun's radiance is obliterated at the time of dusk."

Having spoken thus to Maithili, Ravana, the oppressor of his foes, looked at those female titans of formidable appearance, some of whom had a single eye or ear, some enormous ears and some the ears of kine or elephants. Some had ears that hung down and some none at all, some had the feet of elephants, some of horses, some of kine, some were hairy, others possessed but a single eye and foot, some had enormous feet and others none at all. Some had heads and necks of inordinate size, some enormous chests and bellies, some disproportionately large mouths and eyes or long tongues and nails and some had no nose or possessed jaws like lions, some had mouths like oxen or snouts like pigs.

Then Ravana, transfiixing those titans with his glance, said to them :—" Ye Titans seek by fair or foul means, by threats or persuasion or honeyed words or gifts to induce Sita to look on me with favour."

Repeating his command again and again, the King of the Titans filled with desire and anger began to inveigh against Janaki, whereupon a female titan named Dhanyamalini, approaching Dashagriva, embraced him and said :—

" O Great King, enjoy thyself with me, what need hast thou for this human being who is wretched and whose countenance is pale? O King of the Titans, it is not with her that the Gods have destined thee to taste the exquisite pleasures that are the reward of the strength of thine arms. He who loves one who is unwilling exposes himself to torment, whereas he whose love is reciprocated, enjoys perfect happiness."

Having said this, the female titan drew Ravana away but he, resembling a mass of cloud, turned back, laughing scornfully. Then Dashagriva strode away, causing the earth to tremble, and returned to his palace that shone with the brilliance of the orb of day.

Surrounding Ravana, the daughters of the Gods and Gandharvas as well as those of the Serpent Race returned to that sumptuous abode with him. Thus Ravana, distracted with desire, left the Princess of Mithila of irreproachable virtue trembling and entered his own dwelling.

SUNDARA KANDA

CHAPTER 23

The Female Titans seek to persuade Sita to wed Ravana

HAVING spoken thus to Maithili and issued his commands to the titan women, Ravana, the scourge of his foes, went away. And that Sovereign of the Titans having returned to his inner apartment, those women of hideous appearance bore down on Sita and, filled with ire, addressed her in harsh tones, saying:—

" Thou dost not fully value an alliance with the offspring of Poulastya the illustrious Ravana, the magnanimous Dashagriva, O Sita."

Thereafter, one among them named Ekjata, her eyes inflamed with anger addressed Sita of small belly, saying :— "According to tradition, Poulastya is the fourth of the six Prajapatis, a mind-born son of Brahma renowned in all the world, O Sita, and that glorious Ascetic Vaishravas sprang from the mind of that great Rishi whose glory equalled the Prajapatis. O Large-eyed Princess, his son was Ravana, the scourge of his foes; it behoveth thee to become the consort of that King of Titans. Why dost thou not consent, O Thou of Lovely Form ? "

Thereupon another titan called Harijata, rolling her eyes that resembled a cat's, said furiously : " It is for thee to become the wife of one who defeated the thirty-three Celestials and their king in combat ; dost thou not desire to be united with him who is heroic, of indomitable prowess and never turns back in battle ? Renouncing his cherished and beloved Queen Mandodari, that mighty King Ravana will be thine, and seek the gorgeous inner apartment, enriched by thousands of women adorned with jewels, and thou wilt be the object of his worship ! "

There followed another titan by name Vikata, who said : " He who again and again triumphs over the Gandharvas, Nagas and Danavas by his valour in battle has made advances to thee, why dost thou not wish to be the wife of that illustrious Lord of Titans, Ravana, who is endowed with riches ?"

Thereafter the titan, Durmukhi spoke saying :—" O Lady of Lovely Lashes, why dost thou not yield to him, in fear of whom the sun dares not shine nor the wind blow, at whose command the trees shower down their blooms and the hills and clouds loose their floods.

" O Beautiful One, why dost thou not consent to be the consort of that King of kings, Ravana ? We speak thus for thy welfare ; accede to our request, O Goddess of Sweet Smiles or thou shalt surely die."!

CHAPTER 24

Their Menaces

THEREUPON all those titans of hideous appearance, unitedly reproached Sita in harsh and unpleasing words, saying :—

" Why dost thou not consent to dwell in that inner apartment abounding in costly couches ? O Lady, thou prizest union with a mere man ; dismiss Rama from thy thoughts for assuredly thou wilt not see him more. Live happily with Ravana, the Lord of the Titans as thy consort who owns the treasure of the Three Worlds. Thou art a woman, O Irreproachable Beauty, and for this dost mourn a man who is banished from his kingdom and who leads a life of misery."

Hearing the words of those titans, Sita, her lotus eyes filled with tears, answered them, saying :—" What you have uttered is immoral and wholly reprehensible and will never find acceptance with me. A mortal woman may not become the wife of a demon. Devour me, if you wish, I will never accede to your request. Poor or deprived of his kingdom, he who is my husband is my spiritual preceptor and I shall ever follow him, as Suvarchala follows the sun or the blessed Sachi remains at Indra's side or Arundhati near Vasishtha or Rohini by Shashin or Lopamudra by Agastya, Sukanya by Syavana,

Savitri by Satyavat, Shrimati by Kapila, Madayanti by Sandasa, Keshini by Sagara and Damayanti, the daughter of King Bhima by her Lord Naishada."

These words of Sita infuriated those titan women, who had been sent by Ravana nd they overwhelmed her with hard and bitter reproaches while Hanuman crouched silently in the Shingshapa tree. And that monkey heard those demons threatening Sita in this wise.

Surrounding Sita on every side, licking their burning lips again and again and, armed with spears, they menaced her in a paroxysm of rage, saying :

" Dost thou think that the great King of the Titans, Ravana, is not worthy to be thy lord ? "

Threatened by those terrible looking titan women, the lovely Sita, wiping away her tears, took refuge beneath the Shingshapa tree, where, surrounded by those women, that large-eyed princess, overcome with distress, seated herself. And all those hideous demons overwhelmed her with reproaches, as, clad in a mud-stained sari, reduced to the last extremity, her countenance wan, she remained absorbed in her grief.

Thereupon, a grim-visaged demon, named Vinata, having hideous teeth, and a protruding belly, cried out angrily :—

" O Sita, thou hast demonstrated thy devotion to thy lord sufficiently but all excess leads to suffering. May good betide thee ! We are satisfied, thou hast preserved the conventions common among men, now hear what I say to thee for thy good ! Do thou take Ravana for thy lord, he, the chief of the titan host who, like unto Vasava, triumphs over his enemies and is brave, liberal and gracious to all beings. Forsaking that wretched wight, Ramachandra, take Ravana as thy husband ! Thy person, sprinkled with celestial perfume and adorned with excellent ornaments, do thou, O Vaidehi, like unto Swaha, the consort of Agni or the goddess Sachi, wife of Indra, from to-day become the Queen of the Worlds ! What shalt thou do with Rama who is wretched and has but a short time to live ? If thou dost not follow my counsel, that very instant we shall devour thee."

Thereafter, another titan, named Vikata, with pendulous breasts, clenching her fists angrily addressed Sita, saying :—

"O Foolish Daughter of Mithila's King, out of compassion and forbearance, we have endured thy harsh speech and yet thou dost not follow our sage and expedient counsel. Thou hast been transported to the further shore of the ocean which is inaccessible to others; Ravana has imprisoned thee in his private apartments to be guarded by us, O Maithili, not even Indra himself can liberate thee. Cease from weeping and lamenting and yield thyself up to pleasure and delight, O Sita; disport thyself with the King of the Titans. O Timid Damsel, dost thou not know how swiftly the youth of women is gone? Ere it fades, pass thy days happily. Till then range the enchanting woods, groves and hills with the sovereign of the titans, O Thou of Sparkling Eyes! Thousands of women will attend on thee if thou dost take the lord of all the titans as thy consort, but if thou dost not follow my counsel, I will tear thy heart out and feast on it, O Maithili."

Then another titan of ferocious looks, named Chandari, brandishing a great spear, said: "Seeing this youthful woman, with the eyes of a young doe who was carried away by Ravana and brought hither, whose breast is now trembling with fear, I feel an intense desire to feast on her liver, spleen, breast, heart, limbs and head."

At this, a female titan called Praghasa, said: "Of what use to argue about her? Let us stop the breath in the throat of this heartless woman and inform Ravana of her death. He will undoubtedly say: 'Do ye devour her'."

The titan, Ajamukhi then said: "Let us divide her equally; disputation is unpleasing to me; let our favourite drink and different garlands be brought hither speedily."

At that moment the demon Shurpanakha said: "I am in full accord with Ajamukhi's words, let wine that dispels all anxiety be brought without delay. Gorged with human flesh, we will dance in the Nikumbhila Grove."

Hearing the monstrous titan's threats, Sita, who resembled the daughter of a God, her endurance at an end, burst into tears.

CHAPTER 25

Sita gives way to Despair

THE many barbarous threats of the titan women, caused the daughter of Janaka to give way to tears and the noble Vaidehi, terror stricken, in a voice broken by sobs, answered them, saying :—

" A mortal woman may not be the wife of a titan ; tear me to pieces if you will but I shall never follow your counsels."

Surrounded by those demons and threatened by Ravana, Sita, who resembled the daughter of a God, could find no refuge anywhere and, seized with violent trembling, she shrank away from them, as a fawn in the forest, separated from the herd, surrounded by wolves. Clinging to the flowering branch of an Ashoka tree, sunk in grief, Sita bethought herself of her lord. Streams of tears bathed her lovely breast and overcome with affliction, she could see no end to her distress. Like a plantain tree uprooted by the storm, she lay, the fear that the titan women inspired in her blanching her cheek ; her long thick plait moving to and fro as she shook, resembling a gliding serpent.

Groaning in her grief and overcome with indignation, Maithili, weeping, began to lament, exclaiming sorrowfully:— " O Rama ! " and again, " O Lakshmana ", " O My Mother Kaushalya ", " O Sumitra ". " True indeed is the saying of the sages : ' neither man nor woman can die ere the hour strikes ', since tormented by the savage titans and separated from Rama, I am still able to survive an instant. Alas ! A woman of little virtue and wretched, I am about to die far from my protector as a laden vessel founders in the midst of the waves driven by the blast of the tempest. In the absence of my lord, I am sinking under the load of my affliction, like a river bank undermined by the current. Happy are those who are able to look upon my lord, whose eyes resemble the petals of the blossoming trees, whose gait is like a lion's and who is full of gratitude and gentle of speech. Deprived of the presence of Rama of subdued soul, it is as hard for me to breathe as for him who has swallowed a virulent poison and henceforth my life is forfeit. What heinous fault have I committed in a previous existence that I should now have to suffer such cruel misfortune? So intense is my grief that I long to die, but alas, I am surrounded by these titan women and cannot be reunited with Rama. Cursed is the human state, cursed is dependence on others, since one may not yield up one's life when one so desires it."

CHAPTER 26

Sita prophesies the Titan's Destruction

HER face bathed in tears, with bowed head the daughter of Janaka began to lament once more and, distracted with grief, beside herself, she rolled on the earth like a colt as though she had lost her senses, crying:—

"I, the spouse of Raghava, who allowed himself to be deceived by the titans able to change their form at will, was seized by the ruthless Ravana who bore me away. Having been made captive by the titans, subject to their insults and menaces, sunk in grief and anxiety, I am no longer able to endure life. Of what use is existence, wealth or jewels to me, living amidst the demons far from Rama of the great Car? Assuredly my heart must be of iron, ageless and imperishable, since it does not break under mine affliction. Woe is me, vile and wicked creature that I am, since I still breathe, in the absence of my lord. Even my left foot shall not touch that Ranger of the Night, how should I feel any love for Ravana, a titan? He, who in his perversity seeks to seduce me, is not conversant with my nature, nor my race, nor the aversion in which he is held by me. Torn to pieces, rent limb from limb or cast into the fire, I shall never submit to Ravana, what use is there in further discussion?

"It is well known that Raghava is righteous, grateful and compassionate; that he has become pitiless is due to mine evil karma. Will he not deliver me, he who in Janasthana destroyed fourteen thousand titans singlehanded? Even were Lanka in the midst of the sea and inaccessible, Raghava's arrows would transcend all obstacles. What can prevent the valiant Rama from rejoining his beloved wife, who has been borne away by a titan? I fear that the elder brother of Lakshmana does not know that I am here, for if he did, that warrior would not endure this affront.

"The King of the Vultures, who would have informed Rama of mine abduction, was slain by Ravana in the struggle. Great indeed was the courage manifested by Jatayu in coming to mine aid and, despite his age, seeking to destroy Ravana. Did Raghava know that I was here, this very hour, he would rid the world of titans with his flaming shafts; he would burn up Lanka, swallow the ocean and blot out the might of Ravana. From each dwelling the groans and cries of the female titans, their husbands slain, would have risen, as mine do now or even louder, and Rama, aided by Lakshmana would range the city, slaughtering the titans, for the foe instantly yields up his life, who comes face to face with them. Then Lanka, its streets filled with smoke issuing from the funeral pyres, encircled by wreaths of vultures, would soon resemble a charnel house. Soon shall I be avenged! This matter will cost you all dear, for such inauspicious omens are to be seen in Lanka, that she will soon be shorn of her splendour.

The King of the Titans, the vicious Ravana having been slain, Lanka, now prosperous and happy, will resemble a widow. Assuredly I shall soon hear the wailing of the daughters of the titans in every dwelling, mourning in their sorrow. Plunged in darkness, deprived of her glory, her valiant titans slain, the city of Lanka will perish. consumed by Rama's arrows, when that hero, the corners of whose eyes are red, learns that I am held captive in the titan's abode. The time fixed by that cruel and wicked Ravana is at hand and that vicious wretch has resolved to destroy me. To ignore what is prohibited, is the practice of these base demons. Terrible is the calamity which will follow this outrage; those titans who live on flesh are ignorant of virtue. Assuredly that titan intends me for his morning repast; I am helpless, what can I do in the absence of my beloved? Deprived of my lord's presence, stricken with grief, not beholding Rama, the corners of whose eyes are red, may I soon see the God Vaivasvata! Nay, the elder brother of Bharata is unaware that I still live, else he and Lakshmana would have scoured the earth for me. Without doubt, overwhelmed by my foes, that warrior, the elder brother of Lakshmana has renounced his body and repaired to the Celestial Region.

Happy are the Gods, Gandharvas, Siddhas and the great Rishis who are able to look on the heroic Rama. It may be that the sagacious and royal Sage Rama, has been absorbed in the Absolute and hath no longer any need of a consort or that one who is present inspires joy, but the absent are forgotten. Perchance the fault is mine, and I have lost the right to happiness, I, the lovely Sita, separated from the illustrious Rama. Death to me is preferable to life, bereft of that magnanimous One, that great hero of imperishable exploits, the destroyer of his foes! It may be that the two brothers, those chiefs of men have laid down their arms, they who feed on the roots and woodland fruits, passing their lives in the forest or they have been put to death through treachery by the vile Ravana, the last of the titans. If that be so, then with all my heart I long for death nor is it forbidden me in my distress. Blessed are those high-souled ascetics who are illumined, their senses subdued, for whom there is neither desire nor aversion; for them, neither love nor hate gives rise to joy or pain; they are free; salutations to those great beings! Forsaken by the beloved Rama, versed in the science of the soul and having fallen into the power of the wicked Ravana, I shall yield up my life."

CHAPTER 27

Trijata's Dream

THESE words of Sita roused the female titans to great fury and some hurried away to repeat them to that vile creature, Ravana.

Then those monsters of hideous aspect approached her and began to threaten her in the same way as before with as little success and some said:

"O Wretched Sita, to-day those demons whose destruction thou hast planned, will devour thy flesh at their pleasure."

Seeing Sita threatened by those vile demons, Trijata, who was aged and prudent, said to them: "Ye Wretches, devour me, but do not lay hands on Sita, the daughter of Janaka and the beloved daughter-in-law of King Dasaratha. Last night, I had a terrible dream causing my hair to stand on end, foretelling the overthrow of the titans and the triumph of this woman's husband."

Hearing these words uttered by Trijata, all those titan women, filled with ire, terrified, demanded that she should speak further, saying:—"Do thou relate the manner of thy dream and what thou didst behold last night."

Hearing those words, falling from the lips of the titan women, Trijata began to relate the dream that had come to her in the early hours, saying:—

"I beheld a celestial chariot made of ivory, drawn by a hundred swans traversing the ethereal regions in which Raghava accompanied by Lakshmana stood clad in dazzling raiment, adorned with garlands. And I saw Sita wearing the purest white, standing on a snow-white mountain surrounded by the sea and she was re-united with Rama, as the light with the sun. And again I beheld Raghava seated on a mighty elephant possessing four tusks, resembling a hill, as also Lakshmana, whereupon those two lions among heroes, ablaze with their own effulgence, approached Janaki arrayed in dazzling robes and decked with garlands. Upon this, she mounted on the shoulders of an elephant led by her lord, appearing in the sky near the summit of that mountain! Thereafter, that lotus-eyed one, rose into the air from her husband's embrace and I beheld her wiping the sun and moon with her hand. Then that foremost among elephants with those two princes and the large-eyed Sita stood over Lanka.

"And again, in dream, I saw Rama, clothed in brilliant attire, wearing garlands, accompanied by Lakshmana, in a chariot drawn by eight white bullocks and I beheld that foremost of men, Rama, whose essence is valour with his brother Lakshmana and Sita ascending a celestial flowery car, bright as the sun, driving towards the northern regions.

"Then I saw Ravana, lying on the earth covered in oil, shaven, attired in red, garlanded with oleander flowers, intoxicated and still drinking. And I beheld him falling from the flowery chariot, Pushpaka, on to the earth, shorn, wearing a black cloth, dragged hither and thither by a woman. Thereafter I saw him seated in a chariot drawn by asses, robed in red, with his body stained likewise, quaffing sesamum oil, laughing and dancing, his mind confused, his senses clouded, speeding towards the south. Again I saw Ravana, the Lord of the Titans, stricken with fear, fall headlong on the earth, thereafter leaping up suddenly, terrified, bemused with liquor, staggering about naked like a madman, incapable of speech yet babbling continuously, stinking and foul, resembling hell itself. Then, proceeding towards the south, he entered a lake where even the mud had dried up and a dark woman clad in red, besmeared with mud, placed a rope round the neck of Dashagriva dragging him to the region of death.

"There I beheld the mighty Kumbhakarna and all the sons of Ravana, their heads shaven, besmeared with oil. Dashagriva riding a boar, Indrajita a porpoise and Kumbhakarna a camel; only Bibishana appeared to me standing in space. under a white canopy, accompanied by four ministers. Thereafter a great company of titans wearing red garlands and raiment filed past, playing on stringed instruments, dancing and drinking. And I beheld the enchanting city of Lanka, filled with elephants, chariots and horses, her gateways and arches shattered, falling into the sea. And in Lanka, crimson with flames, the female titans were laughing and creating a terrible clamour, quaffing oil. I saw Kumbhakarna and all the other titans, dark-hued, wearing scarlet robes, falling headlong into a cesspool.

"Do ye now depart since Raghava is about to be re-united with Sita and, in extreme ire, will exterminate you all with the titans. If his beloved and revered consort, who, for his sake, followed him to the forest, is threatened and tormented by you, Raghava will never brook the insult. Enough therefore of these invidious threats, occupy yourselves in consoling her and crave her forgiveness; you should seek to influence Vaidehi by persuasion. That unfortunate one, on whose account I had so significant a dream, is about to be delivered from her woes and re-united to her beloved and illustrious lord once more. Even after the menaces you have uttered, let us give up all harsh words and implore her forgiveness. In truth, a terrible disaster for the titans will proceed from Raghava. By casting yourselves at her feet, you may placate Maithili, the daughter of Janaka, who is able to preserve us from a great calamity. Furthermore, I do not find any blemish in that lady of large eyes nor the least defect in any of her limbs. Verily I deem the misfortune that has befallen this goddess, who does not merit adversity, has no more substance than a shadow.

" I foresee the immediate attainment of Vaidehi's desires, the destruction of the King of the Titans and the imminent triumph of Raghava. Behold the indications of great joy, held in check by that lady, in the twitching of her left eye large as a lotus petal and without apparent cause ; the slight trembling of the left arm of that virtuous daughter of Videha, her left thigh too resembling an elephant's trunk is quivering, as if Raghava himself stood before her and the winged creatures nesting in the branches above her are pouring forth their song as if to announce the advent of an auspicious hour."

Thereupon, that modest and youthful woman, greatly delighted at the prospect of her husband's victory, said to them : " If this prove true I will be your protector."

CHAPTER 28

Sita's Lament

HEARING the harsh speech of that King of the Titans, Ravana, the unfortunate Sita began to tremble, as a she-elephant attacked by a lion on the edge of the forest.

Threatened by Ravana and encircled by the titans, that timid damsel gave way to despair like a young girl abandoned in a wood.

She reflected : " The sages affirm truly that death does not come before the appointed hour since, worthless creature that I am, I still live after these insults. Bereft of happiness, filled with misery, my heart must be hard indeed that it does not break into a hundred pieces this day, like the crest of a mountain struck by lightning. Nay, I am not to blame for this —I may be slain by that dreadful monster but I can no more give him my affection than a brahmin can impart the teachings of the Veda to one of low caste. If that Lord of the Worlds does not appear at the appointed hour, that vile King of the Titans will cut me to pieces with his sharp weapons as a surgeon cuts the foetus from the heart of its mother. Two months will quickly pass away and I shall have to suffer the pain of death, unhappy creature that I am, like a thief, who having disobeyed his sovereign is bound and being led to execution when the night is over.

" O Rama, O Lakshmana, O Sumitra ! O Mother of Rama ! O My Mothers ! I am about to perish miserably as a ship foundering in the sea battered by the storm. Assuredly those two valiant princes must have fallen under the blows of that creature disguised as a deer, like a bull or lion struck by lightning. There is no doubt that it was fate in the form of a deer that deluded me, unfortunate creature that I am and in my folly I sent those two princes, Rama and Lakshmana to capture it. Alas ! O Rama, O Thou of truthful vows and long arms ! O Thou, whose countenance shines like the full moon ! O My Life, thou, the benefactor and friend of all beings, art not aware that I am about to be put to death by the titans. For me, who have no other God than my lord, my patience, my sleeping on the bare ground, my observance of duty, my devotion to my husband have all been in vain, as a service rendered to one who is ungrateful. Vain has it been, that I have fulfilled my duty and that I am wholly devoted to thee alone since I do not behold thee and in thine absence, wasting away, pale and weak, have given up all hope of being re-united with thee. Having courageously carried out the behests of thy sire, having fulfilled thy vow, returning from the forest, thou shalt sport with many large-eyed ladies in peace. O Rama, I, who conceived a lasting love for thee, to mine own destruction was wholly attached to thee; having practised asceticism and observed my vows, I am about to lose my life, woe unto me, unfortunate wretch that I am! Gladly would I take my life by means of poison or by sharp weapons but there is none who will bring them to me in this city of the titans."

Overcome by sorrow, reflecting for a long time, Sita undid the cord that tied her hair, saying:—"I shall hang myself with this cord and reach the abode of death."

Then the lovely Sita, whose form was full of grace, took hold of a branch of the tree under which she stood and became absorbed in the thought of Rama, Lakshmana and her kinsfolk; and many auspicious signs removing her grief and lending her courage, well-known in the world, appeared to her, indicating the advent of future well-being.

CHAPTER 29

Sita observes auspicious Portents

WHILST the irreproachable and lovely princess remained bereft of joy and full of anxiety, she beheld auspicious portents on every side, resembling willing servants attendant on a wealthy man. And the large left eye of that lady of lovely looks, with its dark pupil, began to twitch like a lotus set spinning by a fish. And her beautiful plump and rounded arm, sprinkled with sandal and aloes which ere this, had served her lord as a pillow, began to tremble again and again. Her left thigh, like unto the tapering trunk of an elephant, moved convulsively foretelling that she would soon behold Rama and the golden sari, now covered with dust, of the large-eyed Maithili, whose teeth were like the seeds of a pomegranate, slipped from her beautiful shoulders.

Comforted by these signs and others also, that foretold a happy ending, Sita of lovely lashes resembling a plant dried by the wind and sun, reviving under tardy rain, experienced a great felicity. Then her countenance, her lips like Bimba fruit, her beautiful eyes, the curve of her lashes and her sharp teeth, recovered their beauty once more as the moon issuing from the mouth of Rahu.

Her despair and exhaustion removed, her fever allayed, her grief was assuaged and her heart filled with joy and that noble lady looked as beautiful as the moon of cool rays in its waxing period.

CHAPTER 30

Hanuman's Reflections

The valiant Hanuman who had heard all that Sita, Trijata and the titans had said, gazed on that illustrious damsel who resembled a celestial being from the Nandana Gardens and many thoughts flitted through the mind of that monkey.

He reflected: "She, who was sought in every place by thousands and millions of monkeys, is here and it is I who have found her. Engaged as a skilful spy to discover the strength of the enemy I have stolen into the city and know everything concerning the might of Ravana and the resources of the titans as also of their capital. It is for me to console the consort of that immeasurably illustrious prince, who is compassionate to all beings, for she is pining for her lord. I shall seek to gain the confidence of this lady, whose countenance resembles the full moon, who formerly was unacquainted with suffering and who cannot see any end to her woes. If I return, without having comforted that virtuous lady whose soul is overwhelmed with grief, my journey will have been in vain. In sooth, when I have departed, that illustrious Princess Janaki, giving up all hope of deliverance, will yield up her life and that long-armed warrior, whose countenance resembles the full moon, anxious to behold Sita is equally worthy of consolation.

To speak to her in the presence of these titans is impossible, what then shall I do? I am in a great dilemna. If I do not give her some reassurance in the last hour of the night, she will undoubtedly give up her life and if Rama enquires of me, 'What did Sita of slender waist say?' what answer can I give to him if I have had no converse with her? If I return without having achieved my purpose regarding Sita, Kakutstha will consume me with his fiery glance, then it were vain to urge my master to take action for Rama's sake, by placing himself at the head of his forces.

"I shall take the first opportunity offered by these titan women to reassure that sorely tried lady, yet in this insignificant form and monkey shape, if I assume a human voice and speak in sanskrita like a sage, Sita will deem me to be Ravana and she will be terrified! It is essential however that I express myself in the human tongue, how otherwise can I inspire this irreproachable lady with courage? Seeing my shape and hearing me speak, Janaki, who has been terrorised by the titans, will be seized with an even greater fear and that illustrious and large-eyed Sita will cry out, imagining me to be Ravana, who is able to change his form at will.

"Hearing her cry, the whole company of titans, armed with every kind of weapon, will form themselves into a great mass resembling death itself and, hideous and indomitable, will rush on me from every side and seek to destroy me or take me captive. Then, beholding me leap from branch to branch and climb to the tops of the highest trees, they will become exceedingly alarmed and will fill the woods with their wild cries; thereafter they will call the titans who are engaged in guarding the king's palace to their aid and, on account of their native excitability, will seize hold of every kind of weapon, spears, darts, and swords and hasten to join in the fray. Surrounded by them on all sides, if I slay that host of titans, exhausted, I shall be unable to cross the ocean or they, outnumbering me, will succeed in capturing me and, being a prisoner, that lady will reap no benefit from my attempt.

"Alternatively, in their passion for evil doing, they may even slay the daughter of Janaka, which will completely defeat the great design of Rama and Sugriva! Janaki dwells in an inaccessible and secret place surrounded by the sea, guarded on all sides by the titans with all its approaches closed. If I am slain or captured by the titans in combat, I know of no other monkey who can cross the four hundred miles of sea. Even if I destroy thousands of titans, I should not then be able to reach the other shore of the vast ocean. Battles are hazardous and I do not like to engage in so uncertain an enterprise ; what wise person would take any risk in a matter of trust ? It would be a great error to frighten Vaidehi by addressing her, yet if I do not do so, she will surely perish. Undertakings often fail through an incompetent messenger unable to take advantage of time and place, as darkness is overcome by the rising sun ; in such cases, whether it concerns the accomplishment or avoidance of any matter, the most widely planned projects do not succeed. Assuredly a presumptuous messenger ruins all ! How shall I act therefore, so that my mission does not prove vain ? How shall I show myself equal to this charge ? How shall the crossing of the ocean not prove to have been useless ? How can I persuade Sita to listen to me without inspiring fear in her ? "

Having put all these questions to himself, Hanuman formed the following resolution :

" I shall speak to her of Rama of immortal exploits, for then his dear consort will not be afraid of me since she is wholly absorbed in the thought of her lord. In a gentle voice, uttering the name of Rama, the foremost of the Ikshwakus of subdued soul and, lauding his piety and renown in sweet accents, I shall induce Sita to listen to me. There is nothing I will not do to inspire her with confidence."

Thereupon, the mighty Hanuman, looking down on the consort of the Lord of the World from the branches of the tree where he sat concealed, spoke to her in melodious and candid tones.

CHAPTER 31

Hanuman praises Rama

HAVING examined the matter from every aspect, that intelligent monkey began to pour sweet words into Vaidehi's ear, saying :—

" There was a king named Dasaratha, the possessor of chariots, horses and elephants, one by nature devout and illustrious, the glory of the Ikshwakus. To harm none was his delight and he was high-minded and compassionate, a true hero of his race that found its splendour and the growth of its prosperity in him. Clad in all the insignia of royalty and majesty, that lion among kings, renowned in the four regions, shed the felicity he enjoyed over all. His beloved eldest son, whose countenance was as bright as the moon, was called Rama, possessor of a keen intellect and the most skilled of archers. Faithful to his vows, the defender of his people, the protector of all beings, upholder of justice, he was the scourge of his foes.

" At the command of his aged sire, his word his bond, that hero accompanied by his consort and his brother was banished to the forest. Whilst giving himself up to the chase in that vast solitude, he slew large numbers of valiant titans who were able to change their form at will.

When Ravana learnt that he had destroyed Janasthana and killed Khara and Dushana, he in fury, bore Janaki away, having lured her lord far into the forest by the aid of Maricha in the form of a deer.

" Whilst searching everywhere to discover the divine and irreproachable Sita, Rama found a friend in the forest, the Monkey Sugriva, Bringing about the destruction of Bali, Rama, the conqueror of hostile cities, conferred the monkey kingdom on the magnanimous Sugriva and by his decree, thousands of monkeys, able to change their form at will, set out to search for that goddess in every region. I am one of those who, at the instance of Sampati, crossed the sea four hundred miles in width, on account of that large-eyed beauty. Hearing of her comeliness, her grace and distinguishing characteristics from Rama, I have been enabled to find her at last."

Having spoken thus, that bull among monkeys fell silent.

And Janaki was extremely astonished, hearing that speech and brushing aside her lovely tangled locks which concealed her face, she looked up into the Shingshapa tree.

Hearing the words of that monkey, Sita glanced enquiringly to the four quarters and other regions, whilst an extreme delight flooded her whole being as she remembered Rama. Then, glancing from side to side and up and down, she espied the son of Vata, who resembled the rising sun, that minister of the King of the Monkeys of incomparable wisdom.

CHAPTER 32

Sita sees Hanuman

BEHOLDING that monkey of pleasing speech, clad in white raiment, resembling a flash of lightning, crouching concealed among the branches, bright as a cluster of Ashoka flowers and like gold refined in the crucible, Sita was greatly agitated.

Observing that foremost of monkeys of humble mien, Maithili said to herself in extreme surprise: "Ah! What a terrible looking monkey, unacceptable and hideous to behold." Thinking thus, her fears increased and she broke into countless plaintive lamentations. Then the lovely Sita cried out in her terror: " O Rama, O Rama, O Lakshmana ! " and the voice of that virtuous princess grew fainter and fainter till, casting her eyes on that excellent monkey once more, who had assumed a reverent attitude, Maithili said to herself: " It must be a dream."

Observing the face of that Indra among Monkeys with its deep scars as has been described and, looking on that excellent ape, the most honourable son of the Wind, the first of the wise, Sita lost consciousness and became like one dead. Thereafter, slowly regaining her senses, she said to herself: " This vision of a monkey is condemned by the scriptures and is an inauspicious dream! Can all be well with Rama, who is accompanied by Lakshmana and my father King Janaka ? Yet it can be no dream for, in the grief and misfortune that overwhelms me, I am no longer able to sleep and, far from him whose countenance resembles the full moon, no joy remains for me. Through constantly thinking and calling on Rama, I imagine I hear and see only those things which are related to Rama. For my love is a torment, my whole being flows towards him, ever absorbed in his rememberance I see and hear him alone. Is it an illusion? This is what perturbs me and makes me uneasy. I deem this to be but a phantom of the mind yet thinking thus, I still behold it, while an imaginary object can never have a form and he who is thus addressing me has a distinct form. Salutations to Vachaspati who is accompanied by the God who bears the Thunderbolt! Salutations to Swyambhu and the God who partakes of offerings! May they grant that the creature who has spoken in my presence, be real and not illusory!"

CHAPTER 33

Hanuman's Converse with the Princess Sita

SLIPPING down from the tree, Hanuman, whose face was the colour of coral, attired in a humble guise, approached Sita and that mighty son of the Wind with joined palms addressed her in gentle tones, saying:

"Who art thou, O Lady, whose eyes resemble lotus petals, who, wearing a soiled silken garment art supporting thyself by the branch of the tree? O Irreproachable One, why are tears of suffering falling from thine eyes, that resemble the lotus, as water flows from a broken vessel? O Fair One, who art thou among the Celestials, Titans, Nagas, Gandharvas, Rakshas, Yakshas and Kinneras? Or do the Rudras claim that thou art born of them or the Wind-gods or the Vasus, O Lady of exquisite features? To me thou appearest to be of divine origin. Art thou Rohini, foremost and most brilliant of stars, who, separated from the moon has fallen from the abode of the immortals? Or art thou the lovely dark-eyed Arundhati, who hath fled in wrath or in pride from her lord, Shri Vasishtha? Is it for a son, a father, a brother or a husband, whose departure from this world thou art mourning, O Lady of slender waist? By thy tears and sighs and thy lying on the earth, it seems to me that thou art not a celestial being and further thou dost ever and again call on the name of a king. From the marks on thy person I deem thee to be the consort or the daughter of a monarch. Art thou not Sita, who was ruthlessly borne away by Ravana from Janasthana? May prosperity attend thee! From thy wretched plight, thine unrivalled beauty and thine ascetic garb, I deem thee to be Rama's consort."

Hearing Hanuman's words and filled with joy at the sound of Rama's name, Vaidehi answered him, as he stood beneath the tree, saying:

"I am the daughter-in-law of Dasaratha, foremost among the kings of the world, a knower of the Self, the destroyer of hostile armies. I am the daughter of King Janaka, the magnanimous sovereign of Videha and my name is Sita, the consort of the highly intelligent Rama, who is endowed with wisdom. For twelve years I dwelt in Raghava's abode, experiencing every earthly delight and satisfying every desire. In the thirteenth year, the king, with the approval of his ministers, resolved to install Rama, the joy of the House of Ikshwaku on the throne. As they were preparing to anoint Rama as heir-apparent, Queen Kaikeyi addressed her lord, saying:—

"'I will neither eat nor drink of that which is served to me each day but shall put an end to my existence if Rama be installed. Let the boons that, in gratitude, thou didst grant me, be redeemed and let Raghava repair to the forest'.

"The king, faithful to his bond, recollected the boons made to the queen and hearing those cruel and unpleasing words was lost in grief. Then that aged monarch, adhering firmly to his vow, weeping, besought his eldest son to renounce the throne. That illustrious prince to whom the words of his sire were more to be prized than the throne, inwardly assenting, promised to obey. Rama, ever a giver, seeking no return, truthful, never uttering a falsehood even were his life to be made forfeit, is essentially brave. Laying aside his costly attire, the highly glorious Rama with his whole heart, renounced the kingdom and gave me into his mother's keeping, but I, assuming the garb of an ascetic, quickly prepared to accompany him to the forest, for, separated from him, I could not bear to dwell even in the celestial regions. Then the fortunate Saumitri, the enhancer of his friends' delight, donning robes of bark and kusha grass also prepared to follow his elder brother. In deference to the will of our sovereign, firm in our vows, we entered the dark and unknown forest. While that one of immeasurable effulgence was dwelling in the Dandaka Forest, I, his consort, was carried away by the Titan, Ravana of perverse soul. Two months is the time fixed by him, after which I am to die."

CHAPTER 34

Sita's Uncertainty on seeing Hanuman

HEARING the words of Sita, who was stricken with grief, Hanuman, the foremost among monkeys, in order to reassure her, said :—

" O Divine Vaidehi, by Rama's decree I have come as a messenger to thee; he is safe and enquires as to thy welfare. Rama, the son of Dasaratha, who is versed in the Veda, conversant with the use of the Brahmastra, the foremost of the learned, offers salutations to thee, O Queen! The highly resplendent Lakshmana too, the most powerful and cherished companion of thy lord, in the midst of his burning anxieties, bows before thee and wishes thee well."

Hearing of the welfare of those two lions among men, Sita, trembling with delight, said to Hanuman :—" Verily the wise say that happiness visits a man even if it be at the end of a hundred years."

Thereupon Sita and Hanuman began to converse with delight and mutual confidence. Hearing Sita speak in this wise, Hanuman, the son of Maruta drew nearer to her who had been overwhelmed with grief and, as he did so, she grew apprehensive and reflected :—"Alas! Why have I entered into converse with him? It is Ravana in another guise!" Thereupon, letting go the Ashoka branch, Maithili of faultless limbs, exhausted with suffering, sank down on the earth.

Then that long-armed monkey bowed unto Janaka's daughter, who, filled with terror, did not dare raise her eyes to him, yet, seeing him bowing humbly before her, Sita, whose face resembled the moon, sighed deeply and said to him in gentle accents :—

"If thou art Ravana's self, who has assumed a perfidious guise in order to increase my distress, it is a vile act. Thou art he, who, renouncing his own shape, appeared to me in Janasthana as a mendicant, O Ranger of the Night. O Thou, wearing shapes at will, it doth not behove thee to torment me, who am distressed and emaciated with fasting.

"Yet thou canst not be he whom I fear, since my heart feels delight in seeing thee. If thou art truly Rama's messenger, may good betide thee! Thou art welcome, O Best of Monkeys for it is sweet to me to hear of Rama. Set forth the virtues of Rama, O Monkey, and ravish my soul, O Gentle One, as the current of a river bears away its banks. O how sweet a dream does an inhabitant of the woods bring to me so long after mine abduction! If I might only see the valiant Raghava accompanied by Lakshmana once more but even a dream denies me this delight. Can it be a dream? To see a monkey in dream does not give rise to happiness yet I am happy now! Is my mind not deranged or has fasting disturbed the humours of my body and caused this delusion or is it perchance a mirage? Nay, it cannot be an hallucination for I am in full possession of my senses and perceive this monkey clearly."

Such were the thoughts that haunted Sita, as also that the titans were able to change their form at will, which convinced her that this was the King of the Titans himself. Having arrived at this conclusion, the daughter of Janaka, of slender waist, ceased to converse with the monkey but Hanuman, divining what was passing through her mind, consoled her with sweet words, enhancing her delight saying:—

"Bright as the sun and like the moon, beloved of all, that sovereign of the world is as munificent as Kuvera. In valour resembling the glorious Vishnu, of sweet and truthful speech like unto Vachaspati, handsome, illustrious and fortunate like the God of Love, the just dispenser of punishment to evil-doers, he is the foremost of car-warriors in the world.

"He in whose arms the whole world takes refuge, that magnanimous Raghava was lured away from the hermitage by means of Maricha in the form of a deer, thus allowing Ravana to bear thee away. Soon shall that mighty hero destroy Ravana in combat with his fiery shafts discharged in anger. It is he, who has sent me with these tidings. Worn with grief at thy separation, he enquires as to thy welfare, as also the highly resplendent Lakshmana, enhancer of Sumitra's delight, who offers salutations to thee. The king of the monkey hosts, Sugriva by name, who is Rama's friend, also pays homage to thee; Rama, Lakshmana and Sugriva have thee ever in mind; though subject to the titans, by good fortune thou dost still live, O Vaidehi. Ere long thou shalt behold Rama and Lakshmana of the great car with Sugriva of limitless prowess.

"I am Sugriva's minister, the monkey Hanuman, I have entered the city of Lanka, having crossed the ocean, thus setting my foot on the head of Ravana of perverse soul. I have come here to see thee, depending on my own prowess, I am not he whom thou deemest me to be. Do thou renounce thy doubts, and have confidence in my words."

CHAPTER 35

Hanuman makes himself known to Sita

HEARING that lion among monkeys discoursing on Rama, Vaidehi spoke to him in sweet and gentle accents, saying :—

"Where didst thou encounter Rama and how didst thou come to know Lakshmana ? How did men and monkeys come to form an alliance ? O Monkey, describe the distinctive characteristics of Rama and Lakshmana once again and so dispel my grief. Speak to me of Rama's grace and form, his arms and thighs, as well as Lakshmana's."

To these questions of Vaidehi, Hanuman, born of Maruta, began to give a detailed description of Rama and said :—

"By good fortune, recognising me to be a messenger of Rama, O Vaidehi, whose eyes are as large as lotus petals, thou hast asked me to describe the person of thy lord as well as that of Lakshmana. O Large-eyed Lady, hear me while I tell thee of those marks of royalty I have observed in the persons of Rama and Lakshmana. O Daughter of Janaka, Rama has eyes like unto lotus petals, his countenance resembles the moon and he is endowed with great beauty and virtue. In radiance like the sun, in patience resembling the earth, in wisdom like unto Brihaspati, in renown equal to Vasava, he is the protector of all beings and the upholder of his race, the guardian of law and tradition and the scourge of his foes. O Lovely One, Rama is the preserver of the people and the four castes, he inaugurates and establishes the social order, he is worshipped by all like the sun and is an observer of pious vows; he knows well the proper time to pay honour to holy men and is conversant with the path of right action.

"Born with royal prerogatives, the servant of the brahmins, learned, endowed with nobility, humble, he is the scourge of his foes. Versed in the Yajur Veda, honoured by those conversant with the Vedas, he is proficient in archery and possesses a thorough knowledge of the Vedas and Vedangas. Broad shouldered, long-armed, handsome, possessing a conch-shaped neck his ribs are well covered and muscular and his eyes are red; such is Rama renowned among men. The tone of his voice resembles the Dundubhi, his skin is smooth, his three limbs, thigh, fist and wrist are hard, and the others, long, his navel, abdomen and breast are well-proportioned and high. The rims of his eyes, his nails and palms are red, his voice and gait grave; there are three folds in the skin of his body and neck; the lines on the soles of his feet and breast are deep; his neck, back and thighs are muscular; his hair is coiled in three circles; his thumb is marked with four lines indicating his deep knowledge of the Vedas; there are four lines on his forehead, the sign of a long life; he is four cubits in height; his arms, thighs and cheeks are plump; wrists, knee-joints, hips, hands and feet are well-proportioned, his four front teeth have auspicious marks; his gait is like a lion's, a tiger's, an elephant's or a bull's; his lips and jaws are fleshy, his nose long, his face, speech, down and skin, cool; his two arms, little fingers, thighs and legs, slender; his countenance, eyes, mouth, tongue, lips, palate, breast, nails and feet resemble lotuses; his forehead, neck, arms, navel, feet, back and ears are ample. He is gifted with grace, renown, and radiance; his lineage is pure on both sides; his armpits, abdomen, breast, nose, shoulders and forehead are elevated; his fingers, hair, down, nails, skin, eyesight and intellect, clear and sharp. Raghava delights in what is just and true, he is filled with energy and is well able to judge how to act under all circumstances; he is benevolent to all.

"His brother Saumitri, whose mother is second in rank among the queens, whose glory is immeasurable, resembles him in beauty, devotion and good qualities; he is of a golden complexion whereas Rama is dark of hue. Those two tigers among men, who yearn to see thee once more, scouring the earth for thee, met with us in the forest. Ranging the earth in search of thee they beheld the King of the Monkeys, who had been banished by his elder brother, at the foot of the Rishyamuka Mountain that is covered by innumerable trees. We were in attendance on the handsome Sugriva, Lord of the Monkeys, who had been driven from the kingdom by his elder brother and, beholding those foremost of men, clad in bark, bearing splendid bows in their hands, that monkey fled to the summit of the mountain, distracted with terror. Thereafter he sent me out to meet them in all haste and, at Sugriva's command, I approached those two princes, those lions among men, with joined palms.

"Distinguished by their handsome features, those two heroes, being informed of what had taken place, were well pleased and I, placing them on my shoulders, transported them to the crest of the hill where the magnanimous Sugriva was to be found. There I related all to Sugriva and they conversed together and a great friendship grew up between those illustrious persons, the King of the Monkeys, and those monarchs among men. Then they comforted each other, narrating their respective misfortunes and Lakshmana's elder brother consoled Sugriva who had been banished by Bali of great prowess on account of the love of a woman. Thereafter, Lakshmana related the suffering and loss that had befallen Rama to Sugriva, who, hearing this recital from his lips, was bereft of his radiance like the sun under eclipse. Then gathering together all the ornaments that thou didst let fall on the earth when the Titan bore thee away, the monkeys brought them to Rama with delight, but they were ignorant of where thou wert.

" All those ornaments which had fallen tinkling to the ground, and had been collected by me, I gave over to Rama, who was beside himself with grief and, clasping them to his breast, that God of divine beauty, the son of Dasaratha, inflamed with grief, with many groans bewailed his loss. For a long time that magnanimous hero lay crushed under the weight of his affliction and I addressed many words of comfort to him, persuading him to rise. Whereupon Rama with Saumitri, gazing again and again on those precious objects, gave them over to Sugriva. In thine absence, O Noble Lady, Raghava is consumed with grief, like a volcano burning with perpetual fire. On account of thee, sleeplessness, sorrow and care consume the magnanimous Rama, as the sacred fires burn down a temple in which they are enclosed. The pain of thy separation has shattered him as a violent earthquake shatters a great mountain. O Daughter of a King, he wanders among the enchanting woods, on river banks and by the side of waterfalls but nowhere finds delight. O Daughter of Janaka, ere long, Ramachandra will undoubtedly bring about the destruction of Ravana with all his kith and kin, and that foremost of men will soon liberate thee.

" It was thus that Rama and Sugriva entered into a friendly alliance to encompass Bali's destruction and institute a search for thee. Thereupon, returning to Kishkindha with those two heroic princes, that lord of monkeys slew Bali in battle and having struck him down by his prowess in fight, Rama made Sugriva king of all the monkeys and bears. Such was the alliance between Rama and Sugriva, O Goddess, know then that I am Hanuman who have come as their deputy. When he had recovered his kingdom, Sugriva, gathering all the great and powerful monkeys together, sent them forth to every region to seek for thee. Under the commands of their king, Sugriva, those mighty monkeys, equal to the Indra of Mountains, scoured the land on every side. Since that time, in fear of Sugriva, those monkeys have been exploring the whole earth; I am one of those. The mighty and illustrious son of Bali, Angada by name, set out with a third part of the army under him; many were the days and nights we spent overwhelmed with distress, having lost our way on the foremost of mountains, Vindhya. Despairing of accomplishing our purpose and the time appointed having passed, in fear of that lord of the monkeys, we resolved to give up our lives. Having searched the mountains and the inaccessible fastnesses, the rivers and waterfalls without finding any trace of thee, we made up our minds to die. Thereafter we began our final fast on the summit of the mountain.

"Submerged in an ocean of grief, Angada lamented unceasingly, reflecting on thine abduction, O Vaidehi, on the death of Bali, on our resolution to die of hunger and on the death of Jatayu. Whilst we were fasting thus, waiting for death, having given up all hope of carrying out the behests of our lord, to the good fortune of our enterprise, there appeared, a mighty vulture, the brother of Jatayu, by name Sampati. Hearing of his brother's death, he cried out in anger:—

"'By whom was my younger brother slain and where does he dwell? I wish to hear this from you, O Excellent Monkeys!'

"Thereupon, Angada related all in detail to him and how that Titan of terrible form destroyed Jatayu on thine account in Janasthana. In his grief for Jatayu's death, that son of Aruna told us that thou wast to be found in Ravana's abode, O Exquisite Damsel!

"Hearing the words of Sampati, our joy was extreme and led by him we all rose up and, leaving the Vindhya Mountain came to the shores of the sea. There a cruel anxiety seized the monkeys anew, eager as they were to find thee, but I was able to dispel that sharp anguish of the monkey host, who beholding the main had lost heart. Then, removing their fear I leapt a hundred leagues over the sea and entered Lanka by night, which was filled with titans; there I beheld Ravana and saw thee overcome with grief, O Irreproachable Lady!

"Now I have told thee all, do thou, in thy turn speak to me, O Goddess! I am the messenger of the son of Dasaratha and have come here to thee, to carry out Rama's purpose. Know me to be Sugriva's minister and the Wind-god's son! All is well with thy lord, Kakutstha, the foremost of those bearing weapons, as also with Lakshmana possessed of auspicious marks and ever engaged in the worship of his superiors and the well-being of his lord.

"I have come here at Sugriva's command and have accomplished the journey alone. Changing my form at will, I have scoured the southern region and, in my eagerness to find thee, have sought thee on every side. With tidings of thee, I shall by divine grace be able to dispel the grief of the monkey host, who have been lamenting on thy account and my crossing the ocean will not have been in vain. I shall win renown for having found thee, O Goddess and the highly powerful Raghava will rejoin thee without delay, having first slain Ravana, the king of the Titans with his sons and relatives.

"Mount Malyavat is the highest of mountains, O Vaidehi, and there dwells my sire, Kesarin. Obedient to the will of the divine Sages, he once repaired to Gokarna and at that sacred spot belonging to the Lord of the Rivers, brought about the destruction of the Titan, Samvasadana. I was born of the consort of Kesarin, O Maithili and my name is Hanuman; I am known throughout the world for my exploits. To inspire thee with confidence, I have described the virtues of thy lord. Ere long, O Goddess, Raghava will certainly take thee hence."

Reassured by the proofs given to her, Sita, exhausted by suffering, recognised Hanuman to be Rama's messenger.

Then Janaki, in an excess of joy, allowed tears of felicity to fall from her eyes fringed with dark lashes. The gentle countenance of that large-eyed damsel with her reddened eyes shone like the moon released from Rahu's hold.

Taking him for a real monkey at last, she reflected in herself: "How could it be otherwise?"

Then Hanuman again addressed that lady of charming mien, saying:—

"I have told thee all, now have confidence in me, O Maithili! What more can I do for thee and what is thy pleasure, ere I return? When the Asura, Samvasadana was destroyed in combat by the foremost of monkeys at the behest of the celestial sages, I was born of Vayu, O Maithili, and though a monkey, I am his equal in prowess!"

SUNDARA KANDA

CHAPTER 36

Sita questions Hanuman

The exceedingly mighty son of Pavana, Hanuman, in order to increase Sita's confidence in him, again addressed her in reassuring words, saying :—

" O Fortunate One, I am a monkey, the messenger of the sagacious Rama; behold this precious ring on which his name is engraved! O Goddess, it was given to me by that magnanimous hero so that thou shouldst have faith in me. Take heart therefore, may good betide thee! Soon shall there be an end to thy grief!"

Then Janaki, taking the jewel that had adorned the finger of her lord, was overcome with joy, as if he himself were present. Her gentle countenance with its large eyes began to sparkle with delight resembling the moon released from Rahu's hold. Blushing with pleasure on receiving this token from her lord, that youthful woman, in her satisfaction, began to look on that great monkey as on a friend and paid tribute to him in the following wise :—

" O Foremost of Monkeys, verily thou who have entered this city of Ravana's alone, art full of courage, valour and address. With admirable tenacity thou hast traversed the ocean, four hundred miles in breadth, the abode of great monsters, reducing it to the measure of a cow's hoof. I do not look on thee as an ordinary monkey, O Lion among Forest Dwellers, since thou dost not stand in awe of Ravana. O Best of Monkeys, thou hast merited associationship with me, since Rama the knower of Self has dispatched thee as his messenger. It is certain that the invincible Rama would never have sent thee to me without first testing thy prowess. By good fortune the virtuous and truthful Rama as also the illustrious Lakshmana, enhancer of Sumitra's delight, are well, yet if Kakutstha live untouched by ill, how is it that he does not burn up the earth encircled by the sea in his wrath like the fires at the dissolution of the worlds ? Those two heroes are able to subdue the Gods themselves and yet they refrain from action ; I deem therefore that my sufferings are still not at an end ! Is Rama not disquieted ; is he not torn with anxiety on my account ? Is that son of a king making every preparation to deliver me ? Is he sorrowful and pre-occupied ? Has he lost sight of his ultimate purpose ; is he fulfilling his duty with fortitude ? Is that slayer of his foes, desirous of victory, propitiating his friends with forbearance and gifts and employing the threefold means of dealing with his enemies ? Does he show goodwill to his friends and have they confidence in him ? Does he ally himself with those of good repute and do they pay him honour ? Does that son of a king seek the favour of the Gods; does he depend on them for his power and fortune ? Has Rama's affection for me decreased as a result of my living far from him ? Will he deliver me from this peril ? Is he not unstrung by this extreme misfortune, being accustomed to felicity and unused to adversity? Has he received frequent good tidings of Kaushalya, Sumitra and also Bharata ? Is not Raghava, worthy of honour, overcome with grief at my absence ? Is he reflecting on how he may rescue me ? Will not Bharata, ever devoted to his brother, send out a great army led by experienced generals for my sake ? O Foremost of Monkeys, will not the King of the Monkeys, the fortunate Sugriva, come to mine aid at the head of a host of valiant monkeys using their teeth and nails ? Will not the heroic Lakshmana, the increaser of Sumitra's delight, skilled in the use of weapons, destroy the titans with his shafts ? Shall I not see Rama strike down Ravana on the battlefield ere long with his friends and kinsfolk by means of Rudra's weapon ? Is the golden countenance of Raghava, fragrant with the scent of lotuses, not dimmed under adversity, like a lotus deprived of water under the burning sun ? Does he still retain his fixity of purpose, he who, for the sake of righteousness, without regret renounced the throne and on foot entered the forest with me ? Neither for his mother nor his father nor for any other does he bear the love that he cherishes for me. I shall only live as long as I hear of him."

Having addressed these words, full of meaning and sweetness to that monkey, that charming lady became silent so that she might hear more of her lord.

And listening to Sita, Maruti, of immeasurable prowess, with joined palms paid obeisance to her and spoke again, saying:

" O Illustrious Princess, the lotus-eyed Rama does not know that thou art here and for this reason has not delivered thee as Purandara rescued Sachi. Learning this from me, Raghava will instantly come hither with his great army of bears and monkeys and, having triumphed over the invincible ocean, the abode of Varuna with his terrible shafts, Kakutstha will rid the city of Lanka of all the titans. Even if death himself or the Gods or the mighty titans seek to bar his passage, he will destroy them all. O Princess, in thine absence, Rama stricken with grief is no longer able to find rest, like an elephant who is attacked by a lion. O Goddess, I swear to thee by the Mandara, Malava, Vindhya, Meru and Dardura Mountains and all the fruits and roots, that thou shalt soon behold Rama's lovely countenance with his beautiful eyes, lips like unto the Bimba fruit, and charming earrings, who resembles the risen moon. Soon thou shalt see Rama on Mount Prasravana, O Vaidehi, like Shatakratu seated on Airavata. Eschewing flesh and wine, Rama subsists on the fruits and roots of the forest alone, carefully prepared by Lakshmana of which he partakes at the fifth period of the day. So absorbed is he in the thought of thee that he no longer drives away flies, insects and worms from his body. Sunk in his reflection, lost in grief, he is wholly absorbed in thy contemplation. Rama, the foremost among men no longer sleeps but should his eyelids close in weariness he starts up crying: 'O Sita!' in gentle accents. Whenever he beholds a fruit or flower or any other object dear to women, he sighs 'O My dear Love!'. O Goddess, that prince unceasingly calls on thee, crying: 'O Sita', and in order find to thee has resorted to every means."

Hearing Rama's praises, Sita was greatly delighted, but grieved also to learn of his pain so that she resembled the autumn moon entering a dark cloud to re-appear once more.

CHAPTER 37

Sita refuses to be rescued by Hanuman

THE moon-faced Sita, hearing this speech, addressed Hanuman in words, fraught with piety and sound judgment:—

" O Monkey, thou hast revealed to me that Rama is wholly pre-occupied with my remembrance and also that he is plunged in grief, which is as nectar mingled with poison. Whether man be at the height of his power or in the abyss of sorrow, death draws him as with a cord. Living beings are unable to escape their destiny, O Excellent Monkey, behold how I, Rama and Saumitri are sunk in misery! As a wreck floating on the waters seeks to reach the shore, so does Raghava seek to come to the end of his woes.

" After destroying the titans, slaying Ravana and laying Lanka waste, will not my lord see me once again? Do thou tell him to hasten, for at the end of this year I must die. This is the tenth month and two alone remain, that is the term fixed for me by that evil wretch, Ravana. His brother Bibishana made great entreaty to him to restore me, but he paid no heed to his proposals. Ravana does not look with favour on my release for death lies in wait for him, driven on, as he is, by fate. O Warrior, on her mother's request, Kala, Bibishana's eldest daughter told me of this. There is an old and trusty titan, named Avindha, full of wisdom, virtue, intelligence and nobility, highly revered by Ravana, who prophesied the imminent destruction of the titans by Rama, but that perverse wretch disregarded his salutory words. O Best of Monkeys, I still hope that my lord will soon be re-united with me, for my heart is pure and Rama's virtues are infinite. He is endowed with endurance, courage, compassion, gratitude, energy and strength, O Monkey. What foe would not tremble before him, who slew fourteen thousand demons in Janasthana without his brother's aid? That lion among men cannot be surpassed by the titan warriors; I am conversant with his powers as

Sachi is with Indra's. O Monkey, that sun, Rama, with his innumerable arrows as his rays. will dry up the lake of hostile titans ! "

Speaking thus, Sita, overwhelmed with grief at the thought of Rama, her face bathed in tears, was again addressed by Hanuman, who said to her :—

" No sooner shall I have spoken to Raghava, than he will hasten hither at the head of a powerful army composed of bears and monkeys or shall I deliver thee this very day from the grasp of those titans and these present afflictions ? Do thou climb upon my back, O Irreproachable Lady, and bearing thee on my shoulders, I will cross over the sea ; verily I am able to carry away the City of Lanka together with Ravana himself. This day, as Anila bears the sacrificial offerings unto Shakra, I shall bring thee back to Raghava on the Prasravana Mountain, O Maithili ! To-day thou shalt behold Rama, who is accompanied by Lakshmana, preparing to destroy the enemy, as Vishnu engaged in the destruction of the Daityas and thou shalt see that mighty hero, eager to behold thee, on that solitary mountain, resembling Purandara on the head of the King of the Serpents.

" O Lovely Goddess, mount on my shoulders, do not hesitate and be united with Rama, as Rohini is restored to Shashanka, as Sachi to Indra, or Savarshala to the Sun. I shall cross the ocean by the aerial path ! O Fair One, bearing thee away from here, none of the dwellers in Lanka will be able to follow me. I shall return as I came, O Vaidehi, bearing thee through space."

Hearing these astonishing words, Maithili, trembling with joy, said to Hanuman : " How canst thou hope to carry me so great a distance, O Hanuman ? This demonstrates thy monkey nature ! How dost thou deem it possible that thy little body should convey me from here to my lord, that king among men, O Monkey ? "

At these words Hanuman reflected : " This is the first affront I have suffered ! Vaidehi is unaware of my prowess and strength. She shall learn that I am able to assume any shape at will ! " Thinking thus, that foremost of monkeys, Hanuman, the scourge of his foes, showed himself to Sita in his true form.

In order to inspire Sita with confidence, leaping down from the tree, that monkey began to expand in size and grew equal to the Meru or Mandara Mountain or a flaming brazier and that lion among monkeys, of a coppery countenance, his body like a mountain, with nails and teeth like diamonds, standing before Sita, said :—

" I am capable of uprooting Lanka with its hills, woods, fields, palaces, ramparts and gates and its monarch also! Take heart therefore O Queen, do not delay further, O Vaidehi! Come and dispel the grief of Raghava as also Lakshmana's."

Seeing the son of the Wind-god grow to the size of a mountain, the daughter of Janaka, whose eyes resembled lotus petals, said to him :—

" O Mighty Monkey, now I recognise the extent of thy powers and thy speed which equals the wind, also thy radiance like unto fire. How should an ordinary monkey have reached this land beyond the infinite ocean ? I know that thou art able to take me from here and bear me away, but, O Foremost of Monkeys, I must consider if the consequences are to mine advantage. Furthermore, is it fitting for me to go with thee ? Thy speed equal to the wind may render me giddy and I might fall from thy back whilst thou wert proceeding high over the ocean. Flung into the sea filled with sharks, crocodiles and giant fish, I should certainly become the chosen prey of those monsters. Nay, I cannot go with thee, O Destroyer of Thy Foes and for thee undoubtedly there is also grave danger. When the titans see thee bearing me away, they will pursue thee at the wicked Ravana's command and, surrounded by those warriors furnished with spears and maces, carrying a woman, thou wilt be beset with peril, O Hero! Fully armed, in great numbers, those titans would pursue thee, who art unarmed ; how couldst thou then resist them and protect me ? And when thou art engaged in combat with those terrible demons, O Foremost of Monkeys, I, stricken with fear, will slip from thy back. Those terrible, huge and powerful titans would then end by overcoming thee in the conflict, O Excellent Monkey. Or turning my head, whilst thou art engaged in fight, I should fall and those wicked titans would bear me away and bring me hither or, wresting me from thy grasp, tear me to pieces. Victory or defeat is uncertain in combat! If I died under the threats of the titans, O First of the Monkeys, all thine efforts to deliver me will have been in vain. Though thou art well able to destroy all the titans, Rama's fame would thereby suffer decrease or the titans, bearing me away, would confine me in a secret place unknown to the monkeys or to Rama. Then, all thine efforts to rescue me will have been fruitless, but if Rama returns with thee, great will be the chances of success.

"O Great-armed Warrior, the lives of Raghava, of his two brothers and of King Sugriva depend on me. Having given up hope of delivering me, worn out with grief and anxiety, those two brothers with all the bears and monkeys would end their existence. O Monkey, furthermore, being wholly devoted to my lord, I am unable to touch the body of any save Rama. When I was forced into contact with Ravana's limbs, I was helpless and without a defender and was no longer in control of my person. If Rama comes to destroy Ravana and the titans and takes me away from here, it will be a feat worthy of him! I have heard of that hero's great exploits and have myself witnessed them, nor can Devas, Nagas nor titans equal Rama on the field of battle!

"Who, having beheld him in combat, wielding his marvellous bow, endowed with a valour and strength like unto Indra's, could withstand Rama who is accompanied by Lakshmana and who resembles a fire fanned by the wind? O Foremost of Monkeys, who would seek to oppose Rama, accompanied by Lakshmana, resembling elephants intoxicated with Mada juice, showering shafts like the rays of the sun at the time of the dissolution of the worlds? O Best of Monkeys, do thou bring my dear one and Lakshmana with the Lord of the Monkey Hosts, here with all speed. On account of separation from Rama, I have long been consumed with grief, now, O Valiant Monkey, make me happy once more."

CHAPTER 38

She gives Hanuman her Jewel

HIGHLY gratified by Sita's words, that lion among monkeys answered thus :—

"O Fair Lady of auspicious presence, thou hast spoken in accord with thy feminine nature and with the modesty of one devoted to her lord ! As a woman, it would not be possible for thee to cross the sea, four hundred miles in width on my back and the plea that thou hast made, saying 'I may not touch the body of any save Rama' is worthy of thee, O Goddess, consort of that magnanimous One. Who but thou would utter such words, O Janaki ? Truly Kakutstha shall hear from beginning to end all thou hast said and done in my presence, O Princess. For many reasons did I speak to thee thus, O Lady, anxious as I was to compass Rama's design, and my heart troubled with feelings of affection. Further it was with great difficulty that I penetrated into the City of Lanka and traversed the ocean and debating what was meet for me to do, I addressed thee in this wise. I wished to bring thee back to the one who is the delight of the House of Raghu this day ! It was my devotion for him and in regard for thee, that I uttered those words. As, however, thou art unable to come with me, O Irreproachable Lady, do thou give me some token which will inspire Rama with faith in me."

Being thus addressed by Hanuman, Sita, who resembled the daughter of the Gods, answered him in faint accents, her voice broken with sobs :—"This is the most perfect token thou canst take to my dear lord ! Do thou say this to him :— 'O Rama, when we formerly resided at the foot of the Chittrakuta Mountain in the eastern region, not far distant from where the ascetics dwelt, in a place rich in roots, fruit and water near the river Mandakini, whilst ranging the flowery groves, redolent with fragrance, thou, having sported in the lake, rested all dripping on my breast. At that moment a crow, approaching, sought to peck me and I threw a stone at it; nevertheless that ferocious devourer of offerings, determined to wound me, would not leave its prey and in my wrath I removed my girdle, in order to strike the bird and my robe slipped down. On seeing this, thou didst laugh at me, whereat I blushed with shame and indignation. Harassed by that crow, who was wild with hunger, I took refuge with thee, and exhausted, threw myself into thine arms as thou wert seated there. Though I was still vexed, thou didst pacify me by thy laughter and my face being bathed in tears, gently dried my eyes; thus I was seen by thee, greatly enraged by the crow, O Lord. Exhausted, O Rama, I slept for a long time on thy breast, and thou in thy turn, didst sleep on mine, O Elder Brother of Bharata. Then, as I awoke, that crow approached me once more and, as I rose from thine arms, tore my breast with its beak, O Raghava. Thereupon, at the shedding of blood, thou didst wake and beholding my breast lacerated, O Long-armed Hero, highly incensed and hissing like a serpent, thou didst speak thus:—

"O Thou, whose thighs resemble the trunk of an elephant, who has wounded thy breast? Who seeks to play with an angry five-headed serpent?"

"Thereafter, looking round, thou didst perceive that crow, who, with sharp and bloody talons stood before me. That bird, prince of winged creatures, was the son of Indra and with the swiftness of the wind, it disappeared into the earth. Then thou, O Long-armed Warrior, thine eyes rolling in fury, resolved to destroy that crow and, plucking a blade of kusha grass, from where thou hadst lain, transformed it into Brahma's shaft and it burst into flame, like unto the fire of death before the bird. Hurling that fiery brand, it followed that bird high into the sky and, pursued by the fiery dart, the crow flew this way and that, thus traversing many regions and ranging through the Three Worlds, repulsed by his sire and the sages; at last it sought refuge with thee, falling on the earth and beseeching mercy of thee. Though worthy of death, thou, O Kakutstha, ever willing to succour all beings, out of compassion, spared him. Then, speaking unto the one who was exhausted and distressed, thou didst say:—"This weapon of

Brahma may never remain ineffective, therefore say what is now to be done?" Then the crow answered:—" I will give up my right eye," whereupon Ramachandra destroyed the right eye of that crow. Having sacrificed the right eye, his life was spared and, paying obeisance to Rama, as also to King Dasaratha, the crow, delivered by that warrior, returned to his abode. O Thou, who, on my behalf, didst discharge the Brahma-weapon, even at a crow, why dost thou leave him who bore me away, unpunished? O Foremost of Men, show thy compassion to me and inspire me with hope. I am conversant with thy great energy, thine immense endurance, thine amazing strength, thine irresistible power unfettered by the limitations of time and space, incapable of being disturbed, thou who art deep like the ocean, lord of the earth and the equal of Vasava himself! Thou, the first among bowmen, who art full of ardour, and courage, wherefore dost thou not direct thy weapons against the titans? Neither Nagas, Gandharvas, Gods nor Maruts can resist thee in combat'.

" If that warrior still retains any regard for me, why does he not exterminate the titans with his whetted shafts, or why does not Lakshmana, the repressor of his foes, endowed with energy, deliver me at his brother's behest? Since those two tigers among men, equal to Vayu and Indra are invincible even against the Celestials, why do they disregard me?

" Alas! I must be guilty of some heinous sin, since those twin scourges of their foes, though able to do so, fail to come to my rescue!"

Hearing Vaidehi's piteous words, uttered with her eyes full of tears, the mighty Hanuman, foremost of the monkeys, said:—" O Exalted One, I swear to thee that Rama's features are altered on account of the sorrow he feels for thee and, seeing his brother overwhelmed with grief, Lakshmana too is filled with distress, this is the truth, O Goddess. Since I have now found thee, there is no cause to lament further and thou shalt soon see an end to thy woes, O Lovely One. Those two tigers among men, those princes of incalculable energy, in their eagerness to see thee, will burn the worlds to ashes. Having slain that formidable warrior, Ravana with his kinsfolk, Raghava shall return with thee to the palace.

" Now tell me what I shall say to Rama and Lakshmana, who are filled with valour and the illustrious Sugriva and all the assembled monkeys ? "

Hanuman having uttered these words, Sita answered him saying :—

" Bowing low to that Lord of the World, enquire after the welfare of that protector of men, whom Kaushalya has brought forth and wish him all prosperity from me. Then offer salutations to the one of whom Sumitra is the happy mother, he, who renounced garlands, jewels, his beloved consort, the dominion of a vast realm hard to attain and his father and mother, after bidding them a tender farewell, in order to follow Rama. That virtuous prince, who, in his devotion, sacrificed unsurpassed felicity, accompanied his brother Kakutstha to the forest, watching over him ; he who is great, wise and pleasing to look upon, possessing broad shoulders and who looks on Rama as his father and reverences me as his mother, that valiant Lakshmana, who did not know that I was being borne away. Full of deference for the aged, dignified and brave, measured in speech, the foremost of those dear unto that king's son and worthy of his father-in-law, he who even undertaketh these tasks to which he is not equal, whose presence causes Rama to forget his sire, who is dearer to him than I ; Lakshmana, the brother of Rama, to him do thou offer obeisance from me and repeat my words to him. May that noble and virtuous one, beloved of Rama, ever mild and pure, bring an end to my sufferings, O Best of Monkeys ! O Chief of the Monkeys, do thou bring about the success of this undertaking. May Rama, on thine instigation, make a supreme effort on my behalf. Further, do thou repeat these words of mine again and again to him :—

" ' I have but one month to live, O Son of Dasaratha! After that month I shall die ; I swear to thee that this is the truth I speak ! Deliver me from the hands of that cruel and wicked Ravana, O Hero, as Kaushiki was delivered from hell '."

Saying this, Sita drew from her robe the pearl which formerly adorned her forehead, which shone with celestial radiance, and bestowing it on Hanuman, said : " Give this to Raghava."

Then the valiant Hanuman, taking the priceless jewel, placed it on his finger, it being too small for his arm and, that foremost of monkeys, having received the pearl, paid obeisance to Sita, circumambulating her from left to right. Filled with delight on having found the princess, Hanuman had already returned to Rama and Lakshmana in thought.

And taking that costly and superb ornament that the daughter of King Janaka had carried carefully concealed in her sari, Hanuman, as if delivered from a hurricane that had overtaken him on a high mountain, his heart full of serenity, once more prepared to set out on his return journey.

CHAPTER 39

Hanuman calms Sita's Fears

HAVING given the jewel to Hanuman, Sita said to him :—

" This token is well known to Raghava and seeing this pearl, the valiant Rama will call three people to mind, my mother, myself and King Dasaratha. O Best of Monkeys, thy heroism being further stimulated by this enterprise, consider carefully what fresh efforts are needed ; thou art capable of undertaking this task, think therefore what course Rama should adopt to bring my misfortunes to an end. O Hanuman seek by thine exertions to terminate my sufferings ! "

Thereupon the son of the Wind-god of immense energy, replied : " So be it," and making obeisance to Vaidehi, prepared to depart, but that exalted one, Videha's daughter, seeing Hanuman about to leave, her voice strangled with sobs, said unto him :—

" O Hanuman, do thou communicate my desires for the happiness of Rama, Lakshmana, Sugriva, his ministers and all the other monkeys and, O Best of Monkeys, in consonance with righteousness, wish them well. It behoveth thee to do that which will cause the long-armed Rama to deliver me from the ocean of affliction in which I am plunged. O Hanuman, do thou speak so that the illustrious Rama rescue me from here while I am yet alive and thereby reap the fruits of virtue. Listening to that which thou shalt relate to him of me, that son of Dasaratha, ever filled with valour, will feel his daring increased a hundredfold in the thought of reunion with me. The heroic Rama, hearing the appeal I have charged thee to deliver to him will be inspired to display increasing prowess."

Listening to Sita's words, Hanuman, born of Maruta, with joined palms, made answer to her saying :—

" Soon shall Kakutstha, surrounded by the foremost monkeys and bears, come, and vanquishing his enemies in fight, dispel thy grief. I know of none among mortals, titans or Gods, who can withstand him when he discharges his arrows. Wert thou the price of victory, he would be able to challenge the Sun or Parjanya or Vaivasvata or Yama himself in conflict and would prepare to conquer the whole earth that is bounded by the sea, O Delight of Janaka."

Hearing these pleasing, true and sweetly expressed words, Janaki addressed Hanuman with respect, who had spoken out of devotion to his master, and said :—" O Hero, if thou judgest it to be wise, then tarry here for one day more and, having rested in some hidden spot, set out to-morrow ! Thy presence, O Monkey, will cause me to forget my great misfortune awhile, I who have experienced so little happiness. But shouldst thou depart to-day, O Lion among Monkeys, my life will be in danger till thy return, this is certain. Furthermore, not seeing thee will prove an increased torment, afflicted as I am with grief and, O Hero, this doubt haunts me continually,—' How will that powerful King, in the midst of the forces of his monkeys and bears and those two sons of a monarch, cross the impassable ocean ? ' In all the worlds, three beings alone have the power to traverse the sea ; Garuda, thou and Maruta ! In the face of this insurmountable obstacle, what means to success canst thou see, O Most Skilled of Beings ? Undoubtedly thou art able to encompass this undertaking unaided, O Destroyer of Hostile Warriors but thou alone wouldst then reap the glory. If Rama, however, together with his armies vanquished Ravana and, delivering me, returned to his own city, that exploit would be worthy of him. If, crossing the sea and besieging Lanka, that destroyer of hostile forces Kakutstha, bore me hence, he would have accomplished what is natural to him. Do thou therefore act in such wise that that valiant warrior may be able to manifest his prowess ! "

Hearing these words, fraught with sense and reason, full of affection, Hanuman replied mildly :—

" O Queen, the leader of the forces of bears and monkeys, Sugriva, full of energy, has resolved to liberate thee. Surrounded by millions of monkeys, that destroyer of titans will come hither without delay. There are, under his command, monkeys endowed with valour, energy and extreme prowess, swift as thought, able to go upward or downward and to every side, nothing can impede their course, no task, however hard, defeats their immeasurable courage. Nay, more than once, by their amazing endurance, they have encircled the entire earth with its seas and mountains on every side, by resorting to the wind's path. Among those Rangers of the Woods, some are equal to me and some superior and, in the whole of Sugriva's company, there is none who is less so. Since I have reached this place, how much more are those valiant monkeys able to do so ! Nor are the superior ones sent on errands but those of less account. O Queen, have no anxiety and abandon thy grief; with a single bound, those foremost of monkeys will reach Lanka and those two brothers, resembling the sun and moon about to rise, will speed to thy side, riding on my back. Having slain Ravana and his hordes, Raghava, the delight of the House of Raghu, will take hold of thee, O Lady of Lovely Limbs, in order to bring thee back to thine own city. Therefore let courage and happiness attend thee, have faith in the dawning of that hour ; ere long, thou shalt behold Rama shining like a flame.

" That Indra of the Titans, his sons, counsellors and kinsfolk, being slain, thou shalt be re-united with Rama as Shashanka with Rohini. Soon thou shalt see the end of thy woes, O Divine Maithili, and Ravana will fall under Rama's blows before thine eyes ! "

Having thus sought to comfort Videha's daughter, Hanuman, born of Maruta, preparing to depart, spoke yet again, saying :—

" Thou shalt soon behold the destroyer of his foes, Raghava of subdued soul, as also Lakshmana, bearing his bow in his hand at the gates of Lanka. Ere long thou shalt see those valiant monkeys, endowed with the courage of lions and tigers, resembling the lord of elephants, fighting with their nails and teeth. O Noble One, innumerable companies of monkeys will be seen by thee, resembling hills or clouds, roaring on the plateaus of Malaya and Lanka. Like an elephant attacked by a lion, Rama is deeply wounded by the formidable shafts of the God of Love! O Goddess, weep no more, but banish fear and sorrow from thy heart; thou shalt be reunited with thy consort, O Beautiful One, as Sachi was to Indra.

" Who can overcome Rama? Who is equal to Saumitri? Those two brothers, resembling the wind and fire, are thy support. O Goddess, thou shalt no' have to dwell long in this place inhabited by formidable titans; thy beloved will not delay his coming; have patience till I return!"

CHAPTER 40

He takes leave of Sita

HEARING the words of that magnanimous son of Vayu, Sita, who resembled a daughter of the Gods, replied in significant words, saying :—

"As the rain, ripening the grain, rejoiceth the earth, so am I gladdened on seeing thee, O Monkey, who speaketh sweetly of my beloved. In compassion for me, who am emaciated with suffering, do that which will enable me to meet with that tiger among men, soon. O Foremost of Monkeys, call to his remembrance, that reed the crow destroyed in his anger, having been deprived of an eye and also how, when my tilaka mark was effaced, he painted another on my cheek, which he will surely remember. Say: ' O Thou who resemblest Indra, how, with thy valour, canst thou suffer Sita to be borne away and set in the midst of the titans? That celestial pearl which adorned my forehead, I have preserved with care. In my misfortunes, I have oft looked on it with delight as on thyself, O Irreproachable Hero! Yielding up this jewel, I shall not live long, being overwhelmed with grief. For thy sake, O Rama, I endure insufferable misery and the menaces of the titans which cleave my heart! O Destroyer of thy Foes, I shall live for one more month, after which, bereft of thee, I shall yield up my life. The King of the Titans is a source of dread to me; if I learn that thou dost hesitate in coming to mine aid, I shall instantly give up my life'."

Witnessing Vaidehi's tears and lamentations, the mighty Hanuman, born of Maruta, answered:—

"O Goddess, thy misfortunes have rendered Rama's features wan, I swear to thee this is the truth and seeing Rama overcome with sorrow, Lakshmana too is deeply distressed. Now that I have found thee, there is no cause for despair! Soon, soon, thou shalt see an end to thy woes, O Lovely Princess! Those blameless princes, foremost of men, eager to see thee, will reduce Lanka to ashes. Having slain Ravana in combat, those two scions of the House of Raghu will take thee back to their own city, O Large-eyed Lady! O Irreproachable Damsel, it is now for thee to give me such a token, that Rama will instantly recognise and that will delight his heart."

Sita answered:—"I have already furnished thee with an excellent token. Seeing that jewel, Rama will instantly believe thy words."

Receiving the marvellous pearl, the Prince of the Monkeys inclined his head to that exalted one and prepared to depart.

Beholding that foremost of monkeys expanding his form and, charged with energy, preparing to leap, her face bathed in tears, in a voice choked with sobs, Sita said to him:—

"O Hanuman, do not fail to offer my good wishes for their welfare to those two brothers, Rama and Lakshmana, who resemble two lions and to Sugriva also and his court. Do that which will cause the long-armed Raghava to deliver me from this ocean of affliction, where I am held prisoner. On thy return, when thou art near him, tell him of my harsh and bitter affliction and the threats of the titans! May prosperity attend thee, O Chief of the Monkeys."

Having received these instructions from the princess, the monkey, his purpose accomplished, exceedingly exultant, reflecting that little remained for him to do, had already crossed the northern region in thought.

CHAPTER 41

Hanuman destroys the Ashoka Grove

Having been honoured by Sita, the monkey, leaving that place, began to reflect on what little remained for him to do since he had discovered that dark-eyed Princess.

Dismissing the three means to success, the fourth now appeared to him as appropriate and he reflected in himself: "Because of their nature, one may not enter into negotiation with the titans nor do gifts avail with the wealthy; one is unable to sow dissension among those who are proud of their strength, there remains therefore prowess as applicable here. In these circumstances, valour is the only resource. When these titans see the foremost of their warriors fall in combat, their martial ardour will be subdued. He who accomplishes his main purpose and compasses innumerable other engagements without jeopardising the original enterprise, is a skilful messenger. He who employs all his resources to execute a minor task, has no sagacity, but the one who uses countless means with the minimum effort, is wise. Though my mission has been fulfilled, yet if, returning to the abode of the King of the Monkeys, I have ascertained the strength of the foe and ourselves in the field, I shall have truly carried out his commands. How shall I act so that my presence here proves fruitful? How can I provoke an encounter with the titans and what can I do so that that Ten-necked One will be made to measure his strength with mine own? Coming face to face with Dashagriva on the field accompanied by his counsellors, his army and charioteer, I shall easily read his intentions and then take my leave.

" I shall now proceed to lay waste this magnificent grove, resembling the Nandana Gardens, that ravishes the eye and where every variety of tree and creeper, is found, as the forest fire consumes the dead trees and this destruction will incite Ravana's fury. Thereafter the King of the Titans will call upon his immense army furnished with tridents and iron pikes, and the horsemen, chariots and elephants, of which it is composed, and a formidable struggle will ensue. Then I shall fight with all my strength against those titans and having defeated the assembled forces of Ravana, I shall return safely to the King of the Monkeys."

Thinking thus, Maruti, like a raging tempest, with immense energy began to root up the trees with his powerful and sinuous thighs, breaking them down, as also the creepers of that grove, where the trumpeting of maddened elephants could be heard.

With its trees uprooted, its foundations shattered, the crests of the hills broken away and all that was fair laid waste, the copper-tinted buds, the trees and creepers withering away, that grove appeared as if a fire had consumed it and the flowering sprays blown hither and thither, resembled women with their robes in disarray. With its grassy dells and charming pavilions ruined, tiger, deer and birds emitting cries of fear and the edifices crumbling, that great demesne was bereft of beauty. And that grove, belonging to the women of the inner apartments, where they were wont to sport, with its avenues of Ashoka trees and its creepers, now laid waste by that monkey, was transformed by him into a heap of ruins.

Then having given that powerful lord of the earth cause for severe displeasure, that monkey, eager to fight against those countless valiant titans single-handed, stationed himself at the gate, blazing with effulgence.

CHAPTER 42

He destroys the Kinkaras

MEANWHILE the cries of birds and the crash of falling trees, struck terror into the hearts of the inhabitants of Lanka. Wild beasts and birds fled hither and thither in terror on every side and inauspicious omens appeared.

Waking from sleep, those grim-visaged titan women beheld the grove devastated by that mighty and heroic monkey and, in order to inspire them with fear, that long-armed one, full of energy, began to increase in size and they, observing that immense ape, as high as a hill, of unimagined power, enquired of Janaka's daughter, saying :—

" Who is this being ? From whence and wherefore has he come hither ? Why did he converse with thee ? Tell us, O Large-eyed Lady, have no fear O Dark-eyed Lovely One."

Thereupon, the virtuous Sita, of faultless limbs, answered them saying :—" Since the titans are able to change their form at will, by what means should I be able to recognise them ? Ye know what he is and what he is about ! Without doubt, serpents know the secret of the serpent's tail ! As for me, I am terrified nor do I know what he is but believe him to be a titan, who has come hither, able to change his form at will."

Hearing Vaidehi's words, the titan women fled with all speed, a few only remaining, whilst some hastened to inform Ravana of what had taken place.

Thereafter those female titans of hideous aspect, approached the King of the Titans and informed him of that monstrous and formidable monkey in the Ashoka grove, saying :—

" O King, there is a monkey of immense size, endowed with immeasurable strength, who, having held converse with Sita, remains there. We besought the daughter of Janaka whose eyes resemble a doe's, to inform us who this monkey was but she would not disclose it. It may be that he is an emissary of Indra or Kuvera or even of Rama himself, who is anxious to discover where Sita is. This being of strange aspect, has completely destroyed thy wonderful pleasure garden that was filled with beasts of every kind. There is not a single quarter that has not been laid waste by him, save the place where the divine Janaki abides, whether to preserve her or for reasons of exhaustion, we know not, but since he is a stranger to fatigue, we deem it is on account of this woman. And the Ashoka tree, covered with buds and lovely foliage, under the shade of which Sita is sheltering, has been spared by him. It behoveth thee to inflict some severe penalty on this formidable being, who has held converse with Sita and destroyed the grove. O Lord of the Hosts of Titans, who would dare to converse with her for whom thine heart yearns without suffering death ?"

Hearing the words of the demons, Ravana, the King of the Titans, his eyes rolling in rage, flamed up like a funeral pyre and, in his wrath tears fell from his eyes like drops of burning oil from a lighted lamp.

Then that mighty monarch ordered those titans named Kinkaras, whose strength equalled his own, to seize Hanuman whereupon eighty thousand of those retainers speedily issued from the palace, bearing maces and iron hooks in their hands. Possessing huge stomachs and large teeth, formidable to look upon, filled with valour and martial ardour, they were all burning to lay hold of that monkey. Approaching Hanuman who was standing at the gate ready to fight, those powerful titans rushed upon him like moths on a flame. Equipped with maces of different kinds and gold-encircled bracelets, with arrows bright as the sun, hammers, axes, spears, darts and lances, they surrounded Hanuman and began their attack. Then he, full of strength and courage, resembling a hill, lashing his tail, began to roar, waving it to and fro, and expanding in size, that son of the Wind-god filled Lanka with his bellowing. On account of the noise of the swishing of his tail and his roaring, the birds began to fall from the air and he proclaimed in a loud voice :—" Victory to the mighty Rama and the valiant Lakshmana ! Victory to Sugriva, protected by Raghava ! I am the servant of the Sovereign of Koshala, Rama, of imperishable exploits, I am Hanuman, the destroyer of hostile armies, the offspring of Maruta. A thousand Ravanas cannot stand before me in combat, when I crush them beneath a myriad trees and rocks ! Under the very eyes of the titans, I shall destroy the City of Lanka and, paying obeisance to Maithili, depart, my purpose being accomplished ! "

On hearing his shouts, the titans were seized with terror and they beheld him standing aloft like a great evening cloud and, knowing now that that monkey had been despatched by his master, under the command of their lord they began to assail him on all sides with every kind of formidable weapon.

Surrounded by those warriors, that mighty monkey seized hold of an iron bar that stood near the gate, and lifting it, struck those Rangers of the Night, and he appeared like Vinata's offspring carrying away a struggling serpent. Grasping the weapon, that valiant monkey began to destroy those demons, moving here and there in the air, as Indra of a thousand eyes crushed the Daityas with his thunderbolt.

Having slain the titans, that heroic and powerful son of Maruta, thirsting for combat, stationed himself at the gate.

Thereafter the few titans, who had escaped, informed Ravana of the destruction of his servants and, hearing that a mighty host of demons had been slain, the king, his eyes rolling in wrath, commanded the son of Prahasta, who was endowed with matchless courage, invincible in battle, to go forth.

CHAPTER 43

He burns the Temple and Monument

HAVING slain the Kinkaras, Hanuman, reflecting awhile, thought to himself :—" I have laid waste the grove but I have not destroyed the sacred temple, I shall now demolish this sanctuary."

Thinking thus, the son of Maruta, displaying his prowess, bounded to the temple that was as high as the peak of Mount Meru, and scaling that edifice, that resembled a mountain, that chief of the monkeys, manifested a great effulgence, equal to the radiance of the sunrise. Thereafter he began to destroy that lofty sanctuary which shone with a glory equal to the Pariyatra Mountain. Assuming immense proportions, the illustrious son of Maruta, in his intrepidity, caused Lanka to tremble, filling it with his roaring and, at that terrifying and deafening clamour, the birds and the guardians of the temple, fell to the ground, their senses overcome.

Thereupon Hanuman cried out: "Victory to Rama, skilled in the use of weapons and to the courageous Lakshmana! Victory to King Sugriva, Rama's henchman! I am Hanuman, the destroyer of hostile armies, son of Maruta, and the servant of Rama, King of Koshala, of immortal exploits! When I hurl down trees and rocks, not even a thousand Ravanas can withstand me in combat. Having destroyed the City of Lanka and paid my obeisance to the daughter of the King of Mithila, my purpose fulfilled, I shall depart."

Having spoken thus, the colossal leader of the monkeys, standing on that edifice, emitted a roar and the hideous clamour struck terror into the hearts of the titans.

In consequence of that great tumult, a hundred temple guards sallied forth, bearing every kind of weapon, dart, scimitar, arrow and axe; and surrounding Maruti struck him with clubs and bars encircled with golden bands. Hurling themselves on that excellent monkey with arrows bright as the sun, that host of titans resembled a mighty whirlpool in the Ganges.

Thereat the son of the Wind, the mighty Hanuman, waxing wrath, taking on a formidable aspect and tearing up from that sanctuary a huge pillar plated with gold, which emitted a hundred rays, spun it round rapidly with great energy, so that the fire generated therefrom set the temple ablaze. Seeing that monument in flames, the leader of monkeys having despatched a hundred titans, resembled Indra slaying the demons with his thunderbolt and, standing in space, he cried out exultingly:—

"Thousands of leaders of monkeys, resembling myself, valiant and brave, are scouring the whole earth under Sugriva's command. Among these, some are as strong as elephants, others ten times as strong, some have the energy of a thousand elephants, some of a whole herd and some have the strength of the wind, while a few possess a strength that may not be measured. Such are the monkeys, armed with teeth and claws, that in hundreds and thousands and millions, will accompany Sugriva when he comes to exterminate you all. Then neither the city of Lanka nor any of you nor Ravana himself will survive, since they have incurred the wrath of that hero of the House of Ikshwaku."

CHAPTER 44

The Death of Jambumalin

UNDER the order of the King of the Titans, the valiant son of Prahasta, Jambumalin of large teeth, went out bearing his bow. Wearing garlands and red attire with a crown and brilliant ear-rings, that invincible warrior of immense stature, rolling his eyes ferociously drew his great bow, furnished with shining arrows, equal to Indra's, with a noise like thunder. Then the entire sky and the four quarters at once re-echoed to the sound of the stretching of that bow.

Beholding him advance in a chariot yoked to asses, Hanuman, endowed with great vigour, emitted cries of exultation. Thereat the highly powerful Jambumalin riddled him with whetted shafts, piercing the face of that leader of monkeys with a crescent-shaped arrow, his head with one furnished with plumes and his arms with ten having iron tips. Struck by those arrows, his coppery countenance shone like an autumn cloud lit by the rays of the sun and his ruddy face, stained with vermilion, resembled a red lotus in the sky, sprinkled with drops of gold.

Wounded by those shafts, that mighty monkey was enraged and seeing a great rock of vast size lying near, he raised it up and hurled it against his adversary with violence, who countered it with ten of his shafts. Perceiving this feat brought to nought, Hanuman, in fury, tore up a mighty Sala tree and began to whirl it in the air, whereupon the highly powerful Jambumalin, seeing that great monkey spinning the Sala tree, let loose innumerable shafts, severing it with four arrows and piercing the arms of that monkey with five others, his belly with a further dart, thereafter piercing him between the breasts with ten more.

His body, covered with darts, a prey to violent anger, Hanuman, seizing a club, spun it with extreme velocity, allowing it to fall on the huge chest of his adversary, whereupon neither his head, arms, thighs, bow, his chariot, his steeds nor arrows could be distinguished, and that mighty car warrior, Jambumalin, dropped to the earth, like an oak that has been felled, his limbs and ornaments crushed.

Then Ravana, hearing that Jambumalin had been slain, as also the powerful Kinkaras, was overcome with wrath. Rolling his eyes inflamed with fury, that Lord of the Titans instantly issued a command that the sons of his ministers, who were endowed with exceeding valour and strength, should go forth to the attack.

CHAPTER 45

Hanuman slays the Sons of Ravana's Ministers

THEN under the command of that Indra of Titans, the sons of his ministers, seven in number, resembling the fire in splendour, set out from the palace. Escorted by a large army, furnished with bows, full of energy, skilled in the use of weapons, they, the flower of warriors, were each burning for victory. Mounted in great chariots plated with gold, surmounted by banners, yoked to horses, they created a noise resembling thunder. Of unequalled courage, stretching their bows inlaid with refined gold, like unto flashes of lightning athwart the clouds, those warriors sallied forth.

Their mothers nevertheless, knowing of the death of the Kinkaras, were overcome with anxiety as also their friends and kinsfolk.

And, exhorting one another, clad in golden armour, they rushed on Hanuman, who stood erect at the gate. From their thundering cars, they loosed innumerable shafts like clouds in the rainy season, and, covered by that hail of missiles, Hanuman's body was concealed, as the King of the Mountains is obscured by rain.

Then that monkey evaded those arrows and their swiftly moving chariots by executing countless skilful evolutions in the air and appeared like Indra sporting with his archers, the clouds. Sending up a mighty shout which struck terror into the great host, that valiant monkey leapt on the titans. The scourge of his foes struck some of them with the palm of his hands and others with his feet; some he hit with his fists and some he tore with his nails, striking them down with his chest and thighs, while some fell to the ground by the force of his cry. Felled to the earth, those warriors lay dying and the entire army fled to the four quarters, filled with terror. Elephants trumpeted and horses fell slain; the ground was strewn with the broken fragments of chariots, seats, banners and canopies; rivers of blood could be seen flowing on the highways and Lanka re-echoed with fearful cries.

Having slaughtered those mighty titans, that heroic monkey, burning with courage, desiring to measure his strength against other demons, stationed himself at the gate once more.

CHAPTER 46

He annihilates five Generals and their Forces

LEARNING that the sons of his ministers had fallen under the blows of that great monkey, Ravana, with a darkened countenance, concealing his fears, formed a resolution which he deemed would prove decisive.

Thereupon Dashagriva commanded the leaders of his forces, Virupaksha, Yupaksha, Durdharsha, Praghasa and Basakarna, masters of strategy, endowed with the speed of the wind, brave and skilful warriors, to take Hanuman captive, saying:—

"Ye Generals, who are full of valour, set out at the head of your troops with your fleet of horses, chariots and elephants and take this monkey prisoner. Approaching that dweller of the woods, exercise great circumspection and act with due consideration for time and place. Having regard to his conduct, I do not judge him to be a monkey, he being endowed with extraordinary prowess. I deem him to be a higher being and not a monkey; perchance he is an emissary created by Indra by virtue of his penances in order to destroy us. Under my command, ye have all triumphed over Nagas, Yakshas, Gandharvas, Devas, Asuras and great Rishis; undoubtedly they are plotting some treachery against us, therefore seize this being by force. O Generals, let each go forth at the head of a mighty host, attended by horses, chariots and elephants and take this monkey prisoner. In former times I have seen monkeys endowed with immense energy, like Bali, Sugriva, the exceedingly powerful Jambavan, the General Nila and others, such as Dvivida, yet there was nothing alarming in their gait, their energy, their prowess, their intelligence, their conduct or their capacity to assume different forms, this, however, is some great being masquerading as a monkey. Even though the Three Worlds with Indra, the Gods, the titans and men cannot resist you on the field of battle, great efforts will be needed to lay hold of him. Nevertheless, even a seasoned warrior, desiring to triumph in combat, is not able to defend his life without exertion, for the outcome of a battle is uncertain."

Obedient to the commands of their lord, all those valiant titans, resplendent as fire, attended by their troops, threw themselves in all haste into their chariots with sharp and pointed weapons and on to their swift steeds and elephants maddened with ichor.

Then those warriors beheld that mighty monkey, shining like the sun that rises with its diadem of sparkling rays, and seeing him stationed at the gate, possessed of immense strength and speed, highly intelligent and brave, with his vast stature and huge arms, they were afraid and assailed him from all sides with their dreadful weapons.

Then Durdharsha discharged five white iron, and yellow pointed arrows at Hanuman's forehead, possessing the lustre of lotus petals, and his head being pierced with those shafts, that monkey leapt into the air making the ten cardinal points ring with his cry, whereupon that powerful and heroic warrior Durdharsha, standing in his chariot with his bow stretched, advanced, letting fly a hundred arrows at once. Thereupon, Hanuman, like unto the wind driving away clouds, intercepted those arrows while coursing in the sky, and sore beset by

Durdharsha, the offspring of the Wind expanded in size, emitting loud roars, and thereafter, with a great bound swooped on the chariot of Durdharsha with extreme force, like a succession of lightning flashes striking a mountain. Thrown from his car, his eight steeds mangled, the pole and the shaft broken, that warrior fell to the earth, slain.

Then Virupaksha and Yupaksha, seeing him lying on the ground, waxing wrath sprang up and advanced on Hanuman dealing blows with their maces, striking the chest of that long-armed monkey as he stood in space; whereupon he meeting the shock of their assault, evaded their arrows and, that exceedingly powerful monkey, the son of Anila, swooped down on the earth like an eagle; thereafter seizing and uprooting a Sala tree, assailing those two titans with blows, that offspring of the Wind-god slew those two mighty and heroic demons.

Then learning that those three titans had been slain by the monkey, endowed with great swiftness, the courageous Praghasa rushed upon him laughing scornfully and the audacious Basakarna enraged, armed with a spear, also advanced towards him. Then each from his side attacked that lion among monkeys. Praghasa assailing him with a sharp-edged axe and Basakarna with his spear and, with his body streaming with blood, his limbs lacerated by their blows, that monkey, highly enraged looked like the rising sun.

Thereafter that heroic monkey, Hanuman, breaking off the peak of a mountain, together with its beasts, snakes and trees, crushed those titans, grinding them to dust; and having slain those five generals, that monkey proceeded to destroy the remaining host. As the Thousand-eyed Deity destroyed the Asuras, so did Hanuman, the horses with horses, the elephants with elephants, chariots with chariots, and warriors with warriors and the pathways were choked with elephants, shattered chariots and the bodies of the titans. Having destroyed those heroic generals with their forces and vehicles, that hero, resembling Time, pausing at the destruction of the worlds, rested at the gate.

CHAPTER 47

The Death of Aksha

Hearing that those five generals with their forces and vehicles had been struck down by Hanuman, the King of the Titans glanced at the youthful Aksha, who full of martial ardour sat before him; and that impetuous warrior, armed with a bow inlaid with gold, responding to his glance, leapt up like a flame that blazes forth when fed with clarified butter by the foremost of sages in the sacrificial chamber.

And he ascended a chariot, acquired at the price of accumulated sacrifice, plated with refined gold, dressed with flags embroidered with pearls, yoked to eight steeds swift as thought, unconquerable by Gods or titans, surmounting every obstacle, flashing like lightning, of superb workmanship, able to travel through space, equipped with quivers, arrows, eight swords, darts and lances in orderly array, bound with golden ropes, shining with its myriad weapons, bearing golden garlands, rivalling the radiance of the sun and moon. Filling the firmament, the earth and its mountains with the sound of horses, elephants and great chariots, Aksha, at the head of his forces, advanced on that monkey, who was stationed on the gate.

Coming before that monkey, Aksha, with the gaze of a lion, in which admiration and respect were mingled, measured Hanuman with his glance, who resembled the fire at the dissolution of the worlds intent on destroying all creatures. Thereafter that mighty son of Ravana, reflecting on the exceeding valour of that monkey, his prowess in regards to the enemy and on his own strength, swelled up with pride and resembled the sun at the end of the world cycle. Then summoning up his courage, enraged, he took his stand resolutely in the field, and with concentrated mind challenged Hanuman, irresistible in combat and of unimaginable prowess, directing three whetted shafts upon him.

Observing that audacious monkey, indifferent to fatigue, accustomed to overcoming his foes and proud, Aksha took up his bow, holding his arrows in his hand. Wearing a corselet and bracelets of gold, with marvellous earrings, endowed with martial ardour, Aksha rushed on that monkey and a terrific struggle ensued which was unparalleled on earth and struck terror even in the Gods and titans. Witnessing that mighty conflict between the monkey and the youthful titan, the earth cried out, the sun ceased to pour down its warming rays, the wind no longer blew and the mountains shook; the whole firmament was filled with the sound and the ocean was convulsed. Then that hero, skilled in directing his aim, fixed his shafts and loosing them pierced that monkey in the forehead with three steel pointed winged arrows plated with gold and resembling venomous snakes.

Wounded by those murderous darts, his eyes blinded by the blood flowing from his brow, Hanuman resembled the rising sun, having arrows for its rays. Beholding that offspring of the foremost of monarchs with his splendid weapons upraised and his marvellous bow, that valiant counsellor of the Lord of the Monkeys rejoiced and in his ardour put forth his whole strength. Resembling the sun crowned with an aureole of rays as it rises over the peak of the Mandara Mountain, Hanuman, inflamed with ire, filled with strength and energy, consumed the youthful Aksha with his forces and vehicles by his fiery glances.

Thereupon that titan, from his bow equal unto Indra's charged with innumerable darts, let fall a mighty shower of arrows on the foremost of monkeys in the fight, as a cloud looses its waters on a lofty mountain.

Seeing the youthful Aksha on the field, seething with wrath and filled with valour, energy and strength, furnished with arrows, that monkey shouted aloud in exultation and, as an elephant draws near to a pit concealed in the grass, so did Aksha, in the inexperience of his youth, giving rein to his fury, proud of his valour, approach that incomparable warrior in conflict. Hanuman struck by those shafts, emitted a loud roar resembling a thunder cloud and, assuming a formidable aspect, full of vigour, agitating his legs and arms, churned up the air.

Leaping upwards, that valiant titan, raining arrows, hurled himself upon Hanuman and that foremost of titans, exceedingly skilled, greatest of car-warriors, Aksha, burning with courage, covered him with a hail of shafts, as a cloud covers the mountains with hailstones. Evading those arrows by darting between them, that heroic monkey, with the speed of the wind, swift as thought, began to range the path of the air. Casting glances full of pride on Aksha, who was armed with bow and arrows, burning to fight and, filling the sky with his countless excellent shafts, that offspring of the Wind-god became thoughtful and his breast, pierced by the shafts of that youthful and powerful hero, he emitted a great shout. Recognising the skill of Aksha, he pondered on the warlike qualities of that warrior, reflecting :—

"This great and powerful warrior, like an infant sun in splendour, has accomplished deeds incapable of being performed by a boy ; I am loath to slay one who has shown himself equal to every martial feat ; he is high-souled, filled with valour, concentrated and able to endure extreme hardship in war, worthy of being honoured by the great Sages, Nagas and Yakshas ; his strength and courage lend him a noble assurance and standing before me, he looks me straight in the eyes. Forsooth the heroism of this audacious being would shake the soul of the Gods and titans themselves. Verily he is an adversary not to be despised, his prowess increases as he fights ; if I disregard him, he will defeat me, therefore I must destroy him for a spreading fire may not be neglected."

Reflecting thus on the strength of his foe and his own, that powerful one, endowed with energy, resolved to slay his adversary. Thereafter that valiant monkey, born of Pavana, coursing through the air, struck those eight excellent steeds of immense size capable of bearing a heavy burden in combat with the palm of his hand and, that great chariot, overturned by the blow administered by the counsellor of the King of the Monkeys, its pole shattered, the shafts riven, the steeds slain, fell to the earth from the sky.

Thereupon, abandoning his car, bearing his bow and sword, that warrior leapt into the air, as an ascetic consequent on his penances ascends to heaven on leaving the body.

Rising into the sky frequented by the King of the Birds, the wind and the Celestials, that monkey, with a single bound, seizing hold of his legs, as Garuda catches hold of a snake, with a strength equal to his sire's, spun him round and round and threw him violently on the earth. With his arms, thighs and chest crushed, vomiting blood, his bones and eyes pulverised, his joints dislocated, his sinews torn, he fell to earth slain by the Son of the Wind.

Thereupon that mighty monkey trod his rival underfoot, striking terror into the heart of the King of the Titans, and all the Rishis, Cakracaras, Bhutas, Yakshas, Pannagas and Suras assembled with their leader Indra, who gazed with wonder on the simian slayer of that youthful titan. And Hanuman, having destroyed the stripling Aksha, whose eyes were inflamed with blood on the field of battle, returned to the gate once more and waited there like Death at the time of the destruction of all creatures.

CHAPTER 48

Hanuman allows himself to be taken captive by the Titans

THE youthful Aksha having been slain by Hanuman, Ravana, controlling his agitation, filled with anger, commanded Indrajita, who resembled a god, to take the field, saying :—

" Thou art the foremost of those bearing arms and hast afflicted even the Gods and Asuras in war ; thou art renowned among warriors and hast acquired divine weapons by the grace of Brahma ; thou art invincible in combat, even against the Maruts led by Indra himself. There is none in the Three Worlds who does not tire in battle, save thou. Thou art preserved by thy prowess in arms and thy valour is thy shield ; being versed in the knowledge of time and place, thou art exceedingly experienced and no feat is impossible for thee to accomplish in the field, who art full of forethought ; there is none in the Three Worlds but is conversant with thine austerities equal to mine own, as also thy prowess and the strength of thine arms in combat, nay, depending on thee, I have no anxiety regarding the outcome of the fray.

"In truth I did not put the same reliance on those who have succombed that I now place in thee, O Destroyer of Thy Foes, neither in the Kinkaras nor in Jambumalin, the son of my counsellor nor in the five generals going forth at the head of their troops with innumerable forces, accompanied by horses, elephants and chariots nor in the youthful, dearly beloved, Aksha, slain by that monkey. O Hero, thou surpassest them all, therefore, reflecting on thine own strength, with all haste act in such a manner that the destruction of the army may be avoided. O Foremost of those bearing arms, considering thine own prowess and that of thine adversary, who now reposes quietly after creating carnage among these hostile hosts, act so that his might may be subdued. Powerful forces can serve no purpose here, for great armies flee before Hanuman nor do maces avail; the speed of Maruti is irresistible and, like unto Agni, he may not be slain by weapons. Therefore, revolving all these things in thy mind and reflecting on the divine quality of thy bow, with the intention of bringing about a successful issue, strive with determination to overcome thy foe by frustrating his attacks. Assuredly it was not my will to expose thee to this hazard, O Foremost among those endowed with intelligence, yet this course of action is approved by warriors and is in accord with the duty of kings. In war one must be versed in the traditions as also in the rules of military science in order to emerge triumphant from the struggle."

Hearing the words of his sire, Indrajita, whose prowess was equal to that of the son of Daksha, circumambulated him and inspired with martial ardour, prepared to fight. Overwhelmed with homage by his cherished companions, who had assembled there, he set out for battle. And the resplendent son of the King of the Titans, whose eyes resembled the petals of a lotus, bounded impetuously forward, like the ocean at the time of the full moon. Thereafter, Indrajita of matchless prowess, equal unto Indra, ascended his chariot, swift as the eagle or the wind, moving freely, drawn by four lions with pure white teeth.

Standing in his chariot, that most skilled of archers, fully conversant with the use of weapons, the foremost of warriors drove rapidly to where Hanuman was to be found.

Hearing the rumbling of wheels and the twanging of the bowstring, the delight of that monkey was redoubled, whereupon Indrajita, seizing his bow and steel-pointed arrows, versed in the art of warfare, proceeded towards Hanuman and as he advanced light-heartedly, his weapons in his hand, the four quarters grew dark and jackals set up a hideous howling. Nagas, Yakshas, Maharishis, Cakracaras and Siddhas assembled and the sky was filled with birds emitting piercing cries.

Seeing that chariot bearing down on him, the standard of Indra unfurled, that monkey raised a great shout and expanded his body; whereupon, Indrajita in his celestial car, drew back his marvellous bow, emitting a sound like thunder and those two powerful heroes closed in conflict, the monkey and the son of the King of the Titans, like unto God and demon.

Indifferent to danger they began to fight and that mighty monkey evaded the impetuous army of that valiant archer and consummate warrior in his great car, by executing a myriad evolutions in the air with indescribable agility. Thereupon, the heroic Indrajita, slayer of his foes, began to discharge his marvellous superbly-fashioned sharp steel-pointed and winged arrows, tipped with gold, swift as lightning. Hearing the rumbling of that chariot, the rolling of the drums together with the sound of the stretching of the bow, Hanuman leapt hither and thither and that mighty monkey, evading the rain of arrows, skilfully eluded that dexterious bowman, whose target he was, and stretching out his arms, Hanuman, the son of Anila, turning aside from those missiles, leapt into the sky. Thus those skilful and spirited warriors, exceedingly swift in motion and versed in the art of warfare, engaged in combat to the wonder of all beings. Nor was the titan able to take Hanuman unawares nor Maruti surprise Indrajita, as they hurled themselves on one another with a courage worthy of the Gods.

Observing him unscathed although the target of his infallible arrows, Indrajita, controlling his senses, engaged in profound concentration of thought on Hanuman, and finding him incapable of being slain, he began to consider how he could be bound fast and that most experienced of warriors, full of exceeding energy, discharged that powerful weapon conferred on him by Brahma on that illustrious monkey. Knowing him to be incapable of being slain, Indrajita, skilled in strategy, bound that offspring of the Wind-god with the aid of that weapon.

Struck by the titan with the Brahma-weapon, that monkey fell to the earth unconscious, but knowing himself to be bound by a shaft belonging to the Lord, he did not experience the least pain and though bereft of strength, that monkey bethought himself of Brahma's blessing. Then that heroic monkey began to recollect the boons conferred on him by Brahma and thinking of that weapon bestowed by the Self-create, consecrated by mantras, he reflected: "I may not release myself from these bonds in virtue of the power of that Guru of the World. Further, this subjugation has been ordained by Him and must be endured by me."

Thereupon, reflecting on the power of that weapon and the compassion of the Grandsire of the World towards him, also of the possibility of deliverance, that monkey submitted himself to Brahma's decree.

He thought: "Though made fast by this weapon, I experience no fear; the Grandsire of the World, Mahendra and Anila will protect me; in sooth I deem it to be to mine advantage to fall into the hands of the titans and thus come face to face with their great king, therefore let mine enemies take me captive!"

Having thus resolved, that destroyer of his foes, full of circumspection, lay motionless and being ruthlessly pinioned by the titans, he responded to their threats and abuses by leonine roars. Beholding that subduer of his foes lying motionless, the titans bound him with plaited ropes of hemp and bark and he willingly allowed himself to be tied and insulted by his foes in order that he might converse with the King of the Titans, should he, out of curiosity, desire to see him. Bound with ropes, the monkey was no longer under the sway of the Brahma-weapon, for, he being secured by other bonds, it was rendered void. Beholding that excellent monkey bound with bark, the valiant Indrajita recognised him to be freed from that supernatural weapon and became pensive, saying aloud :—

" Alas, those titans have rendered my exploit useless, not being conversant with the power of mantras and that Brahma-weapon being rendered void, no other is effective, thus we are all placed in a great predicament for this weapon may not be loosed twice."

Though delivered from the power of that weapon, Hanuman betrayed it by no sign, despite the suffering caused by the fetters that bound him and he allowed himself to be ill-treated by the titans and assaulted by those cruel demons who struck him with their fists and dragged him before Ravana. Freed from the Brahma-weapon, yet bound by hempen ropes, that powerful and heroic monkey was paraded by Indrajita before Ravana and his court. And those titans related to the king everything concerning that foremost of monkeys, who resembled a maddened elephant that has been bound.

On seeing the foremost of monkeys made captive, those warlike titans enquired saying :—"Who is this? Who has sent him? From whence has he come? What is his mission? Who are his supporters?" and others exclaimed angrily: " Kill him! Burn him! Devour him!"

Having come some way, Hanuman observed elderly attendants seated at the feet of their sovereign and he gazed with admiration on the palace decorated with gems.

Then the exceedingly powerful Ravana beheld that foremost of monkeys dragged hither and thither by those hideous titans, and Hanuman gazed at the Lord of the Titans, who was like unto a blazing sun in his might and glory.

Seeing Hanuman, that Ten-headed One issued orders to his chief ministers, distinguished for their lineage and character, who stood before him and commanded them to interrogate that monkey. Thereupon, questioned in turn by them concerning the purpose of his coming, Hanuman answered :— " I am a messenger, I come from King Sugriva."

CHAPTER 49

His Astonishment on beholding Ravana

PONDERING on the exploits of that one of exceeding prowess, Hanuman gazed with wonder on the King of the Titans, whose eyes were red with anger and who was blazing with rare and dazzling gold, adorned with a splendid diadem studded with pearls and excellent ornaments of diamonds and precious stones created by the power of concentrated thought. Attired in costly linen, daubed with red sandalpaste painted with variegated devices, he looked splendid with his reddened eyes, fierce gaze, brilliant sharp teeth and protruding lips.

To that monkey, that Ten-Headed One, who was resplendent and of great energy, resembled the Mandara Mountain with its summits infested with innumerable snakes or a mass of blue antimony. A string of pearls gleaming on his breast, his countenance possessing the lustre of the full moon, he resembled a cloud illumined by the rising sun. With his great arms laden with bracelets, smeared with sandal paste, his fingers, like five-headed serpents covered with sparkling rings, he was seated on a superb and marvellously inlaid crystal throne studded with gems and covered with rich hangings. Women, sumptuously attired, surrounded him, chowries in their hands and he was attended by four experienced counsellors, Durdhara, Prahasta, Mahaparshwa and the minister Nikumbha who stood round him like the four seas surrounding the earth; and other counsellors too waited upon him as do the Gods on their King.

Then Hanuman gazed on the Lord of the Titans, clothed in extreme splendour, resembling the peak of Mount Meru surrounded by thunder clouds and, though suffering at the hands of those titans of dreadful prowess, Hanuman experienced extreme astonishment at the sight of that monarch and beholding the effulgence of that Lord of the Titans, dazzled by his magnificence, he became absorbed in thought.

'What splendour, what power, what glory, what majesty,' he reflected, 'nothing is lacking! Were he not evil, this mighty monarch of the titans could be the protector of the celestial realm and Indra himself, but his cruel and ruthless deeds, abhorrent to all, render him the scourge of the worlds as also of the Gods and demons; in his anger he could make an ocean of the earth!'

Such were the diverse thoughts of that sagacious monkey on beholding the immeasurable power and might of the King of the Titans.

CHAPTER 50

Hanuman is questioned by the Titans

BEHOLDING that tawny-eyed one standing before him, the mighty-armed Ravana, the terror of the worlds, was seized with violent rage. Gazing on that lion among monkeys radiating splendour, his mind filled with apprehension, he reflected:—

"Is this the blessed Nandi, who has come hither, he who formerly cursed me when, on Mount Kailasha, he became the object of my mockery? Or is he perchance Vana Bali's son in the form of a monkey."

His eyes red with anger, the king then addressed the foremost of his counsellors, Prahasta, in words that were opportune and fraught with good sense, saying:—

"Demand of this perverse wretch, whence he has come, for what reason he laid waste the grove and why he slew the titans? What is his purpose in entering this impregnable citadel and why did he attack my retainers? Interrogate this scoundrel concerning these matters!"

At these words of Ravana, Prahasta said to Hanuman:— "O Monkey, be of good courage, thou hast nought to fear! If it be Indra who has sent thee to Ravana's abode, tells us frankly! Have no anxiety, thou shalt be liberated! If thou art from Vaishravana, Yama or Varuna and have penetrated into our city disguising thy real form or if thou hast been dispatched by Vishnu, hungry for conquest, then tell us. Thy form alone is that of a monkey, not thy prowess. Unfold all this unto us faithfully, O Monkey and thou shalt instantly regain thy freedom but if thou liest, thou shalt pay for it with thy life! Therefore tell us why thou hast entered Ravana's abode."

Thus addressed, the foremost of monkeys answered the Lord of the Titans, saying:—

"I am not from Shakra nor Yama nor Varuna nor am I allied to Kuvera nor am I sent by Vishnu. I am truly a monkey as I appear to be, who have come here in order to behold the King of the Titans and for this purpose I destroyed the grove. To preserve my life I fought with the titans who, full of valour, presented themselves before me. Neither weapons nor chains can subdue me, even those of the Gods and titans themselves, I having received this boon from the Grandsire of the World. It was because I desired to see the king that I suffered myself to be overcome by the Brahma-weapon. Though I was not under the spell of that weapon, yet I permitted the titans to capture me in order to further Rama's design for which purpose I have entered the king's presence. Knowlng me to be the messenger of Raghava, whose power is limitless, listen to my words, which will prove to thine advantage, O Lord."

CHAPTER 51

His Words

SEEING the mighty ten-headed Ravana, that intrepid monkey addressed him fearlessly, in words fraught with penetration, saying:—

"I have come here at the command of Sugriva, O Lord of the Titans! As a brother, that Sovereign of the Monkeys offers salutations to thee. Hear the counsel of a brother, the magnanimous Sugriva; his words are in accord with justice, advantageous and salutary both in this world and hereafter.

King Dasaratha, the master of chariots, elephants and horses, in splendour equal to Indra, was the friend of all and like unto a father to his subjects. His eldest son, mighty-armed, the darling of his sire, at his command, entered the Dandaka Forest with his brother Lakshmana and his consort Sita. His name is Rama and he is exceedingly valiant and ever abides in the path of virtue. His faithful consort, Sita, the illustrious daughter of the high-souled Janaka, King of Videha, vanished in the forest of Janasthana. Seeking for that princess, the king's son with his younger brother came to Rishyamuka and met with Sugriva. That King of the Monkeys promised to undertake the search for Sita and Rama agreed to aid him in recovering the monkey kingdom. Thereupon, slaying Bali in combat, that king's son established Sugriva on the throne, as lord of all the bears and monkeys. Bali, that bull among monkeys, formerly known to thee, was slain by Rama with a single arrow in the fight, whereupon the Lord of the Monkeys, Sugriva, true to his vow, eager to find Sita, dispatched monkeys in all directions. Hundreds, thousands and millions of monkeys are exploring every region high and low, even up to the heavens and some resemble Vainataya and some the wind and those highly energetic monkeys course hither and thither without rest, incapable of being stayed. I am named Hanuman, the beloved son of Maruta and, in order to find Sita, I have crossed four hundred miles of sea. Having passed over the ocean, wandering through thy palace, I observed Janaka's daughter.

" It does not become thee, who art conversant with what is meet and proper and hast enriched thyself by thy penances, to bear away another's wife, O Eminently Sagacious One. Intelligent beings, such as thou, should not commit acts prohibited by the law of righteousness which lead to ruin! Who, even among the Gods and titans, can withstand the shafts loosed by Lakshmana or those of Raghava in his wrath? Nay, in the Three Worlds, there is none who may affront Rama with impunity. Following the path of duty and profit, do thou ponder these words fraught with advantage to thee in the three divisions of time and restore Janaki to Rama, that lion among men!

" I have seen Sita and achieved that which was difficult to compass, as for what remaineth to be done, Rama himself shall accomplish it. I have beheld her in thine abode, suffering grievously; thou art seemingly unaware that thou harbourest a five-headed serpent in thy mansion. Even as food mixed with poison may not be digested even by Gods or titans, so is she. It is not worthy of thee to bring to nought that merit acquired by extreme mortification, as also a long and prosperous life. Thou deemest thyself by thy penances, to have won immunity from death even from Gods, Immortals or titans, but Sugriva is neither a God nor an Immortal nor a titan. Raghava, O King, is a mortal and Sugriva, the Lord of Monkeys, therefore how wilt thou preserve thy life? The fruits of virtue do not blend with those of vice nor does equity destroy iniquity, Till to-day thou hast plucked the fruit of thy merits but soon thou wilt reap the fruit of thine evil deeds. Having learnt of the destruction of Janasthana, the death of Bali and the alliance of Rama and Sugriva; ponder on these things to thine own advantage. I am undoubtedly able to destroy Lanka with its horses, chariots and elephants single-handed yet I have not received the mandate to do so. In the presence of the troops of monkeys and bears, Rama vowed to slay his foes, those who bore Sita away. Assuredly, in doing injury to Rama, even Indra himself could not dwell in peace, how much less one like thee. This Sita, who is known to thee and who stays in thine abode is the night of death that will bring about thine end and that of Lanka. Beware of placing thy neck in the noose of death in the form of Sita. Consider how thou mayest save thyself. Thou shalt behold this marvellous city with its palaces and highways consumed by Sita's power and the flames fed by Rama's wrath. Do not therefore abandon friends, ministers, kinsfolk, brothers, sons, servants, wives and Lanka to this fate. O Indra among Titans, follow this good counsel since it is offered to thee by one who is a monkey, the servant and messenger of Rama.

"Having wholly annihilated the worlds and their inhabitants with all that moves or does not move, the illustrious Raghava could re-create them all. Among the chiefs of the Gods, Titans, Yakshas, Danavas, Nagas, Vidyadharas, Gandharvas, wild beasts, Siddhas Kinneras or birds, in no way nor anywhere, at no time, among any beings, has any been found, who could stand against Rama whose valour is equal to Vishnu's.

Since thou hast offered that lion among kings, Rama, this affront, thy life is forfeit!

"Devas, Daityas, Gandharvas, Vidyadharas, Nagas and Yakshas are all unable to hold their own in combat with Rama, the Protector of the Three Worlds, O King of the Titans! Even were it the Four-headed Brahma, Swyambhu Himself or the Three-eyed Rudra, the destroyer of Tripura, or the mighty Indra, Chief of the Gods, not one of them could withstand Raghava in the field."

Hearing this distasteful yet excellent speech of that bold and fearless monkey, the Ten-Necked One, his eyes rolling in anger, ordered him to be put to death.

CHAPTER 52

Bibishana pleads for Hanuman

HEARING the words of that high-souled monkey, Ravana, in a transport of fury, ordered him to be put to death. This decree however, issued by the King of the Titans in his perversity on one who had proclaimed himself to be a messenger, did not meet with the approval of Bibishana.

Knowing that Lord of the Titans to be exceeding wrath and the affair about to be concluded, that prince, firm in justice, began to consider what should now be done and that subduer of his foes, having resolved how to act, addressed his elder brother in words which were essentially true and mild, saying :—

"O King of the Titans, control thine anger and with a tranquil mind hear me, extend thy favour to me. Righteous monarchs, being conversant with the laws of cause and effect, do not take the life of a messenger. O Valiant Prince, it is contrary to justice, opposed to social usage, and unworthy of thee to bring about the death of this monkey. Thou art versed in the moral code, dost recognise an obligation, canst distinguish between high and low, dost carry out thy kingly duties and art aware of the ultimate purpose of life. If the wise, such as thou, suffer themselves to be mastered by anger, then the study of the scriptures is only a weariness of the flesh. Be pacified therefore, O Slayer of thine Enemies, O Unconquerable Sovereign of the Titans and consider what is meet and just in dealing out punishment to a foe."

Hearing Bibishana's words, Ravana, the Lord of the Titans, in a violent rage, answered him saying :—

" O Scourge of Thy Foes, to slay an evil-doer is no sin, therefore I shall make an end of this worker of iniquity."

Hearing this infamous and unscrupulous speech, essentially perverse, Bibishana, who was the foremost of those endowed with wisdom, answered in words fraught with integrity, saying :—

" O Lord of Lanka, King of all the Titans, be gracious unto me and listen to that which embodies the significance of virtue and profit. Under no conditions is an envoy put to death, this is the unanimous verdict of the good. Undoubtedly this is a formidable adversary and he has inflicted immeasurable injury on us, yet men of honour do not sanction the slaying of a messenger though innumerable punishments have been ordained for them. Mutilation of the body, the whip, stripes, shaving of the head, branding, one or all of these may be inflicted on a messenger but of punishment by death, none has ever heard. How can a hero such as thou art, whose mind is swayed by a sense of duty and who is discriminating and conversant with what is noble and ignoble, suffer himself to be overcome by anger ? The virtuous do not give way to wrath ! Thou hast no equal among those who rule over a people and thou art able to comprehend the import of the scriptures ; thou surpasseth the titans and the Gods. Invincible to the Gods and titans who are endowed with prowess, martial ardour and intelligence, thou hast oft-times in battle routed the King of the Celestials and other monarchs. Fools who, even in thought seek to injure thee, who art a great and intrepid warrior, who hast fought with Daityas and Devas, heroic, intrepid and unconquerable, are already deprived of their lives. I see no justification for putting this monkey to death. It is on those who sent him, that the punishment should fall. Whether he be honest or not, the responsibility rests with them. Advocating another's interests and dependent on them, an envoy does not merit death. Further if this one be killed, no other sky-ranger may present himself to us, therefore, O Conqueror of Hostile Citadels, do not seek to take his life; direct thine efforts against the Gods and their leader. O Thou who lovest warfare, if he be slain, I see none who can incite those two haughty princes to take arms against thee. It is not fitting for thee, whom the Gods and titans cannot conquer, to rob the Nairritas, whose delight thou art, of the opportunity of witnessing that encounter! They are devoted to thy welfare, courageous, disciplined warriors distinguished for their great qualities, intelligent, renowned for their burning ardour and fine bearing. Therefore let some of these, setting out under thine orders to-day, seize those two princes and establish thy supremacy among thy foes."

On this, Ravana, that sagacious Lord of the Titans, the formidable foe of the celestial realm, recognised the wisdom of the inspired words uttered by his younger brother.

CHAPTER 53

Hanuman is led bound through the City

HEARING the words of his high-souled brother, spoken in consonance with time and place, Dashagriva answered him saying:—

"Thou hast spoken truly, the slaying of a messenger is to be deprecated, it is therefore necessary to inflict some punishment other than death on him. In the case of monkeys, the tail is unquestionably the most cherished embellishment, therefore let it be set on fire and, having been burnt let him go, whereafter his friends, kinsfolk and allies as all those dear to him shall behold him degraded and mutilated."

Then the Lord of the Titans issued this command: "With his tail in flames, let him be led through the city of Lanka and its highways."

Hearing his words, the titans in their savage fury began to wrap the tail of Hanuman in cotton rags and thus swathed, that colossal monkey increased in size like unto a fire in a forest fed by dry wood. And having soaked the cloths in oil, the titans set them on fire and Hanuman, filled with rage and indignation, his face shining like the rising sun, lashed out at them with his blazing tail, whereupon that lion among monkeys was secured more tightly by the assembled demons. Accompanied by women, children and the aged, those rangers of the night gathered to enjoy the spectacle and the valiant Hanuman, who was bound, began to reflect on the matter and thought to himself :—

" Assuredly, though fettered, the titans are not able to prevent me from breaking my bonds and leaping amongst them creating fresh carnage, still it is in the interest of my master that I have taken this journey and it is under the orders of their lord that they have bound me, I shall not therefore resist them. From the point of view of stature, I am well able to engage all these titans in battle but for love of Rama I shall suffer this outrage. I shall survey Lanka anew, since during the night I was not able to view the fortifications, it proving too difficult. The night having passed I shall behold Lanka by day. Let them bind me anew; even though they inflict pain on me by the burning of my tail, my mind is not troubled."

Meanwhile the titans seizing hold of that great monkey of formidable aspect who was full of courage, an elephant among apes, exultant, advanced joyfully, proclaiming his misdeeds with conches and trumpets and those demons of cruel exploits dragged Hanuman, the conqueror of his foes, through the city, he willingly submitting himself to them.

Thereupon, passing through the titan's capital, that great monkey surveyed those marvellous palaces, covered highways, well laid out squares and streets flanked with mansions and cross roads, lanes and alleys, as also the interior of the dwellings and on the terraces and roads and along the royal highways all those titans cried out : " This is a spy ! "

Then those hideous titan women informed the divine Sita of these unpleasant tidings, saying :—" O Sita, that red-faced monkey, who had converse with thee, is being led through the streets, his tail ablaze." And hearing those words, Vaidehi remembering her own abduction, overcome with grief, having duly purified herself, called upon that God who nourishes himself on the sacrifices and urgently implored him to show his favour to that mighty monkey. And the large-eyed Sita, standing before the fire said: "If I am possessed of true devotion to my lord and have practised penances, if I have been a chaste wife, then do thou prove cool to this monkey. If the sagacious Rama still has any compassion for me, if my merits are not wholly exhausted, then do not burn Hanuman."

Whereupon Anala of ardent rays, as if communicating with that lady, whose eyes were like a doe's, blazed up and, at the same time, Hanuman's sire, in order to please that goddess, blew on that flaming tail with ice-cold breath and the monkey, whose tail was ablaze, thought:—"How is it that this fire, blazing up, does not burn me? I see a great flame, yet feel no pain, even as if the snow had fallen upon it. In sooth this is a wonder due to Rama's power which I witnessed when crossing the main. If the ocean and the virtuous Mainaka acted in such a manner, in reverence for him, what will the God of Fire not do? It is on account of Sita's virtue, Raghava's power and my sire's affection for me, that Pavaka does not burn me."

Thereafter that elephant among monkeys reflected:— "Why should a warrior such as I, suffer himself to be bound by these vile titans? It is meet that I should manifest my valour and avenge myself!"

Then that impetuous and mighty monkey snapped his bonds and springing into the air uttered a shout and that offspring of the Wind-god reached the gate of the city which was as high as the peak of a mountain and where no titans were to be found. Then, he who resembled a great hill, assumed a diminutive form and casting off his fetters became free, whereupon he expanded to the size of a mountain once more. Looking about him he observed an iron bar lying at the gate and the long-armed Maruti, seizing hold of that weapon, employed it for slaying the guards. Having destroyed them, in his ardour, that one of exceeding prowess, with the burning plume of his tail resembling an aureole, looking like the glorious sun surrounded by rays, cast his eyes over Lanka.

CHAPTER 54

He sets fire to Lanka

SURVEYING Lanka, that monkey, having attained his purpose, began to consider what he should do further and reflected in himself:—"What more remains for me to do to afflict the titans? The grove laid waste, those vile titans slain, a part of the army destroyed, nothing is left for me but to demolish their citadel. With their fort destroyed, it were easy to bring my labours to an end; with a little effort I can complete my task and obtain the price of my trouble. The Bearer of Sacrificial Offerings that flames on my tail must be propitiated by me, I shall therefore burn up these excellent buildings."

Thereat, with his tail in flames, which lent him the appearance of a cloud charged with lightning, that great monkey began to range the roofs of the dwellings of Lanka. Glancing round, passing from mansion to mansion, with a calm mind he encircled those stately edifices and gardens and leaping impetuously towards the palace of Prahasta, that one of exceeding prowess in strength resembling the wind, set fire to it. Thereafter the mighty Hanuman bounded to the mansion of Mahaparshwa lighting a fire equal to that at the end of the world. Then that monkey of immense energy leapt on the residence of Vajradanshtra and on those belonging to Shuka and the intelligent Sarana. In the same way that leader of monkeys burnt down the habitations of Indrajita, Jambumalin and Sumali and those of the titans Rashmiketu, Suryashatru, Hrasvakarna, Damshtra, Romasha, Yuddhonmatta, Matta, Dwajagriva, Vidyujjihva and Hastimukha and the dwellings of Karala, Vishala, Shonitaksha, Kumbhakarna, Maharaksha, those of Narantaka, Kumbha, Nikumbha and the magnanimous Yajnashatru and Brahmashatru.

That mighty bull among monkeys thereafter set fire to the accumulated treasure of those affluent titans and having passed over the other dwellings that powerful and auspicious one approached the residence of the King of Titans. Then the virtuous Hanuman, emitting loud cries, resembling a cloud at the dissolution of the world, with the tip of his blazing tail set fire to that foremost of buildings decorated with every variety of gems resembling Mount Meru or Mandara, enriched with sumptuous decoration.

Fanned by the wind, the flames spread everywhere, casting livid gleams like the Fires of Time and those palaces, enriched with gold, decorated with pearls and gems, richly bejewelled, toppled to earth, crumbling to dust like the mansions of the Celestials, who have fallen from heaven their merit exhausted. Then there arose a mighty uproar among the titans, who fled in all directions unable to preserve their dwellings, bereft of their treasure, crying out :—" Verily it is the God of Fire himself in the form of a monkey ! "

Some of the titan women with babies at their breasts ran shrieking from their homes and some, enveloped in flames, their hair in disorder, fell from the high balconies like flashes of lightning in the sky. And Hanuman saw various metals flowing in a molten mass, mixed with diamonds, coral, emeralds, pearls and silver, streaming from the palaces and, as fire is not sated in consuming wood and straw, neither did Hanuman weary of slaying those leaders of titans nor the earth from receiving their corpses. As Rudra consumed the Demon Tripura so did that impetuous and mighty monkey burn up Lanka and, from the summit of that mountain where Lanka stood, that dreadful conflagration kindled by the intrepid Hanuman shot forth in tongues of flame. Resembling the fires at the destruction of the world, the smokeless conflagration, lit by Maruta blazed up to the skies aided by the wind, feeding on the dwellings of the titans and their bodies like sacrificial offerings and, with the fierce ardour of a million suns, it consumed Lanka wholly as with increasing volume the fire cleaves the mundane Egg with a sound resembling innumerable thunderclaps. That fire of incalculable fury, rising into the sky, with its flames resembling Kimshuka flowers, its clouds of smoke like unto the blue lotus, looked exceedingly beautiful.

"Verily this is the God who bears the thunderbolt, Mahendra, the Chief of the Thirty or Yama or Varuna or Anila. This is no monkey but the God of Death himself who has come! Or perchance it is a manifestation of Brahma's wrath, the four-faced God who, in the form of a monkey has come hither to destroy the titans or is it the supreme power of Vishnu, unimaginable, unutterable, infinite and unsurpassed, which, by his Maya, has assumed the form of a monkey?"

Thus did the chief titans speak, being assembled and, seeing their city suddenly consumed by fire with its inhabitants, horses, chariots, flocks of birds, beasts and trees they began to lament, crying:—"O My Father, O My beloved Son, O My dear One, O My Friend! Woe, alas! O My Lord, our spiritual merit is exhausted!" Thus amidst, a frightful clamour, did the titans cry aloud, and Lanka, encircled with flames, her heroes slain, her warriors succumbing to the swift wrath of Hanuman, appeared to have fallen under a curse. In the midst of the tumult Hanuman with pride, surveyed Lanka bearing the marks of that violent blaze and its terror-stricken demons as Swyambhu surveys the final destruction of the world.

Having demolished the grove planted with rare trees and slain those powerful titans in combat and burned that city filled with splendid palaces, that monkey born of Pavana rested.

Having dispatched those titans in great numbers, destroyed the dense woods and spread the fire amongst the titan dwellings, the illustrious Hanuman became absorbed in the thought of Rama.

Thereupon all the Celestials lauded that prince among monkey warriors endowed with immense energy, equal to Maruta in swiftness, that sagacious and excellent son of Vayu. And all the Gods, the foremost of the Ascetics, the Gandharvas, Vidyadharas, Pannagas and Bhutas experienced an exceeding and indescribable joy.

And having devastated the forest, slain the titans in conflict and burnt the great city of Lanka, that mighty monkey, seated on the roof of the foremost of buildings, spreading the rays of his flaming tail like a aureole, resembled the sun encircled with a nimbus. Then having consumed the city of Lanka, that great monkey quenched the fire of his tail in the sea.

Beholding Lanka consumed by fire, the Gods, Gandharvas, Siddhas and great ascetics were struck with amazement.

CHAPTER 55

Hanuman's Anxiety concerning Sita

SEEING Lanka consumed by fire and that city with its terror-stricken titans filled with tumult, the monkey Hanuman became thoughtful and a great anxiety invaded his mind.

He reflected :—" In burning Lanka, I have without doubt done something reprehensible! Blessed are those great souls, who, in their wisdom extinguish the anger born within them as a fire is quenched by water. What evil is not committed by those who give way to wrath? In anger one may even slay one's spiritual preceptor; nor does he who is enraged, refrain from affronting virtuous men. He who gives way to wrath is unable to discriminate as to when it is fitting to speak or when to be silent; there is no iniquity that cannot be perpetrated by him. He is truly said to be a man, who, controlling himself, subdues the anger rising within him as a snake casts off its slough. Woe is me, wretched and shameless doer of evil that I am, who, forgetting Sita, have slain my lord by fire. Should that noble daughter of Janaka have perished in this conflagration, which has wholly consumed the city of Lanka, I have frustrated the purpose of my master; Sita having been burnt, I have marred my lord's design. To burn down Lanka is a trifling occurrence, but suffering myself to be overcome by anger I have cut at the very root of my mission. Assuredly Janaki has perished for there remains no corner of Lanka that has not been laid waste, the entire city lies in ashes. Since I have sacrified everything through my lack of understanding, I shall yield up my life this instant, either I shall throw myself into the fire or into the jaws of Vadava, or give my body to the denizens of the deep. Living, I am not able to face the King of the Monkeys or those two tigers among men, having marred their purpose. Through my culpable anger I have manifested my undisciplined simian nature to the Three Worlds. Woe to the unbridled passion, uncurbed and unrestrained, under which I failed to protect Sita when it was in my power to do so. She, having perished, those two heroes will die also and on their ceasing to exist, Sugriva will yield up his life with all his kinsfolk. On hearing these tidings, how shall the virtuous Bharata, devoted to his brother or Shatrughna, survive? Then on the extinction of the illustrious race of Ikshwaku, their subjects will be overcome with grief.

"Unfortunate am I, whose merits have been annulled through being false to the ties of duty and advantage, suffering myself to be dominated by a corrupting passion, thus becoming the destroyer of creatures!"

Immersed in these melancholy reflections, Hanuman recollected certain auspicious signs that he had previously observed and said to himself:—

"Is it possible that that Lovely One, protected by her own spiritual merit, has happily escaped death? Fire cannot burn fire! Nay, Pavaka would not dare to approach that virtuous one, preserved by her own purity, who is the consort of one of immeasurable glory. That Bearer of Sacrificial Offerings has not burned me owing to Rama's power and the virtue of Vaidehi. How should she therefore, the object of worship of those three brothers, Bharata and the others and the beloved of Rama's heart, perish? Since it is the nature of fire to burn, he who reigns invincible as master everywhere yet who has not burned my tail, why should he consume that exalted One?"

Thereafter Hanuman remembered with wonder how the Mainaka hill had appeared to him in the ocean and he reflected: "By virtue of her asceticism, sincerity and undeviating devotion to her lord, she is able to consume fire itself but it cannot consume her."

Pondering thus on the magnitude of the divine Sita's spiritual merit, Hanuman heard the high-souled Charanas conversing thus:—

"Assuredly Hanuman has accomplished a difficult feat in igniting a fierce and terrible fire in the dwellings of the titans.

The hosts of women, children and the aged are fleeing away and the tumult re-echoes as in a cavern; the city of Lanka with its towers, walls and gateways is wholly consumed but Janaki still lives, a great wonder!"

Such were the words, resembling ambrosia, which fell on Hanuman's ears and from that instant, happiness flooded his heart once more. On account of the auspicious portents, his own conclusions, the merits of Sita and the words of the saints, Hanuman was delighted beyond measure. Thereupon that monkey, having attained his end, knowing the princess to be safe, resolved to leave Lanka after seeing her once more.

CHAPTER 56

He takes leave of Sita

PAYING obeisance to Janaki seated at the foot of the Shimshapa tree, Hanuman said to her: "By the grace of heaven I find thee unharmed!"

Looking on him again and again as he stood ready to depart, Sita, inspired by conjugal affection, said to him:—

"If, O Child, thou judgest it opportune, then, O Irreproachable Friend, remain here in some hidden spot to-day; to-morrow, having rested, do thou set out. Thy proximity, O Monkey, will make me forget mine overwhelming grief awhile. Thou wilt go, O Great Monkey and it is doubtful whether I shall still be living on thy return, O Foremost of Monkeys! In thine absence my torments will increase and falling into one misfortune after another, I shall be consumed with grief and sorrow. Further, O Hero, this fear is ever present with me; how will the most valiant Sugriva or that host of bears and monkeys cross the impassable ocean or those two sons of men supported by those powerful monkeys? Three beings alone are able to bound over the deep, Vainateya, thou and Maruta.

"In the face of this insurmountable obstacle, in thy consummate experience dost thou see any possibility of success?

O Destroyer of Hostile Warriors, thou alone art competent to perform this task, thou shalt attain renown by thy prowess; yet, if Kakutstha, the scourge of his foes were able to lay Lanka waste with his forces and bear me away, it would be worthy of him. Therefore do that which will enable the magnanimous Rama to manifest his prowess in conformity with a warrior's nature."

Hearing these words full of loving solicitude, reason and significance, the valiant Hanuman answered :—

"O Noble Lady, that lord and foremost of monkeys, Sugriva, endowed with power, has resolved to deliver thee. Attended by thousands of billions of powerful monkeys, he will not delay in coming hither, O Vaidehi, and those foremost of men, the flower of the human race, Rama and Lakshmana, coming here, will afflict Lanka with their arrows. Having destroyed the titans and their adherents, the son of Raghu, O Exceedingly Fair One, shall bear thee away and bring thee to his capital. Take heart, therefore, O Gentle One and await that hour! Soon shalt thou see Rama strike down Ravana on the field of battle. The Lord of the Titans slain with his sons, ministers and people, thou shalt be re-united with Rama, as Rohini with the moon. Ere long Kakutstha will appear accompanied by the foremost of monkeys and bears and, triumphing in the fight, shall remove thy grief."

Having thus consoled Vaiḍehi, Hanuman, born of Maruta, prepared to depart, offering salutations to her and, having comforted her and displayed his surpassing strength by rendering that city desolate, having thwarted Ravana and exhibited his immeasurabke power, Hanuman, paying obeisance to Vaidehi, intent on returning, resolved to cross the ocean once more.

Then the repressor of his foes, that powerful monkey, eager to see his lord, ascended the foremost of mountains, Arishta, covered with dark groves of Padmaka trees, resembling a mantle which, with the clouds clinging to its sides, seemed to expand with joy under the sun's rays; the metals scattered here and there appeared to be its eyes and the solemn sound of its torrents resembled its voice chanting the Veda; the waterfalls, the singing of its song and the tall Devadaru trees caused the mountain to resemble a giant with uplifted arms, the thundering of the torrents were its cries re-echoing round about and the autumnal woods agitated by the wind made it appear as if it trembled; as the breeze whistled through the reeds, it seemed to be piping while great and venomous serpents created the illusion of its hissing in anger. With its ravines shrouded in mist, investing it with a solemn air, as if it were deeply absorbed in contemplation and the clouds moving here and there on its slopes lending it the appearance of walking; with its peaks towering heavenwards, so that it appeared to be yawning, it was bristling with escarpments and filled with innumerable caves. Planted with Sala, Tala. Kharjura, Tamala, Karna and Vanisha trees with a myriad creepers laden with flowers and abounding in herds of deer and containing innumerable streams, with countless crags, rich in minerals, intersected by rills, frequented by Maharishis, Yakshas, Gandharvas, Kinneras and Uragas, impenetrable on account of the thorns and briars, its caves were filled with lions, and tigers and other beasts abounded there and that mountain was furnished with trees having delicious fruit and roots.

Then the foremost of monkeys, the son of Anila, ascended that mountain burning to behold Rama once more and, wherever he placed his foot on those enchanting slopes, the rocks crumbled and broke away with a thundering sound.

Having scaled the Indra of Mountains, that mighty monkey gathered up his strength, desirous of crossing from the southern to the northern shore of the salty sea and, reaching the summit, he beheld that formidable expanse of water inhabited by dreadful monsters. Then the son of Maruta, with the swiftness of the wind as it blows through space, leapt from the southern region to the northern shore and, pressed under foot by that monkey, the mountain giant re-echoing to the cries of countless denizens sank into the bosom of the earth with its peaks toppling and its trees overturned. Borne down by Hanuman's prodigious bounds, trees laden with blossom fell to the ground as if struck by Indra's thunderbolt and the dreadful roar of great lions lurking in the caverns rent the skies as they were crushed by the falling mountain. Vidyadharas, their raiment torn and their ornaments in disorder, fled in terror from that place and large and powerful serpents, filled with poison, shooting out their tongues, lay in coiled heaps, their heads and necks crushed. Kinneras, Uragas, Gandharvas, Yakshas and Vidyadharas, deserting that mountain, returned to the celestial realm and that mighty hill, measuring forty miles in extent and thirty in height, was levelled to the earth with its trees and lofty summits

Then that monkey, desirous of crossing over the salty sea, whose shores were threatened by the tides, rose into the air.

CHAPTER 57

The Return of Hanuman

LIKE a winged mountain, with one impetuous bound, Hanuman sailed over the airy sea, whose serpents were the Yakshas and the full-blown lotuses; the Gandharvas the moon was the lily on those enchanting waters, the sun its waterfowl, Tishya and Shravana its swans and the clouds its reeds and moss; Purnavasu was the whale and Lohitanga the crocodile; Airavata the spacious island; Swati, its decoration in the form of a swan; the breezes were its billows and the rays of the moon its cool and peaceful waves.

Unwearyingly, Hanuman swallowing up that space adorned with the sun and stars, skimmed past the King of the Planets. Cleaving the clouds and crossing that ocean without fatigue, he beheld great masses of cloud, white, roseate, purple, blue, yellow and black, looking exceedingly beautiful and he, entering and re-emerging from them, looked like the moon, when it is lost to sight and becomes visible again. Coursing through those massed clouds in his white attire, that hero could at times be seen and again was hidden in the sky, like unto the moon. Borne through space, that son of the Wind constantly dispersed the groups of clouds, sailing on and on, emitting loud roars resembling thunder and, having slain the titans, rendered his name famous, laid the city of Lanka waste, harassed Ravana, inflicted defeat on those mighty warriors and paid homage to Vaidehi, he was now returning full of glory, across the sea.

And that one endowed with prowess, paid homage to the foremost of mountains, Mainaka, as he sped on like an arrow loosed from the bowstring. Approaching from afar, he observed that lofty Mountain Mahendra, like a great cloud and that mighty monkey, having a lusty voice resembling thunder, filled the ten cardinal points with his roars.

Reaching the southern shore, eager to see his friends once again, he began to wave his tail to and fro and emit loud cries and as he proceeded in the path of Suparna, the clamour rent the skies and it appeared as if the firmament and the sun's disc were shattered.

Thereupon those mighty warriors on the northern shore of the ocean, anxiously awaiting the Wind-god's offspring, heard the sound created by the thighs of Hanuman proceeding at great speed, resembling clouds blown by the wind and those rangers of the woods, who had been dispirited, heard the roars of that monkey which were like unto thunder. Hearing that clamour raised by Hanuman, those monkeys who were eager to see their friend once again, were greatly excited and Jambavan, the foremost of the monkeys, his heart exultant, addressing them all, spoke thus :—

" Undoubtedly Hanuman has been wholly successful in his enterprise ; if it were not so he would not have raised this clamour."

Thereupon the monkeys, hearing the violent movements of that magnanimous one, as also his shouts, highly delighted, leapt up and in their joy, bounding from rock to rock and from crest to crest, eager to behold Hanuman, climbed to the tops of the trees waving their clean apparel.

And the roaring of the mighty Hanuman, born of Maruta, resembled the wind whistling through a mountain gorge. Seeing that great ape, who, alighting, shone like a mass of clouds, all the monkeys stood before him with joined palms, whereupon that valiant monkey, high as a hill, leapt down on to the Mahendra Mountain covered with trees and, overflowing with felicity, he alighted on that lofty and enchanting peak, like a winged hill, whose pinions have been clipt and who has fallen from the sky.

Then instantly all the monkeys with glad hearts began to gather round the magnanimous Hanuman, encircling him, their faces shining with joy, drawing near to him in the excess of their felicity. Then offering obeisance to him they brought roots and fruits to that greatest of monkeys, born of Maruta. In their delight, some emitted shouts of joy and the foremost of the monkeys brought branches of trees so that he might be seated.

Meanwhile that mighty ape, Hanuman, paid obeisance to his elders and the aged with Jambavan at their head, as well as Prince Angada. And honoured by them all, as he had merited to be and overwhelmed by courtesies, he informed them briefly :—" I have seen the Goddess ! " Then taking the hand of Bali's son, he sat down in the enchanting grove on the Mahendra Mountain and, questioned by them, he joyfully addressed those foremost of monkeys, saying :—

" In the midst of the Ashoka grove, I observed Janaki; that irreproachable one is guarded by dreadful titan women. That damsel is wearing a single plait of hair and constantly sighs for Rama's presence. She is faint on account of fasting, stained with dust, emaciated, and wears matted locks."

Those foremost of monkeys, hearing the words of Maruti : " I have seen her ", sweet as Amrita, intoxicated with joy began to shout and emitting cries of pleasure raised ululations. Some waved their tails to and fro, others raised them up lashing them or bounded to the summit and with delight touched the fortunate Hanuman, that chief of monkeys.

And when Hanuman had spoken, Angada, in the midst of those valiant monkeys, paid tribute to Hanuman in excellent words, saying :—

" For valour and courage thou hast no equal, O Monkey, since thou hast crossed the immense ocean and hast now returned. Thou alone hast given us back our lives, O Great One. By thy grace, our purpose accomplished, we can rejoin Raghava. O What devotion thou hast shown to thy master ! What prowess ! What endurance ! By the grace of heaven, thou hast seen the divine and glorious consort of Rama. By the grace of heaven, Kakutstha will abandon the grief that Sita's absence has caused him!"

Thereafter, surrounding Angada, Hanuman and Jambavan, the monkeys full of joy brought large rocks and, seated thereon, eager to hear how he had crossed the main and seen Lanka, Sita and Ravana, they waited with joined palms, their eyes fixed on Maruti.

And the youthful Angada, surrounded by innumerable monkeys, resembled the Chief of the Gods enthroned in heaven amidst the myriad hosts.

When the glorious and renowned Hanuman with the illustrious Angada, who was adorned with bracelets were seated, that elevated and mighty peak shone with splendour.

CHAPTER 58

Hanuman recounts his Experiences

THEREAFTER, on the summit of Mount Mahendra, those monkeys, their eyes fixed on the mighty Hanuman were filled with delight and when all those high-souled and happy monkeys were seated, Jambavan, glad at heart, enquired of the great and fortunate offspring of the Wind concerning the success of his mission, saying:—

"How didst thou discover that noble lady; how doth she fare there; how doth that cruel Ten-headed One bear himself towards her? Do thou truthfully relate all this unto us, O Mighty Monkey!

"How wast thou able to trace the divine Sita? What did she reply to thine enquiries? Having learnt all, we can take counsel as to what should be done! Do thou tell us also what, on our return, we should say and what we should conceal, O Thou who art well able to subdue thyself!"

Thereupon, that messenger, his hair standing on end with joy on hearing these words, inclining his head in token of his reverence for Sita, answered:—

" In your presence I leapt from the summit of the Mahendra Mountain into space with a concentrated mind, desirous of reaching the southern shore of the sea. In my course, a formidable obstacle presented itself to my view and I beheld a great mountain having a golden peak, divine and splendid, which obstructed my path. Approaching the sun-like summit of that mighty mountain, reflecting: ' I will shatter this ', I struck it with my tail and that peak which shone like the sun, broke into a thousand fragments. Seeing its condition, that great mountain addressed me in sweet accents, bringing as it were refreshment to my soul, and said:

" ' Know me, O My Son, to be the brother of thy father Matarishvat, famed as Mainaka, dwelling in the deep. Formerly, all the larger mountains were furnished with wings and ranged over the earth causing devastation everywhere. Hearing of the conduct of those mountains, Mahendra, that blessed One, by whom Paka was chastised, with his thunderbolt severed the wings of those mountains by thousands but I was delivered by thine illustrious sire and that high-souled Wind-god cast me into the sea, the abode of Varuna. O Subduer of thy Foes, I am willing to render assistance to Raghava, Rama is the foremost among virtuous men and is as powerful as Mahendra himself '.

" Hearing the words of the magnanimous Mainaka, I confided my purpose to him and he gave me leave to depart. Then, counselling me to proceed, he vanished in his human form and in the shape of a mountain became submerged in the sea.

" For a long time I travelled onward with speed till I observed the divine Surasa, Mother of Serpents, in the midst of the ocean and that Goddess addressed me saying:—

" ' Thou art destined by the Celestials to be my food, O Best of Monkeys, I am about to devour thee since thou hast been assigned to me '.

" Hearing this, I, with humility, turning pale, made obeisance to her with joined palms and uttered these words:—

" ' Rama, the fortunate son of Dasaratha, the Scourge of his Foes, withdrew to the Dandaka Forest with his brother Lakshmana and Sita; his consort was borne away by the wicked

Ravana; I am proceeding to her on Rama's behest. In this matter thou shouldst assist Rama. Having seen Mithila's daughter as also her lord of imperishable exploits, I shall return and enter thy mouth, this I promise thee'.

"Thus accosted by me, Surasa, able to change her form at will, said: 'None is able to pass by me, this is the boon I have received'.

"Thus addressed by Surasa, I attained the magnitude of ten yojanas and then another ten, but her mouth assumed even greater proportions. Seeing her jaws thus dilated, I instantly assumed a tiny form measuring a thumb's size and quickly entered her mouth, emerging immediately, whereupon the divine Surasa, taking on her normal shape, said to me:—

"'O Best of Monkeys, O Dear One, go, accomplish thy mission and restore Vaidehi to the magnanimous Rama. Be thou blessed, O Mighty One! I am pleased with thee!'

"Then all beings praised me saying: 'Excellent! Excellent!' and I again leapt into the infinite blue like unto Garuda, when suddenly, without anything being visible, my shadow was held fast. Stayed in my course, I surveyed the ten cardinal points unable to discover who held me prisoner. Then the thought came to me: 'What is this obstacle that has risen in my path? I cannot discern its nature!' And as I looked down bewildered, I beheld a dreadful demon lying in the waves, thereupon that monster, laughing scornfully, addressed these inauspicious words to me, who though undaunted, remained motionless:—

"'Whither art thou bound, O Thou of gigantic form? Do thou become my food, who am hungry, and gratify this body deprived of sustenance for a long period.' Saying:—'Be it so' I expanded my body to more than the capacity of her mouth but she increased the size of her huge and dreadful jaws in order to swallow me nor could she comprehend that I was able to assume different shapes at will. In the twinkling of an eye, abandoning my vast size, I, extracting her heart, flew into the sky.

"Throwing up her arms, that cruel demon sank under the salty waves like a mountain, whereupon I heard the harmonious voices of those magnanimous beings stationed in the air, saying :—' That dreadful demon Sinhika has been swiftly slain by Hanuman.'

" That monster destroyed, I recalled to mind the urgency of my mission, and the delay that had occurred in discharging it and, after traversing a great distance, I beheld the southern shore of the ocean and the mountain on which Lanka was situated. The sun having set, I penetrated the abode of the titans unnoticed by them and, as I did so, a woman resembling the clouds at the end of the world period rose before me, breaking into laughter. Striking that exceedingly dreadful form, having flames for her hair, who had sought to take my life, with my left fist I thrust her aside and entered there at dusk, whereupon that one, affrighted, addressed me saying :—

" I am the city of Lanka, O Warrior! Vanquished have I been by thy prowess, thou shalt also triumph over all the titans!'

" Meanwhile I sought for Janaka's daughter all through the night, penetrating into Ravana's inner apartments, but did not find her there. Not finding Sita in Ravana's palace, I was submerged in a sea of sorrow and in the midst of my distress I saw an enchanting grove with a mansion surrounded by a lofty golden wall. Having scaled that enclosure I beheld a grove of Ashoka trees in the midst of which a great Shimshapa grew. Ascending it, I observed a thicket of golden aspens and hard by the Shimshapa tree, I beheld that supremely beautiful one, dark blue of hue, whose eyes resembled lotus petals, clad in a single piece of cloth. Emaciated with fasting, her hair soiled with dust, Sita, fixed in devotion to her lord, was surrounded by cruel and hideous titan women living on blood and flesh, as a doe encircled by tigresses. Wearing a single plait, absorbed in the thought of her lord, lying on the earth, her limbs wasted, she resembled a lotus at the advent of winter. Deprived by Ravana of the object of her desire, she had resolved to die.

" Beholding that lady, whose eyes resembled a doe's, the illustrious consort of Rama, I remained seated in the Shimshapa tree.

" Thereafter I heard a great clamour mixed with the jingling of girdles and anklets, issuing from the palace of Ravana and, exceedingly agitated, contracting my body, I concealed myself like a bird in the thick foliage of the Shimshapa tree. Thereupon the mighty Ravana accompanied by his consorts came to the place where Sita was and, seeing the Lord of the Titans, Janaki of lovely hips, shrank into herself, concealing her breasts with her arms and, in great dread and extreme confusion, glancing here and there and finding no refuge, that unfortunate being was seized with violent trembling.

" Then Dashagriva, inclining his head, bowed to the feet of the princess, who was overcome with extreme grief and said to her :—

" ' O Fair One, do thou regard me with favour ! If, O Sita, through pride, thou dost refuse to honour me, at the end of two months I shall drink thy blood ! '

" Hearing these words spoken by the wicked Ravana, Janaki growing exceedingly wrath, answered with dignity :—

" ' O Vilest of Titans, having uttered such a speech to the consort of Rama of immeasurable prowess, to me, the daughter-in-law of Dasaratha of the Ikshwaku line, why has thy tongue not fallen out ? O Vile Wretch, great indeed was thy valour to bear me hence far from the illustrious Rama, in his absence ! Thou art not even worthy to be the slave of Raghava, that invincible, loyal, courageous and illustrious warrior ! '

" Thus addressed in harsh terms, Dashagriva blazed up with wrath like a fire on to which a brand has been cast and, rolling his eyes in rage, clenching his right fist he prepared to strike Mithila's daughter.

" Then all the titan women cried out : ' Hold ! Hold ! ' and from their midst, the wife of that evil wretch, the lovely Mandodari, ran towards him and with gentle words, inspired by the love she bore him, contrived to pacify him.

" She said :—' Thou whose valour is equal to Mahendra's, what need hast thou for Sita ? Divert thyself with me, who am in no way inferior to her or do thou disport thyself with the daughters of the Gods, the Gandharvas or Yakshas. What is Sita to thee ? '

" Thereafter, that company of women raised up that powerful Ranger of the Night and conducted him back to his residence.

" Ravana having departed, those titan women of hideous aspect, railed at Sita in harsh and cruel terms, but Janaki paid no more heed to their speech than to a straw, and their taunts were lost on her; and those titan women, who fed on flesh, failing in their attempts, informed Ravana of Sita's unconquerable resolution, whilst others, tired of tormenting her, giving up hope, exhausted, lay down to rest.

"And while they slept, Sita, devoted to her lord, gave voice to bitter lamentation in the extremity of her distress.

"Thereafter, rising in their midst, Trijata spoke, saying:—

"'Devour me this instant, if you will, but do not lay hands on the dark-eyed Sita, daughter of Janaka, the virtuous daughter-in-law of King Dasaratha. In truth I have had a fearful dream, causing the hair to stand on end, presaging the destruction of the titans and the triumph of this one's lord. It is for us to seek the grace of Vaidehi, who alone I deem, can defend us from Raghava. Let us therefore relate this dream to her, for one who is the object of such a vision, being freed from her distress, will attain the height of felicity. By bowing low in submission, we shall earn the favour of Janaki, who alone can deliver us from this great peril!'

"Thereat that chaste and youthful woman, on hearing of the coming victory of her lord, rejoicing, said:—

"'If Trijata speak truly, then indeed will I protect you all.'

"Observing Sita's unfortunate plight, I became absorbed in thought and my mind was perturbed. Then I cast about as to how I might find some means of speaking to Janaki and I began to extol the race of Ikshwaku.

"Hearing the words I uttered embellished with the praises of those Rajarishis, that exalted lady, her eyes suffused with tears, enquired of me saying:—'Who art thou; how and on whose behest hast thou come hither? From whence comes thine attachment to Rama? It behoveth thee to relate all to me.'

"Listening to her speech, I made answer to her in this wise:—

"'O Goddess! Rama, thy consort, hath found an ally endowed with supreme prowess, named Sugriva, who is the redoubtable and powerful King of the Monkeys. Know me to be his servant, Hanuman, who has come hither to thee, dispatched by thy lord of imperishable exploits. O Illustrious

Lady, that highly effulgent son of Dasaratha, foremost of men, hath sent this ring as a token to thee. O Queen, what is thy behest? Shall I bring thee back to Rama and Lakshmana on the northern shore of the ocean?'

" Hearing this, Sita, the delight of Janaka, reflected within herself awhile and said :—

" ' Suffer Raghava to destroy Ravana and himself carry me hence.' Inclining my head to that noble and irreproachable lady, I requested some token from her which might enhance the delight of Raghava, whereupon Sita said to me :—

" ' Take this excellent jewel for which thou shalt be highly regarded by that One of mighty arms.'

" Thereupon, that princess of lovely limbs gave me a marvellous jewel and in a voice strangled with sobs, bade me farewell. I bowed to that daughter of a king with deep respect and, circumambulating her began to consider returning home, but she, having searched her heart, addressed me once again, saying :—

" ' O Hanuman, do thou relate my story to Raghava in such wise that those two heroes, Rama and Lakshmana, will come here instantly accompanied by Sugriva, or else, having but two months to live, Kakutstha will see me no more, like one without a protector.'

" Hearing these dreadful words, a wave of anger surged over me and I instantly resolved on what I should do. Thereupon, expanding my body to the size of a mountain, burning to fight, I laid waste the grove. Then all the beasts and birds began to flee away in fear and those terrible titan women awoke and beheld the devastation. Observing me, they all assembled and instantly ran in haste to inform Ravana, saying :—

" ' O Valiant Sovereign, this thine inviolable grove has been destroyed by a wretched monkey who sets thy prowess at nought. Slay that perverse creature instantly, who thus affronts thee, lest he escape!'

" On this, the King of the Titans, Ravana, sent out innumerable warriors called Kinkaras and eighty thousand of those titans, armed with spears and maces, were slain by me in the grove with an iron bar. Then a few, who survived, quickly went to Ravana to inform him of the destruction of his troops.

" Thereupon I resolved to destroy the marvellous palace with its monument and slew the guards stationed there. In my fury I laid this building, the ornament of Lanka, low, whereupon Ravana sent out the son of Prahasta, Jambumalin with a company of titans of grim and fearful aspect.

" With my formidable mace I slew that mighty and skilful warrior with his retinue and Ravana, the Lord of the Titans, on hearing this, dispatched the highly powerful sons of the ministers followed by a regiment of infantry but with my iron bar I sent them all to the abode of death.

" Learning that, despite their ardour, I had struck down the sons of his ministers on the field, Ravana quickly ordered five of his heroic commanders to set out at the head of their troops, but I slew them all, whereupon Dashagriva sent out his highly powerful son, Aksha, with countless titans, to engage me in combat. Then that youthful son of Mandodari, a skilful warrior sprang into the air and I seized him by the feet, whirling him round and throwing him on the earth.

" Thereat the ten-necked Ravana, full of ire, hearing of the downfall of Aksha, sent his second son Indrajit, full of courage and martial ardour, against me and I, rendering the prowess of all those titans ineffectual, experienced extreme delight. Nevertheless, that long-armed warrior in whom Ravana had supreme confidence, inflamed with wine, continued to fight at the head of his warriors.

" And he, realising that I was invincible and seeing his forces routed, made me captive by aid of the Brahma-weapon, whereupon the titans bound me with ropes and taking hold of me brought me before Ravana. Then that One of vicious soul entered into conversation with me and enquired of me regarding my coming to Lanka and why I had slain the titans, whereto I replied :—

" ' I have done all this for Sita ! To find her I came hither ! I am the son of Maruta, the monkey Hanuman ! Know me to be Rama's messenger and the minister of Sugriva. It is to carry out Rama's design that I stand before thee ! Hear me now O Lord of the Titans ! The King of the Monkeys offers thee salutations and enquires as to thy welfare, O Mighty Hero ! He has commissioned me to communicate this message in words that are both fitting and in accord with duty, legitimate pleasure and profit.

" ' While sojourning on Rishyamuka, that mountain covered with trees, I entered into an alliance with Raghava, that great warrior, invincible in combat, and he spoke to me saying :— ' O King, my consort has been borne away by a titan ; it behoves thee to assist me in this matter ! ' Thereafter, in the presence of fire, the Lord, Raghava, who was accompanied by Lakshmana, allied himself to me in friendship, who had been deprived of my royal prerogatives by Bali.

" ' And he hath made me lord over all the monkeys, after slaying Bali in combat with a single arrow. It is therefore fitting that we should assist him by every means and by virtue of this contract I have despatched Hanuman unto thee as envoy. Do thou therefore speedily return Sita to Rama, ere those valiant monkeys overthrow thy forces. Who is not conversant with the monkeys' prowess, whose aid has been solicited even by the Gods themselves ? '

" Speaking thus to Ravana, he bent his furious glances on me as if he would consume me and that ruthless titan ordered me to be put to death, being unaware of my power.

" Meanwhile his high-souled brother Bibishana, endowed with great sagacity, interceded for me in the following wise ; saying : ' O Thou Foremost of the Titans, abandon thy resolve, which is not in accord with the royal code. The death of an envoy is not sanctioned by royal tradition, O Titan. A messenger simply communicates the mandate of his master ! O Thou of incomparable prowess, there is no warranty for his destructon, yet, if his guilt be considerable, he may be mutilated.'

" At these words of Bibishana, Ravana issued this command to the demons : ' Set fire to the monkey's tail ! '

" On this behest, those titans wrapped my tail in hemp and cotton rags and they, in well-wrought armour struck me with their clenched fists and sticks and set fire to my tail. Bound and fettered with ropes by the titans, I submitted to it, resolving to set fire to the city. Thus pinioned and enveloped in flames, those warriors, shouting, led me along the royal highway to the gates of the city. There, contracting my body I assumed a diminutive form and casting off my bonds, I seized an iron bar and assailed those titans, thereafter with one bound vaulting the gate, I rapidly burnt down the whole city and its gates and towers with my flaming tail, resembling the fire that consumes all beings at the end of the world.

"Seeing Lanka in flames I reflected with anxiety that Janaki must without doubt have perished since there was no corner of the city that had not been reduced to ashes. Thinking thus, overcome with grief, I overheard the Charanas saying in auspicious accents :—

"'Janaki has not perished in the flames!' and hearing these wonderful words, proclaimed by their enchanting voices, I regained my courage. I was thereafter reassured by many auspicious signs, that Janaki had been saved from the flames and though my tail was on fire, I had not been consumed! My heart was filled with joy and the wind spread its delicious perfumes. By virtue of these propitious manifestations, by my confidence in Rama's prowess and in Sita and the words pronounced by the great sages, felicity filled my soul. Then, re-visiting Vaidehi once again, I took leave of her and, scaling the Mount Arishta, leapt in this direction in order to see you all once more. Following the path of the wind, sun, moon and the Siddhas and Gandharvas, I found you here.

"By the grace of Rama and your prowess, I have carried out Sugriva's charge to the uttermost. I have related all to you in detail and it now remains for you to accomplish what is still to be done."

CHAPTER 59

Hanuman appeals to the Monkeys to rescue Sita

HAVING completed his narrative, Hanuman, born of Maruta, added these significant words :—"Fruitful have been the endeavours of Rama and Sugriva! Having witnessed Sita's constancy, I am happy at heart! By the power of her penances, the most illustrious Sita is able to uphold the earth or consume it with her ire, O Monkeys. The power of Ravana also, created by austerities, is great and it is because of this that he was not destroyed when he laid hands on Sita. Nay, the flame to which one reaches out is not so greatly to be feared as is Sita's wrath.

"It now behoveth all the mighty monkeys and others, with Jambavan at their head to take part in this expedition, the purpose of which is now known to you, in order to behold Vaidehi re-united with those two princes.

"Alone I was able to enter Lanka, inhabited by titans and have afflicted that city by my prowess, as also Ravana and his people. What more could I not do therefore with the courageous and powerful Plavagas, endowed with heroism and martial prowess, strong and eager for victory?

"I shall destroy Ravana with his entire army, his sons, brothers and followers in combat. I shall destroy all the titans and circumvent those invisible weapons and other missiles, bestowed on Indrajita by Brahma, Rudra, Vayu, Varuna, scattering them and slaying the titans; with your sanction my prowess will bring them under restraint. Hills and mountains torn up by me will I discharge continuously, which even the Gods themselves cannot withstand, how much less those rangers of the night? Were the sea to overflow or Mount Mandara move from its place, Jambavan will never be daunted by an enemy host in conflict. And that heroic monkey, the son of Bali, is alone able to destroy the entire host of Rakshasas. With the movement of his vigorous thighs, the powerful Nila could overthrow Mount Mandara itself, how much more the titans on the field of battle. Amongst the Celestials, the Titans, Yakshas, Gandharvas, serpents or birds, show me any who could withstand Dvivida? Nor do I know any who could resist those two sons of the Ashwins, endowed with supreme energy, the foremost of monkeys, in the arena.

"Single-handed I have laid Lanka low and, setting it on fire have reduced it to ashes. On every highway I proclaimed aloud: 'May Victory crown the invincible Rama and Lakshmana! May the King Sugriva, whose support is Raghava, prosper. I am the servant of the King of Koshala, the offspring of Pavana! I am Hanuman!' I have announced this everywhere.

" In the centre of the Ashoka grove of the vicious-souled Ravana, the virtuous Sita waits forlornly at the foot of the Shimshapa tree surrounded by titan women, emaciated with sorrow and suffering, resembling the orb of the moon bereft of its splendour in the midst of cloud. Spurning Ravana, whose powers have rendered him arrogant, Vaidehi, the daughter of Janaka of fair limbs, remains undeviatingly faithful to her lord. Wholly devoted to Rama, the lovely Vaidehi, thinks of him alone, as Poulomi, Purandara. Clad in a single garment, soiled with dust, I beheld her in the grove surrounded by titan women who were heaping insults upon her. Her hair, dressed in a single braid that unfortunate being was absorbed in the thought of her lord. Lying on the earth, pale as a lotus at the approach of winter, separated by Ravana from the object of her love, she had resolved to yield up her life.

" With difficulty I was able to re-kindle Sita's hopes by addressing that damsel, whose eyes resemble a doe's, and relating all to her. And she, hearing of the alliance between Rama and Sugriva became happy and, fixed in her devotion, her conjugal affection reached its zenith. Fortunate is that ten-necked demon that she has not destroyed him, due to the boon he received from Brahma ; but it is for Rama that the destruction of that monster is reserved.

" Already greatly reduced, Janaki grows frailer every day, in Rama's absence, as learning wanes that is prosecuted on the first day of the lunar fortnight.

" Thus liveth Sita worn out by grief! It is for you to take counsel as to what it is proper to do in the matter."

CHAPTER 60

Jambavan rejects Angada's Project

HEARING these words, the son of Bali, Angada, said :—

" The sons of the Ashwins are exceedingly powerful and proud of the boon conferred on them by the Grandsire of the World, who in order to honour the Ashwi rendered those two monkeys incapable of being slain by any. This unique privilege inflamed their pride and those two powerful warriors, having overcome the mighty celestial host, drank up the nectar of immortality. These two, inflamed with ire, are able to destroy the entire city of Lanka with its horses, chariots and elephants, what of other monkeys? I myself am capable of destroying the city with its titans and the mighty Ravana! How much more so if I am accompanied by powerful warriors, masters of themselves, well-armed, skilful and desirous of victory?

"We have heard that the courageous son of Vayu alone set fire to Lanka. He has seen the divine Sita but has not brought her back. I deem it unfitting that warriors as renowned as you are acquaint Rama of this. There are none in leaping and in prowess, whose skill and bravery equal yours in the worlds of the Immortals or amongst the Daityas, O Foremost of Monkeys. Few have escaped the carnage wrought by Hanuman, therefore it only remains for us to slay Ravana and the rest of the titans and bring back the daughter of Janaka, placing her between Rama and Lakshmana! What need have we to trouble those other residents of Kishkindha? It is for us to proceed to Lanka and, having slain the titans, return to Rama, Lakshmana and Sugriva."

Such was the project of Angada, whereupon Jambavan, the foremost of monkeys, in his wisdom, cheerfully made answer in words fraught with good sense, saying:—

"O Great Monkey, O Thou of supreme understanding, we have received a mandate from the King of the Monkeys and the virtuous Rama to explore the southern region to its utmost confines, but we have not been commanded to bring back Sita nor would it find favour with that lion among monarchs, Rama, if we did so, for he, proud of his lineage, has vowed before all the leading monkeys that he will himself deliver her. How should his words be rendered null and void? What is the use of undertaking that which is not conducive to his pleasure? This display of our prowess will prove fruitless, O Foremost of Monkeys! Let us therefore return to where Rama, with Lakshmana and the illustrious Sugriva can be found and inform them of the result of our quest.

What thou hast proposed finds favour with us, O Prince, yet it is by adhering to Rama's design that thou shouldst look for success."

CHAPTER 61

The Devastation of Madhuvana

ALL the heroic monkeys headed by Angada and the great ape Hanuman highly approved Jambavan's words and, those foremost of monkeys led by the son of Vayu leaping down from the summit of the Mahendra Mountain, bounded forward. Resembling the mountains Meru and Mandara, they appeared like elephants maddened with ichor, covering the whole of space as it were with their shadow, their eyes fixed on the highly powerful Hanuman gifted with velocity, having control of his senses and honoured by the Siddhas. Resolved on bringing about the success of Rama's design, proud of the results obtained, desirous of communicating their auspicious tidings, all those virtuous inhabitants of the forest, eager to assist Rama and avid for combat, jumping and frisking, reached Madhuvana.

And they came to that celestial grove protected by Sugriva, planted with countless trees, enchanting to look upon, where none might enter. And Sugriva's maternal uncle, the mighty monkey Dadhimukha guarded that picturesque and spacious garden belonging to the Lord of Monkeys. Extremely anxious to partake of the fruits of that beautiful orchard, those tawny-coloured monkeys, greatly delighted, craved permission of the prince to taste the honey, yellow as they. Then he graciously allowed those venerable monkeys, headed by Jambavan, to drink of the honey.

Thereupon, under Angada's command, authorised by that youthful son of Bali, those monkeys ascended the trees, swarming with bees, feasting on the fruit and roots and, in an access of intoxication, began to frolic here and there.

Singing, laughing, dancing, bowing, declaiming, running, capering and clapping their hands, some supported others, some quarrelled and some talked at random. Some leapt from tree to tree, springing down from the highest branches, some bounded into the air or chased each other round the trees from rock to rock, responding to each other's songs and laughter, groans and lamentations, exchanging blow for blow.

Then a general confusion arose amongst that host of monkeys and there were none who were not inebriated or inflamed with excitement.

Seeing the wood laid waste, the trees stripped of their leaves and flowers, Dadhimukha was filled with anger and sought to restrain them. But that heroic and elderly monkey, the protector of the wood, was in turn upbraided by those insolent monkeys whereupon he grew even more determined to defend the forest that was entrusted to his care against them. Thereafter he spoke to some in harsh terms without fear or forethought and struck others with the palm of his hands, approaching some threateningly and others with soothing words.

They, however, excited with liquor, restrained by Dadhimukha, began to ill-treat him brazenly without reflecting that the fault lay with them, scratching him with their nails, biting him with their teeth, assailing him with blows of their hands and feet, and knocking him senseless laid waste to the whole of Madhuvana.

CHAPTER 62

The Fight between Dadhimukha and the Intruders

THEN Hanuman said to those monkeys: "O Monkeys, gather honey undisturbed! I will drive away anyone who hinders you!"

Hearing these words, Angada, that prince of monkeys, gaily echoed his advice, saying: "Do you all drink honey. We should be guided by all that Hanuman does, who has accomplished his purpose; even if it be improper, I am in accord with it!"

Listening to Angada, those foremost of monkeys all cried out:—"Excellent! Excellent!", praising the prince again and again. Thereafter they surged into the Malin wood with the violence of a torrent and, having penetrated into those orchards, they drove away the guards by force. Happy in the thought that Hanuman had discovered Maithili and having had tidings of her, with the consent of Angada they drank the honey and feasted on the fruits.

Hurling themselves on the guardians of that orchard who approached them in hundreds, they overwhelmed them with blows and beat them off. Collecting honeycombs, a drona in size with their hands, those monkeys, yellow as honey themselves, drank the nectar and threw away the combs; some in frolic pelted each other with wax or piling up the branches sat down under the trees; some, heavy with drink, heaped leaves on the earth and lay down exhausted whilst others, stimulated by the intoxicating nectar, reeling, struck out at their companions wildly. Singing at the top of their voices, some imitated the roar of lions and some whistled like birds, others, drunk with honey, slept on the ground; some roared with laughter or burst into tears, some babbled wildly whilst others tried to interpret their utterances.

Meanwhile the guards of the forest, the servants of Dadhimukha, set upon by those terrible monkeys, crushed between their knees, fled in all directions. Wrought up with fear, they approached Dadhimukha and said:—"Empowered by Hanuman, those terrible monkeys have, despite us, laid waste to Madhuvana and, crushed between their knees, we all but gave up our lives."

Highly incensed, Dadhimukha, beholding the destruction in the Madhu Wood, which had been entrusted to his guards, consoled his subordinates, saying:—"Proceed to that place and fall upon those insolent monkeys; I myself shall soon follow and drive away by force those who are drinking the honey."

Hearing the words of their master, those valiant monkeys returned to Madhuvana and Dadhimukha, in their midst, accompanied them with great speed, bearing huge trees. Arming themselves with rocks, trees and stones, all those monkeys, highly incensed, proceeded to where the Plavamgamas were to be found, where, biting their lips in anger, they remonstrated with them again and again, seeking to suppress them by force.

Then all those monkeys, headed by Hanuman, beholding Dadhimukha greatly enraged, drove him back with violence and, as the mighty Dadhimukha of huge arms advanced bearing a tree in his hands, the powerful Angada incensed, intercepted him with his hands and, beside himself with inebriation, without showing the least mercy, though he merited it being his great-uncle, threw him to the ground with violence. Then that monkey, his arms and thighs broken and his face mutilated, bathed in blood, fell senseless for a space, thereafter, disengaging himself with difficulty, that foremost of monkeys withdrew to a distance and addressed his attendants, saying :—

"Let us all proceed with haste to where the thick-necked Sugriva, resides with Rama. I shall relate all Prince Angada's misdeeds to him and filled with ire that Sovereign will punish all the monkeys. The enchanting Madhu Wood, enjoyed by his forefathers, inviolate even to the Gods, is greatly beloved by Sugriva and he will mete out heavy punishment to those perverse wretches avid for honey and will slay those who have disobeyed their sovereign, with their friends and kinsfolk. Then shall my wrath, which I am unable to restrain, be appeased."

Speaking thus to the guards of the forest, Dadhimukha, their leader, departed with them with all speed and in the twinkling of an eye, reached the place where that sagacious offspring of the Sun, Sugriva, was.

Beholding Rama, Lakshmana and Sugriva, that great and heroic monkey, Dadhimukha, descending from the sky, alighted on the ground and with a sorrowful mien placing his joined palms to his forehead, touched Sugriva's feet.

CHAPTER 63

Dadhimukha relates how Madhuvana has been laid waste

SEEING that monkey prostrating himself, his forehead touching the earth, Sugriva, his heart moved, said to him :—

"Rise, Rise ! Why art thou lying prostrate at my feet ? Speak without fear ! Why hast thou come hither ? It behoveth thee to make thy purpose plain. Is all well in Madhuvana? I wish to know everything, O Monkey!"

Thus reassured by the magnanimous Sugriva, the highly sagacious Dadhimukha rose and spoke as follows:—

"O Lord, that wood which neither thou nor Bali suffered to be enjoyed by the monkeys, has been laid waste by them! Seeking to drive them away with my attendants, they, disregarding me, continued to feast there merrily. I resisted their depredations with the assistance of my guards, but without showing any consideration for me, O Prince, those savages continued their orgy. These attendants of mine, assaulted by them, were driven from the wood and those countless powerful monkeys. their eyes inflamed with anger, broke their arms and feet and, crushing them between their thighs, flung them into the air. Thou art the living lord of these warriors who have been assaulted by those monkeys, who even now are pillaging Madhuvana and quaffing the honey."

While Sugriva listened to these tidings, the sagacious Lakshmana, Slayer of his Foes, enquired of him saying:—"O King, who is this monkey, the guard over the forest who has come to thee and what distress has led him to speak thus?"

Being thus addressed by the high-souled Lakshmana, Sugriva, skilled in converse, answered:—

"O Noble Lakshmana, this is Dadhimukha and this heroic monkey informs me that those war-like forest dwellers led by Angada have drunk the honey and eaten the fruits of the orchard. Such an escapade would not have been indulged in by those who had failed in their mission. Assuredly they have been successful since they have devastated the wood. It is for this reason that they have beaten with their knees those who have obstructed their revelry and have disregarded the valiant Dadhimukha whom I myself appointed as guardian to my orchard. In sooth, Hanuman and none other must have discovered the divine Sita. Hanuman alone could accomplish such a feat. The success of that enterprise depended on the sagacity of that foremost of monkeys endowed with courage, strength and learning. Where Jambavan and Angada are the leaders and Hanuman the moving spirit, success is assured. Assuredly Madhuvana has been laid waste by those heroic monkeys led by Angada. Having explored the southern region, on their return this orchard excited their cupidity, whereupon they plundered it and drank the honey, assaulting the guards and beating them with their knees. This monkey, the gentle-voiced Dadhimukha, renowned for his prowess has come to communicate these tidings to me. O Mighty Saumitri, undoubtedly Sita must have been found else these monkeys would never have destroyed the wood bestowed on us by the Gods."

Hearing these words pleasant to the ear falling from Sugriva's lips, the virtuous Lakshmana and Raghava were overcome with joy and the illustrious Sugriva, exultant on receiving these tidings from Dadhimukha, answered that guardian of the forest, saying :—

" Highly gratified am I that those warriors, being successful, have eaten the honey and fruit! One should bear with the arrogance of those who have been victorious. Return to the Madhu Wood immediately and send all those monkeys with Hanuman at their head, here! With these two descendants of Raghu, I wish to interrogate those deer of the branches without delay, who, with the boldness of lions have fulfilled their task, in order to learn if they have discovered Sita."

Beholding those two princes, their eyes dilated with joy, in the height of felicity, the King of the Monkeys, realising the success of his enterprise was near, experienced extreme satisfaction.

CHAPTER 64

Sugriva consoles Rama

THUS addressed by Sugriva, the monkey Dadhimukha cheerfully offered obeisance to him and gave salutations to Raghava and Lakshmana. Thereafter, having honoured Sugriva and those powerful sons of the House of Raghu, escorted by his attendants, he sprang into the air. Departing with the same speed by which he had come, he descended from the sky and, alighting on the earth, entered the Madhu wood. There he beheld those foremost of monkeys, now sober, spending the hours happily, having relieved themselves, the outcome of drinking honey, and approaching them, that hero with joined palms addressed Angada in the following words :—

" O Noble Prince, do not harbour any ill-feeling towards the guards, who, enraged, sought to drive thee away by force. May peace attend thee ! O Thou of great strength, do thou partake of the honey freely which is thine by right, since thou art the heir-apparent and owner of the wood. It behoveth thee to pardon us for our wrath, arising out of ignorance ! Like unto thy sire formerly and Sugriva, so art thou Lord of the monkey host ! O Irreproachable Prince, I have related all unto thine uncle, who, hearing of the presence of the monkeys here, of thine arrival and also of the devastation of the forest, was not the least incensed, rather was he gratified. Highly pleased, thy paternal uncle, Sugriva, King of the Monkeys, said : ' Send them all here without delay ! ' "

Hearing those words of Dadhimukha, Angada, Prince of the Monkeys, skilled in speech, addressed all his companions, saying :—

" O You Leaders of the Monkey Host, undoubtedly all these events have been related to Rama. This may be inferred by Dadhimukha's tidings. It does not behove us to linger here further, our mission having been accomplished, O Slayers of your Foes ! You have all drunk honey in full measure, O Heroic Forest Dwellers, nothing remains for us but to rejoin Sugriva. Whatever all of you counsel me to do, I shall put into effect. I am your servant and, though the heir-apparent, it is not for me to issue orders to you. You have all accomplished your task ; it would therefore be unfitting for me to treat you arbitrarily."

Hearing these admirable words of Angada, those monkeys, full of delight, spoke thus :—

" Who, of thy status, O Foremost of Monkeys, would speak thus ? Drunk with power, each says : ' I am the leader ! ' None but thee would utter words of such felicity. Thine humility augurs well for us. We are all ready to return to

Sugriva the King of the Monkeys without delay, but without thy word of command none among us is able to advance a single step."

On this, Angada answered them, saying:—"It is well, let us go!", whereupon all those warriors sprang into the air and the space was entirely filled as if by stones shot from a mortar.

Preceded by Angada, who was followed by Hanuman, those Plavamgamas bounded tempestuously into the air with a great clamour, like clouds driven before the wind.

Angada having arrived near to Sugriva, the King of the Monkeys addressd the lotus-eyed Rama, who was consumed with grief, and said:—

"Be of good courage! Rest assured the divine Sita has been found! These monkeys would not have returned otherwise, the time fixed by me being already past; I infer this from Angada's joy! Had the long-armed Angada, the foremost of monkeys not been successful, he would not have come back to me. If they had not succeeded in their enterprise, after such an escapade, that youthful prince, his mind troubled, would have appeared dejected. Without having seen the daughter of Janaka, they would not have dared to destroy Madhuvana which was obtained from my forbears or attacked that venerable monkey who guards it. O Noble Son of Kaushalya, O Thou fixed in thy vow and faithful to thine obligations, in sooth Hanuman and none else has discovered Sita. No other is qualified to encompass this end. O Thou, the foremost of the virtuous, the means to success are intelligence, resolution, valour and knowledge and Hanuman is endowed with all these. Where Jambavan with Angada leads and Hanuman directs the work, there can be but one outcome. O Thou of immeasurable prowess, have no anxiety! Those dwellers of the wood, having reached the height of insolence, would not have entered into an escapade of this kind had they failed in their mission. They have laid waste Madhuvana and taken the honey, I infer therefore that they have been successful."

At that instant, cries of "Kilakila" resounded in the sky from those inhabitants of the woods, who, proud of Hanuman's exploit, were proceeding towards Kishkindha, thus proclaiming their trumph.

Hearing that tremendous clamour, the King of the Monkeys, curling and uncurling his tail, became greatly excited, whilst those monkeys, eager to see Rama, with Angada at their head and Hanuman before them, drunk with joy, alighted from the sky in front of their sovereign and Raghava.

Thereafter the mighty-armed Hanuman, inclining his head in salutations, informed Rama of Sita's physical and spiritual well-being. And hearing from Hanuman the auspicious words sweet as Amrita: " I have seen Sita ", the joy of Rama and Lakshmana was extreme and Lakshmana gazed on Sugriva, who had placed the matter in the hands of the son of Pavana, with profound respect, whilst Raghava, the destroyer of his foes, in extreme felicity looked on Hanuman with veneration.

CHAPTER 65

Hanuman tells Rama of his Meeting with Sita

HAVING reached the Mount Prasravana with its many woods, Hanuman paid obeisance to the mighty Rama and Lakshmana. Preceded by the heir-apparent, Angada and bowing to Sugriva and the monkeys, he began to recount the story of Sita and her confinement in Ravana's harem, of the threats of the female titans, of her unflinching devotion to Rama and the time fixed for her execution. All this did the monkey relate in Rama's presence.

And hearing of Vaidehi's well-being, Rama said:—" O Monkeys, where is the illustrious Sita to be found and what are her feelings towards me ? Do ye relate everything unto me! "

Hearing Rama's words, the monkeys requested Hanuman, conversant with the matter, to describe all in detail. And he, versed in the art of speech, acquiescing in their desire, inclining his head in salutation to the divine Sita, turning to the south described his meeting with her and bestowed on Rama the heavenly jewel, blazing in its own effulgence; then the son of Maruta offered obeisance to him and said :—

" Anxious to behold Sita, I crossed the ocean four hundred miles in extent and after a time reached Lanka, that city belonging to the wicked Ravana which is situated on the southern shore of the sea. There I beheld Sita in the inner apartments of Ravana and there she dwells, O Rama, centring all her thoughts on thee. I observed her reviled by hideous titan women who are guarding her in the grove and that noble lady, accustomed by thee to felicity, is now stricken with grief in thine absence, O Hero. Imprisoned in Ravana's inner apartments under the strict surveillance of those female demons, wearing a single plait, forlorn, that unfortunate being is absorbed in the thought of thee! Lying on the earth, emaciated, resembling a lotus on the approach of winter, spurning Ravana, she is resolved to yield up her life.

" O Kakutstha, O Guileless Prince, with considerable difficulty I discovered that princess of whom thou art in some sort the very soul and, narrating the glories of the Ikshwaku Race, I succeeded in gaining her confidence, whereupon I told her all.

" Hearing of the alliance between thee and King Sugriva, she was greatly delighted and she remains constant to thee in faith and love. O Foremost of Men, it was in this condition that I discovered her engaged in severe penances with her heart fixed on thee. Bestowing this jewel upon me, she requested me to relate to thee what happened on Chittrakuta concerning the crow, O Sagacious One and, addressing me thus, she said :—

" ' O Son of Vayu, do thou describe all that thou hast seen here to Rama and present him with this jewel, which has been preserved by me with care. Do thou remind him of the mark traced with red powder on my countenance! Say :— ' O Sinless One, seeing this unique pearl formed by the waters that I send to thee, meseems I see thee before me and I rejoice in the midst of my distress. O Son of Dasaratha, I shall live but for a month, after which, being in the power of the titans, I shall die! ' "

" Such were the words addressed to me by Sita of emaciated limbs, whose eyes resemble a doe's, imprisoned in Ravana's apartments. I have related all faithfully to thee, O Raghava, now take counsel in order to bridge the ocean."

Seeing those two princes filled with renewed hope, the son of Vayu having presented the jewel as a token of recognition to Raghava, described everything to him from beginning to end.

CHAPTER 66

Rama's Grief

AT these words of Hanuman, Rama, born of Dasaratha, pressing the jewel to his heart, wept with Lakshmana. And beholding that marvellous gem, Raghava, stricken with grief, his eyes suffused with tears, said to Sugriva :—

"As milk flows from the udders of a cow on beholding its calf, so does my heart brim over on beholding this jewel! This pearl was conferred on Sita by my father-in-law on the occasion of our nuptuals and she wore it on her brow, thus enhancing her beauty. Obtained from the waters and reverenced by the Gods, it was conferred on Janaka by the sagacious Shakra, gratified by his adoration at a sacrifice.

"Seeing this magnificent gem, I recall the presence of my sire and my father-in-law, the King of Videha. This lovely ornament appeared beautiful on the forehead of my beloved and seeing it, it seems as if she herself were present here. As if sprinkling water on one who has lost consciousness, do thou relate to me what Vaidehi hath said, again and again, O Friend! What could be more poignant, O Saumitri, than seeing this pearl obtained from the waters, without Vaidehi? If she survive one month more, she will live long, but it is hard for me to exist an instant without Sita! Do thou lead me to where thou hast seen my beloved; after hearing these tidings, I cannot brook a moment's delay. How can that lady of lovely hips, who was ever timorous, endure life amidst those grim and fearful demons? As the autumnal moon, enveloped in cloud is unable to shine forth, so Sita's countenance is no longer resplendent. O Hanuman, do thou relate unto me again and again what Sita said to thee. These words will revive me as the sick are cured by medicine. O Hanuman, what did my gentle, sweet-spoken and beautiful lady, who is separated from me, say to thee? How is that daughter of Janaka able to survive in her dire misfortune?"

CHAPTER 67

Hanuman describes his Interview with Sita

BEING thus addressed by the high-souled Raghava, Hanuman began to relate all that Sita had said to him:—

"O Lion among Men, in order to give credence to my report, the divine Sita described what took place on Mount Chittrakuta. Sleeping happily at thy side, Janaki one day was the first to wake, when suddenly a crow wounded her breast with its beak. O Rama, thou wert then asleep on Sita's lap and that crow again attacked her, pecking her cruelly, and, being bathed in blood and suffering, she did arouse thee. O Slayer of thy foes, seeing her breast wounded, thou, like an angry serpent didst enquire, saying:—'Who, O Timid One, hath with his claws wounded thee? Who hath dared to play with a five-headed snake?' Then, looking here and there, thou didst perceive the crow with its talons sharp and bloody standing before thee. And that foremost of birds was Indra's son, who with the speed of the wind disappeared into the earth. Then thou, O Mighty-armed One, didst roll thine eyes furiously and resolve to destroy that crow. Taking a tuft of Kusha grass from where thou hadst lain, pronouncing the Brahma-mantra, thou didst hurl the blade that blazed up like the fire at the dissolution of the world at the bird and that flaming grass followed in its wake.

"Forsaken by the Gods, who were terrified, that crow traversed the Three Worlds without finding a protector and returned to thee, O Subduer of thy foes, seeking refuge in thee and falling on the earth before thee. Thereupon, O Kakutstha, thou in thy compassion didst pardon it, albeit it merited death. But thinking it improper that the purpose of the weapon should be rendered void, thou didst destroy the right eye of that crow, O Raghava. Then paying homage to thee and to King Dasaratha, that bird, thus delivered, returned to its abode.

"Sita said :—'O Raghava, thou art the foremost of those skilled in weapons, mighty and full of integrity, why dost thou not discharge thy shafts against the titans? Neither the Gods, Gandharvas, Asuras or Maruta can withstand thee in battle. If thou in thy magnanimity hast any regard for me, then with thy well-directed shafts destroy Ravana without delay. Under the behest of his brother, why does not Lakshmana, the scourge of his foes and the foremost of men, fly to my defence?

"'How is it that those two mighty lions among men, the equals of Vayu and Agni in valour, whom the Gods themselves are unable to overcome, have forgotten me? Assuredly I have committed a great sin, since those two scourges of their foes, who are able to do so, do not unite to deliver me!'

"To those plaintive and gentle words of the noble Vaidehi, I answered : 'O Illustrious Lady, Rama is sorely stricken on account of thine absence and seeing his brother a prey to sorrow, Lakshmana too is suffering, I swear it. Since I have found thee at last, the time for lamentation is past. In an instant thou shalt see the end of thy woes, O Lovely Princess. Those two sons of a king, the foremost of men and subduers of their foes, eager to see thee once more, will reduce Lanka to ashes. Having slain the cruel Ravana with his kinsfolk in battle, Raghava will take thee back to his capital, O Charming One! O Irreproachable Lady, do thou bestow some token on me that is known to Rama and will bring him delight.'

"Thereat Sita, glancing round on every side, drew from her robe an excellent jewel which had fastened her locks and bestowed it on me, O Mighty One.

"Then I, inclining my head in salutation, took the gem into my hands and made ready to depart, O Beloved of the Raghu Race! Whereupon, seeing me about to take my leave expanding my body, Sita, the beautiful and unfortunate daughter of Janaka, her face bathed in tears, addressed me in a voice strangled with sobs and, in the intensity of distress at my departure, said to me :—

" ' Happy art thou, O Monkey, since thou shalt behold the mighty Rama whose eyes resemble lotuses and the long-armed Lakshmana, my illustrious brother-in-law ! '

" To these words of Maithili, I made answer :—' Climb on my back without delay, O Noble Lady, and this very day I will show thee Sugriva, Lakshmana and thy consort Rama, O Fortunate Dark-eyed Princess ! '

" Then that Goddess answered me, saying :—' It is not proper for me to climb on thy back of mine own accord, O Great Monkey ! Although before this I was touched by the demon, it was on account of my helplessness, subject as I was to destiny. Do thou thyself repair to where those two princes are ! ' After this she added :—

" ' O Hanuman, do thou greet those two lions among men with Sugriva and his ministers ! Do thou describe unto Rama and Lakshmana of immeasurable prowess the intensity of my despair and the insults heaped on me by the titans. May thy journey be prosperous, O Foremost of Monkeys ! '

" Thus did that illustrious princess speak to me in the midst of her grief. Reflecting on my narrative, have faith in the integrity of the virtuous Sita."

CHAPTER 68

He repeats his Words of Consolation to Sita

" O Foremost of Men, that Goddess then addressed me in the midst of her grief out of love for thee and solicitude on my account, saying :—

" ' Do thou repeat all this to the son of Dasaratha, so that he may come with all speed and, having slain Ravana in combat, take me hence. O Hero, O Subduer of thy foes, if it find approval with thee, rest concealed here in some secret spot for one more day to relieve thy fatigue and to-morrow thou canst make ready to depart ! O Hanuman, in thy company I am able to forget my sufferings awhile. O Thou gifted with great prowess, I shall await thy return but doubt if I shall be living then. Beholding thee no more, I shall be consumed with fear, unfortunate creature that I am, overwhelmed with affliction ! Moreover I am filled with doubt regarding thy companions, the bears and monkeys and how in effect, they and those two princes will be able to cross the impassable ocean. O Irreproachable Warrior, there are only three creatures qualified to traverse the sea—Garuda, Vayu and thyself. In view of this insurmountable obstacle, what possibility of success dost thou see, O Thou foremost of those skilled in the art of converse ? True it is, that thou art able to accomplish this work single-handed, O Subduer of thy foes, but such a manifestation of prowess would benefit thee alone. If Rama however, with his forces, slaying Ravana in fight, were to bring me back in triumph to his capital, it would redound to his glory. It would not be worthy of Raghava to capture me by stealth as did Ravana, who under a disguise bore me away from the forest. Truly it would prove a feat of signal excellence, worthy of him, if Kakutstha, the conqueror of his foes, should destroy Lanka and deliver me. Do thou so act that that high-souled hero may display his prowess ! '

" Hearing these words, full of good sense, reasonable and affectionate, I replied for the last time :—

" ' O Goddess, Sugriva, the Leader of the bears and monkeys, gifted with valour, has resolved to deliver thee. He hath under his command innumerable powerful and courageous monkeys gifted with prowess, who are as swift as thought, able to go upwards or downwards and to every side, whom nothing can impede nor may they be daunted by the hardest tasks. Moreover those great and powerful monkeys, endowed with vigour, have circled the earth again and again, coursing through the air. Sugriva has many monkeys equal to me and greater ; none are inferior. If I am able to cross the sea, how much more these heroes ? The great ones are never sent out on a mission but those of inferior merit only.

" O Lady, now abandon grief ; in one bound those leaders of the monkey hosts will reach Lanka and these two lions among men, like unto the sun and moon, will present themselves to thee, O Princess. Soon shalt thou see at Lanka's gate, Raghava, resembling a lion and Lakshmana, bow in hand. And thou shalt soon behold those monkey warriors, endowed with the strength of lions and tigers, whose weapons are their nails and teeth, resembling the lords of the elephants, hastening here without delay. Ere long thou shalt hear the roaring of those leaders of monkeys on the summit of the Mount Malaya, resembling the rumbling of clouds. Soon thou shalt see Raghava, the Slayer of His foes, returning from his exile in the forest, installed on the throne with thee in Ayodhya.'

"Thereafter the daughter of the King of Mithila, though profoundly afflicted by thine absence, was comforted by these auspicious words and experienced great peace."

END OF SUNDARA KANDA

GLOSSARY

(For Flowers, Trees and Weapons, see separate Glossaries)

A

ABHIJIT. The twenty-second Nakshatra q.v.

ABIKI. A sheep.

ACHAMANA. A purificatory rite at which water is taken in the palm of the hands and poured over the head and breast and the mouth rinsed. It also includes touching various parts of the body.

ACHARYA. A spiritual Preceptor.

ADAMBARA. A drum.

ADITI. Mother of the Gods, who represents space and infinity.

ADITYAS. Sun Gods or sons of Aditi.

AGARU. Agallochum, a species of sandal or Indian Aloe Exorcaria. Used as incense or for perfuming purposes.

AGASTYA. A great Rishi, the reputed author of several hymns in the Rig-Veda. This Sage, whose miraculous powers are described in the great classics, entertained Rama, Sita and Lakshmana in his hermitage during their exile.

AGNEYA. A mountain. Also the south-eastern quarter, of which Agni is Regent.

AGNI. The God of Fire.

AGNIHOTRA. The Fire Sacrifice.

AGRAHAYANA. A Feast similar to the Harvest Festival.

AHALYA. Wife of the Rishi Gautama, who was transformed into a rock by her husband's curse and ultimately restored by Rama to her natural state.

AIRAVATA. The sacred elephant that transports the God, Indra.

AJA. A king of the dynasty of Ikshwaku, father of Dasaratha.

AJAS. A class of hermits. See note on Ascetics.

AKAMPANA. The Titan who informed Ravana of the destruction of Janasthana and persuaded him to abduct Sita.

ALAKA. Kuvera's capital.

AMARAVATI. Indra's capital, also called Vitapavati.

AMBARISHA. A king whose story is told in Balakanda.

AMRITA. The " Nectar of Immortality " produced by the churning of the ocean by Gods and Demons.

ANANGA. Lit.: " Bodiless "—a name given to Kandarpa, the God of Love.

ANANTA. The thousand-headed serpent or Shesha on which the Lord Vishnu rests during the withdrawal of the worlds.

GLOSSARY

ANASUYA. Wife of the Rishi Atri.

ANDHAKA. A demon, son of the Sage Kashyapa and Diti—Andhaka was said to have a thousand arms and heads and was slain by Shiva.

ANGA. The kingdom ruled over by King Lompada, probably Bengal. A part or limb. An army may be divided into angas and in this context has been translated as divisions.

ANGADA. The son of Bali, a monkey warrior.

ANGARAKA. A female demon.

ANILA. The God of the Wind.

ANJALI. A salutation made with joined palms.

ANJANA. A nymph with whom the God of the Wind became enamoured and who subsequently gave birth to Hanuman.

ANSHUMAN. Son of Asamanjas. See Balakanda for his story.

ANTAKA. A name of Yama, the God of Death.

ANTIGAS. A measure implying the utmost number.

ANUHLADA. The son of Hiranya-kashipu, a Daitya and the father of Prahlada whose story is told in the Vishnu Purana. Hiranyakasipu was slain by Vishnu in his incarnation of Nrsingha, half man, half lion.

APSARA. "Ap" meaning water and "sara" to emerge from; the name means a water-sprite or nymph. The Apsaras were the wives of the Gandharvas.

ARANYA. A forest.

ARBUDHA. A number approximating to a hundred million.

ARGHYA. A traditional offering of water, milk, kusha grass, rice, Durva grass, sandalwood, flowers, etc.

ARISHTANEMI. A name of Garuda's meaning "The Felly of whose wheel is unhurt".

ARTHA. Dharma, Artha and Kama—duty, prosperity and legitimate pleasure, which are said to be the three ends of life.

ARTHA-SHASTRA. The science of moral and political government. The Artha Shastras are ancient Hindu treatises summarizing the main duties of man in the field of politics and economics, where the subjects are treated from the individual and not the universal point of view.

ARUNA. Brother of Garuda.

ARUNDHATI. Wife of the Rishi Vasishtha, a model of conjugal excellence. Also the morning star.

ARYAMANA. Chief of the Pittris or Ancestors.

ASAVA. Wine made of sugar and honey or the blossom of Bossia Latifiloia or, according to some, grapes.

ASCETICS. Sages who practised austerities, of which the following are specially cited :—

Ardrapatavasa. Those practicing silent prayer.

Asmakuttas. Those who lived in stone huts on uncooked food.

Dantolukhalis. Those who took raw food such as grain crushing it between their teeth.

Gatmasayyas. Those who slept on the ground without making a bed.

Marichipas. Those who lived by absorbing the rays of the sun or moon.

Pancagni. Those practising asceticism between five fires, i.e.: four fires and the sun above.

Patraharas. Those who lived on the leaves of trees.

Sampraksalas. Those said to be born of the water in which Brahma's feet were cleansed.

Vaikhanasas. Born from the nails of the Creator, Brahma.

Valakhilyas. Born from the body of Brahma.

ASHADHA. The month that covers part of June and July.

ASHOKA. One of King Dasaratha's counsellors. For the tree of this name see separate Glossary.

ASHRAMA. Hermitage or forest retreat.

ASHWAYUJ. The month September—October.

ASHWINS or ASHWINI-KUMARAS. Celestial horsemen, precursors of the dawn, twin offspring of the sun and patrons of medicine.

ASURA. A Demon or Titan, enemy of the Gods.

ASWAMEDHA. Horse sacrifice of Vedic times, performed only by kings.

ATHARVA VEDA. The fourth Veda.

ATIBALA. See Bala and Atibala.

ATODYAS. A musical instrument.

ATRI. One of the Seven Immortal Sages.

ATYARTHA SADAKA. One of King Dasaratha's counsellors.

AUM or OM. The sacred syllable, said to have been the first sound in creation. Its import can be studied in the Mandukya Upanishad.

AURVA. A great Rishi, the grandson of Bhrigu. His name is derived from "uru" or thigh as he was said to have been produced from his mother's thigh. His austerities alarmed the Gods and his anger against the warrior class, who had slain his forbears, was unparalleled. Eventually it was mitigated by the intervention of the Pittris and he cast the fire of his wrath into the sea, where it became a being with a horse's head named Haya-shira.

AYODHYA. The capital of Koshala, ruled over by King Dasaratha, possibly Oudh.

AYOMUKHA. A mountain.

AYOMUKHI. A female Titan or Demon.

AYURVEDA. The "Veda of Life". A work on medicine attributed to the Sage Dhanwantari who rose from the ocean when it was churned by Gods and Titans.

AYUTA. A number not to be counted, a myriad or sometimes said to be a thousand plus a hundred.

GLOSSARY

B

BAHADUR. A title of honour, conferred by Mohammedan kings, similar to a knighthood.

BALA and ATIBALA. The Science of Sacred Formulas, given to Rama by the Sage Vishwamitra.

BALI or VALI. King of the Monkeys, slain by Rama. His brother was Sugriva.

BALHIKAS or VALHIKAS. Bactrians or people of the North and West of India.

BHAGA. A Deity mentioned in the Vedas, who was an Aditya presiding over love and marriage. The name means "Wealthy Master", "Gracious Lord", "Bestower of Wealth".

BHAGIRATHA. A descendant of King Sagara, who by his penances brought the sacred river Gunga down to earth. A name of the river Gunga or Ganges, so called after the Sage Bhagiratha.

BHARADWAJA. A Sage who entertained Rama, Sita and Lakshmana in the forest and subsequently created a great feast for Bharata. See Balakanda. Many Vedic hymns are attributed to him.

BHARATA. The younger brother of Rama and son of Queen Kaikeyi.

BHARATVARSHA. Ancient India.

BHASA. A vulture or bird of prey.

BHASKARA. Father of Sugriva. A name of the Sun.

BHERIS. A kettledrum.

BHOGAVATI. The voluptuous subterranean capital of the Serpent Race also called Putkari.

BHRIGU. A Vedic Sage, said to be the son of Manu, the progenitor of mankind.

BHRINGARAJA. A shrike or a bee.

BHUR, BHUVAH, SWAH. The Lower, Middle and Upper Worlds.

BHUTAS. Ghosts, imps or goblins, malignant spirits.

BHUTI. The mother of the nymph Manu.

BIBISHANA or VIBISHANA. Brother of Ravana but a devotee of Rama, who conferred the Kingdom of Lanka on him after Ravana's death.

BISHAKA or VISHAKA. A devotee who constantly contemplates the Deity. Also one of the Nakshatras q.v.

BRAHMA. The creative aspect of Divinity, Shri Vishnu being the maintaining aspect and Shiva the destructive aspect.

BRAHMACHARI. Religious student living in the house of a spiritual teacher, having taken certain vows.

BRAHMACHARINI. The female equivalent of Brahmachari.

BRAHMACHARYA. Religious studentship, implying the taking of certain vows.

BRAHMA-JNANA. Knowledge of Brahman, Truth or the highest Reality.

BRAHMA-LOKA. The abode or region of Brahma.
BRAHMAN. The Absolute or highest Reality. Attributeless Being.
BRAHMAPUTRA. Son of Brahma.
BRAHMARSHI. A constellation said by some to be Shravana q.v.
BRATASURA, VRATASURA or VRITRA. A Titan slain by Indra.
BRIHASPATI or VRIHASPATI. The spiritual Preceptor of the Gods, also said to be the Regent of the planet Jupiter which is called by the same name.
BUDHA. The planet Mercury.

C

CAITYA. Tombstone, column, or pile of stones.
CAKRACARA. Lit.: Going in a circle. A class of heavenly beings.
CASTES. The four: Priest, Warrior, Merchant and those who serve these three.
CELIKA. Musical instrument.
CHAITARATHA or CHITARATHA. King of the Gandharvas q.v.
CHAKRATUNDA. A fish resembling a wheel in appearance.
CHAKRAVAKA. Brahmany duck or ruddy goose.
CHAMARA. Chowrie, a fan made of Yaks' tails, insignia of royalty.
CHAMARA. A Yak, Bos Grunniens, highly prized for its bushy tail.
CHANDALA. An outcaste.
CHANDRA. The moon.
CHARANAS. The Panegyrists of the Gods.
CHITRA. The planet Spica. The month Chitra or Chaitra is part of February and March.
CHITTRAKUTA. A sacred mountain where Rama and Sita dwelt while in exile. It is still a holy retreat.

D

DAITYAS. Titans.
DAKSHA. Son of Shri Brahma. His daughter Uma became Shiva's consort.
DAKSHINA. Traditional offering made after a sacred ceremony.
DANAVAS. A race of giants, enemies of the Gods.
DANDAKA. A vast forest lying between the rivers Godaveri and Narmada, the scene of Rama and Sita's exile.
DANU. A name of the Demon Kabandha q.v.
DASHAGRIVA. "The Ten-Necked One." A title of Ravana.
DASHANANA. "Ten-Faced One." A name of Ravana.
DASARATHA. King of Koshala, father of Rama, Lakshmana, Bharata and Shatrughna.
DATYUHAKA. A small gallinule resembling a cuckoo.

DEVARISHI. See under Rishi.
DEVAS. The Gods or Shining Ones.
DEVI. A title given to Parvati q.v.
DHANADA. A name of Kuvera, the God of Wealth, "Giver of Wealth."
DHARA. Wife of the Sage Kashyapa.
DHARMA. Traditionally ordained course of conduct or duty. The Law of Righteousness. Dharma is personified in one of the Prajapatis, God of moral and religious duty. Also the four ends of life: Legitimate enjoyment, prosperity and duty, the fourth being the attainment of spiritual bliss.
DHARMABRIT. A Sage whom Rama encountered near the Lake of the Four Nymphs.
DHATAR OR DHATRI. Creator, Author or Founder, a name given to Vishnu or Brahma and others.
DHRISHTI. One of the chief counsellors of King Dasaratha.
DHUMA. The God of smoke.
DHUMAKETU. A meteor, comet or falling star. The personified descending node.
DHUNDUMARA. Slayer of the Demon Dhundu, a title of the King Kuvalayashwa.
DILIPA. Father of the Sage Bharadwaja.
DINDIMA. A musical instrument.
DITI. Daughter of Daksha, wife of Kashyapa, mother of the Daityas.
DIVISIONS OF TIME, the Three. Past, present and future.
DRONA. A measure approximating to 92 lbs.
DUKULA. Woven silk or very fine cloth made of the inner bark of the plant of the same name.
DUNDHUBI. A giant slain by Bali. Also a kettledrum.
DUSHANA. A General of Khara's army, slain by Rama.
DYUMATSENA. Prince of S'abra, father of Satyavanta.

E

EKASHALYA OR EKACALYA. An aquatic creature. The word means "having a tip or point". Possibly a shark, or swordfish.

G

GADHI. Father of the Sage Vishwamitra, the son of King Kushanaba, hence the patronymic Kaushika.
GANDHAMANDANA. A general of the monkey army, killed by Indrajita, also the name of a mountain, "The Mount of Intoxicating Fragrance".

GANDHARVAS. Celestial Musicians.

GANGES. The sacred river Gunga, also known under many other names such as Bhagirathi, Harasekhara, or the "Crest of Shiva," Khapaga, "Flowing from Heaven," Tripathaga, "Three-way Flowing," Mandakini, Gently Flowing, Jahnavi, after the Sage Jahnu, etc.

GARUDA. King of the Birds, the vehicle of Shri Vishnu and the destroyer of serpents, sometimes portrayed as an eagle or jay.

GAUTAMA. A great sage, the husband of Ahalya q.v.

GAYATRI. The most sacred prayer of the Rig-Veda. A Goddess, wife of Brahma, mother of the Four Vedas.

GODAVERI. A river close to the Dandaka Forest.

GODHA. A piece of leather or metal worn on the left arm to protect it from the bow-string.

GOHA. A soft leather, possibly cow or doeskin.

GOLANGULA. A black monkey that has a tail like a cow's.

GOLOBHA. A giant.

GOSHPADA. A measurement equal to a cow's hoof.

GRANDSIRE OF THE WORLD. A title of Brahma.

GRIDHIRAS. Birds of prey.

GRIHI. A person who, having finished his education, marries and becomes a householder. Also known as Grihasta.

GUHA. King of the Nishadas, a mountain tribe. A great devotee of Rama.

GUHYAKAS. Hidden Beings, attendants on Kuvera q.v.

GUNAS. "Guna" literally means a thread or strand. It is also used for a quality, attribute or property: for instance, the air has tangibility and sound for its "guna". According to the Sankhya Philosophy, nature consists of the equipoise of the three gunas Sattwa, Rajas and Tamas, or goodness, passion and darkness, which are the characteristics of all created things.

GURU. A traditional Teacher of the spiritual science. One who dispels ignorance.

H

HALA HALA. The poison churned from the ocean by Gods and Demons.

HAMSA. Swan, flamingo or heron.

HANUMAN OR HANUMAT. A monkey minister of Sugriva, the King of the Monkeys. Hanuman was the son of Pavana, the God of the Wind and Anjana. He became a devotee of Rama's and was an ideal disciple. He is also known as Maruti, Anjaneya, Yogachara, for his magic and healing powers, and Rajata-dyuti, "The Brilliant".

HARI. The name of the Lord Vishnu, meaning "captivating" or "pleasing".

HARIVAHANA. A name of Garuda meaning " Bearer of Vishnu ".
HASTA. A star, the thirteenth lunar asterism identified as Corvus.
HAWAN. A particular offering to the Gods ; an ancient fire-ceremony.
HAYAGRIVA. Lit. : " horse-necked ". According to one legend, Vishnu himself assumed this form to recover the Veda which had been carried off by two Daityas, Madhu and Kaitabha.
HEMA. A nymph ; also a kind of gold.
HIMAPANDARA. One of the Elephants of the Four Quarters, supporting the earth.
HIMAVAT. Lit. : " The Abode of Snows ". The King of Himalaya.
HIRANYA-KASIHPU. Lit. : " Golden Dress ". A Daitya who obtained the sovereignty of the Three Worlds from Shiva, for a million years, and persecuted his son Prahlada, a devotee of Vishnu.
HOMA. The Homa sacrifice is the act of making an oblation to the Gods by pouring butter into the fire, to the accompaniment of prayers and invocations. It is regarded as one of the five great sacrifices called " Deva-yajnas ".

I

IKSHNAKU. Son of Manu, founder of the Solar Race of Kings who reigned in Ayodhya.
ILVALA. A demon subdued by the Sage Agastya.
INDRA. The King of the Gods, who is known under many other names, such as : Mahendra, or Great Indra, Shatakratu, or " He of a hundred sacrifices ", Purandara, " Destroyer of Cities", Vajrapani, " Of the Thunderbolt hand ", " Lord of Sachi ", Maghavan, " Possessor of Wealth ".
INDRALOKA. The Abode of Indra or the Celestial Realm.
IRAVATI. Mother of the elephant Airavata.

J

JABALI. A Brahmin of King Dasaratha's court.
JAGARI. Coarse brown sugar made of palm sap.
JAHNAVI. A name of the sacred River Gunga.
JAHNU. The Sage who drank up the Gunga.
JAMBAVAN or JAMBAVAT. King of the Bears, an ally of Rama.
JAMBU. A river.
JAMBUDWIPA. One of the seven continents of which the world was said to be composed.
JANAKA. King of Mithila, father of Sita.
JANAKI. A name of Sita.

JANASTHANA. The colony of Titans in the Dandaka Forest.
JAPA. Silent repetition of a prayer or sacred formula.
JATARUPA. Gold in its original purity.
JATAYU. The King of the Vultures, who attempted to prevent Ravana from carrying Sita away.
JAYA. A Goddess, producer of weapons.
JAYANTA. King Dasaratha's minister.
JUTA. The matted locks of a devotee.

K

KABANDHA. An Asura or Demon, slain by Rama and Lakshmana.
KADAMVARI. Natural wines which require no preparation.
KADRU. A daughter of Daksha and wife of the Rishi Kashyapa; she was the mother of the many-headed serpents, including Shesha and Vasuki.
KAIKEYA. The Kingdom ruled over by King Kaikeya.
KAIKEYI. Favourite Queen of King Dasaratha and mother of Bharata.
KAILASHA. Sacred mountain, said to be the abode of Shiva.
KAKUTSTHA. A title used for the descendants of Kakutstha in the House of Ikshwaku, also for Puranjaya, a prince of the Solar race, whose story is told in the Vishnu Purana. From "KAKUD", an emblem of royalty and "STHA"—residing—meaning a prince, a grandson of Ikshwaku.
KALAGURU. Aloes or Agallochum, a species of sandal.
KALAHAMSA. A kind of duck or goose, Gallinula Porphyria.
KALAKA. Wife of the Rishi Kashyapa, mother of the Danavas.
KALINDI. Wife of King Asit.
KALMASHI. A titan, demon or goblin.
KAMA or KANDARPA. The Indian Cupid, or God of Love.
KAPILA. A great Sage who destroyed the sons of King Sagara.
KARANDA or KARANDAVA. A species of duck.
KARKA. The sign of Cancer.
KARMA. The law governing the behaviour of matter in all its gross and subtle forms, according to the divine purpose.
KARTTIKA. The month October—November. When the sun enters Libra.
KARTTIKEYA. The God of War, the son of Shiva, also called Skanda and Mahasena "Great Captain,"
KASHI. The sacred City of Benares.
KASHYAPA. The great Vedic Sage, grandson of Brahma and father of Vivaswat.
KATYAYANA. An ancient writer of great celebrity, author of the Dharmashastra.
KAUPIN. A loin-cloth.
KAUSHALYA. Chief Queen of King Dasaratha and mother of Rama.

KAUSHIKA. Title of Vishwamitra after his grandfather. Also a devotee who went to hell for having pointed out a road to robbers, by which they pursued and killed some persons who were fleeing from them.
KAUSHIKI. A river said to be Vishwamitra's sister.
KAUSTUBHA. Celebrated jewel churned from the ocean and worn by Shri Vishnu.
KAVYAHANAS. A class of Celestial Beings.
KESHNI. Chief Queen of King Sagara.
KHARA. The brother of Ravana. A demon, slain by Rama,
KHIVA or KHEEVA. Frumenty, hulled wheat boiled in milk and sweetened.
KINNERAS. Celestial Beings attendant on Kuvera q.v.
KIRTI. A celestial Nymph, personifying fame and glory.
KISHKINDHA. The country ruled over by Bali, possibly Mysore. This Kingdom was given to Sugriva by Rama.
KNOWER OF SELF. Knower of Truth or Reality. An illumined being.
KOSHALA. The kingdom ruled over by King Dasaratha.
KOTI. Ten million.
KOYASHTIKA. The lapwing.
KRAUNCHA. A species of heron, Ardea Jaculator.
KRAUNCHACHARYA. A Sage.
KRAUNCHARANYA. A forest. Lit.: "The Forest of the Heron".
KRAUNCHI. The daughter of Kashyapa and Tamra, mother of owls and birds of prey.
KRIKALA. A partridge.
KAITABHA and MADHU. Two Daityas who carried off the Vedas and were slain by Vishnu.
KRITTIKAS. The Pleiades, nurses of the God of War.
KSHIRODA. The Ocean of Milk.
KUBIJA. A hunchback servant of Queen Kaikeyi.
KUMBHAKARNA. Brother of Ravana, a monster killed by Rama.
KUNJARA. Maternal grandfather of Hanuman.
KURARA. An osprey.
KUSHA. One of the sons of Rama and Sita.
KUVERA. The God of Wealth.

L

LAGNA-KARKA. The sign of Cancer.
LAGNA-MEENA. The sign of Pisces.
LAGNAS. The twelve signs of the Zodiac are considered as rising above the horizon in the course of the day. The Lagna has the name of the sign; its duration is from the first rising of

the sign till the whole is above the horizon. Lagna literally means the point where the horizon and the path of the planet meet.

LAKSHMANA. Son of King Dasaratha and Queen Sumitra, favourite brother of Rama who accompanied him in his exile. Lakshmana was said to be the incarnation of the thousand-headed Shesha, the serpent who upholds the world.

LAKSHMI. The consort of Shri Vishnu, also known as " Shri ", signifying prosperity. Sita was said to be an incarnation of Lakshmi.

LAMBA. A mountain.

LANKA. The kingdom ruled over by Ravana, the King of the Titans, probably Ceylon.

LOHITANGA. The planet Mars.

LOKAPALAS. The Guardians of the Four Quarters.

LOMAPADA. A King whose story is told in Balakanda.

LOSHTHA. A vessel of coconut or metal used for begging or ceremonial purposes.

M

MADA. The temporal juices of an elephant in rut.

MADANA. God of Love, Kama or Kandarpa.

MADHA. A spiritous liquor, made of honey and molasses or the blossom of Bassia Latifolia.

MADHU. A Demon.

MADHUCCHANDA. Vishwamitra's son, cursed by his father for disobedience.

MADHUPARKA. A mixture of curds, butter, honey and the milk of the coconut, a traditional offering.

MADHUSUDANA. Name of Shri Vishnu, meaning the " Destroyer of the Demon Madhu ".

MAGADHA. A kingdom ; now South Bihar.

MAGDA-PHALGUNI. The season from the middle of January to the middle of March.

MAHADEVA. 'Great God,' a title of Shiva.

MAHAPADMA. One of the Elephants of the Four Quarters.

MAHARATHAS. Car Warriors.

MAHARATHRAS. Great Warriors.

MAHATMA. 'Great-souled One,' a title given to a Sage or Rishi.

MAHAVANA. ' Great Forest.'

MAHODARA. A son of Vishwamitra's. Also a general in Ravana's army.

MAHODAYA. An ascetic who was transformed into one of the lowest caste by Vishwamitra's curse.

MAINA. Mina or Mynah, a small percher about the size of a swallow which can be taught to repeat words.
MAINAKA or MINAKA. A golden mountain, north of Kailasha. Also a numph who tempted Vishwamitra.
MAIREYA or MIREYA. Liquor extracted from the blossom of the Lythrum Fructicosum tree, mixed with sugar.
MAITHILA or MITHILA. The kingdom ruled over by King Janaka.
MAITHILI. A name of Sita, as daughter of the King of Mithila.
MAITRA. Period of the early morning.
MAKARA. A kind of sea monster, sometimes confounded with a shark, crocodile or dolphin.
MALAYA. A mountain.
MANASAROVA. A lake on Mount Kailasha, lit.: " The Lake of the Mind ", said to be hollowed out of the mind of Brahma.
MANDAKINI. A river near Mt. Chittrakuta.
MANDARA. A mountain used in the churning of the ocean by Gods and Titans.
MANDARKANI. A Sage who created the Lake of Five Nymphs.
MANDAVI. Bharata's wife, daughter of King Kushadwaja.
MANDHATA or MANDHATRI. A king.
MANDODARI. The wife of Ravana.
MANKUKA. A musical instrument.
MANMATHA. A name of Kama, the God of Love.
MANTHARA. The hunchbacked maid of Kaikeyi.
MANTRA. Mantras or mantrams are sacred formulas.
MANU. The First Man who was given the Holy Truth by his father Vivaswat—see Bhagawadgita, Chapter IV, opening verses.
MARICHA. A demon who, disguised as a deer, lured Rama from his hermitage.
MARICHIPAS. A class of ascetics who derive their nourishment from particles of light.
MARKANDEYA. A Sage, remarkable for his austerities.
MARUTI. A name of Hanuman as son of Maruta, the God of Wind.
MARUTS. The Wind-Gods, or Gods of the Tempest.
MASHAS. A class of Sages or Hermits.
MATALI. Indra's charioteer.
MATANGA. A great Sage.
MATARISHWAN. An aerial being, mentioned in the Rig-Veda as bringing down fire to earth.
MAYA. The deluding power of the Lord, by which the universe has come into existence and appears to be real. A Giant who created a magical cave dwelling.
MAYAVI. A giant killed by Bali.
MEGHA. The Regent of the clouds.
MERU. A great and sacred mountain.
MERUSAVARNI. A great ascetic.
MLECCHAS. Foreigners, barbarians, eaters of flesh. A people said

to be born of the sacred cow Shabala for her protection. See Balakanda.

MRIDANGA. A kind of drum.

MRIGI. Daughter of Krodhavasha, mother of elephants.

MRITYU. The God of Death, another name for Yama.

MUHURTA. An instant, a moment, an hour, according to the context.

MUNI. A holy Sage, a pious and learned person, a title applied to Rishis and others.

MURAGA. A tambourine.

MUSHTIKAS. People cursed by Vishwamitra who assumed the lowest caste.

N

NABHAGA. The son of Yayati and father of Aja, who was Dasaratha's father.

NAGAS. The Serpent Race.

NAHUSHA. The father of King Yayati, Nahusha's curious story is found in the Mahabharata and Puranas.

NAIRRITAS. A race of Demons, offspring of Nairriti or Niritti.

NAKAPRISHTA. The highest heaven (from Naka—vault) in which there is no unhappiness.

NAKSHATRAS. The Hindus, beside the common division of the Zodiac into twelve signs, divided it into 27 Nakshatras, two to each sign. Each Nakshatra has its appropriate name :—

1. Aswini. 2. Bharani. 3. Krittika. 4. Rohini. 5. Mr'gashriras. 6. Ardea. 7. Purnavasu. 8. Pushya. 9. Alesha. 10. Magna. 11. Purva-phalguni. 12. Uttaraphalguni. 13. Hasta. 14. Chitra. 15. Svati. 16. Vishaka. 17. Anuradha. 18. Jyasatha. 19. Mula. 20. Purvashadha. 21. Uttarashraddha. 22. Abijit. 23. Shravana. 24. Shravishtha or Dhanishta. 25. Shatabhishaj. 26. Purva Bhadrapada. 27. Uttara-Bhadrapada. 28. Revati.

(The last is used if Abijit is omitted.)

NALA. A monkey chief, a general in Sugriva's army.

NALINI. A river.

NAMUCHI. A demon slain by Indra.

NANDANA. Indra's celestial garden.

NANDI. Sacred bull, the vehicle of Shiva, symbolising the Sattwaguna, q.v.

NANDIGRAMA. The city from which Bharata ruled in the absence of Rama.

NARADA. A divine Sage who appeared to Valmiki, see Balakanda.

NARAKA. Hell, a place of torture where the wicked are sent. Manu enumerates twenty hells.

NARAYANA. A name of Shri Vishnu, so called because the waters (nara) were his first place of motion.
NARMADA. A river.
NATYUHA. A bird. A small galliuile.
NIDHIS. The personified Treasures of the God of Wealth, Kuvera.
NIKUMBHILA. A grove on the outskirts of Lanka.
NILA. A monkey chief, general in Sugriva's army.
NIMI. A royal ancestor of King Janaka.
NISHADAS. A mountain tribe dwelling in the Vindhya Mountains, living on hunting.
NISHKA. A gold piece or nugget, sometimes worn as an ornament.

O

OM. See Aum.
OSHADI or OSHADI-PRASTHA. " The Place of Medicinal Herbs ", a city in the Himalayas mentioned in ' Kumara-Sambhava.'

P

PADMA. A measurement, a thousand billions.
PAHLAVA. Warriors born from the sacred cow Shabala, possibly Persians. See Balakanda.
PAKA. A demon slain by Indra.
PAMPA. A lake by which Rama and Lakshmana rested in their exile.
PANAVA. A tabor or cymbal.
PANCHAPSARAS. 'The Lake of Five Nymphs' created by the Sage Mandarkarni.
PANCHAVATI. A district near the source of the Godaveri River where Rama passed a period of his exile.
PANNAGAS. Celestial serpents, offspring of Kadru.
PARAMARISHIS. Great or Supreme Rishis, q.v.
PARAMATMAN. The Absolute, Brahman.
PARANTAPA. A title meaning " Oppressor of the Foe ".
PARASURAMA. 'Rama with the axe,' the sixth incarnation of Shri Vishnu, son of Yamadagni and Renuka.
PARIHARYAS. A bracelet.
PARIPLAVA. A spoon used in sacrifices.
PARIYATRA. One of the principal mountain ranges of India.
PARJANYA. A Vedic Deity or Rain God. Sometimes this title is used for Indra.
PARVAN. The period of the moon's change.
PARVATI. Shiva's consort, also known under many other names, such as Bahravi, Devi, Girija, Kanya, Sati, Padma-Lanchana,

Shiva-Duti, Uma and countless others.

PASHUPATI. Lord of Creatures, a title of Shiva.

PATAGAS. Winged creatures.

PATAHA. A kind of drum.

PATALA. The infernal regions.

PAULASTYA. See Poulastya.

PAULOMA. Wife of Kashyapa, mother of the Danavas.

PAVAKA. A name of Agni, the God of Fire.

PAVANA. The God of the Wind, father of Hanuman.

PAYASA. A preparation of rice and milk.

PHALGUNI. A Nakshatra, q.v.

PINAKA. Sacred bow.

PINGAS. " Tawny Ones ", a name given to the monkey race.

PISACHAS. Ghosts or evil spirits.

PITTRIS. Manes or Ancestors.

PLAVAGAS or PLAVAMGAMAS. Those who move by leaps and bounds; a title given to the Monkey Race.

POULASTYA. One of the Seven Immortal Sages, Grandfather of Ravana.

PRABHA. The consort of the Moon, also the personification of the light of the Sun.

PRABHAKARA. The Sun.

PRABHAVA. A minister of Sugriva's.

PRADAKSHINA. Circumambulation in a reverent manner from left to right.

PRAHASTA. Father of Jambavan, a general in Sugriva's army.

PRALAMBA. A mountain.

PRALAYA. Period of the dissolntion of the world.

PRAMATHIN. A monkey renowned for his courage.

PRANA. The vital air or breath.

PRASRAVANA. A mountain.

PRATYAKSTHALI. A sacred grove, a site facing the West.

PRAUSTHAPADA. August—September.

PRAYAGA. The confluence of the Ganges and the Yamuna, a sacred spot.

PRISHATA. Spotted deer, cow or piebald horse.

PRIYAKA. A spotted deer.

PULOMAN. A Danava, father of Sachi, consort of Indra.

PUNARVASU. The seventh and most auspicious Nakshatra, q.v.

PURANAS. Legends and tales of ancient times in epic form. There are eighteen chief Puranas.

PURANDARA. Destroyer of Cities, a title of Indra.

PUROHITA. A family priest.

PURURAVAS. A king who wedded the nymph Urvashi.

PURUSHA. The supreme Spirit, the highest Reality.

PUSHAN. The Sun.

PUSHPAKA. A celestial aerial chariot which was so vast that it contained palaces and their precincts.

PUSHPITAKA. A mountain.
PUSHYA. A constellation of three stars considered auspicious. Also the sixth lunar mansion.
PUTTRA. A son who is said to deliver his father from hell.
PUTTRESTI. A ceremony performed for the extending of the race by the birth of sons.

R

RAGHAVA. A title of those belonging to the House of Raghu to which King Dasaratha and his forbears belonged.
RAHU. A mythical demon said to cause the eclipse of the sun and the moon.
RAJAHAMSA. Royal Swan or Flamingo.
RAJAS. See Guna.
RAJASUYA Sacrifice. A great sacrifice performed in ancient times at the installation of a monarch.
RAKSHASAS. Demons or Titans.
RAKSHASI. Female Titan or Demon.
RAMA or RAMACHANDRA. The Incarnation of Shri Vishnu and the eldest son of King Dasaratha. It is round this great figure that the 'Ramayana' was created.
RAMA-KATHA. The recitation of 'Ramayana' which has been a tradition in India for thousands of years.
RAMBHA. A nymph symbolising the perfection of beauty from Indra's realm; often sent to distract Sages from their pious practices.
RATHA. A chariot.
RATI. The Consort of the God of Love.
RATNA. A necklace.
RAVANA. A Titan, the King of Lanka who carried off Sita and was slain by Rama. The name means the 'Vociferous' 'One who roars.'
RAVI. The Sun.
RENUKA. The wife of Yamadagni and mother of Parasurama.
RIKSHABHA. A mountain.
RIKSHABILA. The magical cave where the monkeys stayed for a time, when searching for Sita.
RIKSHARAJAS. The father of Bali and Sugriva, a King of the Monkeys.
RIKSHAS. The Bears.
RISHI. A great Sage or illumined being of which there are four classes :—
Rajarishi—A royal Rishi,

Maharishi—A great Rishi,
Brahmarishi—A sacred Rishi,
Devarishi—A divine Rishi.

RISHYAMUKA. A mountain on which Sugriva took refuge.

RISHYASHRINGA. The " Deer-horned " Son of the Sage Vibhandaka who married the daughter of King Lomapada, Shanta, and later performed the Puttresti ceremony (q.v.) for King Dasaratha

RITVIJS. Priest officiating at the installation ceremony.

ROHI. A fish, Cyprinus Rohita Ham.

ROHINI. The star Aldebaran.

ROHITA. A kind of deer.

ROHITAS. Name of the horses of the sun, also a Deity celebrated in the Atharva Veda, probably a form of Fire or the Sun.

RUDRA. A name of Shiva.

RUDRAS. The sons of Kashyapa and Aditi.

RUMA. Sugriva's Consort.

RUMANA. Sugriva's general, a monkey chief.

RURU. A deer.

S

SACHI. Indra's Consort.

SADHYAS. The personified rites and prayers of the Vedas who dwell between heaven and earth, a class of Deities.

SAGARA. A King whose history is told in Balakanda.

SAMPATI. A vulture, brother of Jatayu.

SAMUDRA. Lord of Rivers, the Ocean.

SANATKUMARA. One of the mind-born sons of Brahma.

SANTANA. One of the five trees in Indra's Paradise.

SAPINDI. The Sapindi Ceremony is for the establishing of a connection with kindred through funeral offerings.

SAPTAJANAS. The 'Hermitage of the Seven Sages.'

SARABHA or SHARABHA. Legendary animal with eight legs.

SARANGA. A bird.

SARASWATI. The Goddess of speech and learning, also a river named after her.

SARAYU. Sacred river, the Sarju.

SARVABHAUMA. The elephant that carries Kuvera q.v.

SATARHADA. Mother of the Demon Viradha.

SATYAVATI. The sister of the Sage Vishwamitra; she became the Kaushika river.

SATYA-YUGA. The Golden Age or Yuga. There are four Yugas which make up a Kalpa or world cycle :—
The Satya Yuga or Golden Age.
The Treta Yuga or Silver Age.
The Dwapara Yuga or Copper Age.

The Kali Yuga or Black Age, also called the Iron Age.

SAUMANASA. One of the elephants of the four quarters.

SAUMITRI. Sumitra's son, Lakshmana.

SAURA. A divine potion. Lit. : " Relating to the Sun ".

SAUVARCALA. Sochal salt or alkali.

SHABARI. A female ascetic, devotee of Rama.

SHAKRA. A name of Indra's.

SHALMALI. A fabulous thorny rod of the cotton tree used for torturing the wicked in hell.

SHALYAKA. A Porcupine. See also Weapons.

SHAMBARA. The Demon of Drought, represented in the Rig Veda as the enemy of Indra.

SHANKHAS. A measurement, a hundred billions or a hundred thousand crores. (A crore is ten millions).

SHANKU. Ten billions.

SHANTA. The daughter of King Lomapada who was wedded to the Sage Rishyashringa.

SHARABANDA. The mother of the Demon Viradha.

SHARABHANGA. A Sage visited by Rama and Sita in the Dandaka Forest.

SHASANKA. The Consort of Rohini or the moon.

SHASI. The moon. Lit. : " Hare-marked ".

SHASTRAS. Teachings of divine and recognised authority.

SHATANANDA. Son of the Sage Gautama and spiritual director to the King Janaka.

SHATAPATRA. " Having a hundred petals ". (See Lotus, under 'Flowers and Trees Glossary.') 'Having a hundred feathers,' said of a peacock or crane. 'Having a hundred wings' or conveyances, said of Brihaspati, q.v.

SHATRUGHNA. King Dasaratha's fourth son, whose mother was Sumitra.

SHISHUMARA. Lit. : 'Child-killer', a word used for crocodile, porpoise or dolphin.

SHIVA. The Lord as Destroyer of Ignorance, also Lord of Bliss.

SHIVYA or SHIVI. A King of the Raghu Dynasty who rescued the God Agni when he had transformed himself into a pigeon and was pursued by Indra, in the form of a hawk.

SHONA. A sacred river.

SHRAVANA. The month of July—August. Also a Nakshatra, q.v.

SHRI. A title of courtesy, also the Consort of Vishnu, Lakshmi, who is the Goddess of Prosperity.

SHRUTA-KIRTI. The Consort of Shatrughna.

SHRUTI or SRUTI. Holy teachings lit. : " What is heard ".

SHUDRA. The lowest of the four castes.

SHUKRA. The planet Venus. Said to be the son of Brighu.

SHUNAKA. Son of the Sage Richika.

SHUNASHEPA. Son of the Sage Richika, offered as a sacrifice and saved by the Sage Vishwamitra.

SHURPANAKHA. Sister of Ravana, a female Titan mutilated by Rama and Lakshmana.

SHVADAMSHTRAS. Earrings.

SHVASANA. A name of the Wind-god. Also of the Demon of Drought slain by Indra.

SHYENAS. Falcons, hawks, eagles, etc., the offspring of Shyeni.

SHYENI. Daughter of Kashyapa and Tamra, mother of birds of prey.

SHVETA. A mountain.

SIDDHARTA. One of King Dasaratha's counsellors.

SIDDHAS. Semi-divine beings, who dwell between the earth and the sun.

SIDHU. A kind of rum distilled from molasses.

SIMHIKA, SINHIKA or SINGHIKA. A female demon who caught hold of Hanuman's shadow.

SINDHU. The river Indus. Also a country east of Koshala.

SITA. Daughter of King Janaka, King of Mithila, and Rama's consort.

SIX KINDS OF TASTE. Sweet, bitter, acid, salt, pungent, acrid and harsh.

SMRITI. Tradition. Lit.: " What is remembered ".

SOMA. The fermented juice of ' Asclepias-acida ', used as a beverage or libation in sacred ceremonies.

SOMADATTA. Daughter of Urmila and mother of Brahmadatta.

SOMAGIRI. A mountain.

SOURA
SOURASHTRA. } Countries east of Koshala.

SRIMARAS. Marine monsters.

STHULASHIRA. A Sage harassed by the Demon Kabandha.

SUBAHU. A demon who disturbed the sacrifices of the Sage Vishwamitra.

SUBHADRA. A sacred tree.

SUCHENA. Son of Varuna, the Lord of the Waters.

SUDAMANA. One of King Janaka's ministers.

SUGRIVA. King of the Monkeys and Rama's ally.

SUMANTRA. The Prime Minister of King Dasaratha.

SUMATI. Younger wife of King Sagara, who gave birth to sixty-thousand sons.

SUMERU. A sacred mountain.

SUMITRA. Mother of Lakshmana and Shatrughna.

SUNABHA. Lit.: " Having a beautiful navel ", a title of the mountain Mainaka.

SUNDA. Father of Maricha.

SUPARNA. A name of Garuda, meaning " Chief of Birds ".

SUPARSHWA. Son of the Vulture Sampati.

SUPRABHA. A Goddess who created celestial weapons, daughter of Daksha.

SURABHA. Daughter of Krodhavasha, consort of Kashyapa.

SURAS. A name of the Gods. In the Vedas it applied to offspring of the Sun.
SURASHTRAS. One of King Dasaratha's ministers.
SURYA. The Sun, one of the three chief deities of the Vedas.
SUSHENA. The father of Tara, Bali's consort.
SUTIKSHNA. A Sage who dwelt in the Dandaka Forest and entertained Rama, Lakshmana and Sita during their wanderings.
SUTA. Khara's charioteer.
SUTRAS. Poetical rhythms or stanzas.
SUVARHALA. The consort of the Sun.
SUYAJNA. Spiritual Director of King Dasaratha.
SVADANGSTRAS. Ornaments worn in the ears.
SVAHA. Word of power or invocation.
SVARBHANU. The Demon Rahu, q.v.
SVATI. The star Arcturus.
SVAVIDH. A Porcupine or Hedgehog.
SWYAMBHU. The Self-Existence, a name of the Creator, Shri Brahma.
SWYAMPRABHA. The Daughter of the Sage Merusavarni.
SWYAMVARA. The ceremony of choosing a consort.
SYANDARA. A river.

T

TALA. A leather strap used by archers. A clapper used in music.
TAMASA. A river.
TAMRA. One of the wives of the Sage Kashyapa.
TAPAS. Penance or austerity.
TAPOVANA. A forest.
TARA. The consort of Bali.
TARAKA. A female demon.
TARKSHYA. In ancient times considered as the personification of the sun in the form of a bird. Later it became a name for Garuda.
TARKSHYAS. Father of the Monkeys.
TEJAS. Lustre, energy or radiance, often used for spiritual power.
THIRTY THE, TRI-DASA. This title applies to the Gods. In round numbers, thirty-three—Twelve Adityas, eight Vasus, eleven Rudras and two Ashwins.
THREE WORLDS THE. Bhur, Bhuvah, Swah, the Lower, Middle and Upper Worlds, also called Tri-Loka and Tri-Bhuvana. Heaven, Earth and Hell.
TILAKA. A mark of auspiciousness placed on the forehead.
TIMINGILA. Lit.: "Swallowing even a Timis", a name of a fabulous fish.
TIMIS. A whale.

TISHYA. An asterism shaped like an arrow, containing three stars, also called Pushya and Sidhya.

TRIJATA. A Brahmin whose story is told in Balakanda. Also a female titan who spoke in defence of Sita.

TRIKUTA. " Three-Peaked ", the mountain on which Lanka was built.

TRIPATHAGA. " Three-way flowing ", the Traverser of the Three Worlds, a name of the Ganges.

TRIPURA. A demon slain by Shiva. A city burnt by the Gods.

TRISHANKU. A King of the Solar Race, whose story is told in Balakanda.

TRISHIRAS. A demon slain by Rama.

TRIVIKRAMA. The name of Shri Vishnu, when taking the three strides covering the earth.

TRIVISTAPA. The world of Indra.

TRYAMBAKA. " Three-eyed " a name of Shiva.

TWICE-BORN. Only a brahmin can strictly be termed " twice-born ", but the term came to be extended to the warrior and agricultural classes.

TUMBURU. A Gandharva cursed by the God Kuvera and born as the Demon Viradha.

U

UCCHAIHSHRAVAS. The white horse of Indra's, produced from the churning of the ocean. It is said to be fed on ambrosia and be the King of Horses.

UDAYA. A golden mountain.

UMA. A name of Parvati, daughter of Himavat and consort of Shiva.

UPA-NAYA. The ceremony of investiture of the sacred thread, by which act spiritual birth is conferred on a youth and he is considered a member of the Brahmin or Twice-born class. The age at which this ceremony takes place is between eight and sixteen years.

UPANISHAD. Esoteric doctrine. The third division of the Vedas, forming part of the revealed World.

UPENDRA. Name of Shri Vishnu or Krishna.

URAGAS. Great Serpents.

URMILA. Consort of Lakshmana.

URVASHI. A nymph mentioned in the Rig-Veda. Many legends are told about her in the classics.

USHANAS. Another name of Shukra or the planet Venus.

USHIRAS. A hair like grass growing on the golden trees in hell. See also Flowers and Trees Glossary.

UTTARA-KURUS. Northern Kurus, a people with whom the Sages took refuge.

UTTARA-PHALGUNI. A constellation, under which Sita was said to have been born.

V

VACHASPATI. Mother of the Gods, Goddess of speech and learning.
VADABA or VADAVA. Lit.: 'Mare's Fire', the subterranean fire or fire of the lower regions, fabled to emerge from a cavity called the 'Mare's mouth' under the sea at the south pole.
VAGARINASAKA. A bird, dark throated and white winged. Also a species of food.
VAIDEHA or VIDEHA. The kingdom ruled over by Janaka.
VAIDEHI. A name of Sita as daughter of the King of Videha.
VAIKHANASAS. A class of Rishi or Hermit.
VAIROCHANA. A name of Bali.
VAISHNAVA. Sacrifice in honour of Shri Vishnu.
VAISHRAVANA. A name of Kuvera, Ravana's brother.
VAISHVANARA. A name of the God Agni.
VAISHYAS. The merchant or agricultural class.
VAITARANI. The River of Hell.
VAIVASWAT. A name of the God Yama.
VAJAPEYA. A sacrifice at which an acetous mixture of meal and water is offered to the Gods.
VAJRADHARA. "Wielder of the Thunderbolt", a name for Indra.
VALAKHILYAS. Divine Beings, the size of a thumb, sixty thousand of whom sprang from the body of Brahma and surround the chariot of the sun.
VALI. See Bali.
VALLAKI. A small crane, also an Indian lute.
VALMIKI. Poet, Sage, author of Ramayana.
VAMANA. The Holy Dwarf, fifth divine Incarnation of Shri Vishnu.
VAMADEVA. A great Rishi, present at Rama's installation.
VANA. Forest.
VANAPRASTHA. A festival similar to a Harvest Festival.
VANARAS. 'Dweller in the Forest,' a title given to the Monkey Race, also called 'Deer of the Trees'.
VANARIS. Female Monkeys.
VANCULAKA. A mythical bird.
VARUNA. The Indian Neptune, Lord of the Waters.
VARUNI. Daughter of Varuna, the personification of Wine.
VASAVA. A name for Indra.
VASISHTHA. The spiritual preceptor of King Dasaratha.
VASUDEVA. A name of the Lord.
VASUKI. The Serpent King.
VASUS. Sons of Kashyapa and Aditi. The eight Vasus were originally personifications of natural phenomena, Apa, Dhruva, Soma, Dhara, Anila, Anala, Pratyusha and Prabhasa.
VASVOKASARA. Another name for Amaravati, Indra's capital.

VATA. A name of Vayu, q.v.

VATAPI. A demon consumed by the Sage Agastya.

VAYU. The God of the Wind.

VEDA. The Holy Scriptures of the Hindu religion. Fountain of Divine Knowledge.

VEDANGAS. A sacred science considered subordinate to and in some sense a part of the Vedas—six subjects come under the denomination :—

1. Siksha—pronunciation. 2. Kalpa—religious rites. 3. Vyakarana—Grammar. 4. Chandas—Prosody. 5. Jyotish —Astronomy. 5. Nirukti—Explanation of difficult words.

VEDI. An altar of Kusha grass. Place of sacrifice.

VIBHANDAKA. Son of the Sage Kashyapa and father of Rishyashringa.

VIBISHANA. See Bibishana.

VIBHUDHAS. Celestial Beings.

VIDARBHA. A country, probably Birar, whose capital was Kundinapura.

VIDEHA. See Vaideha.

VIDHATAR. " Arranger ", " Disposer ", " Creator ". Name of Brahma.

VIDHYADHARAS. Lit. : " Magical knowledge holder ". Particular good or evil spirits attendant on the Gods.

VINA. An Indian lute.

VINATA. The mother of Garuda.

VINDHA. The auspicious hour for finding what has been lost.

VINDHYA. A mountain ordered by Agastya not to increase in height.

VIPANCI. An Indian lute.

VIRADHA. A demon, son of Java and Shatarade who was slain by Rama and had formerly been the Gandharva Tumburu.

VIROCHANA. A giant, father of Bali.

VIRUPAKSHA. Elephant of one of the Four Quarters.

VISHAKAS. One of the lunar asterisms, also a month of the flowering season.

VISHNU. The Lord in His aspect of Maintainer of the Universe.

VISHRAVAS. Son of Poulastya and father of Ravana and Kuvera.

VISHWADEVAS. All the Gods, said to be " Preserver of Men and Bestowers of Rewards ".

VISHWAKARMA. Architect of the Gods.

VISHWAMITRA. A great Sage whose story is told in Balakanda.

VISHWARUPA. A title of Vishnu meaning " wearing all forms " " Omnipresent." Also the son of Vishwakarma slain by Indra.

VISHWATAM. The God of the Wind.

VITAPAVATI. The celestial city of Kuvera.

VIVASWAT. 'The Brilliant One', a title given to the Sun.

VRINDA. A large number, a multitude.

VRITRASURA or VRITRA. A demon slain by Indra.

GLOSSARY

Y

YADU. The son of Yayati and Devayani. Yayati was the founder of the Yadavas in which line Krishna was born.

YAJNA. A sacrifice or penance.

YAJURVEDA. The part of the Veda that treats of ceremonies and rites.

YAKSHAS. Supernatural Beings attendant on the God Kuvera.

YAMA. The God of Death.

YAMUNA. A sacred river.

YATUDHANAS. Evil spirits that assume various forms.

YAVANAS. A people said to have been born of the sacred cow Shabala.

YAYATI. The son of Nahusha, a forbear of King Dasaratha. His story appears in the Mahabharata and Vishnu Purana.

YOGA. A School of Philosophy of which the most important is Adwaita, the non-dualist system elaborated by Shri Shankaracharya.

YOJANA. A measurement. Approximately four or five miles.

YUGA. A world age or period. The Yugas are four in number and their duration several thousands of years. Between each of the periods there is a time of Sandhya or Twilight when creation is withdrawn and lies latent or potential in the Supreme Spirit or Brahman. The Yugas are called Krita, Treta, Dwapara and Kali.

FLOWERS AND TREES

(Wherever possible an English equivalent has been given or some description of the plant or tree ; some however could not be traced)

A

AGNIMUKHA. Semicarpus Anancardium Zeylanica, the Plumbago or Plumbago Zeylanica. A white flowered shrub, that blooms in June or July; its flowers are set in spikes. The plant is medicinal.

AGNIMUKHYA. The Marking Nut plant.

AMLAKA. Phyllanthus Emblica. A many branched shrub resembling Hemlock.

AMRA. Mango Mangifera Indica. A short-trunked tree covered with evergreen foliage, which flowers from January to March, the blossom being partly white and partly greenish yellow with an orange stripe on each petal.

ANKOLA or ANKOTA, ANGOLATA, ANKOTHA. Alangium Hexapetalum. A poison, Ankola-sara, is prepared from this plant.

ARAVINDA. Nymphoea Nelumbo, a water-lily.

ARISTA. Sapindus Saponeria, the Soap plant.

ARJUNA or ARJUNAKA. Terminalia Arjuna, a species of Nimba tree. A tall evergreen tree usually found on the banks of streams. The leaves cluster at the end of the branches and the flowers are tiny. The Arjuna-Jarul, is the Queens flower or Crepe flower.

ASANA. Terminalia Tormentosa or, the plant Marsilla Quadrifolia. The first is a common forest tree yielding excellent timber similar to the Arjuna tree and rarely seen outside forest areas.

ASHOKA. Saraca Indica. A small evergreen tree which produces a profusion of orange and scarlet clusters in January and February with deep green shining foliage. Buddha was said to have been born under an Ashoka tree and Sita was kept by Ravana in an Ashoka Grove. Both Buddhists and Hindus regard it as sacred. It is medicinal.

ASHWA-KARNA. Vatica Robusta.

ASHWA-LAGNA. The Saul Tree.

ASHWATTHA. The Fig Tree, of which there are many varieties :—
Ficus Bengalensis—The Banian Tree.
Ficus Religiosa—The Pipal or Peepal or Bo Tree.
Ficus Glomerata—Rumbal or Umbar.
Ficus Elastica—The Indian Rubber Tree.

GLOSSARY

ATIMUKHA. Premna Spinoza. The wood by which attrition is produced.

ATIMUKTAS. Gaertnera Racemosa.

B

BADRI or VADRI. Zixyphus Jujuba. The Jujube Plant.

BAKULA or VAKULA. Mimisops Elengi.

BALALAKA. Flacourtia Cataphracta. A shrub with hairy leaves and edible fruit; the fine grained wood is used for turnery and combs. Flowers in March or April.

BANJULA or VANJULA. Hibiscus Mutabilis.

BANDHUJIVA. Pentapetes Phoenicea. A plant with a red flower which opens at midday and withers away next morning at sunrise.

BHANDIRA. Mimosa Seressa, a lofty fig tree.

BHANDUKA. Calosanthes Indica.

BHAVA. Indian Laburnum. Monkeys are particularly partial to the sweet pulp in which the seeds lie.

BHAVYA. Dillenia Indica alias Dillenia elliptica speciosa. A tree that grows to forty feet; it is an evergreen; the flowers are large, white with yellow antlers and appear at the end of the branches. This tree is found in dense forests in the north and is much cultivated round temples. The bark and leaves are medicinal and the juice from the acid fruit mixed with sugar forms a cooling drink. There is another small fruit tree allied to the 'Magnolia Speciosa' of this name.

BHAYA. Trapa Bispinosa.

BIJAPURA. Citrus Medica. Citron Tree.

BILWA. Aegle Marmelos, commonly called Bel. Wood apple which bears a delicious fruit that unripe is used for medicinal purposes; its leaves are used in the ceremonies of the worship of Shiva.

BIMBA or VIMBA. Momordica Monadelpha. A plant bearing a bright red gourd.

C

CHAMIKARA. Thorn apple.

CHAMPAKA. A species of Magnolia.

CHANDAKA. Clove.

CHANDANA. Sirium Folium. Red or False Sandalwood. It bears straw-coloured flowers changing to deep purple.

CHANDATA. Nerium Odorum. Sweet-scented Oleander Rosebay.

CUTA. Mango.

D

DADIMA. Common Pomegranate. Bears double flowers.

DADINA. Punica Granatum. Pomegranate. A shrub with large red flowers and hard globose fruit.

DEVADARU, A variety of pine.

DEVA PARNA. The Divine Leaf. A medicinal plant.

DHANVANA. Grewia Asiatica. Also, under different spellings, various other plants.

DHANWARIA. Echites Antidy Senterio. A Twining Plant.

DHARA. Woodfordia Florebunda. A small spreading shrub from which red dye is obtained from the bright red flowers. Also a species of Acacia.

DHATRI. Sterospermum Aciderifolium.

DHATURA. Datura Stramonium L. (Solanaceae) Thorn apple. A poisonous drug is made from this tree.

DHUVA. One of the Acacia family.

DURVA GRASS. Panicum Dactylon. Bent Grass.

E

F

G

GAJAPUSHPI. Elephant Flower. A sort of Arum.

GOSHIRSHAKA. A Sandal-tree.

GULAR. A resinous tree, fragments of which are put into the water in a loshta for ceremonial purposes.

H

HARISHYAMA. See Shyama.

HINTALA. Phoenix Sylvestus. The Marshy Date Tree.

I

J

JAMBU. Eugenia Jambolana. The Rose Apple or Java Plum.

JAMNU. Prunus Padus L. Bird Cherry.

GLOSSARY

K

KADALA. Musa Sapientum. A plantain. It has a soft perishable stem and is poetically as a symbol of the frailty of human life.

KADAMBA. Nauclea Cadumba, a plant.

KAHLARA. A white water lily.

KAKUBHA. Terminalia Arjuna. A tall evergreen tree with a smooth grey bark often tinged with green or red; usually found on the banks of streams. The creamy honey-scented flowers appear from March to June.

KAMANARI. A species of Mimosa.

KAMRANGA. Averrhoa Carambola.

KANYA. The name given to several plants, one of which is a tuberose plant growing in Kashmir. Also the Aloe Perfoliata.

KAPIMUKA. The Coffee plant.

KAPITHA. The Jack Fruit.

KARAVIRA. Another fragrant Oleander, common in many parts of India in the rocky stream beds and the lower Himalayas, fringing roads and rivers. The foliage is evergreen throughout the year but at its height during the rains, the colours are deep rose, pink and white, single and double. The sap is poisonous.

KARNIKARA. Pterospternum Acerfolium also called Cassia Fistula commonly called Kaniyar.

KARPURA. Ficus Glomerata or Wild Fig. In April the new leaves of shining dark red, lend it a beautiful appearance.

KASANARI. Gmelina Arborea. The Liquorice plant.

KASHAS. Reeds or Rushes.

KASHASTHALI. Bignonia Suaveolens. The Trumpet Flower.

KEDUMBRA. A Tree with fragrant orange-coloured flowers.

KETAKA. Pandanus Odoratissimus.

KHADIRA. Acacia Catechu. The Areca or Betel-nut Palm, which grows in the hot damp coastal regions of southern India and Ceylon. Betel nut is the fruit universally chewed by Asian peoples.

KHARJURA. Phoenix Sylvestris. Wild Date Palm or Toddy Palm. The leaves are greyish green; the scented flowers appear in March. The fruit is used for preserves and palm wine.

KICHAKAS. Arundo Karka. A reed. The name is also given to a hollow bamboo or rattling cane and a tree.

KIMSHUKA or KUMSHUKA. Butea Frondosa. Having beautiful orange flowers and a quantity of milky sticky juice. This tree is called the "Flame of the Forest" or the "Parrot Tree". From January to March it is a mass of orange and vermilion; the flowers are unscented.

KOVIDARA. Banhinia Variegata, also the "Tree of Paradise." One of the loveliest of Indian trees with a dark brown smoothish bark. The leaves fall in the cold season and the large sweetly scented flowers open on the bare branches. Their colour varies from magenta, mauve, pink with crimson markings or white with a şplash of yellow.

KRITAMALA. Cassia Fistula. Indian Laburnum. Also the common Bottle Flower.

KUAYRAL. Mountain Ebony.

KUJAJA. Wrightia Awtidy Senterica. A medicinal plant.

KUMUDA. A white water lily.

KUNDA. Jasmine Multiflorum.

KURAKA. Boswellia Thorifera. Olivanum Tree.

KURANDA. A plant commonly called Sakarunda.

KURUBAKA. Dronapushpi. The Drona flower. Drona meaning a vessel, cup or pot, it probably produces a gourd.

KUSHA GRASS. Demostachya Bipennata. Sacred Grass used for religious ceremonies. This grass has long stalks and pointed leaves like rushes.

KUVALA. A water lily.

L

LAKUCA. or Lakuka. Artocarpus Lacucha. The same genus as the Jack Fruit, cultivated in the plains of Northern India.

LOHDRA. Simplocos Racemosa. The bark of this tree is used as a dye.

M

MADHAVA. A Mango.

MADHAVI. Bassia Latifolia. A species of leguminous plant. Also Basil and a kind of Panic grass.

MADHUKA. Bassia Latifolia. Illipi Butter Tree. A large deciduous tree with thick grey bark found in dry rocky hill regions. Valuable for its delicious and nutritive flowers which bloom at night and fall to the ground at dawn. They taste something like figs and are much sought after by bears, birds and deer, so that the natives have to guard the trees in order to collect flowers for themselves.

MADHURA. Perennial Jasmine.

MADURA. A tree reminiscent of Cassia which has long sprays of pale pink flowers.

MALLIKA. Evening Jasmine.

MUCHUKUNDA. Pterospernum Suberifolium. A white variety of Thorn Apple.

MUCHULINDA. Possibly connected with the Muchi wood or Coral Tree.

N

NAGA. Mesua Ferrea. A small tree.
NAGAVRIKSHA. A mountain shrub.
NAKTAMALA or NAKTAMALLAKA. Caleduba Arborea or Dalbergia Arborea or Pongamia Glabra.
NALINA. Nelumbium Speciosum. A water lily.
NARCAL GRASS. Phragmites Karka Trin. A species of Reed.
NARIKELA. Coconut Palm.
NICHULA. Barringtonia Acutangola commonly called Hijjal.
NILASHOKA. An Ashoka with blue flowers.
NILOTPALA. The Blue Lotus.
NIMBA. Azadirachta Indica. A tree with bitter fruit, the leaves of which are chewed at funerals.
NIPA, NIPAKA. A species of Kadamba Tree.
NIVARA or NAIVARA. Wild Rice.
NYAGRODHA. Ficus Indica. Indian Fig Tree.

O

P

PADMA. A pink lotus.
PADMAKA. Costus Speciosus or Arabicus, a kind of Fir.
PANASA. Arto Carpus Intergrifolia. Jack-fruit Tree, bearing the largest edible fruit in the world, weighing up to 100 lbs., oblong or round and irregular. This fruit is in great demand but less favoured than the mango or plantain. This tree grows in the forests in the Western Ghats.
PARABHADRAKA. Erythrininina Fulgens. Coral Tree, which bears angular spikes of rich red blooms along its bare branches from January to March.
PATALA. Tropical evergreen climbing plant.
PATALI or PATALIKA. Bynaria Suaroleus, a tree with sweet scented blossom (possibly the red Lodhra).
PINJARA. Mesua Roxburghii.
PIPPALA. Sacred Fig Tree.
PIYALA or PRIYALA or PRYALA. Commonly called Piyal. Found in Central India. Broad-leafed Mohwah. Common oil plant. Also a vine-like plant.
PLAKSHA. Ficus Infectoria. Wavy-leafed Fig Tree.
PRIYAKANYA. Terminalia Tormentosa.
PRYANKARA. Various plants.
PUNNAGA. Rottleria Tinctoria. The flowers of this tree produce a yellow dye.
PURNA. A Cypress.
PURNASA. Sacred Basil.

GLOSSARY

Q

R

RAKTACHANDAN. The red Sandal Tree.
RAJIVA. A red Lotus.
RANJAKA. Barbadoes Pride. The Red Wood or Coral Pea Tree.

S

SALA. Shorea Robusta. The Sal Tree.
SALLAKA. Bignonia Indica. The Gum Tree.
SANGANDHIKA. The White and Blue Water-lily.
SAPTA. A kind of grass. Sacharum Cylindricum.
SAPTACCHADA. Seven-leafed Milk Plant or Poon Tree or Devil's Tree.
SAPTAPARNA. Alstonia or Echites Scholaris. Lit.: Seven-leafed Tree.
SARALA. Pinus Longifolia. A species of Pine.
SARJA. White Murdah.
SARPAT GRASS. Saccharium Bengalense Retz. (S. Sara Roxb.). One of the sugar canes.
SHAMI. Acacia Suma. This tree possesses very tough and hard wood supposed to contain fire—it is employed to kindle the sacred fires by rubbing two bits together. Also the shrub Serratula anthelmintica.
SHAIVALA. Vallisneria Octandra or Bexica. An aquatic plant.
SHALMALI. The Silk Cotton Tree.
SHIMSHAPA or SHINGSHAPA. Dattergia Sisu. An Ashoka.
SHIRASHAKA. Probably a form of fragrant Sirissa.
SHIRIBILWA, see BILWA.
SHIRISHA. Acacia Sirissa.
SHIRISHKAPIR. One of the Sirissas. Bears a small white flower which is fragrant at night. This tree yields a gum similar to Gum Arabic. Its seeds are used for opthalmic diseases and are useful in leprosy.
SHYAMA. An extensive dark-blue climber. Also Datura Metel. A Thorn apple.
SILLEA. Cephalostashyum Capitatum Munro. A large Bamboo.
SIMHAKESARA. Cassia Sianica.
SINDHUVARA. Vitex Negundo, a small tree.
SURA. A Sal tree.
SVADAMSHTRA. Astercantha Longifolia.
SYANDARA. Dalbergia Ougeninensis.

GLOSSARY

T

TAKKOLA. Pinieta Acris.

TALA. Borassus Flabelliformis. A kind of Palm.

TAMALA. Phyllanthus Emblica. The name Myrabolan is applied to the fruit which with that of another tree makes a tonic called Tregala Churan.

TILAKA. Commonly called Tila. A tree with beautiful flowers similar to the Sesamum plant.

TIMIDA. The Sesamum plant.

TIMIRA. An aquatic plant.

TIMISHA or TINISHA. A kind of pumpkin or water-melon. Also a climber with purple flowers.

TINDUKA. Diospyros Glutinosa or Diospyros Embryopteris. A sort of Ebony.

TINDURA. Persimmon.

TUNGA. Rottleria Tinctoria. Coconut.

U

UDDALA or UDDALAKA. The plant Cordia Myxa or Latifolia also Paspalum Frumentaceum. Uddalaka—pushpa—bhanjika or the " Breaking of Uddalaka flowers " is a sort of game played by people in the eastern districts.

USHIRAS. Spikenard or a grass a small Saccharum. Also the fragrant root Andropogan Muricatus.

UTPALA. Any water-lily, the blue lotus and also the plant Costus Speciosum.

V

VANIRA. Calamus Rotang. A Reed.

VANDHIRA. Memisa Sirissa.

VANJULA. Hibiscus Mutabilis.

VARANA. Craetova Tapia. A sacred medicinal Tree.

VASANTA KUSUMA. Cordia Myxa or Latifolia. " Having blossoms in Spring ".

VASANTA DUTA. Gaetnera Racemosa. A creeper. Also a trumpet flower.

VASANTA DRU. A Mango.

VATA. A species of Banian.

VETRA. An ornamental Palm.

VETTAS. The Rattan Cane.

VIBHITA or VIBHITAKA. The Tree 'Terminalia Belerica.'

VIJAKA. The Citron Tree.

GLOSSARY

W

X

Y

Z

WEAPONS

A

AGNEYA. The Fire Weapon.
AINDRA. Indra's Weapon.
AISHIKA. An Arrow.
ALAKSHYA. A Weapon that cannot be followed in its course.
ANKUSHA. A Goad.
ARDEA. The Web (See Shuska).
ARHANI. The Thunderbolt.
AVANAGMUKHA. Weapon with a bent or curved head.
AVARANA. The Weapon of Protection.

B

BHINDIPALA. A short Dart or Arrow thrown from the hand or shot through a tube. Also an iron Spear or Dart or a stone fastened to a string.
BIBHITAKA. A Weapon that breaks through, pierces or penetrates.
BRAHMA-PASHA. Net or noose of Brahma (Pasha meaning a rope).
BRAHMASHIRA. Brahma-headed, probably four-headed.
BUSHUNDI. A kind of Mace.

C

D

DANDA or DUNDA. Lit.: Staff. As a Weapon, the Rod of Punishment. ("Dundadhara" being the title of the God of Death, who bears the "Rod of Chastisement.")
DARANA. A Weapon that tears or splits asunder.
DARPANA. The Drying-up Weapon.
DASHAKSHA. The Ten-eyed Weapon.
DASHA-SHIRSHA. The Ten-headed Weapon.
DHANA. The Weapon of Wealth.
DHANYA. The Rice Weapon.
DHARMA DISCUS or DHARMA PALA. The Noose of the God of Justice.
DHARMA-NABHA. The Weapon of sacred navel.

DHARMA-PASHA. The Weapon that has the power of entangling the Foe.
DHRISHTA. The active Weapon.
DHRITI. The Weapon of forbearance.
DISC OF DHARMA. The Disc of Virtue.
DISC OF KALA. The Disc of Time in the form of death.
DITYA. The Titan.
DRIRNABHA. The Weapon of firm navel.
DUNDA-NABHA. The Dunda-navelled.

E

F

G

GANDHARVA. The Weapon of the Gandharvas.

H

HALA. A Weapon shaped like a plough-share.
HAYA-SHIRA. The Horse-headed Weapon.

I

ISHIKA. The ardent Weapon.

J

JYOTISHMA. The luminous Weapon.

K

KAMARUCHI. A Weapon that is bright and able to go where it will.
KAMARUPA. A Weapon able to assume any form at will.
KANDARPA. A Weapon creating sex desire.
KANKANA. A Weapon protecting the side, possibly a kind of armour.
KAPALA. A Helmet.
KARAVIRA. The Weapon of the valiant hand.
KARNIS. Arrows with two sides resembling ears.

KASHA. A Whip.
KOUMODAKI. A Weapon giving joy to the earth.
KROUNCHA or KRAUNCHA. A Weapon named after the bird of that name.
KSHAPANI. An oar or net. Something that destroys the destroyer.
KSHURA. An arrow with a razor-like edge.
KSHURAPRA. A Crescent-shaped arrow.
KUNTALA. A Sickle-shaped Weapon.
KUTA. A Poniard.
KUTAMUDGARA. A concealed Weapon, similar to a Hammer.

L

LAKSHYA. A Weapon that can be followed in its course.
LOHITA MUKHI. The Bloody-mouthed Weapon.

M

MAHA-NABHA. The Large-navelled Weapon.
MAHA VAHU. The Great-armed or handed Weapon.
MALI. The Chain Weapon. That which holds or binds.
MANAVA. The Weapon of Manu.
MATHANA. The Weapon that inflicts injury and suffering.
MAYADHARA. The Great Deception or Illusion.
MODANA. The Weapon of Inebriation.
MOHA. The Weapon that causes loss of Consciousness.
MOHAN. The Weapon of attraction.
MUSHALA or MOUSHALA. A Club.

N

NALIKA. An Iron Arrow or Dart; also a Pike or Javelin.
NANDANA. The Joy-producing Weapon.
NARACHA. An Iron Arrow.
NARAYANA. Lit.: " Residing in water ".
NIRASHYA. The Discourager.
NISHKALI. The Peaceful.
NISHTRINSHA. A Sword, Scimitar or Falchion more than thirty fingers in lengt.
NIVATA KAVACHA. Impenetrable Armour.

O

GLOSSARY

P

PAISHA ASTRA. The Ghostly Weapon, belonging to the Pisachas, ghosts or demons.
PARAMO DARA ASTRA. The Supreme Clearing Weapon.
PARASAVA. An Axe or Hatchet.
PARIGHA. An Iron Bludgeon or Iron-studded Club.
PASHUPATI. The Weapon sacred to Shiva.
PATH. A kind of Sword.
PINAKA. The Bow sacred to Shiva.
PITRIYA. The Weapon of the Pittris (Ancestors).
PRAMA THANA. The Churner.
PRASHA. A Bearded Dart.
PRASHAMANA. The Weapon of Destruction.
PRASHWAPRANA. A Weapon dealing with the vital airs.
PRATIHARDARA. That which neutralizes the effects of other weapons.
PURANG MUKHA. A Weapon that has its face averted.

Q

R

RABHASA. The Desolator.
RATI. The Weapon of Enjoyment.
RUCHIRA. The Approving Weapon.
RUDRA. The Weapon sacred to Rudra (Shiva).

S

SALA. An Arrow with short leads.
SAMVARTTA. The Covering Weapon.
SANDHANA. The Arm Weapon.
SANTAPANA. The Weapon that scorches or burns up. One of Kamadeva's Arrows.
SARICHIMALI. That which has force or power.
SARPA-NATHA. The Weapon sacred to the Lord of Serpents.
SATYA-ASTRA. The Weapon of Existence.
SATYAKIRTI. The Justly-famed.
SAURA. The Heroic Weapon.
SHAKUNA. The Vulture-shaped Weapon.
SHANKARA. The Cause of Welfare. A Weapon of Shiva's.
SHARNGA. The Bow of Vishnu.

SHATAGNI. Either a spiked mace or a stone set round with iron spikes.
SHATAVAKTRA. The Hundred-mouthed Weapon.
SHATODARA. The Hundred-bellied Weapon.
SHITESU. A sharp Arrow.
SHOSHANA. A Weapon used to dry up water and counteract the Varshana Weapon.
SHUCHIVANU. The Pure-handed Weapon.
SHUSHKA. The Dry Weapon.
SILIUMKHA. An Arrow resembling a heron's feathers.
SINHADANSHTRA. A Weapon resembling lion's teeth.
SOMASTRA. The Dew Weapon.
SOUMANVA. The Weapon of the controlled mind.
SUNABHUKA. The Fine-navelled Weapon.
SWAPANA. To do with the act of sleeping.
SWANABHUKA. The Rich-navelled Weapon.

T

TOMARA. An Iron bar, crow-bar, lance or javelin.
TRIMBHAKA. The Gaper.
TWASHTRA. A Weapon possessing the power of Twashtra, the Architect of the Gods.

U

USIRATNA. A Scimitar.

V

VARSHANA. The Rain-producing Weapon.
VARUNA PASHA. The Net of Varuna.
VATRA. The Weapon caused by the Wind (Vatri—The Blower).
VATSADANTA. A Weapon resembling a calf's teeth.
VAYUVYA. A Weapon having the power of the Wind.
VIDDANA. The Weapon that rends or tears asunder.
VIDHUTA. The Strongly-vibrating Weapon.
VIPATRA. A Weapon resembling the Karavira.
VIDYA DHARA. The Weapon of the Demi-Gods.
VILAPANA. The Weapon causing wailing.
VIMALA. The Pure.
VINIDRA. The Somniferous.
VISHNU DISCUS. The Discus of Vishnu.

W

X

Y

YAMIYA. The Weapon of Death.
YOGANDHARA. The United.

Z